# *The* WORLD WAR I DATABOOK

## The Essential Facts and Figures for All the Combatants

# JOHN ELLIS & MICHAEL COX

AURUM PRESS

First published 1993 by Aurum Press Ltd
25 Bedford Avenue, London WC1B 3AT
Copyright © 2001 by John Ellis and Michael Cox

A catalogue record for this book is available from the British Library.

ISBN 1 85410 766 6

5    4    3    2    1
2005    2004    2003    2002    2001

Book designed and typeset by Philip Mann, ace@cha.forthnet.gr

Printed and bound in Great Britain by MPG Books Ltd, Bodmin

# CONTENTS

# SECTION 2
# COMMAND STRUCTURES

# SECTION 3
# ORDERS OF BATTLE

## PART I COMBAT DIVISIONS

## PART II CAMPAIGNS

# SECTION 5 STRENGTHS

## PART I MILITARY MANPOWER AND ARMIES

## PART II NAVIES AND MERCHANT MARINE

## PART III AIR FORCES

# Contents

# SECTION 8
# HARDWARE

# PREFACE

This book is intended to serve as a natural 'prequel' to John Ellis's earlier solo effort *The World War II Databook* (Aurum, 1993) and as such shares much of the earlier book's rationale. Two aspects of this are especially noteworthy. Firstly, despite the continuing proliferation of books about the First World War, very few of them attempt to offer any kind of systematic and comprehensive presentation of basic details about the organisation and deployment of all the various armies, navies and air forces, or about their relative success in getting men and material to the battle fronts. Monographs on such topics do exist, as shown in Bibliography, but these are mostly long out of print, deal with a single belligerent only, are in a foreign language, or are published by small specialist presses.

Secondly, such literature as is available at the present time, in English at least, tends to be rather parochial, over-emphasising the British (or American) contribution to the war and dwelling almost exclusively on the battlefields of northern France and Flanders. A keen debate is now underway about the military competence of British generals, supposedly vindicated by the victories of summer and autumn 1918, but few of the new generation of historians involved have yet looked for 'better 'oles' beyond the Western Front, and begun to give proper coverage to the Russian, Balkan, and Turkish fronts, to the enormous sacrifices of the populations of states such as Austria-Hungary, Serbia, Bulgaria, Rumania and Turkey, or even to the contribution to the Allied effort made by British and French colonial troops.

Hence this second *Databook* which strives above all to present a reasonably all-embracing database of the essential facts and figures about the military conduct of the First World War. Inevitably some of the data is familiar. However, whilst old favourites like British divisions on the Somme or the technical specifications of the Sopwith Camel, a dreadnought battleship or a German U-boat are here, so too, for example, are thumbnail combat records for every Austro-Hungarian division, full orders of battle for the Kerensky Offensive of 1917, T.O. & E.s for French tank units, details on U.S. naval aviation in Europe, iron ore production in occupied Luxemburg, cabinet changes in Bulgaria, comparative casualties in Africa, etc. It has always been known that the events of 1914-18 were the first *world* war - this book endeavours to give this concept a database to stand on.

A few other specific points merit brief explanation. The book contains no biographical entries as it was felt that this was one aspect of First World War history that *had* been fully covered by existing alphabetically-sequenced encyclopedias/dictionaries/almanacs and the like. This is not to say, however, that there are no names in this book and Section 2 on Command Structures is largely given over to them.

Most surprising, probably, is the absence of an index. At first sight this might seem like a remarkable omission, but in fact the decision stemmed from the realisation that an index would be largely redundant. It became clear that for most readers' queries it would be self-evident which section and sub-section must contain the relevant information, and in those cases where there was a possibility of a misunderstanding, a detailed Contents list would provide exact page guidance just as easily as an index. It is to the *front* of this book, then, that those seeking to focus their enquiries should turn.

This book contains several question marks which indicate where we have been unable to track down a particular detail. Each such mark represents a minor failure and we would be most grateful to anyone who could, care of the publisher, provide an answer. We would be equally grateful, though rather more embarrassed, to anyone who can correct any of the (hopefully few) mistakes that must inevitably creep into a work of this nature. Any such information or amendments will be duly acknowledged in subsequent editions.

John Ellis's first *Databook* was under his own name but nevertheless owed much to Mike Cox's prodigious order of battle database and so vital was this source to the present work that it was felt that only joint authorship could give adequate credit. Whether concerning divisional listings, orders of battle (military and naval), or air forces generally, the Cox database has been the prime source for the tables and lists that follow and a *sine qua non* of the book as a whole. As regards the preparatory ordering of the data on the page, Sections 1, 2, 4, 5, 6, and 7 were done by John Ellis. Sections 3 and 8 were split, with Mike Cox contributing the core Parts II and III of the Orders of Battle section and Part III of the Hardware section.

Mike Cox also brought to this enterprise a group of like-minded experts who made a fundamentally important contribution with regard to several key topics. Duncan Maclean was indefatigable in exploring his peerless First World War air force database and unstintingly generous in providing us with the fruits of his research. Without his help our air force coverage would have been skimpy indeed. Eugen Pinak, in Kiev, also conducted tireless research on our behalf and the fact that our Russian tables and orders of battle are much more complete than in any English source hitherto, is largely attributable to Mr Pinak and some of his like-minded compatriots. Our coverage of Austria-Hungary, especially, and of Germany was enormously helped by the staff of the Goethe Institute in Manchester, whose Director and librarians, most especially the tireless and supremely efficient Gabriele Reinsch, who made available to us numerous key books from German libraries. (The authors are appalled to hear that the Institute in Manchester is to be axed and wonder just how such an act of cultural vandalism squares with pan-European ideals). The authors would also like to thank Peter Abbott who supplied us with some invaluable data on colonial armies and those of the minor players of the First World War; the staff of the Naval Historical Branch (Ministry of Defence) and its erstwhile Director David Brown, who made available confidential copies of First World War Navy Lists, Movements of H.M.Ships Books, and staff monographs; Phil McCarty who supplied a huge tranche of vital details about French divisions; the Office of the Greek Defence Attaché who copied some official maps for us and Nick Sekunda who helped in their translation; Suzy Harrison in the Imperial War Museum Department of Printed Books who provided details from an elusive French naval source; the staff of Manchester Central Reference Library who struggle valiantly on to provide a first-class academic resource in the face of constant penny-pinching in local government. Last, but most assuredly not least, we would like to thank our publisher, Piers Burnett, for his remarkable forbearance in the face of some spectacularly missed delivery dates, and Philip Mann of Spiti Campana, Crete, who actually typeset this book, working from original manuscript and typescript that would have defeated the scholars who deciphered the Dead Sea Scrolls. It is he alone who should take credit for the austerely attractive and eminently functional layouts that adorn each page.

John Ellis
Mike Cox
Manchester 2001

# ABBREVIATIONS and GLOSSARY

Abbreviations explained in individual Map keys (Section 1) and Organigrams (Section 2) are not repeated here. The Glossary portion of this list is limited to a few terms that might be problematical even for the informed reader.

## A

| | |
|---|---|
| A.A. | *Anti-aircraft* |
| Abschnitt | Sector (in the Austro-Hungarian army a sub-division of a Rayon) |
| Abt. | *Abteilung* |
| AC & A/Cr. | *Armoured Cruiser* |
| A.D. | *Armée d'Orient* |
| A.E.F. | *American Expeditionary Force* |
| A.F. | *Air Force* |
| A.F.O. | *Armée Francaise d'Orient* |
| A.Gp. | *Army Group* |
| A-H | *Austro-Hungarian* |
| A.L.H. | *Australian Light Horse* |
| Alp. Gp. | *Alpine Group* |
| A.M.C. | *Armed Merchant Cruiser* |
| ANZAC | *Australian and New Zealand Corps* |
| A.O.K. | *Armee Oberkommando* (Austrian) *any Army HQ* (German) |
| Armee-Abteilung | Small Army-sized formation, often assigned to a quiet sector |
| Armeegruppe | An ad hoc formation, usually smaller than an Army and not to be confused with a full Army Group (Heeresgruppe) |
| A.U.S. | *Armee des U.S.* (*sic.*) |
| A.W. | *Armée de Woevre* |

## B

| | |
|---|---|
| B. | *Bantam* |
| Ban | *1st, 2nd etc wave of the general mobilisation* |
| BAR. | *Browning Automatic Rifle* |
| Batt. | *Battalion* |
| Bav. | *Bavarian* |
| B.B. | *Battleship* |
| B.C. & B/Cr. | *Battle-cruiser* |
| Bde. | *Brigade* |
| B.E.F. | *British Expeditionary Force* |
| B.I.L.A. | *Bataillon d'Infanterie Legere d'Afrique* |
| B.I.C. | *Bataillon d'Infanterie Coloniale* |
| Bn. | *Battalion* |
| Bogohl | *Bombengeschwader der O.H.L.* |
| Br. | *British* |
| Brdg. | *Bridging* |
| B.S.A. | *British Salonika Army* |
| B.T.S. | *Bataillon de Tirailleurs Senegalais* |
| Bty. | *Battery* |
| Bulg. | *Bulgarian* |

## C

| | |
|---|---|
| C. | *Cruiser* |
| C.A.A. | *Commandement des Armées Alliées en Orient* |
| C.A.C. | *Corps d'Armée Coloniale* |
| Cas. | *Casualties* |
| Cau. & Cauc. | *Caucasian* |
| Cav. | *Cavalry* |
| Cav. à p. | *Cavalerie à pied* |
| C.C. | *Cavalry Corps* |
| C.D. | *Cavalry Division* |
| C.d.D. | *Chemin des Dames* |
| Cdn. | *Canadian* |
| C.E.D. | *Commandement Expéditionnaire des Dardanelles* |
| C.E.O. | *Commandement Expéditionnaire d'Orient* |
| C.E.S. | *Commissioned Escort Ship* |
| C.G.S. | *Chief of the General Staff* |
| Cmd. | *Command* |
| Col. | *Colonial* or *column* |
| Comb. | *Combined* |
| Comp. | *Composite* |
| Coop. | *Cooperation* |
| Coss. | *Cossack* |
| Coy. | *Company* |
| C.Powers | *Central Powers* (Germany, Austria-Hungary, Bulgaria and Turkey) |
| Cr. | *Cruiser* |
| C.S.I. | *Corpo di Spedizione Italiani* |
| C.S.N. | *Commandement Superieur du Nord* |
| Cwt. | *Hundredweight* |

## D

| | |
|---|---|
| D.A.B. | *Détachement d'Armée de Belgique* |
| D.A.L. | *Détachement d'Armée de Lorraine* |
| D.A.N. | *Détachement d'Armée du Nord* |
| D.A.V. | *Détachement d'Armée des Vosges* |
| Det. & Dét. | *Detachment* |
| Dest. | *Destroyer* |
| D.I. | *Division d'Infanterie* |
| D.I.C. | *Division d'Infanterie Coloniale* |
| Dismtd. | *Dismounted* |
| D.I.T. | *Division d'Infanterie Territoriale* |
| Div. | *Division* |
| Div. de M. | *Division de Marche* |
| D.M. | *Division Marocaine* |
| D/n. | *Dreadnought* |
| D.1 etc | *Destroyer Flotilla 1* etc. (the Senior Officer's ship) |
| Druzhina | A Cossack or Militia battalion |

## E

| | |
|---|---|
| E.F. | *Expeditionary Force* |
| Eng. | *Engineers* |
| Ers. | *Ersatz* |
| Ersatz Division | Formation made up of replacement units originally intended as reinforcements for existing divisions |

## F

| | |
|---|---|
| F. | *Flagship* |
| Feldjäger | An Austro-Hungarian jäger |
| Finn. | *Finnish* |
| Fl.Abt. | *Flieger Abteilung* |
| F.Ldr. | *Flotilla Leader* (large destroyer with staff accommodation) |
| Fr. | *French* |
| Front | Russian Army Group |
| Ftr.Gd. | *Frontier Guard* |

## G

| | |
|---|---|
| G. | *German* |
| G.A.C. | *Groupe d'Armées du Centre* |
| G.A.E. | *Groupe d'Armées de l'Est* |
| G.A.F. | *Groupement d'Armées de Flandres* |
| G.A.N. | *Groupe d'Armées du Nord* |
| G.A.R. | *Groupe d'Armées de Réserve* |
| G.B. | *Gunboat* |
| Gd. & Gds. | *Guard(s)* |
| G.D.R. | *Groupe de Divisions de Réserve* |
| G.D.T. | *Groupe de Divisions Territoriales* |
| Gib. | *Gibraltar* |
| G.H.Q. | *General Headquarters* |
| Gen.Kdo.& G.Kdo. | *General Kommando.* Temporary h.q.with corps-level responsibilities |
| G.M.P. | *Gouvernement Militaire de Paris* |
| G.P.E. | *Groupe Provisoire de l'Est* |
| G.P.N. | *Groupe Provisoire du Nord* |
| G.Q.G. | *Grand Quartier Général* |
| G.Q.G.A. | *Grand Quartier Général des Armées Alliées* |
| Gr. | *Graduated* |
| Gren. | *Grenadier* |
| Grenzjäger | *Border rifleman* |

## H

| | |
|---|---|
| H. | *Hours* |
| Halbregiment | Half-regiment (dismounted cavalry) |
| H.C.D. | *Honved Cavalry Division* |
| Heeresfront | Army Group (Austro-Hungarian) |
| Heeresgruppe | Army Group (German) |
| H.K.K. | *Höheres Kavallerie Kommando* (equivalent to a cavalry corps) |
| Honved | Originally Hungarian Home Defence troops. Later simply used to denote Hungarian formations |
| How. | *Howitzer* |
| Hvy. | *Heavy* |

## I

| | |
|---|---|
| I.D. | *Infantry Division* |
| I.E.F. | *Indian Expeditionary Force* |
| Imp. | *Improved* |
| in. | *Inch* |
| Ind. | *Indian* |
| Indep. | *Independent* |
| It. | *Italian* |

## K

| | |
|---|---|
| k. & km. | *Kilometre* |
| Kagohl | *Kampfgeschwader der O.H.L.* |
| K.A.R. | *King's African Rifles* |
| Kav.Sch.Div. | *Kavallerie Schützen Division* |
| kg. | *Kilogram* |
| K.J.D. | *Kaiserjäger Division* |

## L

| | |
|---|---|
| L. | *Labour* |
| Landwehr | Austro-Hungarian: originally Austrian home-defence troops. Landwehr divisions gradually became indistinguishable from ordinary line divisions. German: initially third-line troops to back up the regular army upon mobilisation. Such divisions gradually became indistinguishable from other types of line division. |
| Landsturm | 4th-line troops mainly employed on secondary fronts or line-of-communication duties. |
| L.C. | *Light Cruiser* |
| Ldr. | *Leader* (of destroyer flotilla) |
| L.E. | *Légion Etrangère* |
| Lehr | Training or demonstration unit |
| l.m.g. | *Light machine gun* |
| L.ofC. | *Lines of Communication* |
| Lst. & L.St. | *Landsturm* |
| LW | *Landwehr* |

## M

| | |
|---|---|
| m. | *Metre* |
| M.D. | *Military District* |
| m.g. | *Machine gun* |
| M.G.C. | *Machine Gun Corps* |
| M.of W. | *Ministry of War* |
| M.T. | *Motor Transport* |
| Mtd. | *Mounted* |
| Mtn. | *Mountain* |

## N

| | |
|---|---|
| N. | *Northern* (Front) |
| N.A. | *(not known)* |
| No. | *Number* |
| N.W. | *North-West* (Front) |
| N.Z. | *New Zealand* |
| N.Z.M.R. | *New Zealand Mounted Rifles* |

## O

| | |
|---|---|
| O.B. & O.O.B. | *Order of Battle* |
| Obs. | *Observation* |
| O.H.L. | *Obersterheeresleitung* |
| Opolchenie | Russian militia |

## P

| | |
|---|---|
| P. | *Pioneer* |
| Pascha | Codename for German units with the Ottoman armies in Palestine. (Also Pasha or Pasa) |
| P.B.B. | *Pre-Dreadnought Battleship* |
| P.C. | *Protected Cruiser* |
| Pk. | *Park* |
| Plastun | Cossack infantry unit |
| Plat. | *Platoon* |
| Pol. | *Polish* |
| Port. | *Portugese* |
| P.o.w. | *Prisoner-of-war* |
| Prov. | *Provisional* |

## R

| | |
|---|---|
| R.A.C. | *Régiment d'Artillerie Coloniale* |
| R.A.F. | *Royal Air Force* or *Royal Aircraft Factory* |
| R.A.N. | *Royal Australian Navy* |
| Rayon | Military defence area, larger than an Abschnitt (sector) |
| R.C.N. | *Royal Canadian Navy* |
| R.de M. | *Régiment de marche* |
| Rds. | *Roads* |
| R.E. | *Régiment Etrangère* |
| Recce. | *Reconnaissance* |
| Res. | *Reserve* |
| R.F.A. | *Royal Field Artillery* |
| R.F.C. | *Royal Flying Corps* |
| R.F.V. | *Region Fortifie de Verdun* |
| R.G.A. | *Royal Garrison Artillery* |
| Rgt. or regt. | *Regiment* |

R.I.C.     *Régiment d'Infanterie Coloniale*
R.M.I.C.     *Régiment de Marche d'Infanterie Coloniale*
R.M.C.M.     *Régiment de Marche Colonial du Maroc*
R.N.     *Royal Navy* or *Royal Naval Division*
R.N.A.S     *Royal Naval Air Service*
R.T.A.     *Régiment de Tirailleurs Algériens*
R.T.An.     *Régiment de Tirailleurs Annamites*
R.T.S.     *Régiment de Tirailleurs Sénégalais*
R.T.T.     *Régiment de Tirailleurs Tunisiens*
R.T.Ton.     *Régiment de Tirailleurs Tonkinois*
Rum.     *Rumanian*
Russ.     *Russian*

## S

S.     *Sloop*
S.A.     *South African*
Sch.     *Schützen*
Schützen Divisions Austrian Landwehr (q.v.) divisions
Schutztruppen     German native colonial troops (askaris)
Sect.     *Section*
Sib.     *Siberian*
Siebenbürgen     Transylvania
S.N.O.     *Senior Naval Officer*
S.O.     *Senior Officer*
Sotnia     Cossack cavalry squadron
Sp/B.     *Sperrbrecher* (auxiliary minesweeper, lit. 'barrier breaker')
Sqn.     *Squadron*
St.Sch.Abt.     *Standschützen Abteilung* (originally a volunteer sharpshooter unit)
S.W.     *South-West* (Front)

## T

T.     *Turkish*
Tabor     Bunch of Albanian cutthroats
T-A.     *Trans-Amur*
T.A.N.     *Troupes Auxiliares Marocaines*
T-B.     *Trans-Baikal*
T-C.     *Trans-Caspian*
Tel.     *Telegraph*
T.G.B.     *Torpedo Gunboat*
T.T.     *Torpedo Tube*
Turk.     *Turkestan*

## U

U.K.     *United Kingdom*
U.S.     *United States*
U.S.N.     *United States Navy*

## V

verst.     *Verstärken* (reinforced)

## W

W.     *Western* (Front)
W.A.F.F.     *West African Frontier Force*
W.F.F.     *Western Frontier Force*

## Y

Yeo.     *Yeomanry*

## Z

z.b.v.     *Zur besonderen Verwendung* (for special employment)

# SECTION 1

# THE WAR IN MAPS

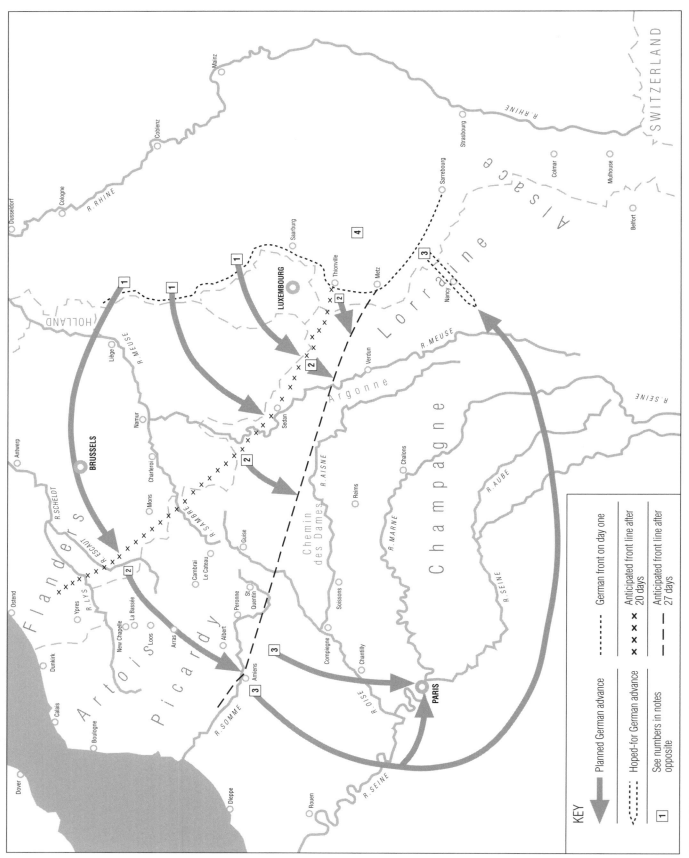

**Map 1 Western Front: Germany's Schlieffen Plan for the Conquest of France 1905-14**

KEY

| | |
|---|---|
| ➤ | Planned German advance |
| ▪▪▪▪ | Hoped-for German advance |
| 1 | See numbers in notes opposite |
| ⋯⋯ | German front on day one |
| × × × | Anticipated front line after 20 days |
| – – – | Anticipated front line after 27 days |

• **MAP 1** • WESTERN FRONT •

## NOTES TO MAP 1

[1] The Schlieffen Plan, drawn up in 1905, proposed defeating France by a surprise attack through Belgium, probably a neutral. The element of surprise was deemed worth the international opprobrium because it was hoped that it would permit a speedy and crushing victory over France before her likely Russian allies could bring significant forces to bear in the east. By the time the Russians would pose a significant threat, it was held, the Germans should be able to shift most of their divisions from west to east. The railways would perform a vital role here, just as they would in the initial massing on the Belgian frontier.

   The initial German attack, therefore, hinging on Metz, was to be as swift as possible, reaching a line roughly along the Franco-Belgian frontier in the first twenty days.

[2] In the next week the Germans were to drive into France itself, with their right wing drawing up to the River Somme.

[3] Even greater things were expected of this wing thereafter. According to Schlieffen it would need to be up to eight times stronger than the defensive left wing, enabling it to make a forced march to the west of Paris and then wheel eastwards to crush the French against the Metz-Saarburg hinge. Complete victory over the French was to be achieved within six weeks.

[4] Schlieffen's successor as Chief of the Imperial General Staff, von Moltke the Younger, whilst perforce adhering to the Schlieffen timetable, was extremely nervous about the weakness of his left wing, where the French themselves were most likely to attack (see Map 2). He therefore redistributed his forces to buttress the defence south-east of Metz. But this left the right wing now only three times stronger than the left and much less assured of making Schlieffen's enormous offensive wheel from Liège to the east bank of the Marne.

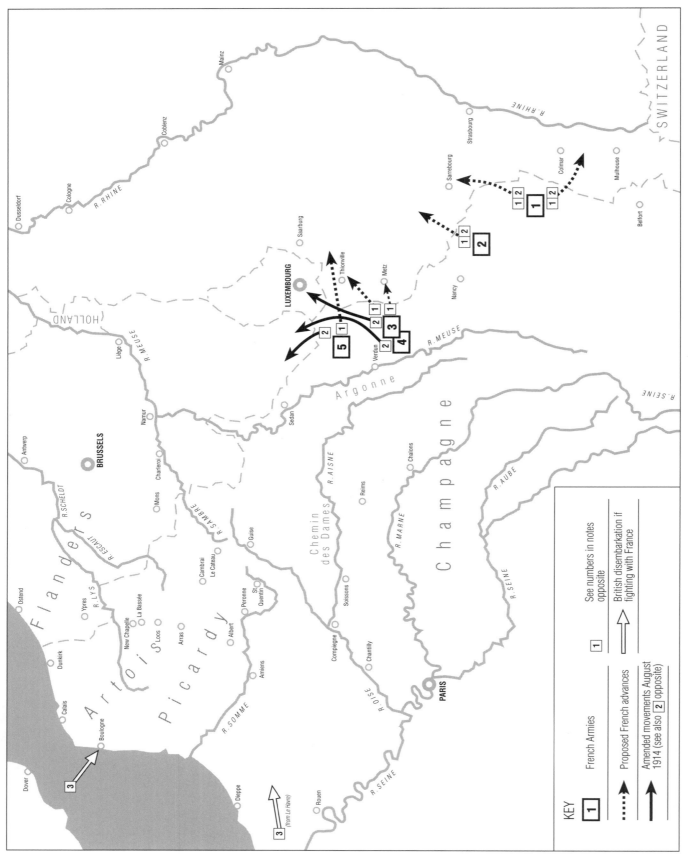

**KEY**

| | |
|---|---|
| **1** | French Armies |
| → | Proposed French advances |
| ⇢ | Amended movements August 1914 (see also **2** opposite) |
| **1** | See numbers in notes opposite |
| ⇨ | British disembarkation if fighting with France |

**Map 2 Western Front: French Plan XVII in the Event of a German Invasion and Initial Amendments August 1914**

## NOTES TO MAP 2

**1** Though the French were not entirely convinced that Germany would respect Belgium and Luxembourg's neutrality, they expected, at worst, nothing more than an ancillary flanking attack through the Ardennes. Therefore their basic strategy, as enshrined in Plan XVII finalised by Joffre in 1913, was based upon a broad-front counter-offensive along the Franco-German frontier. French eyes had been firmly fixed here since the loss of Alsace-Lorraine to the Germans in 1871, at the end of the Franco-Prussian War.

**2** Once it became known that Belgium and Luxembourg had been invaded in strength, Plan XVII was amended with the French left being turned north-west into the Ardennes. South of Metz, however, the *idée* remained *fixe* upon the reconquest of the 'occupied' territories.

**3** France and Britain had been engaged in staff talks about a possible war with Germany since 1906, but by 1914 all that had emerged was that a British expeditionary force, if it did intervene, would take up positions somewhere on the French left. Exactly where remained most uncertain. In the event, because of the need to confront German forces in Belgium, the BEF concentrated just south of Mons rather than being marched towards Sedan, as some French generals had anticipated, or deploying around Amiens, which had been War Minister Kitchener's preference.

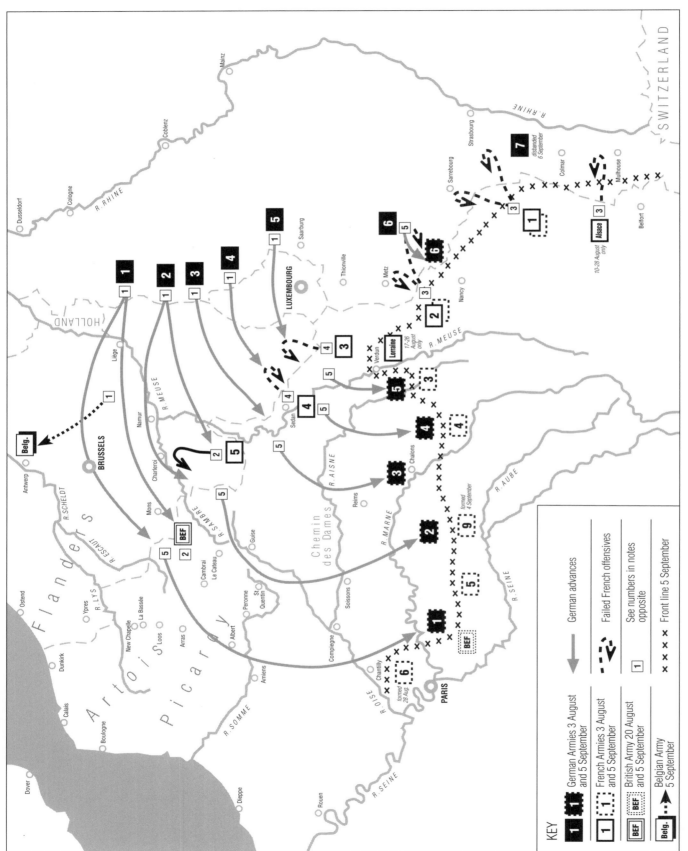

Map 3 **Western Front: The Battle of the Frontiers and the German Advance to the Marne 3 August–5 September 1914**

KEY

| | |
|---|---|
| **1** **1** | German Armies 3 August and 5 September |
| **1** **1** | French Armies 3 August and 5 September |
| BEF BEF | British Army 20 August and 5 September |
| Belg. | Belgian Army 5 September |
| → | German advances |
| ⟿ | Failed French offensives |
| 1 | See numbers in notes opposite |
| × × × | Front line 5 September |

• **MAP 3** • WESTERN FRONT •

## NOTES TO MAP 3

**1** German cavalry patrols crossed into Belgium on 3 August and soon the Belgian Army was being forced back towards Antwerp as the main German forces approached the French frontier. Liège was occupied on 7 August and its forts pounded into submission by the 16th. Namur was similarly reduced between the 21st and the 25th, whilst Brussels fell on the 20th. The Belgian government had already moved to Antwerp on the 17th and two days later the Belgian Army began to withdraw into this bastion.

**2** The BEF had begun landing in France on 9 August and by the 20th was concentrated south of Mons. Here they were confronted by Schlieffen's hammer-head, the German First Army under von Kluck. Any hope of sustained resistance had to be given up once French Fifth Army, which itself had advanced into Belgium, was unable to hold the line of the Sambre and on the 24th, hearing of the imminent fall of Namur, began to withdraw. The British had no option but to follow suit.

**3** Up to this point, however, the French had been giving most of their attention to the lost provinces of Alsace and Lorraine that featured so prominently in Plan XVII (see Map 2). A minor French advance here on 7 August was repulsed two days later but on the 12th a general offensive was launched. Saarburg was taken on the 18th as other French troops pushed into Alsace. On the 20th, however, rash assaults by French Second Army were repulsed and their retreat soon degenerated into a rout, and made it necessary for the First Army to pull back as well. By the 26th most of the ground gained had been lost.

**4** On 21 August the French launched an offensive in the Ardennes, with the aim of surprising the Germans in what was assumed to be a fairly static sector. However, on the 22nd, the French Fourth Army's left flank bumped into a general German advance conforming to the great wheel of First and Second Armies. With German strategic intentions becoming clearer, the French commander-in-chief, Joffre, determined to shift as many units as he dared northwards and on the 25th ordered a general withdrawal by all attacking armies.

**5** Joffre now intended to hold a line from the Somme to Verdun, prior to launching a counter-offensive. The French and British did manage to delay the Germans at Guise and Le Cateau, between the 26th and the 29th, but it proved impossible to actually halt the Allied retreat until they had fallen back across the Marne, on 4 September. Various factors helped Joffre to rally on this new line between the Seine and Verdun. Firstly he had ruthlessly stripped the Alsace-Lorraine sector to create a new Sixth Army around Paris, a new Ninth Army to the right of the sorely tried Fifth, and two extra corps for Third Army around Verdun. Secondly, the commander of the BEF, Sir John French, had been persuaded by the Minister of War, Lord Kitchener, to hide his great misgivings about his main ally and to keep his forces at Joffre's disposal. Thirdly, though the Germans had pressed across the Oise and the Aisne by 2 September, they were increasingly feeling the effects of Moltke's dilution of the Schlieffen Plan. Intense heat, exhausting forced marches and heavy casualties made it difficult for First and Second Armies to adequately man their ever-widening front. As gaps appeared von Kluck was now ordered to march to the *east* of Paris so that he could maintain contact with von Bülow's right flank. But in so doing Kluck now exposed his own left flank to the army that was being hastily assembled around Paris.

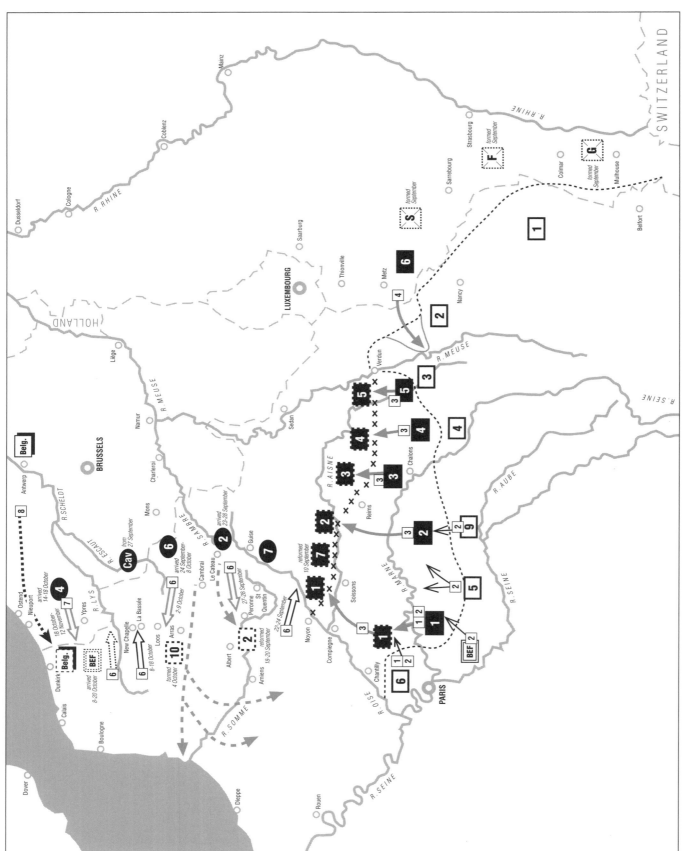

Map 4 Western Front: The Battles of the Marne, the Aisne, the Race to the Sea and First Ypres 6 September–12 November 1914

• **MAP 4** • WESTERN FRONT •

## KEY

| | |
|---|---|
| ▮1 ▦1 | German Armies 6 September and 14 September |
| □1 □BEF □Belg. | French, British and Belgian Armies 6 September |
| ⬤1 | German Armies 18 September and 18 October * |
| ⦙1⦙ ⦙BEF⦙ ⦙Belg.⦙ | French, British and Belgian Armies 18 September to 18 October |
| ⦙S⦙ ⦙F⦙ ⦙G⦙ | German Army Detatchments Stranz, Falkenhausen and Gaede |
| ◄ - - - | Proposed German advances 21 September |
| ◄——— | German withdrawals and advances |
| ◄——— | French and British advances |
| ◁=6 ◁=6 ◁····=6 | See Note 6 in Notes |
| ◄········ | Belgian withdrawal |
| □1 | See number in Notes |
| × × × × × | Front line 6 September |
| - - - - - - - - - | Front line 14 September |

\* Cav. = I, II and IV Cavalry Corps, **not** a formal Army grouping

## NOTES TO MAP 4

**1** On 4 September Joffre issued orders for a counter-offensive to begin two days later, spearheaded by Sixth Army and the BEF and followed up by Fifth Army. Ninth Army was to remain on the defensive. In fact, the French and Germans clashed at the extreme eastern end of the front on the 5th and von Kluck began to send troops eastwards to bolster his flank.

**2** On the 6th the Allies slowly moved forwards, including Foch's Ninth Army which had chosen to ignore its defensive brief. Fortuitously, the Allies were now applying pressure at the weakest part of the German line, as von Kluck was pulled eastwards to counter French Sixth Army and von Bulow was becoming hemmed in by the steady pressure from Fifth and Ninth Armies. A gap between the two German armies was already apparent on the 6th and by the night of the 8th, as von Bülow withdrew his right flank, was becoming critical.

**3** The Allies slowly pressed forward but Moltke remained largely ignorant of these developments and on the 8th a staff officer was sent to assess German progress. It was immediately clear to him that the German advance was in considerable disarray and he had no alternative but to sanction the withdrawal order that von Bülow had already issued to his own army. Kluck's First Army also had to pull back and a little later Moltke ordered Third Army to follow suit. The remaining armies were held in place but after a personal visit Moltke ordered a general retreat to a line Noyon–Verdun. By 14 September the Germans were organising strong positions along the Aisne, and on that same day Moltke was replaced by von Falkenhayn. It took the Allies some time to catch up to the retreating Germans and they never mustered sufficient forces to force the Aisne before the Germans were properly dug in. By 18 September their attacks, comprising the First Battle of the Aisne, had petered out. Nor were the Germans content to simply remain on the defensive, with their Third, Fifth and Sixth Armies all launching vigorous offensives of their own.

**4** The Germans' only success, however, was on the 24th with the creation of a troublesome salient at Saint Mihiel, on the Meuse, south of Verdun.

**5** The impasse on the Aisne prompted one last flurry of movement in the West. Both sides took note of the much weaker positions west of the Oise and on 18 September began a series of mutual attempted flanking movements that came to be known as the Race to the Sea. In fact, the Germans were mainly attempting to head the Allies off short of the Channel ports and rather than a race the ensuing campaign resembled two American football teams attempting successive end-runs nearer and nearer the sidelines. On the whole, the Allies got the better of it as the over-stretched German right was forced back to Nieuport, thwarting the original German intention to hold the line of the Somme.

**6** These operations necessitated substantial redeployments and the major offensives are shown by the thick outline arrows with attached dates.

**7** The final effort was by the Germans, attacking between the coast and the Yser. This was the First Battle of Ypres and by then the Allies had established a firm defensive line, solidly anchored on the coast.

**8** On 6 October, with the Germans preparing for a devastating artillery assault on Antwerp, the Belgians withdrew and from the 15th began to take up positions on the extreme left of the Allied line.

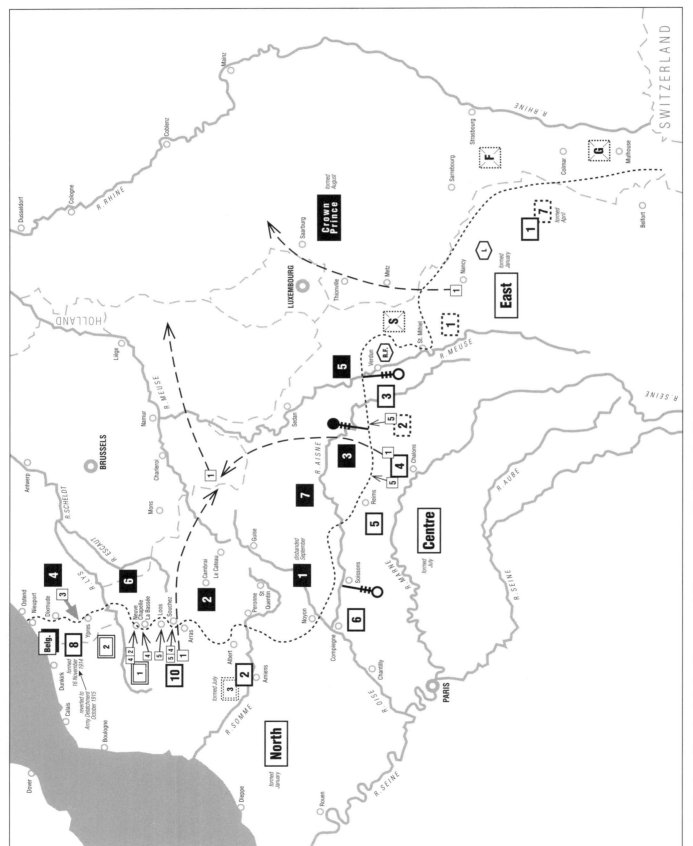

Map 5 **Western Front: Artois, Ypres and Champagne: the Front in 1915**

• **MAP 5** • WESTERN FRONT •

KEY

| | |
|---|---|
| ▆▆▆ | German Army Groups |
| ▭ | Allied Army Groups |
| ●╍╍╍ | German Army Group boundary |
| ○╍╍╍ | Allied Army Group boundary |
| **1** | German Armies |
| 1  ⌐1⌐ | French Armies January and July |
| 2  ⌐2⌐ | British Armies January and July |
| **Belg.** | Belgian Army |
| S  F  G | German Army Detatchments Stranz, Falkenhausen and Gaede |
| (R.F.) | Région Fortifié |
| ⬡ L | Army Detatchment Lorraine |
| – – –> | Joffre's intended breakthrough and advance September 1915 |
| ◄─── | German offensives |
| ───> | Allied offensives |
| 1 | See number in Notes |
| - - - - - | Front line 1915 |

## NOTES TO MAP 5

**1** The creation of a solid trench line from the Channel to Switzerland did little to curb the offensive ambitions of Allied commanders. Not entirely without reason, they saw this stretching of enemy manpower as an invitation to concentrated offensives against narrow sectors of the front. In early 1915, therefore, Joffre was hoping that two such concerted assaults would nip out the huge German salient between Arras and Reims and thereafter allow an advance towards the Rhine.

**2** Actual gains, however, were meagre. At the northern end of the salient, in Artois, the British were committed around Neuve Chapelle. They jumped off on 10 March, aiming for Aubers Ridge a mile and a half to the east. Despite achieving complete surprise and a swift initial breakthrough, the attack soon stalled, due mainly to poor communications, and by the 13th the British had been held, having gained only some 1,000 yards of ground.

**3** At this time the Germans were mainly concerned with operations in the East (see Maps 15 & 16) but not enough to prevent their own fixation upon an enemy salient, in this case the British one at Ypres. On 22 April, therefore, they marched against the northern end of this salient, behind clouds of chlorine gas. Some progress was made but by the 24th, after desperate fighting, the Germans had been checked. But it was clear that the salient was still far too exposed and on 1 May the British pulled back to a more defensible front line three miles east of Ypres.

**4** On 9 May the British resumed their assault on Aubers Ridge but to even less effect. On the 15th they attacked again at Festubert but lost at least three times as many men as the Germans for only minimal gains. These attacks, which lasted until 26 May, were in support of French efforts just north of Arras, in the Second Battle of Artois. Repeated attacks by the latter between 9 May and 20 June, towards Souchez and Vimy Ridge, gained perhaps 1,000 yards of ground at the cost of appalling casualties.

**5** In September Joffre attempted the converging offensive that had been in his mind all year. The French once more attacked in Artois, between 25 September and 14 October, and were supported by a simultaneous British effort at Loos (on 25–26 September and 13 October). Gains, especially in the French sector, were again minimal. The second arm of the offensive, in Champagne, east of Reims, involved two French armies along a seven-mile front. Here too the French jumped off on 25 September and after some impressive initial breakthroughs, soon ran up against recently constructed reserve trench lines. By the 30th large-scale operations had been halted.

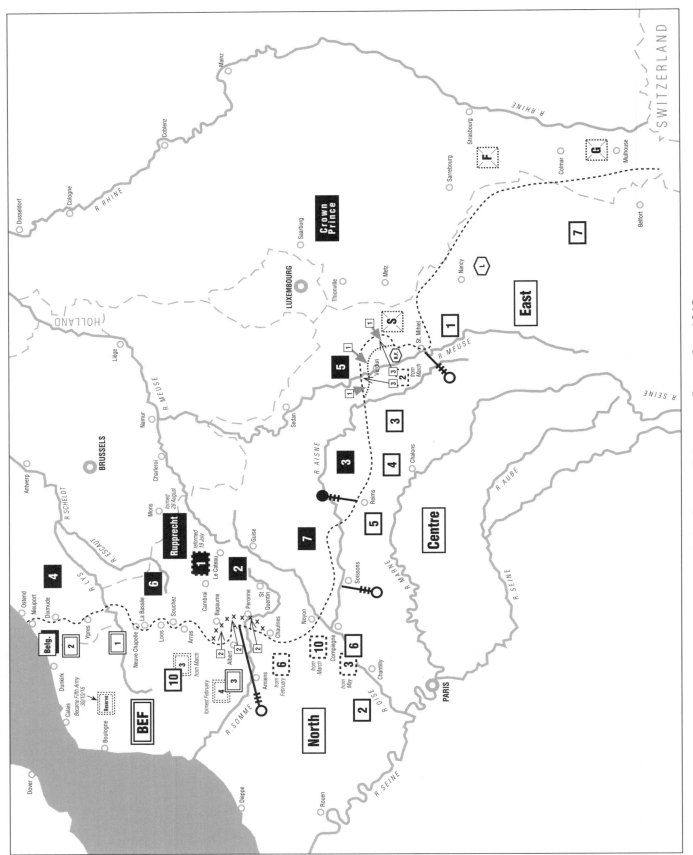

Map 6 **Western Front: The Battles of Verdun and the Somme February – December 1916**

KEY

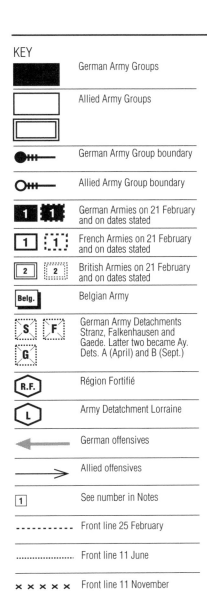

| | |
|---|---|
| | German Army Groups |
| | Allied Army Groups |
| ●⊞━ | German Army Group boundary |
| ○⊞━ | Allied Army Group boundary |
| **1** ▓ | German Armies on 21 February and on dates stated |
| 1 ⸬1⸬ | French Armies on 21 February and on dates stated |
| 2 ⸬2⸬ | British Armies on 21 February and on dates stated |
| **Belg.** | Belgian Army |
| ⸬S⸬ ⸬F⸬ ⸬G⸬ | German Army Detachments Stranz, Falkenhausen and Gaede. Latter two became Ay. Dets. A (April) and B (Sept.) |
| **R.F.** | Région Fortifié |
| L | Army Detatchment Lorraine |
| ⬅ | German offensives |
| ⟶ | Allied offensives |
| 1 | See number in Notes |
| ---------- | Front line 25 February |
| ................. | Front line 11 June |
| × × × × × | Front line 11 November |

## NOTES TO MAP 6

**1** After the stalemated battles of 1915 it became clear that modern warfare was likely to involve huge butchers' bills. Commanders on both sides tried to incorporate this grisly truth into their plans and to devise attritional scenarios which could somehow be expected to sap the enemy's will to fight quicker than their own. For Joffre such *batailles d'usure* were a preparatory stage, conducted as much as possible by his allies, to bleed the Germans prior to his own decisive, breakthrough offensive. For Falkenhayn, on the other hand, attrition was an end in itself, with the French being lured into a perpetual mincing machine that would utterly grind down their military capability. The British remained extremely wary about the role that Joffre envisioned for them and at the Chantilly Conference in December 1915 would only agree to *simultaneous*, coordinated offensives. The first of these was to be a 65-division effort on the Somme in March but the Allies' unpreparedness after the losses of 1915 caused it to be put back until June.

But, to the Allies' complete surprise, the Germans acted first. Falkenhayn had been seeking a sector of the front in whose defenses the French would willingly bleed themselves white and he found it at Verdun, a fortress on the Meuse that had long been a jewel in the necklace of France's eastward defences. The German assault began on 21 February and on the 25th the greatest of the Verdun forts, Douaumont, fell. But the French quickly fed in Petain's Second Army, established strong artillery positions on the west bank of the Meuse, and by the end of February had halted the German advance. At the beginning of March the Germans were themselves able to strike along the west bank and by early May had slowly pushed forward to take several key features. On 1 June the renewed the east bank attacks. Fort Vaux fell on the 7th and on the 21st German units employing gas shells came within striking distance of Verdun itself. By then, however, Falkenhayn had already been forced to start closing down his mincing machine to provide reinforcements in the east where the Central Powers were reeling under the shock of the Brusilov Offensive (see Map 17).

**2** The British also played their part in relieving pressure on the French when on 1 July they took on the lion's share of the long-planned Somme offensive. British gains were extremely limited but were sufficient to persuade Falkenhayn, on the 2nd, to halt the Verdun attacks completely. Haig took this as his own summons to attritional warfare and his appalling casualties only seemed to convince him that the next attack must be the one that would snap German morale. The battle, in fact, dragged on until mid-November and despite major attacks at Delville Wood (15 July – 3 September), Pozières (23 July – 3 September), Flers-Courcelette (15 – 22 September), Thiepval (26 – 28 September) and the Ancre (1 October – 11 November), gains for the whole battle where nowhere more than seven miles.

**3** Yet British pressure had undoubtedly helped end the bloodbath at Verdun. Falkenhayn was replaced on 28 July and his successors, Hindenburg and Ludendorff, immediately reduced the German forces there to the bare minimum. Too bare, as it turned out, for from early September the French began to nibble away at German gains, recapturing Douaumont on 24 October and Vaux on 2 November. A major offensive on 15 December pushed the Germans back almost to their February start lines. Suddenly attrition seemed a dead letter and the organiser of these latest attacks, the self-styled innovator Nivelle, replaced Joffre as French Commander-in-Chief on 26 December.

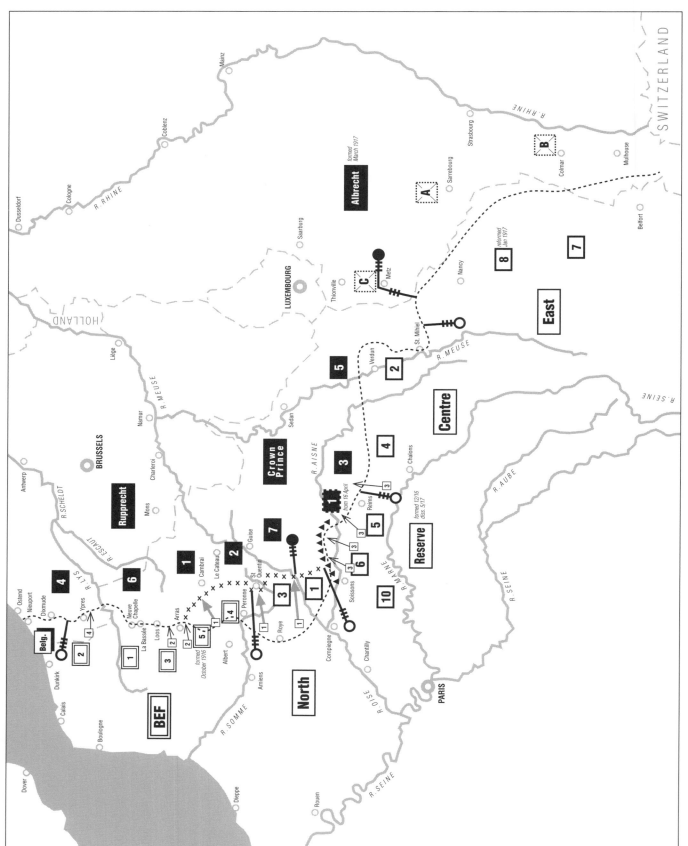

Map 7 **Western Front: German Withdrawal to the Siegfried Line, and the Battles of Arras/Vimy Ridge and 2nd Aisne, March – April 1917**

• **MAP 7** • WESTERN FRONT •

## KEY

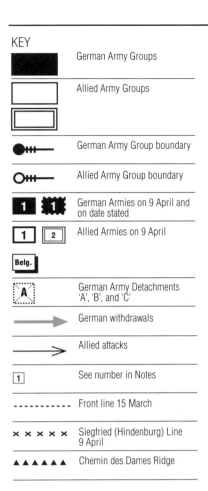

| | |
|---|---|
| ▆ (black box) | German Army Groups |
| ▢ (open box) | Allied Army Groups |
| ▣ (double box) | |
| ●━━━ | German Army Group boundary |
| ○━━━ | Allied Army Group boundary |
| **1** / **1** | German Armies on 9 April and on date stated |
| 1 / 2 | Allied Armies on 9 April |
| **Belg.** | |
| **A** | German Army Detachments 'A', 'B', and 'C' |
| ➡ | German withdrawals |
| ⟶ | Allied attacks |
| 1 | See number in Notes |
| - - - - - - - - | Front line 15 March |
| × × × × × | Siegfried (Hindenburg) Line 9 April |
| ▲▲▲▲▲▲ | Chemin des Dames Ridge |

## NOTES TO MAP 7

**1** Before his removal at the end of 1916, Joffre had been planning to turn the Somme sector into his own version of Falkenhayn's Verdun and grind the Germans down with ceaseless Allied offensive pressure. When combined with other Allied attacks on the Eastern, Salonika and Italian fronts (see Maps 18, 23 and 26), this pressure would, Joffre hoped, utterly exhaust the German war machine. Nivelle, on the other hand, fresh from his triumphant counter-offensive at Verdun, was contemptuous of such an attritional strategy and convinced the credulous politicians that he had an infallible tactical blueprint for a sudden, decisive breakthrough. His *point d'appui* was to be along the Chemin des Dames ridge, between Soissons and Reims, where his French divisions were to simply smash their way through previously impregnable defences. But the British, too, had their part to play, with major attacks between Arras and Bapaume to draw in German reserves just before the main offensive along the Aisne. Other French units would also launch similar pinning attacks between Roye and the Oise.

However, just as at Verdun in 1916, the Germans in 1917 had a February surprise for the Allies and between the 25th and the beginning of April they withdrew from most of the Soissons-Arras salient. In so doing they not only left Nivelle's subsidiary offensives flailing at thin air, but also considerably shortened their own front and so freed more reserves to counter the main Allied attacks.

**2** The subsidiary attacks were called off except for limited French efforts at St Quentin and north-east of Soissons (not shown) and a limited British one at Arras. The latter jumped off on 9 April and thanks to heavy preliminary shelling and the use of a new type of gas shell, the whole front line was taken in less than an hour. The most notable success was that of the Canadian Corps at Vimy Ridge. Thereafter, however, despite a supporting attack south of Arras on the 11th, the British were unable to make any more real gains and the offensive was halted on the 14th.

**3** But so convinced was Nivelle of his strategic genius that he barely noticed the British failure to make any real headway. Nor did he worry when he learned that the Germans were fully informed about his plans, and on 16 April his troops jumped off on schedule. The front line was taken, despite appalling casualties, but the Germans had only recently transferred their First Army to the east of the Chemin des Dames ridge and their strong counter-attacks and crushing artillery concentrations prevented any further French advance. A small German salient east of Soissons was evacuated but without in any way compromising the front as a whole. On 15 May, Nivelle was dismissed and replaced by Pétain.

**4** French failure on the Aisne only served to persuade Haig that the Germans must now have used up their main reserves and would be too stretched to contain another major British offensive in Flanders. First he wished to straighten out the small German salient south of Ypres and ordered the seizure of Messines Ridge. The attacking troops jumped off on 7 June, in the wake of a concentrated bombardment and the blowing of 19 huge mines laid by tunnellers under the German Front. The whole ridge was taken and consolidated in eight hours, before the Germans could organise any serious counter-attacks. Many of the staff of Second Army recognised their victory for what it was – a testimony to meticulous planning in pursuit of limited tactical objectives. To Haig, however, it was just further proof that the whole German front would crumble in the face of a last major offensive.

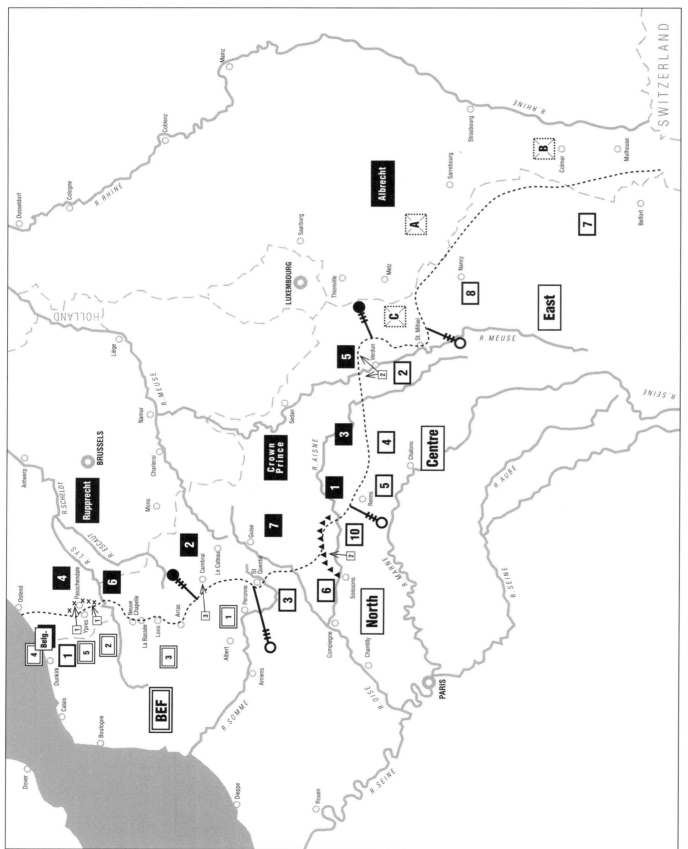

Map 8 **Western Front: The Third Battle of Ypres, Second Verdun and Cambrai 31 July – 7 December 1917**

• **MAP 1** • WESTERN FRONT •

## KEY

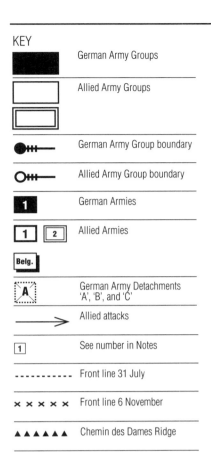

| | |
|---|---|
| ■ | German Army Groups |
| ▢ | Allied Army Groups |
| ▢▢ | |
| ●╫━ | German Army Group boundary |
| ○╫━ | Allied Army Group boundary |
| **1** | German Armies |
| **1** ▢2 | Allied Armies |
| **Belg.** | |
| A | German Army Detachments 'A', 'B', and 'C' |
| ⟶ | Allied attacks |
| ▢1 | See number in Notes |
| ---------- | Front line 31 July |
| × × × × × | Front line 6 November |
| ▲▲▲▲▲▲ | Chemin des Dames Ridge |

## NOTES TO MAP 8

**1** Flushed with the success at Messines, Haig entertained high hopes for his Fifth Army divisions as they embarked on the main offensive out of the Ypres salient, on 31 July. Some high ground was taken on the left but with the ground already sodden after days of continuous rain the attackers soon bogged down in the mud. This allowed the Germans ample time to bring up reserves and further British assaults towards the Ghelulvelt Plateau (10 August), Langemarck (16 August) and St Julien (22 August) all failed to pierce the enemy lines. On the 25th, Haig decided to transfer control of the battle to Plumer's Second Army, the victors at Messines, and on 20 September it made the first of a series of meticulously planned tactical bounds, with precise, limited objectives. The front for each was kept narrow and a pause allowed before the next one, to bring up the guns, supplies and reserves. At Ghelulvelt Plateau (Menin Road Ridge) (20 September), Polygon Wood (26 September) and Broodseinde (4 October) these methods paid dividends but thereafter the Flanders mud made a mockery of any attempt at tactical finesse. The final one-mile push to the village of Passchendaele, repulsed on 12 October, was not brought to a horribly Pyrrhic conclusion until 6 November.

**2** The leading British role in Allied operations in summer and autumn was not solely attributable to Haig's extravagant optimism. The French Army, in fact, was in crisis after the carnage of the Chemin des Dames had finally provoked the *poilus* to widespread mutiny. Few men suggested quitting the front altogether but they did refuse to take part in any more futile mass attacks, forcing Pétain to introduce a much more effective system of rests and reliefs and to consider only the most limited and parsimonious offensive plans. Two such attacks took place at Verdun, between 20 August and 9 September, and along the Aisne, at La Malmaison, between 23 October and 1 November. It was only during this last battle that the French actually took full possession of the Chemin des Dames ridge, a fact hitherto concealed from the public.

**3** A British secret weapon, the tank, had not had an auspicious debut in the Somme battles and had been an irrelevance in the mud of Third Ypres. But Haig kept faith with the clumsy machines and in November saw the possibility of using them west of Cambrai, in a limited operation to seize better observation points over the enemy. But Haig's for once modest ambitions were too limited for the Third Army commander, Byng, who saw the possibility of a full-scale breakthrough to Cambrai. This would seal off German Second Army and permit a parallel advance towards Valenciennes. On D-Day, 20 November, the tanks were almost completely successful and the German front was breached to a depth of five miles. But Byng had failed to provide the necessary reserves to keep up the momentum of the attack, either fresh tanks, or men to support them. By 28 November not even the observation points had been taken, let alone Cambrai, and on the 30th the Germans launched a powerful counter-attack. Much of the ground gained was retaken as the battle petered out in the first week of December.

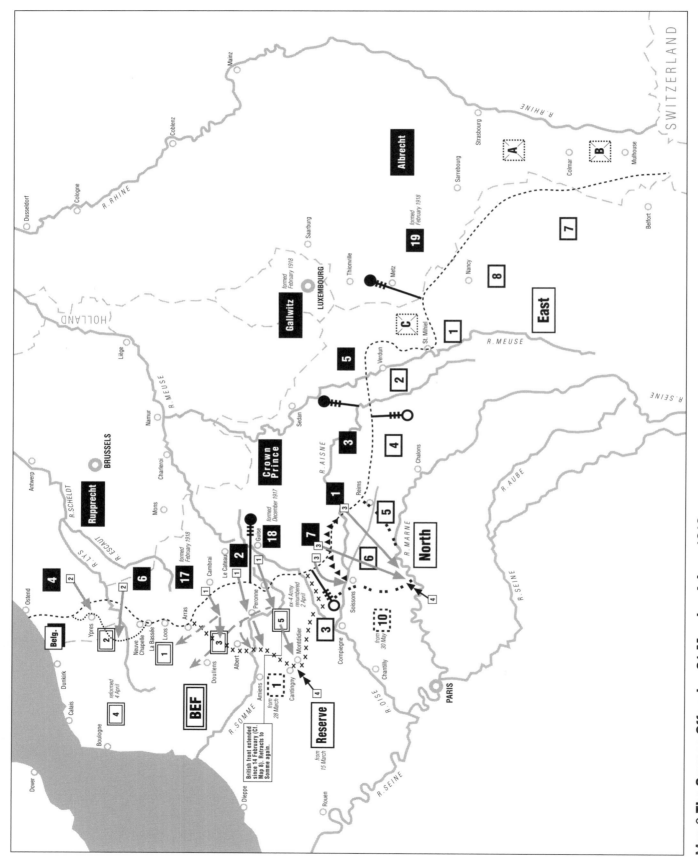

Map 9 **The German Offensive 21 March – 4 June 1918**

## KEY

| | |
|---|---|
| ▮ | German Army Groups |
| ▯ | Allied Army Groups |
| ◲ | |
| ●▬ | German Army Group boundary |
| ○▬ | Allied Army Group boundary |
| **1** | German Armies 21 March |
| 1  ⌐1⌐ | French Armies 21 March and on date stated |
| 1  Belg. | British and Belgian Armies |
| ⌐A⌐ | German Army Detachments 'A', 'B', and 'C' |
| ◄ | German advances |
| ◄ --- | Proposed German axis of advance 21 March |
| ➤➤ | US advances |
| 1 | See number in Notes |
| ---------- | Front line 21 March |
| × × × × × | Front line 4 April |
| ............. | Front line 30 April |
| ▪▪ ▪▪ ▪▪ ▪▪ | Front line 4 June |
| ▲▲▲▲▲▲ | Chemin des Dames Ridge |

## NOTES TO MAP 9

**1** By the last weeks of 1917 even Haig was beginning to have doubts about the efficacy of prolonged offensive operations and in early 1918 both he and Pétain began to establish the same elaborate defensive networks in depth that characterised German trench lines. Ironically, however, the Germans themselves, notably the joint commander-in-chief Ludendorff, had reluctantly concluded that Germany's best chance for an honourable peace lay in quickly establishing a position of strength from which to initiate negotiations. This could only be achieved by large-scale offensive operations that forced the Allies back, and in divergent directions.

Ludendorff chose as his main axis of advance to move south-west towards the Somme, before hooking north-west to roll up the British line. German Eighteenth Army was to maintain a defensive left flank on the Somme. This attack jumped off on 21 March and by the 25th had already taken the intermediate objectives of Péronne and Bapaume. On the 26th German troops marched into Albert. Yet Ludendorff had already made a fateful decision that was to vitiate his whole offensive. British Fifth Army had in fact collapsed so completely that instead of concentrating his operations north of the Somme and sealing his southern flank, Ludendorff made the Eighteenth Army front his main axis and allowed these troops to be drawn into a strategic vacuum. In theory, of course, they threatened Paris but the Germans were simply not logistically prepared for such a major thrust, especially after having had to traverse the war-torn Somme battlefields. By 4 April their attacks had simply run out of steam. Moreover, the Allies had bolstered their own resolve by sacking the commander of Fifth Army, naming Foch as Supreme Allied Commander-in Chief, and transferring many French units from the Meuse.

**2** Belatedly realising that his push south of the Somme was minimising the pressure on British Third Army, Ludendorff launched a subsidiary attack in Flanders. This began on 9 April but despite early successes up to the 15th, the British were already fashioning much more adroit counter-measures than on the Somme. Even on the 12th German attacks were waning and on the 17th they suffered severe reverses. Ypres, into which many British troops had retreated, held firm and by the 30th this offensive, too, had run out of steam.

**3** On 30 April the German Supreme Command decided to launch a large diversionary attack against the French, along the Chemin des Dames ridge, to draw Allied reserves away from Flanders. Once this was accomplished Rupprecht's Army Group was to deliver his *coup de grâce* against the BEF. The assault divisions began concentrating on 15 May and finally jumped off on the 27th. Early advances were spectacular, with 13 miles being gained in the first 24 hours, the biggest advance since 1914. Soissons fell on the 28th, putting the Germans well beyond their objective line along the Vesle. Once again Ludendorff was unable to resist the opportunity offered and he urged his troops forward so that by 3 June they had drawn up to the Marne in strength. But once again he had completely overtaxed his armies' logistical resources and on the very next day the offensive had to be halted.

**4** An omen for the future were two attacks by recently arrived US divisions, both at the tip of two of the biggest German salients. One was by 1 US Division at Catigny, on 28 May, and the other by 2 US Division at Belleau Wood, on 2 June.

*German Codenames during the 1918 Offensives*
Attacks beginning 21 March codenamed MICHAEL
Attacks beginning 9 April codenamed GEORGETTE
Attacks beginning 27 May codenamed BLÜCHER-YORCK

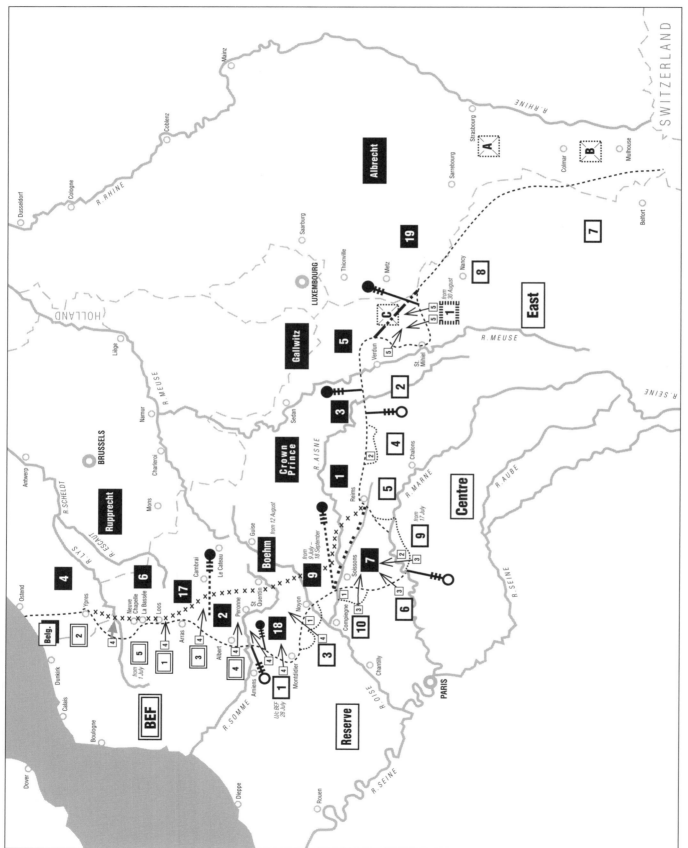

Map 10 **Western Front: The Allied Counter-Offensive: the Reduction of the Salients 15 July – 25 September 1918**

## KEY

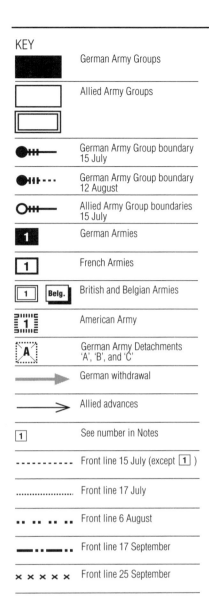

| | |
|---|---|
| | German Army Groups |
| | Allied Army Groups |
| | |
| | German Army Group boundary 15 July |
| | German Army Group boundary 12 August |
| | Allied Army Group boundaries 15 July |
| **1** | German Armies |
| 1 | French Armies |
| 1 Belg. | British and Belgian Armies |
| 1 | American Army |
| A | German Army Detachments 'A', 'B', and 'C' |
| | German withdrawal |
| | Allied advances |
| 1 | See number in Notes |
| - - - - - - - - | Front line 15 July (except 1 ) |
| ............. | Front line 17 July |
| ▪▪ ▪▪ ▪▪ ▪▪ | Front line 6 August |
| ▬▪▪▬▪▪ | Front line 17 September |
| × × × × × | Front line 25 September |

## NOTES TO MAP 10

**1** An important feature of Ludendorff's newly expanded Aisne salient was the railway running through Soissons and along the salient's western edge. In an effort to fully control this line, the Germans launched yet another offensive, to reach a line Compiègne-Montdidier, between 9 and 12 June. Progress was disappointing, however. Eighteenth Army's effort had been stymied by French counter-attacks on the 11th and by the 13th the whole effort was abandoned.

**2** Ludendorff next tried on either side of Reims, aiming to consolidate a line Chateau Thierry-Chalons. The threat to this heavily-fortified French sector would hopefully draw in reserves from Flanders and so facilitate Ludendorff's long-cherished *coup de grâce* against the BEF. This latter operation was already being planned in detail by Rupprecht's staff and was timed to begin in early August. But the effort in Champagne, east of Reims, was most disappointing, with assault troops jumping off on 15 July but losing all momentum as early as 11 o'clock that morning. West of Reims the Germans did manage to force the Marne in some strength but the French began to rally the next day and by the 17th were masters of the situation.

**3** Nor were the French simply content to contain the Germans. Railways had also been prominent in Foch's thoughts and his plans for future operations centred around three railway supply axes: the Marne portion of the Paris-Verdun line, the Paris-Amiens line, and that part of the Paris-Nancy line running through the St Mihiel salient. These plans were not formally endorsed by the Allies until 24 July but the first of the attacks, against the Aisne-Marne salient, was already underway by the 18th, a date Foch had resolutely refused to alter even when pre-empted by the Germans' own attack on the Marne. The main effort was by French Tenth Army, pitted against inferior static units, and German positions soon became untenable. On the 19th they pulled back across the Marne and soon abandoned the Reims offensive entirely. On the 20th, Ludendorff bit the bullet and cancelled the planned Flanders offensive, whilst also allowing Seventh Army to begin an organised withdrawal behind the Vesle. This took until 6 August, with French troops reoccupying Soissons on the 2nd.

**4** By now the Allies were fully committed to full-scale offensive operations and on 8 August, dubbed by Ludendorff 'the Black Day of the German Army', they unleashed probably the most decisive offensive of all. On the first day Fourth British and First French Armies attacked south of Albert. The town itself did not fall until the 22nd but so substantial were British gains elsewhere on their front that, on the 10th, Haig had his troops pause to regroup. French Third Army then took up the running, to the south, before halting to await a

renewed Allied offensive, beginning on the 21st, when it and British Third Army took the lead. On the 22nd, British Fourth Army joined in once more, along with French First Army and, from the 26th, British First Army. On the 26th, in fact, the Germans began a ten-mile withdrawal to a line Noyon-Lens and on 13 September a further 13-mile withdrawal was sanctioned. In Flanders, moreover, the evacuation of the Lys salient had been under way since 29 August. On this same day Noyon and Bapaume were occupied, with Peronne falling for the last time on 2 September

By now the Germans had been pushed back almost to their spring start lines along the Siegfried Line. From 2 September, repeated attacks between Arras and Soissons kept the Germans off-balance, with their troops showing an increasing disinclination to defend the vital outpost lines in front of the main defences and thus finding themselves unable to significantly blunt the momentum of the British attacks against these *Stellungs*. First to fall was part of the Wotan Line, covering Douai, which was breached by British First and Third Armies whilst in the south French Tenth Army nibbled away at the defences on the St Gobain massif, north of Soissons and east of Noyon. In the centre, on 18 September, British Third and Fourth and French First Armies thrust forward between Cambrai and St. Quentin, and by the 24th were on the very fringes of the Siegfried Line proper. Gruelling as this fighting was, the daily advances of the Allies made the Western Front of 1914-17 look like another war.

**5** But Foch was not done with salient-busting. On 12 September, whilst the advance to the Siegfried Line was gathering pace, newly formed US First Army, with some French colonial troops under command, hit the St Mihiel salient from north and south, just as the Germans were preparing to withdraw. The two thrusts met on the 13th, but from the 17th the new front across the base of the salient began to congeal. Nevertheless, the fact that Ludendorff had been prepared to voluntarily give up this salient, even without an Allied attack, was a measure of German manpower problems. Not only did it cover vital steel-making plants north-west of Metz as well as the Saar coalfields, but it also offered excellent artillery positions from which to disrupt French movements west of the Meuse.

*German Codenames during the 1918 Offensives*
Attacks beginning 9 June codenamed GNEISENAU
Attacks beginning 15 July codenamed MARNE-RHEIMS

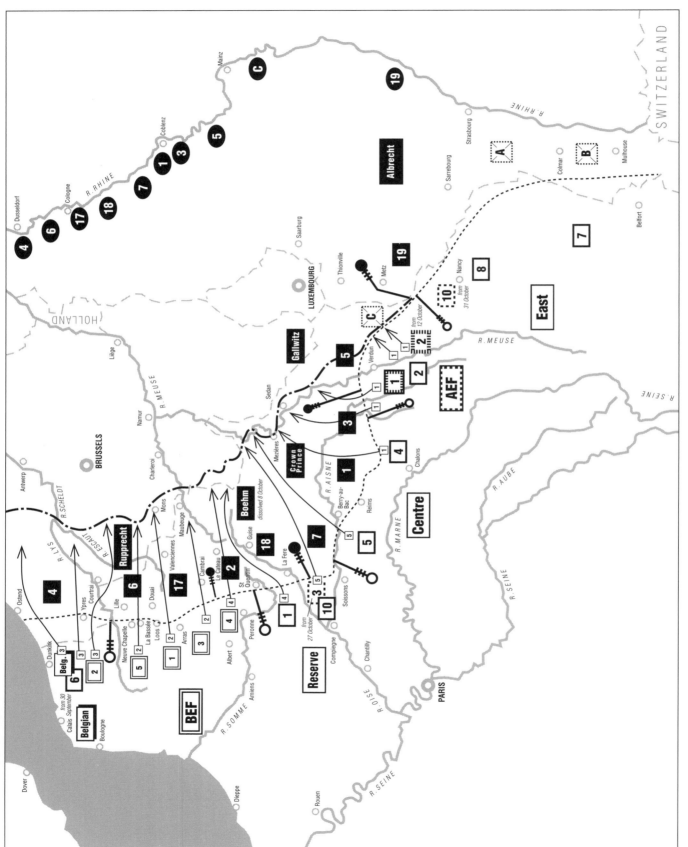

Map 11 Western Front: The Allied Counter-Offensive: Advance to Armistice 26 September – 11 November 1918

• **MAP 11** • WESTERN FRONT •

KEY

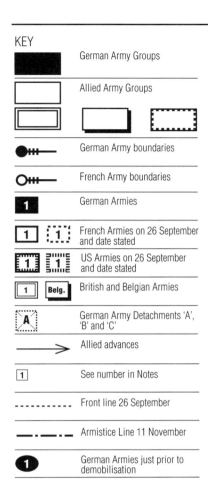

German Army Groups

Allied Army Groups

German Army boundaries

French Army boundaries

German Armies

French Armies on 26 September and date stated

US Armies on 26 September and date stated

British and Belgian Armies

German Army Detachments 'A', 'B' and 'C'

Allied advances

See number in Notes

Front line 26 September

Armistice Line 11 November

German Armies just prior to demobilisation

## NOTES TO MAP 11

**1** With the main defence of the Siegfried Line still in front of his northern and central armies, Foch reactivated plans for a French flanking offensive in Lorraine. It was to begin on 14 November and in late October the experienced Tenth Army HQ was moved south-east to spearhead operations. But this is not to say that the rest of the front was to remain quiescent, especially as the north-south railways by which the Germans might withdraw from Lorraine, or be reinforced, lay within reasonable striking distance of much of the new front line.

Thus, prior to the one in Lorraine, fully four preparatory offensives were envisaged – between the Argonne and the Meuse by the Americans and the French; between the Lys and Cambrai by the BEF; in Flanders by an Allied army group under King Albert; and on each side of the Somme by the French and the British. The French-American offensive began on 26 September with the latter finding it slow going until replaced by veterans from the St Mihiel salient, on 4 October. By the 18th the Americans had broken through the last significant German defences, the Kriemhilde Line, which permitted the French to pull up alongside and along the Aisne. On 1 November, the offensive was renewed, taking the French across the Aisne on the 2nd, the Americans to the outskirts of Sedan on the 6th, and the French just south of Mezières on the 10th.

**2** The River Lys-Cambrai attack jumped off on 27 September, with Fifth Army joining in on the 29th. By 5 October the Siegfried Line had been decisively breached, with Cambrai falling on the 9th. But even before this, on the 8th, both Boehm and Rupprecht's army groups had been ordered to fall back to the Hermann Line. On the 20th, this, too, was breached and on 4 November the British launched major attacks towards the Sambre. The Germans pulled back once more. By the 9th the British were in Mauberge and on the following day had advance parties in Mons.

**3** The Flanders offensive began on 28 September. The Belgians took Ostend on 17 October and by the 20th had cleared the whole of the Belgian coast. The French were temporarily baulked at Ypres, early in October, but on the 15th British Second Army crossed the Lys to take Courtrai and on the 31st reached the Escaut. Belgian troops were now pressing inland and by 10 November had reoccupied Ghent.

**4** Along the Somme, St Quentin did not fall until 20 October but attacks to the north and south had taken Le Cateau on the 10th, La Fère on the 13th, and Guise on the 29th. By this time, though, British Fourth Army was coordinating its efforts with its northern neighbours in the Battle of the Selle (not shown) and the Sambre.

**5** The Aisne front was not entirely quiescent. French Fifth Army had attacked on 30 September and on 5 October, because British successes to the north had forced a German withdrawal there, the latters' First, Third and Seventh Armies also began to fall back to the Hunding-Brunhild position. On the 7th, the French took Berry-au-Bac and by 10 November were in Mezières. French Tenth Army (later Third Army) launched its big attack on 8 October, taking Laon on the 13th and bursting through the Hunding Line on the 18th.

Post-Armistice

The Armistice, signed on 11 November, required that the German armies pull back to the Rhine within the next 14 days. This withdrawal began on 16 November and by the 18th the last German soldier had quit France, had done likewise in Luxembourg by the 22nd, and in Belgium by the 26th. The Allies began to move into their occupation zones around Cologne (British), Koblenz (US) and Mainz (French) on the 6th, 8th and 11th December respectively.

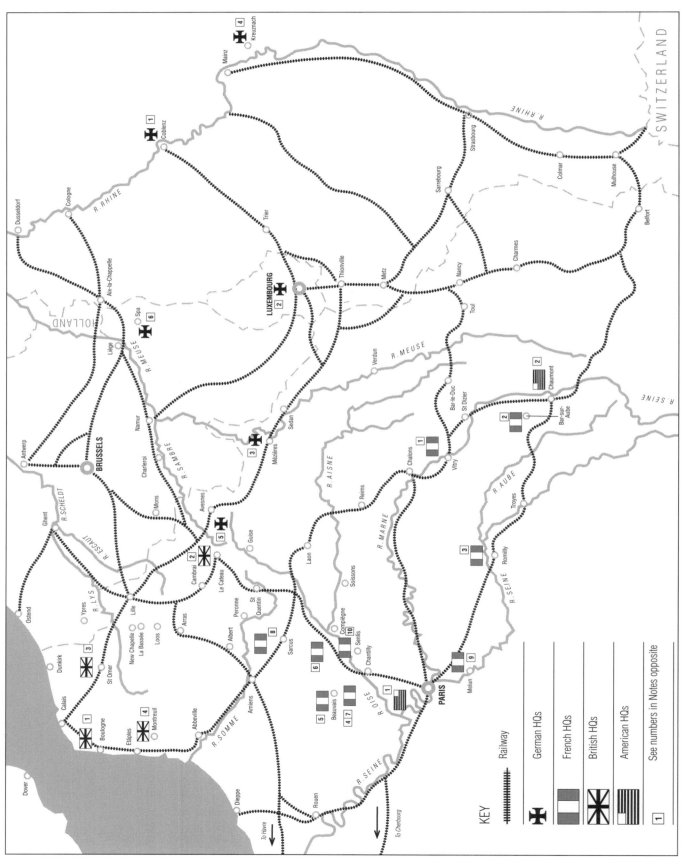

Map 12 Western Front (Supplementary): Main Railways, between the Seine and the Rhine, and Main German and Allied HQs 1914 – 1918

• **MAP 12** • WESTERN FRONT (SUPPLEMENTARY) •

## NOTES TO MAP 12

### French Headquarters

[1] *Grand Quartier Generale* (GQG) at Vitry-le-Francois to 1/9/14.

[2] GQG at Bar-sur-Aube to ?

[3] GQG at Romilly-sur-Seine to ?/11/14.

[4] GQG at Chantilly to 6/1/17.

[5] GQG at Beauvais to 3/4/17.

[6] GQG at Compiègne to ?/3/18. Then returns to Chantilly.

[7] From early April 1918, however, overall command of the French (and Allied) armies passes to the headquarters of the French Chief-of-Staff, Foch, now named as Allied generalissimo. His headquarters at Sarcus from 7/4/18 to 5/6/18.

[8] Foch's HQ at Château Bombon (near Melun) to 18/10/18.

[9] Foch's HQ at Senlis.

### British Headquarters

[1] GHQ British Expeditionary Force landed at Boulogne and remained there until 15/8/14.

[2] GHQ moved to Le Cateau and was thereafter almost continuously on the move, occupying a further twelve locations until settling at St Omer on 8/10/14.

[3] GHQ at St Omer to 20/3/16.

[4] GHQ at Montreuil to Armistice. (It should be noted, however, that Haig often resided with an Advanced GHQ, usually on a special train, which stayed at two other locations in 1915, one in 1916, three in 1917 and seven in 1918.

### American Headquarters

[1] GHQ American Expeditionary Force at Paris from 13/6/17 to 31/8/17.

[2] GHQ at Chaumont-en-Bassigny to Armistice.

### German Headquarters

[1] Kaiser's *Grosse Hauptquartier* (GHQ) and the *Oberste Heeresleitung* (OHL) at Coblenz 7-30/8/14.

[2] GHQ and OHL at Luxembourg to 24/9/14.

[3] GHQ and OHL in Mézières to 19/9/16 but Chief-of-Staff, Chief of Operations and Kaiser, along with some staff officers, in the East (Pless) from 9/5/15 to 15/2/16 and 16/8-19/9/16. From this latter date GHQ and OHL were formally stationed at Pless but Mezières still functioned as the Western Front HQ (although no overall C-in-C. West was appointed). GHQ and OHL remain at Pless to 10/2/17.

[4] GHQ and OHL at Kreuznach from 17/2/17 to 7/3/18.

[5] OHL only in Avesnes to 7/9/18.

[6] GHQ in Spa 8/3-18/11/18 and joined by OHL 8/9/18.

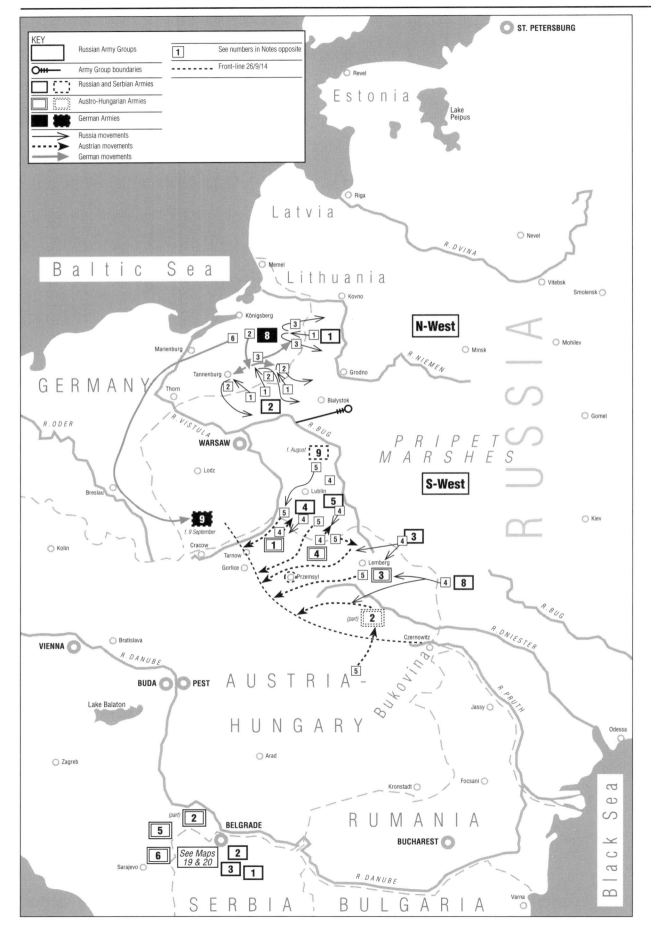

• **MAP 13** • EASTERN FRONT •

## Map 13 **Eastern Front: East Prussia and Galicia 13 August–26 September 1914**

### NOTES TO MAP 13

**1** On 13 August, Russian First and Second Armies advanced into East Prussia with the intention of attacking German Eighth Army and using their own Second Army to cut off its retreat. Things began promisingly and the Germans were worsted at Gumbinnen on 20 August.

**2** The Germans then decided to disengage on this front and concentrate their main forces against Russian Second Army. By 26 August this concentration was complete, whereas the Russians had become dispersed in their efforts to catch up with the 'retreating' Germans. By the 31st, at the Battle of Tannenberg, Second Army had been destroyed in detail.

**3** The Germans then immediately marched against Russian First Army, launching their main attack on 5 September. At the ensuing Battle of the Masurian Lakes the Russians just managed to avoid encirclement through a well-timed counter-attack, but the whole army was nevertheless obliged to retreat back over the frontier, which was accomplished by 13 September.

**4** The other main front in the east was in Galicia, where four Russian armies faced three Austro-Hungarian. Both sides advanced immediately war was declared, the main Russian effort being towards Lemburg and the main Austrian northwards, towards Lublin. At first the Austrians had the best of it, defeating the Russian Fourth Army at Krasnick (23–25 August) and Komarow (26 August–1 September). On the Lemberg front, however, Austrian Third Army was decisively defeated by two Russian armies at the Battle of Gnila Lipa (26–30 August).

**5** At the beginning of September, Austrian Fourth Army, thinking that the Russians in the Lemberg front were in retreat, turned south to face the advancing Russian Third Army which threatened its rear. An indecisive engagement took place at Rawa Ruska (8–10 September) but then Russian Fifth Army also began to advance, posing a new threat to the Austrian rear. But this was just one in a series of Austrian setbacks. By 6 September part of their Second Army, marching up from the Serbian Front (see Map 19), had been repulsed by Russian Eighth Army, whilst at the other end of the front their First Army was driven back by the newly-formed Russian Ninth Army, which had begun its advance on 6 September. Austrian Third and Fourth Armies were now threatened with encirclement and on the 11th the whole Austrian front began to pull back, not halting until the 26th when it reached the Carpathian passes and the River Dunajec, to the east of Cracow.

**6** Between 17 and 27 September important elements of the German forces in East Prussia were redeployed, forming a new Ninth Army to march on Warsaw.

• **MAP 14** • EASTERN FRONT •

Map 14 **Eastern Front: German Advance on Warsaw 28 September–10 November 1914**

## NOTES TO MAP 14

**1** By 23 September the major portion of the Russian armies facing the Austrians had withdrawn to a line south-east of Tarnow (see map). On this day, however, in response to urgent appeals from the French, they began redeploying to a start line behind the Vistula, south of Warsaw, prior to an attack into Silesia that would hopefully draw in German divisions from the Western Front. As the redeployment began, however, German and Austrian forces, coordinated by Hindenburg, began an advance of their own whose main axis was that of German Ninth Army, itself now secretly redeployed (see Map 13), and of Austrian First Army, towards Warsaw. On 28 September the whole Austro-German front began to advance and by 12 October Ninth Army was only 12 miles from Warsaw.

**2** To counter this threat the Russians moved their First and Second Armies to the Warsaw area and by mid-October they were exerting telling pressure on the Germans' northern flank. The Germans, moreover, were encountering growing problems in maintaining liaison with the Austrians. On the 17th, therefore, despite having almost perfect radio intelligence of Russian intentions, Hindenburg decided to withdraw and by 1 November the Central Powers forces were all back to their start lines, with the Russians following close in their wake.

**3** Knowing that the Russians were still keen to begin their aborted offensive into Silesia, Hindenburg redeployed Ninth Army south of Thorn, between 4–10 November, so that it would be able to strike the Russian advance in the flank.

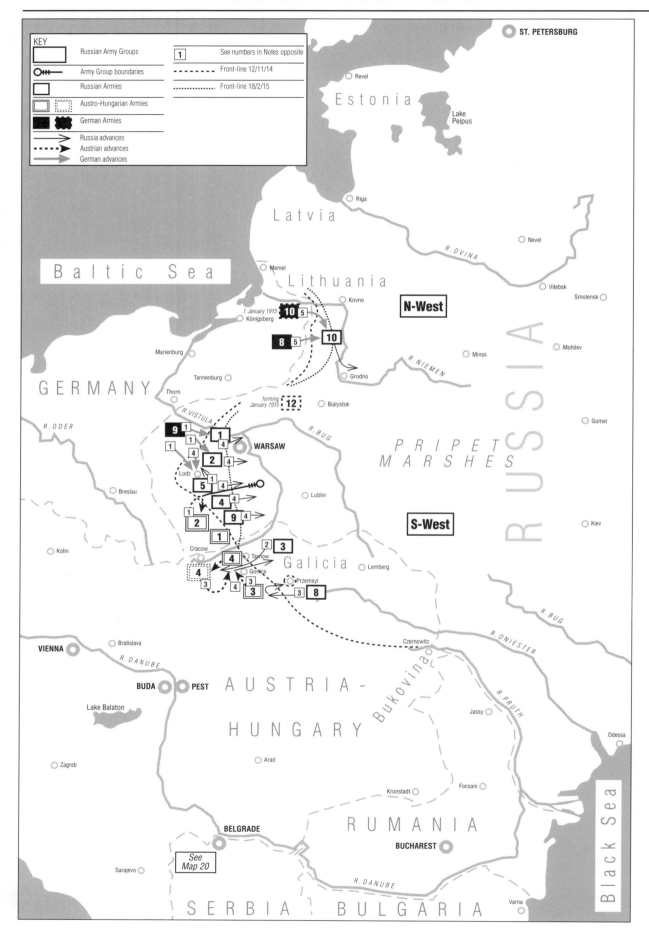

• **MAP 15** • EASTERN FRONT •

Map 15 **Eastern Front: Russians Defeated at Lodz and Limanowa 11 November 1914–18 February 1915**

**NOTES TO MAP 15**

**1** On 11 November, the regrouped German Ninth Army began its offensive against Russian First and Second Armies. The Germans were very soon pressing towards Lodz and Warsaw and only the timely intervention of Russian Fifth Army, rushing northwards from 17 November, prevented Second Army being surrounded in front of Lodz. By the 23rd Lodz was saved and the German spearheads pushed back, but German reinforcements hurried over from the Western Front did manage to force the Russians back to the River Bzura-Ravka, just to the west of Warsaw. These attacks had been supported in the south by Austrian Second Army, which had recently moved up from the Carpathians, but its attacks met with little success. On the whole, however, the Germans had achieved a significant strategic victory in forcing the Russians to abandon their Silesian offensive, which was never renewed.

**2** On 1 December, the Russians launched an offensive along their original Galician axis, south of Cracow (see Map 13), and pushed back Austrian Fourth Army.

**3** This drive was assisted by the transfer westwards of two corps from Eighth Army, but despite the threat this presented the Austrians were able to assemble forces for an attack on the southern flank of Russian Third Army, in the Battle of Limanowa which began on 1 December.

**4** This attack was not sufficient in itself to force the Russians back, but when the Germans renewed their own drive against Lodz the Russian front began to waver. Lodz was evacuated on the 6th December and from the 15th the Russian armies in Poland began pulling back to a new line west of the Vistula. This in turn obliged Russian Third Army to withdraw its increasingly isolated units back to their start lines.

**5** Early in 1915 the German command in the East, against the advice of the Chief-of-Staff, Falkenhayn, resolved to attempt a major encirclement offensive in Galicia and East Prussia. This opened on 7 February but the supporting attacks by Austrian Third and Fourth Armies (not shown) were a dismal failure. The Germans' own effort in East Prussia, the Battle of Masuria, was much better organised, with a frontal pinning attack by Eighth Army being coordinated with a flanking attack by newly-formed Tenth Army, whose existence was unknown to the Russians. Heroic resistance by a single Russian corps in the Forest of Augustow allowed the other three corps to escape and all German attempts to achieve a breakthrough with their northern pincer failed. For the moment the Germans had to be content with having created a deep salient in the northern end of the Russian front.

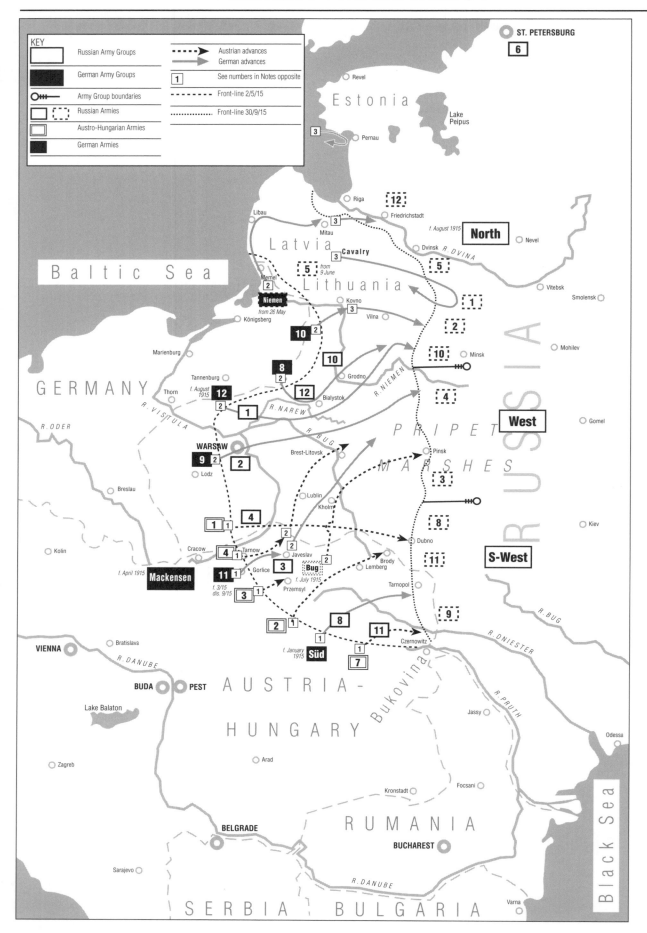

• **MAP 16** • EASTERN FRONT •

## Map 16 **Eastern Front: The Russians lose Galicia, Poland and Courland 2 May–30 September 1915**

### NOTES TO MAP 16

**1** By spring 1915 the Germans were becoming increasingly fearful about Italian intervention in the was as their forces would be almost entirely directed against the Austrians. The latter's abject performance in Galicia, in February, heightened German fears and they resolved to take the offensive again, seeking a decisive victory that would deter the Italians. To improve Austrian capabilities the Germans inserted some of their own formations into the line. The attack opened on 2 May and by the next day Mackensen, commanding German Eleventh and Austrian Fourth Armies, had torn a ten-mile gap in the Russian front between Tarnow and Gorlice. Tarnow itself fell on 6 May and Jaroslav on the 16th. Further south the Austrians were able to take advantage of Mackensen's successes and throughout the summer advanced steadily across the Dniester and the Bug, taking Przemsyl (which had fallen to the Russians in March) on 3 June, Lemberg (Lvov) on 22 June, Brody on 1 September and Dubno on the 7th.

**2** The Russian retreat in Galicia soon exposed a deep salient in Poland, increasingly vulnerable to German encirclement. Hindenburg, and his Chief-of-Staff Ludendorff, pressed for a strategic encirclement closing in from Vilna in the north and Tarnopol in the south. But Falkenhayn, supported by the Kaiser, decided in early July on a more limited effort in Poland itself, linking up at Brest-Litovsk. Fourth, Eleventh and Bug Armies had already begun to turn north in early July and on the 13th, Ninth and Twelfth attacked towards Warsaw. Twelfth Army was first across the Narew on the 25th, by which time the Russians had already decided to evacuate the Polish capital. It was entered by German Ninth Army on 5 August. By this time the Austro-German drive from the south, between the Bug and the Vistula, had taken Lublin and Kholm (30-31 July). By mid-August the two Austro-German pincers had joined near Brest-Litovsk and the city itself was taken on the 25th. Bug Army went on to take Pinsk on 16 September but the Russians, despite heavy casualties, had once again managed to elude a strategic encirclement. North of the Bug, Twelfth, Eighth and Tenth German Armies pressed on eastwards, taking Kovno, Bialystok and Grodno between 17 August and 2 September. In the far north, from 15 July, Niemen Army advanced up the coast to Libau, taken a few days later, and then turned eastwards towards Mitau and Riga. The former fell on 1 August but the drive to Riga then stalled, with an attempted supporting landing at Pernau, on 17 August, being an ignominious failure.

**3** Despite the failure at Pernau, the Niemen Army's advance towards Dvinsk and the River Drina continued, with Kovno falling on 17 August. The main body finally halted in early September but a substantial cavalry force probed forward around the enemy's rear in the direction of Minsk. These horsemen were meant to form the northern pincer of yet another attempted encirclement, the southern arm being provided by Hindenburg's long-cherished thrust through Vilna. Progress here was very slow, however, with Vilna not falling until 18 September, and when the cavalry were repulsed south of Dvinsk, the Russians were once more able to extricate the major part of the threatened force, this time Fifth and Tenth Armies. By the end of September the whole eastern front had congealed.

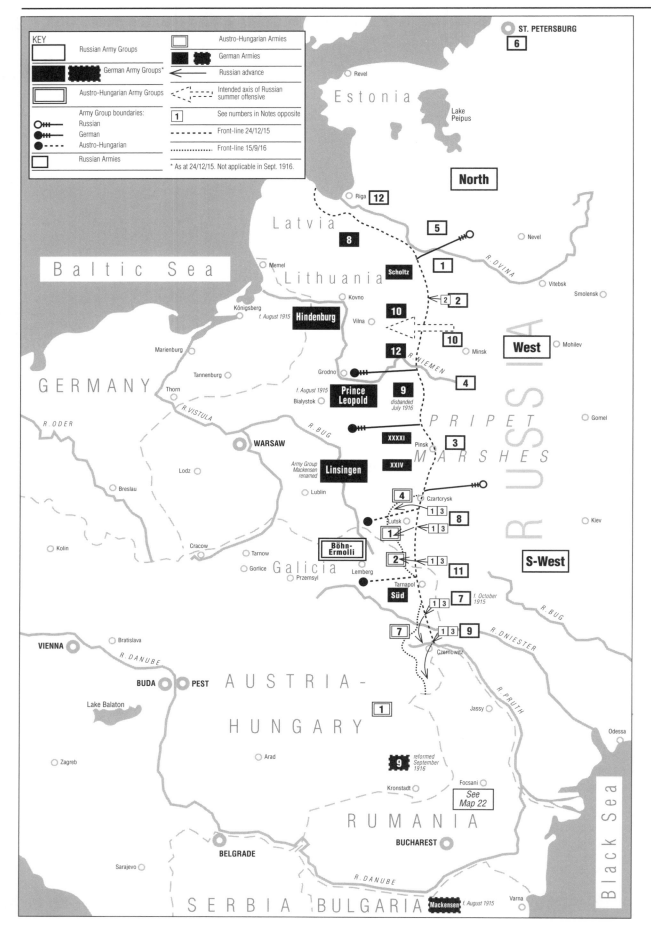

• MAP 17 • EASTERN FRONT •

## Map 17 **Eastern Front: The Russian Diversions: the Ivanov Offensive, Lake Narotch and the Brusilov Offensive 24 December 1915–15 September 1916**
### NOTES TO MAP 17

1 Despite the stalemate in the east in autumn 1915, the Russians remained responsive to the requests of their allies. By early winter the situation in the Balkans had become critical, with the Rumanians seemingly about to throw in their lot with the Central Powers, and with the latter concentrating forces against the Allied landing at Salonika (see Map 22). On Christmas Eve, therefore, South-West Front, under Ivanov, launched a full-scale diversionary offensive between Czartorysk and Czernowitz. In the north Czartorysk was taken but the main push against Czernowitz was halted almost at the gates of the city whilst Seventh Army's enveloping attack across the Dniester failed to secure any viable crossing points. Heavy snow began to fall and on 15 January the offensive ground to a halt. Nevertheless, it had obliged the Germans to buttress their Austrian allies with five divisions brought up from the Balkans.

2 Despite the disappointing results of this offensive, the Russians pressed ahead with plans for a major offensive to coincide with French and British operations on the Western Front in summer 1916. The main Russian effort was to be made by West Front in a drive on Vilna but when the French began to come under heavy pressure at Verdun, from February (see Map 6), the Russians again laid in a diversionary offensive. West Front was still the chosen instrument but only one of its armies, Second, was to be used, in a two-pronged attack around Lake Narotch. It jumped off on 17 March but, sadly, the preliminary two-day bombardment had only served to aggravate the effects of the spring thaw and by the 24th the Russians had been halted. Little ground had been gained and casualties had been five times heavier than those of the Germans.

3 Preparations for the full-scale summer offensive continued but in May the Russians were once again asked to jump the gun to relieve pressure on another part of the Allies front. The threat this time was on the Trentino front in Italy (see Map 25) but in the east only Brusilov's South-West Front was able to contemplate an immediate attack. He attacked on 4 June and thanks to his insistence on all his armies making simultaneous attacks, backed by scrupulously planned artillery bombardments, significant breakthroughs were soon made.

By the 7th, Lutsk had been taken whilst to the south an aggressive drive between the Pruth and the Dniester swept over most of the Bukovina region, taking Czernowitz on the 17th. By the end of the month many units had advanced up to sixty miles beyond their start lines and had taken over 350,000 prisoners. The Central Powers were forced to divert 7 1/2 divisions from the Italian and Western Fronts and five from Hindenburg's Army Group. But this was the highwater mark of Brusilov's effort. Casualties on both sides had been heavy and the Russians were badly outclassed in their ability to bring up replacements. By July the retreat of German Süd Army slowed to a measured withdrawal and over the next weeks the whole front began to stabilise. But the Russian High Command, understandably elated by the initial successes, refused to pause to consolidate. They stripped other Army Groups of men and equipment stockpiled for the summer offensive but only managed to worsen the traffic bottlenecks. Moreover, they were now funnelling troops into just the sector where the enemy were most prepared, rather than creating major diversions elsewhere on the eastern front to tie up his reserves. Desperate attacks in August and September were all repulsed at terrible cost and by the middle of September the front had congealed once more. The Russians had lost upwards of one million men and the elation of June was giving way to a profound crisis of morale that verged on open mutiny.

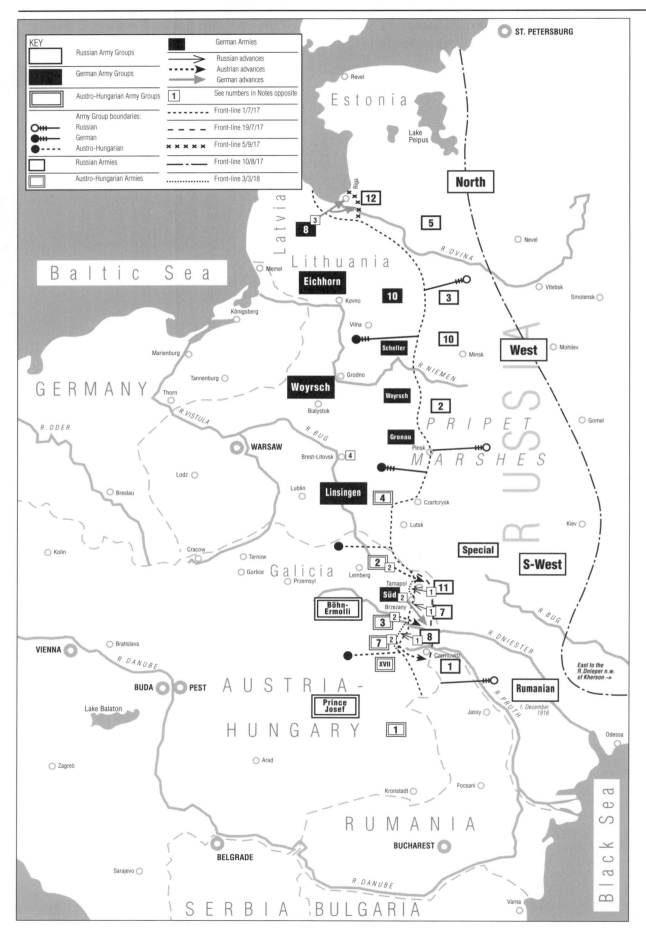

• **MAP 18** • EASTERN FRONT •

## Map 18 **Eastern Front: Russian collapse: the Kerensky Offensive, the loss of Riga and the Treaty of Brest-Litovsk July 1917– March 1918**
## NOTES TO MAP 18

1 The slow collapse of the Brusilov Offensive in August and September 1916 sounded the death knell of the Imperial Russian Army. By early 1917, its plummeting morale had affected even the Tsar's most loyal units and in March, after riots in Petrograd, he agreed to abdicate. The Petrograd Soviet, as usual acting in defiance of Prince Lvov's Provisional Government, issued an order stripping all officers of their disciplinary authority. Within a few weeks upwards of 50 per cent of the officer corps had been removed and mass rank-and-file desertions were an everyday occurrence. Germany immediately suspended offensive operations so as not to provoke any patriotic backlash but, remarkably, the Minister of War, Kerensky, did succeed in organising one last coordinated offensive. Brusilov's South-West Front was again the instrument and it jumped off on 1 July, making early headway against the Austrian Second, Third and Seventh Armies. On *Süd Armee's* front, however, Russian Seventh Army broke itself in head-on assaults on the fortified town of Brzezany.

2 A German counter-offensive on 19 July threw the Russians back all along the line, with Tarnopol falling on the 26th and Czernowitz on 1 August.

3 On 1 September, the Germans opened a new offensive in the north where Eighth Army pushed across the Dvina. Riga was surrounded and fell on the 5th, upon which Russian Twelfth Army largely disintegrated. This defeat sealed the fate of the Provisional Government and Kerensky fled to Moscow, leaving Petrograd at the mercy of Lenin and the Bolsheviks, who duly seized power in October.

4 They immediately opened peace negotiations with the Germans and signed a preliminary agreement in December, at Brest-Litovsk. Such was the military weakness of the new regime that when peace was concluded, in March 1918, the Germans were able to insist on a new demarcation line up to 250 miles further to the east.

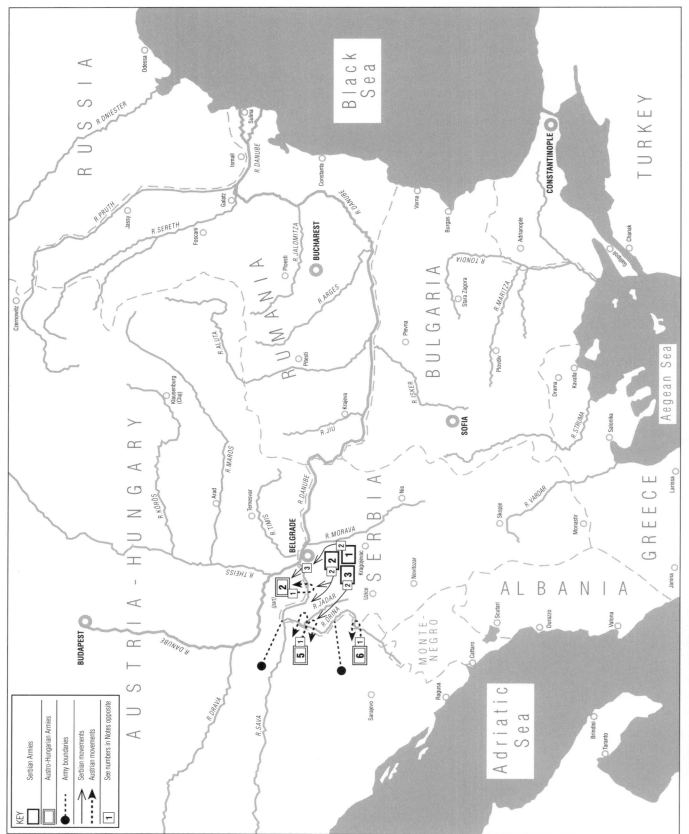

Map 19 **The Balkans: Austro-Hungarian Invasion of Serbia Repulsed 12 August–6 September 1914**

• **MAP 19** • THE BALKANS •

## NOTES TO MAP 19

**1** The Austro-Hungarian mobilisation plan, put into motion on 25 July, assumed a concentric attack on Serbia by three armies. However, when the offensive actually began, on 12 August, Second Army in the north had already been reassigned to operations against the Russians in Galicia. Of the remaining two armies, Sixth soon became bogged down in a war of detachments in the mountains and only Fifth was able to make any decisive advance, on either side of the River Jadar.

**2** The Serbians had kept their own three armies concentrated, away from the frontiers, until they could discern the main axis of Austrian advance. Once Austrian Fifth Army was recognised as the most threatening, the Serbs moved their Second and Third Armies against it and in the Battle of the Jadar, from 15–20 August, drove the Austrians back. Serbian First Army marched north to screen Belgrade.

**3** By 24 August all Austrian troops had withdrawn from Serbia and the latter's Chief-Of-Staff, Putnik, despatched First Army north across the Sava to try and foment unrest in Syrmia as a prelude to a general invasion of Bosnia.

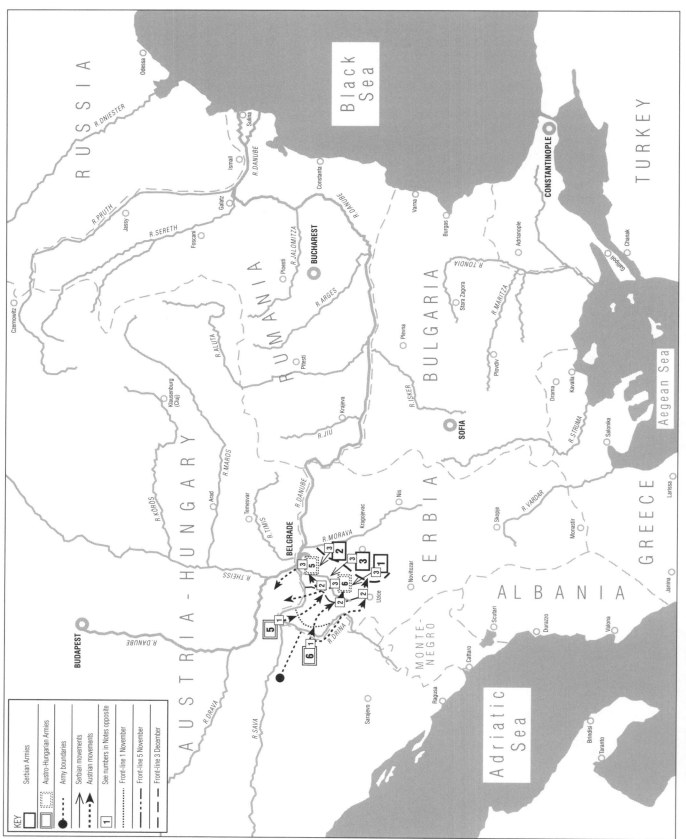

**Map 20 The Balkans: Second Austro-Hungarian Invasion of Serbia Repulsed 8 September–15 December 1914**

KEY

| | |
|---|---|
| | Serbian Armies |
| | Austro-Hungarian Armies |
| | Army boundaries |
| | Serbian movements |
| | Austrian movements |
| 1 | See numbers in Notes opposite |
| | Front-line 1 November |
| | Front-line 5 November |
| | Front-line 3 December |

• MAP 20 • THE BALKANS •

# NOTES TO MAP 20

**1** Stung by the incursion into Syrmia, the Austrians marched into Serbia once more on 8 September. The Serbs were forced to give up ground but after recalling First Army to the southern portion of their line on the 11th (movement not shown on map) were able to halt the Austrians by the 17th. The invaders persevered with increasingly costly attacks but were finally forced to give these up on the 28th. Operations were stalemated throughout October but on 1 November, battered by superior Austrian artillery, and fearful for their vulnerable right flank, the Serbs made a voluntary withdrawal to more defensible positions.

**2** On 5 November the Austrians sent Sixth Army forward in a renewed offensive. At first the Serbs tried to hold the enemy on the River Kolubara, reached on the 16th, but ammunition shortages obliged them to fall back. On 22 November the Austrians broke through south of the Kolubara and on the 25th crossed its lower reaches. By the end of the month the Serbs had been forced to pull their whole line south of Belgrade. The capital was evacuated and the Austrians marched in on 1 December.

**3** Their occupation was short-lived. On 3 December the Serbs, now being supplied with French ammunition brought in through Salonika, launched a counter-offensive. Thinking their enemy already defeated, the Austrians were taken completely by surprise. A decisive breakthrough was made by First Army in the south and on the 9th the Austrians ordered a general withdrawal. Their retreat remained fairly orderly but by 13 December the Serbs were on the lower reaches of the Drina. Two days later they reoccupied Belgrade and the last Austrian troops had once again been forced back across the frontier. But at a heavy cost: 70,000 Serbs had been killed or died of sickness and in the following weeks a typhus epidemic spread throughout the civilian population.

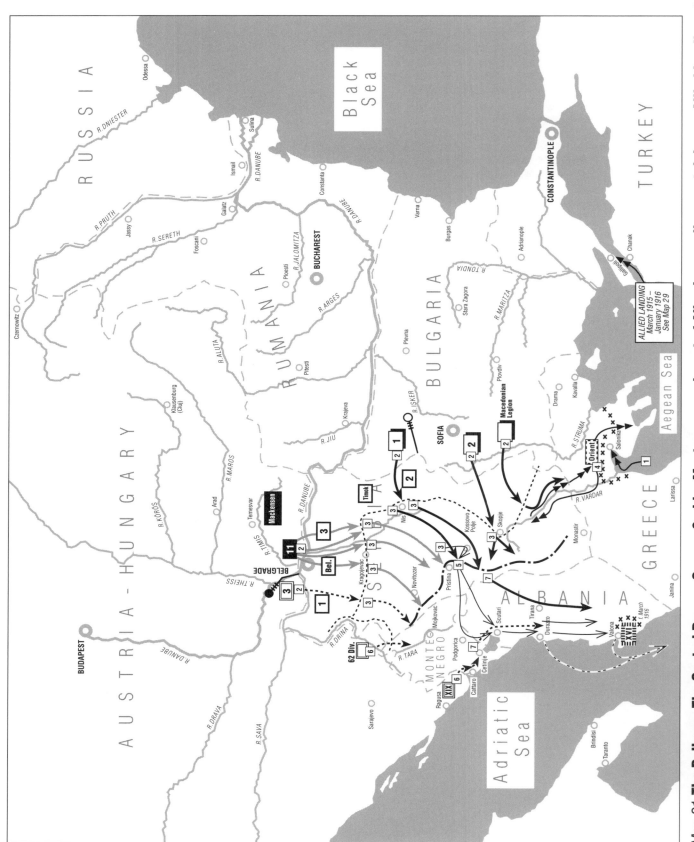

Map 21 **The Balkans: The Central Powers Occupy Serbia, Montenegro and most of Albania as well as containing an Allied Landing at Salonika 7 October 1915–March 1916**

• **MAP 21** • THE BALKANS •

## KEY

| | |
|---|---|
| ☐ | Serbian Armies |
| ▬ | German Army Groups |
| **1** | German Armies |
| ☐ | Austro-Hungarian Army |
| ☐ | Bulgarian Army |
| ⬚ | Franco-British Army |
| ⁞⁞⁞⁞ | Italian troops |
| ●⊪━ | Austro-Hungarian Army Boundary |
| ○⊪━ | German Army Group Boundary |
| ⟶ | Serbian movements |
| ⟶ | Central Powers movements |
| •••••▶ | |
| ━▶ | |
| ━▶▶ | Franco-British movements |
| - ·· --▷ | Serbian evacuation |
| 1 | See number in Notes |
| ·········· | Front line 1/11/15 |
| ━·━·━·━ | Front line 22/11/15 |
| × × × × × | Front line 1/3/16 |

## NOTES TO MAP 21

**1** In autumn 1915, the Austrians finally persuaded their German ally to help with a renewed invasion of Serbia. The Germans were keen to open up a rail link through the Balkans with the Turks, to provide much-needed munitions, and had also persuaded the Bulgarians to assist in a virtual encirclement of the Serbian forces. To this end First Bulgarian Army was under the direct control of Army Group Mackensen. The Allies had also tried to woo the Bulgarians and, learning of their rebuff, despatched forces to Salonika to protect the Serbian rear. This Army of the Orient came ashore on 3 October but was only made up of scratch divisions and was commanded by generals with little enthusiasm for their mission.

**2** Mackensen's own offensive was launched in two stages, the Germans and Austrians jumping off on 7 October and the main Bulgarian forces on the 14th. German Eleventh Army, operating down the relatively accessible Morava valley, was able to make the best progress, making ruthless use of a large artillery train that methodically blasted away Serb strong-points. However, progress on the Austrian and Bulgarian wings was nowhere near as good and although the Serbs were always in retreat in the centre, with Belgrade falling on 9 October and Kragujevac on 1 November, neither enemy on their flanks was able to get behind them to cut off their retreat.

**3** Nevertheless, by mid-November the Bulgarians had effectively cut the Serb's line of retreat through Skopje, by which they might have hoped to join up with the Allies at Salonika. An attempt to break through Bulgarian blocking positions at Kossovo Polje, between 19 and 24 November, failed and from the 21st the Serbs were already under orders to begin withdrawing into Albania. Pristina fell on the 23rd and by 4 December Central Powers forces had drawn up to the Albanian border where Mackensen ordered them to halt.

**4** Allied efforts to aid the Serbs had achieved little. A force was sent up the Vardar valley into Serbia, on 12 October, and this was halted by the Bulgarians on the 21st. A reinforced push north was begun on 3 November but this was pulled back as soon as it was realised that the Serb's eastern line of retreat had been cut. The Allies withdrew first to the Macedonian frontier and Lake Doiran and later, from 12 December, all the way back into the Salonika perimeter (up to 14 miles inland along an 80-mile perimeter).

**5** The Serbs, meanwhile, had been conducting an agonising retreat through the Montenegrin and Albanian mountains towards the coast. The main columns made for Scutari, reaching the coastal plain by mid-December. From 12 January 1916 most of these men were evacuated by the Allies to Corfu. This evacuation, mainly concentrated at Durazzo, was completed by 9 February, with some 75,000 Serbs being disembarked at Corfu. Between 11 April and 31 May, the 70,000 or so that had not died were transported to Salonika to join King Peter who had arrived there on New Year's Day.

**6** Although Allied with the Serbs, the Montenegrins had played little part during the three Austrian invasions. But their troops did play an important role during the final Serbian retreat. Based mainly around Mt. Lovcen, overlooking Cattaro, they provided a flank-guard against any Austrian attacks from Bosnia or along the Dalmatian Coast. A limited Austrian offensive from Bosnia was launched on 30 November but by Christmas this had stalled at the River Tara. On 8 January a more powerful offensive was launched and after only two days the supposedly impregnable Mount Lovcen defences were given up. The capital, Cetinje, fell on the 11th and the King fled to Italy. Retreating Montenegrin troops put a stout resistance on the Tara, especially at Mojkovac, but on 17 January the army capitulated.

**7** With the collapse of Montenegro the Austrians quickly moved into Albania. On 21 January they entered Scutari, though by then the Serb evacuation had already shifted to Durazzo and Valona. Similarly, the evacuation from Durazzo had been completed more than a fortnight before the Austrians marched into the port on 27 February. Northern Albania was then handed over to the Bulgarians but the Allies did retain a southern foothold around Valona where an Italian Corps was created in March.

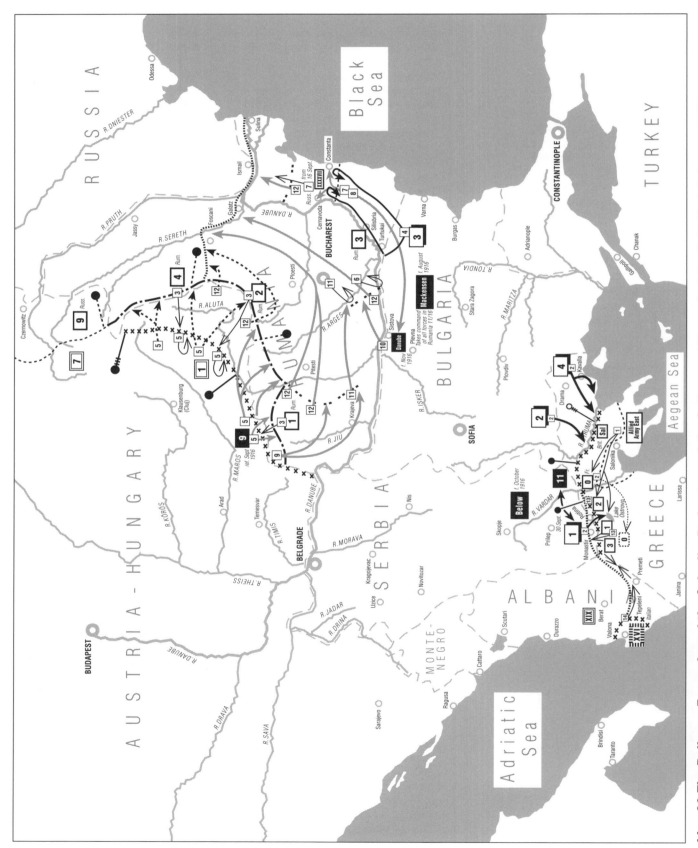

Map 22 **The Balkans: Expansion of the Salonika Perimeter and the Collapse of Rumania 1 April 1916–1 February 1917**

• **MAP 22** • THE BALKANS •

## KEY

| | |
|---|---|
| ▭ | Allied Army Groups |
| ▭1 | Allied Armies* |
| ▬ | German Army Groups |
| ▪1 | German Armies |
| ▯ | Austro-Hungarian Armies |
| ▱ | Bulgarian Armies |
| ⊟ | Italian troops |
| ●━ | German Army Boundary |
| ●╫ | Austro-Hungarian Army Boundary |
| ○╫ | Bulgarian Army Boundary |
| ●····· | Allied Army Boundary |
| ⟶ | Allied movements |
| ⟶ | Central Powers movements |
| ▪▪▪▪▶ | |
| ━━▶ | |
| 1 | See number in Notes |
| ---------- | Front line 1/4/16 |
| × × × × × | Front line Macedonia 17/8/16 Front line Rumania 18/9/16 |
| ━·━·━ | Front line 20/10/16 |
| ▪▪ ━ ▪▪ ━ ▪▪ | Front line 26/11/16 |
| ···············| Front line 18/2/17 |

\* 1, 2, and 3 Armies in Macedonia are Serbian.
*Abbreviations:*
O = Army of the Orient
Sal = Salonika Army

## NOTES TO MAP 22

**1** In April the Allies began cautiously expanding the Salonika perimeter and from mid-July were able to use the re-formed Serbian armies to help man the line. The Allied Commander, Sarrail, began planning an offensive up the Vardar valley, in August, but postponed this so that it would coincide with Rumania's expected entry into the war.

**2** However, the Bulgarians pre-empted the Allies by launching an offensive of their own at both ends of the Macedonian front, beginning on 17 August. In the east they merely marched into unoccupied Greek territory, but in the west they succeeded in pushing back the weak Serbian Third Army. But the Serbs rallied on the eastern side of Lake Ostrovo and by the 26th the Bulgarian offensive had petered out. To guard against future attacks a large part of the French Army of the Orient was moved over to this flank.

**3** Just as the Bulgarian attacks were faltering south of Monastir, Rumania finally declared war on the Central Powers and on 27 August launched an offensive into Transylvania with three of their four armies. This made good early progress, with advances of up to 50 miles, but in mid-September the attacks began to lose momentum.

**4** To make matters worse, the Rumanians were also under considerable pressure in the south where, on 1 September, Mackensen's Army Group had attacked into the Dobruja, the south-eastern portion of Rumania. Turtekai fell on the 6th and Silistria on the 9th as Rumanian Third Army fell back in disarray. Only the arrival of a Russian Corps allowed the creation of a firm defensive line just south of Constanta.

**5** But success in the south was more than offset by disasters in Transylvania. Here German Ninth Army had come into the line and on 18 September it went on to the offensive against Rumanian First Army. By the 26th the Rumanians had begun pulling back over the border. On the 29th, Rumanian Second and Fourth Armies attempted diversionary counter-attacks but these were soon repulsed and when Second Army itself was counter-attacked on 4 October, it too began to fall back. Fourth Army was soon obliged to follow suit to maintain any kind of cohesive front.

**6** On 1 October, Rumanian Third Army attempted a diversionary assault crossing of the Danube but sudden floods prevented all but a handful of units reaching the far bank.

**7** On 20 October, now reinforced with two Turkish divisions, Mackensen resumed the Dobruja offensive. On the 23rd Constanta was taken and on the 25th the important railhead at Cernavoda, thus depriving the Rumanians of a crucial logistical link with Russia.

**8** Having followed the retreating Russians a little further north, Mackensen halted and began to move forces to Sistova in preparation for an assault across the Danube.

**9** On 10 November, Falkenhayn's Ninth Army attacked through the last of the Rumanian-held mountain passes, where their positions were surprisingly weak, and he soon drove forward into eastern Wallachia, taking Kraiova on the 21st.

**10** On 23 November, Mackensen crossed the Danube with little difficulty and soon pressed forwards to the lower reaches of the River Arges.

**11** The German advance did offer the Rumanians one glimmer of hope for Mackensen's forces had outstripped Falkenhayn's right wing and so left their own left and rear exposed. The Rumanians swiftly tried to exploit the gap but the forces allotted were too weak. Mackensen's line held against the initial attacks on 1 December and when a reinforcement from Ninth Army arrived on the following day the Rumanians reeled back in panic.

**12** This defeat marked the end of any serious Rumanian resistance. Their whole line now started to withdraw and within a little more than a month the Rumanian 'sock' had been chopped off from the ankle down. Pitesti fell on 29 November, Ploesti and Bucharest on 6 December. The lower Jalamitsa was crossed on 14 December and Focsani taken on 8 January 1917. In the Dobruja, in mid-December, the Russians had begun pulling back to the far bank of the Danube.

**13** In Macedonia, meanwhile, Allied forces had begun a renewed offensive, on 12 September, to try and upset any Central Powers response to the Rumanian declaration of war. Diversionary operations were undertaken all along the front but the main effort was that of Serbian First Army at Mt. Kajmakcalan, directly north of Lake Ostrovo, intended as a prelude to an advance up the Vardar valley. A supporting British attack towards the valley failed but on 2 October the Serbs took Kajmakcalan. However, a complementary Franco-Serb attack on their left, towards Monastir, made only very slow progress. Florina was not taken until 17 September and further progress up the Kenali valley proved impossible with German Eleventh Army taking over this sector at the end of September. After weeks of stalemate the Serbs again took up the running, this time in the loop of the River Crna, to the north of Kajmakcalan. They jumped off on 10 November and by the 15th had forced the Germans to pull back from the Kenali valley so as to shorten their line. On the 19th Monastir was given up but the Allied attempt to hustle the enemy back to Prilep, and perhaps beyond, soon faltered. On 11 December the whole Allied front was ordered on to the defensive.

**14** In August the Italians had begun advancing out of their Valona bridgehead, taking Tepeleni at the end of the month and Premeti on 9 September. Over the next months the Allies in Albania and Macedonia gradually edged towards each other, with their advance guards finally linking up on 18 February 1917.

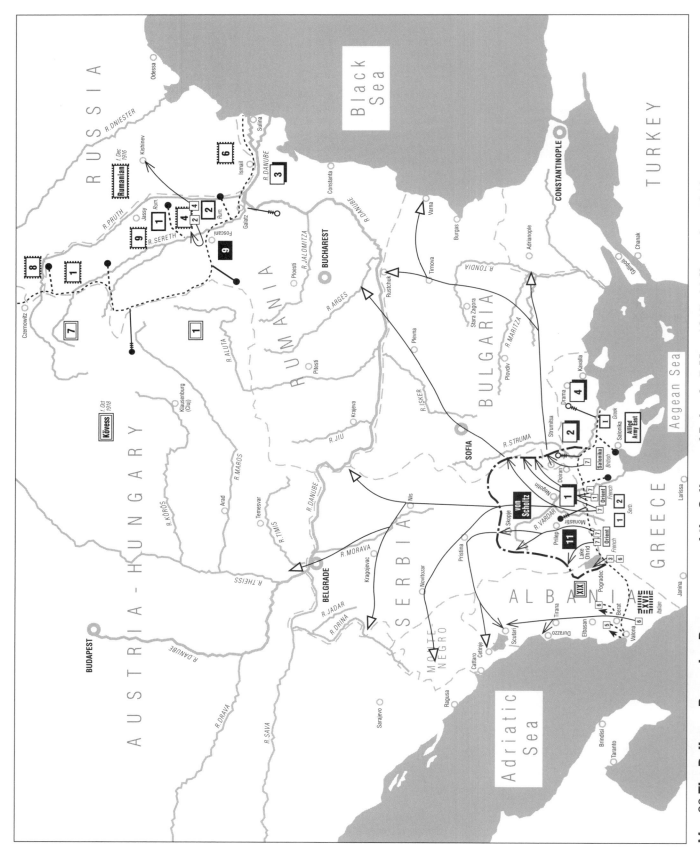

Map 23 **The Balkans: Rumanian Resurgence and the Collapse of Bulgaria 5 May 1917–11 November 1918**

• **MAP 23** • THE BALKANS •

## KEY

| | |
|---|---|
| ☐ | Allied Army Groups |
| 1 | Allied Armies |
| 7 | Russian Army Groups and Armies September 1917 |
| 7 | |
| ■ | German Army Groups |
| 1 | German Armies |
| ☐ | Austro-Hungarian Army Groups |
| ☐ | Austro-Hungarian Armies |
| ☐ | Bulgarian Armies |
| ●····· | Army Boundaries 9/17 |
| ●⊪ | Army Boundaries 9/18 |
| ○⊪ | |
| → | Allied movements |
| 1 | See number in Notes |
| ---------- | Front line May 1917 |
| —·—·—·— | Front line 30/9/18 |
| ▷ | Furthest Allied advance 11/11/18 |

## NOTES TO MAP 23

**1** On 5 May the Allies in Macedonia opened an offensive in the Vardar/Crna sector but this broke down on the 17th when Serbian First Army refused to attack. The whole operation was halted on the 21st.

**2** After the debacle of 1916 the Rumanian Army was reduced to a mere five active divisions, with most of the line in Moldova being taken over by the Russians. By mid-1917, however, fifteen new divisions had been created with French help, and on 23 July Rumanian Second Army launched an offensive at Marasesti, north of Foscani. Despite initial successes along a 20-mile front, Russian Fourth Army resolutely refused to lift a finger in support and the advance gradually bogged down. A second offensive was planned for 7 August but this was pre-empted by a German counter-offensive on the 6th. The Russians promptly turned tail and on the 9th the Germans crossed the Sereth, prompting the Rumanian royal family to evacuate to Jassy. But the Rumanians continued to cling on at Marasesti and by mid-September the front had pretty much stabilised.

**3** On 7 September a French division recently arrived in Albania began to push towards Pogradec which was taken on the 10th. This advance was halted on the 10th.

**4** In January 1918, having the previous month signed a three-month armistice with the Central Powers, the Rumanians decided to take advantage of the growing chaos in revolutionary Russia and marched troops into Bessarabia. They entered Kishinev on the 26th. Despite this irredentist flourish most of southern Rumania continued to be occupied by the Central Powers right up to November 1918.

**5** In early 1918 the Austrians undertook several attacks against the Allied front in Albania (now manned by French as well as Italian units). The most serious of these, against Valona, was finally repulsed by the end of March.

**6** In June 1918 the Allies launched their own offensive in Albania. On the 9th French and Albanian troops took Mt. Karnia, south-west of Lake Ohrid, and on 6 July the Italians attacked, taking Berat a few days later. An Austrian counter-offensive on 20 August succeeded in briefly retaking the town before the Allies rallied on the 26th. Reinforcements began to arrive and in late September the Allies resumed the offensive. Berat was reoccupied on 1 October and Elbasan on the

7th. On the 14th the Allies reached Tirana but the Austrians had already evacuated the town, and the port of Durazzo on the 11th. By the end of the month Italian troops had entered Scutari.

**7** By autumn 1918 Allied positions in Macedonia were faced almost entirely by Bulgarian troops, albeit commanded by a German Army Group. But the Bulgarians were too starved of reserves to adequately man such an extensive front and the troops' morale had been steadily undermined by the withdrawal of their allies to other fronts. Thus, though the Allies chose to concentrate their last offensive to one of the most rugged parts of the line, between the Vardar and Crna rivers, the French and Serb attackers were able to make remarkable progress. The offensive began on 15 September, with a subsidiary British attack towards Doiran on the 18th, and quickly penetrated up to five miles along a twenty-mile front. On the 20th the Bulgarians were ordered to pull back to a new defensive line, but with no reserves to cover this withdrawal the fragmented front broke completely and the disorganised units dispersed into the mountains. By the 22nd the Serbs had reached the Vardar near Negotin. The main axis of advance was north-west, towards the Bulgarian frontier, but a bold French cavalry brigade probed directly northwards into Serbia, entering Prilep on 23 September and Skopje on the 29th. By then the British had crossed the Bulgarian frontier, taking Strumitsa on the 26th as well as encountering a Bulgarian surrender delegation. Talks began on the 28th and hostilities ceased completely on the 30th. Thereafter the Allied forces fanned out at will through Serbia and Bulgaria and on 3 November the Austro-Hungarians, too, conceded defeat.

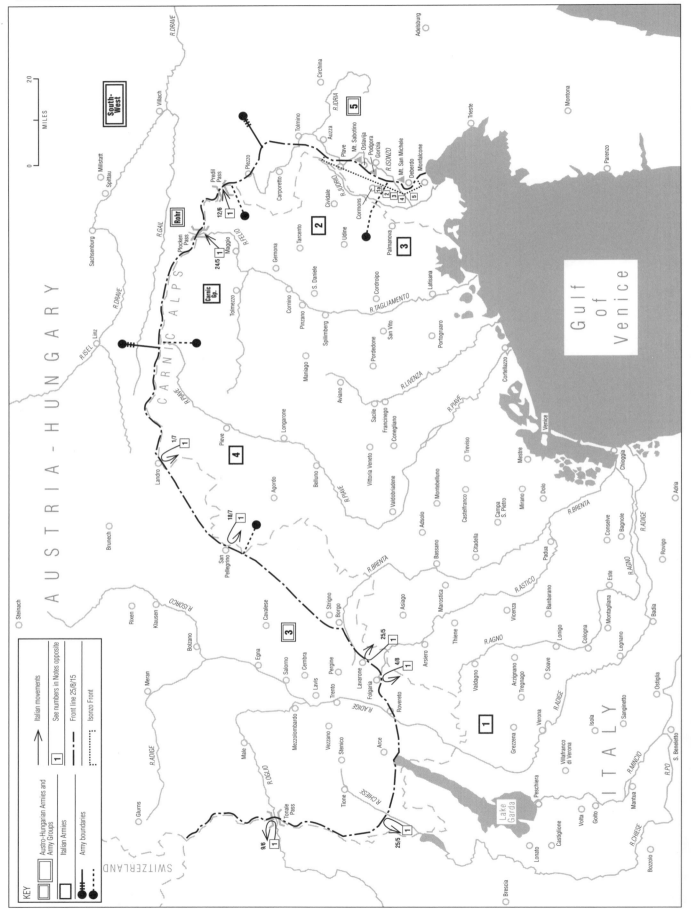

Map 24 **Italy: First Italian Attacks and the Subsequent Focussing of Operations during the First Five Battles of the River Isonzo 25 May 1915–16 March 1916**

• MAP 24 • ITALY•

## NOTES TO MAP 24

**1** During the first months of the war Italy remained neutral, but by May 1915, seeing the way the Austrians were becoming tied down in Galicia and Serbia, her leaders decided that intervening on the side of the Allies offered a real prospect of seizing those Italian-speaking areas still incorporated in the Austrian Empire. War was declared on 23 May and during the next weeks the Italians launched a series of probing attacks at various points along their mountainous, 400-mile frontier with Austria (dates shown on map) but nowhere were they able to make any sort of breakthrough.

**1a** The Italians most important objective was Trieste and thus their main effort had been over the River Isonzo, towards the important communications centre at Gorizia. Attacks here began on 27 May, spread along much of Italian Second and Third Armies' front. In the following month these became somewhat more focussed. On 23 June, after a seven-day bombardment, Italian infantry threw themselves against the Gorizia bridgehead and against the Carso (Karst) plateau north and west of Monfalcone. But hardly any ground was gained despite terrible casualties. The story was exactly the same during a second assault that began on 3 July and had to be called off two days later.

**2** On 18 July, launching the Second Battle of Isonzo, the Italians tried again. The whole of Third Army's front was active but the main effort was against the Doberdo ridge, at the western end of the Carso plateau. The attackers' intention was to hook northwards to take Gorizia from the rear. But the main attack made hardly any progress and though an ancillary drive against Monte San Michele did take the town on the 20th, it was quickly recaptured on the 23rd. A renewed offensive along the whole Third Army front, on the 25th, had been pretty much halted within three days although the Second Battle was not officially ended until 10 August.

**3** The Third Battle of Isonzo began on 21 October and involved both Italian Armies, with the Second aiming for the Bainsizza plateau to the north of Gorizia, as far as the River Idria, and the Third trying to clear the Doberdo ridge. The plan then was for the two Armies to envelop Gorizia in a pincer movement. In the event the fiercest fighting was around Plave and Monte San Michele, with a supporting attack against the Gorizia bridgehead on the 25th. At the northern end of the bridgehead Monte Sabatino was taken, only to be almost immediately lost to an Austrian counter-attack. Everywhere else, the Austrian line, though sorely stretched. was not broken at all. By 4 November the Italians had to call off the Third Battle, too, with almost nothing to show for their soaring casualty lists.

**4** For the Fourth Battle the Italians narrowed the front a little, with the main effort being made between Plave and the Doberdo. They jumped off on 10 November and soon the main fighting was concentrated between Monte Sabatino and Monte San Michele. From 18 November the town of Gorizia was systematically razed to the ground by artillery and on the 27th Oslavija was taken. But no further progress proved possible and during the first fortnight of December the Italian attacks became increasingly desultory, the battle being officially terminated on the 15th. (Oslavija was recaptured by the Austrians on 24 January 1916).

**5** No major offensive was attempted during the winter of 1915–16 and it was not until 11 March that the Italians opened the Fifth Battle of Isonzo. In fact, this was little more than a reconnaissance in force, with the main aim of taking prisoners to be able to identify enemy units.

Attacks were concentrated around Monte San Michele and the Podgora but when they were called off on the 16th the bag of prisoners was disappointingly small. Indeed, there was precious little to show for the previous ten months of carnage during which no more than a mile of ground had been taken along the Isonzo, for the loss of some 200,000 Italian soldiers.

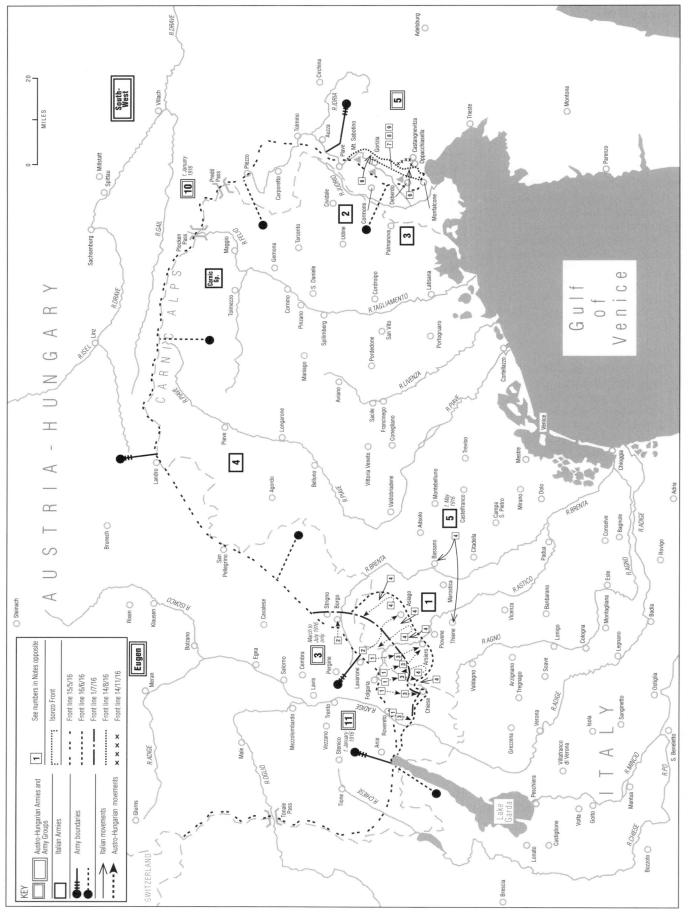

Map 25 Italy: Austro-Hungarian Offensive in the Trentino and Renewed Italian Attacks during the Sixth to Ninth Battles of Isonzo
15 May–4 November 1916

• MAP 25 • ITALY •

## NOTES TO MAP 25

**1** Ever since late 1915, Conrad, the Austrian Chief-of-Staff, had been contemplating sidestepping the Isonzo deadlock and attacking through the Trentino, part of the Tyrol. Concentrating his forces between Roverto and the upper Brenta, he intended to break into the north Italian plain, south of Chiese, Arsiero and Asiago, and move on to cut the Verona-Vicenza and Mantua-Padua railways that supplied the Isonzo front. Possibly, he might even find the opportunity to strike at Venice itself and so cut off the easterly front entirely. Conrad had hoped for German assistance, as many as eight divisions, but when these were not forthcoming he began stripping his own fronts. Eventually he mustered some 14 divisions but the build-up was so slow that the Italians had ample notice of the forthcoming offensive. Worse, the Austrians elected to stagger the attacks of the two leading corps, from Eleventh Army, and thus forfeited any chance of replacing surprise with concerted shock effect. The leading corps, which jumped off on 15 May, did manage to penetrate the first two lines of Italian defence but could not maintain the momentum to breach the third.

**2** On the 20th the Austrians abruptly changed their plan and transferred one of Eleventh Army's corps to Third Army and directed it south-eastwards towards Asiago. Asiago was taken on the 29th but further attacks were dogged by supply difficulties, fierce Italian resistance and the thick, forested terrain. Attacks on Monte Meletta and Monte Lemerle, to the south of Asiago, went on until 15 June but failed to break through into the plain below and advance on Bassano.

**3** Though the Austrians deemed the Asiago-Bassano axis the primary one, there was also a concerted effort towards Arsiero, with a view to approaching Bassano in a more extended hook through Piovene. Arsiero fell on the 27th and Monte Priafora, just to the south, was stormed on the 30th. But the Austrians' flagging attacks proved unable to take Monte Cengio, to the east, whilst attacks on Monte Pasubio, east of Chiese, were also thwarted. By mid-June this whole front had stagnated, though in places only a mile from the northern plain.

**4** On 7 June the newly-formed Italian Fifth Army was ordered up between Thiene and Bassano and on the 16th First Army launched a counter-offensive against the Asiago plateau. The first line of Austrian defences was taken but nowhere was any decisive breakthrough made. On 22 June the Italian left also attacked, at Villarsa, but two days of fierce fighting also failed to make a significant breach in the enemy line. On the night of 25/26 June the Austrians began to withdraw in good order. The Italians only re-established contact on the 27th, by which time the enemy was firmly ensconced in strong, pre-prepared positions. Undaunted, the Italians continued their attacks, mainly against the Val Sugana, Asiago plateau, Val Posino, Vallarsa and Monte Pasubio. Little headway was made, as always at great cost, but the attacks were not called off until 24 July, by which time troops were being transferred to the Isonzo front for a renewed offensive there.

**5** (There is no **5** so as to permit arrow numbers to match with the relevant Isonzo battle).

**6** The Sixth Battle of Isonzo began on 4 August. Initial attacks in the Monfalcone area were only a feint and the main assault opened on the 6th, in the Gorizia bridgehead. Monte Sabatino, the Podgora and Monte San Michele all fell on this same day and patrols were over the Isonzo on the morning of the 9th. They entered Gorizia later that day, the Austrians having been evacuated, and by the 12th the attackers had reached the second line of defences on the Carso plateau. But here the Austrians stood and the offensive was halted on the 14th.

**7** The Seventh Battle began on 14 September with a feint in the north, around Plezzo, and the main attack by Second Army on the Carso plateau. Atrocious weather hampered all movement and only very small gains were made east of Oppachiasella. Within 48 hours the battle was called off.

**8** It was resumed, for the eighth time, on 10 October with the front now extended to the high ground east of Gorizia. Thick mist was now the main problem and only small gains were made south-east of Oppachiasella before operations were halted on the 12th.

**9** The Italian High Command was still determined to break through to Trieste before the onset of winter and on 1 November it opened the Ninth Battle. The front again stretched from east of Gorizia to the sea. The biggest successes were in Second Army's sector where a salient was punched out north-west of Castagnevizza. Much of this ground was taken after the failure of Austrian counter-attacks on the 3rd but by the following day their defences had solidified once more and the Italians were forced to suspend operations for the winter.

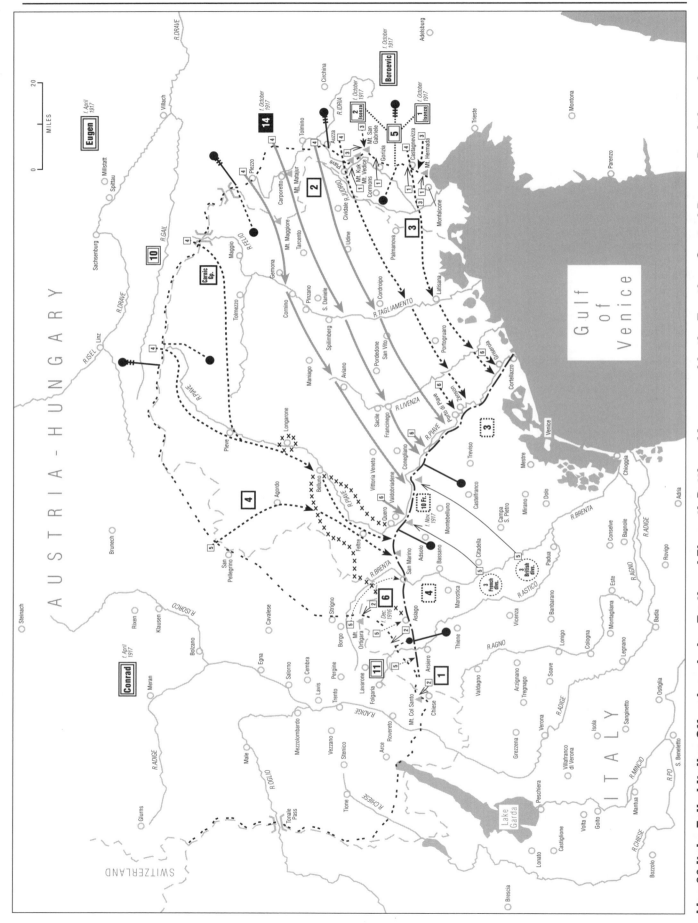

Map 26 Italy: Failed Italian Offensives during Tenth and Eleventh Battles of Isonzo and in the Trentino, Central Powers Breakthrough at Caporetto and Italian Retreat to the Piave 14 May–2 December 1917

• **MAP 26** • ITALY •

## KEY

| | |
|---|---|
| ▭ ▯[1] | Austro-Hungarian Army Groups and Armies 24/10/17 |
| ■[1] | German Armies 24/10/17 |
| [1] [1] | Italian and Allied Armies 14/5/17 and 2/12/17 |
| ●━━ ●···· ● | Central Powers and Allied Army boundaries 14/5/17 and 2/12/17 |
| ━━▶ | German movements |
| ·······▶ | Austro-Hungarian movements |
| ━━▶ | Allied movements |
| [1] | See number in Notes |
| ·· ·· ·· ·· | Front line 14/5/17 |
| × × × × × | Front line 10/11/17 |
| ━·━·━·━ | Front line 2/12/17 |

## NOTES TO MAP 26

**1** In Spring 1917 the attention of the Italian High Command remained focussed on the Isonzo front and the possibility of a breakthrough to Trieste. With Gorizia and half of the Carso plateau taken, their eyes now turned to the coastal sector and the immensely strong Austrian defences on Monte Hermada. However, keen to conceal their main axis of advance, the Italians opened the Tenth Battle of Isonzo, on 14 May, with strong diversionary attacks by Second Army between Plave and Gorizia. These, in fact, succeeded in making important gains in the south-west approaches to the Bainsizza plateau, with Monte Kuk and Monte Vodice falling on 15 and 16 May. Little headway was made, however, against Monte Santo. On 23 May, Third Army began the main offensive in the south. Castagnevizza fell on the 25th and soon after that San Giovanni, in the foothills of Monte Hermada. But no further advances up Hermada proved possible and after a week of heavy casualties the Italians were counter-attacked, on 1 June, losing San Giovanni and the whole of Monte Hermada. By 4 June the Tenth Battle was over.

**2** The Italians continued to strive for a breakthrough towards Trieste but began to worry that its very success might provoke an Austrian thrust into their rear. To forestall this possibility they resolved to 'tidy' the line in the Trentino and push the Austrians back at least to their 1916 start line on the Folgario-Lavarone plateau. The main targets were to be Monte Col Santo and Monte Kempel, at either end of the front, and the northern slopes of the Posina valley, north-west of Arsiero. In the event, the Italians had not provided sufficient reinforcements for such a broad attack frontage so that the offensive, which opened on 10 June, was soon concentrated just against Monte Ortigara in the north. A grim sequence of attack and counter-attack ensued until the 25th when the Austrians cleared Ortigara completely and forced the Italians to abandon this secondary effort.

**3** On 19 August the Italian infantry stormed forward to begin the Eleventh Battle of Isonzo. Attacks were made all along Second Army's front, from Tolmino southwards, but the *point d'appui* this time was the Bainsizza plateau. Attacks from Monte Kuk enjoyed considerable success and on the 24th Monte Santo was taken. Monte San Gabriele proved a tougher nut, however, and subsidiary attacks against Monte Hermada also made little headway. At the end of the month the Italians paused to regroup only to be beset by Austrian counter-attacks on both the Bainsizza and Carso plateaus. In the second week of September the Italians succeeded in reaching the crest of Monte San Gabriele but a major Austrian counter-attack on the 11th dislodged them. By the 13th the front had congealed once more.

**4** During the Isonzo battles the Italians had progressively denuded the front north-west of the River Idria, comforting themselves with the belief that the terrain there was largely impassable. But the enemy were less convinced and in autumn 1917 built up a new German army, the Fourteenth, between Plezzo and Auzza, to spearhead a Central Powers offensive on the Isonzo. Fourteenth Army attacked on 24 October and had soon smashed a fifteen-mile wide hole in the Italian line north of Tolmino, completely destroying Second Army's left wing. By the end of the first day they were in Caporetto and by the 26th most Second Army positions east of the Isonzo had been lost, including Monte Kuk, Monte Santo and Monte Matajur. On the 26th Monte Maggiore was taken, followed by Cividale on the 27th and Udine on the 28th. By this time the whole north-western front was in retreat, with Third Army and the Carnic Group both having to conform with Second Army's headlong withdrawal. By the 31st the Italians were behind the River Tagliamento. On 2 November they lost the bridges at Cemano and Pinzano and by the 4th were streaming back to the Livenza. By the 9th this river line, too, had been lost and the Italians were taking up last-ditch positions behind the Piave. Second Army had virtually ceased to exist but Third Army's much more measured withdrawal had just allowed sufficient time for Italian Fourth Army to also pull back without being cut off by the Austrian forces driving down the upper Piave. By the time Belluno and Longarone fell on 10 and 11 November, most of Fourth Army was already in position between the bend of the Piave and the Brenta.

**5** During this pursuit down the upper Piave, Austrian Eleventh Army in the Trentino also attacked, on 8 November, hoping to get in behind the retreating Italians. Initial advances were impressive with Asiago falling on the 9th and Agordo on the 10th. South of Asiago, Austrian attacks now began to falter but were more successful between the Brenta and the Piave, with Feltre falling on the 12th, the Austrians and Germans linking up at Fonzaso on the 14th, and Querso being occupied on the 18th. But this was the limit of the Central Powers' advance and although fighting continued on this front until late December, the Italians, with Franco-British help from the beginning of December, were able to create a solid defensive line linking Monte Tomba, Monte Grappa, Foza, Asiago and points west.

**6** On 10 June, two days after the start of the Trentino offensive, the Austrians and Germans also attacked at various points along the Piave (First Battle of the Piave). No significant breakthroughs were made although small bridgeheads were seized at Zenson, on the 10th, Griserola on the 13th and Ponte di Piave on the 16th. Another assault on the 23rd was halted two days later and on 2 December this phase of the Piave fighting was formally terminated.

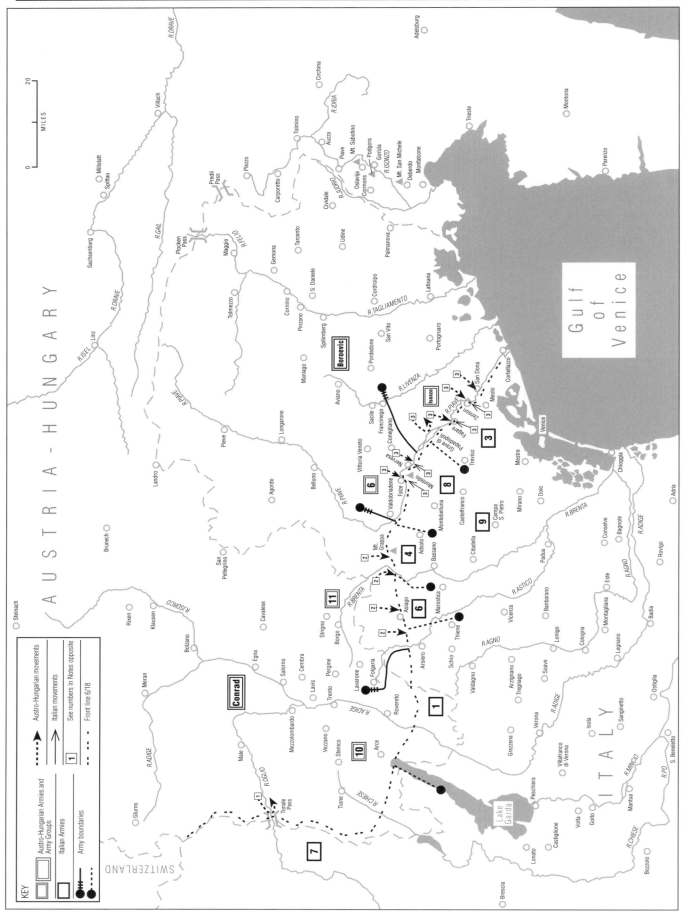

Map 27 **Italy: Failed Austrian Offensive in Trentino and on the Piave 13–24 June 1918**

• **MAP 27** • ITALY •

## NOTES TO MAP 27

[1] The Russian collapse in the second half of 1917 meant that the Austrians were able to transfer many of their divisions away from the Eastern Front (see Map 18 and Table 5.7). The Germans pressed for these to be sent to France and Belgium but the Austrian High Command preferred to reinforce the Italian front where they intended to launch combined offensives on the Asiago plateau and along the Piave. Originally timed for 20 May, this operation was postponed to 15 June, with a preliminary diversionary attack against the Tonnale Pass jumping off on the 13th. This latter was driven back to its start lines by the afternoon of the first day and the isolated success, the taking of the Col de Rosso, was overturned on 30 June.

[2] The Asiago attacks had for their objective the line Schio-Asolo but the Italians were fully informed about Austrian intentions and were able to meet the initial assaults on the 15th with fearsome artillery concentrations. Early Austrian gains west of Monte Grappa were soon recaptured and by nightfall on the 16th almost all the attackers were back at their start lines.

[3] The Piave attacks on the 15th were directed against three main objectives: Monte Montello, the Grave di Popadopoli, an island on the Piave, and San Dona near the coast. Now committed to a much more elastic defence, the Italians willingly gave up their front lines and allowed the Austrians to establish several bridgeheads. By the 17th the Austrians were in possession of two-thirds of Monte Montello and had linked up the Zenson and Fagare lodgements to form a bridgehead twelve miles wide and between three and five miles deep. But heavy rains soon turned the river into a torrent, sweeping away the temporary bridges, and this was soon followed by strong Italian counter-attacks against Zenson-Fagare on the 18th, and Monte Montello on the following day. The Austrians' own counter-attacks, to the 21st, made little headway and on the following two nights they pulled all their troops back across the Piave. This withdrawal, conducted in secrecy, did have the advantage of thwarting an Italian offensive on the 23rd, which found only empty enemy trenches.

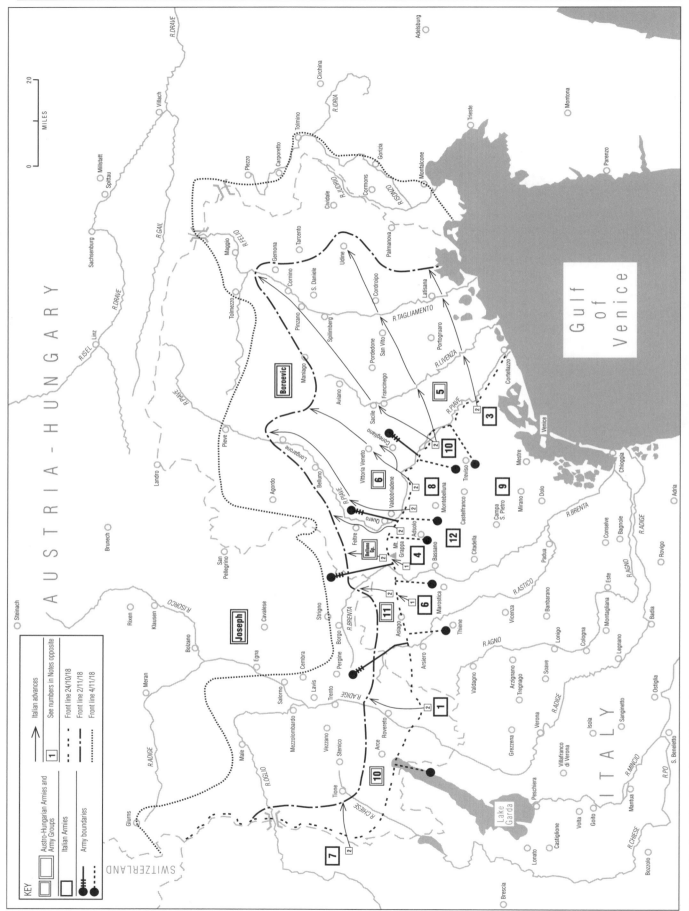

Map 28 Italy: The Battle of Vittorio Veneto and Final Austro-Hungarian Collapse 24 October–4 November 1918

KEY

Austro-Hungarian Armies and Army Groups

Italian Armies

→ Italian advances

1 See numbers in Notes opposite

····· Front line 24/10/18

----- Front line 2/11/18

-··-··- Front line 4/11/18

Army boundaries

• **MAP 28** • ITALY •

## NOTES TO MAP 28

[1] After the Caporetto debacle Italian commanders remained loth to commit their troops to offensive action and for some weeks the High Command firmly resisted Allied pressure for renewed operations on this front. By October 1918, however, after the Bulgarian capitulation (see Map 23), it became clear that the Italians must resume the offensive or risk losing much of their authority at the peace table. Contingency plans for an offensive had been in place since mid-September, envisaging simultaneous pushes on the Asiago and Piave fronts, but sudden and unexpected flooding of the Piave meant that it was the Trentino armies that jumped off first, on 24 October.

[2] Tenth, Twelfth and Eighth Armies followed suit just two days later but in both sectors Austrian resistance was tenacious, with hardly any ground being given up before the 28th. Yet by the following day the Austrians were in full retreat, abandoning in short order Monte Cosen, Quero, Susegana, Conegliano, Vittorio Veneto and the Gravi di Popodopoli. Before the day was out an Austrian delegation appeared with a white flag and was whisked off to Padua to discuss terms. On the 30th the retreat turned into a rout, with Italian First Army joining in the pursuit on 1 November and Seventh Army on the following day. The whole Italian line surged forward, occupying Roverto, Trent, Longarone, Belluno, and crossing the Tagliamento as far as Udine. On the 3rd the Italian Navy steamed into Trieste, already in the hands of Yugoslav nationalists, and an armistice was signed at 6.30 that evening, coming into force 24 hours later.

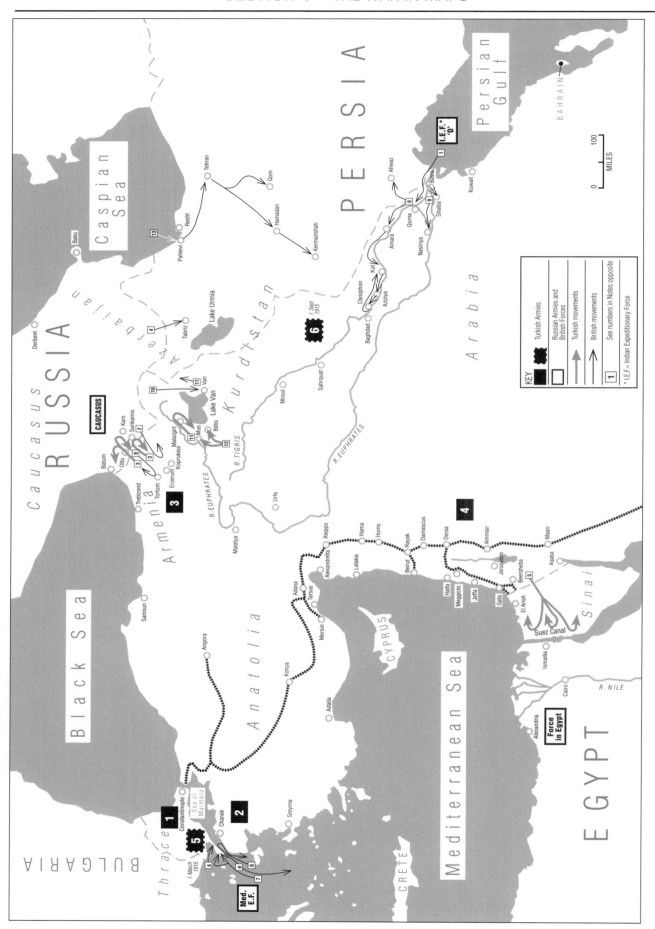

Map 29 **Turkey: War on Four Fronts: Armenia, Mesopotamia, the Suez Canal and Gallipoli 1914-15**

• **MAP 29** • TURKEY •

## NOTES TO MAP 29

**1** When Turkey officially lined up with the Central Powers, on 1 November 1914, the British responded immediately. An Indian Army division was already stationed in the Persian Gulf and this was dispatched to the mouth of the Euphrates the better to protect the vital Abadan oil-fields. The first troops disembarked on 6 November and, with the Turks immediately falling back, were able to occupy Basra on the 22nd and the Qurna on 9 December.

**2** The Russians also responded swiftly, opening an offensive towards Koprukeui on 2 November. But this soon ran into a Turkish counter-offensive and the Russians only narrowly avoided encirclement before the fighting petered out by the middle of the month.

**3** On 12 December, the Turks in Armenia launched a more ambitious offensive, with the main blow aimed at Sarikamis and a flanking attack towards Oltu. But their troops soon began to feel the effects of the harsh winter in the mountains and their attacks were halted more by climatic attrition than by the enemy.

**4** Immediately the Turks declared war the Russians had occupied part of Persian Azerbaijan but in early January 1915 they withdrew, allowing Tabriz to fall on the 14th. But the Russians made amends for their error and retook the city on the 30th. A Turkish counter-attack in April was repulsed.

**5** On 10 January 1915, Fourth Turkish Army crossed into Sinai, heading for the Suez Canal. The first skirmish with the British took place on the 26th and on the night of 2/3 February the invaders launched a three-pronged assault, the main effort being made just south of Ismailia. But all attacks had been decisively repulsed by the 4th and the Turks withdrew.

**6** On 18 March an Allied fleet attempted to force the Dardanelles, hoping the threat to Constantinople might put Turkey out of the war at a stroke. The enemy's coastal batteries were put out of action but seven ships struck mines, laid only ten days earlier. The fleet withdrew.

**7** An amphibious assault was now attempted, with British, French and Anzac troops coming ashore on the Gallipoli peninsula (Cape Helles and Anzac Cove) on 25 April. They were immediately pinned in their small beachheads and after Turkish counter-attacks were narrowly repulsed the campaign quickly settled into the familiar trench deadlock. (**s**) On 7 August fresh Allied divisions were landed at Suvla Bay to try and assist the Anzac Cove forces to force their way out of the peninsula. The plan was thwarted by appalling lack of local initiative and the Suvla troops, too, became prisoners in their narrow beachhead. (**e**) It was then quickly decided to evacuate the whole force. This was achieved, extremely efficiently, between 18-20 December and 8-9 January 1916.

**8** On 27 April 1915, the Russians began a drive towards Tortum but this had been checked by mid-June.

**9** After preliminary operations in mid-April to occupy Shaiba and Ahwaz, to safeguard the oil-fields, the advance along the Tigris was resumed on 11 May. Progress was steady as far as Ctesiphon, with Amara falling on 3 June, Kut on 28 September, Aziziya on 5 October and Ctesiphon on 21 November. Here the British paused, however, allowing the Turks to bring in reinforcements that thwarted subsequent attacks towards Baghdad. On 25 November, the British began pulling back towards Kut. They reentered the town on 3 December only to find themselves completely surrounded there by 7 January 1916. On 5 July 1915, the British had also begun to advance up the Euphrates, occupying Nasiriya, where they halted, on the 25th.

**10** On 20 April 1915, the Turks laid siege to Van which had been seized by Armenian insurgents in the wake of the first Armenian massacres, in February. In early May, however, the Turks withdrew from the Lake Van-Lake Urmia area and Van was occupied by the Russians on 19 May. On the 25th they re-occupied Urmia.

**11** In July a Turkish offensive to the west of Lake Van took Melazgirt on the 26th. Their further drive northwards was thrown back between 4-6 August but not before Van had been evacuate on the 3rd.

**12** Supporting attacks by the Turks, between 2-6 August, permitted them to retain control of Mus and Bitlis.

**13** On 29 October Russian troops landed at Pahlevi (Enzeli), on the Caspian coast, and began a deep thrust into western Persia that was intended to link up with British forces along the Tigris. Tehran was cowed, but not entered, in mid-November, Hamadan was taken on 14 December, Qom on 20th, and Kermanshah on 25 February 1916.

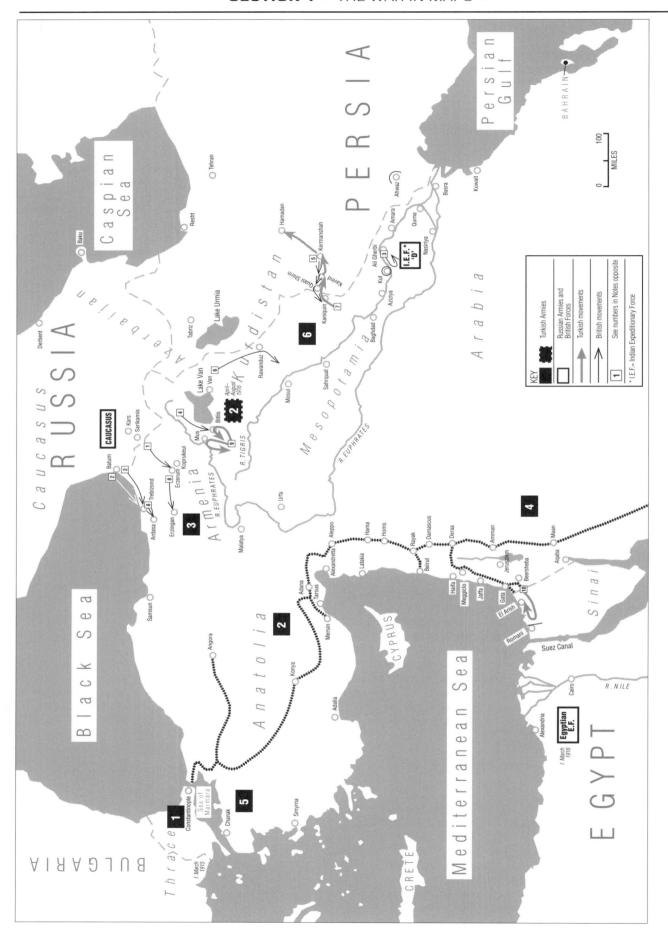

Map 30 **Turkey: Russian Success in Armenia and British Embarrassment in Mesopotamia 1916**

• **MAP 30** • TURKEY •

# NOTES TO MAP 30

**1** On 10 January 1916 the Russians again advanced on Erzerum and Koprukeui. The latter was taken on the 17th and the former was stormed, after a short siege, on 17 February.

**2** The Russians had also opened up another axis of advance along the Black Sea coast, towards Trebizond. Starting out on 18 January from Batum, Russian troops, supported by ships of the Black Sea Fleet, seized half-a-dozen intermediate coastal towns as well as forcing several river crossings, before obliging the Turks to give up Trebizond on 15 April.

**3** In Mesopotamia, on 3 January, the first relief expedition to Kut left Ali Gherbi. After two costly victories, on 9 and 13 January, the British were halted at Hanna defile on the 21st. Later attempts to break through, in March and April, all failed and on 29 April the garrison at Kut surrendered. For the rest of the year the chastened British concentrated on building up stores and an adequate logistic apparatus to support a renewed advance in 1917. (In February 1916, supreme command in this theatre had passed from the Indian government to the War Cabinet).

**4** On 3 March the Russians retook Bitlis.

**5** In March the Russians in Persia resumed their advance towards the Tigris, taking Kavind on 12 March and Qasi Shirin on 7 May.

**6** A complementary Russian advance between Lakes Van and Urmia took Rawanduz on 13 May and pressed on towards Mosul.

**7** The Persian axis was repulsed at Kanaquin, however, and now it was the Turks' turn to advance, retaking Qasi Shirin and Kavind on 9 and 26 June and Kermanshah on 1 July. Here the Turks halted briefly before pressing on to take Hamadan.

**8** Meanwhile, the Russians had continued to concentrate their main effort in Armenia, pushing forward from Trebizond and Erzerum. Ardassa fell on 20 July and on the 25th the Turks suffered a crushing defeat at the Battle of Erzingan.

**9** On 5 and 6 August the Turks retook Bitlis and Mus only to lose them again later the same month.

**10** In the first half of 1916, the British in Sinai pushed their defence line eastward, to Romani, where they dug in. A Turkish force attacked these positions on 4 August but it was repulsed the next day and by the 12th had withdrawn to El Arish.

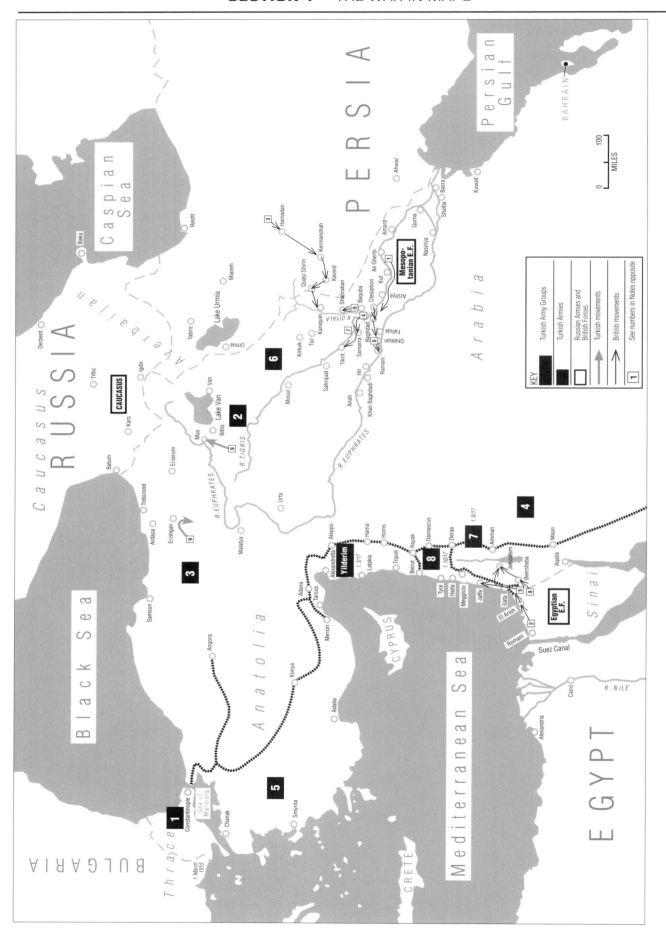

Map 31 **Turkey: Renewed British Pressure in Palestine and Mesopotamia 1917**

## NOTES TO MAP 31

**1** The Tigris offensive was renewed on 13 December 1916 but only got into its administrative stride from 9 January 1917. To 24 February the British pretty much refought the battles of the Kut relief expedition the previous winter. This time, however, they broke down the dour Turkish resistance and on 25 February moved into Kut 24 hours behind the evacuating Turks. Thereafter they met much less concerted Turkish resistance, and occupied Aziziyah on 29 February, Ctesiphon on 6 March and Baghdad on the 11th.

**2** In Sinai, on 20 December, the British began an offensive towards El Arish only to find that the Turks had evacuated the town a few days before. The British entered on the 22nd and the seizure of Rafa, 9 January 1917, marked the complete expulsion of the enemy from Sinai.

**3** In February 1917, Turkish troops in Persia began pulling back from Hamadan and Kermanshah. The Russians followed in their wake, retaking Hamadan on 2 March, Kermanshah on the 11th, Kavind on the 17th and Kaniquin on 3 April.

**4** Once in Baghdad, General Maude divided his forces into three columns, advancing up the Tigris, Euphrates and Diyala rivers. The central axis was the main one, Maude having an eye both on the Mosul oil-fields and on a link-up with the Russians. On the Euphrates, Falluja was taken on 19 March; Baquba on the Diyala fell on the 18th, and Samarra on the Tigris on 24 April. Further advances were made up the Diyala and Euphrates, to Shahraban on 23 March and Ramadi on 12 July, but supply difficulties and Turkish resistance forced both these axes to pull back and sit out the intense summer heat.

**5** After clearing Sinai General Marshall was authorised to undertake a limited offensive into Palestine. However, both his preliminary attacks on Gaza, on 26 March and 19 April, failed and led to his replacement by Allenby, with terse instructions to take Jerusalem by Christmas.

**6** In August and September 1917, the British in Mesopotamia concentrated upon tidying up the subsidiary Euphrates and Diyala axes, reoccupying Shahraban on 20 August and thwarting an attempted Turkish concentration at Ramadi on 29 September.

**7** In October the main task was the clearance of the Jebel Hamrin (not shown), south-east of Tuz. The main attack was launched between 16 and 20 October. This was successful and on 2 November the advance up the Tigris was resumed, with Tikrit being occupied on the 5th.

**8** The Turks were also under attack in Palestine as an assault on the Gaza-Beersheba line got under way on 31 October. Deceiving the Turks that the main effort would be along the coast, against Gaza, Allenby in fact concentrated his main strike force against Beersheba, which was stormed on the very first day. Threatened by a right-hook behind Gaza, the Turks began withdrawing on 7 November. They escaped but had to give up Jaffa on the 16th. Two days later Allenby began the advance on Jerusalem. Despite a bitter stalemate in late November/early December, the Turks finally yielded to a renewed British push on the 8th and began a full-scale withdrawal that same day.

**9** In Armenia, with both sides desperate for men to shore up other fronts and with the Russian army increasingly wracked by revolutionary ferment, there were no major operations. The most notable events in 1917 were a successful Turkish drive on Mus, taken on 1 May, and a failed offensive south of Erzingan, in mid-October.

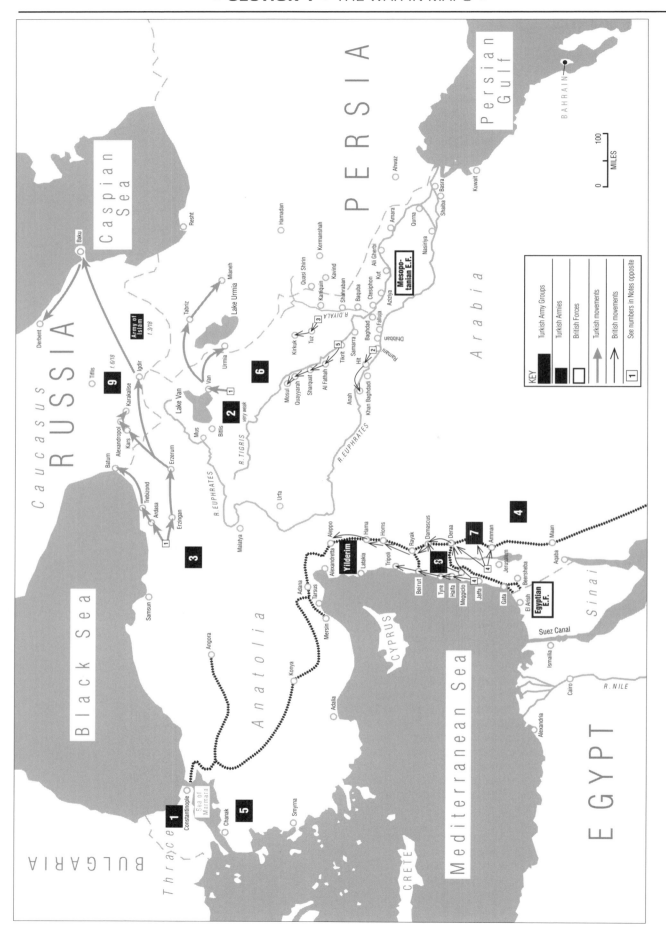

Map 32 **Turkey: Turks Attempt to Profit from Russian Collapse as British Drive Forward in Palestine and Mesopotamia 1918**

## NOTES TO MAP 32

**1** Throughout 1917 the efficiency of the Russian Army had been fast declining and after the Tsar's abdication, in March 1917, the troops began to desert *en masse*. By early 1918 the Turks felt confident enough to resume the offensive in Armenia, where they were mainly faced by scratch indigenous units. Setting forth on 12 February, they took Erzingan on the 14th, Trebizond on the 24th, Erzerum on 12 March. In mid-April they entered Batum and on the 25th Kars. Both Alexandropol and Igdir fell on 18 May and the Armenians were defeated at Karakalise between the 26th and 28th. The Turkish advance led to some tension with the Germans, who had pushed south to Tiflis by 12 June, but Turkish troops were permitted to invest Baku which fell on 14 September after a six-week siege. The Turks then set off towards Dagestan but had only reached Derbent when the armistice with the Allies took effect. The Turks were also active between Lakes Van and Urmia and in north-west Persia. Van fell on 4 April, Tabriz on 14 June and Urmia on 2 August. On 20 August the Turks struck south-east from Tabriz and had reached Mianeh on 9 September before being recalled to Constantinople.

**2** In early 1918 General Marshall in Mesopotamia set about securing his flanks before attempting any further advance up the Tigris. Operations along the Euphrates began on 18 February, aimed at forestalling any attempt by Yilderim Army Group to launch an offensive of its own down this river. The British occupied Hit on 9 March, Khan Baghdadi on the 25th and Anah on the 28th. Here the advance halted for the duration.

**3** From 26 April Marshall looked to his volatile right flank in Kurdistan. Tuz fell on the 29th and Kirkuk on 7 May. The latter had been burnt out and the British were forced to return to Tuz as their advance base, not returning to Kirkuk until 24 October, just prior to the Turkish surrender.

**4** On 19 September the British opened what was to be the last phase of the campaign in Palestine. Again great efforts had been made to deceive the Turks about Allenby's intentions, this time drawing their attention *away* from the coast, towards the Jordan valley. The bait was swallowed eagerly and the Turks had no idea about the size of the force being massed in the coastal plain. Operationally at a loss and tactically panic-stricken, Turkish Seventh and Eighth Armies began to fall back almost immediately and the last day to see any serious resistance was the 21st. By then the British had taken Nazareth and rounded up most of Eighth Army. On 22 September, Fourth Army was also ordered to retreat and found itself sorely harassed by Lawrence and his Arab guerrillas. Thereafter the British advance was more of a procession as Haifa was entered on the 23rd, Amman on the 25th, Devan on the 28th and Damascus on 1 October. By the end of that month the British had also taken Tyre (4th), Beirut (8th), Homs (9th), Tripoli (13th) and Aleppo (26th). On the 31st the Turks accepted Allied armistice terms.

**5** Turkish resistance proved a little more obdurate in Mesopotamia, as Marshall began his final advance on Mosul. Setting out on 18 October, he was obliged to fight three battles at Al Fathah (23rd-26th), Sharquat (28th-30th) and Quayyarah (30th) before finally accepting Sixth Army's surrender on the 30th. It was not until 3 November, in fact, that the first British troops entered Mosul.

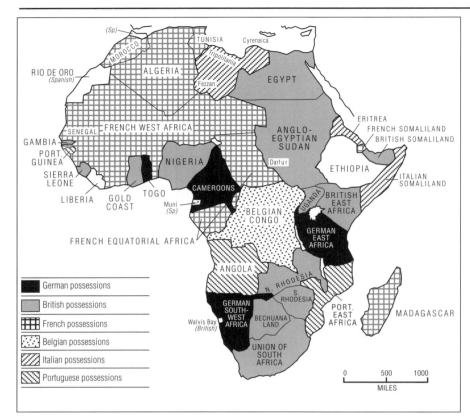

Map 33a **German Possessions in Africa August 1914**

Map 33b **The Campaign in Togoland 6-26 August 1914**

KEY (Maps 33b-d)
- British movements
- French movements
- German movements
- [A] See notes opposite

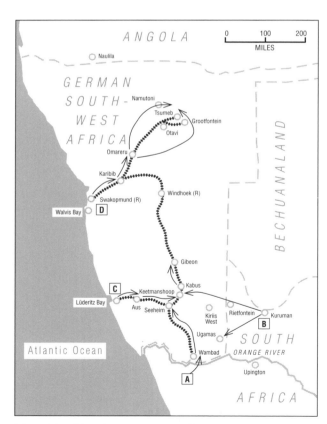

Map 33c **The Campaign in German South-West Africa September 1914–July 1915**

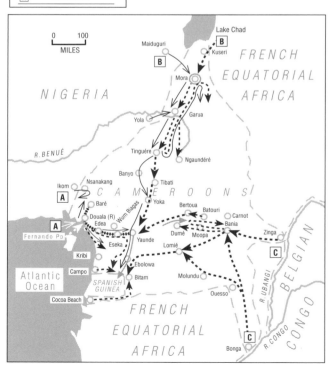

Map 33d **The Campaign in the Cameroons August 1914–February 1916**

• **MAP 33** • AFRICA •

## NOTES TO MAP 33

### 33b Togoland

Traditional imperial rivalries aside, with the outbreak of war the main importance of the German colonies was the powerful radio stations located there which could be used to monitor Allied shipping. The Togoland station was located at Atakpame and on 6 August British troops were already poised to move across the frontiers. They marched from Gambaga, Krachi and Ada and on the 7th the French agreed to also despatch columns from Cheti, Grand Popo and Duagadoudou. The Ada contingent occupied Lomé that same day and set up their main base there. On the 13th these troops began an advance on Kamina. They were held up by the Germans on the 22nd, at Khra, but the latter soon withdrew, falling back to blow up the radio station at Atakpame on the 25th. On the following day they surrendered, just as the Lomé, Krachi and Cheti columns all converged on Kamina and the radio station.

### 33c South-West Africa

Very soon after the outbreak of war the South African government offered to take over responsibility for military operations in German South-West Africa and so free the Imperial Garrison for service in Europe. On 18 September 1914 a force landed at Lüderitz Bay but little exploitation was possible for the rest of the year as Botha's government became embroiled in putting down a rebellion by pro-German Boers. Operations were not resumed until late December with a further landing at Walvis Bay and on 14 January Swakopmund was occupied. Other forces were assembled to the south and east and the campaign became another of the converging columns exercises that typified the First World War African operations. The four columns were as described below:

**A** The southern column crossed the Orange River, at Shuit's Drift, on 6 March and occupied Wambad on 3 April. On 18 April it entered Seeheim and on the 20th Keetmanshoop.

**B** The eastern column, crossing the Kalahari from Kuruman, reached Rietfontein on 31 March and joined up with the southern column at Kabus on 20 April. A subsidiary column had taken Ugamas on 5 April.

**C** The western column left Lüderitz Bay in mid-March and took Aus on the 30th. By the end of April all three of the above columns had united at Keetmanshoop, under Smuts, and were pressing north. Mounted infantry from the western column took the lead, riding into Gibeon on 26 April.

**D** The main northern column, under Botha, had begun its reconnaissance towards Windhoek on 22 February, occupying Rossing on the 23rd. But it was not until 18 March that his main force, divided into three columns, left Swakopmund. After fighting off a German force at Pforteburg, Botha paused to consolidate, only resuming the advance on 27 April after the fall of Gibeon. Karibib fell on 6th May and the capital Windhoek on the 12th. But the Germans had already withdrawn and, refusing Botha's demand for unconditional surrender, fell back to Grootfontein. On 14 June Botha began his final advance northward. Omeraru was taken on the 20th and from there his force split again into three columns, with the eastern and western flanks swinging around through Tsumeb and Namutomi to seal off any further German retreat. These two towns were occupied in 4 and 6 July, respectively, and having been driven out of Otavi on the 1st, the Germans finally surrendered on 8 July. Although they had inflicted less than a thousand battle casualties on the enemy, the Germans had obliged them to put fully 50,000 men into the field to capture this colony and its two radio stations.

### 33d Cameroon

With the British eager to capture the excellent port of Douala and the radio station located there, and the French keen to grab back the large chunk of Equatorial Africa lost to the Germans after the Agadir crisis, the two countries were happy to cooperate in a joint invasion of the Cameroons. As usual the campaign involved converging columns of advance against a German force only concerned with tying down troops who might otherwise be employed in Europe. The three main axes of advance are described below:

**A** The columns in the west began with a failed sortie from Ikom and a successful amphibious landing at Douala on 27 September. The Germans there fled to Edea only to be pushed out again on 26 October and forced to retreat to Yaoundé. The British then cleared the railway north to Baré, taken on 11 December, and the French consolidated at Edea. The advance then ceased until early April. Wum Biagas and Eseka were both taken in May but severe outbreaks of dysentery forced the Franco-British force back to Edea until September. Wum Biagas and Eseka were recaptured in October but the remaining few miles to Yaoundé were bitterly contested. The town finally fell on 1 January 1916 but the Germans had already withdrawn south. The French set off in pursuit but, despite being joined by troops from the other Allied axes, including columns from Spanish Guinea, could not prevent the Germans from themselves crossing into Guinea on 4 February. Here they were interned, the German whites being sent to Spain and the askaris to Fernando Po.

**B** In the north, a British column crossed the frontier on 25 August whilst a French one from the Lake Chad area went on to take Kuseri on 21 September. Attempts to storm Mora in August and early November failed and the garrison was by-passed, with both columns halting in December until the following spring. With the advance resumed, Garoua fell after a short siege on 10 June. Ngaoundéré was taken only 18 days later and on 9 July Tinguere also fell. The Allies then backtracked to attempt another assault on Mora, in late August and early September, but once again they were repulsed. Before they could try again they were summoned south to assist in the push on Yaoundé. Tibal fell on 3 November, the fortified Banyo area was cleared by the 6th, and Yoka entered on 1 December. On 4 January this column, too, reached Yaoundé and afterwards took part in the pursuit south to Ebolowa. The Mora garrison only finally surrendered on 18 February, after an eighteen-month siege.

**C** The eastern axis was almost entirely composed of French colonial troops and two columns set off from Bonga and Zinga in mid-August, meeting at Bania on 15 October. Batouri and Bertoua both fell in December but a German counter-attack forced the French back to Carnot. The advance was not renewed until late April 1915, with Morpa falling on 23 June, Batouri three weeks later, and Bertoua and Doumé a few days after that. Two subsidiary columns had already met at Lomié on 25 June. Another lull in operations followed but the French then took part in the push on Yaoundé, which their leading units reached on 4 January 1917. They then set off south, along with another column from Lomié, to join in the pursuit of the retreating Germans.

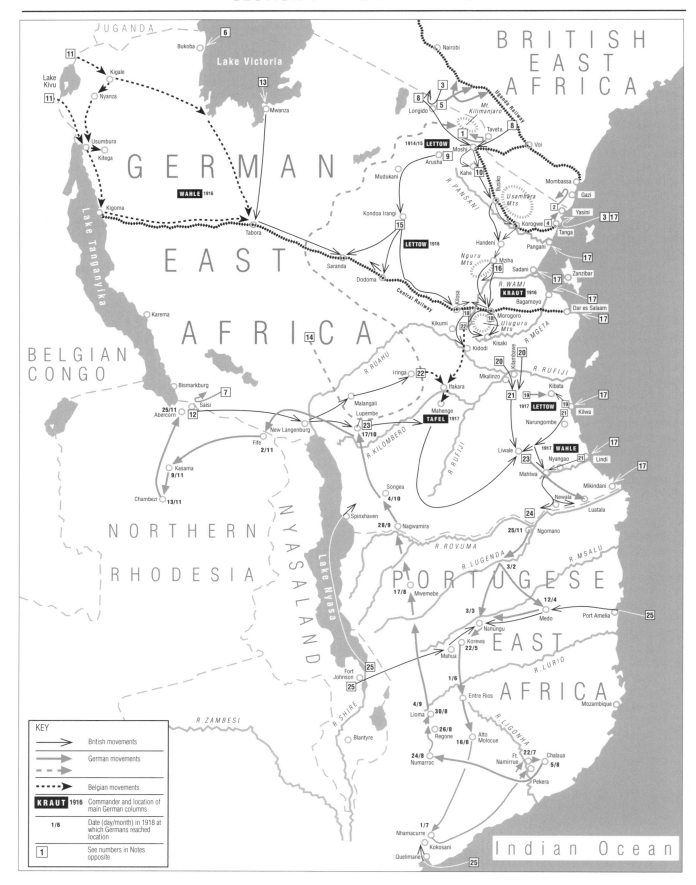

Map 34 **The Campaign in East Africa 1914-18**

• **MAP 34** • AFRICA •

## NOTES TO MAP 34

### 1914

[1] On 15 August the Germans made a strong raid against Taveta but were repulsed.

[2] In late September the Germans switched their attention to the coast, probing towards Mombassa. They were forced back to the frontier after being held at Gazi on 7 October.

[3] On 2 November an Indian expeditionary force attempted a landing at Tanga but by the 5th had been driven back to the boats, in which they retreated to Mombassa. An attack on Mt. Longido, on the 4th, was also repulsed.

### 1915

[4] On 18 January the Germans launched another attack up the coast, on Yasini which was occupied by the British. This was successful but cost so many casualties that the German commander in East Africa, von Lettow-Vorbeck, resolved to limit himself to hit-and-run guerrilla operations thereafter.

[5] These operations were conducted from a base area around Mt. Longido and concentrated upon cutting the Uganda railway from Mombassa. Most of the campaigning in 1915 comprised these raids and the belated British responses to them.

[6] The only other British operation of any note was the seizure of Bukoba, on the western shore of Lake Victoria, on 23 June.

[7] The Germans' only significant foray beyond the railway was an unsuccessful raid on Saisi, in N.Rhodesia, on 24 and 29 July.

### 1916

[8] By early 1916, with all the other campaigns in Africa almost won, the British felt ready to begin offensive operations into German East Africa. The first task was to pinch out Mt. Kilimanjaro and operations began, under Smuts' command, on 5 March. Kilimanjaro was isolated by the 14th when the converging eastern and western columns reached Koshi. Kahe was attacked on the 21st but the Germans simply withdrew and this failure to 'bag' the main German force was to be a recurrent feature of the whole campaign as time and again British pincer and flank attacks failed to cut the German line of retreat ahead of their withdrawal.

[9] On 3 April, having moved most of his eastern column to Arusha, Smuts attacked towards Kondoa Irangi, taking Mudukani on the 10th and Kondoa on the 18th. There this column halted in deference to the rainy season. They beat off a determined German attack on 9 and 10 May although von Lettow-Vorbeck did not finally withdraw from the area until 24 June. The British remained at Kondoa Irangi until 15 July.

[10] Not until 22 May did Smuts' western column set off towards the Usambara Mountains, although they soon entered Busiko on the 31st. After a week's halt Korogwe was entered on 15 June. Smuts now pressed on across the River Pangani and was in Handeni on 18 June. Overcoming stern German resistance on the River Lukigura (not shown) on the 24th, he pushed on to Mziha and halted there on 5 July to allow his logistic 'tail' to reorganise.

[11] In the meantime three other drives had been launched from Rhodesia and Uganda (see [12] and [13]) and from the Belgian Congo. This latter column set off from the southern end of Lake Kivu on 19 April, reaching Usumbara on 6 June and the capital Kitega on the 16th. Taking the surrender of the local king on the 27th, the Belgians pressed south towards the railway, reaching Kigoma on 28 July and turning east along

it from 3 August. A second Belgian column left from the northern end of Lake Kivu on 23 April, reaching Kigale on 6 May, and Nyanza on the 19th. Most of the column then pressed south-east towards Tabora, reaching Lake Victoria on 27 June.

[12] On 25 May the Nyasaland Rhodesia Field Force left N.Rhodesia and struck east, taking Neu Langenburg on the 29th and then marching north-west to link up with Smuts. On the way they took Malangali on 24 July, Lupembe on 18 August and Iringa on the 29th.

[13] A force from the King's African Rifles landed at Mwanza on 11 July and three days later had occupied the town. On 26 August they, too, joined in the march on Tabora, which they reached on 25 September. The Belgians had already taken control of the town on the 19th but only to find that the Germans had secretly pulled out the week before, retreating south-eastwards towards the Iringa-Mahenge region.

[14] The German force retreating before this Belgian-British advance was commanded by retired Major-General Wahle, who had divided his men into four columns. Two of these were finally overcome in October, near Iringa and Mahenge. A third column eventually made contact with von Lettow-Vorbeck south of the Rufiji but the fourth, under Wintgens and later Naumann, marched to Lupembe and then turned back on itself and proceeded to lead its pursuers a merry dance across the north-eastern portion of the German colony until finally surrendering near Mt. Kilimanjaro in October 1917.

[15] Meanwhile, Smuts' main force had resumed its advance towards the Central Railway. Its western columns had moved off first, leaving Kondoa Irangi on 15 July and entering Dodoma on the 28th. At no stage, however, did Smuts succeed in infiltrating a blocking force in the German rear. Smuts then proceeded to take control of the railway, employing one of his columns from Kondoa Irangi to seize Saranda on 31 July and another to take Kilosa on 22 August.

[16] The rest of Smuts' force left Mziha on 1 August. They entered Morogoro shortly afterwards but the attempt to feed a flanking force across the German line of retreat came to nothing.

[17] Between July and September Smuts cooperated with the Royal Navy to organise a series of amphibious operations against the German colony's coastline. Tanga fell on 7 July, Pangani on the 23rd, Sadani and Bagamoyo on 1 and 5 August, and Dar es Salaam, Kilwa, Mikindani and Lindi on 4, 7, 13 and 16 September respectively.

[18] On 31 August Smuts set off once again, sending columns around each side of the Uluguru Mountains. After unsuccessful attacks on 7 and 8 September, the British finally took Kisaki on the 14th, but only after the Germans had again stolen away. Von Lettow-Vorbeck withdrew to the River Mgeta where he established strongly fortified positions. Here Smuts paused and replaced many of his white troops, easy prey to malaria, with Nigerians and East Africans. Another of his columns had meanwhile advanced to the west of the Mgeta to take Kikumi on 3 September and Kidodi on the 10th.

[19] In September, also, a Kilwa Force was created (expanded to a division in November) and on 18 October it took Kibata. However, subsequent attempts to use it as a base for search and destroy missions against the German supply dumps were thwarted when von Lettow-Vorbeck himself attacked Kibata, in early December, and forced the British to concentrate a large garrison to defend it.

### 1917

[20] On 1 Jan, after over three months of static trench warfare along the

flooded Mgeta, Smuts once more began offensive operations. The Germans soon gave up the Mgeta positions and on 3 and 6 January Smuts' two columns crossed the Rufiji. At the same time Kilwa Force began to push north and north-west but yet again the British were unable to trap von Lettow-Vorbeck. Subsequent operations through until May were hampered by a particularly severe and protracted rainy season.

**21** During the second half of the year Smuts and his replacements (Hoskins and later Deventer) made serious but necessarily sporadic attempts to launch a concentrated blow against the Germans. They operated along three axes, the strongest being from Kilwa and Lindi. At one stage Liwale seemed the best place to close the trap but the Germans, despite losing heavily in battles at Narumgombe (19 July) and Nyangao/Mahlwa (15-18 October), continued to evade their pursuers. After reaching Newala, on 17 November, von Lettow-Vorbeck crossed the Rovuma and now entered Portuguese East Africa. British patrols did not follow until late the following month.

**22** The other main Allied operation that year was against German columns under Captain Tafel, operating from a base on the Mahenge plateau. Again, little was done in the first half of the year until the Belgians agreed to resume operations of their own. In August they transferred columns to Kilosa and Iringa and, having been obliged to retake Kidodi on the 18th, advanced towards Mahenge, taking Ifakara on the 28th and occupying the base itself on 9 October.

**23** The Nyasaland Rhodesia Field Force, meanwhile, had been advancing from Lupembe, first assisting in the clearance of the Mahenge plateau and then turning south to pursue the retreating Tafel. He was chased all the way to Liwale, which fell to the NRFF on 29 October, but still managed to break through the attempted pincers by these units and the Kilwa force on 16 November. He then turned south to try and join von Lettow-Vorbeck but was finally brought to bay at Luatala, on the Rovuma, where he surrendered on 28 November.

1918

**24** Once over the Rovuma, with no secure bases and very short of ammunition, von Lettow-Vorbeck's only objective was to keep some kind of force in being and oblige the British to deploy as many men as possible to pursue him. For the rest of the war German resistance was limited to minor rearguard actions. The campaign was now more of a route-march than a military contest and is significant mainly for the German forces' remarkable endurance and discipline. Their extensive peregrinations are marked on the map along with the dates at which they reached a particular town or village. Indeed, it was not until 25 November that von Lettow-Vorbeck finally surrendered at Abercorn, the last German commander in the field to do so.

**25** From the British point of view, operations in the last months of the war were in two main phases. First came an attempted 'squeeze' from the Indian Ocean and from Lake Nyasa, the two forces setting forth in January. Once these columns had failed to close the trap at Nanungu (5 May) and Korewa (22 May), the campaign became simply a vain pursuit of the dwindling German force all the way into N.Rhodesia. There were also small landing operations, one at Quelimane, on 25 June, to support the Portuguese, and one at Spinxhaven, on the eastern shore of Lake Nyasa, on 19 September.

# SECTION 2

# COMMAND STRUCTURES

## Notes to Table 2.1 (opposite)

(1) Coalition Govt. from 5/15.

(2) Previously the Committee of Imperial Defence which became the first War Cabinet in 11/14. Renamed the Dardanelles Committee in 5/15 and the War Committee in 11/16. In its final manifestation, one month later, it comprised the P.M., the Chancellor, the Lord President (*Curzon*), the Minister for Nat. Service (to 8/17) and the Ministers without Portfolio.

(3) Grew out of the Labour Dept. at the Board of Trade.

(4) Responsible to the War Cabinet for the control of their particular services – link not shown.

(5) Formed as Dept. National Service 12/16. Grew partly out of Recruitment Dept. at War Office.

(6) Took charge of merchant shipbuilding from the Navy Controller. Answerable directly to the First Lord.

(7) There was also a Food Production Dept. (f. 1/17), originally part of the Board of Agriculture but later independent.

(8) Grew out of the Foreign Office's Contraband Dept.

(9) Grew out of the Shipping Control Committee (f. 1/16). Absorbed the Admiralty's Transport Div. in 2/17. The Board of Trade, however, held on to its Mercantile Marine Dept. See also Navy Controller and note.

(10) As Air Board from 5/16. From 12/16 the President of the Air Board (*Cowdray*) was given ministerial status.

(11) Had little control over naval or merchant shipping production. Took over army and air force production immediately and design and research from 11/15.

(12) Previously Dir. Air Equipment (*McInnes*). Both its successor and the Dir. Aero. Engine Supplies (below) soon became semi-detached from the Ministry of Munitions, being housed with the Air Council and so forming a virtual Ministry of Aircraft Production.

(13) Also known as the Aeronautical Inspection Dept.

(14) Very much in Kitchener's shadow.

(15) Detached from Military Operations 1/16.

(16) In charge, left to right, of military cryptography, counter-espionage and military espionage – MI5 was known as MO5g to 1/16 and MI1c as the Secret Service Bureau to 5/16.

(17) Duties assumed by 1st Sea Lord 5/17.

(18) Originally referred to as Room 40, in charge of naval cryptoanalysis. Not formally part of Naval Intelligence until 5/17.

(19) Originally known as Enemy Submarine Section (EI) until 6/17.

(20) In charge of both naval and merchant-shipping construction. Prior to this the latter had been in the hands of private industry, to 12/16, and then the Shipping Controller.

(21) Not shown in the organigram are the other Sea Lords: 2nd (Chief of Naval Personnel): *Hamilton* to 6/16, *Gough-Calthorpe* to 12/16, *Burney* to 8/17, *Wemyss* to 9/17, *Heath*; 3rd (Chief of Naval Matériel): *Tudor* to 12/17, *Halsey* to 6/18, *de Bartolmé*; 4th (Chief of Supplies and Transport): *Lambert* to 12/16, *Halsey* to 12/17, *Tothill*; 5th (Chief of Naval Air Service)(f. 12/16): *Paine*. (The descriptive titles in brackets were not formalised until 10/17).

(22) In 1/18, prior to the R.N.A.S. being absorbed into the R.A.F., two new posts were created: Director of the Air Division, to liaise with the Air Council and to supervise aerial ASW (*Scarlett*), and an Admiral commanding Grand Fleet air units (*Phillimore*).

(23) Under Trade Division until 9/17. There was also a Convoy Section (f. 4/17) of the Board of Trade, later moved to the Min. of Shipping Control.

(24) See note 9.

• **TABLE 2.1** • U.K. GOVERNMENT AND HIGH COMMAND •

**Table 2.1 U.K. Government and High Command 1914-18**

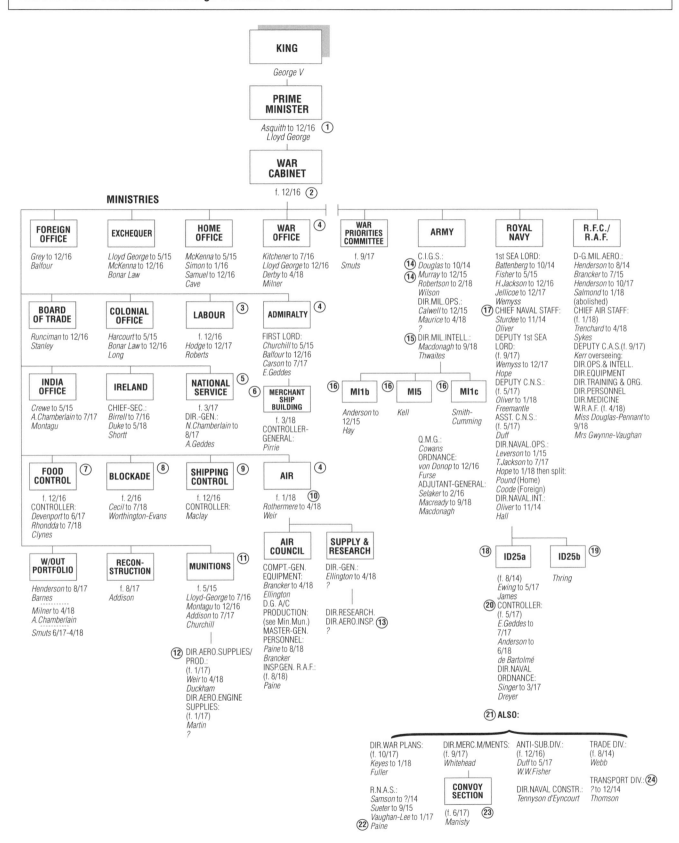

**KING**

*George V*

**PRIME MINISTER**

*Asquith* to 12/16 ①
*Lloyd George*

**WAR CABINET**

f. 12/16 ②

**MINISTRIES**

**FOREIGN OFFICE**

*Grey* to 12/16
*Balfour*

**EXCHEQUER**

*Lloyd George* to 5/15
*McKenna* to 12/16
*Bonar Law*

**HOME OFFICE**

*McKenna* to 5/15
*Simon* to 1/16
*Samuel* to 12/16
*Cave*

**WAR OFFICE** ④

*Kitchener* to 7/16
*Lloyd George* to 12/16
*Derby* to 4/18
*Milner*

**WAR PRIORITIES COMMITTEE**

f. 9/17
*Smuts*

**ARMY**

C.I.G.S.:
⑭ *Douglas* to 10/14
⑭ *Murray* to 12/15
*Robertson* to 2/18
*Wilson*
DIR.MIL.OPS.:
*Calwell* to 12/15
*Maurice* to 4/18
?
⑮ DIR.MIL.INTELL.:
*Macdonagh* to 9/18
*Thwaites*

**ROYAL NAVY**

1st SEA LORD:
*Battenberg* to 10/14
*Fisher* to 5/15
*H.Jackson* to 12/16
*Jellicoe* to 12/17
*Wemyss*
⑰ CHIEF NAVAL STAFF:
*Sturdee* to 11/14
*Oliver*
DEPUTY 1st SEA LORD:
(f. 9/17)
*Wemyss* to 12/17
*Hope*
DEPUTY C.N.S.:
(f. 5/17)
*Oliver* to 1/18
*Freemantle*
ASST. C.N.S.:
(f. 5/17)
*Duff*
DIR.NAVAL.OPS.:
*Leverson* to 1/15
*T.Jackson* to 7/17
*Hope* to 1/18 then split:
*Pound* (Home)
*Coode* (Foreign)
DIR.NAVAL.INT.:
*Oliver* to 11/14
*Hall*

**R.F.C./ R.A.F.**

D-G.MIL.AERO.:
*Henderson* to 8/14
*Brancker* to 7/15
*Henderson* to 10/17
*Salmond* to 1/18
(abolished)
CHIEF AIR STAFF:
(f. 1/18)
*Trenchard* to 4/18
*Sykes*
DEPUTY C.A.S.(f. 9/17)
*Kerr* overseeing:
DIR.OPS.& INTELL.
DIR.EQUIPMENT
DIR.TRAINING & ORG.
DIR.PERSONNEL
DIR.MEDICINE
W.R.A.F. (f. 4/18)
*Miss Douglas-Pennant* to 9/18
*Mrs Gwynne-Vaughan*

**BOARD OF TRADE**

*Runciman* to 12/16
*Stanley*

**COLONIAL OFFICE**

*Harcourt* to 5/15
*Bonar Law* to 12/16
*Long*

**LABOUR** ③

f. 12/16
*Hodge* to 12/17
*Roberts*

**ADMIRALTY** ④

FIRST LORD:
*Churchill* to 5/15
*Balfour* to 12/16
*Carson* to 7/17
*E.Geddes*

**INDIA OFFICE**

*Crewe* to 5/15
*A.Chamberlain* to 7/17
*Montagu*

**IRELAND**

CHIEF-SEC.:
*Birrell* to 7/16
*Duke* to 5/18
*Shortt*

**NATIONAL SERVICE** ⑤

f. 3/17
DIR.-GEN.:
*N.Chamberlain* to 8/17
*A.Geddes*

**MERCHANT SHIP BUILDING** ⑥

f. 3/18
CONTROLLER-GENERAL:
*Pirrie*

⑯ **MI1b**

*Anderson* to 12/15
*Hay*

⑯ **MI5**

*Kell*

⑯ **MI1c**

*Smith-Cumming*

Q.M.G.:
*Cowans*
ORDNANCE:
*von Donop* to 12/16
*Furse*
ADJUTANT-GENERAL:
*Selaker* to 2/16
*Macready* to 9/18
*Macdonagh*

**FOOD CONTROL** ⑦

f. 12/16
CONTROLLER:
*Devenport* to 6/17
*Rhondda* to 7/18
*Clynes*

**BLOCKADE** ⑧

f. 2/16
*Cecil* to 7/18
*Worthington-Evans*

**SHIPPING CONTROL** ⑨

f. 12/16
CONTROLLER:
*Maclay*

**AIR** ④

f. 1/18
*Rothermere* to 4/18 ⑩
*Weir*

⑱ **ID25a**

(f. 8/14)
*Ewing* to 5/17
*James*
⑳ CONTROLLER:
(f. 5/17)
*E.Geddes* to 7/17
*Anderson* to 6/18
*de Bartolmé*
DIR.NAVAL ORDNANCE:
*Singer* to 3/17
*Dreyer*

**ID25b** ⑲

*Thring*

**W/OUT PORTFOLIO**

*Henderson* to 8/17
*Barnes*
----------
*Milner* to 4/18
*A.Chamberlain*
----------
*Smuts* 6/17-4/18

**RECON-STRUCTION**

f. 8/17
*Addison*

**MUNITIONS** ⑪

f. 5/15
*Lloyd-George* to 7/16
*Montagu* to 12/16
*Addison* to 7/17
*Churchill*

⑫ DIR.AERO.SUPPLIES/ PROD.:
(f. 1/17)
*Weir* to 4/18
*Duckham*
DIR.AERO.ENGINE SUPPLIES:
(f. 1/17)
*Martin*
?

**AIR COUNCIL**

COMPT.-GEN. EQUIPMENT:
*Brancker* to 4/18
*Ellington*
D.G. A/C PRODUCTION:
(see Min.Mun.)
MASTER-GEN. PERSONNEL:
*Paine* to 8/18
*Brancker*
INSP.GEN. R.A.F.:
(f. 8/18)
*Paine*

**SUPPLY & RESEARCH**

DIR.-GEN.:
*Ellington* to 4/18
?

DIR.RESEARCH.
DIR.AERO.INSP. ⑬
?

㉑ ALSO:

DIR.WAR PLANS:
(f. 10/17)
*Keyes* to 1/18
*Fuller*

R.N.A.S.:
*Samson* to ?/14
*Sueter* to 9/15
*Vaughan-Lee* to 1/17
㉒ *Paine*

DIR.MERC.M/MENTS:
(f. 9/17)
*Whitehead*

**CONVOY SECTION**

(f. 6/17) ㉓
*Manisty*

ANTI-SUB.DIV.:
(f. 12/16)
*Duff* to 5/17
*W.W.Fisher*

DIR.NAVAL CONSTR.:
*Tennyson d'Eyncourt*

TRADE DIV.:
(f. 8/14)
*Webb*

TRANSPORT DIV.: ㉔
?to 12/14
*Thomson*

**Supplement to Table 2.1:** Other Major British Commands

## THE ARMY
### Theatre/Area Commands:
**1** C-in-C. BRITISH ARMIES IN FRANCE (f.12/14)
Previously BRITISH EXPEDITIONARY FORCE
> *French* to 12/15
> *Haig*
> CHIEF OF STAFF
> *Murray* to 1/15
> *Robertson* to 12/15
> *Kiggell* to 1/18
> *Lawrence*
> CHIEF OF OPERATIONS
> *Harper* 11/14 to 2/15
> *Maurice* to 12/15
> *Davidson* to 3/18
> *Dill*
> CHIEF OF INTELLIGENCE
> *Macdonogh* to 1/15
> *Charteris* to 1/18
> *Cox* to 8/18
> *Clive*
> QUARTERMASTER-GENERAL
> *Robertson* to 1/15
> *Maxwell* to 12/17
> *Clarke*

**2** C-in-C. EGYPT AND PALESTINE (FORCE IN EGYPT to 3/16 then
EGYPTIAN EXPEDITIONARY FORCE)*
> *Byng* to 9/14
> *Maxwell* to 10/15
> *Monro* to 1/16
> *Murray* to 6/17
> *Allenby*

**3** C-in-C. GALLIPOLI (MEDITERRANEAN EXPEDITIONARY FORCE
f.3/16)
> *Hamilton* to 10/15
> *Monro* to 11/15
> *Birdwood*

**4** C-in-C. BRITISH SALONIKA ARMY (f.11/15)
> *Monro* 4/11 to 15/11/15
> *Mahon* to 5/16
> *Milne*

**5** EASTERN MEDITERRANEAN FORCES (f.11/15. A short-lived
umbrella command for the rump Mediterranean Expeditionary Force [see 3
above] and the first arrivals for the British Salonika Army [see 4 above],
themselves coming from Gallipoli.)
> *Monro* to 1/16

**6** C-in-C. MESOPOTAMIA EXPEDITIONARY FORCE (f.2/16.
Previously INDIAN EXPEDITIONARY FORCE 'D' which arrived Basra 11/14.)
> *Nixon* to 1/16
> *Lake* to 8/16
> *Maude* to 11/17
> *Marshall* to 7/18
> *Fanshawe* (acting) to 9/18
> *Marshall*

**7** C-in-C. BRITISH FORCES IN ITALY (f.11/17. Became part of Italian
Tenth Army [see p.86], also commanded by Cavan, in 10/18.)
> *Cavan* 6/11 to 13/11/17
> *Plumer* to 3/18
> *Cavan*

**8** C-in-C. EAST AFRICA (as C-in-C. INDIAN EXPEDITIONARY FORCES
'B' and 'C' to 11/14)
> *Aitken* to 12/14
> *Wapshawe* to 4/15
> *Tighe* to 12/15
> *Tighe* (acting)† to 2/16
> (Thereafter under South African commanders. See p.105.)

**9** C-in-C. INDIA‡
> *Duff* to 10/16
> *Monro*

**10** C-in-C. HOME FORCES
> *Hamilton* to 3/15
> *Rundle* to 12/15
> *French* to 5/18
> *Robertson*

**11** C-in-C. IRELAND
> *Paget* to 4/16
> *Maxwell* to 11/16
> *Mahon* to 5/18
> *Shaw*

### Armies
All numbered Armies served in France and Belgium only.

**1** FIRST ARMY (f.12/14)
> *Haig* to 12/15
> *Rawlinson* to 2/16
> *Monro* to 9/16
> *Horne*

**2** SECOND ARMY (f.12/14) HQ transferred to Italy 11/17 to take
command of the British Forces in Italy (see 7 above).
> *Smith-Dorrien* to 5/15
> *Plumer* to 11/17
> ***Rawlinson*** to 2/18 ◊
> *Birdwood* (acting) to 3/18 ◊
> *Plumer*

**3** THIRD ARMY (f.7/15)
> *Monro* to 10/15
> *Allenby* to 6/17
> *Byng*

**4** FOURTH ARMY (f.2/16) HQ was transferred to Second Army (see
above) in 11/17.
> *Rawlinson* to 11/17
> *Birdwood* (acting) to 12/17
> *Rawlinson* 5/18 to end

**5** FIFTH ARMY (f.11/16) HQ was transferred to reformed Fourth Army
(see above) in 5/18.
> *Gough* to 4/18
> *Rawlinson* to 5/18
> *Birdwood*

**6** RESERVE ARMY (f.5/16 and became FIFTH ARMY [see above]
11/16. Ref. 4/18 and became reformed FIFTH ARMY [see above] on
23/5/18).
> *Gough* to 11/16
> *Birdwood* 4/18 to 5/18

**7** SALONIKA ARMY
> (see Theatre/Area Commands 4 above.)

**8** CAVALRY CORPS (f.10/14 to 2/16 and ref. 9/16.)
> *Allenby* to 12/14
> *Kavanagh*

### Lesser Commands and Expeditionary Forces
**1** ADEN BRIGADE later ADEN FIELD FORCE (GOC and Political
Resident)

* The EEF also
incorporated the
rump Mediterranean
Expeditionary
Force
(see 3 below).

† On behalf of
*Smith-Dorrien* who
had swiftly
succumbed to
pneumonia.

‡ See also separate
entry on p.103.

◊ No divisions under
command

* All acting in the name of the Government of Bombay, except for *Younghusband* who acted for the Government of Egypt.

† For other East Africa commanders see also Table 2.10: India and South Africa.

‡ See also Table 2.10: Japan.

◊ As part of Delta Command (not listed).

• Also C-in-C, except where latter also named.

Δ From 7/18 acting for *Northey*.

** Also Governor British-occupied Togoland from 9/14.

†† Acting for *Mereweather*.

‡‡ Governor of Straits Settlements and High Commissioner of Malay Protectorates.

◊◊ Also Governor British-occupied Cameroons from 2/15.

•• Under High Commissioner South Africa

ΔΔ For *Jackson* and (from 12/17) for *Coryndon*.

*Bell* to ?/14
*Shaw* to 7/15
*Younghusband* to 9/15*
*Price* to 7/16
*Stewart*

**2** Commanding **CAMEROONS EXPEDITION** (see Map 33d)
*Dobell*

**3** Commanding **DUNSTERFORCE** (f.1/18 in Persia) which fought its way into the Caucasus before being forced to evacuate Baku in 9/18.
*Dunsterville*

**4** C-in-C. **FORCE IN EGYPT**. Pre-war name for British troops in Egypt prior to establishment of Egyptian Expeditionary Force (see Theatre/Area Commands 2). Reformed in 1/18.
*Watson* from 1/18

**5** C-in-C. **LEVANT BASE** (f.10/15) at Alexandria to coordinate allocation of supplies to forces in Egypt, Gallipoli and Salonika. Disbanded 4/16.
*Ellison* to 12/15
*Altham*

**6** C-in-C. **NORTH RUSSIA EXPEDITIONARY FORCE** (f.5/18) which landed at Murmansk that month to help safeguard Allied interests in the Arctic Theatre. Helped seize Archangel 7/18. Evacuated 1919.
*Poole* to 2/19
*Briggs*

**7** **PERSIA**. Two separate forces formed:
EAST PERSIA CORDON (f.2/16)
*Dryer* to 10/16
*Tanner*
SOUTH PERSIA RIFLES (Persian levies under British commander, f.3/16)
*Sykes*

**8** **GOC RHODESIA/NYASALAND BORDER** (f.11/15)†
The Rhodesian element of the Allied invasion of German East Africa in 1916.
*Northey*

**9** Commanding **TOGOLAND EXPEDITION** (see Map 33b)
*Bryant* (acting)

**10** Commanding **TSINGTAO EXPEDITION** (9-11/14)‡
*Barnardiston*

**11** Commanding **WESTERN FRONTIER FORCE** (f.11/15)
for hostilities against the Senussi in Cyrenaica (modern Libya).
*Wallace* to 1/16
*Peyton* to 4/16
*Dallas* (acting) to 6/16
*Dobell* to 10/16
*Watson* to 3/17
*Casson* ◊

**Colonial Governors•**
**1** AUSTRALIA
(see Table 2.10)
**2** BAHAMAS
*Haddon Smith* to 2/14
*Allardyce* (arr.6/15)
**3** BARBADOS
*Probyn* to 5/18
*O'Brien*
**4** BRITISH GUIANA
*Egerton* to 6/16
*Clementi* (acting) to 4/17
*Collett*
**5** CANADA
(See Table 2.10)
**6** EGYPT
(See Table 2.10)

**7** EAST AFRICA
*Belfield* to 4/17
*Browning*Δ
**8** GAMBIA
*Cameron*
**9** GIBRALTAR
*Miles* to 9/18
*Smith-Dorrien*
**10** GOLD COAST
*Clifford***
**11** JAMAICA
*Manning* to 5/18
*Probyn*
**12** LEEWARD ISLANDS
*Hesketh-Ball* to 1/16
*Vans Best*††
**13** MALAYA
GOVERNOR‡‡
*Young*
C-in-C
*Ridout*
**14** MALTA
*Rundle* to 2/15
*Methuen*
**15** NEWFOUNDLAND
(See Table 2.10)
**16** NEW ZEALAND
(See Table 2.10)
**17** NIGERIA
*Lugard*◊◊
**18** NYASALAND
*G. Smith*
**19** RHODESIA
RESIDENT COMMISSIONER••
*Burns Begg* to 4/15
*Stanley* to 7/18
*Douglas Jones*
S.AF.COY. ADMINISTRATOR:
N. RHODESIA
*Wallace*
S. RHODESIA
*Milton* to 10/14
*Chaplin*
**20** SEYCHELLES
*O'Brien* to 9/18
?
**21** SIERRA LEONE
*Merewether* to 12/15
*Wilkinson*
**22** SOMALILAND
COMMISSIONER
*Archer*
C-in-C
*Summers*
**23** SOUTH AFRICA
(See Table 2.10)
**24** SUDAN
*Wingate* to 1/17
*Stack*
**25** TRINIDAD & TOBAGO
*Le Hunte* to 10/15
*Chancellor* (arr.6/16)
**26** UGANDA
*Wallis* (acting)ΔΔ to 11/14

*Jackson* to 4/17
*Wallis* (acting)ΔΔ

**27 ZANZIBAR**
as East Africa (see 5 above)

**Other**

**1 GERMAN EAST AFRICA** (Occupied)
CIVIL ADMINISTRATOR
*Byatt* from 1/16

**2 INDIA**
(See Table 2.10)

**3 IRELAND**
LORD LIEUTENANT
*Wimborne* to 5/18
*French*

**4 PALESTINE** (Occupied)
MILITARY GOVERNOR
*Clayton* to 4/18
*Money*

# ROYAL NAVY
**Home Commands**

**1 GRAND FLEET**
COMMANDER-IN-CHIEF
*Jellicoe* to 11/16
*Beatty*
CHIEF-OF-STAFF
*Madden* to 11/16
*O.de B. Brock*
CAPTAIN OF THE FLEET
*Everett* to ?
*Halsey* to 11/16
*Brand*

**2 BATTLE-CRUISER FORCE***
*Beatty* to 11/16
*Pakenham*

**3 CHANNEL FLEET**
*Burney* to 12/14
*Bayly* to 1/15
*Bethell* to 6/15 (disbanded)

**4 HARWICH FORCE**
*Tyrwhitt*

**5 NORTHERN PATROL** (f.2/18).Originally TENTH CRUISER
SQUADRON which was paid off 12/17.
*de Chair* to 3/16
*Tupper* to 8/18 (disbanded)

**6 C-in-C. MINELAYERS** (f.1/18)
*Clinton-Baker*

**7 ADMIRAL OF MINESWEEPING†**
*Charlton* to 12/15
*Fitzherbert* to 3/17 (disbanded)

**8 C-in-C. CONTROLLED MINEFIELDS** (f.6/18)
*Dampier*

**9 ADMIRAL OF PATROLS/PATROL FLOTILLAS**
(see EAST COAST OF ENGLAND 12 below)

**10 SUBMARINE BRANCH**
*Keyes* to 2/15
*Hall*

**11 DOVER PATROL** (f.10/14)
*Hood* to 4/15
*Bacon* to 1/18
*Keyes*

**12 EAST COAST** (f.11/15) Previously ADMIRAL OF PATROLS/PATROL
FLOTILLAS

*Ballard* to 5/16
*Nicholson* to 7/18
*Charlton*

**13 MILFORD HAVEN** (f.2/15)
*Dare*

**14 NORE**
*Poore* to 1/15
*Callaghan* to 3/18
*Doveton Sturdee*

**15 ORKNEY AND SHETLANDS**
*Colville* to 1/16
*F.E.E. Brock* to 1/18
*King-Hall*

**16 PLYMOUTH** (Devonport)
*Egerton* to 4/16
*Warrender* to 12/16
*Bethell* to 8/18
*Thursby*

**17 PORTSMOUTH**
*Meux* to 2/16
*Colville*

**18 QUEENSTOWN** (COAST OF IRELAND)
*Coke* to 7/15
*Bayly*

**19 ROSYTH** (COAST OF SCOTLAND)
*Lowry* to 7/16
*Hamilton* to 10/17
*Burney*

**Foreign Commands**

**1 ADRIATIC FORCE** (f.5/17). Previously [from 3/15] ADRIATIC
SQUADRON
*Thursby* to 5/16
*Kerr* to 8/17
*Meneage* to 3/18
*Kelly*

**2 AEGEAN SQUADRON** (f.8/17) Previously EAST MEDITERRANEAN
SQUADRON
*Carden* to 3/15
*de Robeck* to 6/16
*Thursby* to 8/17
*Fremantle* to 1/18
*Hayes-Sadler* to 2/18
*Lambert* to 9/18
*Culme-Seymour*

**3 AUSTRALIAN FLEET**
*Patey*

**4 CAPE OF GOOD HOPE**
*King-Hall* to 2/16
*Charlton* to 6/18
*Fitzherbert*

**5 CHINA SQUADRON**
*Jerram* to 7/15
*Grant* to 10/17
*Tudor*

**6 EAST COAT OF SOUTH AMERICA**
(See SOUTH EAST COAST OF AMERICA 16 below)

**7 EAST INDIES SQUADRON**
*Peirse* to 1/16
*Wemyss*
*Grant*

**8 EAST MEDITERRANEAN SQUADRON**
(See AEGEAN SQUADRON 2 above)

**9 EGYPTIAN DIVISION** (f.7/17)

* So-called from
11/16. Previously
CRUISER FORCE
A then BATTLE-
CRUISER FLEET.
Often referred to as
Battle-Cruiser
Squadron.

† Originally (from
9/14) C-in-C
EAST COAST
MINESWEEPERS.
New title from
12/15.

* Later Senior
Naval Officer.

† Overall
command in the
Mediterranean
passed to the
French and on
*Milne*'s departure,
*Carden* of East
Mediterranean
Squadron became
the senior British
commander. The
British recreated
their own C-in-C
Mediterranean in
8/17.

‡ Took under
command
*Stoddart*'s North of
Montevideo
Station.

◊ RFC renamed as
RAF 4/18, when it
also took Royal
Naval Air Service
under command.

• Formed to
undertake
'strategic' bombing
missions. These
had previously
been undertaken
by 3 Wing RNAS
(f.10/16).

∆ Contained only
41 Wing (now u/c.
*Baldwin*) until
7/18.

** Previously the
commander of the
first squadron to
arrive in
Mesopotamia
(30th) in 2/16.

†† The first
squadron (17th)
arrived in
Macedonia 7/16.

*Jackson*

**10** GIBRALTAR
*F.E.E. Brock* to 10/15
*Currey* to 7/17
*H.S.Grant*

**11** MALTA
ADMIRAL SUPERINTENDENT*
*Carden* to 9/14
*Limpus* to 9/16
*Ballard* to 10/18
*Bartelot*
REAR-ADMIRAL/ADMIRAL OF PATROLS (f.12/15)
*Marchant* to 11/16
*Lyon* to 9/17
*Fergusson*

**12** C-in-C. MEDITERRANEAN
*Milne* to 14/8/14†
*Gough-Calthorpe* from 8/17

**13** NORTH AMERICA AND WEST INDIES (f.9/14)
*Hornby* to 3/15
*Patey* to 9/16
*Browning* to 1/18
*W.L.Grant*

**14** C-in-C. PACIFIC (f.12/17)
*Colomb*

**15** SOUTH ATLANTIC AND SOUTH PACIFIC (f.10/14)‡
*Sturdee* (dissolved 2/15)

**16** SOUTH EAST COAST OF AMERICA. Later EAST COAST OF SOUTH
AMERICA
*Luce* to 11/16
*A.C.H.Smith*

**17** SYDNEY NAVAL ESTABLISHMENT (f.12/15)
*Henderson* (dissolved 4/17)

**18** WEST INDIES (as separate command 1-3/15)
*Patey*

**19** WHITE SEA (f.?)
*Kemp*

# ROYAL FLYING CORPS/ROYAL AIR FORCE◊

**1** FRANCE AND BELGIUM
GENERAL OFFICER COMMANDING
*Henderson* to 8/15
*Trenchard* to 1/18
*J.Salmond*
CHIEF OF STAFF
*Sykes* to 5/15
*Brooke-Popham* to 4/16
*Game*

**2** INDEPENDENT AIR FORCE (f.6/18)• Originally 41 WING (f.10/17)
then 8 BRIGADE (f.2/18)∆
*Newall* to 5/18
*Trenchard*

**3** MIDDLE EAST COMMAND (f.?/18). Originally 5 WING (f.1/16)
which became MIDDLE EAST BRIGADE (f.7/16)
*W.G.H.Salmond* to 11/17
*Brancker* to 1/18
*W.G.H.Salmond*

**Subordinate Commands**
**a** EGYPT BRIGADE (f.?/18 from Middle East Brigade)
?

**b** PALESTINE BRIGADE (f.10/17)
*Borton*

**c** MESOPOTAMIA WING (31 WING) (f.8/17)

*Tennant***

**d** MACEDONIA WING (16 WING) (f.9/16)††
*Todd*

## Table 2.2: French Government and High Command 1914-18

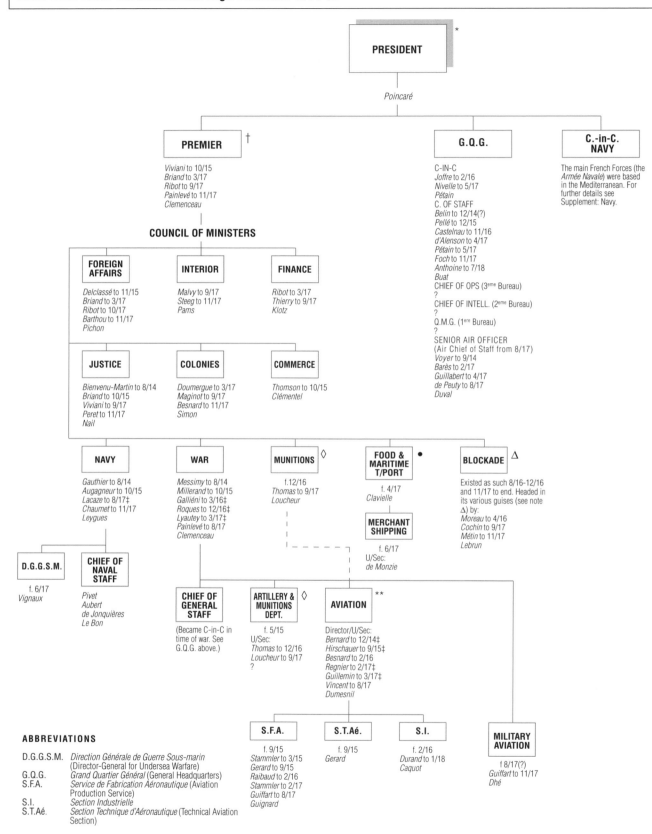

**PRESIDENT** *

*Poincaré*

**PREMIER** †

*Viviani* to 10/15
*Briand* to 3/17
*Ribot* to 9/17
*Painlevé* to 11/17
*Clemenceau*

**COUNCIL OF MINISTERS**

**FOREIGN AFFAIRS**

*Delcassé* to 11/15
*Briand* to 3/17
*Ribot* to 10/17
*Barthou* to 11/17
*Pichon*

**INTERIOR**

*Malvy* to 9/17
*Steeg* to 11/17
*Pams*

**FINANCE**

*Ribot* to 3/17
*Thierry* to 9/17
*Klotz*

**JUSTICE**

*Bienvenu-Martin* to 8/14
*Briand* to 10/15
*Viviani* to 9/17
*Peret* to 11/17
*Nail*

**COLONIES**

*Doumergue* to 3/17
*Maginot* to 9/17
*Besnard* to 11/17
*Simon*

**COMMERCE**

*Thomson* to 10/15
*Clémentel*

**G.Q.G.**

C-IN-C
*Joffre* to 2/16
*Nivelle* to 5/17
*Pétain*
C. OF STAFF
*Belin* to 12/14(?)
*Pellé* to 12/15
*Castelnau* to 11/16
*d'Alenson* to 4/17
*Pétain* to 5/17
*Foch* to 11/17
*Anthoine* to 7/18
*Buat*
CHIEF OF OPS (3eme Bureau)
?
CHIEF OF INTELL. (2eme Bureau)
?
Q.M.G. (1ere Bureau)
?
SENIOR AIR OFFICER
(Air Chief of Staff from 8/17)
*Voyer* to 9/14
*Barès* to 2/17
*Guillabert* to 4/17
*de Peuty* to 8/17
*Duval*

**C.-in-C. NAVY**

The main French Forces (the *Armée Navale*) were based in the Mediterranean. For further details see Supplement: Navy.

**NAVY**

*Gauthier* to 8/14
*Augagneur* to 10/15
*Lacaze* to 8/17‡
*Chaumet* to 11/17
*Leygues*

**D.G.G.S.M.**

f. 6/17
*Vignaux*

**CHIEF OF NAVAL STAFF**

*Pivet*
*Aubert*
*de Jonquières*
*Le Bon*

**WAR**

*Messimy* to 8/14
*Millerand* to 10/15
*Galliéni* to 3/16‡
*Roques* to 12/16‡
*Lyautey* to 3/17‡
*Painlevé* to 8/17
*Clemenceau*

**CHIEF OF GENERAL STAFF**

(Became C-in-C in time of war. See G.Q.G. above.)

**ARTILLERY & MUNITIONS DEPT.** ◊

f. 5/15
U/Sec:
*Thomas* to 12/16
*Loucheur* to 9/17
?

**MUNITIONS** ◊

f.12/16
*Thomas* to 9/17
*Loucheur*

**AVIATION** **

Director/U/Sec:
*Bernard* to 12/14‡
*Hirschauer* to 9/15‡
*Besnard* to 2/16
*Regnier* to 2/17‡
*Guillemin* to 3/17‡
*Vincent* to 8/17
*Dumesnil*

**S.F.A.**

f. 9/15
*Stammler* to 3/15
*Gerard* to 9/15
*Raibaud* to 2/16
*Stammler* to 2/17
*Guiffart* to 8/17
*Guignard*

**S.T.Aé.**

f. 9/15
*Gerard*

**S.I.**

f. 2/16
*Durand* to 1/18
*Caquot*

**FOOD & MARITIME T/PORT** •

f. 4/17
*Clavielle*

**MERCHANT SHIPPING**

f. 6/17
U/Sec:
*de Monzie*

**BLOCKADE** Δ

Existed as such 8/16-12/16 and 11/17 to end. Headed in its various guises (see note Δ) by:
*Moreau* to 4/16
*Cochin* to 9/17
*Métin* to 11/17
*Lebrun*

**MILITARY AVIATION**

f 8/17(?)
*Guiffart* to 11/17
*Dhé*

### ABBREVIATIONS

D.G.G.S.M. *Direction Générale de Guerre Sous-marin (Director-General for Undersea Warfare)*
G.Q.G. *Grand Quartier Général (General Headquarters)*
S.F.A. *Service de Fabrication Aéronautique (Aviation Production Service)*
S.I. *Section Industrielle*
S.T.Aé. *Section Technique d'Aéronautique (Technical Aviation Section)*

* Elected by the National Assembly (Senate and Chamber of Deputies).

† President of the Council of Ministers, chosen by the President of the Republic.

‡ Members of the armed forces.

◊ The Artillery and Munitions Dept. was expanded to become the Ministry of Munitions, but remained a department within the Ministry.

• Originally an Under-Secretary's department for Maritime Transport, also headed by Claveille.

Δ Originally the Committee for Restrictions (f. 3/15) and later an Under-Secretary's department within the Foreign Ministry. When reformed as a Ministry in 11/17 it also dealt with Liberated Territories.

** From 11/17 the Aviation Under-Secretary became answerable to both the Ministry of War and the Ministry of Munitions.

**Supplement to Table 2.2: Other Major French Commands**

# THE ARMY
## Theatre/Area Commands

Operations on the Western Front, which throughout the war occupied the major proportion of French forces were under the control of GQG (see Table 2).*

**1** DARDANELLES EXPEDITIONARY CORPS, originally EXPEDITIONARY CORPS OF THE EAST (f.4/15)

*d'Amade* to 5/15
*Gouraud* to 7/15
*Bailloud* (acting) to 10/15
*Brulard* to 1/16 (dissolved)

**2** ALLIED ARMIES OF THE EAST. Allied forces in Macedonia under a French commander (See Table 2.9: Allied Supreme Command).

**3** ARMY OF THE EAST
See ARMIES 14 below

**4** FRENCH FORCES IN ITALY (f.10/17)

*Duchêne* to 11/17†
*Fayolle* to 2/18‡
*Maistre* to 3/18†
*Graziani*◊

## Army Groups

**1** NORTHERN ARMY GROUP (f.1/15: W. Front). Originally NORTHERN PROVISIONAL GROUP (f.10/14).

*Foch* to 12/16
*Franchet d'Esperey* to 6/18
*Maistre* to 7/18 (dissolved)•

**2** CENTRAL ARMY GROUP (f.6/15: W.Front).
Dissolved 11/17-6/18.

*de Curières de Castelnau* to 12/15
*de Langle de Cary* to 5/16
*Pètain* to 5/17
*Fayolle* to 11/17 (dissolved)
*Maistre* from 7/18∆

**3** EASTERN ARMY GROUP (f.1/15: W.Front)

*Dubail* to 3/16
*Franchet d'Esperey* to 1/17
*Foch* (temp.) to 3/17**
*de Curières de Castelnau*

**4** RESERVE ARMY GROUP (f.12/16: W.Front). Dissolved 5/17-2/18.

*Micheler* to 5/17 (dissolved)
*Fayolle* from 2/18

## Armies

**1** FIRST ARMY (f.8/14: W.Front)

*Dubail* to 1/15
*Roques* to 3/16
*Mazel* in 3/16
*Gérard* to 12/16
*Fayolle* to 5/17
*Micheler* to 6/17
*Gouraud* in 6/17
*Anthoine* to 12/17
*Debeney*

**2** SECOND ARMY (f.8/14: W.Front)

*de Curières de Castelnau* to 6/15)
*Pètain* to 5/16
*Nivelle* to 12/16
*Guillaumat* to 12/17
*Hirschauer*

**3** THIRD ARMY

*Ruffey* to 8/14
*Sarrail* to 7/15
*Humbert*††

**4** FOURTH ARMY (f.8/14: W.Front)

*de Langle de Cary* to 12/15
*Gouraud* to 12/16
*Fayolle* to 12/16
*Roques* to 3/17
*Anthoine* to 6/17
*Gouraud*

**5** FIFTH ARMY (f.8/14: W.Front)

*de Lanrezac* to 9/14
*Franchet d'Esperey* to 3/16
*Mazel* to 5/17
*Micheler* to 6/18
*Buat* to 7/18
*Berthelot* to 10/18
*Guillaumat*

**6** SIXTH ARMY (f.9/14:W Front)
Originally ARMY OF LORRAINE (f.8/14). Renamed FRENCH ARMY IN BELGIUM 10/18.

*Maunoury* to 3/15
*Dubois* to 2/16
*Fayolle* to 12/16
*Mangin* to 5/17
*Maistre* to 12/17
*Duchêne* to 6/18
*Degoutte* to 10/18
*Baucheron de Boissoudy* in 10/18
*Degoutte*

**7** SEVENTH ARMY (f.4/15: W Front).
Originally ARMY DETACHMENT VOSGES (f.11/14).

*Putz* to 4/15
*de Maud'huy* to 11/15
*de Villaret* to 12/16
*Debeney* to 5/17
*Baucheron de Boissoudy* to 10/18
*Humbert* in 10/18
*de Mitry*

**8** EIGHTH ARMY (f.11/14:W Front).
Originally ARMY DETACHMENT BELGIUM (f.10/14). Not in line 1/15 to 1/17.‡‡ Then reformed from ARMY DETACHMENT LORRAINE.◊◊

*d'Urbal* to 2/15
*Gèrard* from 1/17

**9** NINTH ARMY (f.9/14: W.Front).
Not in the line 10/14-7/18

*Foch* to 10/14
*de Mitry* from 7-8/18 (dissolved)

**10** TENTH ARMY (f.10/14: W.Front).
HQ to Italy 11/17-3/18

*de Maud'huy* to 4/15
*d'Urbal* to 4/16
*Micheler* to 12/16
*Duchêne* to 12/17
*Maistre* to 6/18••
*Mangin*

**11** ARMY OF ALSACE (f.8/14)

*Pau* to 8/14 (dissolved)

**12** ARMY OF THE ALPS (f.8/14)

*d'Amade* to 8/14 (dissolved)

---

* However, the GQG, nominally in command of the whole Field Army, did not gain control of the fronts outside France until 12/15. See also Table 2.9: Allied Supreme Command.

† As commander of the Tenth Army staff which controlled French Forces in Italy. Succeeded in this post by *Maistre* in 12/17.

‡ *Fayolle* was an ex-army group commander (see ARMY GROUPS 2 below) who was installed above *Duchêne* in the (vain) hope that his rank would also entitle him to command the British contingent in Italy.

◊ A Corsican who nevertheless was given command of Italian Twelfth Army in 10/18. It may be that he also remained in command of French Forces in Italy.

• Renamed Central Army Group.

∆ Reformed by renaming Northern Army Group.

** Renamed Army Group Foch during his period in command.

†† Commanded Seventh Army for one week in 10/18.

‡‡ Became Army Detachment Belgium once again from 4-5/15, then XXXVI Corps.

◊◊ Army Detachment Lorraine had been reformed in 3/15 (see also Sixth Army above).

•• *Maistre* returned to France in 3/18 with Tenth Army HQ and was replaced in Italy by *Graziani* and staff of XII Corps.

**13** ARMY OF THE DANUBE (f.10/18)
*Berthelot*
**14** ARMY OF THE EAST (f.12/15: Macedonia)
*Sarrail* to 8/16*
*Cordonnier* to 10/16
*Leblois* (temp.) to 2/17
*Grossetti* to 9/17
*Regnault* (temp.) to 12/17
*Henrys*
**15** ARMY OF LORRAINE (f.8/14).
Became SIXTH ARMY 9/14 (see above).
*Durand* to 8/14
*Maunoury*
**16** FRENCH ARMY IN BELGIUM
see Sixth Army above

**Lesser Commands**
**1** MILITARY GOVERNOR OF PARIS (f.8/14).
Retitled PARIS ARMY GROUP 6-9/18.
*Michel* to 8/14
*Galliéni* to 11/15
*Maunoury* to 4/16
*Dubail* to 6/18
*Guillaumat* to 10/18
*Moinier*
**2** FORTIFIED REGION VERDUN (f.8/15).
Replaced by Second Army 2/16.
*Herr*
**3** NORTHERN HIGH COMMAND† (f.12/17)
Dunkirk-Calais-Boulogne). Dissolved 4/18
and reformed 7/18‡
*Putz* to 4/18
*Dumas* from 7/18
**4** FRENCH FORCES IN CAMEROON (8/14-2/16).
*Aymerich*
**5** FRENCH FORCES IN TOGOLAND (8/14).
*Maroix*
**6** FRENCH FORCES IN THE SAHARA (f.3/17)◊
*Laperrine*
**7** FRENCH DETACHMENT IN PALESTINE
(arr. 4/17). In 3/18 became FRENCH DETACHMENT IN PALESTINE AND
SYRIA.
*Bailloud* to ?
*Piépape*
**8** FRENCH FORCES IN RUSSIA
**a** Vladivostock (arr.8/18)•
*Janin*Δ
**b** Archangel (arr.8/18)
*Lucas*

**Colonial Governors****
**1** ALGERIA
*Lutaud* to ?/18
*Jonart*
**2** MOROCCO
*Lyautey* to 12/16
*?* to 5/17
*Lyautey*
**3** TUNISIA
*?*
**4** FRENCH EQUATORIAL AFRICA††
*Merlin* to ?
*?*
**5** FRENCH WEST AFRICA‡‡

*?* to 4/17
*v.Vollenhoven* to ?/18
*?*
**6** INDOCHINA ◊◊
*v.Vollenhoven* to 3/15
*Nestor* to 5/16
*Charles* to 1/17
*Sarraut*

**THE NAVY**
**1** C-in-C. NAVY, C-in-C FIRST FLEET,••
C-in -C. MEDITERRANEANΔΔ
*Boué de Lapéyrère* to 10/15
*Dartige du Fournet* to 12/16
*Gauchet*
CHIEF OF STAFF
*Habert* to ?/15
*Barnouin* to ?/17
*Morin* to ?/18
*Merveilleux du Vigneaux*
**2** C-in-C. ADRIATIC
*Lejay* to 1/16
*de Cacqueray* to 11/16
*Frochot* to 11/17
*d'Adhémar de Cransac*
**3** C-in-C. DARDANELLES
*Nicol* to 9/14
*Guépratte* to 5/15
*Nicol* to 10/15
*Dartige du Fournet* in 10/15
*Gauchet* to 3/16
*?*
**4** C-in-C. AEGEAN (f.1918)
*Darrieu* to 7/18
*Amet****
**5** C-in-C. SYRIAN COAST (f.2/15)
*Dartige du Fournet* to 10/15
*Moreau* to 3/16
*de Spitz* to ?/17
*Varney*
**6** ADMIRAL OF PATROLS (Mediterranean) (f.1916)
*Fatou* to 11/17
*Ratyé*
**7** C-in-C. ENGLISH CHANNEL redesignated NORTHERN ARMIES
NAVAL ZONE 5/16
*Rouyer* to 10/14
*Favereau* to 5/16
*Ronarc'h*
**8** C-in-C. BREST (N.Atlantic)
*Berryer* to ?/15
*Pivet* to ?/17
*Moreau*
**9** C-in-C. WEST COAST AFRICA (S. Atlantic)
*?*
**10** C-in-C. W. AFRICAN COAST (HQ Dakar)
*?*
**11** C-in-C. W.INDIES (W.Atlantic)
*?*
**12** C-in-C. CHINA SQUADRON
*Huguet* to ?/15†††
**13** C-in-C. INDOCHINA
*Boisrouvray* to ?/14
*Fatou* to ?/16
*Estienne*

* *Sarrail* was also
supreme Allied
commander in
Macedonia (see
**Theatre
Commands** 2
above).

† *Commandement
Supérieur du Nord*

‡ Reformed as part
of General
Headquarters.

◊ A unified
command formed
to fight the
Senussi.

• From Indochina.

Δ Also Allied C-
in-C.

** Also
Commanders-in-
Chief.

†† Comprising
Chad, Ubangi-
Chari, Middle
Congo and Gabon.

‡‡ Comprising
Maurentania,
Sudan, Senegal,
Guinea, Upper
Volta, Ivory Coast,
Dahomey and
Niger.

◊◊ Comprising
Cochin China,
Annam, Tonkin,
Cambodia, Laos
and Kwang-Chow-
Wan.

•• *Première
Armée navale.*

ΔΔ Also Allied C-
in-C.
Mediterranean
(see Table 2.9).

*** Allied C-in-C.
from ?/18.

††† Token
command only by
1915.

**Lesser Commands**

Shortage of space does not permit a listing of commanders at the following bases and stations: Cherbourg, Dunkirk, Le Havre, Lorient, Marseille, Rochefort, Toulon, Algeria and Tunisia, Morocco, E. Coast of Africa, E. Indies and E. Pacific

**14** C-in-C. SUBMARINES

*?*

**15** C-in-C. NAVAL AVIATION (*Aviation Maritime*)

*?*

## AIR FORCE *(Aviation Militaire)*

Most routine flying operations (reconnaissance and artillery-spotting) were carried out by squadrons, attached individually to corps or army headquarters. Bomber and fighter squadrons, however, were progressively formed into *groupes* (of two to five squadrons) which could be concentrated at specific sectors of the front or the enemy rear. Ten such *groupes de bombardment* were formed and thirteen *groupes de combat.**

*\* Sometimes referred to as groupes de chasse.*

### Groupes de Bombardment

| | |
|---|---|
| **1** | f.1914 |
| **2, 3, 4** | f.1915 |
| **5, 6** | f.1916 |
| **7, 8, 9** | f.1917 |
| **10** | f.1918 |

*† Not including temporary groupes formed for the Verdun and Somme battles 2 and 7/16.*

### Groupes de Combat†

| | |
|---|---|
| **11, 12, 13** | f.1916 |
| **14, 15** | f.1917 |
| **16** to **23** | f.1918 |

In 2/15 some of the *groupes de combat* were formed into two *escadres* and a few weeks later bomber groups were organised into three *escadres*. In 5/18 all these *escadres* were formed into two mixed *groupements* which were then formed into

*‡ The two groupement commanders were Menard and Fequant.*

**1** DIVISION AERIENNE (f.5/18)

*Duval‡*

*Table 2.3:* **Russian Goverment and High Command 1914-18***

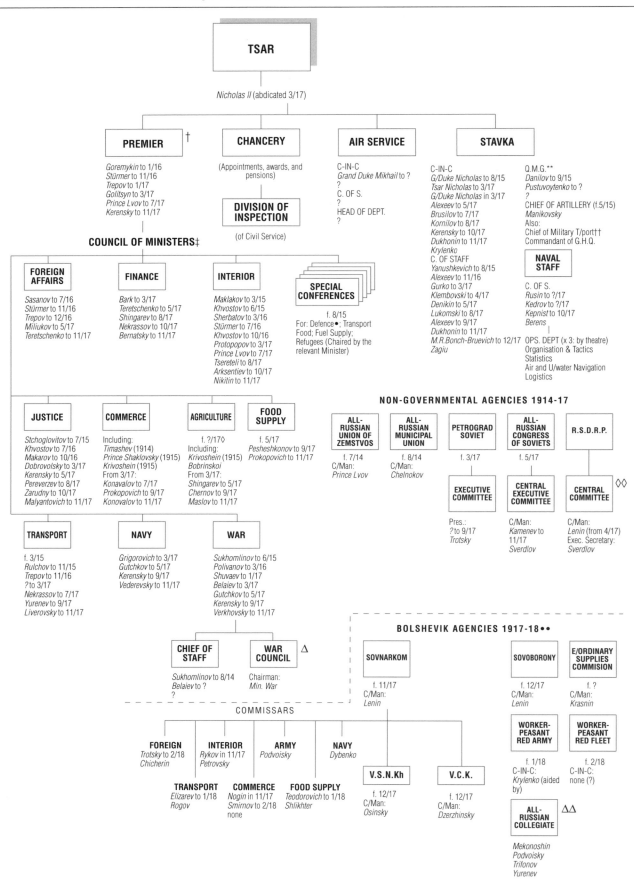

**TSAR**

*Nicholas II* (abdicated 3/17)

**PREMIER** †

*Goremykin* to 1/16
*Stürmer* to 11/16
*Trepov* to 1/17
*Golitsyn* in 3/17
*Prince Lvov* to 7/17
*Kerensky* to 11/17

**COUNCIL OF MINISTERS‡**

**CHANCERY**

(Appointments, awards, and pensions)

**DIVISION OF INSPECTION**

(of Civil Service)

**AIR SERVICE**

C-IN-C
*Grand Duke Mikhail* to ?
?
C. OF S.
?
HEAD OF DEPT.
?

**STAVKA**

C-IN-C
*G/Duke Nicholas* to 8/15
*Tsar Nicholas* to 3/17
*G/Duke Nicholas* in 3/17
*Alexeev* to 5/17
*Brusilov* to 7/17
*Kornilov* to 8/17
*Kerensky* to 10/17
*Dukhonin* to 11/17
*Krylenko*
C. OF STAFF
*Yanushkevich* to 8/15
*Alexeev* to 11/16
*Gurko* to 3/17
*Klembovski* to 4/17
*Denikin* to 5/17
*Lukomski* to 8/17
*Alexeev* to 9/17
*Dukhonin* to 11/17
*M.R.Bonch-Bruevich* to 12/17
*Zagiu*

Q.M.G.**
*Danilov* to 9/15
*Pustuvoytenko* to ?
?
CHIEF OF ARTILLERY (f.5/15)
*Manikovsky*
Also:
Chief of Military T/port††
Commandant of G.H.Q.

**NAVAL STAFF**

C. OF S.
*Rusin* to ?/17
*Kedrov* to ?/17
*Kepnist* to 10/17
*Berens*
|
OPS. DEPT (x 3: by theatre)
Organisation & Tactics
Statistics
Air and U/water Navigation
Logistics

**FOREIGN AFFAIRS**

*Sasanov* to 7/16
*Stürmer* to 11/16
*Trepov* to 12/16
*Miliukov* to 5/17
*Teretschenko* to 11/17

**FINANCE**

*Bark* to 3/17
*Teretschenko* to 5/17
*Shingarev* to 8/17
*Nekrassov* to 10/17
*Bernatsky* to 11/17

**INTERIOR**

*Maklakov* to 3/15
*Khvostov* to 6/16
*Sherbatov* to 3/16
*Stürmer* to 7/16
*Khvostov* to 10/16
*Protopopov* to 3/17
*Prince Lvov* to 7/17
*Tsereteli* to 8/17
*Arksentiev* to 10/17
*Nikitin* to 11/17

**SPECIAL CONFERENCES**

f. 8/15
For: Defence●; Transport
Food; Fuel Supply;
Refugees (Chaired by the
relevant Minister)

**JUSTICE**

*Stchoglovitov* to 7/15
*Khvostov* to 7/16
*Makarov* to 10/16
*Dobrovolsky* to 3/17
*Kerensky* to 5/17
*Pereverzev* to 8/17
*Zarudny* to 10/17
*Malyantovich* to 11/17

**COMMERCE**

Including:
*Timashev* (1914)
*Prince Shaklovsky* (1915)
*Krivoshein* (1915)
From 3/17:
*Konavalov* to 7/17
*Prokopovich* to 9/17
*Konovalov* to 11/17

**AGRICULTURE**

f. ?/17◊
Including:
*Krivoshein* (1915)
*Bobrinskoi*
From 3/17:
*Shingarev* to 5/17
*Chernov* to 9/17
*Maslov* to 11/17

**FOOD SUPPLY**

f. 5/17
*Pesheshkonov* to 9/17
*Prokopovich* to 11/17

**NON-GOVERNMENTAL AGENCIES 1914-17**

**ALL-RUSSIAN UNION OF ZEMSTVOS**

f. 7/14
C/Man:
*Prince Lvov*

**ALL-RUSSIAN MUNICIPAL UNION**

f. 8/14
C/Man:
*Chelnokov*

**PETROGRAD SOVIET**

f. 3/17

**EXECUTIVE COMMITTEE**

Pres.:
? to 9/17
*Trotsky*

**ALL-RUSSIAN CONGRESS OF SOVIETS**

f. 5/17

**CENTRAL EXECUTIVE COMMITTEE**

C/Man:
*Kamenev* to
11/17
*Sverdlov*

**R.S.D.R.P.**

**CENTRAL COMMITTEE** ◊◊

C/Man:
*Lenin* (from 4/17)
Exec. Secretary:
*Sverdlov*

**TRANSPORT**

f. 3/15
*Rulchov* to 11/15
*Trepov* to 11/16
? to 3/17
*Nekrassov* to 7/17
*Yurenev* to 9/17
*Liverovsky* to 11/17

**NAVY**

*Grigorovich* to 3/17
*Gutchkov* to 5/17
*Kerensky* to 9/17
*Vederevsky* to 11/17

**WAR**

*Sukhomlinov* to 6/15
*Polivanov* to 3/16
*Shuvaev* to 1/17
*Belaiev* to 3/17
*Gutchkov* to 5/17
*Kerensky* to 9/17
*Verkhovsky* to 11/17

**CHIEF OF STAFF**

*Sukhomlinov* to 8/14
*Belaiev* to ?
?

**WAR COUNCIL** Δ

Chairman:
*Min. War*

**BOLSHEVIK AGENCIES 1917-18●●**

**SOVNARKOM**

f. 11/17
C/Man:
*Lenin*

**SOVOBORONY**

f. 12/17
C/Man:
*Lenin*

**E/ORDINARY SUPPLIES COMMISION**

f. ?
C/Man:
*Krasnin*

**WORKER-PEASANT RED ARMY**

f. 1/18
C-IN-C:
*Krylenko* (aided by)

**ALL-RUSSIAN COLLEGIATE** ΔΔ

*Mekonoshin*
*Podvoisky*
*Trifonov*
*Yurenev*

**WORKER-PEASANT RED FLEET**

f. 2/18
C-IN-C:
none (?)

**COMMISSARS**

**FOREIGN**
*Trotsky* to 2/18
*Chicherin*

**INTERIOR**
*Rykov* in 11/17
*Petrovsky*

**ARMY**
*Podvoisky*

**NAVY**
*Dybenko*

**V.S.N.Kh**
f. 12/17
C/Man:
*Osinsky*

**V.C.K.**
f. 12/17
C/Man:
*Dzerzhinsky*

**TRANSPORT**
*Elizarev* to 1/18
*Rogov*

**COMMERCE**
*Nogin* in 11/17
*Smirnov* to 2/18
none

**FOOD SUPPLY**
*Teodorovich* to 1/18
*Shlikhter*

---

\* Complete only to March 1918 when the Russians signed the Treaty of Brest-Litovsk. There had in fact been little fighting since December 1917 when an armisitice had come into force.

† Chairman of the Council of Ministers. Appointed by the Tsar, to whom the whole Council was responsible rather than to the twin legislative/ consultative bodies the Council of State and the Duma. These latter exerted little influence, being constrained by their own conservatism (the Council of State) or Tsarist autocracy (the Duma). After the Tsar's abdication the premier became the prime minister in the Provisional Government.

‡ Ministers post-March 1917 are those of the Provisional Government.

◊ Previously Main Administration for Land Tenure and Agriculture.

● The Council for Defence developed out of the Special Committee for the Improved Supply of Essential Munitions to the Army in the Field, f. 5/15.

Δ Composed of aged generals resposible for the financial oversight of the war effort.

\*\* The Quartermaster-General in fact acted as the Chief of Operations. Resposibility for supply and logistics rested with the Chief of Staff.

†† *Ronzhin* to 1916.

◊◊ 21 members. The Politbureau, which may not have actually functioned in this period, comprised *Lenin, Trotsky, Stalin, Karnenev, Zinoviev, Sokolnikov* and *Bubanov*.

●● Organised to maintain Bolshevist grip on power rather than with any thought of resisting the Germans.

ΔΔ All-Russian Collegiate for the Organisation and Administration of the Worker-Peasant Red Army.

---

**Supplement to Table 2.3: Other Major Russian Commands (To November 1917)**

## THE ARMY
### Theatre/Area Commands
**1** C-in-C CAUCASUS

*Vorontsov-Dashkov* to 9/15*

*Grand Duke Nicholai* to 3/17

*Yudenich* to 5/17

*Prjewalski*

**2** C-in-C RUMANIA (f.12/16). Originally DANUBE ARMY (see Armies 17 below)

*King Ferdinand* of Rumania†

DEPUTY COMMANDER

*Saharov* to 4/17

*Shcherbachev*

### Army Groups (Fronts)
**1** NORTHERN FRONT (f.8/15)

*Ruzski* to 12/15

*Plehve* to 2/16

*Kuropatkin* to 7/16

*Ruzski* to 5/17

*Dragomirov* to 7/17

*Klembowski* to 9/17

*Cheremisov*

**2** NORTH-WEST later WESTERN FRONT (f.8/14)

*Zhilinski* to 9/14

*Ruzski* to 2/15

*Alexeyev* to 8/15

*Evert* to 3/17

*Smirnov* in 3/17

*Gurko* to 6/17

*Denikin* to 8/17

*Balyiev*

**3** SOUTH-WEST FRONT (f.8/14)

*Ivanov* to 3/16

*Brusilov* to 6/17

*Gutor* to 7/17

*Kornilov* to 8/17

*Denikin* to 9/17

*Wolodchenko*

**4** RUMANIAN FRONT

see Theatre/Area Commands 2 above

* Nominal. Real command was exercised by his deputy *Myshlaevski* and the latter's Chief-of-Staff *Yudenich*.

† Nominal. Real command was exercised by the deputy commander. HQ also referred to as Rumanian Front.

### Armies◊
**1** FIRST ARMY (f.8/14)

*Rennenkampf* to 12/14

*Litvinov* to 4/17

*Sokovnin* to 7/17

*Vannovski* to 9/17

*v.Notbek*

**2** SECOND ARMY (f.8/14). Destroyed the same month but reformed by the end of the year.

*Samsonov* to 8/14

*Scheidemann* to 12/14

*Smirnov* to 4/17

*Veselovski* to 7/17

*Danilov*

**3** THIRD ARMY (f.8/14)

*Ruzski* to 9/14

*Radko Dmitriev* to 6/15

*Lesh* to 8/17

*Tsikovich* to 9/17

*Odishelidze* to 10/17

*Parski*

**4** FOURTH ARMY (f.8/14)

*Zaltsa* in 8/14

*Evert* to 9/15

*Ragoza*

**5** FIFTH ARMY (f.8/14)

*Plehve* to 2/15

*Churin* to 4/15

*Plehve* to 12/15

*Klembowski* to 1/16

*Dragomirov* to 5/17

*Danilov* to 9/17

*Boldirev*

**6** SIXTH ARMY (f.8/14). Not in the line until autumn 1915. Absorbed Danube Army 12/16 (see below).

*van der Vliet* to 3/15

*Ruzski* to 8/15

*Churin* to 3/16

*Gorbatowski* to 12/16

*Zurikov*

**7** SEVENTH ARMY (f.8/14) Not in the line until autumn 1915.

*Nikitin* to 10/15

*Shcherbachev* to 4/17

*Belkovich* to 7/17

*Selivatchev* to 9/17

*Zihovich*

**8** EIGHTH ARMY (f.8/14)

*Brusilov* to 3/16

*Kaledin* to 5/17

*Kornilov* to 7/17

*Sokovnin*

**9** NINTH ARMY (f.8/14)

*Lechitski* to 4/17

*Stupin* to 8/17

*Cheremisov* to 9/17

*Kelchevski*

**10** TENTH ARMY (f.9/14)

*Pflug* to 10/14

*Sievers* to 2/15

*Radkevich* to 12/16

*Gorbatowski* to 4/17

---

### ABBREVIATIONS used in Table 2.3

| | |
|---|---|
| R.S.D.R.P. | *Rossijska social-democraticeskaja rabocaja partija* (Russian Social Democratic Workers' Party) |
| SOVNARKOM | *Sovet narodnych komissarov* (Council of People's Commissars) |
| SOVBORONY | *Sovet oborony* (Council of Defence) |
| STAVKA | *Shtab glavnogo/verkhovnogo komandovaniya* (Supreme Command H.Q.) |
| V.C.K. (also Vecheka) | *vserossijskaja crezvycajnaja kommissija (po por 'be s kontrrevolivciej i sabotazem)* (All-Russian Extraordinary Commission for Combatting Counterrevolution and Sabotage) |
| V.S.N.Kh (also Vesenka) | *Vyssij sovet narodnogo khozjajstva* (Supreme Council of the National Economy) |

*Kiselevski* to 7/17
*Lamnovski* to 9/17
*Shilinski*

**11** ELEVENTH ARMY (f.10/14)
*Selivanov* to 4/15
*Shcherbachev* to 10/15
*Saharov* to 10/16
*Klembowski* to 12/16
*Gutor* to 5/17
*Erdelli* to 7/17
*Rerberg* to 8/17 (acting)
*Promtov*

**12** TWELFTH ARMY (f.1/15). HQ dissolved and replaced by that from Thirteenth Army 8/15 (see below).
*Plehve* to 4/15
*Churin* to 8/15
*Gorbatowski* to 3/16
*Radko Dmitriev* to 7/17
*Parski* to 9/17
*Yusefovich*

**13** THIRTEENTH ARMY (f.6/15). HQ transferred to Twelfth Army 8/15 (see above).
*Gorbatowski* to 8/15

**14** GUARDS ARMY (f.late 1915) Renamed SPECIAL ARMY in 7/16.
*Bezobrazov* to 8/16
*Gurko* to 11/16
*Balujev* to 7/17
*Erdelli* to 9/17
*Stelnitski*

**15** CAUCASUS ARMY (f.8/14). See Theatre/Area Commands 1. From 4/17 HQ was also that of a larger Front command.
*Vorontsov-Dashkov* to 9/15

**16** DOBRUJA ARMY (f.8/16). Absorbed into Danube Army (see below) 10/16.
*Zhaionchkovski* to 10/16 (dissolved)

**17** DANUBE ARMY (f.10/16). HQ from XLVII Corps. Became Rumanian Front 12/16 (see Army Groups 4 above).
*Saharov* to 12/16

### Lesser Commands
**1** EXPEDITIONARY FORCE IN PERSIA
Began advance through W.Persia 11/15.
*Baratov* to 3/17
*Pavlov* to 8/17
*Baratov*

## THE NAVY
**1** BALTIC FLEET
*Essen* to 5/15
*Kanin* to 9/16
*Nepenin* to 3/17
*Maksimov* to 6/17
*Verderevski* to 7/17
*Razvozov*

**2** BLACK SEA FLEET
*Eberhard* to 7/16
*Kolchak* to 6/17
*Lukin/Smirnov?* to 8/17
*Nemits*

**3** AMUR FLOTILLA
*Bazhenov* to 4/17
*Ogilvie*

**4** ARCTIC FLOTILLA (f.2/16)
*Ougrimov* to ?/16

*Korvin* to ?/17
?
*Vikorst* (from 7/17)

**5** CASPIAN FLOTILLA
*Kluphel*

**6** SIBERIAN FLOTILLA (ex-Pacific Fleet. Token force only).
*Schultz*

## THE AIR FORCE
See Table 2.3 and Section 5, Part III: Russia. We have been unable to find any details on intermediate formations and commanders.

**Table 2.4:** Italian Government and High Command 1915-18

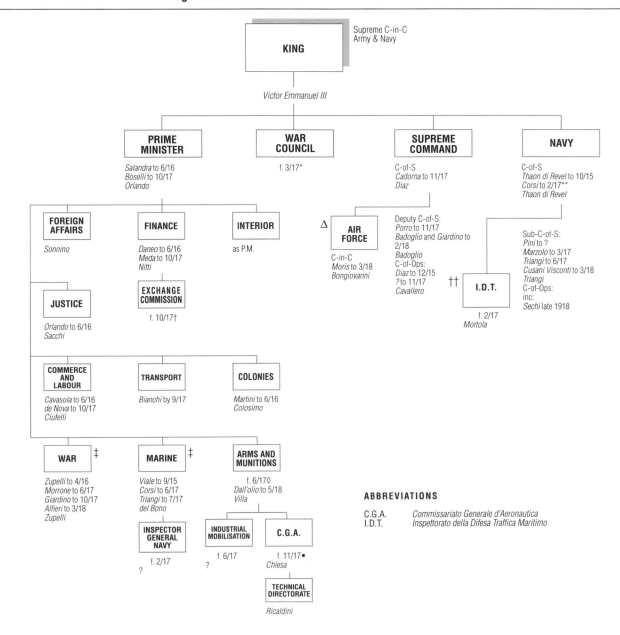

\* To coordinate the military and civilian war effort.

† To control raw materials allocation and industrial production.

‡ All generals or admirals.

◊ Originally the Under-Secretary for Arms and Munitions (f. 6/15), also Dall'olio.

• Originally a General Inspectorate in the War Office and then the General Directorate of Military Aviation in the Ministry of Arms and Munitions.

Δ Successively the *Corpo Aeronautica Militare*, the *Ufficio Servizi Aeronautica* and the *Commando Superiore di Aeronautica*.

\*\* Appointment not official until 2/16.

†† To coordinate anti-submarine warfare

**KING** — Supreme C-in-C Army & Navy

*Victor Emmanuel III*

**PRIME MINISTER**
*Salandra* to 6/16
*Boselli* to 10/17
*Orlando*

**WAR COUNCIL**
f. 3/17\*

**SUPREME COMMAND**
C-of-S
*Cadorna* to 11/17
*Diaz*

**NAVY**
C-of-S
*Thaon di Revel* to 10/15
*Corsi* to 2/17\*\*
*Thaon di Revel*

**FOREIGN AFFAIRS**
*Sonnino*

**FINANCE**
*Daneo* to 6/16
*Meda* to 10/17
*Nitti*

**INTERIOR**
as P.M.

Δ **AIR FORCE**
C-in-C
*Moris* to 3/18
*Bongiovanni*

Deputy C-of-S:
*Porro* to 11/17
*Badoglio* and *Giardino* to 2/18
*Badoglio*
C-of-Ops:
*Diaz* to 12/15
? to 11/17
*Cavallero*

Sub-C-of-S:
*Pini* to ?
*Marzolo* to 3/17
*Triangi* to 6/17
*Cusani Visconti* to 3/18
*Triangi*
C-of-Ops:
inc:
*Sechi* late 1918

**JUSTICE**
*Orlando* to 6/16
*Sacchi*

**EXCHANGE COMMISSION**
f. 10/17†

†† **I.D.T.**
f. 2/17
*Mortola*

**COMMERCE AND LABOUR**
*Cavasola* to 6/16
*de Nova* to 10/17
*Ciufelli*

**TRANSPORT**
*Bianchi* by 9/17

**COLONIES**
*Martini* to 6/16
*Colosimo*

**WAR** ‡
*Zupelli* to 4/16
*Morrone* to 6/17
*Giardino* to 10/17
*Alfieri* to 3/18
*Zupelli*

**MARINE** ‡
*Viale* to 9/15
*Corsi* to 6/17
*Triangi* to 7/17
*del Bono*

**ARMS AND MUNITIONS**
f. 6/17◊
*Dall'olio* to 5/18
*Villa*

**INSPECTOR GENERAL NAVY**
f. 2/17
?

**INDUSTRIAL MOBILISATION**
f. 6/17
?

**C.G.A.**
f. 11/17•
*Chiesa*

**TECHNICAL DIRECTORATE**
*Ricaldini*

**ABBREVIATIONS**

| | |
|---|---|
| C.G.A. | *Commissariato Generale d'Aeronautica* |
| I.D.T. | *Inspettorato della Difesa Traffica Maritimo* |

**Supplement to Table 2.4: Other Major Italian Commands**

## THE ARMY (*L'Esercito*)
### Theatre/Area Commands
Within Italy itself, the main theatre of war, there were no subordinate commands between the Commander-in-Chief and the various armies.

**1**  ALBANIA (arr.12/14). Mainly XVI Corps (f.3/16)*
   ? to 11/15
   *Bertotti* to ?/16
   *Bandini* to 12/16
   *Ferrero*

### Armies
**1**  FIRST ARMY (f.5/15)
   *Brusati* to 5/15
   *Percori-Giraldi*
**2**  SECOND ARMY (f.5/15)
   *Frugoni* to summer 1916
   *Piacantini* to 7/17
   *Capello* to 10/17
   *Montuori* (temp.) to 11/17 (destroyed)
**3**  THIRD ARMY (f.5/15)
   *Duke of Aosta*
**4**  FOURTH ARMY (f.5/15)
   *Nava* to 9/15
   *de Robilant* to ?/18
   *Giardino*
**5**  FIFTH ARMY (f.5/16). Dissolved 7/16 to 2/18
   *Brusati* to 7/16
   *Capello*
**6**  SIXTH ARMY (f.12/16)†
   *Mabretti* to ?/18
   *Montuori*
**7**  SEVENTH ARMY (f.3/18)
   *Tassoni*
**8**  EIGHTH ARMY (f.?/18‡ around remnants of Second Army (see above).
   *Pennella* to 6/18
   *Caviglia*
**9**  NINTH ARMY (f.?/18)‡
   *Morrone*
**10**  TENTH ARMY (f.10/18)
   *Cavan* ◊
**11**  TWELFTH ARMY (f.10/18)
   *Graziani*●

### Lesser Commands
**1**  CARNIC CORPS△ (XII) (f.5/15)
   *Lequio* to ?/17
   *Tassoni* to 11/17 (destroyed)
**2**  WESTERN FRONT (II Corps: in front line from 6/18)
   *Abricci*
**3**  MACEDONIA (35 Inf. Div: arrived 8/16)
   *Petitti*

## THE NAVY (*La Marina*)
**1**  C-in-C FLEET
   *Duke of Abruzzi* to 2/17
   *Thaon di Revel* **
   CHIEF-OF-STAFF
   *Filomarino* to ?/15
   *Lorenzo* to ?/17

   *Morino*
   ACTING C-in-C.††
   *Cutinelli-Rendina* to 6/17
   *Cerri* to 3/18
   *Cusani Visconti*
**2**  FIRST BATTLE SQUADRON‡‡
   *Corsi* in 5/15
**3**  SECOND BATTLE SQUADRON‡‡
   *Presbitero* in 5/15
**4**  BATTLE SQUADRON (Combined)‡‡
   *Corsi* to 3/18
   *Solari*
**5**  SCOUTING DIVISION
   *Millo* to 10/15
   *Patris* to 11/15
   *Belleni* to 5/16
   *Pini* to 9/16
   *Acton* to 2/17 (dissolved?)

### Shore-based Commands
**1**  BRINDISI
   *Finzi* to ?/16
   *Fabrini* to ?/17
   See Acting C-in-C
**2**  LA MADDALENA
   *Corri* to ?/15
   *Magliano*
**3**  NAPLES
   *Cattolica* to ?/16
   *Presbitero* to ?/17
   *Millo*
**4**  LA SPEZIA
   *Carelli* to ?/15
   *Del Bono* to ?/16
   *Filomarino* to ?/17
   *Cagni*
**5**  TARANTO
   *Presbitero* to ?/15
   *Cerri* to ?/18
   *Acton*
**6**  VENICE
   *Cutinelli-Rendina* to 10/15
   *Thaon di Revel* to 2/17
   *Filomarino* to ?/18
   *Marzolo*

## THE AIR FORCE (*L'Aeronautica*)
**1**  From 4/17 the Italians began grouping most of their land air assets in ARMY AVIATION COMMANDS. Those for Second and Third Armies were formed in 4/17, for First and Fourth Armies in 5/17, for Fifth, Sixth and Seventh in 2/18, for Eighth Army in 6/18, and for Tenth and Twelfth Armies in 10/18.◊◊
**2**  From *c*.8/17 there also existed the AVIATION OF THE SUPREME COMMAND, mainly consisting of the Caproni bomber squadrons●●
   *La Polla*
**3**  An ARTILLERY AVIATION COMMAND existed between 4/16 and 4/17△△
   *de Siebert*
**4**  From their entry into the war Italian squadrons were organised in GROUPS, the number of which expanded considerably during the war.***
   I,II,III Groups existed pre-5/15.

---

*   10/15 to 3/16 known as *Corpo d'occupazione dell'Albania.*

†   Not in front-line autumn 1917 to 2/18.

‡   In the line by 6/18.

◊   British.

●   French.

△   Also referred to as Carnic Group and Carnic Zone.

**   With Title Head of Mobilised Naval Forces.

††   Deputising for *di Revel* who doubled as Chief of Naval Staff and so spent much of his time in Rome. With *Cerri*'s appointment the command moved from Taranto to Brindisi.

‡‡   Unfortunately, the changes in Italian fleet organisation are much too complicated to be summarised here and we have limited ourselves to showing battleship organisations at the beginning and end of the war.

◊◊   Details on the commanders of these formations are far from complete.

●●   Originally concentrated in IV Group and later in IV, XI, XIV and X Groups (see below).

△△   V, VI and VII Groups.

***   A full list of Group commanders is available but there is no space here to list the 88 names involved.

* Ex-Artillery
Aviation Group.

The Artillery Aviation Group was formed in 6/15.
IV, V*,VI, VII Groups were formed in 4/16.
VIII Group (Albania) was formed in 12/16.
IX, X, XI Groups were formed in 4/17.
XII Group was formed in 5/17.
XIII, XIV Groups were formed in 11/17.
XV, XVI, XVIII Groups were formed in 12/17.
XIX, XX Groups were formed in 3/18.
XXI Group (Macedonia) was formed in 5/18.
XXII, XXIII, XXIV Groups were formed in 7/18.
XVII Group was formed in 9/18.

**5**  Two **DEFENCE GROUPS** were formed in 9/16 for anti-submarine patrols. One was the Northern Group and the other the Southern, the latter being dissolved in 3/18.

**6**  ALBANIA (See VIII Group above).
*Carta* to 8/17
*de Rada* to 1/18
*Pellegrino* to 6/18
*Livi* (temp.) to 8/18
*Ponis* (temp.) in 8/18
*Liotta*

**7**  MACEDONIA (See XX Group above).
*Lanciano* to 6/18
*Martucci*

**8**  LIBYA (between two and four squadrons).
?

**Table 2.5:** U.S. Government and High Command 1917-18

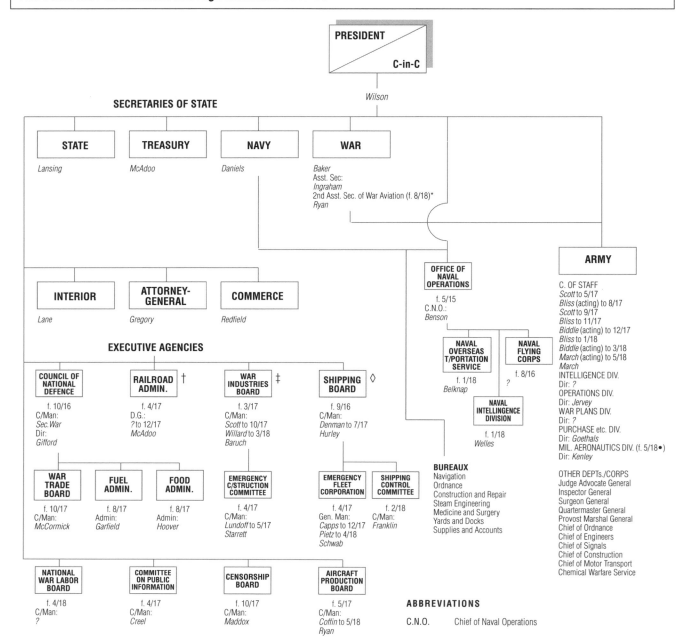

PRESIDENT
C-in-C

Wilson

SECRETARIES OF STATE

STATE — Lansing
TREASURY — McAdoo
NAVY — Daniels
WAR — Baker
Asst. Sec: Ingraham
2nd Asst. Sec. of War Aviation (f. 8/18)* Ryan

INTERIOR — Lane
ATTORNEY-GENERAL — Gregory
COMMERCE — Redfield

EXECUTIVE AGENCIES

COUNCIL OF NATIONAL DEFENCE
f. 10/16
C/Man: Sec.War
Dir: Gifford

RAILROAD ADMIN. †
f. 4/17
D.G.: ? to 12/17
McAdoo

WAR INDUSTRIES BOARD ‡
f. 3/17
C/Man: Scott to 10/17
Willard to 3/18
Baruch

SHIPPING BOARD ◊
f. 9/16
C/Man: Denman to 7/17
Hurley

WAR TRADE BOARD
f. 10/17
C/Man: McCormick

FUEL ADMIN.
f. 8/17
Admin: Garfield

FOOD ADMIN.
f. 8/17
Admin: Hoover

EMERGENCY C/STRUCTION COMMITTEE
f. 4/17
C/Man: Lundoff to 5/17
Starrett

EMERGENCY FLEET CORPORATION
f. 4/17
Gen. Man: Capps to 12/17
Pietz to 4/18
Schwab

SHIPPING CONTROL COMMITTEE
f. 2/18
C/Man: Franklin

NATIONAL WAR LABOR BOARD
f. 4/18
C/Man: ?

COMMITTEE ON PUBLIC INFORMATION
f. 4/17
C/Man: Creel

CENSORSHIP BOARD
f. 10/17
C/Man: Maddox

AIRCRAFT PRODUCTION BOARD
f. 5/17
C/Man: Coffin to 5/18
Ryan

OFFICE OF NAVAL OPERATIONS
f. 5/15
C.N.O.: Benson

NAVAL OVERSEAS T/PORTATION SERVICE
f. 1/18
Belknap

NAVAL FLYING CORPS
f. 8/16
?

NAVAL INTELLINGENCE DIVISION
f. 1/18
Welles

BUREAUX
Navigation
Ordnance
Construction and Repair
Steam Engineering
Medicine and Surgery
Yards and Docks
Supplies and Accounts

ARMY

C. OF STAFF
Scott to 5/17
Bliss (acting) to 8/17
Scott to 9/17
Bliss to 11/17
Biddle (acting) to 12/17
Bliss to 1/18
Biddle (acting) to 3/18
March (acting) to 5/18
March
INTELLIGENCE DIV.
Dir: ?
OPERATIONS DIV.
Dir: Jervey
WAR PLANS DIV.
Dir: ?
PURCHASE etc. DIV.
Dir: Goethals
MIL. AERONAUTICS DIV. (f. 5/18•)
Dir: Kenley

OTHER DEPTs./CORPS
Judge Advocate General
Inspector General
Surgeon General
Quartermaster General
Provost Marshal General
Chief of Ordnance
Chief of Engineers
Chief of Signals
Chief of Construction
Chief of Motor Transport
Chemical Warfare Service

* Not confirmed by 11/18.

† Originally Railways War Board to 2/18.

‡ Originally Munitions Standards Board (to 4/17) then General Munitions Board, nominally under the Council of National Defence, to 5/18.

◊ Powers greatly increased in 7/17.

• Directly under the Secretary of War.

ABBREVIATIONS

C.N.O.        Chief of Naval Operations

**Supplement to Table 2.5:** Other Major US Commands (From April 1917)

## THE ARMY
### Theatre/Area Commands
**1** AMERICAN EXPEDITIONARY FORCE (f.5/17)*
*Pershing*
CHIEF-OF-STAFF
*Hardbord* to 5/18
*MacAndrew*
CHIEF-OF-OPERATIONS (G-3)
*Palmer* to 8/17
*Walker* (acting) to 10/17
*Eltings* (acting) to 11/17
*Conner*
CHIEF-OF-INTELLIGENCE (G-2)
*Nolan*

### Army Groups
See note* above

### Armies
**1** FIRST ARMY (f.8/18:France)
*Pershing* to 10/18
*Liggett*
**2** SECOND ARMY (f.10/18:France)
*Bullard*
**3** THIRD ARMY (formation orderd 7/11/18 but only officially begun on the 15th.)
*Dickman*

### Lesser Commands
**1** SERVICES OF SUPPLY† (f.7/17: France)
*Stanley* to 7/17
*Blatchford* to 11/18
*Patrick*
**2** US FORCES IN RUSSIA
**a** SIBERIA (arr.8/18)‡
*Graves*
**b** ARCHANGEL (arr.9/18)◊
*Stewart*

## THE NAVY
**1** PACIFIC FLEET
*Caperton* (from 8/16)
**2** ATLANTIC FLEET
*Mayo* (from 6/16)
**3** NAVAL FORCES IN EUROPEAN WATERS (f.6/17).
*Sims*
CHIEF-OF-STAFF
*Twining*
**4** 6th BATTLESHIP DIVISION (Ireland from 9/18).
*Rodgers*
**5** 9th BATTLESHIP DIVISION
Became 6th BATTLE SQUADRON, GRAND FLEET on arrival Scapa Flow 12/17.
*Rodman*
**6** DESTROYER FORCE, ATLANTIC FLEET (part: began arriving Ireland 5/17).
*Taussig*
**7** CRUISER AND TRANSPORT FORCE, ATLANTIC FLEET•
*Gleaves*
**8** PATROL SQUADRONS IN FRENCH WATERS (f.6/17: Brest)
*Fletcher* to 11/17
*Wilson* to ?/18△

**9** MINE SQUADRON ONE, ATLANTIC FLEET**
*R. Belknap* to ?/18
*Strauss*
**10** NAVAL FORCES IN MEDITERRANEAN (f.8/17: Gibraltar)
*Niblack*
**11** PATROL FORCE (f.?/18: Key West)
?
**12** SUBMARINE FLOTILLA, ATLANTIC FLEET
*Robinson*
**13** NAVAL FLYING CORPS (f.8/16)
?
**14** NORTHERN BOMBING GROUP (f.9/18: Dunkirk).
*Hanrahan*

## THE AIR FORCE
**1** AIR SERVICE, AMERICAN EXPEDITIONARY FORCE (f.6/17).
*Todd* to 6/17††
*Mitchell* to 8/17
*Kenly* to 11/17
*Foulois* to 5/18
*Patrick*
CHIEF-OF-STAFF
*Whitehead*
ZONE OF ADVANCE (f.9/17)
*Mitchell*
SERVICES OF SUPPLY (f.9/17)‡‡
*Bolling* to 11/17
*?* to 5/18
*Foulois*

---

*Margin notes (left column):*

\* Arrives France 6/17. Becomes an official army H.Q. 9/17 and an army group H.Q. 10/18.

† To 3/18 known as Line of Comunications or Service of the Rear.

‡ Two infantry regiments.

◊ One infantry regiment.

• Responsible for transport of troops.

△ Split between separate commands at Brest, Lorient and Rochefort.

** Laid most of the mines in the Northern Barrage, in 1918.

†† Military aviation still part of US Signal Corps to 6/17.

‡‡ Formed as Zone of Interior and later Lines of Communication.

**Table 2.6:** German Government and High Command 1914-18

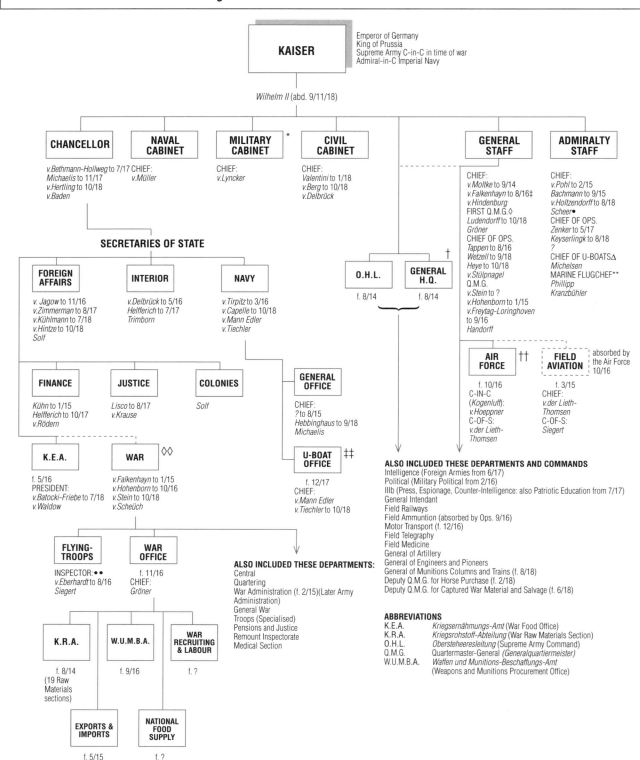

**KAISER**

Emperor of Germany
King of Prussia
Supreme Army C-in-C in time of war
Admiral-in-C Imperial Navy

*Wilhelm II* (abd. 9/11/18)

**CHANCELLOR**

*v.Bethmann-Hollweg* to 7/17
*Michaelis* to 11/17
*v.Hertling* to 10/18
*v.Baden*

**NAVAL CABINET**

CHIEF:
*v.Müller*

**MILITARY CABINET** *

CHIEF:
*v.Lyncker*

**CIVIL CABINET**

CHIEF:
*Valentini* to 1/18
*v.Berg* to 10/18
*v.Delbrück*

**GENERAL STAFF**

CHIEF:
*v.Moltke* to 9/14
*v.Falkenhayn* to 8/16‡
*v.Hindenburg*
FIRST Q.M.G.◊
*Ludendorff* to 10/18
*Gröner*
CHIEF OF OPS.
*Tappen* to 8/16
*Wetzell* to 9/18
*Heye* to 10/18
*v.Stülpnagel*
Q.M.G.
*v.Stein* to ?
*v.Hohenborn* to 1/15
*v.Freytag-Loringhoven*
to 9/16
*Handorff*

**ADMIRALTY STAFF**

CHIEF:
*v.Pohl* to 2/15
*Bachmann* to 9/15
*v.Holtzendorff* to 8/18
*Scheer*•
CHIEF OF OPS.
*Zenker* to 5/17
*Keyserlingk* to 8/18
?
CHIEF OF U-BOATS∆
*Michelsen*
MARINE FLUGCHEF**
*Phillipp*
*Kranzbühler*

### SECRETARIES OF STATE

**FOREIGN AFFAIRS**

*v. Jagow* to 11/16
*v.Zimmerman* to 8/17
*v.Kühlmann* to 7/18
*v.Hintze* to 10/18
*Solf*

**INTERIOR**

*v.Delbrück* to 5/16
*Helfferich* to 7/17
*Trimborn*

**NAVY**

*v.Tirpitz* to 3/16
*v.Capelle* to 10/18
*v.Mann Edler*
*v.Tiechler*

**O.H.L.**

f. 8/14

**GENERAL H.Q.** †

f. 8/14

**FINANCE**

*Kühn* to 1/15
*Helfferich* to 10/17
*v.Rödern*

**JUSTICE**

*Lisco* to 8/17
*v.Krause*

**COLONIES**

*Solf*

**GENERAL OFFICE**

CHIEF:
? to 8/15
*Hebbinghaus* to 9/18
*Michaelis*

**AIR FORCE** ††

f. 10/16
C-IN-C
(*Kogenluft*):
*v.Hoeppner*
C-OF-S:
*v.der Lieth-Thomsen*

**FIELD AVIATION**

f. 3/15
CHIEF:
*v.der Lieth-Thomsen*
C-OF-S:
*Siegert*

absorbed by
the Air Force
10/16

**K.E.A.**

f. 5/16
PRESIDENT:
*v.Batocki-Friebe* to 7/18
*v.Waldow*

**WAR** ◊◊

*v.Falkenhayn* to 1/15
*v.Hohenborn* to 10/16
*v.Stein* to 10/18
*v.Scheüch*

**U-BOAT OFFICE** ‡‡

f. 12/17
CHIEF:
*v.Mann Edler*
*v.Tiechler* to 10/18

**FLYING-TROOPS**

INSPECTOR:••
*v.Eberhardt* to 8/16
*Siegert*

**WAR OFFICE**

f. 11/16
CHIEF:
*Gröner*

**K.R.A.**

f. 8/14
(19 Raw
Materials
sections)

**W.U.M.B.A.**

f. 9/16

**WAR RECRUITING & LABOUR**

f. ?

**EXPORTS & IMPORTS**

f. 5/15

**NATIONAL FOOD SUPPLY**

f. ?
(ancillary to
K.E.A.)

**ALSO INCLUDED THESE DEPARTMENTS:**
Central
Quartering
War Administration (f. 2/15)(Later Army
Administration)
General War
Troops (Specialised)
Pensions and Justice
Remount Inspectorate
Medical Section

**ALSO INCLUDED THESE DEPARTMENTS AND COMMANDS**
Intelligence (Foreign Armies from 6/17)
Political (Military Political from 2/16)
IIIb (Press, Espionage, Counter-Intelligence: also Patriotic Education from 7/17)
General Intendant
Field Railways
Field Ammunition (absorbed by Ops. 9/16)
Motor Transport (f. 12/16)
Field Telegraphy
Field Medicine
General of Artillery
General of Engineers and Pioneers
General of Munitions Columns and Trains (f. 8/18)
Deputy Q.M.G. for Horse Purchase (f. 2/18)
Deputy Q.M.G. for Captured War Material and Salvage (f. 6/18)

**ABBREVIATIONS**
K.E.A.        *Kriegsernähmungs-Amt* (War Food Office)
K.R.A.        *Kriegsrohstoff-Abteilung* (War Raw Materials Section)
O.H.L.        *Oberstesheeresleitung* (Supreme Army Command)
Q.M.G.        Quartermaster-General (*Generalquartiermeister*)
W.U.M.B.A.    *Waffen und Munitions-Beschaffungs-Amt*
              (Weapons and Munitions Procurement Office)

---

\* Controlled all military appointments. Placed under the War Ministry 10/18.

† The iiner circle of General Staff officers (most were posted to the individual field armies and army groups) in their role as the Kaiser's military staff once he took over Supreme command. The exact distinction between the General H.Q. (known as the *Grosse Hauptquartier*) and the O.H.L. remains rather opaque to the present authors. By August 1916, however, it had become somewhat clearer. For then the Kaiser and his personal staff returned to Germany whilst the 'real' staff of the O.H.L. remained in France, mainly concerned with directing operations on the Western Front.

‡ Not offically appointed until 11/16.

◊ In effect, joint C-in-C with *Hindenburg*, a post especially created for *Ludendorff* in 8/16.

• Also C-in-C *Seekriegsleitung* (f. 8/18) which centralised naval command and administration. *Scheer*'s Chief-of-Staff was *v.Levetzow*.

∆ From 11/17, when he took charge of all U-boat operations. (See also Supplement: Naval No.9).

** Titled thus from 8/17. Previously *Befehlshaber der (Marine-) Flieger-Abteilungen*.

†† *Die Luftstreitkräfte*.

‡‡ Formed to oversee U-boat production and deliveries.

◊◊ In charge of military administration. In fact the Prussian War Ministry which took on an imperial role in time of war. The Minister became part of the General H.Q. in 8/14 (*v.Wandel* was named as acting Minister in Berlin) but he returned the capital in summer 1916 and in December was given the title Supreme Commander Berlin. All the Ministers were soldiers.

•• Also C-in-C Flying Troops to 3/15. In 10/16 became subordinate to the *Luftstreitkräfte*.

**Supplement to Table 2.6:** Other Major German Commands

## THE ARMY (*Das Heer*)
### Theatre Commands*

**1** COMMANDER-IN-CHIEF EAST (*Oberbefehlshaber Ost*) (f.11/14)
*v. Hindenburg* to 8/16
*Leopold of Bavaria*†
CHIEF-OF-STAFF
*Ludendorff* to 8/16
*Hoffmann*

### Army Groups (*Heeresgruppen*)‡
Almost all of these commands were identified by the name of the commander and this is not therefore normally listed separately.◊

**1** ARMY GROUP DUKE ALBERT (f.3/17: W. Front)
CHIEF-OF-STAFF•
*Krafft v. Dellmensinger* to 9/17
*Hene* to 9/18
*Hell* to 10/18
*v. Lossberg*

**2** ARMY GROUP BELOW (f.10/16:Macedonia).
Became Army Group Scholtz 4/17 (see 14 below).

**3** ARMY GROUP BOEHN (f.8/18: W.Front).
Dissolved 10/18

**4** ARMY GROUP EICHHORN
**a** 7/16-3/18: E.Front Formed from Army Group Hindenburg (see 7 below).
**b** See Army Group Kiew below.
**c** f.8/18: E.Front

**5** ARMY GROUP STAFF F△ (f.7/17: Mesopotamia and Palestine).
*v. Falkenhayn* to 3/18
*Liman v. Sanders*

**6** ARMY GROUP GALLWITZ
**a** 7/16-8/16: W.Front. Became Army Group Rupprecht (see 13 below).
**b** f.2/18: W.Front,

**7** ARMY GROUP HINDENBURG (f.8/15: E Front). Became Army Group Eichhorn 7/16 (see 4a above)

**8** ARMY GROUP KIEW** (f.4/15: E.Front).
*v. Mackensen* to 9/15
*v. Linsingen* to 4/18
*v. Eichhorn* to 7/18
*Count v. Kirchbach*

**9** ARMY GROUP KIRCHBACH. See Army Group Kiev above

**10** ARMY GROUP LINISINGEN.
**a** See Army Group Kiev above.
**b** f.4/18: E.Front.

**11** ARMY GROUP LEOPOLD OF BAVARIA (f.8/15:E.Front). Became Army Group Woyrsch 8/16 (see 16 below).
CHIEF of STAFF
*Grünert* to 11/15
*v. Lambsdorff*

**12** ARMY GROUP MACKENSEN
**a** See Army Group Kiev (a) above.
**b** 9/15-7/16: Serbia and Macedonia.
**c** f.8/16 Rumania

**13** ARMY GROUP GROWN PRICE RUPPRECHT OF BAVARIA (f.8/16 W.Front). Formed from Army Group Gallwitz (see 6a above)
CHIEF OF STAFF
*v. Kuhl*

**14** ARMY GROUP SCHOLTZ (f.4/17:Macedonia). Formed from Army Group Below (see 2 above).

**15** ARMY GROUP CROWN PRINCE WILHELM (f.8/15: W.Front)
CHIEF-OF-STAFF

*Schmidt v. Knobelsdorf* to 8/16
*v. Lüttwitz* to 11/16
*v. der Schulenburg*

**16** ARMY GROUP WOYRSCH (f.8/16: E.Front). Formed from Army Group Leopold (see 11 above). Dissolved 12/17.

**17** ARMY GROUP YILDERIM. Turkish name for Army Group Staff F (see 5 above).

### Armies

**1** FIRST ARMY (f.8/14)
**a** f.8/14: W.Front
*v. Kluck* to 3/15
*v. Fabeck* to 9/15 (dissolved)
**b** f.7/16: W.Front
*F. v. Below* to 6/18
*v. Mudra* to 10/18
*O. v. Below* to 11/18
*v. Eberhardt*

**2** SECOND ARMY (f.8/14: W.Front)
*v. Bülow* to 4/15
*F. v. Below* to 7/16
*v. Gallwitz* to 12/16
*v.d. Marwitz* to 9/18
*v. Carlowitz*

**3** THIRD ARMY (f.8/14: W.Front)
*v. Hausen* to 9/14
*v. Einem*

**4** FOURTH ARMY (f.8/14: W.Front)
*Duke Albert of Württemberg* to 2/17
*Sixt v. Arnim*
CHIEF-OF-STAFF (to 2/17)
*v. Lüttwitz* to 9/14
*Ilse*

**5** FIFTH ARMY (f.8/14: W.Front)
*Crown Prince Wilhelm* to 11/16
*v. Lochow* to 12/16
*v. Gallwitz* to 9/18
*v.d. Marwitz*
CHIEF-OF-STAFF (to 11/16)
*v. Knobelsdorf* to 8/16
*v. Ledebur*

**6** SIXTH ARMY (f.8/14: W.Front)
*Crown Price Rupprecht of Bavaria* to 8/16
*v. Falkenhausen* to 4/17
*O.v. Below* to 9/17
*v. Quast*
CHIEF-OF-STAFF (to 8/16)
*v. Dellmensingen* to 5/15
*v. Lambsdorff* to 11/15
*v. Ruhl*

**7** SEVENTH ARMY (f.8/14: W.Front)
*v. Heeringen* to 8/16
*v. Schubert* to 3/17
*v. Boehn* to 8/18
*v. Eberhardt* to 10/18
*v. Boehn*

**8** EIGHTH ARMY
**a** f.8/14: E.Front
*v. Prittwitz u. Gaffron* to 8/14
*v. Hindenburg* to 9/14
*v. Schubert* to 10/14

---

* There was no C-in-C. West.

† From 8/16 *Oberost* also took command of all Austro-Hungarian forces to the north of their Seventh Army (see Maps 17 & 18). This arrangement lasted until early 1918.

‡ Not *Armeegruppen*, which HQs were ranked lower than an Army HQ.

◊ It was the German practice to omit the particle "*von*" in such formation titles.

• Army Group and Army Chiefs-of-Staff are listed where the commander was appointed more in deference to his blood than his military competence.

△ *Heeresgruppe-Kommando F.*

** Often known by the name of its commander.

---

*v. Francois* to 11/14
*O. v. Below* to 5/15
*v. Scholtz* to 9/15 (dissolved)

**b** f.9/15: E.Front. Previously NIEMEN ARMY (f.5/15).
*O. v. Below* to 10/15
*v. Fabeck* in 10/16
*v. Mudra* to 1/17
*v. Scholtz* to 4/17
*v. Hutier* to 12/17
*Count v. Kirchbach* to 7/18
*v. Rathen*

**9 NINTH ARMY**

**a** f.9/14: E.Front
*v. Hindenburg* to 11/14
*v. Mackensen* to 4/15
*Prince Leopold of Bavaria* to 7/16 (dissolved)

**b** f.9/16: E.Front
*v. Falkenhayn* to 5/17
*Kolsch* to 6/17
*v. Eben* to 8/18
*v. Carlowitz*

**10 TENTH ARMY** (f.1/15: E.Front)
*v. Eichhorn* to 3/18
*v. Falkenhayn*

**11 ELEVENTH ARMY**

**a** f.3/15: E.Front
*v. Fabeck* to 4/15
*v. Mackensen* to 9/15 (dissolved)

**b** f.9/15: Serbia and Macedonia
*v. Gallwitz* to 3/16
*v. Winckler* to 6/17
*v. Steuben*

**12 TWELFTH ARMY** (f.8/15: E Front)
*v. Gallwitz* to 9/15
*v. Fabeck* to 10/16 (dissolved)

**13 FOURTEENTH ARMY** (f.9/17: Italy)
*O. v. Below* to 1/18 (dissolved)

**14 SEVENTEENTH ARMY** (f.2/18: W.Front)
*O. v. Below* to 10/18
*v. Mudra*

**15 EIGHTEENTH ARMY** (f.12/17: W.Front)
*v. Hutier*

**16 NINETEENTH ARMY** (f.2/18: W.Front)
*v. Bothmer* to 11/18
*v. Fasbender*

**17 BUG ARMY** (f.7/15: E. Front)
*v. Linsingen* to 3/18 (dissolved)

**16 NIEMEN ARMY**
see 8 above

**19 SOUTH ARMY** (*SÜDARMEE*) (f.1/15: E.Front).
*v. Linsingen* to 7/15
*v. Bothmer* to 1/18 (dissolved)

#### Army Detachments (*Armee-Abteilungen*)

**1** 'A' (f.4/16: W.Front). Previously AY. DET. FALKENHAUSEN (f.9/14)
*v. Falkenhausen* to 4/16
*d'Elsa* to 1/17
*v. Mudra* to 8/18
*v. Eben*

**2** 'B' (f.9/16: W.Front) Previously AY. DET. GAEDE (f.9/14)
*Gaede* to 9/16
*v. Gündell*

**3** 'C' (f.2/17: W.Front). Previously AY. DET. STRANTZ (f.9/14)
*v. Strantz* to 2/17

*v. Boehn* to 3/17
*Fuchs*

**4** 'D' (f.1/17: E.Front). Previously AY. DET. SCHOLTZ (f.10/15)
*v. Scholtz* to 1/17
*v. Hutier* to 4/17
*v. Kirchbach* to 10/18 (dissolved)

**5 WOYRSCH** (f.11/14: E.Front)
*Woyrsch* to 12/17 (dissolved)

#### Lesser Commands

**1** EAST AFRICAN *SCHUTZTRUPPE*
*v. Lettow-Vorbeck*

**2** SOUTH-WEST AFRICAN *SCHUTZTRUPPE*
*v. Heydebreck* to 7/15 (surrendered)

**3** CAMEROONS *SCHUTZTRUPPE*
*Zimmerman* to 2/16 (surrendered)

**4** TOGOLAND *POLIZEITRUPPE*
*v. Döring* to 8/14 (surrendered)

**5** TSINGTAO GARRISON*
*Meyer-Waldeck†* to 11/14 (surrendered)

**6** ASIATIC CORPS (f.7/17). Replaced PASHA I (f.early 1916)‡
*?* to 7/17
*v. Frankenberg-Proschlitz* to ?/18
*v. Oppen*

**7** FINLAND: BALTIC DIVISION (f.3/18)
*R. v. d. Goltz*

#### Occupied Territories

**1** BALTIC STATES
See 4 below.

**2** BELGIUM
See entry in Table 2.10.

**3** FRANCE
See entry in Table 2.10.

**4** OBERBEFEHLSHABER OST (see also **Theatre Commands** above). German conquests in the east, to the north of Bialystok (see also Poland below), formed a Zone (*Gebiet*) under the control of *Oberost*.◊ Actual administration was delegated to *Oberost's Oberquartiermeister*.
*v. Eisenhart-Rothe* to 1/17
*v. Brandenstein*

**5** POLAND
See entry in Table 2.10.

**6** RUMANIA
See entry in Table 2.10.

**7** UKRAINE
Invaded by the Germans in 2/18 to ensure the security of food supplies back to the Reich. Under the direct control of Army Group Kiev (see **Army Groups** 8 above) whose authority was barely diluted by the puppet *Hetman Skoropadsky*.
MILITARY GOVERNOR
*Gröner* (A. Gp Kiev Chief-of-Staff)
WIRTSCHAFTSSTELLE•
*Wiedfelt* and *Melchior*
MINISTER AMBASSADOR
*Mumm v. Schwarzenstein*

### THE NAVY (*Kriegsmarine*)

**1** HIGH SEAS FLEET (*Hochseeflotte*)
C-in-C
*v. Ingenohl* to 2/15
*v. Pohl* to 1/16
*Scheer* to 8/18
*v. Hipper*
CHIEF-OF-STAFF

\* Capital of Kiachow colony.

† German Navy.

‡ The *Asien Korps*, which fought with the Turks in Palestine, was also sometimes referred to as Pasha II.

◊ By autumn 1915 this *Giebet* was subdivided into seven districts (*Bezirke*): Bialystok, Grodno, Kurland, Litau (Lithuania), Suwalki and Wilna (Vilna). By 2/18 these had been progressively absorbed into just two military administrations (*Militärver-waltungen*): Litau and Kurland (the latter now also including Estland [Estonia] and Livland [Livonia]). The administration/ exploitation of the Ukraine remained separate (see below). In 8/18 Litau was renamed a *Militär-Gouvernement*.

• Representatives of the Reich Financial Secretary in charge of economic exploitation.

* Included the High Seas Fleet battlecruisers.

† A mainly honourary position, although the Prince did have the ear of his brother the Kaiser.

‡ Retained this name even when its two ships were handed over to the Turkish Navy in 8/14, and even though it thereafter only once briefly ventured into the Mediterranean.

◊ *Bauer*'s title was actually *Führer der U-Boote*. Both he and his successor were only in charge of the U-Boats of the High Seas Fleet until 12/17 when the whole submarine command was centralised.

• HQ and bases at Pola and Cattaro, in the Adriatic.

Δ Land-based Marines stationed at the northern extremity of the German Front.

** Carrier-pigeon Detachment Ostend.

†† Served on the E.Front from 3-7/15. In 12/15 (still under *Siegert*) it became Kampfgeschwader der OHL 1 and became increasingly involved in tactical operations.

‡‡ Became Kagohl 2 in 12/15. See note above.

◊◊ Soon dedicated to bombing attacks on Britain and often referred to as the *Englandgeschwader*.

•• Long distance Airplane Detachment. Latvia to 2/18 then France.

ΔΔ E.Front to 8/17 then Belgium. Under command of Bobohl 3 (see 3 above) until 2/18.

*** Senior German air officer in the Middle East since 2/15.

*Eckermann* to 2/15
*Michaelis* to 2/16
*v. Trotha*

**2** SCOUTING GROUPS (*Aufklärungsgruppe*)*
*v. Hipper* to 8/18
?

**3** C-in-C. BALTIC†
*Prince Heinrich of Prussia* to 1/18 (dissolved)
CHIEF-OF-STAFF
*Capt. Heinrich*

**4** C-in-C. BALTIC STATION
*Bachmann* to 2/15
*v. Ingenohl* to 8/15
*Bachmann*

**5** NORTH SEA STATION
*v. Krosick*

**6** EAST ASIATIC SQUADRON
*v. Spee* to 12/14 (destroyed)

**7** MEDITERRANEAN SQUADRON (*Mittelmeerdivision*)‡
*Souchon*

**8** BLACK SEA STATION (f.1/18)
*Hopman*

**9** *BEFEHLSHABER DER U-BOOTE*
*Bauer* to 6/17◊
*Michelsen*

**10** FLANDERS U-BOAT FLOTILLA (f.2/15)
*Bartenbach* to 10/18 (dissolved)

**11** MEDITERRANEAN U-BOAT FLOTILLA (f.8/15)•
*Adam* to ?
*Kophamel* to 6/17
*Püllen* to 8/18
*Grasshof*

**12** BALTIC U-BOAT HALF-FLOTILLA (f.3/16)
*Schött* to 10/17 (dissolved)

**13** FLANDERS MARINE CORPS (f.11/14)Δ
*v. Schröder*

## THE AIR FORCE (*Luftstreitkräfte*)

(Except for bombers, aircraft units were very much subordinate to Army commanders and there were no significant German air force theatre hqs comparable to the RFC/RAF in France and Belgium. The main commands with some degree of operational autonomy were the strategic bombing units and the "Pascha' squadrons in the Middle East).

**1** BRIEFTAUBEN ABTEILUNG OSTEND** (f.10/14)
Cover-name for FLIEGERKORPS DER OBERHEERESLEITUNG.
*Siegert* to 12/15††

**2** BRIEFTAUBEN ABTEILUNG METZ (f. 8/15)
*Kastner-Kirdorf* to 12/15‡‡

**3** BOMBENGESCHWADER DER OBERHEERESLEITUNG 3 (BOGOHL3) (f.1/17). Previously KAMPFGESCHWADER DER OHL 3 (f.?/16).◊◊
*Brandenburg* to 6/17
*Kleine* to 10/17
*Walter* to 1/18
*Brandenburg*

**4** RIESENFLUGZEUG ABTEILUNG 500•• (f.11/15).
*v. Könitz* to 12/15
*Haller v. Hallerstein* to 11/16
*Schilling* to 8/18
*Borchers*

**5** RIESENFLUGZEUG ABTEILUNG 501 (f.8/16).ΔΔ
*Krupp* to 11/16
*v. Bentavegni*

**6** RIESENFLUGZEUG ABTEILUNG 502 (f.12/16)

? to 9/17 (dissolved)

**7** RIESENFLUGZEUG ABTEILUNG 503 (f.12/16)
? to 9/17 (dissolved)

**8** KOMMANDEUR DER FLIEGER HEERESGRUPPE F (f.7/17: Middle East)
*Serno****

**Table 2.7:** Austro-Hungarian Government and High Command 1914-18

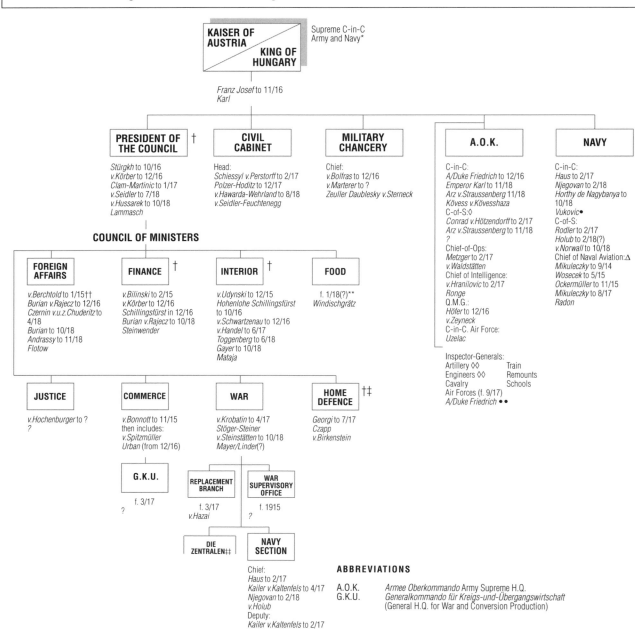

**KAISER OF AUSTRIA / KING OF HUNGARY**

Supreme C-in-C Army and Navy*

*Franz Josef* to 11/16
*Karl*

**PRESIDENT OF THE COUNCIL** †

Stürgkh to 10/16
v.Körber to 12/16
Clam-Martinic to 1/17
v.Seidler to 7/18
v.Hussarek to 10/18
Lammasch

**CIVIL CABINET**

Head:
Schiessyl v.Perstorff to 2/17
Polzer-Hoditz to 12/17
v.Hawarda-Wehrland to 8/18
v.Seidler-Feuchtenegg

**MILITARY CHANCERY**

Chief:
v.Bolfras to 12/16
v.Marterer to ?
Zeuller Daublesky v.Sterneck

**A.O.K.**

C-in-C:
A/Duke Friedrich to 12/16
Emperor Karl to 11/18
Arz v.Straussenberg 11/18
Kövess v.Kövesshaza
C-of-S:◊
Conrad v.Hötzendorff to 2/17
Arz v.Straussenberg to 11/18
?
Chief-of-Ops:
Metzger to 2/17
v.Waldstätten
Chief of Intelligence:
v.Hranilovic to 2/17
Ronge
Q.M.G.:
Höfer to 12/16
v.Zeyneck
C-in-C. Air Force:
Uzelac

Inspector-Generals:
Artillery ◊◊       Train
Engineers ◊◊      Remounts
Cavalry            Schools
Air Forces (f. 9/17)
A/Duke Friedrich ••

**NAVY**

C-in-C:
Haus to 2/17
Njegovan to 2/18
Horthy de Nagybanya to 10/18
C-of-S:
Rodler to 2/17
Holub to 2/18(?)
v.Norwall to 10/18
Chief of Naval Aviation:△
Mikuleczky to 9/14
Wosecek to 5/15
Ockermüller to 11/15
Mikuleczky to 8/17
Radon

**COUNCIL OF MINISTERS**

**FOREIGN AFFAIRS**

v.Berchtold to 1/15††
Burian v.Rajecz to 12/16
Czernin v.u.z.Chuderitz to 4/18
Burian to 10/18
Andrassy to 11/18
Flotow

**FINANCE** †

v.Bilinski to 2/15
v.Körber to 12/16
Schillingsfürst in 12/16
Burian v.Rajecz to 10/18
Steinwender

**INTERIOR** †

v.Udynski to 12/15
Hohenlohe Schillingsfürst to 10/16
v.Schwartzenau to 12/16
v.Handel to 6/17
Toggenberg to 6/18
Gayer to 10/18
Mataja

**FOOD**

f. 1/18(?)**
Windischgrätz

**JUSTICE**

v.Hochenburger to ?
?

**COMMERCE**

v.Bonnott to 11/15
then includes:
v.Spitzmüller
Urban (from 12/16)

**WAR**

v.Krobatin to 4/17
Stöger-Steiner
v.Steinstätten to 10/18
Mayer/Linder(?)

**HOME DEFENCE** ‡‡

Georgi to 7/17
Czapp
v.Birkenstein

**G.K.U.**

f. 3/17
?

**REPLACEMENT BRANCH**

f. 3/17
v.Hazai

**WAR SUPERVISORY OFFICE**

f. 1915
?

**DIE ZENTRALEN**‡‡

**NAVY SECTION**

Chief:
Haus to 2/17
Kailer v.Kaltenfels to 4/17
Njegovan to 2/18
v.Holub
Deputy:
Kailer v.Kaltenfels to 2/17
Rudler to 2/18
v.Teichgräben

**ABBREVIATIONS**

A.O.K.    *Armee Oberkommando* Army Supreme H.Q.
G.K.U.    *Generalkommando für Kriegs-und-Übergangswirtschaft*
          (General H.Q. for War and Conversion Production)

---

\* The Kaiser traditionally delegates the supreme command to the C-in-C. at A.O.K. On 4/11/18 he handed it over completely.

† The Hungarian counterparts of these ministers were:
President of the Ministry: *Tisza de Boros-Jeno* to 6/17; *Esterhazy* to 8/17; *Wekerle* to 4/18; *Serenyi* to 10/18; *Wekerle* to 11/17; *Karolyi v.Nagykaroly* to 11/18; *Hock*
Finance: *Teleszky* to 6/17; *Gratz* to 9/17; *Wekerle* to 2/18; *Popovics* to 10/18; *Karolyi v.Nagykaroly*
Interior: *Sandor* to 6/17; *Ugron* to 1/18; *Toth* to 5/18; *Wekerle* to 11/18; *Batthyany*
Home Defence: *v.Hazai* to 3/17; *v.Szurmay*. Often known as the Honved Ministry.

‡ The Home Defence Ministers were responsible for *Landwehr*, *Honved* and *Landsturm* units.

◊ Also a member of the Military Chancery.

• Navy handed over to putative Yugoslavia.

△ The command was known as the *Seeflugleitung* from 8/16 and the *Seefliegerkorps* from 4/17.

\** Originally the Food Control Office, f. 12/16 under *Höfer*.

†† *von Berchthold von und zu Ungerschitz, Fratting und Pullitz.*

‡‡ Small, often one-man departments set up to oversee production of the 91 raw materials and finished products deemed essential to the war effort.

◊◊ Each with its own specialised staff.

•• Absorbed by the C-in-C. Air Force in 9/18.

| | |
|---|---|
| * For much of 1916 and the second half of 1917 seems to have lost responsibility for forces in Tirol.<br><br>† Invaded in late 1915.<br><br>‡ As commander of Third Army (see Armies below).<br><br>◊ Became *Armeegruppe Albanien* during this period.<br><br>• In effect the old Fifth Army which had been subdivided into First and Second Isonzo Armies which now formed *Boroevic's* army group.<br><br>∆ Often referred to as Army Group Tirol.<br><br>** Sometimes referred to as *Heeresfront Archduke Josef.* (*Josef Augustin* as distinct from sometime army commander *Archduke Josef Ferdinand.*)<br><br>†† Downgraded to become 1 Generalkommando.<br><br>‡‡ *Böhm-Ermolli* had remained in command of Second Army even after he had been given charge of an army group in 9/15 (see **Army Groups** 2).<br><br>◊◊ Merged with Seventh Army (see below).<br><br>•• Downgraded to become 4 Generalkommando.<br><br>∆∆ For *Archduke Josef Ferdinand.*<br><br>*** For *Archduke Josef.*<br><br>††† Downgraded to become 7 Generalkommando. | **Supplement to Table 2.7:** Other Major Austro-Hungarian Commands |

## THE ARMY
### Theatre/Area Commands
**1** SOUTH-WEST FRONT* (f.8/14: Italy).
*Rohr* to 5/15
*Archduke Eugen* to 1/18 (dissolved)
CHIEF-OF-STAFF
*Krauss* to ?
*Konopicky*
**2** BALKANS
**a** *Potiorek* to 12/14
*Archduke Eugen* to 5/15
*Tersztyanszky v. Nadas* to 9/15
**b** f.10/18 (partially)
*Kövess v. Kövesshaza*
**3** MONTENEGRO AND ALBANIA†
*Kövess v. Kövesshaza* to ?/16‡
Then split between:
**a** C-in-C. BOSNIA, HERZERGOVINA AND DALMATIA (f.12/14)
*Sarkotic v. Lovcen*
**b** XIX CORPS (f.?/15)
*Trollman* to 10/17
*v. Koennen-Horak* to 8/18
*v. Pflanzer-Baltin*◊
**c** GENERALGOUVERNEMENT MONTENEGRO
See *Occupied Territories* below

### Army Groups (*Heeresgruppen*)
**1** ARMY GROUP BOROEVIC (f.9/17: Italy)•
**2** ARMY GROUP BÖHM-ERMOLLI (f.9/15: E.Front).
Became OSTARMEE 5/18 (see *Armies* 13 below)
**3** ARMY GROUP CONRAD∆ (f.3/17: Italy).
Became Army Group Archduke Josef 7/18 (see 4 below).
**4** ARMY GROUP ARCHDUKE JOSEF**
**a** 12/16-1/18: E.Front. Formed from Army Group Archduke Karl (see 7 below). Became Army Group Kövess 1/18 (see 5a below).
CHIEF-OF-STAFF
*v. Seeckt* to 12/17
*v. Willerding*
**b** f.7/18: Italy. Became Army Group Krobatin 10/18 (see 6 below).
CHIEF-OF-STAFF
*v. Willerding*
**5** ARMY GROUP KÖVESS
**a** 1/18-4/18: E.Front. Dissolved.
**b** f.10/18: Balkans. Incomplete.
**6** ARMY GROUP KROBATIN (f.10/18: Italy).
From Army Group Archduke Joseph (see 4b above).
**7** ARMY GROUP ARCHDUKE KARL (f.6/16: E.Front).
Became Army Group Archduke Josef 12/16 (see 4a above).
CHIEF-OF-STAFF
*v. Seeckt*

### Armies
**1** FIRST ARMY (f.8/14: E.Front)
*Dankl v. Krasnik* to 5/15
*Puhallo v. Brlog* to 8/16
*Arz v. Straussenberg* to 2/17
*Rohr* to 4/18 (dissolved)††
**2** SECOND ARMY (f.8/14: Balkans then almost immediately E.Front).
*v. Böhm-Ermolli* to 3/18 (dissolved)‡‡
**3** THIRD ARMY (f.8/14: E. Front to 6/15 then to Balkans to 3/16 when moved to Italy. Returned to E.Front 6/16).

*v. Brudermann* to 9/14
*Borevic v. Bojna* to 5/15
*Kövess v. Kövesshaza* to 10/16
*v. Kirchbach* to 2/17
*Tersztyansky v. Nadas* to 7/17
*Kritek* to 1/18 (dissolved)◊◊
**4** FOURTH ARMY (f.8/14: E.Front)
*v. Auffenberg-Komarow* to 9/14
*A/duke Josef Ferdinand* to 6/16
*Tersztyanszky v. Nadas* to 2/17
*v. Kirchbach* to 3/18 (dissolved)••
CHIEF-OF-STAFF∆∆
*Krauss* to ?/15
*v. Paic* to ?
*Berndt*
**5** FIFTH ARMY (f.8/14: Balkans).
To Italy 5/15. Renamed ISONZO ARMY 5/17 and split into 1 and 2 ISONZO ARMIES 10/17. United again as single ISONZO ARMY by 6/16.
*v. Frank* to 5/15
*Boroevic v. Bojna* to 10/17
*v. Wurm*
**6** SIXTH ARMY (f.8/14: Balkans).
Absorbed by Fifth Army (see above) 12/14. Reformed 1918 in Italy.
*Potiorek* to 12/14
*Archduke Josef* to 7/18
*Schönburg-Hartenstein*
CHIEF-OF-STAFF***
*v. Willerding*
**7** SEVENTH ARMY (f.5/15: E.Front).
*v. Pflanzer-Baltin* to 10/16
*Kövess v. Kövesshaza* to 1/18
*Kritek* to 4/18 (dissolved)†††
**8** TENTH ARMY (f.1/16: Italy).
*Rohr* to 6/16
*Scotti* to 4/17
*v. Krobatin* to 12/17 (dissolved)
**9** ELEVENTH ARMY (f.3/16: Italy).
*Dankl v. Krasnik* to 6/16
*Rohr* to ?/17
*Scheuchenstuel*
**10** ISONZO ARMY. See Fifth Army above.
**11** FIRST ISONZO ARMY. See Fifth Army above.
*v. Wurm*
**12** SECOND ISONZO ARMY. See Fifth Army above.
*v. Henriquez*
**13** OSTARMEE (f.5/18: E.Front).
*v. Böhm-Ermolli* to 5/18
*Krauss*

### Lesser Commands
**1** XVIII CORPS (to W.Front 8/18).
*L. Goiginger*
**2** IX CORPS (forming on W.Front 11/18).
*Schneider Edl. v. Manns-Au*

### Occupied Territories
**1** MONTENEGRO
see entry in Table 2.10.
**2** POLAND
see entry in Table 2.10.

**3** SERBIA
see entry in Table 2.10.

## THE NAVY

**1** C-in-C. FLEET
Same as C-in-C. Navy.
See Table 2.7.
CHIEF-OF-STAFF
As above to 2/17 then Fleet
Chief-of-Staff only:
*Holub* to 2/18
*Konek Edler v. Norwall*

**2** FIRST (BATTLE) SQUADRON
*Njegovan* to 2/17
*Willenik* to ?
*Seitz*

**3** SECOND (BATTLE) SQUADRON
*Löfler* to ?
*Seidensachser* to ?
*Lauffer*

**4** CRUISER FLOTILLA*
*Fiedler* to ?/16
*Hansa* to ?/18
*Heyssler* to ?
*Hansa*

**5** U-BOAT FLOTILLA
*v. Thierry*

**6** DANUBE FLOTILLA
*Grund* to 9/14
*Lucich* to 12/17
*Wickerhauser* to ?
*Ratkovic* to ?
*Wulff*

**7** C-in-C. POLA (Ashore)
*v. Chlemarz* to ?/16
*Fiedler* to ?/18
*Cicoli*

\* Became an autonomous command in early 1916 when the battleship squadrons were effectively penned in port.

### THE AIR FORCE (*Luftfahrtruppen*)†

Air force units were not organised under theatre commanders but under officers (*Stabsoffiziere* later *Kommandanten*) attached to each Army. By the end of the war there was also a Giant Bomber Commander attached to Army Group Boroevic in Italy. We have been unable to find the names of these officers.

† By 10/18 officially referred to as *das Luftfahrwesen*.

• TABLE 2.8 • MAJOR TURKISH COMMANDS •

**Table 2.8:** Turkish Government and High Command 1914-18

* Even when not the minister *Djaved* remained the dominant financial administrator.

† Originally Food Board (f. 4/16) and later Supreme Food Commission (f. 3/18).

‡ Mainly in Damascus (as Gov.-Gen. Syria) until 12/17.

◊ Including Logistics and Armaments.

• Had largley superceded the Ministry of War Aviation Branch by 12/16. Became the General Inspectorate for Aviation Affairs in 7/18. Actual operational control of flying units always remained with the local army commanders.

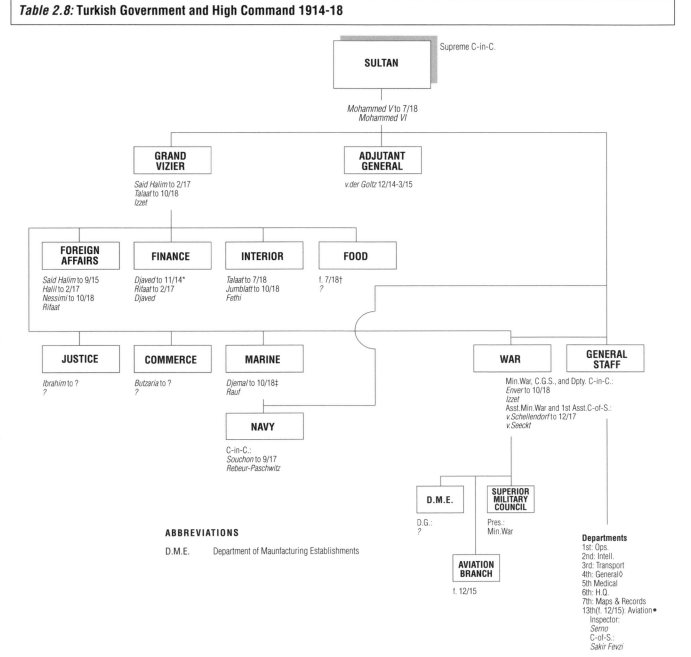

**ABBREVIATIONS**

D.M.E.    Department of Maunfacturing Establishments

---

**Supplement to Table 2.8:** Other Major Turkish Commands

## THE ARMY
### Theatre/Area Commands
**1**   C-in-C. ARMENIA/KURDISTAN (f.3/16)
*Ahmet Izzet Pasha to ?/17*
*Vehip Pasha to 6/18*
*Khalil Pasha*

### Army Groups
**1**   YILDERIM ARMY GROUP (f.7/17).* Originally intended to retake Baghdad, the A.Gp. was soon transferred to Palestine to try and forestall the British advance there.
*v. Falkenhayn to 3/18*
*Liman v. Sanders*

### Armies
**1**   THE FIRST ARMY (f.8/14). Based on Istanbul. Once the Gallipoli landings had been repulsed became little more than a depot formation. Its corps provided the contingents in S.E.Europe (see **Lesser Commands** 1, 2, and 3 below).
*Liman v. Sanders to 3/15*
*C. v. der Goltz to 10/15*
*?*
**2**   SECOND ARMY (f.8/14) Based in Anatolia. Involved in Gallipoli operations from 7/15 and then slowly transferred to Armenia/Kurdistan in the first half of 1916.
*Vehip Pasha to 3/16†*
*Ahmet Izzet Pasha to 10/16*
*Kemal Pasha to 8/17*
*Nihad Pasha‡*
**3**   THIRD ARMY (f.8/14). Armenia/Kurdistan
*Hasan Izzet Pasha to 12/14*
*Enver Pasha to 1/15*
*Hakki Pasha to 3/15*
*Kamil Pasha to 3/16*
*Vehip Pasha to 6/18*
*Essad Pasha*
**4**   FOURTH ARMY (f.9/14). Syria/Palestine. By late 1917 was a reserve and l.of c.h.q. with most of its units taken over by the new Eight Army h.q. (see below).
*Djemal Pasha to 12/17 ◊*
*Djemal 'Kucjuk' Pasha•*
**5**   FIFTH ARMY (f.3/15)/ Dardanelles. From 1916 progressively reduced to just a few divisions.
*Liman v. Sanders to 3/18*
*?*
**6**   SIXTH ARMY (f.9/15). Mesopotamia.
*C.v. der Goltz to 4/16*
*Khalil Pasha to 6/18*
*Ali Ihsan*
**7**   SEVENTH ARMY (f.7/17). Intended to help retake Baghdad as part of Yilderim Army Group (See **Army Groups** above) but transferred to Palestine.
*Kemal Pasha to 9/17*
*Fevzi Pasha to 8/18*
*Kemal Pasha*
**8**   EIGHTH ARMY (f.10/17). Formed in Palestine to control ex-Fourth Army units (see 4 above).
*Kress v. Kressenstein to 12/17*
*Djevad Pasha△*

**9**   NINTH ARMY (f.6/18). Armenia/Kurdistan with a view to operations in N. Persia.
*Sevki Pasha*
**10**   ARMY OF ISLAM (f.3/18). To operate in the Caucasus in the wake of Russian collapse.
*Nuri Pasha*

### Lesser Commands
**1**   ROUMANIA (VI CORPS). Began arriving 9/16 and departed second half 1917.
*Hilmi Pasha*
**2**   GALICIA (XV CORPS). Arrived 8/15 and departed 9/17.
*Sevki Pasha to 9/15*
*Djevad Pasha △*
**3**   MACEDONIA (XX CORPS). HQ arrived 12/16. From 6/17 one div. only and know as RUMELI FIELD DETACHMENT. Departed 4/18.
*Abdulkerim Pasha to ?*
*?*

## THE NAVY
See Table 2.8. The small Turkish fleet remained confined to the Dardanelles and the Black Sea.

## THE AIR FORCE
See Table 2.8. We have no details on any intermediate formations although it was the Turkish practice, as in other air forces, to allocate squadrons piecemeal amongst the armies.

* Known officially to the Germans as Army Group F.

† Sometimes translated as *Wahib Pasha*.

‡ A few battalions only during 1918.

◊ Sometimes translated as *Cemal Pasha*.

• *Djemal* "the Lesser".

△ Sometimes translated as *Cevat Pasha*.

**Table 2.9: Inter-Allied Agencies**

## Military

**1   ALLIED SUPREME WAR COUNCIL** (f.11/17)
Formed at Rapallo as an *ad hoc* response to the crisis on the Italian front. Soon expanded its writ to the Western Front, albeit in a mainly advisory capacity, but was superseded here after the creation of an Allied Supreme commander in 3/18 (see below). Latterly mainly concerned itself with secondary fronts and politically sensitive topics such as the armistice terms. Met usually at Versailles. The representatives were

> FRENCH
> *Foch* to 12/17
> *Weygand* to 4/18
> *Belin*
> BRITISH
> *Wilson* to 2/18
> *Rawlinson* to 4/18
> *Sackville-West*
> ITALIAN
> *Cadorna* to 2/18
> *Giardino* to 4/18
> *de Robilant*
> U.S.
> *Bliss*

*\* Officially Chef des Armées Alliées.*

**2   SUPREME COMMANDER ALLIED ARMIES\***
First appointed 29/3/18 after the shock of the great German offensive that month. Arrived 3/4/18 to 'coordinate' but given official command 14/4/18. Responsibilities extended to Italian front 2/5/18.
> *Foch*

**3   C-in-C. GALLIPOLI**
> See Supplement to Table 2.1: Theatre Commands 3

**4   C-in-C. ALLIED ARMIES IN THE EAST** (Macedonia f.10/15)
> *Sarrail* to 12/17
> *Guillaumat* to 7/18
> *Franchet d'Esperey*

**5   C-IN-C. ALLIED FORCES RUSSIA** (f.8/18: Vladivostok.)
> *Janin*

## Naval

**1   INTER-ALLIED NAVAL CONFERENCE** (f.12/17.) Comprised Navy Ministers and Chiefs of the Naval Staff for France, U.K. and Italy as well as Deputy-C.N.S. for U.S. and Japan.

**2   ALLIED C-IN-C. MEDITERRANEAN** (f.8/14.) As French C-in-C. Mediterranean (see Supplement to Table 2.2: Navy 1.)

**3   FIRST ALLIED FLEET** (f. 5/15: Adriatic.) As Italian C-in-C (see Supplement to Table 2.4: Navy 1).

*† Direction Générale de la Guerre Sous-Marine.*

**4   GENERAL DIRECTORATE†** (f. 6/17: HQ Malta.)
> *Vignaux*

## Air Force

*‡ Began to function 3/18. Oversaw the work of national blockade sub-committees.*

**1   INTER-ALLIED INDEPENDENT AIR FORCE** (f. 10/18). Italian, U.S. and French long-distance bomber squadrons added to the existing British Independent Air Force (see Supplement to Table 2.1: Air Force 2). Never undertook operations.
> *Trenchard*

## Civilian

**1   ALLIES BLOCKADE COMMITTEE‡** (f. 8/17: London).
> *Leverton Harris* (U.K.) (Chairman)
> *Charpentier* (France)
> *Giannini* (Italy)
> *Sheldon* (U.S.)

**2   ALLIED MARITIME TRANSPORT COUNCIL** (f.12/17: London). To coordinate availability of merchant shipping and strategic requirements for imports. Comprised a Ministerial Council and an Executive. The Chairman of the latter was the Director of Shipping Requisitioning in the British Ministry of Shipping.

**3   CENTRAL INTER-ALLIED PROPAGANDA COMMISSION** (f.4/18: Padua). No further details.

**4   COMMISSION INTERNATIONALE DE RAVITAILLEMENT** (f.8/14: London). To mediate Allied and War Office purchasing requirements within the U.K. A British executive led by
> *Wintour* to early 1915
> *Wyldbore Smith*

**5   INTER-ALLIED FOOD COUNCIL** (f.8/18: London). Comprising a Board of the Allied national Food Controllers and a Standing Committee of Representatives. Oversaw the work of international committees for the supply of Cereals; Oils and Seeds; Sugar; Meats and Fats. Chairman of the Standing Committee was
> *Beale* (U.K.)

**6   INTER-ALLIED MUNITIONS COUNCIL** (f.?/18). Oversaw the work of international committees for the supply of Steel; Chemicals; Nitrates; Non-Ferrous Metals; Explosives; Aircraft; Mechanical Transport. No further details.

**7   INTER-ALLIED RAW MATERIALS COUNCIL** Proposed. To oversee the work of international committees for the supply of Coal and Coke; Cotton; Flax, Hemp and Jute; Hides and Leather; Paper and Pulp; Petroleum; Tobacco; Wool.

**8   INTER-ALLIED COUNCIL FOR WAR PURCHASES AND FINANCE** (f.?/17). To regulate and mediate Allied purchases and credits in the U.S.
> CHAIRMAN (London)
> *Crosby* (U.S.)
> SECRETARIES-GENERAL
> *Cook* (British: London)
> *Lazard* (French: Paris)

## Table 2.10: Governments and High Commands in other Belligerent Countries

**AUSTRALIA**
GOVERNOR-GENERAL
  *Munro-Ferguson*
PRIME MINISTER
  *Cook* to 9/14
  *Fisher* to 10/14
  *Hughes*
FOREIGN AFFAIRS
  *Glynn* to 9/14
  *Arthur* to 12/14
  *Mahon* to 10/14
  *none*
FINANCE
  *Forrest* to 9/14
  *Fisher* to 10/15
  *Higgs* to 11/16
  *Poynton* to 2/17
  *Forrest* to 3/18
  *Watt*
INTERIOR
  *Cook* to 9/14
  *Archibald* to 10/15
  *O'Malley* to 11/16
  *Barnford* to 2/17
  *Glynn*
WAR
  *Millen* to 9/14
  *Pearce*
NAVY (became Ministry 7/15)
  *Jensen* to 2/17
  *Cook*
CHIEF OF THE GENERAL STAFF
  *Legge* to 5/15
  *Irving (acting)* to 12/15
  *Forster (acting)* to 9/17
  *Legge*
C-IN-C. AUSTRALIAN IMPERIAL FORCE (AIF) (f.8/14).
  *Bridges* to 5/15
  *Birdwood* to 5/18*
  *White*
ANZAC CORPS (f.12/14). Egypt and then Gallipoli. Back to Egypt 1/16 and then to France 3/16 where became I ANZAC CORPS (see below).
  *Birdwood*
I ANZAC CORPS (f.6/16).† Formed from ANZAC CORPS (see above). France and Belgium. Absorbed into Australian Corps (see below) 12/17.
  *Birdwood*
II ANZAC CORPS (f.6/16). France and Belgium. Absorbed into Australian Corps (see below) 12/17.‡
  *Godley*
AUSTRALIAN CORPS (f.12/17). France and Belgium.
  *Birdwood* to 5/18
  *Monash*
CHIEF OF NAVAL STAFF◊
  *Creswell*

**BELGIUM**
By 10/14 the Belgian army had been completely overrun and the whole country, except for a tiny rump west of the Yser, was under German occupation. The King remained at the front whilst the government moved to Sainte-Adresse near Le Havre.•
HEAD OF STATE

  *King Albert*
PRIME MINISTER
  *de Broqueville* to 6/18
  *Cooreman*
FOREIGN AFFAIRS
  *Davignon* to 7/15
  *Beyens* to 8/17
  *de Broqueville* to 12/17
  *Hyams*
FINANCE
  *van de Vyvere*
INTERIOR
  *Berryer*
WAR
  *de Broqueville* to 8/17
  *de Ceuninck* to ?/18
  *Janson*
C-IN-C. ARMY
  *King Albert*
CHIEF OF THE GENERAL STAFF
  *de Selliers de Moranville* to 9/14
  *Wielemanns* to 1/17
  *Rucquoi* to 4/18
  *Gillain*
FLANDERS ARMY GROUP (f.9/18).
  *King Albert*
CHIEF-OF-STAFF
  *Degoutte*△
COMPAGNIE DES AVIATEURS became AVIATION MILITAIRE 1915.
  *de Saint-Marcq* to ?/??
  *Mathieu* to 3/15
  *Wahis* to early 1916
  *van Crombrugghe*

**Occupied Belgium**
A German Governor-General was appointed on 23/8/14 and in 11/14 two-thirds of the country was allotted to the *Gouvernement Général*, the remaining western third being placed under military control as part of the *Etappengebiet*. In 11/17 the country was partitioned into two, Flandern and Wallonie, and in December the former was declared independent.
GOVERNOR-GENERAL
  *C.v. der Goltz* to 11/14
  *v. Bissing* to 4/17
  *v. Falkenhausen*
CIVIL ADMINISTRATOR
  *Sandt*
COLONIAL GOVERNORS
  CONGO
  *?* to 2/15
  *Henrij*

**BULGARIA**
Declared war on Serbia 9/10/15 and agreed armistice with Allies 29/9/18.
HEAD OF STATE
  *King Ferdinand* to 10/18
  *King Boris III* **
PRIME MINISTER
  *Radoslavov* to 7/18
  *Malinov*
FOREIGN AFFAIRS
  *Radoslavov* to 10/18

* Acting to 9/16.

† In fact, contained no New Zealand units.

‡ Absorbed minus the New Zealand Division.

◊ On the outbreak of war the Royal Australian Navy (f.7/11) became the Australian Squadron under the command of the Royal Navy. Originally commanded by *Patey*, this squadron was soon dispersed to various theatres.

• The government moved from Brussels to Antwerp on 17/8/14, to Ostend on 6/10, and to Le Havre on 13/10. The government moved without most of its administrative staff which remained in Brussels.

△ French.

** Abdicated 1/11/18.

\* All generals.

† From 10/15.

‡ This list may be incomplete.

◊ German.

● Remained as Minister of War Overseas until after the war.

△ Putative until late 1918 and not internationally recognised until 1919.

\*\* For further details on Czech military units, see Section 3: Part I.

†† Rarely actually in Paris. Peripatetic *via* England, Russia and the United States.

‡‡ Latter defected late 1916.

◊◊ And President of the Council of Ministers.

●● Official name for the British army of occupation in Egypt. Soon absorbed into the Expeditionary Force there and title lapsed in 1915.

△△ Stationed in the Sudan.

*Todoroff*
FINANCE
   *Tontchev* to 10/18
   *Liaptchev*
INTERIOR
   *Radoslavov* to 10/15
   *Popov* to 9/16
   *Radoslavov* to 10/18
   *Takev*
WAR\*
   *Fitchev* to 8/15
   *Zhekov* to 10/15
   *Naidenhov* to 10/18
   *Sarov*
C-IN-C. ARMY†
   *Zhekov* to 10/18
   *King Boris*
   CHIEF-OF-STAFF‡
   *Zhostov* by 10/15
   *Lukov* by 12/16
   *Burmov* by 9/18
FIRST ARMY (f.9/15).
   *Bojadjiev* to 9/16
   *v. Winckler*◊ to 10/16
   *Geshov* to ?/18
   *Nerezov*
SECOND ARMY (F.9/15).
   *Todorov* to ?/18
   *Lukov*
THIRD ARMY (f.9/15).
   *Toshev* to early 1917
   *Nerezov* to 8/17
   *Sarov* to ?/17
   *Nerezov* to ?/18
   *?*
FOURTH ARMY (f.?/17).
   *Toshev*
ARMY AVIATION BATTALION (f.4/16).
   *Zlatarov*
   *?*

## CANADA
GOVERNOR-GENERAL
   *Duke of Connaught* to 11/16
   *Duke of Devonshire*
PRIME MINISTER
   *Borden*
FOREIGN AFFAIRS
   *Coderre* to 10/15
   *Blondin* to 8/16
   *Patenaude* to 6/17
   none to 10/17
   *Burrell*
FINANCE
   *White*
INTERIOR
   *Roche*
WAR
   *Hughes* to 11/16
   *Kemp* to 10/17●
   *Mewburn*
MARINE, FISHERIES AND NAVAL SERVICE
   *Hazen* to ?/17
   *Ballantyne*

CHIEF OF THE GENERAL STAFF
   *Gwatkin*
CANADIAN EXPEDITIONARY FORCE (f.8/14). Became CANADIAN CORPS (f.9/15).
   *Alderson* to 5/16
   *Byng* to 6/17
   *Currie*
   CHIEF-OF-STAFF
   *Harington* to 6/16
   *Radcliffe* to 4/18
   *Webber* to 10/18
   *Hayter*
DIRECTOR NAVAL SERVICES
   *Kingsmill*
CANADIAN AIR FORCE (f.9/18).
   (no C-in-C. listed until 1920.)

**CHINA** (from 8/17).
Declared war on the Central Powers 8/17. This was essentially an American-inspired ploy to gain China a seat at the peace conference and China, riven by internal dissension and revolt, was unable to offer any practical aid to the Allies.
HEAD OF STATE
   *Feng Kuo-chang* to 9/18
   *Hsu Shih-chang*
PRIME MINISTER
   *Tuan Chi-jui*

**CZECHOSLAVAKIA**△
Throughout the war Czech and Slovak lands remained part of the Austro-Hungarian Empire. However, by 2/18 Czech emigré units fighting with the Allies had been recognised as forming a Czech Army, albeit dispersed.\*\*
On 14/10/18 the Czech National Council was recognised as the provisional government, on the 17th the Republic was proclaimed, and on the 29th the National Council took over the Hapsburg administration in Prague.
CZECH FOREIGN COMMITTEE (f.11/15) became CZECH NATIONAL COUNCIL in 1/16. Based in Paris.
   CHAIRMAN
   *Masaryk* ††
   DEPUTY CHAIRMAN
   *Stefanik* & *Dürich* ‡‡
   GENERAL SECRETARY
   *Benes*

**EGYPT**
KHEDIVE (to 12/14) then SULTAN
   *Abbas Hilmi* to 12/14
   *Hussein Kamel* to 10/17
   *Ahmed Fuad*
CONSUL-GENERAL (to 12/14) then HIGH COMMISSIONER
   *Kitchener* to 8/14
   *Cheetham* (acting) to 12/14
   *Macmahon* to 1/17
   *Wingate*
PRIME MINISTER◊◊
   *Rushdi Pasha*
C-IN-C. EGYPT AND PALESTINE
See Table 2.1: Theatre/Area Commands 2.
BRITISH FORCE IN EGYPT (ref.1/18)●●
   *Watson*
SIRDAR EGYPTIAN ARMY△△
   *Wingate*

## FINLAND

Began the war as a Grand Duchy of Russia. After the abdication of the Tsar, in 3/17, an executive committee assumed power. In July it declared itself in charge of all its affairs except military and foreign, and in 12/17 it opted for complete independence. A pro-Bolshevik putsch took place the following month and the ensuing civil was was finally won by the whites in 5/18 (with the help of the German Baltic Division).

GOVERNOR-GENERAL*
    *Seyn* to 3/17
    *Stakovich*
REGENT (from 5/18).
    *Svinhufvud*
PRIME MINISTER (from 10/17).†
    *Svinhufvud* to 5/18
    *Paasikivi*
DEFENCE CORPS (f.1/18).
    *Mannerheim* to 5/18
    *Wilkama*

## GREECE

Greece remained neutral during the first years of the war, with its rulers split between the pro-Allied Venizelists and the pro-German monarchists. Eventually, in 9/16, Venizelos left for Crete to set up a Provisional Government of his own. This moved to Salonika in 10/16 and in the following month declared war on Germany and Bulgaria. During the following winter the Venizelists formed their own volunteer divisions to fight with the Allies in Macedonia. Meanwhile, fearful for their lines of communication, the Allies had been putting increasing diplomatic and military pressure on the King and his government and in 6/17 secured his abdication. Venizelos then returned as Prime Minister in Athens and a few days later Greece as a whole declared war on the Central Powers. By spring 1918 regular Greek divisions were coming into the line alongside the Venizelists.

HEAD OF STATE
    *King Constantine* to 6/17
    *King Alexander*
PRIME MINISTER
    *Venizelos* to 3/15
    *Gounaris* to 10/15
    *Zaimis* to 11/15
    *Skouloudes* to 6/16
    *Zaimis* to 9/16
    *Kalogeropoulos* to 10/16
    *Lambros* to 4/17
    *Zaimis* to 6/17
    *Venizelos*
FOREIGN AFFAIRS
    *Venizelos* to 4/15
    *Zografos* to 8/15
    *Venizelos* to 10/15
    *Zaimis* to 11/15
    *Skouloudes* to 6/16
    *Zaimis* to 9/16
    *Karapanos* to 10/16
    *Zalocostas* to 5/17
    *Zaimis* to 6/17
    *Politis*
FINANCE
    *Diomedes* to 3/15
    *Protopapadakis* to 8/15
    *Repoulis* to 10/15
    *Dragoumis* to 4/16
    *Rallis* to 6/16
    *Momferatos* to 10/16

    *Kalogeropoulos* to 10/16
    *Tsanetovleas* to 4/17
    *Drosopoulos* to 6/17
    *Negropontes*
INTERIOR
    *Repoulis* to 4/15
    *Triantaphilakos* to 8/15
    *Kafandaris* to 10/15
    *Gounaris* to 6/16
    *Charalambos* to 9/16
    *Roufos* to 10/16
    *Tselos* to 6/17
    *Repoulis* to 1/18
    *Ractivan*
WAR
    *Venizelos* to 3/15
    *Gounaris* to 8/15
    *Danglis* to 10/15‡
    *Yanakitsas* to 6/16‡
    *Kallaris* to 9/16‡
    *Kalogeropoulos* to 10/16
    *Drakos* to 6/17‡
    *Venizelos* to 9/17
    *Danglis* to 1/18‡
    *Venizelos*
CHIEF OF THE GENERAL STAFF◊
    *Dousmanis* to 8/16
    *Moschopoulos* to 6/17 (?)
    *Braquet* to 12/17•
    *Bordeaux* to 6/18•
    *Granat*•
C-IN-C ROYAL GREEK ARMY (from 6/17)
    *Danglis*
C-IN-C. NAVY∆
    *Kondouriotis*
C-IN-C. AIR FORCE**
    ?

**Provisional Government** (9/16 to 6/17)
PRIME MINISTER
    *Venizelos*
FOREIGN AFFAIRS
    *Politis*
FINANCE
    *Negropontes*
INTERIOR
    *Sofoulis*
WAR
    *Zimbrakakis* to 12/16
    *Miliotis*
CORPS OF NATIONAL DEFENCE††
    *Zimbrakakis*

**Allies in Greece**
ALLIED HIGH COMMISSIONER (from 6/17)
    *Jonnart*

## INDIA
SECRETARY OF STATE (London)
    *Lord Crewe* to 5/15
    *A. Chamberlain* to 7/17
    *Montague*
VICEROY & GOVERNOR-GENERAL
    *Lord Hardinge* to 4/16
    *Lord Chelmsford*

* Russian.

† Officially known as Chairman of the Senate.

‡ All generals.

◊ Seems also to have been the effective Commander-in-Chief, although from 7/17, when the Chiefs-of-Staff were French, *General Danglis*, as a sop to Greek pride, was named nominal C-in-C.

• All French.

∆ Seized by the Allies 10/16 to 8/17. Only slowly returned to Greek control.

** Entirely French-equipped when rebuilt after 6/17.

†† Remained separate from Royal Greek Army even after *Venizelos* had once again become the P.M. in Athens.

• **TABLE 2.10** • GOVERNMENTS/HIGH COMMANDS IN OTHER BELLIGERENT COUNTRIES •

‡‡ Technically there was also a Foreign Affairs Member but this post was traditionally always occupied by the Governor-General.

\* Adopted name Taisho.

† All generals. Had direct access to the Emperor over the head of the Prime Minister.

‡ Both admirals.

◊ Co-equal with War Minister and C.G.S.

• Title was simply Governor until 6/17.

## Council of the Governor-General

Comprising seven members ‡‡ of whom the most important were the Army Member (the C-in-C: see below), and the

FINANCE MEMBER
*Meyer* to ?
HOME MEMBER
*Craddock* to ?
C-IN-C. INDIA
*Duff* to 10/16
*Monro*
CHIEF-OF-STAFF
*Lake* to 1/16
*Kirkpatrick*
DIRECTOR OF MILITARY OPERATIONS
*Kirkpatrick* to 1/16
QUARTERMASTER-GENERAL
*Bunbury* to ?/16
NORTHERN ARMY
*Willcocks* to ?/15
*Nixon* to 4/15
*Barratt*
SOUTHERN ARMY
*Nixon* to ?/15
*?* to 4/17
*Anderson*
DIRECTOR ROYAL INDIAN MARINE
*Lumsden* to ?

## JAPAN

Declared war on the Central Powers 23-25/8/14. Took no part in land operations except for the siege of Tsingtao (autumn 1914) and the Allied intervention against the Bolsheviks in 1918. Made a significant naval contribution, however, helping sweep the Indian and Pacific Oceans and sending a well-trained squadron to the Mediterranean.

HEAD OF STATE
*Emperor Yoshihito\**
PRIME MINISTER
*Okuma* to 10/16
*Terauchi* to 9/18
*Hara*
FOREIGN AFFAIRS
*Kato* to 8/15
*Ishii* to 10/16
*Motono* to 4/18
*Goto* to 9/18
*Ushida*
FINANCE
*Wakatsuke* to 8/15
*Taketomi* to 10/16
*Terauchi* to 12/16
*Katsuta* to 9/18
*Takahashi*
INTERIOR
*Okuma* to 1/15
*Oura* to 8/15
*Ikki* to 12/16
*Goto* to 4/18
*Mizuno* to 9/18
*Tokonami*
WAR†
*Oka* to 3/15
*Oshima* to 9/18
*Tanaka*

NAVY‡
*Yashiro* to 8/15
*Kato*
CHIEF OF THE GENERAL STAFF
*Yamagata* (?)
INSPECTOR-GENERAL OF MILITARY TRAINING◊
?
TSINGTAO EXPEDITIONARY FORCE (Expanded 18 Div: arr.9/14).
*Kanio*
VLADIVOSTOK EXPEDITIONARY FORCE (12 Div: arr.7/18).
*Otani*
CHIEF OF THE NAVAL STAFF
*Ijuin* (to end?)
FIRST FLEET (Japan)
*T. Kato* to ?/15
*Yoshimatsu* to ?/18
*Yamashita*
SECOND FLEET (Tsingtao)
*S. Kato* to ?/15
*Nawa* to ?/16
*Yashiro* to ?
*Yamaya* by 11/18
THIRD FLEET (Formosa)
*Tsuchiya* to ?/15
*Takarabe* to ?/16
*Murakami* to ?/17
*Akima*
1st SOUTH SEA SQUADRON (f.8/14).
*Yamaya* to 12/14 (disbanded)
2nd SOUTH SEA SQUADRON (f.8/14).
*Matsumura* to 12/14 (disbanded)
SOUTH SEA GUARD SQUADRON (f.1915).
*Togo* to ?/17
*Yoshida* to ?/18
*Nagata*
EAST INDIES STATION (Singapore: f.2/16).
*Oguri*
There were also important shore-based commands at KURE, SASEBO. YOKOSUKA (all mainland Japan), CHINHAI (Korea), PORT ARTHUR and the PESCADORES.

## NEW ZEALAND

GOVERNOR-GENERAL•
*Earl of Liverpool*
PRIME MINISTER
*Masset*
FOREIGN AFFAIRS
none
FINANCE
*Allen* to 8/15
*Ward*
INTERIOR
*Bell* to 8/15
*Russell*
WAR
*Allen*
NEW ZEALAND EXPEDITIONARY FORCE (f.8/14). Until the formation of the N.Z.Division (see below), the Expeditionary Force was largely absorbed in the New Zealand and Australian Division in Gallipoli and Egypt. In early 1916 N.Z.E.F. headquarters moved to France.
*Godley*
NEW ZEALAND DIVISION (f.3/16).
To France 4/16.
*Russell*

## POLAND

Ill-starred Poland was divided between Germany, Austria-Hungary and Russia until summer 1915 when the Central Powers overran the whole of the Russian portion, Galicia. This was divided between the conquerors who now placed military governors in their respective sectors. In 11/16, however, a Polish Provisional Council of State was formed, with its own Military Commission and token armed forces. In 9/17 the Council of State became a Regency Council to which was added a premier with his own 12-man cabinet. It was a newly-formed version of this cabinet that declared a Polish Republic in 11/18.

GOVERNOR-GENERAL
German (Warsaw)
  *v. Beseler*
Austrian (Lublin)
  *Steptycki* to 2/18
  *Liposcak*
MILITARY COMMISSION
  *Pilsudski* to 7/17 (dissolved)

### Regency Council

  *Archbishop Kakowski*, *Prince Lubomirski* and *Count Ostrowski*
PRIME MINISTER
  *Kucharzewski* to 2/18
  *Steczkowski* to 9/18
  *Kucharzewski* to 10/18
  *Swiezynski*

## PORTUGAL (from 3/16)

Parliament declared war on Germany 11/14. This had no executive force until 3/16 when the Central Powers reciprocated after the seizure of their ships that had taken refuge in Portugese ports at the beginning of the war.
HEAD OF STATE
  *Machado Guimaraes* to 12/17
  *Paes*
PRIME MINISTER
  *de Almeida* to 4/17
  *Costa* to 12/17
  *Paes*
FOREIGN AFFAIRS
  *Soares* to 12/17
  *Pais* to 5/18
  *Lima* to 10/18
  *Moniz*
FINANCE
  *Costa*
INTERIOR
  *Reis* to 6/16
  *de Albuquerque* to 4/17
  *Ribiero* to 12/17
  *Santos* to 3/18
  *Bessa* to 5/18
  *Barbosa* to 10/18
  *Ferreira*
WAR
  *de Matos* to 12/17
  *Paes* to 5/18
  *Mota* to 10/18
  *Mendonça*
CHIEF OF THE GENERAL STAFF
  ?
PORTUGESE EXPEDITIONARY FORCE (arr. France 2/17).
  *de Abreu*

## RUMANIA (from 8/16)

Declared war on Austria-Hungary 8/16. Signed armistice 12/17 but actual peace treaty never ratified. Declared war again 10/11/18.
HEAD OF STATE
  *King Ferdinand*
PRIME MINISTER
  *I. Bratianu* to 1/18
  *Averescu* to 3/18
  *Marghiloman*
FOREIGN AFFAIRS
  *Porambaru* to 12/16
  *I. Bratianu* to 1/18
  none to 3/18
  *Arion*
FINANCE
  *Continescu* to 12/16
  *Antonescu* to 6/17
  *Titulescu* to 1/18
  none to 3/18
  *Saulescu*
INTERIOR
  *Mortzun* to 12/16
  *Constantinescu* to 1/18
  none to 3/18
  *Marghiloman*
WAR
  *I. Bratianu* to 29/8/16
  *V. Bratianu* 7/17
  *Jancovescu* to 3/18*
  *Harjeu**
C-IN-C. ARMY
  *King Ferdinand* to 12/17
  *Prezan*
CHIEF OF THE GENERAL STAFF
  *Zottu* to 9/16
  *Iliescu* to 12/16
  *Prezan*
FRENCH MILITARY MISSION (arr.9/16).
  *Berthelot* to 3/18 (dissolved)
FIRST ARMY (f.8/16). Largely destroyed by 12/16. Reformed in 3/17 but does not reappear in the front line until summer of that year.
  *Culcer* to 11/16
  *Stratilescu* to 12/16
  *Iliescu* to ?/17
  *Critescu* to 8/17
  *Grigorescu*
SECOND ARMY (f.8/16). The only Rumanian Army to remain in the field up until the armistice of 12/17.
  *Crainiceanu* to 10/16
  *Averescu*
THIRD ARMY (f.8/16). Destroyed by 11/16.
  *Aslan* to 9/16
  *Averescu†*
FOURTH ARMY (f.8/16). Destroyed by 12/16.
  *Prezan*

## SERBIA

Finally overrun by the Central Powers in late 1915, the remnants of the Serbian Army were evacuated to Corfu and later to the Macedonian front.‡ In 10/18 the reconstituted divisions were able to take part in the liberation of their homeland.
HEAD OF STATE
  *King Peter*

\* Both generals.

† Some sources also mention *Valeanu* as a (joint?) commander by 10/16.

‡ The King and much of the government were also evacuated but, whilst the King made the move to Macedonia, the government-in-exile remained on Corfu.

• **TABLE 2.10** • GOVERNMENTS/HIGH COMMANDS IN OTHER BELLIGERENT COUNTRIES •

\* A colonel.

† Both generals.

‡ And annexation by South Africa.

PRIME MINISTER
  *Pasic*
FOREIGN AFFAIRS
  *Pasic*
FINANCE
  *Pachu* to 11/15
  *Nincic* to 6/17
  *Protic*
INTERIOR
  *Protic* to 12/14
  *Jovanovic*
WAR
  *Stefanovic* to 12/14\*
  *Boyovic* to 10/15†
  *Terzic*†
C-IN-C. ARMY
  *Crown-Prince Alexander*
CHIEF OF THE GENERAL STAFF
  *Putnik* to 12/15
  *Boyovic* to 6/18
  *Misic*
FIRST ARMY (f.7/14). Destroyed by 11/15. Reformed in Corfu and Macedonia and back in the line from late 1916.
  *Boyovic* to 12/14
  *Misic* to 6/18
  *Boyovic*
SECOND ARMY (f.7/14). As FIRST ARMY.
  *Stepanovic*
THIRD ARMY (f.7/14). As FIRST ARMY.
  *Vasic* to ?/15
  *Jurisic-Sturm* to ?/16
  *Vasic* to 3/17 (disbanded)

## SOUTH AFRICA

GOVERNOR-GENERAL
  *de Villiers* (acting) to 9/14
  *Lord Buxton*
PRIME MINISTER
  *Botha*
FOREIGN AFFAIRS
  none
FINANCE
  *Smuts* to 2/15
  *Graaf* to 2/16
  *Burton* to 10/17
  *Orr*
INTERIOR
  vacant to 2/16
  *Watt*
WAR
  *Smuts*
C-IN-C. UNION DEFENCE FORCES
  *Beyers* to 9/14
  *Smuts*

**South-West Africa** (arr.9/15)
C-IN-C.
  *Botha* to 7/15 (German surrender)‡
MILITARY GOVERNOR
  *Beves* to 11/15
ADMINISTRATOR
  *Gorges*

**East Africa**
Military operations here were initially the responsibility of the Indian Army until taken over by the War Office (for first commanders see Table 2.1: Theatre/Area Commands). From 10/15, however, commanders were told to deal directly with the South African military authorities and it was their troops that increasingly shouldered the burden during 1916, before being gradually replaced by Africans. From 2/16 this theatre was also put under a S. African field commander.
  *Smuts* to 1/17
  *Hoskins* to 6/17
  *van Deventer*
N.B. For more details on S. African divisions that fought in E. Africa and on the S. African Brigade in France, see Section 3: Part I.

**SUDAN**
Jointly administered by Britain and Egypt. The main theatre of operations for the Egyptian army (see that entry above).
GOVERNOR-GENERAL AND C-IN-C.
  *Wingate* to 11/16
  *Stack*

# SECTION 3

# ORDERS OF BATTLE

The following section comprises two groups of data. In Part I will be found, alphabetically by country, lists of all the divisions, infantry and cavalry, that saw any kind of combat services during the war. Each divisional entry features a brief resume of its combat history, showing both the theatres in which it served and either the armies to which it was attached at various times, or the particular regions in which it was located.* Where army attachments are shown the army number or name is italicised. Dates are shown as M/Y or D/M/Y. Where the complete sequence of divisional movements is known an entry uses the formula x to M/Y. Where we only know the Army attachments at certain dates, and not the complete sequence, the formula x on D/M/Y or x in M/Y is used.

It will be appreciated that normally there has not been space to list units smaller than divisions. However, for a few of the smaller dominions and dependencies even a sub-divisional contribution represented a significant military effort. We have therefore added, at the end of the divisional listings, a Supplement that takes account of these smaller, often largely ignored contributions to the overall war effort. In these entries the units listed are mostly regiments or battalions. The Supplement concludes with a complete listing of British battalions that fought in the war, showing the theatres in which they served and the divisions to which they were attached. We have made this exception to our 'divisions only' rule because of the unique nature of British regimental nomenclature, the enormous emotional significance of regimental affiliation and, frankly, the fact that this book was launched on the British market.

Part II of this section assembles more conventional orders of battle, giving army group/army/corps/division breakdowns of the forces available to both sides at particular dates during the various campaigns. (The reader is also referred to Part I of Section 5, which give summaries of the allocation of divisions to the various theatres.

Details on the size and organisation of the different national divisions listed in this section can be found in Section 4, showing Tables of Organisation and Equipment.

# PART I COMBAT DIVISIONS

## Arabia

The regular, ex-Ottoman component of the Sharifian army, comprising as it did two very small brigades, was sometimes referred to as a 'division'. For further details see p.000.

## Armenia

### INFANTRY DIVISIONS (and others)

Many Armenian regulars had fought with the Russians in 1914-16, in the numerous rifle battalions they manned in the Caucasus theatre. With the fall of the Tsar, in March 1917, the Armenians began to strive for independence and set up the Trans-Caucasian Federation, an independent republic that also included Georgia and Azerbaijan. The Armenians supplied the main military component of the Federation, *1* and *2 Infantry Divisions*, formed from the ex-Russian battalions, and twelve other volunteer battalions from Turkish Armenia.† In February 1918, the Turks moved against the Federation and after the surrender of Batum and Kars, in April, the Armenians were steadily forced back. On 4 June an armistice was agreed although it was some time before this was generally adhered to.

## Australia

### INFANTRY DIVISIONS (total = 6)

| DIVISION | FORMED | COMBAT RECORD |
|---|---|---|
| **1** | 8/14 | **Gallipoli:** 4/15-12/15<br>**W. Front:** *2* 4/16-6/16; *Res.* to 9/16; *2* to 11/16; *4* to 2/17; *5* to ?/??; *3* to 7/17; *2* to 12/17; *4* to 4/18; *2* to 8/18; *4* |
| **2** | 8/15 | **Gallipoli:** 9/15-12/15<br>**W. Front:** as 1 Div. to 4/18 then remains in 4 Army |
| **3** | 1/16 | **W. Front:** *2* 11/16 to 11/17; *4* |
| **4** | 1/16 | **W. Front:** *2* in 6/16; *Res.* to 9/16; *2* to 11/16; *4* to 2/17; *5* to 4/17; *2* to 12/17; *5* to 1/18; *4* |
| **5** | 1/16 | **W. Front:** *2* in 6/16; *1* to ?/??; *2* to 11/16; *4* to 2/17; *5* to ?/??; *3* to 7/17; *2* to 12/17; *4* |
| **Anzac** | 1/15 | **Gallipoli:** 4/15-12/15 ; disbanded 1/16 |

## Austria-Hungary

### INFANTRY DIVISIONS (total = 76)

N.B. In some of the divisional combat records listed below there appear a few italicised Army affiliations that do not appear on the maps nor in the Army listings for each country. These are all *Armeegruppen*, groupings of corps that were not rated as meriting a full army HQ or could not be provided with one. The *Armeegruppen* in question are: Albania, Belluno (Heeresgruppe Boroevic); Bernhardi (HG Linsingen); Eichhorn (HG Hindenburg); Litzmann (HG Linsingen); Marwitz (HG Linsingen); Pflanzer-Baltin (Southern Flank); Rohr (Tirol). Also mentioned are Abschnitt Kovel and Abschnitt Lipa, both part of HG Linsingen.

### CAVALRY DIVISIONS (total = 2)

| DIVISION | FORMED | COMBAT RECORD |
|---|---|---|
| **Anzac Mounted Division‡** | 1/16 | **Egypt & Palestine:** 7/16- end |
| **Australian Mounted Div.** | early 1917◊ | **Palestine:** 3/17- end |

| DIVISION | FORMED | COMBAT RECORD |
|---|---|---|
| **1** | pre-war | **Serbia:** *6* in 8/14; *6* in 10/14; *6* in 12/14; *6* in 2/15; *see Italy below*<br>**Italy:** *5* from 5/15; *5* in 10/15; *10* in 3/16; *5* in 8/16; *5* in 11/16; *5* in 5/17; *Isonzo* in 8/17; *14G* in 11/17; *10* in 6/18; *see below*<br>**W. Front:** • (XVIII Corps) from 7/18; *5G* in 10/18 |
| **2** | | **Russia** Δ: *1* in 8/14; *1* in 10/14; *3* in 1/15; *3* in 5/15; *4* in 9/15; *4* in 1/16; *4* in 7/16; *4* in 11/16; *4* in 3/17; *4* in 7/17; *Ost* in 6/18; *see below*<br>**Italy:** from 7/18; *Isonzo* in 10/18 |
| **3** (Eidelweiss) | | **Russia:** *3* in 8/14; *4* in 10/14; *4* in 1/15; *4* in 5/15; *4* in 9/15; *4* in 1/16; *see below*<br>**Italy:** from 3/16; *11* in 3/16; *11* in 8/16; *11* in 5/17; *14G* in 11/17; *11* in 6/18; *AGp. Res* in 10/18 |
| **4** | | **Russia:** *4* in 8/14; *4* in 10/14; *1* in 1/15; *1* in 5/15; *AGp. Res* in 9/15; *4* in 1/16; *4* in 6/16; *Berhardi* in 8/16; *Berhardi* in 11/16; *Abschnitt Kovel* in 3/17; *ditto* in 7/17; *see below*<br>**Italy:** from 9/17; *Theatre Reserve* in 11/17; *11* in 6/18; *Belluno* 10/18 |
| **5** | | **Russia:** *1* in 8/14; *1* in 10/14; *1* in 1/15; *7* in 5/15; *7* in 9/15; *7* in 1/16; *7* in 6/16; *Marwitz* in 7/16; *3* in 11/16; *3* in 3/17; *3* in 7/17; *7* in 7/17<br>**Italy:** from 4/18; *11* in 6/18; *11* in 10/18 |

*Side notes (left margin):*

* The decision as to whether to list army attachments or regional movements has been dictated solely by the nature of the sources used for different countries' forces.

† Some sources have these twelve battalions organised into a third *Western Armenian Division.*

‡ Includes NZ Mounted Rifle Brigade.

◊ Originally Imperial Mounted Division. Name changed July 1917. From 1918 absorbed Australian elements of Imperial Camel Corps.

• i.e. France

Δ No attempt has been made to regionally subdivide the Russian Front (*cf.* Divisions: Germany [below]) as (a) allocations to Armies are given which can be located on Maps 13–18 and (b) Austro-Hungarian divisions on this front fought almost exclusively in Galicia.

| INFANTRY DIVISIONS continued | | |
|---|---|---|

| DIVISION | FORMED | COMBAT RECORD |
|---|---|---|
| **6** | pre-war | **Russia**: *2* in 8/14; *3* in 10/14; *3* in 1/15; *7* in 5/15; *7* in 9/15; *see below*<br>**Italy**: from 10/15; *Theatre Reserve* in 3/16; *11* in 5/16; *11* in 8/16; *11* in 5/17; *11* in 11/17; *11* in 6/18; *11* in 10/18 |
| **7** | | **Serbia**: *2 & 5* in 8/14; in 10/14; in 12/14; *see Russia below*<br>**Russia**: from 1/15; *3* in 1/15; *Süd* in 5/15; *1* in 9/15; *1* in 1/16; *4* in 6/16; *Marwitz* in 7/16; *Litzmann* in 11/16; *see Italy below*<br>**Italy**: from 2/17; *5* in 5/17; *see Rumania below*; from 7/18; *Isonzo* in 10/18<br>**Rumania \***: from 6/17; *1* in 7/17; *see below*<br>**Interior**: from 6/18; *see Italy above* |
| **8**<br>(Kaiserjäger) | | **Russia**: *3* in 8/14; *4* in 10/14; *4* in 1/15; *4* in 5/15; *see below*<br>**Italy**: from 6/15; *Tirol* in 10/15; *11* in 3/16; *11* in 8/16; *11* in 3/17; *11* in 11/17; *10* in 6/18; *10* in 10/18 |
| **9** | | **Serbia**: *5* in 8/14; *5* in 9/14; *Reserve* in 12/14; *see Russia below*<br>**Russia**: from 2/15; *2* in 5/15; *1* in 9/15; *see Italy below*<br>**Italy**: from 11/15; *5* in 3/16; *5* in 8/16; *5* in 11/16; *5* in 5/17; *Isonzo* in 8/17; *2 Isonzo* in 11/17; *6* in 6/18; *see below*<br>**Macedonia**: from 9/18; *11G* in 10/18 |
| **10** | | **Russia**: *4* in 8/14; *3* in 10/14; *4* in 1/15; *4* in 5/15; *4* in 9/15; *4* in 1/16; *see below*<br>**Italy**: *3* in 3/16; *11* in 8/16; (to Isonzo 10/16); *5* in 5/17; *Theatre Reserve* in 8/17; *1 Isonzo* in 11/17; *Isonzo* in 6/18; *6* in 10/18 |
| **11** | | **Russia**: *2* in 8/14; *3* in 10/14; *4* in 1/15; *3* in 5/15; *GHQ Reserve* in 9/15; *7* in 1/16; *4* in 6/16; *4* in 7/16; *4* in 3/17; *4* in 7/17; *Ost* in 6/18; *Ost* in 10/18 |
| **12** | | **Russia**: *1* in 8/14; *1* in 10/14; *1* in 1/15; *11G* in 5/15; *GHQ Reserve* in 9/15; *7* in 1/16; *7* in 6/16; *Süd* in 7/16; *7* in 11/16; *7* in 3/17; *see below*<br>**Italy**: from 6/17; *Isonzo* in 8/17; *1 Isonzo* in 11/17; *Isonzo Ost* in 6/18; *Isonzo* in 10/18 |
| **13**<br>Schützen† | | **Russia**: *4* in 8/14; *4* in 10/14; *4* in 1/15; *2* in 5/15; *1* in 9/15; *Gerok* in 1/16; *4* in 6/16; *4* in 7/16; *4* in 11/16; *4* in 3/17; *4* in 7/17; *see below*<br>**Italy**: from 9/17; *Theatre Reserve* in 11/17; *6* in 6/18; *Belluno* in 10/18 |
| **14** | | **Russia**: *1* in 8/14; *1* in 10/14; *1* in 1/15; *2* in 5/15; *2* in 9/15; *2* in 1/16; *2* in 6/16; *2* in 7/16; *see below*<br>**Italy**: from 10/16; *5* in 11/16; *5* in 5/17; *Isonzo* in 8/17; *1 Isonzo* in 11/17; *Isonzo* in 6/18; *Isonzo* in 10/18 |
| **15** | | **Russia**: *4* in 8/14; *4* in 10/14; *4* in 1/15; *7* in 5/15; *7* in 9/15; *7* in 1/16; *7* in 6/16; *Süd* in 7/16; *3* in 11/16; *3* in 3/17; *3* in 7/17; *3* in 6/18; *Ost* in 9/18<br>**Macedonia**: in 10/18 |
| **16** | | **Russia**: *2* in 8/14; *2* in 10/14; *2* in 1/15; *Woyrsch* in 5/15; *Woyrsch* in 9/15; *Woyrsch* in 6/16; *Woyrsch* in 7/16; *see Italy below*; from 6/17; *3* in 7/17; *see Rumania below*<br>**Italy**: from 8/16; *5* in 11/16; *5* in 5/17; *see above*; from 5/18; *11* in 6/18; *11* in 10/18<br>**Rumania**: from 7/17; *see Italy above* |
| **17** | | **Serbia**: *2* in 8/14; *see Russia below*<br>**Russia**: *2* in 8/14; *2* in 10/14; *3* in 1/15; *3* in 5/15; *see Italy below*<br>**Italy**: from 5/15 (Carnic Alps); *5* in 10/15; *5* in 3/16; *5* in 8/16; *5* in 11/16; *5* in 5/17; *Isonzo* in 8/17; *1 Isonzo* in 11/17; *6* in 6/18; *Belluno* in 10/18 |
| **18** | | **Serbia**: *6* in 8/14; *6* in 9/14; *6* in 12/14; *see below*<br>**Italy**: from 5/15; *5* in 6/15; *5* in 10/15; *GHQ Reserve* in 3/16; *3* in 4/16; *11* in 8/16; *11* in 3/17; *11* in 6/17; *11* in 11/17; *11* in 6/18; *11* in 10/18 |
| **19** | | **Russia**: *4* in 8/14; *4* in 10/14; *Süd* in 1/15; *11G* in 5/15; *Süd* in 9/15; *Süd* in 1/16; *Süd* in 7/16; *2* in 11/16; *2* in 3/17; *2* in 7/17; *see below*<br>**Italy**: from 9/17; *11* in 11/17; *10* in 6/18; *10* in 10/18 |

| DIVISION | FORMED | COMBAT RECORD |
|---|---|---|
| **20**<br>Honved‡ | pre-war | **Russia**: *2* in 8/14; *2* in 10/14; *3* in 1/15; *11G* in 4/15; *see below*, *Lipa* in 3/17; *Lipa* in 7/17; *see below*<br>**Italy**: from 5/15 (Carnic Alps); *5* in 3/16; *5* in 8/16; *5* in 11/16; *see above*; from 11/17; *2 Isonzo* 11/17; *11* in 6/18; *Belluno* in 10/18 |
| **21**<br>Schützen | | **Serbia**: *5* in 8/14; *5* in 9/14; *Reserve* in 12/14; *see Russia below*<br>**Russia**: from 2/15; *3* in 5/15; *4* in 9/15; *4* in 1/16; *7* in 6/17; *3* in 7/16; *3* in 11/16; *3* in 3/17; *see Italy below*<br>**Italy**: from 6/17; *Isonzo* in 8/17; *11* in 11/17; *see below*, *Belluno* in 10/18<br>**Interior**: in 6/18; *see above* |
| **22**<br>Schützen | | **Russia**: *2* in 8/14; *3* in 10/14; *3* in 1/15; *3* in 5/15; *7* in 1/15; *see below*<br>**Italy**: *5* in 10/15; *GHQ Reserve* in 3/16; *11* in 4/16; *11* in 5/16; *11* in 8/16; *11* in 5/17; *14G* in 10/17; *10* in 11/17; *10* in 6/18; *10* in 10/18 |
| **23**<br>Honved | | **Russia**: *3* in 8/14; *Przemysl garrison* in 10/14; captured at Przemysl 3/15. not reformed. |
| **24** | | **Russia**: *1* in 8/14; *1* in 10/14; *3* in 12/14; *3* in 5/15; *4* in 9/15; *4* in 12/15; *7* in 1/16; *7* in 6/16; *10G* in 7/16; *Eichhorn* in 10/16; *see Rumania below*<br>**Rumania**: from 11/16; *1* in 3/17; *see below*<br>**Italy**: from 5/17; *Isonzo* in 8/17; *2 Isonzo* in 11/17; *L. of C.* in 12/17; *Isonzo* in 6/18; *Isonzo* in 10/18 |
| **25** | | **Russia**: *4* in 8/14; *4* in 10/14; *1* in 1/15; *1* in 5/15; *1* in 9/15; *1* in 1/16; *1* in 6/16; *2* in 7/16; *1* in 11/16; *2* in 3/17; *2* in 7/17; *see Interior below*<br>**Interior**: *4/18* to 7/18; *see below*<br>**Italy**: from 7/18; *6* in 9/18; *Belluno* in 10/18 |
| **26**<br>Schützen | | **Russia**: *4* in 8/14; *3* in 10/14; *4* in 1/15; *3* in 5/15; *4* in 6/15; *1* in 8/15; *4* in 9/15; *2* in 1/16; *HG Linsingen Reserve* in 6/16; *Bernhardi* in 7/16; *Bernhardi* in 11/16; *Kovel* in 3/17; *Kovel* in 7/17; *see below*<br>**Italy**: from 2/18; *11* in 6/18; *Isonzo* in 8/18; *Isonzo* in 10/18 |
| **27** | | **Russia**: *4* in 8/14; *4* in 10/14; *2* in 1/15; *2* in 5/15; *2* in 9/15; *2* in 1/16; *2* in 6/16; *2* in 11/16; *2* in 3/17; *2* in 7/17; *Ost* in 6/18; *see below*<br>**Italy**: by 7/18; *11* in 10/18 |
| **28** | | **Russia**: *2* in 8/14; *3* in 10/14; *3* in 1/15; *3* in 5/15; *see below*<br>**Italy**: from 8/15; *5* in 10/15; *GHQ Reserve* in 3/16; *11* in 5/16; *11* in 8/16; *5* in 9/16; *5* in 5/17; *Isonzo* in 8/17; *2 Isonzo* in 11/17; *11* in 6/18; *Belluno* in 10/18 |
| **29** | | **Serbia**: *2* in 8/14; *5* in 9/14; *Reserve* in 12/14; *see Russia below*<br>**Russia**: from 1/15; *3* in 1/15; *2* in 5/15; *2* in 9/15; *2* in 1/16; *2* in 5/16; *4* in 6/16; *4* in 11/16; *4* in 3/17; *4* in 7/17; *see below*<br>**Italy**: from 9/17; *2 Isonzo* in 11/17; *Isonzo* in 6/18; *Isonzo* in 10/18 |
| **30** | | **Russia**: *3* in 8/14; *3* in 10/14; *4* in 1/15; *7* in 5/15; *7* in 9/15; *7* in 1/16; *7* in 6/16; *3* in 7/16; *7* in 11/16; *7* in 3/17; *7* in 7/17; *Ost* in 6/18; *see below*<br>**Macedonia**: from 10/18; in *11G* |
| **31** | | **Serbia**: *2* in 8/14; *see Russia below*<br>**Russia**: *2* in 9/14; *2* in 10/14; *2* in 1/15; *2* in 5/15; *2* in 9/15; *2* in 1/16; *2* in 6/16; *2* in 7/16; *see Rumania below*; *7* in 8/17; *see Italy below*<br>**Rumania**: *1* in 2/17; *1* in 3/17; *1* in 7/17; *see Russia above*<br>**Italy**: from 2/18; *6* in 6/18; *6* in 10/18; *Belluno* in 11/18 |
| **32** | | **Serbia**: *2* in 8/14; *see Russia below*<br>**Russia**: *2* in 8/14; *2* in 10/14; *2* in 1/15; *2* in 5/15; *2* in 9/15; *2* in 1/16; *Süd* in 6/16; *Süd* in 7/16; *2* in 11/16; *2* in 3/17; *2* in 7/17; *see Italy below*<br>**Italy**: from 3/18; *11* in 3/18; *11* in 6/18; *see Interior below*<br>**Interior**: from 7/18 to 10/18; *see below*<br>**Macedonia**: *11G* in 10/18 |
| **33** | | **Russia**: *1* in 8/14; *1* in 10/14; *3* in 1/15; *2* in 5/15; *2* in 9/15; *2* in 1/16; *2* in 6/16; *1* in 7/16 (part); *2* in 11/16; *2* in 3/17; *2* in 7/17; *see below*<br>**Italy**: from 9/17; *AGp. Reserve* 11/17; *Isonzo* in 6/18; *Isonzo* 10/18 |

\* Includes Transylvania during concentration for Rumanian offensive up to 18 Sept. 1916

† *Schützen* divisions were those belonging to the Austrian *Landwehr*. Originally they were intended as home defence formations but by 1914 had been placed on an equal footing with the regular divisions.

‡ *Honved* divisions were those belonging to the Hungarian *Landwehr* which had the same status as the Austrian *Landwehr* (see note above).

| INFANTRY DIVISIONS continued | | |
|---|---|---|

| DIVISION | FORMED | COMBAT RECORD |
|---|---|---|
| **34** | pre-war | **Russia**: *2* in 8/14; *2* in 10/14; *3* in 12/14; *2* in 5/15; *2* in 9/15; *2* in 1/16; *see below*, *7* in 7/16; *7* in 11/16; *7* in 3/17; *7* in 7/17; *Ost* in 6/18; *see below*<br>**Italy**: from 2/16; *3* in 3/16; *11* in 4/16; *11* in 6/16; *see above*; from 7/18; *6* in 10/18 |
| **35** | | **Russia**: *2* in 8/14; *2* in 10/14; *2* in 1/15; *Woyrsch* in 5/15; *Woyrsch* in 9/15; *2* in 1/16; *Woyrsch* in 6/16; *Woyrsch* in 7/16; *Woyrsch* in 11/16; *Woyrsch* in 3/17; *see below*<br>**Italy**: from 5/17; *Isonzo* in 8/17; *2 Isonzo* in 11/17; *6* in 6/18; *see below*<br>**W. Front**: from 7/18; *Ay. Det. 'C'* in 10/18 |
| **36** | | **Serbia**: *5* in 8/14; *5* in 9/14; *unatt.* in 12/14; *see Russia below*<br>**Russia**: from 1/15; *Pflanzer-Baltin* in 1/15; *7* in 5/15; *7* in 9/15; *7* in 1/16; *7* in 6/16; *Süd* in 7/16; *3* in 11/16; *3* in 3/17; *3* in 7/17; *see below*<br>**Italy**: from 5/18; *11* in 6/18; *AGp. Reserve* in 10/18; to *Piave* sector 10/18 |
| **37**<br>Honved | | **Russia**: *1* in 8/14; *1* in 10/14; *3* from 1/15; *2* then *4* in 5/15; *GHQ Reserve* in 9/15; *4* in 1/16; *4* in 6/16; *4* in 7/16; *see Rumania below*<br>**Rumania**: from 9/16; *1* in 11/16; *1* in 3/17; *1* in 7/17; *1* in 10/17; *1* in 3/18; *see below*<br>**W. Front**: from 9/18; *Ay. Det. 'A'* in 10/18 |
| **38**<br>Honved | | **Russia**: *2* in 8/14; *2* in 10/14; *3* in 12/14; *4* in 1/15; *3* in 2/15; *Süd* in 5/15; *Süd* in 9/15; *Süd* in 1/16; *Süd* in 4/16; *Süd* in 7/16; *Süd* in 11/16; *Süd* in 3/17; *Süd* in 7/17; *see Italy below*<br>**Italy**: from 3/18; *11* in 6/18; *see below*; from 9/18; *11* in 10/18<br>**Interior**: from 7/18 to 9/18; *see Italy above* |
| **39**<br>Honved | | **Russia**: *4* in 8/14; *4* in 10/14; *4* in 1/15; *11G* in 5/15; *GHQ Reserve* in 9/15; *7* in 9/15; *7* in 1/16; *7* in 6/16; *Süd* in 7/16; *see Rumania below*, *Ost* in 6/18<br>**Rumania**: from 9/16; *1* in 11/16; *1* in 3/17; *1* in 7/17; *see Interior below*<br>**Interior**: from 3/18; *see Russia above*<br>**Italy**: from 7/18; *11* in 10/18 |
| **40**<br>Honved | | **Serbia**: *6* in 8/14; *6* in 9/14; *6* in 12/14; *see Russia below*<br>**Russia**: from 1/15; *3* in 1/15; *Süd* in 5/15; *1* in 9/15; *1* in 12/15; *7* in 1/16; *7* in 6/16; *7* in 7/16; *7* in 11/16; *7* in 3/17; *7* in 7/17; *see Interior below*<br>**Interior**: from 3/18 to 7/18; *see below*<br>**Italy**: from 7/18; *Belluno* in 10/18 |
| **41**<br>Honved | | **Russia**: *3* in 8/14; *4* in 10/14; *4* in 1/15; *2* in 2/15; *2* in 4/15; *4* then *1* in 5/15; *GHQ Reserve* in 9/15; *Gerok* in 1/16; *4* in 5/16; *Berhardi* in 9/16; *Berhardi* in 11/16; *see below*<br>**Italy**: from 12/16; *5* in 3/17; *Isonzo* in 8/17; *1 Isonzo* in 11/17; *6* in 6/18; *6* in 10/18 |
| **42**<br>Honved | | **Serbia**: *5* in 8/14; *5* in 9/14; *unatt.* in 12/14; *see Russia below*<br>**Russia**: from 1/15; *unatt.* in 1/15; *7* in 5/15; *7* in 9/15; *7* in 1/16; *7* in 6/16; *3* in 7/16; *3* in 11/16; *3* in 3/17; *3* in 7/17; *see below*<br>**Italy**: from 2/18; *11* in 6/18; *Belluno* in 10/18 |
| **43**<br>Schützen | | **Russia**: *2* in 8/14; *1* in 10/14; *4* in 12/14; *3* in 1/15; *2* in 5/15; *2* in 9/15; *2* in 1/16; *4* in 5/16; *see below*; from 11/17; *Ost* in 6/18; *see below*<br>**Italy**: from 3/16; *3* in 3/16; *5* in 7/16; *5* in 11/16; *Isonzo* in 8/17; *2 Isonzo* in 10/17; *see above*; from 8/18; *6* in 10/18 |
| **44**<br>Schützen | | **Russia**: *3* in 8/14; *3* in 10/14; *3* in 1/15; *2* in 5/15; *see below*; from 6/16; *7* in 6/16; *7* in 7/16; *see below*<br>**Italy**: from 7/15; *Carnic* in 10/15; *10* in 3/16; *see above*; from 8/16; *5* in 8/16; *5* in 11/16; *5* in 5/17; *Isonzo* in 8/17; *1 Isonzo* in 11/17; Training Div. in Spring 1918; *Isonzo* in 6/18; *AGp. Reserve* in 10/18; *Isonzo* in 11/18 |
| **45**<br>Schützen | | **Russia**: *1* in 8/14; *1* in 10/14; *4* in 1/15; *3* in 5/15; *AGp. Reserve* in 9/15; *4* in 1/16; *AGp. Reserve* in 6/16; *Bernhardi* in 7/16; *Bernhardi* in 11/16; *Kovel* in 3/17; *Kovel* in 7/17; *see below*<br>**Bosnia**: 4/18 to end |

| DIVISION | FORMED | COMBAT RECORD |
|---|---|---|
| **46**<br>Schützen | pre-war | **Russia**: *1* in 8/14; *1* in 10/14; *1* in 1/15; *1* in 5/15; *1* in 9/15; *1* in 1/16; *1* in 6/16; *Marwitz* in 7/16; *Litzmann* in 11/16; *Lipa* in 3/17; *Lipa* in 7/17; *see below*<br>**Italy**: from 3/18; *Isonzo* in 6/18; *Isonzo* in 10/18 |
| **47** | | **Montenegro**: (Cattaro/Kotor): *6* in 8/14; *unatt.* in 8/15; *unatt.* in 12/15<br>**Albania**: *3* in 1/16; *3* in 3/16; *unatt.* in 8/16; in 5/17; in 6/18; *Albania* in 7/18; in 9/18; in 11/18 |
| **48** | | **Serbia**: *6* in 8/14; *6* in 9/14; *6* in 12/14; *6* in 2/15; *see Italy below*<br>**Italy**: from 5/15; *5* in 5/15; *Carnic* in 7/15; *Carnic* in 10/15; *11* in 3/16; *see below*; from 11/16; *5* in 5/17; *Isonzo* in 8/17; *1 Isonzo* in 11/17; *11* in 6/18; *Belluno* in 10/18 |
| **49** | 5/15 | The renamed Pustertal Division. See below:<br>**Italy**: *unatt.* in 11/17; *10* in 6/18; *10* in 10/18 |
| **50** | 10/14 | **Serbia**: *6* in 10/14; *6* in 12/14; *6* in 2/15; *see below*<br>**Italy**: from 5/15; *5* in 5/15; *5* in 10/15; *10* in 3/16; *5* in 8/16; *5* in 11/16; *5* in 5/17; *Isonzo* in 8/17; *14G* in 11/17; *11* in 6/18; *Belluno* in 10/18 |
| **51**<br>Honved | 2/15 | The renamed Combined Div. Kornhaber. See below:<br>**Russia**: in 2/15; *2* in 5/15; *2* in 9/15; *2* in 1/16; *2* in 6/16; *3* in 7/16; *see Rumania below*; from 12/16; *7* in 12/16; *7* in 3/17; *7* in 7/17; *see Interior below*<br>**Rumania**: from 8/16; *9G* in 9/16; *9G* in 11/16; *see above*<br>**Interior**: from 3/18 to 5/18; *see below*<br>**Italy**: from 5/18; *6* in 6/18; *6* in 10/18 |
| **52(a)** | 10/14 | **Russia**: *3* in 11/14; *3* in 12/14; disbanded 1/15 |
| **52(b)** | 10/17 | The renumbered 90 Div. See below.<br>**Italy**: *unatt.* in 10/17; *11* in 6/18; *11* in 10/18 |
| **53(a)** | 8/15 | **Serbia**: *3* in 10/15; *3* in 1/16; *see Russia below*<br>**Russia**: from 2/16; *AGp. Reserve* in 6/16; *Bernhardi* in 7/16; *Bernhardi* in 11/16; *Kovel* in 3/17; *Kovel* in 7/17; *see below*<br>**Italy**: from 8/17; *2 Isonzo* in 10/17; see 64 Div. below |
| **53(b)** | 11/17 | The renumbered 71 Div. See below.<br>**Italy**: *2 Isonzo* in 11/17; *11* in 6/18; *11* in 10/18 |
| **54**<br>(Schützen<br>from 10/17) | 10/14 | **Russia**: *Pflanzer-Baltin* in 11/14 and 2/15; (not mentioned again until:) *Süd* in 6/16; *Süd* in 7/16; *Süd* in 11/16; *Süd* in 3/17; *Süd* in 7/17; *Ost* in 6/18; *Ost* in 10/18 |
| **55(a)** | 10/14 | **Russia**: *Süd* in 1/15; *Süd* in 5/15; *Süd* in 8/15; disbanded 10/15; reformed 1/16; *Süd* in 1/16; *Süd* in 6/16; *Süd* in 7/16; *Süd* in 11/16; *Süd* in 3/17; *Süd* in 7/17; renumbered 10/17; see 155 Div. below |
| **55(b)** | 10/17 | The renumbered 93 Div. See below.<br>**Italy**: *14G* in 11/17; *11* in 6/18; *Belluno* in 10/18 |
| **56** | 10/14 | **Russia**: *Pflanzer-Baltin* in 11/14; *3* in 12/14; reduced to brigade 12/14 |
| **56**<br>Schützen | 10/17 | **Italy**: *11* in 11/17; *10* in 6/18; *10* in 10/18 |
| **57(a)** | 2/15 | The renamed Combined Div. Goiginger. See below.<br>**Italy**: *5* in 5/15; *see below*; from 2/16; *11* in 3/16; *11* in 8/16; *5* in 11/16; *5* in 3/17; absorbed into 90 Div. in 7/17; *see below*<br>**Serbia**: from 9/15; *3* in 10/15; *3* in 1/16; *see above* |
| **57(b)** | 8/17 | The renamed Combined Div. Hrozny. See below.<br>**Italy**: *Isonzo* in 8/17; *2 Isonzo* in 11/17; *Isonzo* in 6/18; *Isonzo* in 10/18 |
| **58** | 3/15 | **Italy**: from 5/15; *5* in 5/15; *5* in 10/15; *5* in 3/16; *5* in 8/16; *5* in 11/16; *5* in 5/17; *Isonzo* in 8/17; *1 Isonzo* in 11/17; *Isonzo* in 6/18; *Isonzo* in 10/18 |
| **59** | 3/15 | **Bosnia**: 3/15 to 7/15; *see Italy below*<br>**Italy**: from 7/15; *5* in 8/15; *see Serbia below*; from 2/16; *11* in 3/16; *11* in 5/16; *see Russia below*<br>**Serbia**: from 9/15; *3* in 10/15; *3* in 1/16; *see Italy above*<br>**Russia**: from 6/16; *3* in 6/16; *7* in 11/16; *7* in 3/17; *7* in 7/17; *Ost* in 1/18; *Ost* in 5/18; *Ost* in 10/18; *see below*<br>**Macedonia**: en route 11/18 |
| **60(a)** | 11/14 | **Serbia**: *5* in 12/14; disbanded 12/14 |

## INFANTRY DIVISIONS continued

| DIVISION | FORMED | COMBAT RECORD |
|---|---|---|
| **60 (b)** | 10/17 | The renumbered 73 Div. See below<br>*Italy*: 2 *Isonzo* in 11/17; 11 in 6/18; *Belluno* in 10/18 |
| **61**<br>(Honved<br>from 8/16) | 5/15 | **Serbia**: in 7/15; *see Italy below*<br>**Italy**: from 7/15; 5 in 8/15; 5 in 10/15; 5 in 3/16; *see Russia below*<br>**Russia**: from 6/16; 7 in 7/16; *see below*<br>**Rumania**: from 8/16; 1 in 9/16; 1 in 11/16; reduced to brigade 12/16 |
| **62** | 7/15 | **Russia**: 1 in 8/15; 4 in 9/15; *see Serbia below*<br>**Serbia**: from 9/15; 3 in 9/15; *unatt.* in 10/15; in 1/16; *see Italy below*<br>**Italy**: from 2/16; 5 in 3/16; 5 in 8/16; 5 in 11/16; 5 in 5/17; *see below*<br>**Rumania**: from 6/17; 9G in 7/17; *Mackensen* in 6/18 and 10/18 |
| **63** | 2/16 | **Albania**: 2/16 to 8/16; disbanded<br>**Italy**: reformed 10/17; 1 *Isonzo* in 11/17; *see below*<br>**Rumania**: frontier 3/18; disbanded 4/18 |
| **64**<br>Honved | 10/17 | Renumbered as 53 Div. See 53 Div.(a) above.<br>**Italy**: 2 *Isonzo* in 11/17; *Isonzo* in 6/18; *Isonzo* in 10/18 |
| **65-69** | – | **Not formed** |
| **70**<br>Honved<br>(as Gendarmerie<br>Div. to 10/15) | 6/15 | **Rumania**: frontier to 2/16; *see Russia below*<br>**Russia**: from 2/16; 4 in 6/16; 4 in 7/16; *see Rumania below*<br>**Rumania**: from 10/16; 1 in 3/17; 1 in 7/17; *see below*<br>**Italy**: from 1/18; *Isonzo* in 6/18; *Isonzo* in 10/18 |
| **71** | 8/16 | **Rumania**: from 8/16; 1 in 9/16; 1 in 11/16; 1 in 3/17; 1 in 7/17; 1 in 9/17; renumbered as 53 Div. See 53 Div.(b) above |
| **72** | 8/16 | **Rumania**: from 8/16; 1 in 9/16; 1 in 11/16; 1 in 3/17; 1 in 7/17; 1 in 11/17; frontier in 2/18; disbanded 6/18 |
| **73** | 10/16 | **Rumania**: 9G in 11/16; 9G in 3/17; *see below*<br>**Italy**: from 6/17; *Isonzo* in 8/17; renumbered as 60 Div. 10/17. See 60 Div.(b) above |
| **74**<br>Honved | 4/17 | **Russia**: 7 in 7/17; 7 in 8/17; *see below*<br>**Italy**: from 5/18; 11 in 6/18; *AGp Reserve* in 10/18 |
| **75-80** | – | **Not formed** |
| **81** | 7/18 | **Albania**: 7/18 to end |
| **82-89** | – | **Not formed** |
| **90** | 5/15 | **Italy**: *Tirol* in 10/15; *Tirol* in 3/16; 11 in 8/16; *unatt.* in 3/17; absorbed 57 Div. 7/17 (see 57 Div.(a) above); *Isonzo* in 8/17; renumbered as 52 Div. 10/17. See 52 Div.(b) above |
| **91** | 5/15 | **Italy**: *Rohr* in 6/15; *Tirol* in 10/15; disbanded 11/15 |
| **92** | 5/15 | **Italy**: *Rohr* in 5/15; Carnic Alps in 10/15; 10 in 3/16; 10 in 8/16; 10 in 3/17; *see below*<br>**Rumania**: 9G in 7/17; disbanded 6/18 |
| **93** | 5/15 | **Italy**: 5 in 5/15; 5 in 8/15; disbanded; reformed in 8/16; 5 in 9/16; 10 in 11/16; 10 in 3/17; renumbered as 55 Div. 10/17. See 55 Div.(b) above |
| **94** | 5/15 | **Italy**: 5 in 5/15; Carnic Alps in 10/15; 10 in 3/16; 10 in 8/16; 10 in 5/17; 10 in 11/17; disbanded 5/18 |
| **95**<br>Landsturm | 8/14 | **Russia**: 4 in 8/14; reduced to brigade in 9/14 |
| **96-105** | – | **Not formed** |
| **106**<br>Landsturm | pre-war | **Russia**: 4 in 8/14; 1 in 10/14; 1 in 1/15; 4 in 5/15; *GHQ Reserve* in 9/15; *see below*; from 7/16; 2 in 7/16; 2 in 11/16; 2 in 3/17; *see Italy below*<br>**Italy**: from 9/15; 5 in 10/15; 5 in 3/16; *see above*; from 4/17; *Isonzo* in 8/17; 11 from 11/17 to 2/18; *see Poland below*<br>**Poland**: (Interior): 2/18 to 9/18; *see below*<br>**W. Front**: from 9/18; 5G in 10/18 |

| DIVISION | FORMED | COMBAT RECORD |
|---|---|---|
| **155**<br>Honved | 10/17 | The renumbered 55 Div. See 55 Div.(a) above<br>**Russia**: Ukraine from 1/18; *Ost* in 6/18; *Ost* in 10/18 |
| Combined<br>Division<br>Goiginger | 10/14 | **Serbia**: 6 in 10/14; 6 in 12/14; became 57 Div. in 2/15. See 57 Div.(a) above |
| Combined<br>Division<br>Hrozny | 8/17 | **Italy**: *Isonzo* in 8/17; became a second incarnation of 57 Div. in 8/17. See 57 Div.(b) above |
| Combined<br>Honved<br>Division<br>Kornhaber | 11/14 | **Russia**: in 11/14; became 51 Div. in 2/15. See above |
| Edelweiss<br>Division | | See 3 Div. above. Started using name instead of number in 1918 |
| Gendarmerie<br>Division | | See 70 Div. above. |
| Kaiserjäger<br>Division | | See 8 Div. above. Started using name instead of number in 1918 |
| Kaiserschützen<br>Division | 3/16 | **Italy**: 3 in 3/16; 11 in 8/16; disbanded 10/16 |
| Pustertal<br>Division | 5/15 | **Italy**: Carnic Alps in 8/15; *Tirol* in 3/16; *unatt.* in 5/17; became 49 Div. in 9/17. See above |

## CAVALRY DIVISIONS* (total=12)

* All fought dismounted from spring 1917.

| DIVISION | FORMED | COMBAT RECORD |
|---|---|---|
| **1** | pre-war | **Russia**: 2 in 8/14; 2 in 10/14; 3 in 1/15; 3 in 5/15; 2 in 9/15; *Gerok* in 1/16; *AGp Reserve* in 6/16; *Bernhardi* in 7/16; *see Rumania below*; from 8/17; 7 in 8/17; *see Italy below*; from 7/18; *Ost* in 8/18; *see Rumania below*<br>**Rumania**: from 9/16; 1 in 11/16; 1 in 3/17; 1 in 7/17; *see above*; from 8/18 to 11/18; disbanded<br>**Italy**: from 2/18; *Isonzo* in 6/18; *see Russia above* |
| **2** | | **Russia**: 3 in 8/14; 4 in 10/14; 1 in 1/15; 1 in 5/15; 9G in 9/15; *Gerok* in 1/16; 7 in 6/16; *Süd* in 7/16; 3 in 11/16; 3 in 3/17; 3 in 7/17; *Ost* in 6/18; *unatt.* in 10/18 |
| **3** | | **Russia**: 1 in 8/14; 1 in 10/14; 2 in 1/15; *GHQ Reserve* in 5/15; 7 in 9/15; 7 in 1/16; 7 in 6/16; 7 in 7/16; *GHQ Reserve* in 11/16; *see Rumania below*<br>**Rumania**: from 11/16; 1 in 3/17; 1 in 7/17; *see below*<br>**Italy**: from 4/18; 11 in 6/18; 10 in 10/18 |
| **4** | | **Russia**: 3 in 8/14; 3 in 10/14; 3 in 1/15; 3 in 5/15; 4 in 9/15; *Gerok* in 1/16; 2 in 6/16; 2 in 11/16; 2 in 3/17; 2 in 7/17; *Ost* in 6/18; *see below*<br>**Macedonia**: en route 10/18 |
| **5**<br>Honved | | **Russia**: 2 in 8/14; 2 in 10/14; *Pflanzer-Baltin* in 2/15; 7 in 5/15; 7 in 9/15; 7 in 1/16; 7 in 6/16; 3 in 7/16; 7 in 11/16; 7 in 3/17; 7 in 7/17; Ukraine 1/18 to 5/18; *Ost* in 6/18; *Ost* in 10/18 |
| **6** | | **Russia**: 4 in 8/14; 4 in 10/14; 4 in 1/15; 7 in 5/15; 7 in 9/15; 7 in 1/16; 7 in 6/16; 3 in 7/16; 7 in 11/16; 7 in 3/17; 7 in 7/17; *see below*<br>**Italy**: from 4/18; 11 in 6/18; 11 in 10/18 |
| **7** | | **Russia**: 4 in 8/14; 1 in 10/14; 2 in 1/15; *Woyrsch* in 5/15; 4 in 9/15; *Gerok* in 1/16; 1 in 6/16; *Marwitz* in 7/16; *Bernhardi* in 11/16; *see below*; from 7/17; 7 in 7/17; 1 in 8/17; Ukraine in 5/18; *Ost* in 6/18; *Ost* in 10/18<br>**Rumania**: from 12/16; 9G in 3/17; *see above* |
| **8** | | **Russia**: 2 in 8/14; 2 in 10/14; 3 in 1/15; 7 in 5/15; 7 in 9/15; 7 in 1/16; 7 in 6/16; 7 in 7/16; 7 in 11/16; 7 in 7/17; *see below*<br>**Italy**: from 4/18; 6 in 6/18; *Isonzo* in 10/18 |
| **9** | | **Serbia**: 2 in 8/14; *see Russia below*<br>**Russia**: 2 in 8/14; 2 in 10/14; 2 in 1/15; *Woyrsch* in 5/15; 9G in 9/15; *Gerok* in 1/16; *AGp Reserve* in 6/16; *Bernhardi* in 7/16; *Bernhardi* in 11/16; *unatt.* in 7/17; *see below*<br>**Italy**: from 2/18; *Isonzo* in 6/18; *see below*<br>**Albania**: from 9/18 to end |

## CAVALRY DIVISIONS continued

| DIVISION | FORMED | COMBAT RECORD |
|---|---|---|
| **10** | pre-war | **Russia**: *4* in 8/14; *4* in 10/14; *Süd* in 1/15; *7* in 5/15; *7* in 9/15; *4* in 1/16; *4* in 6/16; *4* in 7/16; *AGp Reserve* in 10/16; *see Rumania below*<br>**Rumania**: from 10/16; *1* in 7/17; *see Italy below*<br>**Italy**: from 4/18; *11* in 6/18; *11* in 10/18; *see below*<br>**Macedonia**: en route 10/18 |
| **11**<br>Honved | | **Russia**: *3* in 8/14; *4* in 10/14; *4* in 1/15; *4* in 5/15; *Bug* in 9/15; *Gerok* in 1/16; *AGp Reserve* in 6/16; *7* in 7/16; *7* in 7/17; *see below*<br>**Italy**: from 4/18; *6* in 6/18; *6* in 10/18 |
| **12**<br>Mounted<br>Schützen | 6/17 | **Russia**: *2* in 7/17; *see below*<br>**Italy**: from 5/18; *6* in 6/18; *6* in 10/18 |

## Belgium

* In January 1918, the six infantry divisions (each of three brigades of two regiments) were cut in half to create twelve infantry divisions of three regiments each.

### INFANTRY DIVISIONS (total = 6*)

| DIVISION | FORMED | COMBAT RECORD |
|---|---|---|
| **1** | pre-war | **W. Front**: 8/14 around Ghent; by 15/10/14 after retiring through Antwerp, the Belgians took positions on the extreme Allied left wing, remaining there until the great Allied advance in late 1918 |
| **2** | | **W. Front**: 8/14 around Antwerp; thereafter see 1 Div |
| **3** | | **W. Front**: 8/14 around Liège; thereafter see 1 Div |
| **4** | | **W. Front**: 8/14 Mons–Charleroi–Namur; thereafter see 1 Div |
| **5** | | **W. Front**: 8/14 as 4 Div.; thereafter see 1 Div |
| **6** | | **W. Front**: 8/14 around Brussels (reserve); thereafter see 1 Div |

### CAVALRY DIVISIONS (total = 2)

| DIVISION | FORMED | COMBAT RECORD |
|---|---|---|
| Cavalry Division (later 1 Cavalry) | pre-war | **W. Front**: 8/14 (reserve); thereafter see 1 Inf. Div. |
| **2** | 1915(?) | Formed by amalgamating the cavalry regiments attached to each infantry division. Not in Order of Battle from 1918. |

## Bulgaria

### INFANTRY DIVISIONS (total = 14)

| DIVISION | FORMED | COMBAT RECORD |
|---|---|---|
| **1** | pre-war | **Serbia**: *1* in 10/15; *1* in 12/15<br>**Rumania**: *3* in 7/16; *3* in 9/16; *3* in 11/16; *3* in 12/16; *9G* in 3/17<br>**Macedonia**: *11G* in 5/17; *11G* in 12/17, 7/18, 9/18 |
| **2** | | **Bulgaria**: (Greek frontier) in 9/15, 10/15, 11/15; *2* in 12/15<br>**Macedonia**: *11G* (part) and *2* (part) in 7/16; *11G* in 9/16, 12/16, 5/17, 12/17, 7/18, 9/18 |
| **3** | | **Serbia**: *2* in 9/15; *2* in 11/15, *1* in 12/15<br>**Albania**: one-third in 3/16<br>**Macedonia**: *1* in 9/16; *11G* in 12/16, 5/17, 12/17, 7/18, 9/18 |
| **4** | | **Serbia**: *3* in 9/15<br>**Bulgaria**: *3* in 10/15; *3* in 12/15<br>**Rumania**: *3* in 7/16, 9/16, 12/16, 3/17, 7/17, 12/17<br>**Macedonia**: *11G* in 7/16; *11G* in 9/18 |

## INFANTRY DIVISIONS continued

| DIVISION | FORMED | COMBAT RECORD |
|---|---|---|
| **5** | pre-war | **Serbia**: part in *3* in 10/15; (rest in GHQ Reserve)<br>**Macedonia**: *2* in 12/15; *11G* in 9/16; *1* in 12/16, 5/17; *1* & *11G* in 12/17; *1* in 7/18; *1* in 9/18 |
| **6** | | **Serbia**: *1* in 9/15<br>**Bulgaria**: in 12/15<br>**Macedonia**: *11G* in 7/16; part in *11G* in 12/16, 5/17, 12/17, 7/18, 9/18<br>**Rumania**: part in *3* in 9/16; part in *9G* in 3/17 and 7/17 |
| **7** | | **Serbia**: *2* in 9/15<br>**Macedonia**: *2* in 10/15, 12/15, 9/16, 12/16, 5/17, 12/17, 7/18, 9/18<br>**Rumania**: part in 7/16 |
| **8** | | **Serbia**: *1* in 9/15, 10/15, 12/15<br>**Albania**: part in 3/16<br>**Macedonia**: *1* in 7/16; *1* in 9/16; *11G* in 12/16; *11G* in 5/17; *2* and *11G* in 12/17; *2* in 7/18; *2* in 9/18 |
| **9** | | **Serbia**: *1* in 9/15; *1* in 12/15<br>**Macedonia**: *11G* in 7/16; *11G* in 9/16 (part); *1* in 12/16, 4/17 (part), 5/17, 12/17, 7/18, 9/18 |
| **10** | | **Macedonia/Thrace**: *3* in 10/15; *2* in 12/15, 9/16, 12/16, 5/17; *4* in 12/17; *4* in 9/18 |
| **11** | 9/15 | **Macedonia**: Reserve in 10/15; *2* in 11/15; *2* in 7/16; *1* and *2* in 12/16, 5/17, 7/18, 9/18 |
| **12** | 9/15(?) | **Bulgaria**: in 12/15 (Rumanian frontier); *3* in 7/16<br>**Rumania**: *3* in 9/16, 11/16, 3/17, 7/17, 12/17 (Location in 1918 not known) |
| Combined | 1916 | **Macedonia**: *11G* in 9/16; *see below*, *11G* in 12/17; *11G* in 9/18<br>**Rumania**: *3* in 11/16; *3* in 12/16; *9G* in 3/17, 7/17; *see above* |
| Bulgarian-Macedonian Mountain | 1917 | **Macedonia**: *11G* in 5/17; *1* in 12/17; *1* in 9/18 |

## CAVALRY DIVISIONS (total = 2)

| DIVISION | FORMED | COMBAT RECORD |
|---|---|---|
| **1** | pre-war | **Macedonia**: *2* in 10/15; *see below*, *4* in 9/18<br>**Bulgaria**: *3* in 7/16 (Rumanian frontier); *see below*<br>**Rumania**: *3* in 9/16, 11/16, 3/17, 7/17; *see Macedonia above* |
| **2** | 1917/18 | **Macedonia**: *4* in 9/18 |

## Canada

### INFANTRY DIVISIONS (total = 4)

| DIVISION | FORMED | COMBAT RECORD |
|---|---|---|
| **1** | 10/14 | **W. Front**: *12*/15–4/15; *2* to *?*/16; *Res.* to 11/16; *1* to 10/17; *2* to 12/17; *1* to 8/18; *4* to *?*/18; *1* |
| **2** | 5/15 | **W. Front**: *2* 9/15–*?*/16; *Res.* to 11/16; *1* to 10/17; *2* to 12/17; *1* to 4/18; *3* to 6/18; *1* to 8/18; *4* to *?*/18; *1* |
| **3** | 12/15 | **W. Front**: *2* 11/16–*?*/16; *Res.* to 11/16; *1* to 10/17; *2* to 12/17; *1* to *?*/18; *3* to 8/18; *4* to 9/18; *1* |
| **4** | 8/16 | **W. Front**: *Res.* in 11/16; *1* to 10/17; *2* to 12/17; *1* to *?*/18; *4* to 9/18; *1* |

In January 1917, 5 Inf. Div. was also formed, in England. But this never left for France and was broken up for reinforcements in early 1918.

## China

### INFANTRY DIVISIONS

Throughout the period 1914–18, China was in a state of near civil war, with the republican Kuomintang in the south pitted against the crypto-imperialist warlord clique in Peking. In fact, it was warlords (technically provincial governors or *tuchuns*) who were in effective control of most of China and when war was declared on Germany in August 1917 it proved impossible to form any sort of expeditionary force to fight with the Allies. Efforts were made, however. It was the northerners who had access to the best cadres, veterans of Yuan Shih-kai's Northern or Peiyang Army which had been formed in 1904 along regularised European lines. Thses were utilised by the northern Premier, Tuan Chi-jui, to establish the New or War Participation Army comprising *three divisions* and four brigades equipped and trained with Japanese assistance. But participate they never did.

## Czechoslovakia

### INFANTRY DIVISIONS (and other)

See Section 2 for background details on what was a 'virtual' country until the peace settlement, as well as for its peculiar tripartite army-in-exile.*

| DIVISION | FORMED | COMBAT RECORD |
|---|---|---|
| **6** (in Italy) | 6/18 † | **Piave**: *9* in 9/18 |
| **7** (in Italy) | ?† | |
| Czech Legion | 8/14 | Formed from Czechs resident in Russia, the 1,000 strong volunteer unit had expanded into a Rifle Regiment by December 1915. It was first attached to Third Army in Galicia and from September 1915 to Brusilov's Eighth Army. In May 1916 it became two regiments united as a Brigade and a third regiment was added in March 1917. It expanded greatly after the fall of the Tsar, fielding 22,000 men in September 1917 and 32,000 in December. During the Kerensky Offensive, in July it distinguished itself at the Battle of Zborow, now fighting with Russian Eleventh Army. A so-called Hussit Division was formed in August and by October a second division had been formed, allowing the creation of a Czech Army Corps. In February 1918, the Bolsheviks came to an agreement with the Allies that the Czech Legion, as it was now known, was officially part of the Czech Army in France (see below) and should be shipped there forthwith. But relations between the Legion and the Bolsheviks soon soured, transport to embarkation ports was refused and the Czechs became embroiled in the Civil War. No more than 2,500 Legionnaires reached France before the Armistice. |
| Czech Army in France | | In February 1918, the French government formally approved the creation of a Czech Army to fight alongside its own troops, but without the transfer of the Czech Legion from Russia (see above) it proved impossible to find the requisite manpower. In the event only three regiments were formed – 21st was already in existence since January 1918 and 22nd and 23rd were formed in May – and the first of these did reach the front, in June 1918. |

## Finland

### INFANTRY DIVISIONS (and other)

Although a Grand Duchy of Russia since 1809, Finland had been allowed to maintain its own army until July 1901 when the tightening Tsarist autocracy effectively merged it with the Imperial Army. In the event few Finnish troops seemed to have been involved in the First World War although some 1,800 volunteers left for Germany where they were formed into 27 Jäger Battalion in July 1916. Finland itself was garrisoned by Russian troops, latterly 40,000 men from XLII Corps and various frontier units. After the abdication of the Tsar in March 1917, the Finns set up a 12-man executive to run the country. At first this body took a pro-Russian line but in November, after the Bolshevik revolution, complete independence was declared. This anti-Bolshevik line angered the militant Social Democrats. Rival White and Red Guards were formed and in January 1918 the former led a putsch in Helsinki. Civil War ensued with the government-in-exile handing over military control of the White Forces to General Mannerheim. When he took command the White Guard was organised into small regional Defence Corps, capable of little more than sporadic guerrilla operations. Mannerheim immediately sought the recall of the 27 Jägers to provide the cadres for a new, elite force of six regiments (18 battalions) of Finnish Jägers. At the same time, efforts were to be made to regularise the remaining Defence Corps into 21 extra infantry regiments.‡ The whole force was to be combined into *nine infantry divisions* though it is unclear how far this had got before the end of hostilities. For the war was a very short one. Russian troops were not in the least eager for combat, the Red Guards remained militarily naive, and Mannerheim received additional support from a small German force, Von der Goltz's composite Baltic Division, which was dispatched from Germany in response to pleas from the overthrown government. In April 1918 both Mannerheim and Von der Goltz won crushing military victories and on 18 May the war was officially declared over. Twelve days later Mannerheim had resigned over what he regarded as a virtual handover of the White Army to the Germans.

*NB. For regular Finnish Rifle Divisions fighting in the Russian Army see that country's entry.*

## France

### INFANTRY DIVISIONS (total = 140)

**REGULAR DIVISIONS**

| DIVISION | FORMED | COMBAT RECORD |
|---|---|---|
| **1** | 8/14 ↓ | **W. Front**: *5* to 12/14; *4* to 3/15; *N.A.* to 4/15; *5* to 7/16; *10* to 8/16; *6* to 10/16; *4* to 3/17; *5* to 6/17; *1* to 12/17; *6* to 3/18; *3, 5* and *6* to 6/18; *10* to 7/18; *3* to 8/18; *7* to 5/11/18; *10* |
| **2** | | **W. Front**: *5* to 12/14; *4* to 3/15; *N.A.* to 4/15; *5, 3* and *1* to 5/15; *5* to 2/16; *4, 3* and *2* to 3/16; *5* to 8/16; *6* to 10/16; *4* to 3/17; *5* to 4/17; *10* and *1* to 6/17; *10* to 7/17; *1* to 12/17; *6* to 5/18; *5* to 6/18; *6* to 8/18; *10* to 9/18; *7* to 8/11/18; *10* |
| **3** | | **W. Front**: *4* to 1/15; *3* to 2/15; *4* to 3/15; *1* to 8/15; *2* to 11/15; *R.F.V.* to 2/16; *2* to 6/16; *6* to 8/16; *10* to 12/16; *8* to 3/17; *10* to 4/17; *5* to 6/17; *4* to 7/17; *2* to 4/18; *1* to 8/18; *4* to 10/18; *8* |
| **4** | | **W. Front**: *4* to 1/15; *3* to 2/15; *4* to 4/15; *1* to 8/15; *R.F.V.* to 10/15; *2* to 11/15; *R.F.V.* to 2/16; *2* to 5/16; *10* to 6/16; *6* to 8/16; *10* to 12/16; *8* to 3/17; *10* to 4/17; *5* to 6/17; *4* to 7/17; *2* to 5/18; *6* to 7/18; *9, 5* and *6* to 8/18; *2* to 9/18; *6* to 10/18; *8* |
| **5** | | **W. Front**: *5* to 3/15; *10* to 10/15; *6* to 3/16; *2* to 3/17; *10* to 5/17; *6* to 7/17; *10* to 9/17; *3* to 1/18; *4* to 6/18; *1* to 7/18; *10, 6* and *3* to 8/18; *10* to 9/18; *G.A.F.* to 10/18; *6* |
| **6** | | **W. Front**: *5* to 3/15; *10* to 10/15; *6* to 3/16; *2* to 2/17; *8* to 3/17; *10* to 5/17; *1* in 5/17; *6* to 7/17; *10* to 8/17; *3* to 1/18; *4* to 6/18; *3* to 9/18; *5* |
| **7** | | **W. Front**: *3* to 9/14; *G.M.P.* and *6* to 9/14; *2* to 12/14; *4* to 1/15; *5* to 2/15; *4* to 10/15; *2* to 1/16; *4* to 8/16; *2* to 12/16; *D.A.L.* to 1/17; *8* to 6/17; *2* to 11/17; *4* to 3/18; *D.A.N.* to 6/18; *5* to 8/18; *4* to 10/18; *5* to 10/11/18; *4* |
| **8** | | **W. Front**: *3* to 9/14; *6* in 9/14; *2* to 12/14; *6* to 10/15; *2* to 1/16; *4* to 7/16; *2* to 8/16; *4* to 10/16; *5* to 11/16; *1* and *3* to 12/16; *10* to 1/17; *3* to 2/17; *2* to 4/17; *4* to 6/18; *5* to 8/18; *4* to 10/18; *5* |
| **9** | | **W. Front**: *3* to 6/16; *2* to 12/16; *5* to 4/17; *10* to 12/17; *6* to 3/18; *3* to 4/18; *7* to 7/18; *1, 9* and *4* in 7/18; *5* |

* At the beginning of the war most Czechs and Slovaks were mobilised into the Austro-Hungarian Army. On the Russian Front I, II and IX Corps were mainly made up of Czechs and on the Serb Front VIII Corps, although Fifth Army as a whole contained a considerable Czechoslovak element.

† The Italian government agreed to the formation of a Czech Army to fight alongside their own troops in April 1918. Within a few weeks 24,000 volunteers had come forward, most of them Austro-Hungarian prisoners-of-war. Two infantry divisions were formed although it remains unclear why they should be numbered 6 and 7.

‡ In all the regularised White Forces numbered around 32,000 men, many of them caught up in the conscription that was introduced in February 1918.

## INFANTRY DIVISIONS continued

### REGULAR DIVISIONS continued

| DIVISION | FORMED | COMBAT RECORD |
|---|---|---|
| **10** | 8/14 | **W. Front**: *3* to 11/14; *4* to 1/15; *3* to 4/16; *2* to 8/16; *6* to 11/16; *4* to 12/16; *5* to 4/17; *10* to 10/17; *6* to 2/18; *3* to 4/18; *7* to 7/18; *1, 9* and *4* in 7/18; *5* |
| **11** | | **W. Front**: *2* to 11/14; *D.A.B.* in 11/14; *8* to 4/15; *10* to 7/15; *D.A.L.* to 8/15; *Gp Pétain* to 9/15; *2* to 12/15; *D.A.L.* to 3/16; *2* to 4/16; *6* to 12/16; *D.A.L.* to 1/17; *8* to 3/17; *6* to 6/17; *8* to 12/17; *2* to 3/18; *4, 3, 4*, and *5* to 5/18; *10* to 10/18; *G.A.F.* in 10/18; *6* |
| **12** | | **W. Front**: *3* to 1/15; *1* to 9/15; *4* to 6/16; *5* to 9/16; *6* to 12/16; *10* and *1* in 12/16; *5* to 1/17; *6* to 6/17; *7* to 3/18; *1* to 4/18; *8* to 7/18; *10* to 10/18; *G.A.F.* in 10/18; *6* |
| **13** | | **W. Front**: *1* to 9/14; *3* and *4* in 9/14; *9* to 10/14; *10* to 1/16; *2* to 2/16; *10* and *3* in 2/16; *2* to 4/16; *4* to 8/16; *10* to 12/16; *7* to 4/17; *1* to 5/17; *6* to 12/17; *7* to 5/18; *4, 6*, and *5* to 6/18; *4* to 10/18; *5* |
| **14** | | **W. Front**: *1* in 8/14; *Alsace* in 8/14; *6* to 8/15; *4* to 12/15; *3* to 1/16; *4* to 2/16; *3* and *R.F.V.* in 2/16; *2* to 3/16; *1* to 4/16; *2* to 5/16; *7* to 7/16; *6* to 9/16; *4* to 1/17; *5* to 8/17; *2* to 1/18; *8* to 4/18; *10* to 5/18; *D.A.N.* to 6/18; *1* to 7/18; *5* to 9/18; *4* |
| **15** | | **W. Front**: *1* to 9/14; *2, 3* and *4* in 9/14; *1* to 9/15; *2* to 12/15; *1* to 6/16; *D.A.L.* to 7/16; *2* to 8/16; *D.A.L.* to 11/16; *10* to 1/17; *4* to 3/18; *3* to 6/18; *10* to 8/18; *3* and *10* in 8/18; *3* to 9/18; *1* |
| **16** | | **W. Front**: *1* to 9/14; *2, 3* and *4* in 9/14; *1* to 2/16; *2* to 9/16; *D.A.L.* to 11/16; *10* to 1/17; *4* to 3/17; *4* in 4/17; *2* to 6/17; *4* to 7/18; *5* |
| **17** | | **W. Front**: *2* in 8/14; *4* in 8/14; *D. Foch* to 9/14; *9* to 10/14; *4* in 10/14; *D.A.B.* to 11/14; *8* to 4/15; *10* to 7/15; *6* to 8/15; *10* to 3/16; *G.A.N.* and *6* to 4/16; *2* to 5/16; *4* to 10/16; *6* to 12/16; *10* to 1/17; *1* to 3/17; *6, 5* and *10* in 3/17; *5* in 4/17; *10* to 8/17; *8* to 3/18; *1* to 4/18; *2* to 7/18; *10* to 10/18; *3* |
| **18** | | **W. Front**: *2* to 9/14; *9* to 10/14; *4* in 10/14; *D.A.B.* to 11/14; *8* to 4/15; *D.A.B.* and *10* to 5/15; *10* to 7/15; *6* to 8/15; *10* to 4/16; *2* to 5/16; *4* to 9/16; *6* to 12/16; *10* to 2/17; *4* to 3/17; *10* to 4/17; *5* in 4/17; *10* to 7/17; *8* to 4/18; *1* to 6/18; *3* to 7/18; *6, 9* and *5* in 7/18; *6* to 8/18; *2* to 9/18; *A.U.S.* to 10/18; *8* |
| **19** | | **W. Front**: *5* to 9/14; *D. Mzud'huy, 10* and *2* to 11/14; *10* to 7/15; *3* to 5/16; *2* to 9/16; *4* to 2/17; *3* to 4/17; *10* and *1* in 4/17; *4* to 5/17; *2* to 3/18; *4* and *5* in 3/18; *6* to 6/18; *10* to 8/18; *2* in 8/18; *7* to 10/18; *3* |
| **20** | | **W. Front**: *5* to 9/14; *2* to 10/14; *10* in 10/14; *2* to 11/14; *10* to 7/15; *3* to 6/16; *6* to 7/16; *10* to 1/17; *3* to 4/17; *10* and *1* in 4/17; *4* to 6/17; *2* to 5/18; *6* to 6/18; *10, 9* and *6* in 7/18; *5* to 9/18; *7* |
| **21** | | **W. Front**: *5, 4* and *D. Foch* to 9/14; *9* and *6* in 9/14; *2* to 8/15; *6* in 8/15; *Gp. Pétain* to 9/15; *2* to 1/16; *4* to 3/16; *3* to 6/16; *2* to 2/17; *4* to 3/17; *6* to 5/17; *3* to 9/17; *6* to 1/18; *7* to 9/18; *4* |
| **22** | | **W. Front**: *5, 4* and *D. Foch* to 9/14; *9* and *6* in 9/14; *2* to 8/15; *6* in 8/15; *Gp. Pétain* to 9/15; *2* to 1/16; *4* to 3/16; *2* to 4/16; *5* to 9/16; *2* to 1/17; *6* to 5/17; *3* to 9/17; *6* to 3/18; *3* to 4/18; *6* to 9/18; *4* |
| **23** | | **W. Front**: *4* to 9/14; *9* to 10/14; *4* to 3/15; *1* to 6/15; *10* to 3/16; *2* to 6/16; *5* to 10/16; *3, 1* and *6* to 11/16; *10* to 1/17; *4* to 10/17<br>**Italy**: *10* to 4/18; *XII* to 10/18; *12 Ital.* |
| **24** | | **W. Front**: *4* to 9/14; *9* to 10/14; *4* to 3/15; *1* to 6/15; *2* to 7/15; *10* to 3/16; *2* to 6/16; *5* to 10/16; *3* in 10/16; *1* to 11/16; *10* to 2/17; *3* in 2/17; *4* to 10/17; *5* to 11/17<br>**Italy**: *10* to 4/18; *XII* to 10/18; *XIII Ital.* |
| **25** | | **W. Front**: *1* to 9/14; *6* in 9/14; *2* to 7/15; *6* to 2/16; *2* to 3/16; *10* to 6/16; *3* to 9/16; *10* to 12/16; *1* in 12/16; *D.A.L.* to 1/17; *1* to 3/17; *3* to 7/17; *4* in 7/17; *2* to 7/18; *10* to 10/18; *3* |
| **26** | | **W. Front**: *1* to 9/14; *2* to 11/14; *D.A.B.* in 11/14; *8* to 12/14; *7* to 7/15; *6* to 2/16; *2* to 3/16; *10* to 12/16; *1* and *D.A.L.* in 12/16; *8* in 1/17; *1* to 3/17; *3* to 7/17; *4* to 8/17; *2* to 5/18; *5* and *10* in 5/18; *6* to 6/18; *2* to 9/18; *A.U.S.* to 11/18; *2* and *10* |

| DIVISION | FORMED | COMBAT RECORD |
|---|---|---|
| **27** | 8/14 | **W. Front**: *3* to 9/14; *2* to 8/15; *Gp. Pétain* to 9/15; *2* to 10/15; *7* to 2/16; *2* to 9/16; *5* to 1/17; *6* and *1* in 1/17; *3* to 5/17; *6* to 6/17; *3* to 8/17; *6* to 12/17; *4* to 1/18; *7* to 4/18; *D.A.N.* to 6/18; *4* to 8/18; *5* in 8/18; *8* |
| **28** | | **W. Front**: *1* to 9/14; *2* to 8/15; *Gp. Pétain* to 9/15; *2* to 10/15; *7* to 2/16; *2* to 1/17; *3* to 5/17; *6* to 6/17; *3* to 8/17; *6* to 12/17; *4* to 1/18; *7* to 4/18; *A.W., G.Q.G.* and *D.A.N.* in 4/18; *4* to 5/18; *5* to 6/18; *8* to 9/18; *5* to 10/18; *4* in 10/18; *5* |
| **29** | | **W. Front**: *2* to 9/14; *3* to 2/16; *R.F.V.* in 2/16; *2* to 4/16; *G.A.N.* to 10/16; *10* to 1/17; *G.A.N.* to 6/17; *1* to 12/17; *C.S.N.* to 4/18; *1* in 4/18; *2* to 8/18; *10* to 10/18; *3* |
| **30** | | **W. Front**: *2* to 9/14; *3* to 8/15; *Gp. Pétain* in 8/15; *5* to 10/15; *4* to 11/15; *5* to 1/16; *2* to 8/16; *5* to 1/17<br>**Macedonia**: *C.A.A.* to 7/17; *A.F.O.* to 10/18; *Danube* |
| **31** | | **W. Front**: *2* to 9/14; *1* to 10/14; *6* and *2* in 10/14; *D.A.B.* to 11/14; *8* to 2/15; *10* and *2* in 2/15; *4* to 8/15; *Gp. Pétain* to 9/15; *2* to 12/15; *5* to 7/16; *2* to 9/17; *7* to 3/18; *5* to 4/18; *D.A.N.* to 5/18; *8* to 8/18; *10* to 10/18; *3* |
| **32** | | **W. Front**: *2* to 9/14; *1* to 10/14; *6* in 10/14; *D.A.B.* to 11/14; *8* to 1/15; *10* to 2/15; *4* to 8/15; *Gp. Pétain* to 9/15; *2* to 11/15; *5* to 7/16; *2* to 10/17; *7* to 4/18; *D.A.N.* to 5/18; *8* to 8/18; *10* to 10/18; *3* |
| **33** | | **W. Front**: *4* to 4/15; *10* to 3/16; *D.A.L.* to 4/16; *4* to 7/16; *2* to 3/17; *4* to 5/17; *2* to 6/18; *6* to 8/18; *10* to 10/18; *1* |
| **34** | | **W. Front**: *4* to 4/15; *10* to 3/16; *2* to 6/16; *4* to 5/17; *2* to 4/18; *5, 10* and *G.Q.G.A.* in 4/18; *D.A.N.* to 5/18; *2* to 8/18; *1* |
| **35** | | **W. Front**: *2* in 8/14; *5* to 4/16; *2* to 6/16; *3* in 6/16; *4* to 12/16; *5, 1* and *3* in 12/16; *10* to 2/17; *3* to 4/17; *10* to 6/17; *7* to 10/17; *4* to 3/18; *3* to 5/18; *10* in 6/18; *3* to 8/18; *1* to 9/18; *10* to 10/18; *1* |
| **36** | | **W. Front**: *2* in 8/14; *5* to 4/16; *2* to 6/16; *3* in 6/16; *4* to 12/16; *5, 1* and *3* in 12/16; *10* to 2/17; *3* to 3/17; *10* to 6/17; *7* to 10/17; *4* to 3/18; *3* to 6/18; *2* to 9/18; *10* to 10/18; *3* |
| **37***<br>Division<br>d'Afrique | | **W. Front**: *5* to 12/14; *6* to 8/15; *4* to 10/15; *G.A.N.* to 1/16; *3* to 2/16; *4, 3* and *R.F.V.* in 2/16; *2* to 3/16; *1* in 3/16; *D.A.L.* to 4/16; *2* to 8/16; *D.A.L.* to 10/16; *2* to 1/17; *4* to 2/17; *5* to 9/17; *2* to 12/17; *8* to 4/18; *1* to 8/18; *3* to 9/18; *1* |
| **38***<br>Division<br>d'Afrique | | **W. Front**: *5* to 10/14; *D.A.B.* to 11/14; *8* to 12/14; *2* to 4/15; *D.A.B.* to 5/15; *G.P.N.* to 5/15; *G.A.N.* to 5/16; *2* to 1/17; *6* to 7/17; *3* to 8/17; *6* to 11/17; *5* to 12/17; *4* to 2/18; *5* to 3/18; *3* to 4/18; *4* to 5/18; *3* to 6/18; *10* to 8/18; *3* to 9/18; *7* |
| **39** | | **W. Front**: *2* to 11/14; *D.A.B.* in 11/14; *8* to 4/15; *D.A.B.* to 5/15; *10* to 7/15; *D.A.L.* to 8/15; *Gp. Pétain* to 9/15; *2* to 12/15; *D.A.L.* to 2/16; *2* to 4/16; *6* to 12/16; *O.A.L.* and *8* in 1/17; *6* to 6/17; *8* to 1/18; *2* to 4/18; *D.A.N.* to 5/18; *6* in 5/18; *2* to 6/18; *10* in 6/18; *6* to 8/18; *2* in 8/18; *A.U.S.* to 10/18; *8* to 11/18; *10* |
| **40***<br>Division<br>d'Afrique | | **W. Front**: *3* to 8/15; *4* to 3/16; *2* to 6/16; *1* to 8/16; *D.A.L.* to 9/16; *6* to 12/16; *4* to 1/17; *5* to 6/17; *4* to 7/17; *2* to 9/17; *8* to 5/18; *5* to 7/18; *8* to 10/18; *4* |
| **41** | | **W. Front**: *1* and *Alsace* in 8/14; *Vosges* to 9/14; *1* to 12/14; *D.A.V.* to 4/15; *7* to 1/16; *D.A.L.* and *6* in 1/16; *10* to 7/16; *6* to 9/16; *4* to 1/17; *5* to 6/17; *4* to 10/17; *2* to 12/17; *8* to 5/18; *D.A.N.* to 6/18; *A.W., 10* and *6* in 7/18; *2* to 8/18; *10* to 9/18; *G.A.F.* to 10/18; *6* |
| **42** | | **W. Front**: *3* in 8/14; *9* to 10/14; *5* in 10/14; *10* to 10/14; *D.A.B.* to 11/14; *8* to 12/14; *2* to 1/15; *3* to 7/15; *2* in 7/15; *4* to 3/16; *2* to 5/16; *1* to 6/16; *D.A.L.* to 9/16; *6* to 11/16; *5* to 12/16; *4* to 1/17; *5* to 4/17; *10* to 5/17; *1* to 6/17; *2* to 10/17; *8* to 1/18; *1* in 1/18; *8* to 4/18; *1* to 8/18; *8* to 10/18; *4* |
| **43** | | **W. Front**: *1* to 9/14; *3, 4* and *9* in 9/14; *2* and *10* in 10/14; *D.A.B.* to 11/14; *8* to 12/14; *10* to 1/16; *2* to 2/16; *10* and *3* in 2/16; *2* to 4/16; *4* to 8/16; *10* to 12/16; *7* to 4/17; *6* to 12/17; *1* to 4/18; *5* to 5/18; *6* to 6/18; *4* to 10/18; *5* |
| **44** | | **W. Front**: *Alpes* and *Alsace* in 8/14; *1* to 9/14. Disbanded 5/9/14 |
| **45***<br>Division<br>d'Afrique | | **W. Front**: *G.M.P.* to 9/14; *6* to 10/14; *10* to 4/15; *D.A.B.* to 5/15; *G.P.N.* to 6/15; *G.A.N.* to 3/16; *5* to 4/16; *2* to 5/16; *D.A.L.* to 8/16; *6* to 9/16; *G.A.N.* to 1/17; *3* to 3/17; *4* to 5/17; *5* to 3/18; *1* to 4/18; *4* to 5/18; *6* and *4* in 5/18; *1* to 6/18; *5* |

* Mobilised in France and Algeria and concentrated in France. Other infantry divisions that at various times included one North African Tirailleur regiment were nos. 8, 17, 25, 34, 48, 52, 56, 58, 68, 74, 126, 129, 166.

## INFANTRY DIVISIONS continued

**REGULAR DIVISIONS continued**

| DIVISION | FORMED | COMBAT RECORD |
|---|---|---|
| **46** | 3/16 | **W. Front**: *7* to 7/16; *6* to 11/16; *7* to 3/17; *5* to 7/17; *10* to 3/18; *5* to 4/18; *10* to 5/18; *D.A.N.* to 6/18; *5* to 7/18; *4* to 8/18; *1* |
| **47** | 1/15 | **W. Front**: *D.A.V.* to 4/15; *7* to 6/16; *6* to 10/16; *7* to 3/17; *10* to 5/17; *1* in 5/17; *10* to 7/17; *2* in 7/17; *8* to 9/17; *4* to 10/17; *see below*, *5* to 4/18; *10* to 6/18; *6* to 7/18; *1* <br> **Italy**: *10* to 3/18 |
| **48** | 2/15 | **W. Front**: *6* in 2/15; *4* to 4/15; *1* to 5/15; *10* to 7/15; *6* to 9/15; *4* to 12/15; *3* to 2/16; *R.F.V.* in 2/16; *2* to 3/16; *1* to 4/16; *2* to 5/16; *5* to 7/16; *6* to 9/16; *D.A.L.* to 1/17; *8* to 5/17; *4* to 7/17; *2* to 1/18; *8* to 3/18; *1* in 3/18; *5* to 4/18; *6* to 5/18; *10* to 6/18; *6* and *Gp. Mangin* in 6/18; *10* to 9/18; *4* |
| **49** | – | **Not formed** |
| **50** | – | **Not formed** |
| **51\*** | 8/14 | **W. Front**: *G.Q.G.* in 8/14; *5* to 5/15; *2* to 7/15; *10* to 8/15; *6* to 10/15; *R.F.V.* to 2/16; *7* to 6/16; *6* to 8/16; *10* to 10/16; *4* to 2/17; *5* to 4/17; *10* to 6/17; *1* to 12/17; *6* to 5/18; *5* in 5/18; *6* to 6/18; *10* to 7/18; *5, 6* and *9* in 7/18; *7* to 10/18; *1* |
| **52** | | **W. Front**: *5* and *4* in 8/14; *Det. Foch* to 9/14; *9* to 10/14; *5* to 6/16; *2* to 7/16; *7* to 9/17; *6* to 9/18; *5* |
| **53** | | **W. Front**: *5* to 8/14; *2* to 4/15; *10* to 7/15; *2* to 10/15; *6* to 4/16; *10* to 5/16; *6* to 8/16; *3* to 10/16; *1* to 5/17; *3* to 8/17; *10* to 10/17; *6* to 3/18; *3* to 6/18; *7* to 9/18; *5* to 10/18; *4* |
| **54** | | **W. Front**: *3* to 10/14. *Disbanded* 27/10/14 |
| **55** | | **W. Front**: *3* in 8/14; *6* to 5/15; *10* to 11/15; *5* to 6/16; *4* to 7/16; *2* to 6/17; *4* to 7/17; *10* to 10/17; *6* to 2/18; *3* to 3/18; *6* to 6/18; *10* to 9/18. *Disbanded* 10/9/18 |
| **56** | | **W. Front**: *3* and *Lorraine* in 8/14; *6* to 10/14; *2* to 7/15; *10* to 9/15; *4* to 5/16; *2* to 6/16; *5* to 9/16; *6* to 12/16; *10* and *12* in 12/16; *5* to 1/17; *6* to 5/17; *7* to 3/18; *1* to 4/18; *8* to 7/18; *1* |
| **57** | | **W. Front**: *1* and *Alsace* in 8/14; *G.Q.G.* to 9/14; *1* to 12/14; *D.A.V.* to 2/15; *7* to 10/15 <br> **Macedonia**: *A.O.* to 8/16; *A.F.O.* |
| **58** | | **W. Front**: *Alsace* in 8/14; *1* to 10/14; *10* to 9/15; *G.A.N.* in 9/15; *10* to 1/16; *G.A.N.* to 5/16; *6* to 6/16; *10* to 11/16; *3* to 12/16; *10* to 1/17; *7* to 8/17; *5* to 1/18; *4* to 5/18; *3* to 7/18; *10* in 7/18; *3* to 9/18; *1* |
| **59** | | **W. Front**: *2* to 9/14; *1* to 1/15; *G.P.E.* to 3/15; *D.A.L.* to 2/16; *2* to 4/16; *D.A.L.* to 10/16; *7* to 12/16; *2* to 4/17; *8* to 5/17; *4* to 7/17; *8* to 3/18; *1* to 5/18; *2* to 8/18; *10* to 10/18; *3* |
| **60** | | **W. Front**: *5* and *4* in 9/14; *9* to 10/14; *4* to 6/16; *2* to 7/16; *4* to 10/17; *2* to 3/18; *6* to 4/18; *1* to 10/18; *7* |
| **61** | | **W. Front**: *G.M.P.* and *G.Q.G.* in 9/14; *6* to 4/16; *10* to 5/16; *6* to 8/16; *10* to 9/16; *3* to 10/16; *1* to 3/17; *3* to 9/17; *6* to 6/18; *7* to 9/18; *4* |
| **62** | | **W. Front**: *G.M.P.* and *G.Q.G.* in 9/14; *6* to 10/14; *2* to 8/15; *6* to 6/16; *10* to 12/16; *3* to 4/17; *G.A.N.* to 5/17; *6* to 6/17; *3* to 1/18; *6* to 2/18; *3* to 4/18; *7* to 8/18; *6* to 9/18; *5* |
| **63** | | **W. Front**: *Alsace* in 8/14; *6* to 8/15; *5* to 5/16; *2* to 6/16; *7* to 9/16; *2* to 4/17; *7* to 6/17; *2* to 7/18; *4* in 7/18; *6*; 8/18 became 1 Polish Division (see entry for Poland). |
| **64** | | **W. Front**: *Alsace* in 8/14; *2* to 9/14; *1* to 10/15; *4* in 10/15; *1* to 5/16; *D.A.L.* to 6/16; *2* to 9/17; *4* to 10/17; *see below*; *10* to 4/18; *1* to 5/18; *8* to 8/18; *10* to 9/18; *1* <br> **Italy**: *10* to 3/18 |
| **65** | | **W. Front**: *Alpes* and *Lorraine* in 8/14; *3* to 11/14; *1* to 12/14; *3* to 1/15; *1* to 5/16; *2* to 9/17; *4* to 10/17; *see below*; *1* to 5/18; *8* to 8/18. *Disbanded* 4/8/18. Becomes 2 Moroccan Inf. Div. <br> **Italy**: *10* to 3/18 |
| **66** | | **W. Front**: *Alsace* to 9/14; *1* to 12/14; *D.A.V.* to 4/15; *7* to 7/16; *6* to 11/16; *7* to 3/17; *5* to 4/17; *10* to 6/17; *6* to 10/17; *7* to 4/18; *6* and *5* in 4/18; *1* to 8/18; *10* to 10/18; *1* |

| DIVISION | FORMED | COMBAT RECORD |
|---|---|---|
| **67** | 8/14 | **W. Front**: *3* to 1/15; *1* to 8/15; *R.F.V.* to 2/16; *2* to 3/16; *5* to 8/16; *2* to 9/16; *1* to 10/16; *D.A.L.* to 1/17; *8* to 7/17; *6* to 2/18; *5* to 3/18; *3* to 6/18; *10* in 6/18; *3* to 9/18; *1* |
| **68** | | **W. Front**: *2* to 9/14; *1* to 1/15; *G.P.E.* to 3/15; *D.A.L.* to 2/16; *2* to 9/16; *D.A.L.* to 1/17; *8* to 6/17; *6* to 7/17; *10* to 8/17; *6* to 9/17; *10* to 6/11/17; *2* to 7/18; *4, 10* and *6* in 7&8/18; *4* to 10/18; *5* in 10/18; *7* |
| **69** | | **W. Front**: *G.Q.G.* in 8/14; *5* to 10/14; *6* to 11/14; *5* to 2/16; *4* to 4/16; *2* to 6/16; *5* to 4/17; *10* to 6/17; *4* to 7/17; *2* to 9/18; *8* to 1/18; *1* to 3/18; *8* to 6/18; *3* to 7/18; *10* to 9/18; *8* |
| **70** | | **W. Front**: *2* to 9/14; *1* in 9/14; *2* to 10/14; *10* to 2/16; *6* to 3/16; *2* to 4/16; *1* in 4/16; *D.A.L.* to 5/16; *1* to 8/16; *6* to 11/16; *1* to 3/17; *3* to 6/17; *6* to 7/17; *7* to 3/18; *4* in 3/18; *3* to 4/18; *7* to 6/18; *10* to 8/18; *3* to 9/18; *1* in 9/18; *G.A.F.* to 10/18; *6* |
| **71** | | **W. Front**: *1* to 12/14; *D.A.V.* to 3/15; *D.A.L.* to 6/16; *2* to 3/17; *4* in 3/17; *2* to 5/17; *4* to 7/17; *5* to 3/18; *6* to 5/18; *D.A.N.* to 6/18; *G.Q.G.A.* and *9* in 7/18; *4* |
| **72** | | **W. Front**: *3* and *Lorraine* in 8/14; *3* to 1/15; *1* to 8/15; *R.F.V.* to 3/16; *1* in 3/16; *7* to 6/16; *6* to 8/16; *10* to 11/16; *3* to 12/16; *10* to 1/17; *2* to 5/17; *4* to 4/18; *3* to 7/18; *10* to 10/18; *3* |
| **73** | | **W. Front**: *G.Q.G., 3, 2* and *Lorraine* in 8/14; *2* to 9/14; *1* to 7/16; *D.A.L.* to 8/16; *2* to 9/16; *D.A.L.* to 1/17; *8* to 6/17; *2* to 7/17; *7* to 5/18; *5, 10* and *3* in 5/18; *6* to 7/18; *9, 5, 6* and *4* to 8/18; *2* to 9/18; *4* to 10/18; *8* |
| **74** | | **W. Front**: *2* to 9/14; *1* to 1/15; *G.P.E.* to 31/15; *D.A.L.* to 9/16; *2* to 3/17; *4* to 6/17; *5* to 3/18; *6* to 6/18; *10* in 6/18; *3* to 9/18; *4* |
| **75** | | **W. Front**: *Alpes* and *Lorraine* in 8/14; *3* to 11/14; *Disbanded* 6/11/14 |
| **76** <br> (Div. de Vassart to 10/14) | 9/14 | **W. Front**: *1* to 3/16; *2* to 5/16; *1* in 5/16; *7* to 12/16 <br> **Macedonia**: *C.A.A.* to 2/17; *A.F.O.* |
| **77** <br> (Div. Barbot then Div. B to 10/14) | 9/14 | **W. Front**: *1* in 8/14; *10* to 3/16; *2* to 4/16; *D.A.L.* to 5/16; *1* to 8/16; *6* in 8/16; *10* to 9/16; *6* to 11/16; *1* to 3/17; *3* to 5/17; *6* to 8/17; *7* to 2/18; *8* to 3/18; *4* and *5* in 3/18; *5* to 5/18; *7* to 6/18; *10* to 7/18; *5* to 8/18; *6* to 9/18; *G.A.F.* to 10/18; *6* |
| **78-80** | – | **Not formed** |

**TERRITORIAL DIVISIONS**

| DIVISION | FORMED | COMBAT RECORD |
|---|---|---|
| **81** <br> (Active Div. from 4/17†) | 8/14 | **W. Front**: *G.Q.G.* to 10/14; *2* in 10/14; *Gp. Bidou* to 2/15; *G.P. Nieuport* to 5/15; *Gp. Nieuport* to 6/15; *G.A.N.* to 9/15; *10* to 2/16; *6* to 6/16; *3* to 10/16; *1* to 12/16; *3* to 2/17; *1* to 3/17; *3* to 5/17; *6* to 8/17; *3* to 1/18; became 1 Foot Cavalry 10/1/18 (see below) |
| **82** | | **W. Front**: *G.D.T.* to 10/14; *2* to 6/15; *Disbanded* 23/6/15 |
| **83** | | **W. Front**: *G.M.P.* to 11/18 |
| **84** | | **W. Front**: *G.D.Q.* to 10/14; *2* in 10/14; *10* to 7/15; *Disbanded* 7/7/15 |
| **85** | | **W. Front**: *G.M.P.* to 12/14; *6* to 6/15; *Disbanded* 14/6/15 |
| **86** | | **W. Front**: *G.M.P.* to 12/14; *2* to 6/15; *Disbanded* 18/6/15 |
| **87** <br> (Active Div. from 4/17†) | | **W. Front**: *Côtes* to 9/14; *Havre* to 10/14; *Dunkirk* and *10* in 10/14; *D.A.B.* to 11/14; *D.A.B.* to 5/15; *G.P.N.* to 6/15; *G.A.N.* to 6/16; *10* in 6/16; *3* to 10/16; *1* to 3/17; *3* to 4/17; *7* to 5/17; *3* to 6/17; *6* to 12/17; *4* to 4/18; *6* and *5* in 4/18; *1* to 6/18; *10* to 8/18; *7* in 4/18; *4* |
| **88** <br> (Active Div. from 3/17†) | | **W. Front**: *G.D.T.* to 10/14; *2* to 11/14; *10* to 3/16; *7* to 4/16; *D.A.L.* to 10/16; *1* to 10/16; *D.A.L.* to 1/17; *8* to 8/17; *6*; *Disbanded* 12/17 |
| **89** | | **W. Front**: *G.M.P.* to 10/14; *G.P.N.* and *Gp. Bidon* in 10/14; *D.A.B.* to 11/14; *8* to 4/15; *D.A.B.* in 4/15; *6* to 8/15; *5* to 6/17; *Disbanded* 17/6/17 |
| **90** | | Never became active; *Disbanded* 9/14 |
| **91** | | **W. Front**: *Alpes* in 8/14; *Intérieur* to 9/14; *G.M.P.* to 10/14; *4* to 6/15; *Disbanded* 15/6/15 |

**\* 51 to 75 Divisions were Reserve Divisions formed upon mobilisation.**

**† The appelation 'active' denoted an official, usually very belated, recognition that the division was fit for front-line service.**

## INFANTRY DIVISIONS continued

### TERRITORIAL DIVISIONS continued

| DIVISION | FORMED | COMBAT RECORD |
|---|---|---|
| **92** | 8/14 | **W. Front**: *G.M.P.* to 10/14; *10* to 7/15; *Disbanded* 7/7/15 |
| **93** | — | **Not formed** |
| **94** | 9/14 | Never became active; *Disbanded* 10/14 |
| **95** | 9/14 | *Formation terminated* 3/10/14 |
| **96** | 10/14 | **W. Front**: *4* to 6/15; *Disbanded* 15/6/15 |
| **97** (Active from 4/17†) | 10/14 | **W. Front**: *G.M.P.* to 9/15; *5* to 1/17; *6* to 4/17; *2* to 8/17; *4* to 1/18; became 2 Foot Cavalry 19/1/18 |
| **98** | — | **Not formed** |
| **99** | 2/15 | **W. Front**: *G.M.P.* to 8/15; *6* to 8/16; *Disbanded* 13/8/16 |
| **100** | 2/15 | **W. Front**: *G.M.P.* to 9/15; *Gp. Pétain* in 9/15; *2* to 10/15; *4* to 8/16; *3* to 9/16; *6* to 12/16; *10* to 1/17; *Disbanded* 5/1/17 |
| **101** | 5/15 | **W. Front**: *Intérieur* to 8/15; *G.M.P.* to 10/15; *R.F.V.* in 10/15; *1* to 10/16; *2* to 11/16; *Disbanded* 26/11/16 |
| **102** | 5/15 | **W. Front**: *Intérieur* to 7/15; *G.M.P.* to 10/15; *6* to 5/16; *Disbanded* 1/5/16 |
| **103** | 8/15 | **W. Front**: *Intérieur* to 9/15; *G.M.P.* to 10/15; *6* to 3/16; *Disbanded* 1/3/16 |
| **104** | 8/15 | **W. Front**: *G.M.P.* to 10/15; *6* to 4/16; *10* to 11/16; *Disbanded* 5/11/16 |
| **105** | 8/15 | **W. Front**: (Formed from Groupement Sud de la Défense Mobile de Belfort – f. 10/14); *7* to 3/16; *Became 133 Inf. Div.* 20/3/16 |
| **106-119** | — | **Not formed** |
| **120** | 6/15 | **W. Front**: *2* to 7/15; *5* to 2/16; *2* to 3/16; *10* to 6/16; *3* to 8/16; *10* to 11/16; *D.A.L.* to 12/16; *1* to 3/17; *3* to 6/17; *2* to 5/18; *5* to 8/18; *2* to 9/18; *4* |
| **121** | 6/15 | **W. Front**: *6* to 4/16; *5* to 5/16; *6* to 8/16; *10* to 10/16; *1* to 3/17; *3* to 8/17; *10* to 10/17; *6* to 4/18; *D.A.N.* to 6/18; *3* to 9/18; *1* in 9/18; *10* to 10/18; *3* |
| **122** (Div. Tassin, then Guérin to 6/15) | 12/14 | **W. Front**: *5* to 10/15; *Intérieur* to 11/15<br>**Macedonia**: *A.O.* to 8/16; *A.F.O.* to 9/16; *C.A.A.* to 11/18 |
| **123** | 6/15 | **W. Front**: *5* to 12/15; *2* to 1/16; *5* to 5/16; *2* to 8/17; *4* to 9/17; *8* to 6/18; *3* to 9/18; *1* |
| **124** | | **W. Front**: *4* to 10/15; *2* to 1/16; *4* to 5/16; *2* to 6/16; *4* to 10/16; *5* to 11/16; *10* to 1/17; *3* to 2/17; *2* to 5/17; *4* |
| **125** | | **W. Front**: *3* to 1/16; *2* to 8/16; *4* in 8/16; *6* to 11/16; *4* to 12/16; *5* to 4/17; *10* to 10/17; *6* to 4/18; *3* to 6/18; *6* to 7/18; *9 and 5* in 7/18; *8* to 9/18; *4* to 11/18; *5* |
| **126** | | **W. Front**: *3* to 8/15; *Gp. Pétain* and *6* in 8/15; *5* to 12/15; *2* to 1/16; *4* to 5/16; *2* to 8/17; *4* to 10/17; *8* to 6/18; *3* to 7/18; *1* |
| **127** | | **W. Front**: *1* to 9/15; *4* to 6/16; *2* to 7/16; *5* to 9/16; *6* to 12/16; *5* to 1/17; *6* to 5/17; *7* to 3/18; *1* to 5/18; *2* to 7/18; *10* to 10/18; *3* to 11/18; *8* |
| **128** | | **W. Front**: *1* to 7/15; *3* to 10/15; *1* in 10/15; *D.A.L.* to 6/16; *2* to 7/16; *1* to 9/16; *2* to 3/17; *4* to 8/17; *2* to 12/17; *8* to 5/18; *5, 1, 3* and *6* to 6/18; *10* to 9/18; *G.A.P.* to 10/18; *6* |
| **129** | | **W. Front**: *7* to 8/15; *D.A.L.* to 9/15; *4* to 10/15; *D.A.L.* to 6/16; *2* to 7/16; *1* to 10/16; *D.A.L.* to 11/16; *10* to 1/17; *8* to 5/17; *6* to 7/17; *3* to 8/17; *6* to 11/17; *G.Q.G.* and *6* to 12/17; *3* in 7/17; *7* to 3/18; *5* to 4/18; *10* in 4/18; *D.A.N.* to 6/18; *3* to 9/18; *8* |
| **130** | 7/15 | **W. Front**: *10* to 3/16; *D.A.L.* to 6/16; *2* to 7/16; *4* in 7/16; *2* to 1/17; *8* to 7/17; *10* to 9/17; *3*; *Disbanded* 11/17 |
| **131** | 7/15 | **W. Front**: *10, 2* and *3* in 7/15; *2* to 7/16; *1* to 10/16; *D.A.L.* to 1/17; *8* to 4/17; *4* to 5/17; *2* to 4/18; *1* to 5/18; *10* in 6/18; *2* to 7/18; *5* to 8/18; *7* to 9/18; *8* |

| DIVISION | FORMED | COMBAT RECORD |
|---|---|---|
| **132** (Div. de Marche de Verdun to 8/15) | 9/14 | **W. Front**: *3* to 1/15; *1* to 8/15; *R.F.V.* to 2/16; *2* to 6/16; *6* to 8/16; *10* to 11/16; *3* to 2/17; *2* to 4/17; *4* to 8/18; *1* to 5/18; *10* to 9/18; *3* and *1* in 9/18; *10* to 10/18; *G.A.F.* in 10/18; *6* |
| **133** | 3/16 | **W. Front**: (f. from 105 Div: see above) *7* to 9/16; *2* to 2/17; *4* to 3/17; *6* to 5/17; *1* to 12/17; *C.S.N.* to 3/18; *1* to 4/18; *5, A.W.* and *G.Q.G.* in 4/18; *D.A.N.* to 5/18; *7* to 6/18; *6* and *Gp. Margin* in 6/18; *3* to 8/18; *1* |
| **134** | 8/16 | **W. Front**: *7* to 6/17; *4* to 8/17; *5* to 10/18; *4* |
| **135-150** | — | **Not formed** |
| **151** | 4/15 | **W. Front**: *2* to 8/15; *6* and *Gp. Pétain* to 9/15; *2* to 1/16; *4* to 5/16; *2* to 8/16; *5* to 7/17; *3* in 7/17; *10* to 9/17; *6* to 6/18; *10* in 6/18; *7* to 8/18; *4* to 10/18; *5* |
| **152** | | **W. Front**: *Intérieur* and *10* in 4/15; *D.A.B.* to 5/15; *G.P.N.* to 8/15; *10* to 4/16; *6* in 4/16; *9* to 9/16; *6* to 12/16; *10* to 2/17; *4* to 3/17; *10* to 4/17; *5* to 8/17; *8* to 3/18; *1* |
| **153** Division d'Afrique | | **W. Front**: *Intérieur* and *10* in 4/15; *D.A.B.* to 5/15; *G.P.N.* to 6/15; *10* to 7/15; *D.A.L.* to 9/15; *2* to 12/15; *D.A.L.* to 2/16; *2* to 4/16; *6* to 12/16; *D.A.L.* to 1/17; *8* in 1/17; *6* to 6/17; *8* to 12/17; *2* to 3/18; *5* to 5/18; *10* to 7/18; *1* to 8/18; *3* to 9/18; *5* to 10/18; *1* |
| **154** | | **W. Front**: *4* and *2* in 4/15; *6* to 9/15; *10* to 12/15; *7* to 4/16; *2* to 8/16; *4* to 12/16; *2* to 1/17; *3* to 3/17; *10* to 8/17; *6* to 11/17; *3* to 1/18; *6* to 2/18; *7* to 3/18; *5* and *4* in 4/18; *D.A.N.* to 5/18; *4* in 5/18; *5* to 6/18; *8* to 9/18; *4* to 10/18; *7* |
| **155** | | *Disbanded* 13/4/15 |
| **156** (2 Div. d'Inf. du C.E.O.* 4/15–10/15) | 3/15 | **W. Front**: *Intérieur* to 4/15<br>**Gallipoli**: *C.E.O.* to 10/15<br>**Macedonia**: *A.O.* to 8/16; *A.F.O.* |
| **157** | 4/15 | **W. Front**: *Intérieur* to 9/15; *6* in 9/15; *4* to 10/15; *7* to 6/17; *5* to 3/18; *6* to 6/18; *2* to 9/18; *4* to 10/18; *7* |
| **158** | 8/15 | **W. Front**: *Intérieur* to 2/16; *G.M.P.* to 3/16; *6* to 4/16; *10* to 8/16; *5* to 1/17; *6* to 7/17; *10* to 8/17; *3* to 11/17; *Disbanded* 5/11/17 |
| **159-160** | — | **Not formed** |
| **161** | 11/16 | **W. Front**: *7* to 7/17; *10* to 10/17; *6* to 4/18; *4* to 10/18; *7* |
| **162** | 10/16 | **W. Front**: *4* to 11/16; *6* to 1/17; *5* to 4/17; *10* to 5/17; *1* to 6/17; *10* to 7/17; *1* to 12/17; *6* to 3/18; *1* to 5/18; *10* to 10/18; *7* |
| **163** | 11/16 | **W. Front**: *4* to 12/16; *1* to 1/17; *2* to 7/17; *4* to 8/17; *2* to 10/17; *4* to 3/18; *1* to 5/18; *4* |
| **164** | 11/16 | **W. Front**: *7* to 3/17; *3* to 4/17; *10* to 7/17; *5* to 11/17; *2* to 12/17; *8* to 5/18; *6* to 9/18; *5* to 10/18; *6* |
| **165** | 12/16 | **W. Front**: *5* in 12/16; *4* to 1/17; *5* to 4/17; *10* to 5/17; *5* to 6/17; *4* to 7/17; *2* to 10/17; *8* to 3/18; *6* and *3* in 4/18; *1* to 6/18; *3* to 9/18; *8* |
| **166** | 1/17 | **W. Front**: *5* in 1/17; *6* to 6/17; *4* to 7/17; *7* to 3/18; *1* to 4/18; *8* to 6/18; *3* to 7/18; *1* |
| **167** | 12/16 | **W. Front**: *D.A.L.* to 1/17; *8* to 4/17; *5* to 8/17; *6* to 12/17; *7* to 5/18; *6* to 7/18; *4* to 10/18; *5* |
| **168** | | **W. Front**: *D.A.L.* to 1/17; *8* to 6/17; *6* to 12/17; *D.A.N.* to 6/18; *10* in 7/18; *5* to 10/18; *1* |
| **169** | | **W. Front**: *10* to 1/17; *4* to 2/18; *2* in 2/18; *4* to 3/18; *3* to 8/18; *1* |
| **170** | | **W. Front**: *7* to 5/17; *6* to 11/17; *7* to 5/18; *5* in 5/18; *10* in 6/18; *4* to 10/18; *5* |

### COLONIAL DIVISIONS

| DIVISION | FORMED | COMBAT RECORD |
|---|---|---|
| **1 Moroccan** (as *Division de Maroc* to 8/18) | 8/14 | **W. Front**: *Intérieur* and *4* in 8/14; *9* to 10/14; *5* to 4/15; *10* to 7/15; *7* to 9/15; *4* to 10/15; *6* to 1/16; *6* to 4/16; *10* to 6/16; *6* to 7/16; *3* to 10/16; *10* to 1/17; *3* to 3/17; *4* to 6/17; *5* to 7/17; *4* in 7/17; *9* to 9/17; *8* to 1/18; *1* to 3/18; *1* to 5/18; *5* in 5/18; *6* to 6/18; *10* to 7/18; *1* to 8/18; *10* to 9/18; *8* |

† The appelation 'active' denoted an official, usually very belated, recognition that the division was fit for front-line service.

* Also known as the Division de Serbie.

## INFANTRY DIVISIONS continued

### COLONIAL DIVISIONS continued

| DIVISION | FORMED | COMBAT RECORD |
|---|---|---|
| **2 Moroccan** (ex-65 Inf. Div.) | 8/18 | **W. Front**: *8* and *3* in 8/18; *10* to 9/18; *5* in 9/18; *4* to 10/18; *7* |
| **1 Colonial** | — | **Not formed** |
| **2 Colonial** | 8/14 | **W. Front**: *4* to 6/15; *10* to 7/15; *4* to 8/15; *Gp. Pétain* to 9/15; *2* to 12/15; *6* to 1/16; *2* in 1/16; *6* to 8/16; *3* to 10/16; *6* to 11/16; *6* to 5/17; *7* to 7/17; *10* to 10/17; *1* to 12/17; *5* to 3/18; *6* to 5/18; *5* |
| **3 Colonial** | 8/14 | **W. Front**: *4* to 5/15; *6* to 6/15; *10* to 7/15; *2* in 7/15; *4* to 8/15; *1* to 9/15; *2* to 12/15; *6* to 1/16; *2* in 1/16; *6* to 8/16; *3* in 8/16; *4* to 10/16; *6* to 11/16; *3* to 3/17; *1* to 4/17; *6* to 5/17; *7* to 7/17; *10* to 10/17; *6* to 11/17; *5* 11/18; *8* |
| **4–9 Colonial** | — | **Not formed** |
| **10 Colonial** | 5/15 | **W. Front**: *4* to 10/15; *6* to 1/16; *2* to 2/16; *6* to 4/16; *10* to 6/16; *3* to 8/16; *10* to 1/17; *6* to 4/17; *1* to 5/17; *8* to 9/17; *2* to 3/18; *8* to 5/18; *6* to 71/18; *9* and *5* in 7/18; *2* to 9/18; *A.U.S.* |
| **11 Colonial** | 1/17 | **Macedonia**: *A.F.O.* |
| **12-14 Colonial** | — | **Not formed** |
| **15 Colonial** | 6/15 | **W. Front**: *3* and *4* to 7/15; *3* to 8/15; *4* to 10/15; *6* to 1/16; *2* to 2/16; *6* to 4/16; *10* to 6/16; *3* to 7/16; *10* to 1/17; *6* to 4/17; *1* to 5/17; *8* to 9/17; *2* to 1/18; *1* to 3/18; *8* to 4/18; *7* in 4/18; *1* to 8/18; *2* to 9/18; *A.U.S.* |
| **16 Colonial** | 6/15 | **W. Front**: *1* to 9/15; *2* to 2/16; *6* to 8/16; *3* to 10/16; *6* to 11/16; *Intérieur* to 12/16 **Macedonia**: *C.A.A.* to 3/17; *A.F.O.* to ?/18; *C.A.A.* to 10/18; *Danube* |
| **17 Colonial** (I Div. d'Inf. du C.E.O. to 1/16) | 2/15 | **Gallipoli**: *C.E.O./C.E.D.* to 1/16 **Macedonia**: *A.O.* to 8/16; *C.A.A.* to 9/16; *A.F.O.* to 10/16; *C.A.A.* to 12/16; *A.F.O.* to 8/18; *C.A.A.* to 10/18; *A.F.O.* |

### OTHER INFANTRY DIVISIONS

| | | |
|---|---|---|
| **'B'** | | *See 77 Inf. Div.* |
| **Barbot** | | *As above* |
| **1 C.E.O.** | | *See 17 Colonial Div.* |
| **2 C.E.O.** | | *See 156 Inf. Div.* |
| **Guérin** | | *See 122 Inf. Div.* |
| **Tassin** | | *See 122 Inf. Div.* |
| **Vassart** | | *See 76 Inf. Div.* |
| **Verdun** | | *See 132 Inf. Div.* |

## CAVALRY DIVISIONS (total=12 [+ 3 temporary])

### REGULAR DIVISIONS

| DIVISION | FORMED | COMBAT RECORD |
|---|---|---|
| **1** | 8/14 | **W. Front**: *G.Q.G., G.M.P., 5* and *6* to 9/14; *2* to 10/14; *10* to 11/14; *8* to 12/14; *10* to 1/15; *2* to 2/15; *4* to 4/15; *1* in 4/15; *2* to 7/15; *10* to 2/16; *6* to 11/16; *1* to 3/17; *3* in 3/17; *10* to 4/17; *3* to 4/18; *5, 6* and *4* to 6/18; *6* to 8/18; *5* to 11/18; *1* |
| **2** | | **W. Front**: *2* to 9/14; *1* to 1/15; *G.P.E.* to 3/15; *D.A.L.* to 9/15; *4* to 10/15; *7* to 6/16; *10* to 7/16; *6* in 7/16; *10* to 11/16; *5* to 1/17; *6* to 2/17; *10* to 4/17; *5* to 1/18; *4* to 2/18; *Intérieur* to 4/18; *1, 10, G.Q.G.* and *G.A.N.* to 5/18; *5* in 5/18; *6* to 6/18; *3* to 7/18; *1* and *5* in 7/18; *10* to 8/18; *1* to 9/18; *G.A.F.* |

| DIVISION | FORMED | COMBAT RECORD |
|---|---|---|
| **3** | 8/14 | **W. Front**: *G.Q.G., G.M.P., 5, 6* and *2* to 10/14; *10* to 11/14; *D.A.B.* in 11/14; *8* to 12/14; *10* to 1/15; *2* to 2/15; *6* to 4/15; *D.A.L.* to 5/15; *2* to 7/15; *10* to 2/16; *6* to 11/16; *1* to 3/17; *10* to 4/17; *3* to 2/18; *6* and *3* in 2/18; *Intérieur* to 4/18; *1, 10, G.Q.G.* and *D.A.N.* to 5/18; *5, 10* and *6* to 6/18; *3, 6* and *5* to 7/18; *4, 9, 5* and *6* to 8/18; *4* to 10/18; *5* |
| **4** | | **W. Front**: *5* to 10/14; *10* in 10/14; *D.A.B.* to 11/14; *8* to 2/15; *10* to 4/15; *2* to 5/15; *5* to 9/15; *4* to 10/15; *5* in 10/15; *4* to 6/16; *10* to 7/16; *6* to 8/16; *10* to 12/16; *5* to 1/17; *6* to 2/17; *10* to 4/17; *1* to 5/17; *5* to 11/17; *G.Q.G.* and *3* to 12/17; *5* to 1/18; *4* to 2/18; *Intérieur* to 3/18; *1* to 4/18; *5* in 4/18; *5, 6, 3* and *1* to 7/18; *10* to 8/18; *1* to 9/18; *G.A.F.* |
| **5** | | **W. Front**: *G.Q.G., 5* and *6* to 9/14; *2* to 10/14; *10* in 10/14; *D.A.B.* to 11/14; *8* to 2/15; *10* to 9/15; *6* in 9/15; *4* to 10/15; *5* in 10/15; *4* to 8/16; *D.A.L.* to 1/17; *7* to 3/17; *6* to 4/17; *3* to 11/17; *G.Q.G.* to 12/17; *3* to 1/18; *6* to 2/18; *3* to 3/18; *1* to 4/18; *5* in 4/18; *6* to 5/18; *4* in 5/18; *6* to 6/18; *4, 5, 9* and *6* in 7/18; *4* to 9/18; *A.U.S.* to 10/18; *5* |
| **6** | | **W. Front**: *1* to 9/14; *9* in 9/14; *4* to 10/14; *10* in 10/14; *D.A.B.* to 11/14; *6* to 1/15; *D.A.V.* to 4/15; *7* to 5/15; *10* to 6/15; *7* to 8/15; *Gp. Pétain* to 9/15; *2* to 10/15; *D.A.L.* to 12/16; *7* to 3/17; *5* to 1/18; *4* to 3/18; *1, 10* and *G.Q.G.* in 4/18; *D.A.N.* to 5/18; *5* in 5/18; *6* to 6/18; *3* to 7/18; *1, 6, 10* and *5* in 7/18; *6* to 8/18; *1* to 9/18; *G.A.F.* |
| **7** | | **W. Front**: *3* to 9/14; *1* to 10/14; *2* and *10* in 10/14; *D.A.B.* to 11/14; *8* to 2/15; *10* to 9/15; *4* to 10/15; *5* in 10/15; *4* to 7/16; *10* to 11/16; *5* to 1/17; *6* to 2/17; *10* to 4/17; *1* to 5/17; *5* to 7/17; *Disbanded 23/7/17* |
| **8** | | **W. Front**: *1* and *Alsace* to 9/14; *5* and *6* in 9/14; *2* to 12/14; *3* to 1/15; *4* to 5/15; *10* to 6/15; *4* to 9/15; *Gp. Pétain* in 9/15; *2* to 10/15; *D.A.L.* to 8/16; *Disbanded 14/8/16* |
| **9** | | **W. Front**: *4* to 9/14; *9* to 10/14; *5* and *2* in 10/14; *D.A.B.* to 11/14; *8* to 12/14; *10* to 1/15; *4* to 5/15; *2* to 6/15; *7* to 8/15; *Gp. Pétain* to 9/15; *2* to 10/15; *D.A.L.* to 6/16; *Disbanded 1/6/16* |
| **10** | | **W. Front**: *2* to 9/14; *5* and *6* in 9/14; *2* to 10/14; *10* to 11/14; *D.A.B.* in 11/14; *1* to 12/14; *D.A.V.* to 4/15; *7* to 6/16; *Disbanded 1/6/16* |

### DISMOUNTED DIVISIONS

| | | |
|---|---|---|
| **1 Foot Cavalry** | 1/18 | **W. Front**: (f. from 81 Div.: see above); *6* to 2/18; *3* to 3/18; *6* to 4/18; *3* to 6/18; *4* |
| **2 Foot Cavalry** | 1/18 | **W. Front**: (f. from 97 Div.: see above); *4* to 3/18; *1* to 4/18; *6* to 6/18; *10, 6* and *3* in 6/18; *2* to 8/18; *A.U.S.* to 11/18; *4* |

### TEMPORARY DIVISIONS (PROVISIONAL)

| | | |
|---|---|---|
| **Cornulier-Lucinière** | 8/14 | **W. Front**: *6* to 9/14; *Disbanded 8/9/14; Reformed 7/11/16; 10* to 27/11/16; *Disbanded* |
| **Beaudemoulin** | 9/14 | **W. Front**: *G.Q.G.* to 10/14; *Disbanded 9/10/14* |
| **Brécart** | 4/17 | **W. Front**: *3* to 5/17; *Disbanded 11/5/17* |

## Germany

| INFANTRY DIVISIONS (total = 241) | | |
|---|---|---|

| DIVISION | FORMED | COMBAT RECORD |
|---|---|---|
| **1 Guards** | pre-war | **W. Front**: Belgium-Marne to 9/14; Artois/Flanders to 1/15; Champagne to 3/15; Alsace to 4/15; *see below*; Artois to 7/16; Somme to 4/17; CdD in 4/17; Argonne to ?/17; *see below*; Champagne to 1/18; Somme to 4/18; Aisne to 6/18; Marne to 9/18; Argonne to 10/18; Champagne<br>**Russia**: Poland to 9/15; *see above*; Galicia and Riga to 10/17; (see above) |
| **1 Guards Reserve** | 8/14 | **W. Front**: Belgium to 9/14; *see below*; Flanders to 5/16; Artois to 7/16; Somme to 9/16; Flanders to 11/17; Somme to 3/17; Artois to 6/17; Flanders in 6/17; Artois to 2/18; Somme to 4/18; Artois to end<br>**Russia**: Poland to 10/15; *see above* |
| **1** | pre-war | **Russia**: E. Prussia to 12/14; Poland to 2/15; Galicia to 2/16; *see below*; Bukovina to 12/17; *see below*<br>**W. Front**: Verdun to 7/16; *see above*; Verdun to 3/18; Somme to 5/18; Champagne to 10/18; Ardennes |
| **1 Reserve** | 8/14 | **Russia**: E. Prussia to ?/14; Poland to 5/15; Lithuania to 7/16; Galicia to 9/16; Lithuania to 10/16; *see below*<br>**W. Front**: Champagne to 4/18; Picardy |
| **1 Landwehr** (orig. 10 L/wehr to 7/15)* | 8/14 | **Russia**: E. Prussia to 10/15; Lithuania to 8/16; Pripet to 2/18; *see below*<br>**W. Front**: Flanders to 7/18; Alsace to 10/18; Lorraine |
| **1 Bavarian** | pre-war | **W. Front**: Lorraine to 9/14; Somme to 10/15; Artois to 5/16; Verdun to 7/16; St Mihiel to 10/16; Somme to 10/16; St Mihiel to 5/17; Picardy to 7/17; Champagne to 12/17; Argonne to 3/18; Somme to 4/18; Champagne |
| **1 Bavarian Reserve** | 8/14 | **W. Front**: Lorraine to 9/14; Artois to 8/16; Somme to 9/16; Aisne to 12/16; Some to 2/17; Artois to 10/17; Flanders to 4/18; Artois to 9/18; Flanders |
| **1 Bavarian Landwehr** (orig. L/wehr Div. Wening to 9/14) | 8/14 | **W. Front**: Lorraine (Chateau-Salins) |
| **1 Marine** | 8/14 | **W. Front**: Flanders coast |
| **2 Guards** | pre-war | **W. Front**: Belgium-Marne to 9/14; Artois/Flanders to 3/15; Alsace to 4/15; *see below*; Flanders to 10/15; Picardy to 8/16; Somme to 4/17; CdD to 7/17; Argonne to 7/17; *see below*; Aisne to 10/17; St Mihiel/Metz to 3/18; Artois to 3/18; Picardy to 5/18; Aisne to 6/18; Marne to 7/18; Somme to 10/18; Flanders<br>**Russia**: Galicia to 9/15; *see above*; Galicia to 8/17; Riga to 9/17; *see above* |
| **2 Guards Reserve** | 8/14 | **W. Front**: Belgium to the Marne to 9/14; Champagne to 2/15; Picardy/Argonne to 5/15; Artois to 5/16; Somme to 3/17; Hindenburg Line to 6/17; Flanders to 2/18; Artois to 10/18; Flanders (?) |
| **2** | pre-war | **Russia**: E. Prussia to 11/14; Poland to 2/15; E. Prussia/Lithuania to 2/17; *see below*; Lithuania to 11/17; *see below*<br>**W. Front**: Flanders to 6/17; *see above*; Champagne to 4/18; Picardy |
| **2 Landwehr** | 8/14 | **W. Front**: Argonne |
| **2 Bavarian** | pre-war | **W. Front**: Lorraine to 9/14; Somme to 10/15; Artois to 5/16; Verdun 7/16; Lorraine to 10/16; Somme to 12/16; St Mihiel to 5/17; CdD to 6/17; Argonne to 11/17; Champagne to 1/18; Lorraine to 3/18; Somme to 5/18; Flanders to 6/18; Somme in 6/18; Champagne |
| **2 Bavarian Landwehr** | 12/16 | **Russia**: Latvia to 2/18; Ukraine |
| **2 Marine** | 11/14 | **W. Front**: Flanders coast |

| DIVISION | FORMED | COMBAT RECORD |
|---|---|---|
| **3 Guards** | 8/14 | **W. Front**: Flanders to 27/8/14; *see below*; Champagne to 6/16; Artois to 7/16; Somme to 8/16; Flanders to 9/16; *see below*; Alsace to 1/17; Lorraine to 4/17; Artois to 6/17; Flanders to 8/17; Alsace to 10/17; Flanders to 11/17; Artois to 3/18; Somme to 4/18; Artois to 5/18; Lorraine to 6/18; Champagne to 9/18; Argonne<br>**Russia**: Galicia to 11/16; *see above* |
| **3** | pre-war | **W. Front**: Belgium-Marne to 9/14; Aisne to 11/14; Flanders in 11/14; *see below*<br>**Russia**: E. Prussia/Poland to 5/15; Poland only to ? subsequent history uncertain but Russian Front to end. |
| **3 Landwehr** | 8/14 | **Russia**: Poland |
| **3 Bavarian** | pre-war | **W. Front**: Lorraine to 9/14; Somme in 9/14; Flanders to 10/15; Artois to 8/16; Somme to 9/16; Artois to 6/17; Flanders in 6/17; Lorraine to 10/17; Aisne to 1/18; Picardy |
| **3 Reserve** | 8/14 | **Russia**: E. Prussia to 5/15; Poland/Lithuania to 5/17; *see below*<br>**W. Front**: Flanders to 6/17; Picardy to 8/17; Flanders 9/17; Alsace to 11/17; CdeD to 4/18; Picardy to 7/18; Champagne to 9/18; Somme in 9/18; Flanders |
| **3 Marine** | 4/17 | **W. Front**: Flanders coast to 3/18; Somme-Scarpe |
| **4 Guards** | 3/15 | **Russia**: Poland/Lithuania to 10/15; *see below*<br>**W. Front**: Artois to 12/15; Flanders to 7/16; Somme to 9/16; Flanders to 11/16; Somme to 3/17; Artois to 9/17; Flanders to 10/17; Artois to 2/18; Somme to 6/18; Lorraine to 7/18; Champagne to 10/18; Ardennes |
| **4** | pre-war | **W. Front**: Belgium-Marne to 9/14; Aisne to 10/14; Flanders to 11/14; *see below*; Ardennes to 11/15; Champagne to 4/16; Verdun to 5/17; Champagne to 10/17; Flanders to 3/18; Ancre to 4/18; Artois/Flanders<br>**Russia**: Poland to 2/15; Galicia to ?/15; Poland to 9/15; *see above* |
| **4 Ersatz** | 8/14 | **W. Front**: Lorraine to 9/14; Flanders to 9/16; Somme to 10/16; Flanders to 12/16; Somme to 3/17; Hindenburg Line to 4/17; Artois to 5/17; *see below*; Artois to 4/18; Lorraine to 6/18; Champagne to 8/18; Artois/Flanders<br>**Russia**: Galicia to 12/17; *see above* |
| **4 Landwehr** | 8/14 | **Russia**: Poland to 4/18; Ukraine |
| **4 Bavarian** | pre-war | **W. Front**: Lorraine to 9/14; Somme to 10/14; Flanders to 9/15; Artois to 8/16; Somme to 9/16; Flanders to 10/17; Lorraine to 3/18; Flanders to 9/18; Champagne |
| **5 Guards** | 2/17 | **W. Front**: Champagne to 7/17; CdD to 1/18; Somme to 5/18; Champagne to 8/18; Flanders in 8/18; Picardy to 9/18; Argonne |
| **5** | pre-war | **W. Front**: Belgium-Marne to 9/14; Aisne to 7/15; Artois to 9/15; Champagne to 12/15; Flanders to 2/16; Verdun to 7/16; Somme to 8/16; Champagne to 12/16; Verdun in 12/16; Alsace to 4/17; Champagne to 6/17; Ardennes to 7/17; Champagne in 7/17; *see below*; Picardy to 3/18; Somme/Avre to 4/18; Champagne to 9/18; Ardennes<br>**Russia**: Galicia to 10/17; *see below*<br>**Italy**: Isonzo-Piave to 1/18; *see W. Front* |
| **5 Reserve** | 8/14 | **W. Front**: Belgium to 12/14; *see below*; Ardennes to 5/17; CdD to 11/17; Picardy to 3/18; Oise/Avre to 6/18; Somme<br>**Russia**: Poland to 4/17; *see above* |
| **5 Ersatz** (Basedow Div. to 6/16) | 9/15 | **W. Front**: Flanders to 10/16; Somme to 11/16; Champagne to 12/16; *see below*<br>**Russia**: Latvia |
| **5 Landwehr** (Waldow Div. to 1/15) | 8/14 | **W. Front**: Lorraine: Woevre to 7/16; St Mihiel |
| **5 Bavarian** | pre-war | **W. Front**: Lorraine to 10/15; Champagne to 12/15; Lorraine to 7/16; Artois to 8/16; Somme to 9/16; Artois to 7/17; Flanders to 3/18; Canal du Nord to 9/18; Somme |
| **5 Bavarian Reserve** | 8/14 | **W. Front**: Alsace to 9/14; Artois to 8/16; Somme to 9/16; Aisne to 12/16; Somme to 2/17; Artois to 4/17; Aisne in 4/17; St Mihiel to 10/17; Flanders/Artois to 4/18; Ancre to 7/18; Alsace to 9/18; Artois in 9/18; Argonne |

* For five months in 1915 there seem to have been two 10 *Landwehr* Divisions.

| INFANTRY DIVISIONS continued | | |
|---|---|---|

| DIVISION | FORMED | COMBAT RECORD |
|---|---|---|
| **6** | pre-war | **W. Front**: Belgium-Marne to 9/14; Aisne to 6/15; Artois to 9/15; *see below*; Picardy to 2/16; Verdun to 3/16; Alsace to 4/16; Verdun to 5/16; Champagne to 10/16; Somme to 11/16; Argonne to 4/17; Alsace in 4/17; Champagne to 5/17; Alsace to 7/17; *see Russia below*; Aisne to 2/18; Flanders to 3/18; Somme to 4/18; Champagne to 8/18; Artois **Serbia**: to 12/15; *see above* **Russia**: Galicia to 10/17; *see W. Front above* |
| **6 Reserve** | 8/14 | **W. Front**: Verdun to 12/14; *see below*; Lorraine to 9/17; *see below*; Somme/Avre to 8/18; *Disbanded* **Russia**: Poland to 9/15; Latvia to 5/17; *see above*; Galicia to 3/18; *see above* |
| **6 Bavarian** | pre-war | **W. Front**: Lorraine to 9/14; St Mihiel to 6/16; Verdun to 8/16; Argonne in 8/16; Somme to 10/16; Artois to 9/17; Flanders to 10/17; Artois to 3/18; Somme to 4/18; Flanders in 4/18; Verdun to 5/18; Somme |
| **6 Bavarian Reserve** | 9/14 | **W. Front**: Flanders/Artois to 9/16; Somme to 10/16; Artois to 6/17; Flanders to 8/17; Alsace to 10/17; Picardy to 4/18; Somme in 4/18; Aisne to 7/18; Artois to 9/18; Flanders |
| **6 Bavarian Landwehr** | 8/14 | **W. Front**: Alsace to 10/14; Flanders to 2/15; split to 4/15; Alsace |
| **7** | pre-war | **W. Front**: Belgium to Marne to 9/14; Aisne in 9/14; Artois to 7/16; Somme in 7/16; Artois to 9/16; Somme to 10/16; Artois to 5/17; Flanders to 7/17; Alsace in 7/17; Artois to 9/17; Flanders to 6/18; Somme to 7/18; Champagne |
| **7 Reserve** | 8/14 | **W. Front**: Belgium-Marne to 9/14; Aisne to 9/15; Champagne to 5/16; Verdun to 7/16; Argonne to 9/16; Somme to 10/16; Argonne in 2/17; Verdun to 5/17; Champagne to 3/18; Somme to 4/18; Champagne to 8/18; Aisne to 9/18; Argonne |
| **7 Landwehr** | 1915 | **W. Front**: Alsace to 2/17; Lorraine to 5/17; *see below* **Russia**: Poland to 2/18; Ukraine |
| **8** | pre-war | **W. Front**: Belgium to Marne to 9/14; Aisne to 10/14; Artois to 7/16; Somme in 7/16; Artois to 9/16; Somme to 10/16; Artois to 8/17; Champagne to 9/17; Flanders/Artois to 9/18; Picardy |
| **8 Landwehr** | 2/15 | **W. Front**: Alsace to 1/17; Lorraine |
| **8 Ersatz** | 8/14 | **W. Front**: Lorraine to 8/16; Somme to 11/16; Lorraine to 5/17 [becomes 243 Div. see that entry] |
| **8 Bavarian Reserve** | 1/15 | **W. Front**: Alsace to 5/15; *see below*; Alsace to 7/16; Somme to 9/16; *see Rumania below*; Flanders to 4/18; Lorraine to 7/18; Champagne to 8/18; Ardennes **Russia**: Galicia to 7/15; *see above*; Galicia/Bukovina to 10/17; *see above* **Rumania**: to 7/17; *see above* |
| **9** | pre-war | **W. Front**: Lorraine to 9/16; Verdun to 11/16; Aisne to 2/17; Lorraine to 4/17; CdD to 12/17; Picardy to 3/18; Somme to 4/18; Picardy to 5/18; Aisne to 6/18; Champagne to 10/18; Picardy |
| **9 Reserve** | 8/14 | **W. Front**: Lorraine to 11/14; Flanders to 12/14; Lorraine to 2/16; Verdun to 4/16; Alsace to 6/16; Champagne to 9/16; Somme to 3/17; Artois to 6/17; Flanders to 9/17; Picardy to 3/18; Somme to 4/18; Artois |
| **9 Landwehr** | 2/15 | **W. Front**: Argonne |
| **9 Bavarian Reserve** | 10/16 | **W. Front**: Aisne to 12/16; Picardy to 1/17; Somme to 2/17; Aisne to 4/17; Lorraine to 8/17; Flanders in 8/17; Lorraine to 10/17; Flanders to 12/17; Picardy to 3/18; Somme/Avre to 5/18; Oise to 6/18; *Disbanded* |
| **10** | pre-war | **W. Front**: Luxembourg/Lorraine to 10/16; Verdun to 12/16; Lorraine to 4/17; Aisne/CdD to 12/15; Picardy to 3/18; Somme to 4/18; Picardy to 5/18; CdD to 6/18; Marne to 8/18; Lorraine |

| DIVISION | FORMED | COMBAT RECORD |
|---|---|---|
| **10 Reserve** | 8/14 | **W. Front**: Lorraine to 2/16; Verdun to 5/16; Alsace to 6/16; Champagne to 9/16; Somme to 10/16; Ardennes to 3/17; CdD to 4/17; Ardennes to 8/17; Champagne to 11/17; Aisne to 3/18; Somme to 4/18; Aisne/Vesle |
| **10 Ersatz** | 8/14 | **W. Front**: Lorraine to 9/16; Somme to 10/16; Champagne to 12/16; Verdun to 4/17; Champagne/Lorraine to 8/17; Flanders to 10/17; *see below*; Artois **Russia**: Galicia to ?/18; *see above* |
| **10 Landwehr** | 2/15 (2nd formation) | **Russia**: E. Prussia/Poland to 7/15; Lithuania to 7/16; Pripet to 12/17; *see below* **W. Front**: Lorraine to 6/18; Marne to 7/18; *Disbanded* |
| **10 Bavarian** | 3/15 | **W. Front**: Flanders to 5/15; Somme to 8/16; *see below*; Alsace to 6/17; Flanders to 10/17; *see below*; Lorraine to 5/18; Aisne/Marne to 8/18; *Disbanded* **Russia**: Galicia to 9/18; *see below*; Galicia to 5/18; *see above*; Poland to 11/17; *see above* **Rumania**: to 2/17; *see Russia above* |
| **11** | pre-war | **W. Front**: Luxembourg/Lorraine to 9/14; Argonne to 1/15; Champagne to 6/15; Artois to 10/15; Somme to 3/17; Hindenburg Line in 3/17; Artois to 4/17; Flanders to 6/17; Lorraine to 10/17; Champagne in 10/17; Flanders to 1/18; Champagne to 4/18; Somme/Picardy |
| **11 Reserve** | 8/14 | **W. Front**: Lorraine/Argonne to 2/16; Verdun to 6/16; Somme to 7/16; Flanders to 9/16; Somme to 11/16; Artois to 3/17; Picardy to 5/17; Artois to 11/17; Flanders |
| **11 Landwehr** (von Einem Div. to 3/15) | 8/14 | **Russia**: E. Prussia to 2/15; Poland/Lithuania to 1/18; Ukraine |
| **11 Bavarian** | 3/15 | **Russia**: Galicia to 6/15; Poland to 9/15; *see below*; Poland to 9/16; *see Rumania below* **Serbia**: to 11/15;(resting in Hungary to 2/16); *see below* **W. Front**: Belgium to 3/16; Verdun to 6/16; *see Russia above*; Alsace to 4/17; Aisne to 9/17; Ardennes to 10/17; Flanders to 10/17; St Mihiel to 1/18; Verdun to 4/18; Flanders in 4/18; Aisne to 8/18; Flanders **Rumania**: to 1/17; *see above* |
| **12** | pre-war | **W. Front**: Lorraine to 9/14; Champagne to 6/15; Artois to 10/15; Somme to 8/16; Artois to 12/16; Champagne in 12/16; *see below*; Flanders to 8/17; Alsace to 9/17; *see Italy below*; Lorraine to 2/18; Alsace to 3/18; Artois to 5/18; Flanders to 7/18; Artois **Russia**: Latvia to 5/17; *see above* **Italy**: Isonzo-Piave to 12/17; *see W. Front above* |
| **12 Reserve** | 8/14 | **W. Front**: Lorraine/Argonne to 3/16; Verdun to 5/16; Artois to 6/16; Somme to 8/16; Flanders to 9/16; Somme to 12/16; Artois/Picardy to 8/17; Flanders to 11/17; Flanders to 2/18; Artois |
| **12 Landwehr*** | 4/15 | **W. Front**: Alsace to 5/17; *see below*; split to c.10/18; Alsace **Russia**: Galicia to c.3/18; *see above* |
| **12 Bavarian** | 7/16 | **Rumania**: 10/16 to 4/18; *see below* **W. Front**: Aisne/Marne to 8/18; Flanders |
| **13** | pre-war | **W. Front**: Belgium-Marne to 9/14; Aisne to 10/14; Artois to 6/16; Somme to 9/16; Verdun to 5/17; Aisne to 10/17; Ardennes to 12/17; Verdun to 2/18; Flanders to 3/18; Somme/Avre to 8/18; Alsace to 10/18; Argonne |
| **13 Reserve** | 8/14 | **W. Front**: Belgium to 9/14; Aisne to 10/15; Flanders to 12/16; Verdun to 12/16; Champagne to 9/17; Verdun to 12/17; Champagne to 4/18; Flanders |
| **13 Landwehr** | 5/15 | **W. Front**: Lorraine to 2/17; Hindenburg Line to 3/18; Picardy to 6/18; Lorraine |
| **14** | pre-war | **W. Front**: Belgium-Marne to 9/14; Aisne to 10/14; Artois to 12/15; Tournai to 6/16; Verdun to 4/17; CdD to 10/17; St Mihiel to 4/18; Somme/Avre to 5/18; Aisne/Marne to 9/18; Picardy |
| **14 Reserve** | 8/14 | **W. Front**: Belgium to 9/14; Aisne to 11/15; Flanders to 12/15; Verdun to 12/16; Champagne to 10/17; Picardy to 5/18; Aisne/Marne to 7/18; Alsace to 9/18; Alsace to 10/18; Champagne |
| **14 Landwehr** | 7/15 | **Russia**: Poland to 2/18; Byelorussia to 5/18; *see below*; reformed 6/18 Byelorussia **W. Front**: Alsace in 5/18; *Disbanded*; *see above* |

* HQ to Finland 3/18 to command Baltic Division (see page 126).

## INFANTRY DIVISIONS continued

| DIVISION | FORMED | COMBAT RECORD |
|---|---|---|
| **14 Bavarian** | 8/16 | **W. Front**: Verdun to 12/16; Somme to 4/17; Artois in 4/17; Flanders in 4/17; *see below*; Champagne to 4/18; Somme/Avre to 9/18; *Disbanded* **Russia**: Poland to 8/17; Latvia to 10/17; Galicia to 12/17; *see above* |
| **15** | pre-war | **W. Front**: Luxembourg-Marne to 9/14; Champagne to 4/15; Artois to 6/15; Aisne to 7/16; Somme to 10/16; Aisne to 11/16; *see below*; CdD to 7/17; Lorraine to 9/17; Verdun to 10/17; Flanders to 3/18; Somme/Avre to 6/18; Picardy to 9/18; Argonne **Russia**: to 4/17; *see above* |
| **15 Reserve** | 8/14 | **W. Front**: Luxembourg-Marne to 9/14; Champagne to 10/15; Aisne to 7/16; Somme to 3/17; Hindenburg Line to 5/17; Artois in 5/17; *see below*; Verdun to 4/18; Artois **Russia**: Galicia to 12/17; *see above* |
| **15 Landwehr** | 3/15 | **W. Front**: Picardy to 3/17; Hindenburg Line in 3/17; *see below* **Russia**: Galicia to 3/18; Ukraine to 5/18; Caucasus |
| **15 Bavarian** | 12/16 | **W. Front**: (from 3/17) Flanders to 4/17; Lorraine to 5/17; Aisne to 7/17; Ardennes to 8/17; Verdun to 7/18; Aisne/Marne to 9/18; Argonne |
| **16** | pre-war | **W. Front**: Luxembourg-Marne to 9/14; Champagne to 4/15; Artois to 6/15; Aisne to 7/16; Somme to 9/16; Aisne to 10/16; Somme in 10/16; Aisne to 11/16; *see below*; Flanders to 4/18; Artois **Russia**: Galicia to 5/17; *see above* |
| **16 Reserve** | 8/14 | **W. Front**: Luxembourg-Marne to 9/14; Champagne to 10/15; Aisne to 10/16; Somme to 12/16; CdD to 4/17; Lorraine to 6/17; Alsace to 7/17; *see below*; Picardy to 3/18; Somme/Ancre to 5/18; Flanders **Russia**: Galicia to 11/17; *see above* |
| **16 Landwehr** (Königsberg Div. to 10/15) | 8/14 | **Russia**: E. Prussia/Lithuania to 3/18; Byelorussia/Ukraine to 9/18; Rumania (via Constantinople) |
| **16 Bavarian** | 1/17 | **W. Front**: Artois to 4/17; Flanders to 12/17; Picardy to 4/18; Flanders to 7/18; Somme/Ancre to 8/18; Flanders |
| **17** | pre-war | **W. Front**: Belgium-Marne to 9/14; Oise to 10/15; Champagne to 6/16; Picardy to 7/16; Somme to 10/16; Artois to 1/17; Somme to 3/17; Artois/Picardy to 6/17; Flanders to 7/17; Picardy to 9/17; Flanders to 10/17; Artois to 7/18; Aisne/Marne to 9/18; Champagne/Ardennes |
| **17 Reserve** | 8/14 | **W. Front**: Belgium to 9/14; Oise to 10/14; Somme to 10/15; Artois to 7/16; Somme to 8/16; Picardy to 9/16; Artois in 9/16; Somme to 10/16; Flanders to 3/17; Artois to 11/17; Flanders to 6/18; Picardy to 9/18; Lorraine to 10/18; Picardy |
| **17 Landwehr** | 12/15 | **Russia**: Lithuania to 3/18; Byelorussia |
| **18** | pre-war | **W. Front**: Belgium-Marne to 9/14; Aisne to 10/15; Champagne to 6/16; Somme to 9/16; Artois to 12/16; Somme to 3/17; Artois to 8/17; Flanders to 10/17; *see below*; Alsace to 2/18; Artois to 3/18; Somme to 5/18; Flanders to ?/18; Aisne to 8/18; Oise **Russia**: Lithuania to 11/14; *see above* |
| **18 Reserve** | 8/14 | **W. Front**: Belgium to 9/14; Oise to 10/14; Somme to 10/15; Artois to 7/16; Somme to 8/16; Artois to 10/16; Somme in 10/16; Flanders to 3/17; Artois to 6/17; Flanders to 8/17; Artois to 10/17; Flanders to 9/18; Artois |
| **18 Landwehr** (Bredow Div. to 12/15) | 8/14 | **Russia**: E. Prussia to 10/14; Poland to 3/18; Byelorussia |
| **19** | pre-war | **W. Front**: Belgium-Marne to 9/14; Champagne to 4/15; *see below*; Champagne to 6/16; *see below*; Picardy to 12/16; Alsace to 1/17; Champagne to 9/17; Verdun to 3/18; Somme/Avre to 8/18; Picardy **Russia**: Galicia to 9/15; *see above*; Poland to 11/16; *see above* |
| **19 Reserve** | 8/14 | **W. Front**: Belgium-Marne to 9/14; Champagne to 4/15; Alsace to 3/16; Verdun to 7/16; Argonne to 10/16; Somme in 10/16; Lorraine to 2/17; CdD to 4/17; *see below*; Flanders to 10/17; Ardennes in 10/17; Verdun to 4/18; Flanders to 5/18; Champagne **Russia**: Lithuania to 8/17; Latvia to 9/17; *see above* |
| **19 Ersatz** | 8/14 | **W. Front**: Vosges/Lorraine to 7/18; Aisne/Marne to 8/18; Picardy to 9/18; Lorraine |
| **19 Landwehr** | 9/16 | **W. Front**: Flanders to 10/17; *see below* **Russia**: Latvia to 7/18; Finland to 8/18; Estonia |
| **20** | pre-war | **W. Front**: Belgium-Marne to 9/14; Champagne to 4/15; *see below*; Champagne to 11/15; Aisne to 6/16; *see below*; Aisne to 2/17; Alsace to 3/17; CdD to 5/17; Champagne to 7/17; *see below*; Flanders to 10/17; Artois to 2/18; Flanders in 2/18; Somme/Ancre to 4/18; Lorraine to 7/18; Aisne/Marne in 7/18; Artois to 10/18; Lorraine **Russia**: Galicia to 9/15; *see above*; Poland to 11/16; *see above*; Galicia/Latvia to 9/17; *see above* |
| **20 Landwehr** | 9/16 | **W. Front**: Flanders to 11/17; Artois in 11/17; *see below* **Russia**: Poland to 3/18; Ukraine |
| **21** | pre-war | **W. Front**: Luxembourg-Marne to 9/14; Champagne to 10/15; Somme to 2/16; Verdun to 5/16; Aisne to 9/16; Somme to 10/16; Lorraine to 11/16; Somme to 2/17; Aisne to 4/17; *see below*; Champagne to 5/18; Somme/Avre to 9/18; Flanders **Russia**: Lithuania to 9/17; *see above* |
| **21 Reserve** | 8/14 | **W. Front**: Luxembourg-Marne to 9/14; Champagne to 6/16; Verdun to 9/16; Champagne to 10/16; Verdun to 1/17; Lorraine to 4/17; Aisne to 6/17; Champagne to 10/17; Somme to 8/18; Flanders to 9/18; Picardy |
| **21 Landwehr** | 4/17 | **W. Front**: Artois to 5/17; *see below*; Vosges **Russia**: Lithuania to 3/18; *see above* |
| **22** | pre-war | **W. Front**: Belgium to 8/14; *see Russia below*; Verdun to 5/18; Aisne/Marne to 8/18; Artois **Russia**: E. Prussia to 10/14; Poland to c.3/16; Lithuania to 6/16; Galicia to 12/16; *see below*; Galicia to 10/17; *see above* **Rumania**: to 1/17; *see Russia above* |
| **22 Reserve** | 8/14 | **W. Front**: Belgium-Marne to 9/14; Aisne/Oise to 10/15; Champagne to 3/16; Verdun to 6/16; Somme to 7/16; Champagne to 11/16; Somme to 12/16; Artois to 2/17; Somme to 3/17; Hindenburg Line to 5/17; Flanders to 8/17; Artois to 11/17; Lorraine/Alsace to 4/18; Flanders to 6/18; Verdun to 7/18; Champagne to 8/18; Somme/Oise to 9/18; Picardy |
| **22 Landwehr** | 3/17 | **Russia**: Latvia to 10/17; Poland to 3/18; Ukraine |
| **23** | pre-war | **W. Front**: Belgium-Marne to 9/14; Aisne to 7/16; Somme to 3/17; Hindenburg Line to 4/17; Ardennes in 4/17; Champagne to 2/18; Picardy to 3/18; Somme/Avre to 4/18; Champagne to 7/18; Aisne/Marne to 8/18; Artois/Flanders |
| **23 Reserve** | 8/14 | **W. Front**: Belgium-Marne to 9/14; Champagne to 7/16; Somme to 8/16; Artois to 10/16; Somme to 12/16; Artois to 4/17; Flanders to 10/17; *see below*; Artois to 6/18; Flanders **Russia**: Lithuania to 3/18; *see above* |
| **23 Landwehr** | 4/17 | **W. Front**: Argonne to 5/17; *see below* **Russia**: Latvia |
| **24** | pre-war | **W. Front**: Luxembourg-Marne to 9/14; Artois to 8/16; Somme to 11/16; Flanders to 10/17; Artois to 3/18; Somme/Ancre to 4/18; Artois to 5/18; Somme/Avre to 8/18; Picardy |
| **24 Reserve** | 8/14 | **W. Front**: Belgium-Marne to 9/14; Champagne to 7/16; Somme to 9/16; Artois to 11/16; Somme to 12/16; Artois to 3/17; Flanders to 4/17; *see below*; Flanders to 11/17; Artois to 3/18; Somme to 6/18; Artois to 7/18; Aisne/Marne to 9/18; Picardy **Russia**: Galicia to 10/17; *see above* |
| **24 Landwehr** | 8/17 | **Russia**: Lithuania to 3/18; Latvia; *Disbanded ?* |

## INFANTRY DIVISIONS continued

| DIVISION | FORMED | COMBAT RECORD |
|---|---|---|
| **25** | pre-war | **W. Front**: Luxembourg-Marne to 9/14; Champagne to 10/14; Somme to 2/16; Verdun to 4/16; Aisne to 9/16; Somme to 3/17; Hindenburg Line to 9/17; Flanders to 3/18; Somme to 4/18; Artois to 8/18; Somme to 9/18; Artois |
| **25 Reserve** | 8/14 | **W. Front**: Luxembourg-Marne to 9/14; Champagne to 10/14; Flanders to 12/14; *see Russia below*; Argonne to 7/16; Verdun to 10/16; Champagne to 2/17; Verdun to 8/17; Vosges to 9/17; Champagne to 4/18; Somme/Avre to 8/18; Picardy; *Disbanded* in 10/18<br>**Russia**: Poland to 2/15; Galicia to 7/15; Poland to 10/15; *see below*<br>**Serbia**: to 11/15; *see W. Front above* |
| **25 Landwehr** | 10/16 | **W. Front**: CdD to 4/17; Alsace |
| **26** | pre-war | **W. Front**: Lorraine/Argonne to 10/14; Flanders to 11/14; *see below*; Flanders to 7/16; Somme to 8/16; Flanders to 11/16; Somme to 3/17; Artois to 8/17; Flanders to 9/17; Lorraine to 10/17; *see Italy below*; Alsace to 3/18; Artois to 5/18; Somme to 7/18; Champagne<br>**Russia**: Poland to 10/15; *see below*<br>**Serbia**: to 11/15; *see W. Front above*<br>**Italy**: Isonzo-Piave to 3/18; *see W. Front above* |
| **26 Reserve** | 8/14 | **W. Front**: Vosges to 9/14; Somme to ?/16; Artois to 3/17; Hindenburg Line to 4/17; Artois to 8/17; Flanders to 3/18; Artois |
| **26 Landwehr** | 1/17 | **W. Front**: Alsace |
| **27** | pre-war | **W. Front**: Lorraine to 9/14; Argonne to 12/15; Flanders to 7/16; Somme to 8/16; Flanders to 11/16; Somme to 1/17; Artois to 8/17; Flanders to 11/17; Alsace to 2/18; Artois to 4/18; Flanders to 7/18; Somme/Ancre to 8/18; Lorraine |
| **28** | pre-war | **W. Front**: Alsace/Lorraine to 10/14; Artois to 6/15; Champagne to 7/16; Somme to 10/16; Champagne to 1/17; Verdun to 9/17; Alsace to 10/17; Artois to 11/17; Ardennes to 2/18; Aisne to 5/18; Aisne/Marne to 9/18; Lorraine to 10/18; Flanders |
| **28 Reserve** | 8/14 | **W. Front**: Alsace to 9/14; Somme to 7/16; Champagne to 10/16; Somme in 10/16; Verdun to 4/17; CdD to 5/17; Verdun to 8/17; Champagne to 2/18; Somme to 4/18; Artois to 5/18; Aisne/Marne to 8/18; Lorraine |
| **29** | pre-war | **W. Front**: Alsace/Lorraine to 10/14; Artois to 6/15; Champagne to 9/16; Somme to 2/17; Hindenburg Line to 4/17; Champagne to 7/17; Verdun to 4/18; Flanders to 7/18; Aisne to 10/18; Picardy |
| **29 Landwehr** | 11/17 | **Russia**: Latvia to 5/18; Estonia |
| **30** | pre-war | **W. Front**: Alsace/Lorraine to 10/14; Flanders to 2/16; Verdun to 9/16; Somme to 11/16; Verdun to 3/17; Champagne to Verdun to 10/17; Artois to 12/17; Champagne to 1/18; Picardy to 6/18; Champagne to 9/18; Picardy |
| **30 Bavarian Reserve** | 8/14 | **W. Front**: Alsace to 4/17; Lorraine to 10/17; Alsace |
| **31** | pre-war | **W. Front**: Lorraine to 9/14; Somme to 1/15; *see below*; Flanders to 7/18; Lorraine to 9/18; St Mihiel to 10/18; Argonne<br>**Russia**: E. Prussia to 2/15; Poland/Lithuania to 12/17; *see above* |
| **32** | pre-war | **W. Front**: Belgium-Marne to 9/14; Champagne to 6/16; Somme to 9/16; Argonne to 10/16; Somme to 3/17; Hindenburg Line in 3/17; Champagne to 6/17; Flanders to 3/18; Artois to 7/18; Lorraine |
| **33** | pre-war | **W. Front**: Lorraine-Marne to 9/14; Argonne to 8/16; Verdun to 9/16; Argonne to 12/16; Somme to 2/17; Argonne to 5/17; Champagne to 6/17; Argonne to 3/18; Somme/Oise to 4/18; Alsace/Marne to 7/18; Verdun |

| DIVISION | FORMED | COMBAT RECORD |
|---|---|---|
| **33 Reserve** | 8/14 | **W. Front**: Lorraine to 8/16; Verdun to 11/16; Lorraine to 4/17; CdD to 5/17; Lorraine to 8/17; Verdun to 9/17; *see below*; Champagne to 5/18; Aisne/Marne to 8/18; *Disbanded*<br>**Russia**: Galicia to ?; *see above* |
| **34** | pre-war | **W. Front**: Lorraine to 9/14; Argonne to 8/16; Verdun to 11/16; Alsace to 2/17; Argonne to 3/17; Champagne to 7/17; Flanders to 8/17; Lorraine to 11/17; Picardy to 3/18; Oise to 4/18; Picardy to 6/18; Aisne to 7/18; Picardy |
| **35** | pre-war | **Russia**: E. Prussia to 9/14; Poland to 10/15; *see below*<br>**W. Front**: Somme to 3/17; Hindenburg Line to 4/17; Artois to 6/17; Flanders in 6/17; Picardy to 10/17; Flanders/Artois |
| **35 Reserve** | 8/14 | **Russia**: E. Prussia/Poland to 1/15; Galicia to 7/15; Poland to 3/18; Ukraine |
| **36** | pre-war | **Russia**: E. Prussia to 9/14; Poland to 10/15; *see below*<br>**W. Front**: Somme to 3/17; Hindenburg Line to 5/17; Artois to 8/17; Flanders to 9/17; Artois to 2/18; Somme/Oise to 5/18; Aisne/Marne to 7/18; Picardy to 8/18; Somme/Artois |
| **36 Reserve** | 8/14 | **Russia**: E. Prussia to 10/14; Poland to 5/15; Latvia to 9/16; Galicia to 5/17; *see below*<br>**W. Front**: Lorraine to 7/17; Artois to 10/17; Flanders to 6/18; Artois to 10/18; Flanders |
| **37** | pre-war | **Russia**: E. Prussia to 9/14; Poland/Latvia to 12/16; *see below*<br>**W. Front**: Alsace to 5/17; CdD to 8/17; Picardy to 3/18; Somme/Oise to 5/18; Aisne/Marne to 8/18; Verdun to 9/18; Argonne |
| **38** | pre-war | **W. Front**: Belgium to 8/14; *see below*<br>**Russia**: Poland to 9/15; *see below*<br>**W. Front**: Artois to 10/15; Oise to 5/16; Verdun to 10/16; Somme to 11/16; Flanders to 12/16; Somme to 4/17; Artois to 6/17; Flanders to 9/17; Artois to 11/17; Flanders to 4/18; Artois to 8/18; Somme/Artois |
| **38 Landwehr** | 4/17 | **W. Front**: Flanders |
| **39** | pre-war | **W. Front**: Alsace to 9/14; Champagne to 10/14; Flanders to 1/16; Verdun to 10/16; Somme to 11/16; Verdun to 12/16; Argonne to 3/17; Champagne to 7/17; Artois to 11/17; Flanders to 12/17; Artois to 3/18; Somme/Ancre to 4/18; Artois to 9/18; Flanders |
| **39 Bavarian Reserve** *(Rekowsky Div. to 12/14)* | 10/14 | **W. Front**: Alsace |
| **40** | pre-war | **W. Front**: Belgium-Marne to 9/14; Flanders to 8/16; Somme to 9/16; Artois to 10/16; Somme to 11/16; Flanders to 8/17; Picardy to 10/17; Flanders to 11/17; *see below*; Lorraine to 6/18; Aisne/Marne to 7/18; Artois to 9/18; Flanders<br>**Russia**: Lithuania to 3/18 |
| **41** | pre-war | **Russia**: E. Prussia to 9/14; Poland to 2/15; Poland/Lithuania to 10/16; *see Rumania below*<br>**Rumania**: to 2/17; *see below*<br>**W. Front**: Lorraine to 5/17; CdD to 11/17; Flanders to 3/18; Artois to 4/18; Somme/Ancre to 7/18; Somme to 9/18; Lorraine to 10/18; Argonne |
| **42** | pre-war | **W. Front**: Lorraine to 9/14; Somme to 1/15; *see below*; Artois to 6/18; Aisne to 8/18; Champagne<br>**Russia**: Poland to 3/15; Lithuania to 4/17; Galicia to 8/17; Latvia to 10/17; Oesel Is. to 11/17; Poland to 12/17; *see above* |
| **43 Reserve** | 10/14 | **W. Front**: Flanders to 4/15; Artois/Flanders to 7/15; *see Russia and Serbia below*; Lorraine to 10/15; *see Serbia below*, Artois to 3/16; Verdun to 5/16; Lorraine to 6/16; *see Russia below*; Champagne to 12/16; Verdun to 1/17; Alsace to 2/17; Champagne to 4/17; Argonne to 7/17; CdD to 8/17; Picardy to 10/17; Aisne/Oise in 10/17; *see Russia below*, (Germany to 2/18); Artois to 6/18; Somme to 9/18; *Disbanded*<br>**Russia**: (one brigade only) Poland to 10/15; *see below*; Poland to 2/18; *see above*<br>**Serbia**: to 1/16; *see W. Front above* |

| DIVISION | FORMED | COMBAT RECORD |
|---|---|---|
| **44** Reserve | 10/14 | **W. Front**: Flanders to 6/15; *see Russia below*; Somme to 3/16; Verdun to 6/16; Ardennes to 7/16; Somme to 3/17; Hindenburg Line to 4/17; Oise to 5/17; Lorraine to 10/17; Flanders to 12/17; Artois<br>**Russia**: Poland to 10/15; *see below*<br>**Serbia**: to 12/15; *see W. Front above* |
| **44** Landwehr | 4/17 | **W. Front**: Lorraine to 10/17; Alsace |
| **45** Reserve | 10/14 | **W. Front**: Flanders to 9/16; Somme to 10/16; Oise to 1/17; Aisne to 5/17; Lorraine to 9/17; Flanders to 10/17; Lorraine to 1/18; Somme to 4/18; Aisne/Marne to 8/18; Alsace in 8/18; Champagne to 10/18; Lorraine |
| **45** Landwehr | 4/17 | **Russia**: Poland to 3/18; Ukraine |
| **46** Reserve | 10/14 | **W. Front**: Flanders to 9/16; Somme to 10/16; Champagne to 1/17; Lorraine in 1/17; Oise to 6/17; CdD to 7/17; Lorraine to 4/18; Somme/Oise to 7/18; Aisne to 8/18; *Disbanded* |
| **46** Landwehr | 5/17 | **Russia**: Lithuania to 1/18; Poland to 3/18; Ukraine to 5/18; Byelorussia |
| **47** Reserve | 10/14 | **W. Front**: Lorraine 11/14; *see below;*\* Lorraine to 6/17; Aisne to 2/18; Picardy to 3/18; Somme/Oise to 4/18; Somme to 6/18; *Disbanded* |
| **47** Landwehr | 10/15 | **W. Front**: Champagne to 2/17; Oise to 5/17; *see below*<br>**Russia**: Poland to 2/18; Ukraine |
| **48** Reserve | 10/14 | **W. Front**: Artois to 11/14; *see Russia below*; Lorraine to 6/17; Verdun to 10/17; Lorraine to 11/17; Alsace to 5/18; Artois<br>**Russia**: Poland to 1/15; Galicia to 10/16; *see below*; Galicia to 5/17; *see above*<br>**Rumania**: to 11/16; *see Russia above* |
| **48** Landwehr | 9/17 | **W. Front**: Lorraine |
| **49** Reserve | 10/14 | **Russia**: E. Prussia/Poland to 10/16; Galicia to 1/17; *see Rumania below*<br>**Rumania**: in 1/17; *see below*<br>**W. Front**: Artois to 6/17; Flanders to 7/17; Artois to 12/17; Flanders to 9/18; Artois |
| **50** | 3/15 | **W. Front**: Aisne to 5/15; Champagne to 4/16; Verdun to 11/16; Argonne to 2/17; Picardy to 4/17; Aisne/CdD to 7/17; Aisne/Oise to 1/18; Picardy to 3/18; Somme to 4/18; Somme/Oise to 5/18; Aisne to 7/18; Aisne/Marne |
| **50** Reserve | 10/14 | **Russia**: Poland to 9/15; *see below*<br>**W. Front**: Champagne to 12/15; Artois to 9/16; Somme to 3/17; Hindenburg Line to 4/17; Artois to 6/17; Flanders to 10/17; Artois to 3/18; Somme to 6/18; Aisne |
| **51** Reserve | 10/14 | **W. Front**: Flanders to 9/16; Somme in 9/16; Champagne to 8/17; Lorraine to 9/17; Champagne to 3/18; Somme/Avre to 5/18; Aisne/Marne to 9/18; Champagne to 10/18; Oise in 10/18; Champagne |
| **52** | 3/15 | **W. Front**: Artois to 9/16; Somme to 11/16; Alsace to 4/17; Aisne to 7/17; CdD to 11/17; Champagne to 3/18; Somme/Avre to 4/18; Ardennes to 5/18; Aisne/Marne to 6/18; Ardennes in 6/18; Artois to 9/18; Argonne |
| **52** Reserve | 10/14 | **W. Front**: Flanders to 9/16; Somme to 10/16; Champagne to 7/17; Flanders to 8/17; Champagne to 4/18; Flanders to 9/18; Artois in 9/18; Flanders |
| **53** Reserve | 10/14 | **W. Front**: Flanders to 10/15; Champagne to 11/15; Flanders to 3/16; Artois to 8/16; Somme to 9/16; Artois to 10/16; Champagne to 11/16; *see below*; Flanders to 3/18; Somme/Avre to 4/18; Verdun to 6/18; Aisne/Marne to 8/18; Argonne to 10/18; *Disbanded*<br>**Russia**: Galicia to 11/17; *see above* |
| **54** | 3/15 | **W. Front**: Champagne to 7/15; *see below*; Oise to 5/16; Verdun to 11/16; Lorraine to 4/17; Aisne to 5/17; Champagne to 7/17; Flanders to 8/17; Artois to 11/17; Lorraine to 3/18; Somme/Avre to 9/18; Artois<br>**Russia**: Poland to 10/15; *see above* |

\* *Addendum*:
**Russia**: Poland to 12/14; Galicia to 4/15; Poland to 9/15; Byelorussia to 5/17.

| DIVISION | FORMED | COMBAT RECORD |
|---|---|---|
| **54** Reserve | 10/14 | **W. Front**: Flanders to 3/16; Artois to 8/16; Somme to 9/16; Lorraine to 11/16; Verdun to 1/17; Champagne to 8/17; Verdun to 10/17; Flanders to 3/18; Somme/Ancre to 9/18; *Disbanded* |
| **55** | — | **Not formed** |
| **56** | 3/15 | **W. Front**: Champagne to 5/15; *see below*; Artois to 7/15; Lorraine to 9/15; Champagne to 4/16; Ardennes to 5/16; Verdun to 7/16; Artois to 8/16; Somme to 9/16; Champagne to 11/16; Somme to 3/17; Hindenburg Line to 4/17; Artois to 6/17; Lorraine to 4/18; Flanders |
| **57** | — | **Not formed** |
| **58** | 3/15 | **W. Front**: Artois to 6/15; *see below*; Lorraine to 3/16; Verdun to 4/16; Champagne to 9/16; Somme in 9/16; Flanders to 10/16; Somme to 11/16; Flanders to 1/17; Verdun to 3/17; Champagne to 4/17; *see below*; Flanders to 8/18; Artois<br>**Russia**: Poland/Lithuania to 10/15; *see above*; Lithuania to 10/17; *see above* |
| **59-74** | — | **Not formed** |
| **75** Reserve | 1/15 | **Russia**: E. Prussia/Poland/Lithuania to 8/16; Pripet to 11/16; Galicia to 7/17; Latvia to 12/17; *see below*<br>**W. Front**: Aisne to 3/18; Picardy/Artois to 11/18; Lorraine |
| **76** Reserve | 1/15 | **Russia**: Poland to 10/15; Lithuania to 12/15; Latvia to 9/15; *see Rumania below*<br>**Rumania**: to 3/18; *see below*<br>**W. Front**: Somme/Avre to 5/18; Verdun to 7/18; Aisne/Marne to 9/18; Argonne |
| **77** Reserve | 1/15 | **Russia**: E. Prussia to 5/15; Latvia to 6/15; Poland/Lithuania to 8/17; Latvia to 4/18; *see below*<br>**W. Front**: Somme/Avre to 7/18; Lorraine to 10/18; *Disbanded* |
| **78** Reserve | 1/15 | **Russia**: Poland to 5/15; Latvia to 4/17; *see below*<br>**W. Front**: Alsace to 5/17; Aisne to 8/17; Verdun to 10/17; Lorraine to 5/18; Aisne/Marne to 8/18; *Disbanded* |
| **79** Reserve | 1/15 | **Russia**: E. Prussia/Poland/Lithuania to 11/16; *see below*<br>**W. Front**: Artois to 7/17; Flanders to 9/17; Artois to 3/18; Somme to 4/18; Artois to 8/18; Picardy |
| **80** Reserve | 1/15 | **Russia**: E. Prussia/Poland to 7/15; Poland/Lithuania to 12/16; *see below*<br>**W. Front**: Artois to 5/17; Flanders to 6/17; Lorraine to 8/17; Verdun to 9/17; Champagne to 10/17; Argonne to 3/18; Somme/Avre to 4/18; Champagne to 8/18; Aisne |
| **81** Reserve | 1/15 | **W. Front**: Somme to 3/15; *see below*; Artois to 7/18; Lorraine to 10/18; Picardy<br>**Russia**: Galicia to 7/15; Poland to 12/17; *see above* |
| **82** Reserve | 1/15 | **W. Front**: Somme to 3/15; *see below*; Lorraine to 4/18; Somme/Avre-Picardy<br>**Russia**: Galicia to 3/15; Poland to 12/15; *see above* |
| **83** | 6/15 | **Russia**: Poland/Lithuania to 4/17; Poland to 6/17; Galicia to 9/17; Bukovina to 4/18; *see below*<br>**W. Front**: Flanders to 8/18; Somme/Ancre to 9/18; Lorraine |
| **84** | 6/15 | **Russia**: Poland/Lithuania to 12/17; *see below*<br>**W. Front**: ? to 5/18; Somme/Avre to 8/18; Oise/Aisne |
| **85** Landwehr (Breugel Div. to 8/15) | 8/14 | **Russia**: Poland/Lithuania to 10/17; Latvia to 5/18; Ukraine |
| **86** (Wörnitz Div. to 6/15) | 8/14 | **Russia**: Poland/Lithuania to 7/16; Pripet to 1/18; *see below*<br>**W. Front**: Aisne/Marne to 10/18; Picardy |
| **87** | 6/15 | **Russia**: Poland/Lithuania to 10/17; Latvia to 12/17; Lithuania to 3/18; *see below*<br>**W. Front**: Champagne to 6/18; Aisne/Marne to 7/18; Ardennes to 8/18; Picardy |
| **88** (Menges Div. to 9/15) | 3/15 | **Russia**: Poland/Lithuania/Latvia to 1/18; *see below*<br>**W. Front**: Picardy to 3/18; Somme/Avre to 4/18; Champagne to 9/18; Lorraine to 10/18; Argonne |
| **89** (Westernhagen Div. to 10/15) | 8/14 | **Russia**: Poland to 8/16; *see below*<br>**Rumania**: to 11/18 |

## INFANTRY DIVISIONS continued

| DIVISION | FORMED | COMBAT RECORD |
|---|---|---|
| **90** | — | Not formed |
| **91**<br>(Clausius Div.<br>to 9/16) | 7/16 | **Russia**: Pripet to 3/18(?); Ukraine |
| **92**<br>(Rusche Div.<br>to 9/16) | 7/16 | **Russia**: Pripet to 8/17; Galicia to 4/18; Ukraine |
| **93** | 10/16 | **Russia**: Lithuania to 12/17; Byelorussia to c.4/18; Ukraine |
| **94** | 6/17 | **Russia**: Lithuania to 5/18; dissolved; reformed Latvia 9/18; *see below*<br>**W. Front**: Lorraine (from 10/18) |
| **95** | 7/17 | **Russia**: Pripet to c.3/18; Ukraine |
| **96** | 7/17 | **Russia**: Galicia to 4/18; *see below*<br>**W. Front**: Alsace |
| **97-100** | — | Not formed |
| **101** | 5/15 | **Russia**: Poland to 6/15; *see Serbia below*; Galicia/Poland to 10/16; *see Serbia below*<br>**Serbia**: Frontier in 6/15; *see above*; to 2/16; *see below*<br>**Macedonia**: to c.1/18; *Disbanded* |
| **102** | — | Not formed |
| **103** | 5/15 | **Serbia**: Frontier to 6/15; *see Russia below*, to 1/16; *see Macedonia below*<br>**Russia**: Galicia to 10/15; *see above*<br>**Macedonia**: to 4/16; *see below*<br>**W. Front**: Champagne to 6/16; Verdun to 8/16; Lorraine to 9/16; Champagne to 10/16; Somme to 11/16; Champagne to 1/17; Verdun to 5/17; CdD to 10/17; Oise to 12/17; Picardy to 3/18; Somme/Oise to 4/18; Aisne/Marne to 9/18; Champagne |
| **104** | — | Not formed |
| **105** | 5/15 | **Serbia**: Frontier to 6/15; *see Russia below*, to 12/15; *see Bulgaria below*<br>**Russia**: Galicia/Poland to 10/15; *see above*, Galicia/Bukovina to 10/16; Latvia to 11/17; *see W. Front below*<br>**Bulgaria**: Rumanian border to 5/16; *see Russia above*<br>**W. Front**: Champagne to 4/18; Somme/Oise to 5/18; Aisne/Oise to 9/18; Picardy |
| **106** | — | Not formed |
| **107** | 5/15 | **Russia**: Galicia/Poland to 10/15; *see Serbia below*, Latvia to 3/16; Lithuania to 6/16; Pripet to 3/17; *see W. Front below*<br>**Serbia**: to 11/15; *see above*<br>**W. Front**: Picardy to 3/18; Somme/Ancre to 9/18; Lorraine to 10/18; Argonne |
| **108**<br>(Beckmann Div.<br>to ?/??) | 7/15 | **Russia**: Lithuania to 12/15; Latvia to 6/16; Pripet to 12/17; *see below*<br>**W. Front**: Picardy to 1/18; Aisne to 4/18; Somme to 8/18; *Disbanded* |
| **109** | 5/15 | **Russia**: Latvia to 11/16; *see Rumania below*<br>**Rumania**: to 3/18; *see below*<br>**W. Front**: ? to 4/18; Somme/Avre to 8/18; *Disbanded* |
| **110** | — | Not formed |
| **111** | 3/15 | **W. Front**: Lorraine to 8/15; Artois to 8/16; Somme to 9/16; Lorraine to 10/16; Somme to 3/17; Hindenburg Line to 7/17; Flanders to 8/17; Lorraine to 10/17; Flanders to 11/17; Artois to 3/18; Somme/Ancre to 8/18; Artois |
| **112** | — | Not formed |
| **113** | 3/15 | **W. Front**: Lorraine to 2/16; Verdun to 4/16; Oise to 7/16; Somme to 8/16; Aisne to 9/16; Somme to 10/16; Lorraine to 2/17; Alsace to 4/17; CdD to 5/17; Oise to 8/17; Picardy to 3/18; Aisne/Picardy to 3/18; Somme in 3/18; ? to 5/18; Aisne/Marne to 8/18; Artois |

| DIVISION | FORMED | COMBAT RECORD |
|---|---|---|
| **114** | — | Not formed |
| **115** | 4/15 | **W. Front**: Artois to 6/15; Aisne to 7/15; *see Russia below*; Flanders to 5/18; Aisne/Marne to 7/18; Verdun to 9/18; Argonne<br>**Russia**: Poland/Lithuania to 8/16; Galicia to 10/16; Pripet to 12/16; *see below*<br>**Rumania**: to 2/18 |
| **116** | — | Not formed |
| **117** | 4/15 | **W. Front**: Champagne to 5/15; Artois to ??/15; Flanders to 7/16; Somme to 8/16; *see Russia below*; Lorraine to 4/18; Artois to 6/18; Flanders to 8/18; Somme to 9/18; Argonne<br>**Russia**: Bukovina to 5/17; *see Rumania below*<br>**Rumania**: to 10/17; *see below*<br>**Italy**: Isonzo-Piave to 3/18; *see W. Front above* |
| **118** | — | Not formed |
| **119** | 4/15 | **Russia**: Galicia/Poland to 3/16; Lithuania to 6/16; Galicia to 5/17; *see below*<br>**W. Front**: Flanders to 11/17; Artois to 3/18; Somme/Ancre to 4/18; Artois to 7/18; Picardy to 10/18; Flanders |
| **120** | — | Not formed |
| **121** | 4/15 | **W. Front**: Lorraine to 3/16; Verdun to 5/16; Somme to 7/16; *see below*; Artois to 8/17; Flanders to 9/17; Lorraine to 4/18; Flanders to 8/18; Somme to 9/18; Picardy<br>**Russia**: Poland to 1/17; Lithuania to 5/17; *see above* |
| **122** | — | Not formed |
| **123** | 4/15 | **W. Front**: Champagne to 6/15; Artois to 11/15; Flanders to 7/16; Somme to 8/16; *see below*, Verdun to 6/18; Aisne/Marne to 7/18; Verdun to 9/18; St Mihiel/Argonne<br>**Russia**: Lithuania to 11/17; *see above* |
| **124-182** | — | Not formed |
| **183***  | 6/16 | **W. Front**: Somme to 7/16; Artois to 10/16; Somme to 11/16; Lorraine to 4/17; CdD to 5/17; Alsace to 8/17; Flanders in 8/17; Picardy to 4/18; Somme/Ancre to 5/18; Lorraine to 7/18; Somme/Ancre to 8/18; Artois; *Disbanded* 9/18 |
| **184** | — | Not formed |
| **185***  | 6/16 | **W. Front**: Aisne to 9/16; Somme to 12/16; Artois to 2/17; Flanders to 4/17; Artois to 10/17; Flanders to 12/17; Somme to 1/18; Artois to 8/18; Picardy |
| **186** | — | Not formed |
| **187***  | 6/16 | **W. Front**: Alsace to 9/16; *see below*, Lorraine to 4/17; Champagne to 9/17; Flanders to 1/18; Artois<br>**Rumania**: to 2/17; *see above* |
| **188-191** | — | Not formed |
| **192***  | 6/16 | **W. Front**: Verdun to 10/16; Lorraine to 12/17; Verdun to 4/18; Oise to 8/18; St Mihiel/Argonne |
| **193-194** | — | Not formed |
| **195** | 7/16 | **Russia**: Galicia to 4/17; *see W. Front below*<br>**W. Front**: Flanders to 7/17; Somme to 10/17; Flanders in 10/17; Lorraine to 11/17; *see below*; Alsace to 2/18; Somme/Ancre to 7/18; Aisne/Marne to 8/18; Lorraine to 9/18; St Mihiel/Argonne<br>**Italy**: to 12/17; *see W. Front above* |
| **196** | — | Not formed |
| **197** | 8/16 | **Russia**: Galicia to 2/18; *see below*<br>**W. Front**: CdD to 5/18; Aisne/Marne to 6/18; Verdun to 8/18; Oise to 10/18; *Disbanded* |
| **198** | 8/16 | No further information |
| **199** | 8/16 | **Russia**: to 11/16; *see below*<br>**W. Front**: Somme to 3/17; Hindenburg Line to 4/17; Artois to 5/17; Somme to 6/17; Flanders to 2/18; Artois to 3/18; Somme to 5/18; Artois to 6/18; Champagne |

\* Brigades from spring 1915. Upgraded by allotment of extra artillery.

## INFANTRY DIVISIONS continued

| DIVISION | FORMED | COMBAT RECORD |
|---|---|---|
| **200** (Jäger) | 7/16 | **Russia**: Bukinova to 7/17; *see Italy below* <br> **Italy**: Isonzo-Piave to 2/18; *see below* <br> **W. Front**: Alsace to 3/18; Somme/Avre to 5/18; Artois to 6/18; Aisne/Marne to 10/18; Picardy |
| **201** | 7/16 | **Russia**: Poland to 12/17; *see below* <br> **W. Front**: Lorraine to 5/18; Aisne/Marne to 8/18; Argonne to 9/18; Somme/Artois to 10/18; *Disbanded* |
| **202** | 10/16 | **Russia**: Latvia to 11/17; *see below* <br> **W. Front**: Lorraine to 5/18; Oise to 8/18; Champagne/Lorraine; *Disbanded* 11/18 |
| **203** | 9/16 | **Russia**: Latvia to 12/17; *see below* <br> **W. Front**: Champagne and Aisne/Marne |
| **204** | 7/16 | **W. Front**: Flanders to 6/17; Alsace to 8/17; Flanders to 9/17; Artois to 11/17; Flanders to 2/18; Artois to 3/18; Somme/Avre to 6/18; Oise/Avre to 8/18; Lorraine to 10/18; Artois |
| **205** | 12/16 | **Russia**: Lithuania to 1/17; Latvia |
| **206** | 9/16 | **W. Front**: Flanders to 10/16; Somme to 11/16; Alsace to 1/17; Lorraine to 4/17; CdD to 6/17; Lorraine to 7/17; Verdun to 8/17; Champagne to 11/17; Somme to 3/18; Somme/Avre to 5/18; Oise to 9/18; Somme to 10/18; Artois |
| **207** | 9/16 | **W. Front**: Flanders to 4/17; Artois to 6/17; Flanders to 10/17; Artois to 10/18; Flanders |
| **208** | 9/16 | **Russia**: Galicia to 11/17; *see below* <br> **W. Front**: Somme to 12/16; Flanders to 4/17; Artois to 5/17; Oise to 8/17; Flanders to 9/17; St Mihiel to 11/17; Somme to 3/18; Somme/Avre to 5/18; Lorraine to 7/18; Oise to 10/18; Artois |
| **209-210** | — | **Not formed** |
| **211** | 9/16 | **W. Front**: Somme to 11/16; Artois to 6/17; Oise to 7/18; Aisne/Marne to 8/18; *Disbanded* |
| **212** | 9/16 | **W. Front**: Somme to 11/16; Champagne to 3/17; *see Rumania below* <br> **Rumania**: to 5/18; *see below* <br> **Russia**: Ukraine |
| **213** | 9/16 | **W. Front**: Somme to 10/16; Aisne to 1/17; Oise to 3/17; Aisne to 6/17; Lorraine to 8/17; Verdun in 8/17; Champagne to 10/17; Aisne to 5/18; Aisne/Marne |
| **214** | 9/16 | **W. Front**: Somme to 2/17; Champagne to 5/17; Argonne to 8/17; Flanders in 8/17; Artois to ?/??; Flanders to 5/18; Artois |
| **215** | 9/16 | **W. Front**: Champagne to 11/16; *see below* <br> **Russia**: Pripet to 3/18; Ukraine |
| **216** | 7/16 | **Russia**: Galicia to 10/16; *see Rumania below* <br> **Rumania**: to 4/18; *see below* <br> **W. Front**: Flanders to 7/18; Aisne/Marne to 10/18; Champagne |
| **217** | 8/16 | **Russia**: Poland to 10/16; *see Rumania below*; Ukraine/Crimea/Georgia to 10/18; *see Serbia below* <br> **Rumania**: to 4/18; *see above* <br> **Serbia**: to 11/18 |
| **218** | 9/16 | **Russia**: Galicia to 12/16; *see below* <br> **Rumania**: to 11/18 |
| **219** | 1/17 | **W. Front**: Lorraine to 6/17; Artois to 9/17; *see Russia below* <br> **Russia**: Latvia to 10/18; *see below* <br> **Serbia**: to 11/18 |
| **220** | 12/16 | **W. Front**: Artois to 10/17; Flanders in 10/17; Artois |
| **221** | 10/16 | **W. Front**: Somme to 3/17; Hindenburg Line to 4/17; Artois to 7/17; Flanders to 8/17; Champagne to 11/17; Flanders in 11/17; Artois to 7/18; Oise to 8/18; Oise/Avre to 9/18; Picardy |
| **222** | 9/16 | **W. Front**: Alsace to 10/16; Somme to 12/16; Aisne/Oise to 3/17; Aisne to 12/17; Picardy to 4/18; Somme/Avre to 7/18; Aisne to 9/18; *Disbanded* |

| DIVISION | FORMED | COMBAT RECORD |
|---|---|---|
| **223** | 10/16 | **W. Front**: Somme to 1/17; Champagne to 5/17; *see below*; Aisne to 3/18; Oise to 8/18; Aisne to 9/18; *Disbanded* <br> **Russia**: Galicia to 1/18; *see above* |
| **224** | 10/16 | **Russia**: Pripet to 3/18; Byelorussia/Ukraine to 10/18; *see below* <br> **W. Front**: Lorraine |
| **225** | 9/16 | **Russia**: Poland to 11/16; *see Rumania below* <br> **Rumania**: to 11/17; *see below* <br> **W. Front**: Lorraine to 5/18; Somme/Avre to 6/18; *Disbanded* |
| **226** | 12/16 | **Russia**: Lithuania to 6/18; *Disbanded* |
| **227** | 3/17 | **W. Front**: Argonne to 6/17; Aisne to 10/17; Flanders in 10/17; Champagne to 4/18; Avre/Oise to 6/18; Lorraine to 8/18; Aisne to 9/18; Picardy |
| **228** | 5/17 | **W. Front**: Verdun to 8/17; Lorraine to 3/18; Somme to 4/18; Artois to 5/18; Champagne to 9/18; Lorraine |
| **229-230** | — | **Not formed** |
| **231** | 1/17 | **W. Front**: (Germany to 3/17); Lorraine to 5/17; Champagne to 3/18; Somme/Avre to 4/18; Aisne/Marne to 6/18; Verdun to 8/18; Picardy |
| **232** | 1/17 | **Russia**: (Germany to 4/17); Latvia to 7/17; Lithuania in 7/17; Galicia to 3/18; *see below* <br> **W. Front**: Aisne to 5/18; Aisne/Marne to 8/18; Somme to 9/18; Artois to 10/18; Oise |
| **233** | 1/17 | **W. Front**: (Germany to 4/17); Oise to 5/17; Flanders to 8/17; Picardy to 10/17; Flanders in 10/17; Lorraine to 4/18; Flanders to 5/18; Somme/Ancre to 8/18; *Disbanded* |
| **234** | 1/17 | **W. Front**: (Germany to 3/17); Somme to 9/17; Flanders to 10/17; Artois to 2/18; Somme to 8/18; Artois |
| **235** | 1/17 | **W. Front**: (Germany to 2/17); Picardy to 3/17; Flanders to 8/17; Aisne to 11/17?; Alsace to 4/18; Flanders to 5/18; Lorraine to 8/18; *Disbanded* |
| **236** | 1/17 | **W. Front**: (Germany to 4/17); Somme to 6/17; Artois to 9/17; Flanders to 10/17; Artois to 3/18; Somme/Sensée to 4/18; Flanders 9/18; Lorraine |
| **237** | 1/17 | **Russia**: (Germany to 3/17); Lithuania to 6/17; Galicia to 1/18; *see below* <br> **W. Front**: Argonne to 5/18; Aisne/Marne to 6/18; Argonne to 8/18; Oise |
| **238** | 1/17 | **W. Front**: (Germany to 4/17); Artois to 10/17; Flanders to 11/17; Picardy to 3/18; Somme/Oise to 4/18; Aisne/Marne to 10/18; Picardy |
| **239** | 1/17 | **W. Front**: (Germany to 2/17); Aisne to 3/17; Champagne to 10/17; Flanders to 9/17; Artois to 4/18; Lorraine to 6/18; Aisne/Marne |
| **240** | 1/17 | **W. Front**: (Germany to 3/17); Alsace to 8/17; Lorraine to 9/17; Flanders to 10/17; Artois to 5/18; Argonne to 7/18; Aisne/Marne to 10/18; Lorraine |
| **241** | 1/17 | **Russia**: (Germany to 3/17); Poland to 4/17; Lithuania to 6/18; Galicia to 2/18; *see below* <br> **W. Front**: Picardy to 3/18; Oise to 10/18; Lorraine |
| **242** | 1/17 | **W. Front**: (Germany to 3/17); Lorraine to 5/17; Champagne to 8/17; Lorraine to 9/17; Aisne to 12/17; ? to 3/18; Oise/Avre to 4/18; Champagne to 5/18; Aisne/Marne |
| **243** | 5/17 | [Formed from 8 Ersatz Div.: see that entry] <br> **W. Front**: Aisne to 8/17; Verdun to 10/17; Lorraine to 3/18; Somme/Avre to 5/18; Somme/Ancre to 9/18; Alsace to 10/18; Artois |
| **244-254** | — | **Not formed** |
| **255** | 5/17 | **W. Front**: Lorraine |
| **256-300** | — | **Not formed** |
| **301** | 6/17 | **W. Front**: Lorraine |
| **302** (Hippel Div. to ?/??) | 10/16 | **Macedonia**: to 11/18 |

## INFANTRY DIVISIONS continued

| DIVISION | FORMED | COMBAT RECORD |
|---|---|---|
| **303** | 9/17 | H.Q. only in command of assorted Landsturm battalions in Germany |
| **Alpine Corps** | 3/15 | [Operated as a division.]<br>**Italy**: to 10/15; *see W.Front below*; Isonzo-Piave to 1/18; *see W. Front below*<br>**W. Front**: Aisne in 10/15; *see Serbia below*; Aisne to 6/16; Verdun to 8/16; Argonne to 9/16; *see Rumania below*; Alsace to 8/17; *see Rumania below*; Lorraine to 4/18; Flanders to 8/18; Somme to 10/18; *see Serbia below*<br>**Serbia**: to 3/16; *see W. Front above*; to 11/18<br>**Rumania**: to 4/17; *see W. Front above*; to 9/17; *see Italy above* |
| **Baltic Division** | 3/18 | **Finland**: 4/18 to end |
| **Basedow Division** | | *see 5 Ersatz Div.* |
| **Bavarian Ersatz** (Benzino Div. to 11/15) | 8/14 | **W. Front**: Alsace to 9/14; Lorraine to 10/16; Somme to 11/16; Aisne to 9/17; Flanders to 10/17; *see below*; Verdun to 7/18; Artois to 9/18; Champagne to 10/18; *Disbanded*<br>**Russia**: Galicia to ?/??; *see above* |
| **Beckmann Division** | | *see 108 Div.* |
| **Benzino Division** | | *see Bavarian Ersatz Div.* |
| **Bredow Division** | | *see 18 Landwehr Div.* |
| **Breugel Division** | | *see 85 Landwehr Div.* |
| **Clausius Division** | | *see 91 Div.* |
| **von Einem Division** | | *see 11 Landwehr Div.* |
| **Franke Division** | 7/16 | **W. Front**: Somme to 9/16; *Disbanded.* (Elements of 23 and 32 Divs.) |
| **Guards Ersatz** | 8/14 | **W. Front**: Lorraine to 4/16; Verdun to 8/16; Lorraine to 1/17; Champagne/Aisne to 6/17; Lorraine to 7/17; *see below*;* Lorraine to 2/18; Flanders to 3/18; Somme/Avre to 4/18; Artois to 6/18; Champagne in 6/18; Aisne/Marne to 8/18; Alsace to 9/18; Flanders |
| **Hippel Division** | | *see 302 Div.* |
| **Jäger Division** | 11/17 | **Italy**: Piave to 3/18; *see below*;<br>**W. Front**: Artois to 4/18; Somme to 5/18; Somme/Oise to 6/18; Picardy in 6/18; Alsace to 7/18; Aisne/Marne to 10/18; Artois |
| **Menges Division** | | *see 88 Div.* |
| **Rekowsky Division** | | *see 39 Bavarian Reserve Div.* |
| **Rusche Division** | | *see 92 Div.* |
| **Waldow Division** | | *see 5 Landwehr Div.* |
| **Wening Landwehr Division** | | *see 1 Bavarian Landwehr Div.* |
| **Westernhagen Division** | | *see 89 Div.* |
| **Wörnitz Division** | | *see 86 Div.* |

## CAVALRY DIVISIONS (total = 11)

| DIVISION | FORMED | COMBAT RECORD |
|---|---|---|
| **1** | 8/14 | **Russia**: inc. Latvia 11/15-8/17 and Ukraine from 3/18 |
| **2** | | **W. Front**: to 11/14; *see Russia below*; to 9/17 (mainly Dutch Frontier); *see Russia below*<br>**Russia**: to 11/16; *see Rumania below*; Pripet to 3/18; Ukraine<br>**Rumania**: to 12/16; *see W. Front above* |
| **3** | | **W. Front**: to 12/14; Belgian occupation to 4/15; *see below*<br>**Russia**: to 11/16; *Disbanded* |
| **4** | | **W. Front**: to 11/14; *see below*; Alsace<br>**Russia**: to 3/18; (dismounted 10/16); *see above* |
| **5** | | **W. Front**: to 10/14; *see below*<br>**Russia**: to 2/18; (dismounted 10/16); *Disbanded* |
| **6** | | **W. Front**: to 10/14; *see Russia below*; Alsace to 7/18 (dismounted from 7/18); Flanders to 8/18; Artois to 9/18; Flanders<br>**Russia**: to 10/16; *see below*<br>**Rumania**: to 2/17; *see W. Front above* |
| **7** | | **W. Front**: to 10/15; Belgian occupation to 10/16; *see below*; Alsace to 5/18; Flanders to 8/18; Artois to 10/18; Flanders<br>**Rumania**: to 1/17; *see above* |
| **8** | | **W. Front**: to 30/8/14; *see below*<br>**Russia**: to 4/18 (dismounted 1917); *Disbanded* |
| **9** | | **W. Front**: to 11/14; *see below*<br>**Russia**: to 3/18 or 7/18 (dismounted 10/16); *Disbanded* |
| **Bavarian** | | **W. Front**: Belgian occupation to 1/15; Germany (?) to 4/15; *see Russia below*<br>**Russia**: to 11/17; *see below*; Ukraine/Crimea<br>**Rumania**: to 4/18; *see above* |
| **Guards** | pre-war | **W. Front**: to 12/14; Dutch Frontier to 6/15; *see Russia below*; Artois to 5/18; Champagne/Aisne<br>**Russia**: to 3/18; (Germany to 4/18: dismounted); *see above* |

## Greece

Intense political divisions within Greece prevented its taking either side in August 1914. Even when the Army was eventually mobilised, in October 1915, the King refused to commit it to the Allied cause and, once they had grabbed a strategic foothold at Salonika, the French and British began to insist that the army be demobilised. This began to happen in June 1916 but by then some Greeks had begun to form a pro-Allied army of their own at Salonika. The arrival of Venizelos accelerated this process and eventually the new Corps of National Defence comprised three divisions. It had been hoped to raise these mainly on the Greek mainland but in the event most of the volunteers came from Crete and the other Greek islands. These divisions, all infantry, were

*\* Addendum.*<br>**Russia**: Lithuania to 9/17.

| DIVISION | FORMED | COMBAT RECORD |
|---|---|---|
| **Archipelago** | early 1917 | **Macedonia**: 10/17 on British Front; 2/18 attached to French First Group of Divisions; 7/18 ditto; 9/18 ditto; 10/18 attached to British XVI Corps |
| **Cretan** | early 1917 | **Macedonia**: 10/17 on British Front; 2/18 attached to French First Group of Divisions; 7/18 ditto; 9/18 in reserve British Salonika Army; 10/18 attached to French First Group of Divisions |
| **Seres** | early 1917 | **Macedonia**: 2/17 on French Front; 2/18 in reserve (?); 7/18 attached to French First Group of Divisions; 9/18 attached to British XII Corps; 10/18 ditto |

Once Venizelos became Prime Minister again, in June 1917, the fifteen divisions of the Royal Greek Army began to mobilise once more. Almost all of their equipment had to be supplied by the Allies and only eight divisions were actually sent to the front. These are listed below. Again, all are infantry divisions.

## INFANTRY DIVISIONS continued

| DIVISION | FORMED | COMBAT RECORD |
|---|---|---|
| **1** Larissa | by 3/18 | **Macedonia**: 3/18 attached to British Salonika Army; 7/18 ditto; 9/18 ditto; 10/18 ditto |
| **2** Athens | by 3/18 | **Macedonia**: 7/18 attached to British Salonika Army; 9/18 ditto; 10/18 ditto |
| **3** Patras | by 7/18 | **Macedonia**: 7/18 attached to French Army of the Orient; 9/18 ditto; 10/18 ditto; 11/18 the only Greek division to operate beyond the Greek frontier – reached Pirot in E. Serbia |
| **4** Napulia | by 6/18 | **Macedonia**: 7/18 in reserve British Salonika Army; 9/18 attached to French First Group of Divisions; 10/18 ditto |
| **8** Preveza | ? | **Epirus**: to 11/18 (Brigade-size only) |
| **9** Yannina | by 3/18 | **Epirus**: to 8/18(?); *see below* **Macedonia**: 9/18 in reserve French Army of the Orient; 10/18 ditto |
| **13** Chalcis | by 3/18 | **Macedonia**: 7/18 attached to British Salonika Army; 9/18 ditto; 10/18 ditto |
| **14** Kalamata | by 6/18 | **Macedonia**: 9/18 in reserve British Salonika Army; 10/18 in reserve French Army of the Orient |

Six other infantry divisions (5, 6, 7, 10, 11, 12) may have existed in Greece at various periods of the war, though none of these saw combat.

## India

### INFANTRY DIVISIONS (total = 10)

| DIVISION | FORMED | COMBAT RECORD |
|---|---|---|
| **3** (Lahore) | pre-war | **W. Front**: *BEF* 9/14-12/14; *Ind. Corps* to 1/15; *1* to 11/15 **Mesopotamia**: 1/16-3/18 **Palestine**: 4/18 to end |
| **6** (Poona) | pre-war | **Mesopotamia**: 10/14-4/16 (surrendered at Kut) |
| **7** (Meerut) | pre-war | **W. Front**: *BEF* 10/14-12/14; *Ind. Corps* to 1/15; *1* to 11/15 **Mesopotamia**: 12/15-12/17 **Palestine**: 1/18 to end |
| **10** | 12/14 | **Egypt**: 12/14 -2/15; *Disbanded*; Reformed 1/16; *Disbanded* 2/16 |
| **11** | 12/14 | **Egypt**: 12/14 -5/15; *Disbanded* 1/16 |
| **12** | 3/15 | **Mesopotamia**: 3/15-3/16; never at full strength; *Disbanded* 4/16 |
| **14** | 5/16 | **Mesopotamia**: 5/16 to end |
| **15** | 5/16 | **Mesopotamia**: as 14 Div. |
| **17** | 10/17 | **Mesopotamia**: 10/17 to end |
| **18** | 11/17 | **Mesopotamia**: 1/18 to end |

Also in existence throughout the war were 1 (Peshawar), 2 (Rawalpindi), 4 (Quetta), 5 (Mhow), 8 (Lucknow), 9 (Secunderabad) and Burma Infantry Divisions, all of which remained in India and Burma. In addition there were the so-called 3 (Lahore), 6 (Poona) and 7 (Meerut) Divisional Areas in which divisional cadres that had remained in India commanded miscellaneous brigades assigned to their home administration area. During the war there was formed 16 Infantry Division (late 1916) which remained in India. A 19 Infantry Division was mooted but never formed whilst no 13 Infantry Division was ever formed.

### CAVALRY DIVISIONS (Total = 3)

| DIVISION | FORMED | COMBAT RECORD |
|---|---|---|
| **1** | pre-war | **W. Front**: *BEF* 10/14-11/14; *Ind. Cav. Corps* to 7/15; *3* to 10/16; *Cav. Corps* in 11/16; renamed 4 Cav. Div. (see UK) (Had suffered hardly any casualties) |
| **2** | pre-war | **W. Front**: *Ind. Cav. Corps* 11/14-7/15; *3* to 5/16; *4* to 9/16; *3* to 11/16; renamed 5 Cav. Div. (see UK) (Had suffered hardly any casualties) |
| **Indian Mounted** | 12/16 | **Mesopotamia**: 12/16 to 4/18 when disbanded |

Though never organised into divisions, Indian troops also made a significant contribution to East African operations. Between 9/14 and 2/18, one cavalry regiment, 16 Indian Army battalions and 3 battalions and 4 half-battalions of the Indian States Forces all served at various times in this theatre.

## Italy

### INFANTRY DIVISIONS (total = 69)

| DIVISION | FORMED | COMBAT RECORD |
|---|---|---|
| **1** | pre-war | **Carnic Alps\***: *4* in 4/15; *4* in 5/15; *4* in 10/15; *4* in 3/16; *4* in 6/16; *4* in 8/16; *4* in 5/17; *4* in 10/17; *see below* **Tirol†**: *4* in 12/17; *4* in 6/18; *see below* **Piave‡**: *8* in 10/18 to end |
| **1** Assault | 6/18 | **Piave**: *9* in 6/18; *8* in 10/18 |
| **2** | pre-war | **Carnic Alps**: *4* in 4/15; *4* in 5/15; *4* in 10/15; *4* in 3/16; *4* in 6/16; *4* in 8/16; *see Isonzo below* **Isonzo**: *3* in 5/17; *3* in 8/17; *see Tirol below* **Tirol**: *1* in 10/17; *4* in 12/17; *6* in 6/18; *see below* **Piave**: *8* in 10/18 |
| **2** Assault | 6/18 | **Piave**: *8* in 10/18 (Formed one week after 1 Assault Div.; *see above*) |
| **3** | pre-war | **Isonzo**: *2* in 4/15; *2* in 5/15; *2* in 12/15; *2* in 3/16; *2* in 6/16; *2* in 8/16; *2* in 11/16; *Gorizia* in 5/17; *2* in 8/17; *2* in 10/17; *see Tirol below* **Tirol**: *1* in 12/17; *see below* **W. Front**◊: 4/18 to end (with *5 Fr., 10 Fr., and 3 Fr.*) |
| **4** | | **Isonzo**: *2* in 4/15; *2* in 5/15; *2* in 10/15; *2* in 12/15; *3* in 3/16; *see below*; *3* in 8/16; *3* in 11/16; *3* in 5/17; *3* in 8/17; *3* in 10/17; *see Piave below* **GHQ Reserve**: *5* in 6/16; *see Tirol below* **Tirol**: *1* in 7/16; *see Isonzo above*; *4* in 6/18; *7* in 10/18 **Piave**: *3* in 12/17; *see Tirol above* |
| **5** | | **Tirol**: *1* in 4/15; *1* in 5/15; *1* in 10/15; *1* in 3/16; *1* in 6/16; *1* 5/17; *1* in 10/17(?); *1* in 12/17; *7* in 6/18; *7* in 10/18 |
| **6** | | **Tirol**: *as above* to 10/18; *1* in 11/18 |
| **7** | | **Isonzo**: *2* in 4/15; *2* in 5/15; *2* in 10/15; *2* in 12/15; *2* in 3/16; *2* in 6/16; *2* in 8/16; *2* in 11/16 (reinf.); *Gorizia* in 5/17; location uncertain in 8/17; *2* in 10/17; *see Tirol below* **Tirol**: *4* in 12/17; *see below*; *7* in 10/18; *6* in 11/18 **Piave**: *9* in 6/18; *see Tirol above* |
| **8** | | **Isonzo**: *2* in 4/15; *2* in 5/15; *2* in 10/15; *2* in 12/15 (reinf.); *2* in 3/16; *2* in 6/16; *2* in 8/16; *2* in 11/16 (reinf.); *Gorizia* in 5/17; *2* in 8/17; *2* in 10/17; ● *see below* **W. Front**: 4/18 to end (with *5 Fr., 10 Fr., and 3 Fr.*) ● Post-Caporetto does not appear in 12/17 O.B. |
| **9** | | **Tirol**: *1* in 4/15; *1* in 5/15; *1* in 9/15; *see Isonzo below*; *1* in 8/16; *1* in 5/17; *1* in 10/17; *1* in 12/17; *1* in 6/18; *see Piave below* **Isonzo**: *GHQ Res.* in 10/15; *GHQ Res.* in 12/15; *GHQ Res.* in 3/16; *see Tirol above* **Piave**: *8* in 10/18 |

---

\* In other words, Fourth Army's front which in fact extended into eastern Tirol.

† From the Tonnale Pass to the River Piave. Includes Trentino region.

‡ Taken to mean the lower Piave, as far north as Valdobriadene. (See Map 24).

◊ i.e. France.

| DIVISION | FORMED | COMBAT RECORD |
|---|---|---|
| | | **INFANTRY DIVISIONS continued** |
| **10** | pre-war | **Carnic Alps**: 4 in 4/15; 4 in 5/15; 4 in 9/15; *see Isonzo below*<br>**Isonzo**: 2 in 10/15; *GHQ Res.* in 12/15; *GHQ Res.* in 3/16; *see Tirol below*; *GHQ Res.* in 8/16; 2 in 11/16; *Gorizia* in 5/17; 2 in 8/17; 2 in 10/17; *see Tirol below*<br>**Tirol**: 1 in 5/16; 1 in 8/16; *see Isonzo above*; 4 in 12/17; 6 in 6/18; *see below*<br>**Piave**: 8 in 10/18 |
| **11** | | **Isonzo**: 3 in 4/15; 3 in 5/15; 2 in 10/15; 2 in 12/15; 3 in 3/16; 3 in 6/16; 3 in 8/16; 2 in 11/16; *Gorizia* in 5/17; 2 in 8/17; *see Tirol below*<br>**Tirol**: 1 in 10/17; 4 in 12/17; *see below*; 7 in 10/18<br>**Piave**: 9 in 6/18; *see Tirol above* |
| **12** | | **Isonzo**: 3 in 4/15; 3 in 5/15; 2 in 10/15; 2 in 12/15; 3 in 3/16; 3 in 8/16; *AGp. Res.* in 11/16; *see Tirol below*<br>**Tirol**: 6 in 5/17; 1 in 10/17; 4 in 12/17; 1 in 6/18; *see below*<br>**Piave**: 8 in 10/18 |
| **13** | | **Isonzo**: 3 in 4/15; 3 in 5/15; 2 in 10/15; 2 in 12/15; 2 in 3/16; *see GHQ Reserve below*; 2 in 8/17; 2 in 10/17•; *see Piave below*<br>**GHQ Reserve**: 5 in 6/16; *see Tirol below*<br>**Tirol**: 1 in 8/16; 6 in 5/17; *see Isonzo above*<br>**Piave**: 9 in 6/18; *see below*<br>**Albania**: *XVI* in 10/18<br>• Post-Caporetto does not appear in 12/17 O.B. |
| **14** | | **Isonzo**: 3 in 4/15; 3 in 5/15; 3 in 10/15; 3 in 12/15; 3 in 3/16; 3 in 6/16; 3 in 8/16; 3 in 11/16; 3 in 5/17; 3 in 8/17; 3 in 10/17; *see below*<br>**Piave**: 3 in 12/17; *see below*<br>**Tirol**: 6 in 6/18; 6 in 10/18 |
| **15** | | **Tirol**: 1 in 4/15; 1 in 5/15; 1 in 10/15; 1 in 3/16; 1 in 6/16; 1 in 8/16; 6 in 5/17; 4 in 10/17; 4 in 12/17; 4 in 6/18; 4 in 10/18 |
| **16** | | **GHQ Res** in 4/15; 5/15; *see below*<br>**Isonzo**: 3 in 10/15; 3 in 12/15; 3 in 3/16; 3 in 6/16; 3 in 8/16; 3 in 11/16; 3 in 5/17; 3 in 8/17; 3 in 10/17; *Disbanded* 12/17 |
| **17** | | **Carnic Alps**: 4 in 4/15; 4 in 5/15; 4 in 10/15; 4 in 3/16; 4 in 6/16; 4 in 8/16; 4 in 5/17; *see Tirol below*<br>**Tirol**: 4 in 10/17; 4 in 12/17; 4 in 6/18; 4 in 10/18 |
| **18** | | As 17 Div. above |
| **19** | | **Isonzo**: 2 in 4/15; *AGp. Res.* in 5/15; 3 in 10/15; *AGp. Res.* in 12/15; *AGp. Res.* in 3/16; *see below*; 3 in 9/16; 3 in 11/16; 2 in 5/17; 2 in 8/17; 2 in 10/17•; *Disbanded* 11/17<br>**Tirol**: 1 in 6/16; 5 in 8/16<br>• Post-Caporetto does not appear in 12/17 O.B. |
| **20** | | **Isonzo**: 2 in 4/15; *AGp. Res.* in 5/15; 3 in 10/15; *AGp. Res.* in 12/15; *AGp. Res.* in 3/16; *see Tirol below*; 3 in 5/17; 3 in 8/17; 3 in 10/17<br>**Tirol**: 1 in 8/16; *see Isonzo above*; 1 in 12/17; 7 in 6/18; *see below*; 6 in 11/18<br>**Piave**: 9 in 10/18; *see Tirol above* |
| **21** | | **Isonzo**: 3 in 4/15; 3 in 5/15; *AGp. Res.* in 10/15; 3 in 12/15; 3 in 3/16; 3 in 6/16; 3 in 8/16; location uncertain in 11/16; 3 in 5/17; 3 in 8/17; 3 in 10/17; *see Piave below*<br>**Piave**: 3 in 12/17; *see below*; 9 in 10/18; *see below*<br>**Tirol**: 7 in 6/18; *see Piave above*; 4 in 11/18 |
| **22** | | As 21 Div. above except 2 in 8/17 and 10/17• (Isonzo)<br>• Post-Caporetto does not appear in 12/17 O.B. |
| **23** | | **Isonzo**: *AGp. Res.* 4/15; 2 in 5/15; 3 in 10/15; 3 in 12/15; 3 in 3/16; *see GHQ Reserve below*; 3 in 9/16; location uncertain in 11/16; *Gorizia* in 5/17; 2 in 8/17; 2 in 10/17; *see GHQ Reserve below*<br>**GHQ Reserve**: 5 in 6/16; *see Tirol below*; in 12/17; *see Piave below*<br>**Tirol**: 5 in 8/16; *see Isonzo above*<br>**Piave**: 3 in 6/18; 10 in 10/18; 3 in 11/18 |

| DIVISION | FORMED | COMBAT RECORD |
|---|---|---|
| **24** | pre-war | **Isonzo**: *AGp. Res.* in 4/15; 2 in 5/15; *see Carnic Alps below*; 3 in 9/16; 2 in 11/16; *Gorizia* in 5/17; 2 in 8/17; 2 in 10/17; *see GHQ Reserve below*<br>**Carnic Alps**: in 10/15; in 3/16; *see GHQ Reserve below*<br>**GHQ Reserve**: 5 in 6/16; *see Tirol below*; in 12/17; *see Tirol below*<br>**Tirol**: 1 in 8/16; *see Isonzo above*; 4 in 6/18; *see Piave below*<br>**Piave**: 12 in 10/18 |
| **25** | | **Isonzo**: *AGp. Res.* in 4/15; *AGp. Res.* in 5/15; *AGp. Res.* in 10/15; 3 in 12/15; 3 in 3/16; *see Tirol below*; 2 in 8/17; 2 in 10/17; *see Piave below*<br>**Tirol**: 1 in 6/16; 1 in 8/16; 6 in 5/17; *see Isonzo above*<br>**Piave**: 3 in 6/18; 3 in 10/18 |
| **26** | | **GHQ Reserve**: in 4/15; in 5/15; *see Carnic Alps below*<br>**Carnic Alps**: in 10/15; in 3/16; in 6/16; in 8/16; *see Isonzo below*, in 10/17•; *see Tirol below*<br>**Isonzo**: 2 in 5/17; *see Carnic Alps above*<br>**Tirol**: 1 in 6/18; 1 in 10/18<br>• Post-Caporetto does not appear in 12/17 O.B. |
| **27** | | **GHQ Reserve**: in 4/15; in 5/15; *see Isonzo below*, in 3/16; *see Tirol below*<br>**Isonzo**: 2 in 10/15; 2 in 12/15; *see above*; 3 in 8/17; *see Tirol below*<br>**Tirol**: 1 in 6/16; 1 in 8/16; 1 in 5/17; *see Isonzo above*; 1 in 10/17; 1 in 12/17; *see Piave below*<br>**Piave**: 9 in 6/18; 6 in 10/18 |
| **28** | | **GHQ Reserve**: in 4/15; in 5/15; *see Isonzo below*<br>**Isonzo**: 3 in 10/15; *AGp. Res.* in 12/15; *AGp. Res.* in 3/16; *see Tirol below*; 3 in 11/16; 3 in 5/17; 3 in 8/17; 3 in 10/17; *see Piave below*<br>**Tirol**: 1 in 6/16; 1 in 8/16; *see Isonzo above*; 6 in 6/18; *see Piave below*<br>**Piave**: 3 in 12/17; *see Tirol above*; 9 in 10/18 |
| **29** | | **GHQ Reserve**: in 4/15; in 5/15; *see Isonzo below*<br>**Isonzo**: 3 in 10/15; 3 in 12/15; 3 in 3/16; *see Tirol below*<br>**Tirol**: 1 in 6/16; 1 in 8/16; 6 in 5/17; 1 in 10/17; 1 in 12/17; 1 in 6/18; 1 in 10/18 |
| **30** | | **GHQ Reserve**: in 4/15; in 5/15; *see Isonzo below*, 2 in 8/17; 2 in 10/17•; *Disbanded* 11/17<br>**Isonzo**: 3 in 10/15; *AGp. Res.* in 12/15; *AGp. Res.* in 3/16; *see below*<br>**Tirol**: 1 in 6/16; 1 in 8/16; 6 in 5/17; *see Isonzo above*<br>• Post-Caporetto does not appear in 12/17 O.B. |
| **31**<br>(as Bersaglieri Div. to 3/16) | | **GHQ Reserve**: in 4/15; in 5/15; in 10/15; *see Isonzo below*<br>**Isonzo**: 3 in 12/15; 3 in 3/16; 3 in 6/16; 3 in 8/16; location uncertain in 11/16; 3 in 5/17; 3 in 8/17; 3 in 10/17•; *see Piave below*<br>**Piave**: 3 in 6/18; 10 in 10/18<br>• Post-Caporetto does not appear in 12/17 O.B. |
| **32** | | **Isonzo**: 2 in 4/15; 2 in 5/15; 2 in 10/15; 2 in 12/15; 2 in 3/16; *see below*<br>**Tirol**: 1 in 6/16; 1 in 8/16; 1 in 5/17; 1 in 10/17; 1 in 6/18; 1 in 10/18 |
| **33** | | **Isonzo**: 2 in 4/15; 2 in 5/15; 2 in 10/15; 2 in 12/15; 2 in 3/16; *see Tirol below*; 3 in 11/16; 3 in 5/17; 3 in 8/17; 3 in 10/17; *see Tirol below*<br>**Tirol**: 1 in 6/16; 1 in 8/16; *see above*; 4 in 12/17; *see below*<br>**Piave**: 9 in 6/18; 10 in 10/18 |
| **34** | | **Tirol**: 1 in 4/15; 1 in 5/15; 1 in 10/15; 1 in 3/16; 1 in 6/16; 1 in 8/16; *see Isonzo below*; 1 in 6/18; *see Piave below*<br>**Isonzo**: 3 in 11/16; 3 in 5/17; 3 in 8/17; 2 in 10/17•; *see Tirol above*<br>**Piave**: 9 in 10/18<br>• Post-Caporetto does not appear in 12/17 O.B. |
| **35** | | **Tirol**: 1 in 4/15; 1 in 5/15; 1 in 10/15; 1 in 3/16; *see below*<br>**Macedonia**: in 6/16 to end. (Became Eastern Infantry Corps – *CSI d'Oriente* – 7/18) |
| **36** | 3/16 | **Isonzo**: 2 in 3/16; *see Carnic Alps below*; 2 in 5/17; *see Carnic Alps below*<br>**Carnic Alps**: *XVI* in 6/16; *XII* in 8/16; *see above*; in 8/18; in 10/17; *see below*<br>**Albania**: *XVI* in 6/18 to end |
| **37** | | **Tirol**: 1 in 3/16; 1 in 6/16; 1 in 8/16; 1 in 5/17; 1 in 10/17; 1 in 12/17; *see below*<br>**Piave**: 9 in 6/18; 10 in 10/18 |

## INFANTRY DIVISIONS continued

| DIVISION | FORMED | COMBAT RECORD |
|---|---|---|
| **38** | 3/16 | **Albania**: 3/16 to end |
| **39-42** | — | **Not formed** |
| **43** | 3/16 | **Albania**: 3/16 to 5/16; *see Tirol below* <br> **Tirol**: *5* in 8/16; *see below* <br> **Isonzo**: *3* in 9/16; *2* in 11/16; *2* in 5/17; *2* in 8/17; *2* in 10/17; *Disbanded* 11/17 |
| **44** | 3/16 | **Albania**: 3/16 to 5/16; *see Tirol below* <br> **Tirol**: *1* in 6/16; *1* in 8/16; *1* in 5/17; *see below* <br> **Isonzo**: *3* in 8/17; *2* in 10/17; *Disbanded* 11/17 |
| **45** | 5/16 | **Isonzo**: *3* in 6/16; *3* in 8/16; *3* in 11/16; *3* in 5/17; *3* in 8/17; *3* in 10/17; *see below* <br> **Piave**: *3* in 12/17; *3* in 6/18; *3* in 10/18 |
| **46** | | **GHQ Reserve**: *5* in 6/16; *see Tirol below* <br> **Tirol**: *5* in 8/16; *see below* <br> **Isonzo**: *3* in 9/16; *2* in 11/16; *2* in 5/17; *2* in 8/17; *2* in 10/17; *Disbanded* 11/17 |
| **47** | | **GHQ Reserve**: *5* in 6/16; *see Isonzo below*, in 12/17; *see Piave below* <br> **Isonzo**: *2* in 8/16; *3* in 11/16; *Gorizia* in 5/17; *2* in 8/17; *2* in 10/17; *see GHQ Reserve above* <br> **Piave**: *8* in 6/18; *4* in 10/18 |
| **48** | 6/16 | **Tirol**: *5* in 8/16; *see Isonzo below* <br> **Isonzo**: *2* in 11/16; *Gorizia* in 5/17; *2* in 8/17; *2* in 10/17; *see below* <br> **Piave**: *3* in 12/17; *8* in 6/18; *8* in 10/18 |
| **49** | 6/16 | **Isonzo**: *3* in 8/16; *3* in 11/16; *Gorizia* in 5/17; *2* in 8/17; *2* in 10/17; *Disbanded* 11/17 |
| **50** | 11/16 | **Isonzo**: *2* in 11/16; *2* in 5/17; *2* in 8/17; *2* in 10/17; *see Tirol below* <br> **Tirol**: *4* in 12/17; *see below*, *4* in 10/18 <br> **Piave**: *8* in 6/18; *see Tirol above* |
| **51** | 11/16 | **Tirol**: *6* in 5/17; *4* in 10/17; *4* in 12/17; *see below* <br> **Piave**: *8* in 6/18; *8* in 10/18 |
| **52** <br> **Alpine** | 1/17 | **Tirol**: *6* in 5/17; *1* in 10/17; *4* in 12/17; *6* in 6/18; *see below* <br> **Piave**: *12* in 10/18 |
| **53** | 2/17 | **Isonzo**: *Gorizia* in 5/17; *2* in 8/17; *2* in 10/17; *see GHQ Reserve below* <br> **GHQ Reserve**: in 12/17; *see below* <br> **Piave**: *3* in 6/18; *3* in 10/18 |
| **54** | 1/17 | **Isonzo**: *3* in 5/17; *3* in 8/17; *3* in 10/17; *see Tirol below* <br> **Tirol**: *3* in 12/17; *1* in 6/18; *see below* <br> **Piave**: *3* in 10/18 |
| **55** | 1/17 | **Tirol**: *1* in 5/17; *1* in 10/17; *1* in 12/17; *1* in 6/18; *1* in 10/18 |
| **56** | 12/16 | **Carnic Alps**: *4* in 5/17; *see Tirol below* <br> **Tirol**: *4* in 10/17; *4* in 12/17; *4* in 6/18; *4* in 10/18; *see below* <br> **Piave**: *8* in 10/18; *10* in 11/18 |
| **57** | 2/17 | **Tirol**: *6* in 5/17; *1* in 10/17; *4* in 12/17; *see below* <br> **Piave**: *9* in 6/18; *8* in 10/18 |
| **58** | | **Isonzo**: *3* in 5/17; *3* in 8/17; *3* in 10/17; *see below* <br> **Piave**: *3* in 12/17; *8* in 6/18; *8* in 10/18 |
| **59** | | **Tirol**: *1* in 5/17; *see Isonzo below* <br> **Isonzo**: *2* in 8/17; *2* in 10/17•; *see below* <br> **Piave**: *4* in 6/18; *4* in 10/18 <br> • *Post-Caporetto does not appear in 12/17 O.B.* |
| **60** | 4/17 | **Isonzo**: *Gorizia* in 5/17; *2* in 8/17; *2* in 10/17; *see Tirol below* <br> **Tirol**: *4* in 12/17; *see below* <br> **Piave**: *9* in 6/18; *8* in 10/18 |
| **61** | | **Isonzo**: *3* in 5/17; *3* in 8/17; *3* in 10/17; *see below* <br> **Piave**: *3* in 12/17; *3* in 6/18; *3* in 10/18 |
| **62** | | **Isonzo**: *3* in 5/17; *2* in 8/17; *2* in 10/17; *Disbanded* 11/17 |
| **63** | | **Isonzo**: *3* in 5/17; *3* in 8/17; *3* in 10/17; *Disbanded* 11/17 |

| DIVISION | FORMED | COMBAT RECORD |
|---|---|---|
| **64** | 7/17 | **Isonzo**: *2* in 8/17; *2* in 10/17; *Disbanded* 11/17 |
| **65** | | **Isonzo**: *2* in 8/17; *2* in 10/17; *Disbanded* 11/17 |
| **66** | | **Isonzo**: *2* in 8/17; *2* in 10/17; *see Tirol below* <br> **Tirol**: *4* in 12/17; *see below* <br> **Piave**: *8* in 6/18; *8* in 10/18 |
| **67** | | **Isonzo**: *2* in 8/17; *2* in 10/17; *Disbanded* 12/17 |
| **68** | | **Isonzo**: *3* in 8/17; *2* in 10/17; *Disbanded* 11/17 |
| **69** | | **Isonzo**: *3* in 8/17; *see below* <br> **Tirol**: *1* in 10/17; *1* in 6/18; *1* in 10/18 |
| **70** | 11/17 | **GHQ Reserve**: in 12/17; *see Tirol below* <br> **Tirol**: *4* in 6/18; *see below* <br> **Piave**: *12* in 10/18 |
| **71-74** | — | **Not formed** |
| **75** | 6/18 | **Tirol**: *7* in 10/18 |
| **76-78** | — | **Not formed** |
| **79** | 10/16 | *Disbanded* 12/16 |
| **80** <br> **Alpine** | 9/18 | **Tirol**: *4* in 10/18 |
| **Bersaglieri Division** | pre-war | See 31 Div. above. (A second Bersaglieri Div. formed in October 1917 was disbanded the following month.) |

See also Czeckoslavakia: Divisions.

## CAVALRY DIVISIONS (total = 4)

| DIVISION | FORMED | COMBAT RECORD |
|---|---|---|
| **1** | pre-war | **Isonzo**: *2* in 4/15; *3* in 5/15; *see GHQ Reserve below*, *3* in 8/16 (dismounted); *3* in 11/16; *3* in 8/17; *see below* <br> **GHQ Reserve**: in 10/15; in 3/16 (dismounted); *see Isonzo above*; in 10/17; in 6/18; in 10/18 |
| **2** | | **Isonzo**: *2* in 4/15; *3* in 5/15; *see GHQ Reserve below*, *2* in 8/17; *see GHQ Reserve below* <br> **GHQ Reserve**: in 10/15; in 3/16 (dismounted); *see Tirol below*; in 10/17; *see Piave below*; in 10/18 <br> **Tirol**: *1* in 6/16; *1* in 8/16; *see Isonzo above* <br> **Piave**: *3* in 6/18; *see GHQ Reserve above* |
| **3** | | **Isonzo**: *3* in 4/15; *see GHQ Reserve below*, *3* in 5/17; *see GHQ Reserve below* <br> **GHQ Reserve**: in 5/15; in 10/15; in 3/16; *see Tirol below*, in 10/17; in 6/18; in 10/18 <br> **Tirol**: *1* in 8/16; *see Isonzo above* |
| **4** | | **GHQ Reserve**: in 4/15; in 5/15; in 10/15; in 3/16 (dismounted); *see Isonzo below*, in 10/17; *see Piave below*, in 10/18 <br> **Isonzo**: *2* in 8/16 (dismounted); *2* in 11/16 (dismounted); *see above* <br> **Piave**: *9* in 6/18 |

# Japan

## INFANTRY DIVISIONS (total = 1)

The Japanese Army of 1914-18 consisted of one Guards and twenty infantry divisions, as well as four independent cavalry brigades. Only one division took part in military operations against the Central Powers.

| DIVISION | FORMED | COMBAT RECORD |
|---|---|---|
| **18** | pre-war | **Tsingtao**: 8-11/14 (Reinforced with one brigade from 15 Infantry Div.) |

One other division, 12 Infantry, did join the Allied intervention against the Bolsheviks, landing at Vladivistok in August 1918.

## New Zealand

| INFANTRY DIVISIONS (total = 1) | | |
|---|---|---|
| DIVISION | FORMED | COMBAT RECORD |
| 1 | 1/16 | **W. Front**: 2 4/16 to 8/16; 4 to 10/16; 2 to 12/17; 4 to 4/18; 3 |

Prior to the formation of 1 Division, in Egypt, one of its brigades, the 1st, had already fought at Gallipoli, as part of the Anzac Division (see Australian Divisions).

### CAVALRY
The largest New Zealand cavalry formation was the Mounted Rifles Brigade, which arrived in Egypt in December 1914. It was sent to Gallipoli, dismounted, in May 1915, and shortly after its return to Egypt, in March 1916, it became part of the Anzac Mounted Division (see Australian Divisions) with which it served in Egypt and Palestine until the end of the war.

## Poland

| INFANTRY DIVISIONS (and others) | | |
|---|---|---|
| DIVISION | FORMED | COMBAT RECORD |
| **Polish Legion** (Austria) | pre-war | Comprising some six battalions at the beginning of the war, the Legion formed its first brigade within the Austro-Hungarian Army in November 1914, the second in September 1915 and the third in October. At this time all three brigades were united on the Volhynia Front. Fears about their political reliability led the Austrians to demand that they swear an oath of allegiance to the Emperor and wear Austrian insignia on their uniforms. Many legionnaires refused to do this and in July 1917 the brigades were disbanded. At its peak the Legion had contained roughly 20,000 men. |
| **Polish Legion** (Russia) | 10/14 | Formed from volunteers in the so-called Kingdom of Poland, the Legion was always held in suspicion by the autocratic Russian government and in February 1915, having reached approximately brigade strength, it was disbanded. Later that year, however, desperate for seasoned units, the Legion was reformed as a brigade and in January 1917 became a *Rifle Division*. After the fall of the Tsar, in March, the Provisional Government sanctioned the creation of a separate Polish Army from the estimated 20,000 Polish officers and ?00,000 other ranks estimated to be serving in Russian Units.* Three Corps were eventually formed, at Minsk, on the Rumanian Front and around Odessa, but all were variously overrun, in February 1918, during the Central Powers' advance in the wake of the Treaty of Brest-Litovsk (see Map ??). The first of these Corps is known to have been made up of 1, 2 and 3 Divisions but 4 and 5 Divisions were independent formations, the former based around the Kuban and the latter in Siberia. Strengths are uncertain but it is thought that I (Eastern) Corps, as it was sometimes known, comprised some 23,500 men. |
| **Polish Army** (France)† | | Eager for Allied recognition and a foot under the peace-table, the Poles strove to create some sort of national army to fight on the Western Front, alongside the major Allies. In June 1917, the French authorised the formation of such an army on their soil and thirteen months later a Polish General arrived to take command of the fledgling army (only one regiment ready for combat). Fully six divisions were envisaged but by the end of the war only one of these, listed below, had actually arrived at the front. |
| 1 | 6/17 | **W. Front**: 7 Fr. 10/18 to end |
| **Royal Polish Army** (Germany) | 1916/17 | Formed in the 'Kingdom of Poland', a rump state created by Central Powers in November 1916. Both Austria and Germany created a local military force, respectively the Polish Auxiliary Corps and the Royal Polish Army. The former was disbanded in July 1917, along with the Legions, and the latter attracted less than 3,000 recruits. Three regiments strong by October 1918 it was taken over by the Polish Regency Council. It had not been called to the front. |

## Portugal

| INFANTRY DIVISIONS (total = 2) | | |
|---|---|---|

The Portugese Army was partially mobilised in August 1914 and eight infantry divisions were formed. There were also three independent infantry regiments and a cavalry brigade. Once Germany declared war on Portugal in March 1916 (fully sixteen months after Portugal had agreed to cooperate in military operations with the British in Africa) the Portugese began organising a *Corpo Expedicionário*, of two divisions, to the Western Front. These divisions are listed below but an equal military effort was made in Africa where over a dozen infantry battalions were sent as well as seven cavalry regiments (See p. 148).

| DIVISION | FORMED | COMBAT RECORD |
|---|---|---|
| 1 | 1915 | **W. Front**: 1 3/17-7/18; BEF to 8/18; 5 |
| 2 | 1917 | **W. Front**: 1 3/17-9/18; 5 |

## Rumania

| INFANTRY DIVISIONS (total = 25) | | |
|---|---|---|

No Rumanian divisions fought outside the home country and therefore it has not been thought necessary to distinguish fronts in each entry. Further details on the location of the various armies can be found on Maps 22-23. Divisions which reappear after the disasters of December 1916 are those that were reorganised and re-equipped by a French Military Mission under General Berthelot.

| DIVISION | FORMED | COMBAT RECORD |
|---|---|---|
| 1 | pre-war | 1 in 8/16; 1 in 12/16 [as 1/17‡]; 2 in 3/17; Marasti/Oituz 7-9/17◊; Disbanded |
| 1 Rifle | mid-1918 | Not fully mobilised until 10/11/18 |
| 2 | pre-war | 1 in 8/16; 1 in 12/16 [as 2/5‡]; 1 in 3/17; known to be in line 7-9/17◊; Disbanded |
| 2 Rifle | mid-1918 | See 1 Rifle Div. above |
| 3 | pre-war | 2 in 8/16•; 2 in 3/17; Marasti 7-8/17◊; Disbanded 5/18 |
| 4 | | 2 in 8/16; 2 in 12/16 (?); 1 in 3/17; known to be in line 7-9/17◊; Disbanded 5/18 |
| 5 | | 2 in 8/16; 1 in 12/16 [as 2/5‡]; 1 in 3/17; Marasesti 8-9/17◊; Disbanded 5/18 |
| 6 | | 2 in 8/16•; 2 in 3/17; Marasti/Oituz 7-9/17◊; Disbanded 5/18; reformed 10/11/18 |
| 7 | | 4 in 8/16; 1 in 12/16; 2 in 3/17; Oituz 8-9/17◊; Disbanded 5/18; reformed 10/11/18 |
| 8 | | 4 in 8/16; 1 in 12/16; 2 in 3/17; Marasti/Oituz 8-9/17◊; Disbanded 5/18; reformed 10/11/18 |
| 9 | | 3 in 8/16; 1 in 12/16 [as 9/19‡]; 1 in 3/17; Marasesti 8-9/17◊; still active 11/18 |
| 10 | | GHQ Reserve in 8/16; 1 in 12/16; 1 in 3/17; Marasesti 8-9/17◊; still active 11/18 |
| 11 (Reserve) | 8/16 | 1 in 9/16; 1 in 12/16; 1 in 3/17; known to be in line 7-9/17◊; Disbanded 3/18 |
| 12 (Reserve) | | 1 in 9/16; 2 in 12/16; 2 in 3/17; known to be in line 7-9/17◊; Disbanded 3/18 |
| 13 (Reserve) | | 1 in 9/16; 1 in 12/16 [as 13/14‡]; 1 in 3/17; Marasesti 8-9/17◊; Disbanded 3/18; reformed 10/11/18 |

* It has been estimated that over one million Poles were mobilised by the various belligerents.

† Often known as 'Haller's Army' or the 'Blue Army'.

‡ Where two divisional members are divided by a slash, this signifies that e.g. 1 and 17 divisions had been amalgamated after suffering very heavy losses.

◊ Signifies that the Division was present at Battle(s) of Marasti, Marasesti or Oituz in July to Spetember 1917. Army attachments unfortunately unknown.

• Not shown as being present in the line in 12/16 and presumably largely destroyed.

◊ Signifies that the Division was present at Battle(s) of Marasti, Marasesti or Oituz in July to Spetember 1917. Army attachments unfortunately unknown.

• Not shown as being present in the line in 12/16 and presumably largely destroyed.

## INFANTRY DIVISIONS continued

| DIVISION | FORMED | COMBAT RECORD |
|---|---|---|
| **14** (Reserve) | 8/16 | *4* in 9/16; *1* in 12/16 [as *13/14*‡]; *1* in 3/17; Marasesti 8-9/17◊; *Disbanded* 3/18; reformed 10/11/18 |
| **15** (Reserve) | ↓ | *GHQ Reserve* in 9/16; •; *1* in 3/17; Marasesti 8-9/17◊; *Disbanded* 3/18; reformed 10/11/18 |
| **16** (Ersatz) | mid-1916 | *3* in 8/16; *2* in 12/16; *Disbanded* 25/12/16 |
| **17** (Ersatz) | 8/16 | *3* in 9/16; *1* in 12/16 [as *1/17*‡]; not reformed |
| **18** (Ersatz) | | *3* in 9/16; *1* in 12/16; *Disbanded* 25/12/16 |
| **19** (Ersatz) | | *3* in 9/16; *1* in 12/16 [as *9/19*‡]; not reformed |
| **20** (Ersatz) | ↓ | *3* in 9/16; •; *Disbanded* 25/12/16 |
| **21** (Ersatz) | 9/16 | *2* in 9/16; *1* in 12/16; *Disbanded* 25/12/16 |
| **22** (Ersatz) | | *2* in 9/16; *2* in 12/16; *Disbanded* 25/12/16 |
| **23** (Ersatz) | ↓ | *1* in 9/16; *2* in 12/16; *Disbanded* 25/12/16 |

## CAVALRY DIVISIONS (total = 2)

| DIVISION | FORMED | COMBAT RECORD |
|---|---|---|
| **1** | pre-war | *2* in 8/16; *1* in 12/16; *1* in 3/17; Oituz 8-9/17◊; still active 11/18 |
| **2** | pre-war | *4* in 8/16; *1* in 12/16; *1* in 3/17; Marasesti 8-9/17◊; still active 11/18 |

## Russia

As with Eastern Front Orders of Battle this section has caused us more problems than any other due to difficulty of obtaining reliable data on the Russian Army.

### Sources available

We were confined to using Austrian and German official histories, German Intelligence sources and secondary English language sources of which the most useful were Knox and Muratoff & Allen. Our only input from Russian sources was from Eugen Pinak who provided some very useful data from Russian language sources.

### Problem areas

1   We were unable to obtain precise dates when war-raised divisions were formed, nor could we discover precise dates as to when rifle brigades were raised to divisional status. ('Around Autumn 1915' seemed to be the general consensus).

2   Whilst we found comprehensive O.B.s for the opening months of the war right across the Eastern Front there was a dearth of material after early 1915 for the North Western sector.

3   Austrian coverage of the South Western sector was consistently good throughout the war up to and including the Kerensky Offensive in the summer of 1917. Similarly coverage of the Army of the Caucasus was good throughout the war in Muratoff & Allen.

### Brief Summary of War Formed Divisions

Details of divisions at the outbreak of war are given Table 3.4 of the Order of Battle Section. The following divisions were formed during the war between 1915-1917.

INFANTRY
    5, 6, 2 Caucasus Grenadier Divisions
    100-127 Inf. Divisions (3rd Line)
    128-138, 151-194 Inf. Divisions (4th Line)
    6-8 Rifle Divisions
    12-22, Composite Siberian Rifle Divisions
    3-7 Caucasus Rifle Divisions
    7-10 Turkestan Rifle Divisions
    5-6 Finnish Rifle Divisions
    1-5 Trans-Amur Border Guard Divisions
    1-2 Naval Infantry Divisions (Baltic, Black Sea)
    6 Non-Russian Volunteer Divisions

CAVALRY
    3 Guards Cavalry Division
    16-17, Combined Cavalry Divisions
    3-6 Don Cossack Divisions
    4-5 Caucasus Cossack Divisions
    3-4, Combined Kuban Cossack Divisions
    2 Terek Cossack Divisions
    Orenburg Cossack Division
    Ural Cossack Division
    Siberian Cossack Division
    1-2 Trans-Baikal Cossack Divisions
(Some Cossack Divisions were formed "on paper" with component regiments operating independently).

Mounted Divisions ('National' Troops)
    Trans-Amur Mounted Border Guard Division
    Caucasus 'Native' Volunteer Division
    Ussuri Mounted Division
Some of the above divisions were formed by expanding brigades existing pre-war.

There were also a number of Independent Brigades the most important of which are mentioned at the end of the divisional section. There were also many Cossack Regiments outside the organisation of divisions and brigades.

### Divisional Service Records

As a result we are satisfied we have fairly comprehensive coverage of divisions which served on the South Western Front, the Rumanian Front and in the Armt of the Caucasus. For the Northern and Western Fronts/Army Groups coverage is largely confined to 1914 and early 1915. Therefore we fell back on what we would call 'inherent military probability'.

### Inherent Military Probability

We are fairly confident in saying that for the many divisions showing very little dated information as to location the strong probability is that such divisions were serving on the northern sectors of the Eastern Front largely against the Germans. The inherent military probability is that they were in either the Northern Front (Northern Army Group) or the Western Front (Western Army Group) of the Russian armies.

### Notes on Reading the Tables

1   Given the multiplicity of divisional types in the Russian Army in World War One we have set these out differently from the other armies. In this section they are arranged by type and then numerically within type. Divisions are listed in the following order:

Infantry
    Guard Infantry and Rifle Divisions
    Grenadier Divisions
    Line Infantry Divisions – Regular, Reserve, 3rd Line, 4th Line

Rifle Brigades/Divisions – European, Finnish, Caucasian,
Turkestan, Siberian
Frontier Guard Divisions
Marine Division
Miscellaneous Divisions
Cavalry
Guard Cavalry
Line Cavalry
Cossack Divisions – Don, Caucasus, Orenburg, Kuban, Terek,
Ural, Turkestan, Siberian, Trans-Baikal
Mounted Divisions

**2   Fronts** – Russian Divisions served on 3 major geographical fronts:
Eastern Front
Sub-divided into 2, then 3 "fronts" (Russian equivalent of
western Army Groups)
North Western subdivided in August 1915 into
Northern and
Western
South Western
Rumanian Front
(formed December 1916)
Armenia-Kurdistan
(Term used by us, officially it was called the Caucasus Front).

**3   Service Records**

All dates are "as at" unless stated otherwise. We have quoted every date for
which we have a positive identification. Where little information is given
post-1915 we again refer readers to our note as to 'inherent military
probability' (i.e. a division was probably on Northern or Western Front if nor
shown as South Western Front, Rumania or Army of the Caucasus).

*Abbreviations*

N.W.   North Western Front (until divided in August 1915)
N.    Northern Front  } Created Aug. 1915 by dividing N.W. Front
W.    Western Front  }
S.W.   South Western Front (in existence throughout the war)

*Reading Divisional Record – e.g. 1 Grenadier Division on this page*
**Eastern Front**   S.W./4 = South Western Front, 4th Army, as at dates given;
W./4 = Western Front, 4th Army, as at dates given;
W./3 = Western Front, 3rd Army, as at date given

Where no Army is given after the Army Group the division is at the disposal
of Army Group H.Q.
e.g. S.W. 5.6/15 = at disposal of S.W.Front H.Q. in May-June 1915.

### INFANTRY DIVISIONS (total = 243)

### GUARD INFANTRY DIVISIONS

| DIVISION | FORMED | COMBAT RECORD (where known) and formation details where appropriate |
|---|---|---|
| **1** | pre-war | **E.Front** *N.W./9/S.W.4* 8-9/14; *S.W./9* 10/14; *N.W./2* 1-2/15; *W./Reserve* 10/15; *G.H.Q. Reserve* 6/16; *S.W./Special* 7/16, 11/16, 3/17; *S.W./11* summer 17 |
| **2** | | **E.Front** *N.W./9/S.W.4* 8-9/14; *S.W./9* 10/14; *N.W./2* 1-2/15; *W./Reserve* 10/15, winter 15/16; *G.H.Q. Reserve* 6/16; *S.W./Special* 7/16, 11/16, 3/17; *S.W./11* summer 17 |
| **3** | ↓ | **E.Front** *N.W./2* 8-9/14, 10/14; *N.W.5* 1-2/15; *S.W./8* 5-6/15; *W./Reserve* 10/15, winter 15/16; *G.H.Q. Reserve* 6/16; *S.W./Special* 7/16, 11/16, 3/17; *S.W./7* summer 17 |

### GUARD INFANTRY DIVISIONS continued

| DIVISION | FORMED | COMBAT RECORD (where known) and formation details where appropriate |
|---|---|---|
| **Guard Rifle** | pre-war | (Brigade, raised to Division Autumn 1915 [?]) **E.Front** *S.W./9* 8-9/14, 10/14; *N.W./2* 1-2/15; *W./Reserve* 10/15; *G.H.Q. Reserve* 6/16; *S.W./Special* 7/16, 11/16, 3/17; *S.W./7* summer 17 |

### GRENADIER DIVISIONS

| DIVISION | FORMED | COMBAT RECORD (where known) and formation details where appropriate |
|---|---|---|
| **1** | pre-war | **E.Front** *S.W./4* 8-9/14, 10/14, 1-2/15, 5-6/15; *W./4* 10/15, winter 15/16; *W./3* 6/16 |
| **2** | | **E.Front** *as for 1 Grenadier Div. above* |
| **3** | | **E.Front** *S.W./5* 8-9/14, 10/14; *S.W./9* 1-2/15; *S.W./4* 5-6/15; *W./4* 10/15, winter 15/16; *W./3* then *4* 6/16; *S.W./Special* 11/16, 3/17; *S.W./11* summer 17 |
| **Caucasus** | ↓ | (N.B. Regarded as 4 Grenadier Division) **Armenia/Kurdistan** *Army of the Caucasus* 8-9/14, then to E.Front **E.Front** *N.W./1* 1-2/15; *S.W./8* 5-6/15; *W./10* 10/15, winter 15/16; *N./4* 6/16 |
| **5** | Autumn 1916-1917 | (Formed from 4th Bns. Grenadier Corps Regiments) **E.Front** *W./2* summer 17 |
| **6** | | (152 ID re-designated) (Noted as of particularly low combat/morale value) **E.Front** *S.W./Special* 3/17; *S.W./11* summer 17 |
| **2 Caucasus** | ↓ | (176 ID re-designated) (Noted as of particularly low combat/morale value) **E.Front** *W./10* summer 17 |

### LINE INFANTRY DIVISIONS (1st Line Regular)

| DIVISION | FORMED | COMBAT RECORD (where known) and formation details where appropriate |
|---|---|---|
| **1** | pre-war | **E.Front** *N.W./2* 8/14; destroyed Tannenberg 8/14; not fully reconstituted until 1916; *N./12* 6/16 |
| **2** | | **E.Front** *N.W./2* 8-9/14, 10/14; *N.W./12* and *5* 1-2/15; *W./Reserve* 10/15, winter 15/16; *N./4* 6/16 **Rumanian Front** *4* 3/17 |
| **3** | | **E.Front** *S.W./5* 8-9/14, 10/14; *S.W./9* 1-2/15; *S.W./8* 5-6/15, 9/15, winter 15/16; *S.W./11* 6/16; *S.W./3* 7/16; *S.W./11* 7/16, 11/16, 3/17, summer 17 |
| **4** | | **E.Front** *N./2* 8-9/14; *N.W./New 1* 10/14; *N.W./2* 1-2/15; *S.W./11* 9/15, 10/15, winter 15/16, 6/16; *S.W./7* 7/16; *S.W./11* 11/16, 3/17, summer 17 |
| **5** | | **E.Front** *S.W./3* 8-9/14, 10/14, 1-2/15, 5-6/15; *W./3* 10/15, winter 15/16, 6/16 |
| **6** | | **E.Front** *N.W./2* 8-9/14; *N.W./12* 1-2/15; *W./4* 10/15, winter 15/16; *W./2* 6/16 |
| **7** | | **E.Front** *S.W./5* 8-9/14, 10/14; *N.W./5* 1-2/15; *W./2* 10/15, winter 15/16, 6/16; *S.W./11* 7/16; *S.W./Special* 11/16, 3/17; *S.W./11* summer 17 |
| **8** | | **E.Front** *N.W./2* 8-9/14; *N.W./12* 1-2/15; *S.W./3* 5-6/15; *W./4* 10/15, winter 15/16; *W./2* 6/16 |
| **9** | | **E.Front** *S.W./3* 8-9/14, 10/14, 1-2/15, 5-6/15; *W./3* 10/15, winter 15/16; *W./3* then *4* 6/16 |
| **10** | | **E.Front** *S.W./5* 8-9/14, 10/14; *N.W./5* 1-2/15; *W./2* 10/15, winter 15/16, 6/16; *S.W./11* 7/16; *S.W./Special* 11/16, 3/17; *S.W./11* summer 17 |
| **11** | | **E.Front** *S.W./3* 8-9/14, 10/14, 1-2/15; *S.W./9* 5-6/15; *S.W./11* 10/15, winter 15/16; *S.W./9* 6/16; *S.W./11* 7/16-To *9*, late 7/16 *S.W./8* 11/16, 3/17, summer 17 |
| **12** | ↓ | **E.Front** *S.W./8* 8-9/14; *S.W./11* 10/14; *S.W./8* 1-2/15; *S.W./3* 5-6/15, *S.W./9* 9/15, 10/15, winter 15/16; *S.W./9* 6/16, 7/17; *S.W./8* 11/16, 3/17 |

## LINE INFANTRY DIVISIONS (1st Line Regular) continued

| DIVISION | FORMED | COMBAT RECORD (where known) and formation details where appropriate |
|---|---|---|
| 13 | pre-war | E.Front S.W./8 8-9/14; S.W./3 10/14; S.W./8 1-2/15, 5-6/15, 9/15, 10/15, winter 15/16; S.W./11 6/16, 7/16, 11/16 |
| 14 | | E.Front S.W./8 8-9/14, 10/14, 1-2/15, 5-6/15, 9/15, 10/15, winter 15/16, 6/16; S.W./11 7/16; S.W./8 late 7/16; S.W./Reserve 11/16 **Rumanian Front** 4 3/17 |
| 15 | | E.Front as for 14 Inf. Div. **Rumanian Front** as for 14 Inf. Div. |
| 16 | | E.Front N.W./2 8-9/14; N.W./New 1 10/14; N.W./2 1-2/15; S.W./11 9/15, 10/15, winter 15/16, 6/16; S.W./7 7/16; S.W./11 11/16, 3/17, summer 17 |
| 17 | | E.Front S.W./5 8-9/14, 10/14; N.W./5 1-2/15; N./5 10/15, winter 15/16; N./1 then 5 6/16 |
| 18 | | E.Front S.W./9 8-9/14, 10/14; S.W./4 1-2/15, 5-6/15; W./1 10/15, winter 15/16; N./1 6/16 |
| 19 | | E.Front S.W./8 8-9/14; S.W./11 10/14; S.W./8 1-2/15; S.W./3 5-6/15; S.W./8 9/15; S.W./9 6/16, 7/16; S.W./7 late 7/16, 3/17; S.W./8 summer 17 |
| 20 | | **Armenia/Kurdistan** Army of the Caucasus 8-9/14, 10/14, to main E.Front 2/15 E.Front W. 5-6/16; S.W./8 7/16; S.W./Special 11/16 |
| 21 | | E.Front S.W./3 and 9 8-9/14; S.W./4 10/14, 1-2/15; S.W./3 5-6/15; W./3 10/15, winter 15/16; W./10 6/16; S.W./7 11/16, 3/17, summer 17 |
| 22 | | E.Front N.W./9 then 2 8-9/14; N.W./2 10/14: N.W./5 1-2/15; W./1 to 10/15, winter 15/16; N. 6/16; S.W./8 7/16; S.W./Special 7/17, 11/16 |
| 23 | | E.Front N.W./9 8/14; S.W./9 9/14, 10/14, 1-2/15; S.W./8 5-6/15; S.W./11 9/15, 10/15, winter 15/16, 6/16; S.W./7 7/16, 10/16, 3/17, summer 17 |
| 24 | | E.Front N.W./9 then 2 8-9/14; N.W./2 10/14: N.W./5 1-2/15; W./1 to 10/15, winter 15/16; N. 6/16; S.W./8 7/16; S.W./Special 7/16, 11/16 |
| 25 | | E.Front N.W./1 8-9/14; N.W./1 to 10 10/14; N.W./2 1-2/15; W./2 to 10/15, winter 15/16, 6/16; S.W./9 11/16 **Rumanian Front** 9 3/17 |
| 26 | | E.Front N.W./1 8-9/14; N.W./1 to 2 10/14; N.W./1 1-2/15; W./10 9/15, to New 7 11/15; S.W./7 11/15, winter 15/16; S.W./9 6/16, 7/16; S.W./9 11/16 **Rumanian Front** 9 3/17 |
| 27 | | E.Front N.W./1 8-9/14; N.W./1 to 10 10/14; N.W./10 1-2/15; W./3 10/15, winter 15/16; W. 6/16; S.W./3 6/16, 7/16; S.W. to W. 1916/17 (?); S.W./3 3/17 |
| 28 | | E.Front N.W./1 8-9/14, 10/14; N.W./10 1-2/15; W./2 10/15, winter 15/16; W./4 to 3 6/16 |
| 29 | | E.Front as for 28 Inf. Div. above |
| 30 | | E.Front N.W./1 8-9/14; N.W./1 to 2 10/14; N.W./5 1-2/15; W./1 10/15, winter 15/16, 6/16 **Rumanian Front** Danube 11/16 (became 6 Army 12/16), 3/17 |
| 31 | | E.Front S.W./3 8-9/14, 10/14, 1-2/15, 5-6/15; W./9 10/15, winter 15/16; W./3 then 4 6/16 |
| 32 | | E.Front S.W./3 8-9/14, 10/14, 1-2/15; S.W./11 5-6/15; S.W./9 9/15; S.W./11 10/15, winter 15/16; S.W./9 6/16, 7/16; S.W./8 11/16, 3/17; W./3 then 4 6/16 |
| 33 | | E.Front S.W./3 8-9/14, 10/14, 1-2/15, 5-6/15; N./5 10/15, winter 15/16; N./1 6/16 |
| 34 | | E.Front S.W./8 8-9/14; S.W./3 10/14; S.W./8 1-2/15, 5-6/15, 9/15, 10/15, winter 15/16; S.W./11 6/16, 7/16, 11/16 |
| 35 | | E.Front N.W./5 8-9/14, 10/14; S.W./9 1-2/15; S.W./8 5-6/15, 9/15, 10/15, winter 15/16; S.W./11 6/16, 7/16, 11/16, 3/17, summer 17 |
| 36 | | E.Front N.W./2 8-9/14, destroyed 8/14, not fully re-constituted until 1916; N./12 6/16 |
| 37 | | E.Front N.W./9 8/14; S.W./9 9/14, 10/14, 1-2/15; S.W./11 5-6/15, 9/15, 10/15, winter 15/16, 6/16; S.W./7 7/16; S.W./8 8/16; S.W./8 11/16, 3/17 |

| DIVISION | FORMED | COMBAT RECORD (where known) and formation details where appropriate |
|---|---|---|
| 38 | pre-war | E.Front S.W./5 8-9/14, 10/14; N.W./5 1-2/15; N./5 10/15, winter 15/16; N./1 then 5 6/16 |
| 39 | | **Armenia/Kurdistan** Army of the Caucasus 8-9/14 through to 3/17 |
| 40 | | E.Front N.W./1 8-9/14; N.W./1 to 2 10/14; N.W./5 1-2/15; W./1 10/15, winter 15/16, 6/16 **Rumanian Front** Danube (became 6 Army 12/16) 11/16, 3/17 |
| 41 | | E.Front S.W./4 8-9/14, 10/14, 1-2/15, 5-6/15; W./4 9/15, 10/15; to S.W./New 7 11/15; S.W./9 6/16; to S.W./7 6/16; S.W./7 7/16, 11/16, 3/17; S.W./8 summer 17 |
| 42 | | E.Front S.W./3 8-9/14, 10/14, 1-2/15, 5-6.15; W./3 10/15, winter 15/16. 6/16 |
| 43 | | E.Front N.W./1 8-9/14: N.W./1 to 2 10/14; N.W./1 1-2/15; W./10 9/15, 10/15; to S.W./New 7 11/15, winter 15/16, 6/16; S.W./7 7/16; S.W./9 8/16; S.W./8 11/16, 3/17 |
| 44 | | E.Front S.W./3 8-9/14, 10/14, 1-2/15, 5-6/15; N./5 10/15, winter 15/16; N./1 6/16 |
| 45 | | E.Front S.W./9 8-9/14, 10/14; S.W./4 1-2/15, 5-6/15; W./2 10/15, winter 15/16; 6/16 |
| 46 | | E.Front S.W./5 8-9/14, 10/14; S.W./9 1-2/15; S.W./4 5-6/15; W./4 10/15, winter 15/16; W./3 then 4 6/16; S.W./Special 11/16, 3/17; S.W./11 summer 17 |
| 47 | | E.Front S.W./4 8-9/14, 10/14, 1-2/15, 5-6/15; W./4 9/15, 10/15; S.W./New 7 11/15, 6/16, 7/16, 11/16, 3/17; S.W./8 summer 17 |
| 48 | | E.Front S.W./8 8-9/14, 10/14, 1-2/15; S.W./3 5-6/15; W./3 9/15, 10/15; S.W./8 11/15; W./10 6/16; S.W./9 7/16 **Rumanian Front** 9 3/17 |
| 49 | | E.Front as for 48 Inf. Div. above **Rumanian Front** as for 48 Inf. Div. above |
| 50 | | E.Front G.H.Q. Disposal/6 8-9/14: to N.W./2 10/14; N.W./2 then New 1 10/14; N.W./1 1-2/15; W./4 10/15, winter 15/16; N. 6/16; S.W./8 then 9 6/16; S.W./8 7/16; S.W./11 late 7/16, 11/16, 3/17; S.W./8 summer 17 |
| 51 | | **Armenia/Kurdistan** Army of the Caucasus 8-9/14, transferred to main E.Front 9/14 E.Front N.W./1 1-2/15; S.W./8 5-6/15; W./10 10/15, winter 15/16; W./4 6/16 |
| 52 | | E.Front S.W./3 8/14; S.W./4 9/14, 10/14, 1-2/15; S.W./3 5-6/15; W./3 10/15, winter 15/16; W./10 6/16; S.W./7 11/16, 3/17, summer 17 |

## RESERVE INFANTRY DIVISIONS* (2nd Line)

| DIVISION | FORMED | COMBAT RECORD (where known) and formation details where appropriate |
|---|---|---|
| 53 | on mobilisation | (Parent division – 1 Grenadier) (Moscow MD) E.Front N.W./1 8-9/14; N.W./1 to 10 10/14; N.W./10 1-2/15; W. 6/16; S.W./8 7/16; S.W./Special 11/16, 3/17 |
| 54 | | (Parent division – 2 Grenadier) (Moscow MD) E.Front N.W./1 8-9/14, destroyed Masurian Lakes 9/14, disbanded, not reformed |
| 55 | | (Parent division – 3 Grenadier) (Moscow MD) E.Front Moscow/Brest-Litovsk 8/14; to S.W./5 8/14; to N.W. 9/14; G.H.Q.Reserve/6 10/14; N.W./2 1-2/15; S.W./8 5-6/15; W./4 6/16 |
| 56 | | (Parent division – 1 Inf. Div.) (Moscow MD) E.Front N.W./1 8-9/14; N.W./1 to 10 10/14; N.W./10 1-2/15; W./2 10/15, winter 15/16; S.W./Special 11/16, 3/17; S.W./8 summer 17 |
| 57 | | (Parent division – 3 Inf. Div.) (Moscow MD) E.Front N.W./1 8-9/14; N.W./10 1-2/15; W./10 10/15, winter 15/16 **Rumanian Front** 6 3/17 |
| 58 | | (Parent division – 5 Inf. Div.) (Kiev MD) E.Front S.W./3 8-9/14; S.W./11 10/14, 1-2/15, 5-6/15; S.W. to N.W. 7-8/15, destroyed Modlin 8/15 |

* Cadres from parent division in home military district.

## RESERVE INFANTRY DIVISIONS* (2nd Line) continued

| DIVISION | FORMED | COMBAT RECORD (where known) and formation details where appropriate |
|---|---|---|
| 59 | on mobilisation | (Parent division – 7 Inf. Div.) (Moscow MD)<br>**E.Front** *N.W./2* 8/14; *Warsaw* 9/14; *N.W./10* 10/14; *N.W./2* 1-2/15; *W./10* 10/15, winter 15/16; *N.* 6/16; *N./5* to *S.W./9* 8/16; *S.W./9* 11/16, 3/17 |
| 60 | | (Parent division – 9 Inf. Div.) (Kiev MD)<br>**E.Front** *S.W./8* 8-9/14; *S.W./11* 10/14; *S.W./8* 1-2/15, 5-6/15; *S.W.–N.W.* 7-8/15; *N./5* 10/15, winter 15/16, 6/16 |
| 61 | | (Parent division – 10 Inf. Div.) (Moscow MD)<br>**E.Front** *S.W./5* 8-9/14, 10/14; *S.W./3* 1-2/15, 5-6/15; *W./10* 10/15, winter 15/16; 6/16; from *10* to *Dobrudja Detachment* 8/16<br>**Rumanian Front** *Dobrudja Det.* 8/16; *Danube* 10/16, 11/16 (*Danube* became *6 Army* 12/16); *6* 12/16, 3/17 |
| 62 | | (Parent division – 13 Inf. Div.) (Odessa MD)<br>*Odessa Area/7* 8-9/14, 10/14; to main E.Front<br>**E.Front** *N.W./5* 1-2/15; *S.W./8* 5-6/15; *W./10* 10/15, winter 15/16, 6/16 |
| 63 | | (Parent division – 14 Inf. Div.) (Odessa MD)<br>*Odessa Area/7* 8-9/14; to main E.Front<br>**E.Front** *N.W./Warsaw & Narew Group* 10/14; *N.W./2* 1-2/15; *S.W./3* 5-6/15; *destroyed Modlin* 8/15 |
| 64 | | (Parent division – 15 Inf. Div.) (Odessa MD)<br>*Odessa Area/7* 8-9/14; to main E.Front<br>**E.Front** *N.W./10* 1-2/15; *W./10* 10/15, winter 15/16; 6/16; from *W./4* to *S.W./9* 8/16; *S.W./8* 11/16, 3/17 |
| 65 | | (Parent division – 19 Inf. Div.) (Kiev MD)<br>**E.Front** *S.W./8* 8-9/14, 10/14, 1-2/15, 5-6/15; from *S.W.* to *N.W.* 7-8/15; *W./4* to 6/16; *S.W./9* 11/16<br>**Rumanian Front** *9* 3/17 |
| 66 | | (Parent division – 21 Inf. Div.) (Caucasus MD)<br>**Armenia/Kurdistan** *Army of the Caucasus* 8-9/14 throughout summer 17 |
| 67 | | (Parent division – 22 Inf. Div.) (St. Petersburg MD)<br>**E.Front** *G.H.Q. Reserve/6* 8-9/14, 10/14; *N.W./2* 1-2/15; *W./4* 10/15, winter 15/16, 6/16 |
| 68 | | (Parent division – 24 Inf. Div.) (St. Petersburg MD)<br>**E.Front** *N.W./1* 8-9/14; *N.W./1* to *10* 10/14; *N.W./10* 1-2/15; *W./2* 10/15, winter 15/16, 6/16; *S.W./9* 11/16<br>**Rumanian Front** *6* 3/17 |
| 69 | | (Parent division – 31 Inf. Div.) (Kiev MD)<br>**E.Front** *S.W./3* 8-9/14; *S.W./11* 10/14; *S.W./8* 1-2/15, 5-6/15; *S.W.* to *N.W.* 7-8/15; *W./10* 10/15, winter 15/16, 6/16 |
| 70 | | (Parent division – 33 Inf. Div.) (Kiev MD)<br>**E.Front** *S.W./5* 8-9/14; *S.W./9* then to *5* 10/14; *S.W./3* 1-2/15, 5-6/15; *W./10* 10/15, winter 15/16; *N./1* 6/16<br>**Rumanian Front** *4* 3/17 |
| 71 | | (Parent division – 34 Inf. Div.) (Odessa MD)<br>**E.Front** *S.W./8* 8-9/14, 10/14, 1-2/15; *S.W./9*, 5-6/15, 9/15; *S.W./8* 10/15, winter 15/16, 2/16, 7/16; *S.W./Special* late 7/16, 11/16 |
| 72 | | (Parent division – 35 Inf. Div.) (Moscow MD)<br>**E.Front** *N.W./1* 8-9/14; destroyed Masurian Lakes 9/14; *disbanded, not re-formed* |
| 73 | | (Parent division – 36 Inf. Div.) (Moscow MD)<br>**E.Front** *N.W./1* 8-9/14; *N.W./1* to *10* 10/14; *N.W./10* 1-2/15; *N./5* 10/15, winter 15/16; *N./?* 6/16; *S.W./3* 7/16; *W.* during 1916/17 date unknown; *S.W./3* 3/17 |
| 74 | | (Parent division – 37 Inf. Div.) (St. Petersburg MD)<br>**E.Front** *G.H.Q. Reserve/6* 8-9/14, 10/14; *S.W./3* 1-2/15; *S.W./9* 5-6/15, 9/15, 10/15, winter 15/16, 6/16, 7/16; *S.W./7* 11/16, 3/17, summer 17 |
| 75 | | (Parent division – 38 Inf. Div.) (Warsaw MD)<br>**E.Front** *S.W./9* 8-9/14; *S.W./4* 10/14; *S.W./9* 1-2/15; *S.W./4* 5-6/15; *W./3* 10/15, winter 15/16, 6/16; *S.W./3* 7/16; *W.* during 16/17 date unknown; *S.W./3* 3/17 |
| 76 | | (Parent division – 40 Inf. Div.) (Vilna MD)<br>**E.Front** *N.W./1* 8-9/14; *N.W./10* 10/14; *N.W./2* 1-2/15; *W./2* 10/15, winter 15/16, 6/16 |
| 77 | | (Parent division – 41 Inf. Div.) (Kazan MD)<br>**E.Front** *N.W./2* 8/14; *N.W./Warsaw* 9/14; *N.W./Warsaw* to *Narew Group* 10/14; *N.W./12* 1-2/15; *S.W./3* 5-6/15; *W./3* to *S.W./8* 9/15; *W./3* 10/15, winter 15/16; *S.W./6* 6/16; *S.W./3* 7/16, 3/17 |

| DIVISION | FORMED | COMBAT RECORD (where known) and formation details where appropriate |
|---|---|---|
| 78 | on mobilisation | (Parent division – 42 Inf. Div.) (Kiev MD)<br>**E.Front** *S.W./3* 8-9/14; *S.W./11* 10/14; *S.W./8* 1-2/15; *S.W./9* 5-6/15; *S.W.* to *N.W.* 7-8/15; *N./5* 10/15, winter 15/16; *N./1* 6/16; *S.W./37* 7/16; *S.W./9* 11/16<br>**Rumanian Front** *9* 3/17 |
| 79 | | (Parent division – 44 Inf. Div.) (Kiev MD)<br>**E.Front** *N.W./2* 8-9/14; *N.W./2 - Narew Group* to *New 1* 10/14; *N.W./1* 1-2/15; *N./12* 10/15, winter 15/16; *S.W./7* 7/16; *S.W./7* to *S.W./9* late 7/16; *S.W./11* 11/16, 3/17 |
| 80 | | (Parent division – 45 Inf. Div.) (Odessa MD)<br>**E.Front** *S.W./4* 8/14; *S.W./9* 9/14, 10/14, 1-2/15; *S.W./11* 5-6/15; *S.W./9* 9/15; *S.W./8* 10/15, winter 15/16, 6/16, 7/16; *S.W./Special* late 7/16, 11/16<br>**Rumanian Front** *4* 3/17 |
| 81 | | (Parent division – 46 Inf. Div.) (Moscow MD)<br>**E.Front** *S.W./5* 8-9/14; *S.W./4* 10/14; *S.W./11* 1-2/15; *S.W./3* 5-6/15; *W./4* 10/15; *W./3* 6/16 |
| 82 | | (Parent division – 47 Inf. Div.) (Kazan MD)<br>**E.Front** *S.W./4* 8-9/14; *S.W./11* 10/14, 1-2/15; *S.W./9* 5-6/15; *S.W./9* to *8* 10/15; *S.W./8* 10/15, winter 15/16; *S.W./9* 6/16, 7/16; *S.W./8* 11/16, 3/17; *S.W./11* summer 17 |
| 83 | | (Parent division – 48 Inf. Div.) (Kazan MD)<br>**E.Front** *S.W./4* 8-9/14; *S.W./9* 10/14, 1-2/15; *S.W./4* 5-6/15; *W./3* to *S.W./8* 9/15; *W./3* 10/15, 6/16; *S.W./3* 7/16; *W.* 1916/17 date unknown; *S.W./3* 3/17 |
| 84 | | (Parent division – 49 Inf. Div.) (Kazan MD)<br>**E.Front** *G.H.Q.Reserve/6* 8-9/14; *G.H.Q.Reserve/6* to *N.W./10* 10/14; *N.W./10* 10/14, 1-2/15; *W./10* 10/15, winter 15/16; 6/16; *S.W./8* 11/16<br>**Rumanian Front** *9* 3/17 |
| 85-98 | – | **Not formed** |
| 99 | ? | This division was never completed. The two regiments formed were converted to Turkestan Rifle Regiments (24 & 25) (originally 393 & 394 IR) |

## INFANTRY DIVISIONS (3rd Line)

Usually formed from *Opolchenie* (militia type) brigades. *Opolchenie* were 2nd reserve manpower – older recruits. Usually 2 militia brigades and reduced artillery ( 1 battalion). Divisions marked thus § were later raised to full artillery brigades status 1916/1917.

| DIVISION | FORMED | COMBAT RECORD (where known) and formation details where appropriate |
|---|---|---|
| 100§ | spring 1915† | Known as Black Sea Division (*Tchernomorskaja Divisia*) (Formed from 13 Militia Bde.)<br>**E.Front** *S.W./8* 6/16; *S.W./3* 7/16, 3/17 |
| 101 | | (Formed from 29 & 36 Militia Bdes.)<br>**E.Front** *S.W./9* 9/15, 10/15, winter 15/16; *S.W./8* 6/16; *S.W./11* 7/16, 11/16, 3/17 |
| 102 | | (Formed from 10 & 34 Militia Bdes.)<br>**E.Front** *S.W./8* 9/15, 10/15, winter 15/16, 6/16, 7/16; *S.W./Special* 11/16, 3/17 |
| 103 | | (Formed from 30 & 86 Militia Bdes.)<br>**E.Front** *S.W./9* 9/15, 10/15, winter 15/16, 6/16, 7/16, 11/16<br>**Rumanian Front** *9* 3/17 |
| 104 | | (Formed from 2 & 12 Militia Bdes.)<br>**E.Front** *W./2* 10/15, winter 15/16, 6/16; *S.W./Special* 11/16, 3/17; *S.W./7* summer 17 |
| 105 | | (Formed from 11 & 38 Militia Bdes.)<br>**E.Front** *S.W./8* 9/15, 6/16; *S.W./11* 7/16, 11/16, 3/17 |
| 106§ | | (106-110 divisions formed from 57, 58, 60, 62, 69, 88 & 108 Militia Bdes.)<br>**Finland** 6/16 |
| 107 | | **Baltic Ports** 6/16 |
| 108§ | | **E.Front** *N./6* 10/15, winter 15/16; *N./12* 6/16; *N.* to *S.W./7* 7/16; *S.W./7* 7/16 11/16, 3/17 |
| 109§ | | **E.Front** *N./6* 10/15, winter 15/16; *N./12* 6/16 |

* Cadres from parent division in home military district.

† In some cases not completed until 1916.

## INFANTRY DIVISIONS (3rd Line) continued

| DIVISION | FORMED | COMBAT RECORD (where known) and formation details where appropriate |
|---|---|---|
| 110§ | spring 1915-1916 | E.Front N./5 10/15, winter 15/16 |
| 111 | | (Formed from 5 & 17 Militia Bdes.) E.Front W./10 10/15, winter 15/16, 6/16 |
| 112§ | | (Formed from 19 & 22 Militia Bdes.) No information as to service record |
| 113§ | | (Formed from 32 & 82 Militia Bdes.) E.Front S.W./7 7/16, 11/16, 3/17, summer 17 |
| 114 | | (Formed from 9 & 18 Militia Bdes.) E.Front destroyed Modlin 8/15, made P.O.W. |
| 115§ | | (Formed from 24 & 84 Militia Bdes.) E.Front service not known Rumanian Front Danube (became 6 Army 12/16); 7/16, 3/17 |
| 116 | | (Formed from 4 & 8 Militia Bdes.) as for 112 Inf. Div. |
| 117 | | (Formed from 31 & 96 Militia Bdes.) E.Front 7/16; to S.W./9 7/16; S.W./9 7/16; S.W./7 11/16, 3/17; S.W./8 summer 17 |
| 118§ | | (Formed from 95 & 102 Militia Bdes.) E.Front destroyed Modlin 8/15, made P.O.W. (According to Russian sources) However, Knox shows it as in existence in 3/17. No other record found in O.B.s. |
| 119 | | (Formed from 98 & 99 Militia Bdes.) E.Front destroyed (before formation completed) Modlin 8/15, made P.O.W. |
| 120§ | | (Formed from 7 & 16 Militia Bdes.) as for 112 Inf. Div. |
| 121§ | | (Formed from 28 & 103 Militia Bdes.) as for 112 Inf. Div. |
| 122§(?) | | (Formed from 26 & 35 Militia Bdes.) (Formation not completed until autumn 1916) E.Front S.W./11 11/16; to Rumanian Front 1916/17; returned to S.W./11 summer 17 Rumanian Front 9 3/17; summer 17; to S.W. |
| 123§ | | (Formed from 20 & 97 Militia Bdes.) Armenia/Kurdistan Army of the Caucasus 6/16 through to summer 17 |
| 124 | | (Formed from 1 & 14 Militia Bdes.) E.Front W./2 6/16 Rumanian Front 6 3/17 |
| 125 | | (Formed in Odessa Military District, Militia Bdes. unknown) E.Front S.W./Army Gp. Reserve 9/15; S.W./8 10/15, winter 15/16, 6/16, 7/16; S.W./Special 11/16, 3/17 |
| 126 | | (Formed from 73 & 74 Militia Bdes.) E.Front S.W./Army Gp. Reserve 6/16; S.W./11 7/16, 11/16; returned to S.W./11 summer 17 Rumanian Front 9 3/17, summer 17; to S.W. |
| 127 | | (Formed from 81 Militia Bde.) Armenia/Kurdistan Army of the Caucasus 6/16 through to summer 17 |

## INFANTRY DIVISIONS (4th Line)

4th wave divisions were formed within each corps by taking 4th battalions from each regiment in the corps, together with "March Companies" of reinforcements. These divisions had *no* artillery. Most were of extremely low morale and combat value.

| DIVISION | FORMED | COMBAT RECORD (where known) and formation details where appropriate |
|---|---|---|
| 128 | autumn 1916-1917 | (Formed with 4th Bns. regiments of XLII Corps) Finland summer 17 |
| 129 | | (Formed with 4th Bns. regiments of X Corps) E.Front W./3 summer 17 |

## INFANTRY DIVISIONS (4th Line) continued

| DIVISION | FORMED | COMBAT RECORD (where known) and formation details where appropriate |
|---|---|---|
| 130§ | autumn 1916-1917 | (Formed with 4th Bns. regiments of XXXI Corps) E.Front W. to S.W./3 3/17; S.W./Special summer 17 |
| 131 | | (Formed in Minsk) no other information |
| 132 | | (Formed with 4th Bns. regiments of II Caucasus Corps) E.Front W./10 summer 17 |
| 133 | | (Formed with 4th Bns. regiments of XX Corps) E.Front W./3 summer 17 |
| 134 | | (Formed in Mohilev) no other information |
| 135 | | (Formed from Kaluga Opolchenie [Militia] Bde.) no other information |
| 136 | | (Formed with 4th Bns. regiments of XIV Corps) E.Front N./5 summer 17 |
| 137 | | (Formed from Kharkov Opolchenie [Militia] Bde.) no other information |
| 138 | | (Formed with 4th Bns. regiments of XIV Corps) E.Front N./5 summer 17 |
| 139-150 | | Not formed |
| 151 | | (Formed with 4th Bns. regiments of V corps) E.Front S.W./Special 3/17; S.W./11 summer 17 |
| 152 | | (Formed from ex-convicts settled in Siberia) Became 6 Grenadier Div. q.v. E.Front S.W./Special 3/17; S.W./11 summer 17 |
| 153 | | (Formed with 4th Bns. regiments of XXXIV corps) E.Front S.W./Special 3/17; S.W./7 summer 17 |
| 154 | | (Formed with 4th Bns. regiments of XXXIV Corps) E.Front as for 153 Inf. Div. |
| 155 | | (Formed with 4th Bns. regiments of VI Corps) E.Front S.W./11 summer 17 |
| 156 | | (Formed with 4th Bns. regiments of XVII Corps) E.Front S.W./11 3/17, summer 17 |
| 157 | | (Formed with 4th Bns. regiments of XXXII Corps) E.Front as for 156 Inf. Div. |
| 158 | | Redesignated as 22 Siberian Rifle Div. q.v. E.Front S.W./11 3/17; S.W./8 summer 17 |
| 159 | | (Formed with 4th Bns. regiments of 20 & 108 Inf. Divs.) E.Front S.W./7 summer 17 |
| 160 | | (Formed with 4th Bns. regiments of XVI Corps) E.Front S.W./7 3/17; S.W./8 summer 17 |
| 161 | | (Formed with 4th Bns. regiments of I Corps) E.Front N./1 summer 17 |
| 162 | | (Formed with 4th Bns. regiments of III Caucasus Corps) E.Front S.W./7 summer 17 |
| 163 | | (Formed with 4th Bns. regiments of VI Corps) Noted as of particularly low combat/morale value E.Front S.W./11 3/17; Mutinied in May 1917 and disbanded |
| 164 | | (Formed with 4th Bns. regiments of XII Corps) E.Front S.W./8 summer 17 |
| 165 | | (Formed with 4th Bns. regiments of XI corps) E.Front S.W./8 summer 17 |
| 166 | | (Formed with 4th Bns. regiments of XVIII Corps) E.Front S.W./8 3/17, summer 17 |
| 167 | | (Formed with 4th Bns. regiments of XXIII Corps) E.Front as for 166 Inf. Div. |
| 168 | | (Formed with 4th Bns. regiments of IX Corps) E.Front S.W./8 3/17; W./2 summer 17 |
| 169 | | (Formed with 4th Bns. regiments of X Corps) Noted as of particularly low combat/morale value E.Front W./3 summer 17 |
| 170 | | (Formed with 4th Bns. regiments of XXXV Corps) E.Front W./3 summer 17 |
| 171 | | (Formed with 4th Bns. regiments of III Corps) E.Front W./10 summer 17 |

## INFANTRY DIVISIONS (4th Line) continued

| DIVISION | FORMED | COMBAT RECORD (where known) and formation details where appropriate |
|---|---|---|
| 172 | autumn 1916-1917 | (Formed with 4th Bns. regiments of XXXI Corps) **E.Front** *S.W./Special* summer 17 |
| 173 | | (Formed with 4th Bns. regiments of XLVI Corps) **E.Front** *S.W./Special* summer 17 |
| 174 | | (Formed with 4th Bns. regiments of XX Corps) **E.Front** *W./3* summer 17 |
| 175 | | (Formed with 4th Bns. regiments of XXXVIII Corps) **E.Front** *W./10* summer 17 |
| 176 | | Redesignated as 2 Caucasus Grenadier Div. q.v. **E.Front** *W./10* summer 17 |
| 177 | | (Formed with 4th Bns. 27 Inf. Div. and Composite Border Guard Division) **E.Front** *W./3* summer 17 |
| 178 | | (Formed with 4th Bns. regiments of I Corps) **E.Front** *N./1* summer 17 |
| 179 | | (Formed with 4th Bns. regiments of VII Corps) **Rumanian Front** *4* summer 17 |
| 180 | | (Formed with 4th Bns. regiments of XIV Corps) **E.Front** *N./5* summer 17 |
| 181 | | (Formed with 4th Bns. regiments of XV Corps) **E.Front** *W./3* summer 17 |
| 182 | | (Formed with 4th Bns. regiments of XIII Corps) **E.Front** *N./5* summer 17 |
| 183 | | (Formed with 4th Bns. regiments of XIX Corps) **E.Front** *N./5* summer 17 |
| 184 | | (Formed with 4th Bns. regiments of XXVIII Corps) **E.Front** *N./5* summer 17 |
| 185 | | (Formed with 4th Bns. regiments of XXI Corps) **E.Front** *N./12* summer 17 |
| 186 | | (Formed with 4th Bns. regiments of XLIII Corps) **E.Front** *N./12* summer 17 |
| 187 | | (Formed with 4th Bns. regiments of XXVII Corps) **E.Front** *N./5* summer 17 |
| 188 | | (Formed with 4th Bns. regiments of XXIV Corps) **Rumanian Front** *9* 3/17, summer 17 |
| 189 | | (Formed with 4th Bns. regiments of XXVI Corps) **Rumanian Front** *9* summer 17 |
| 190 | | (Formed with 4th Bns. regiments of XXX Corps) **Rumanian Front** *4* 3/17, summer 17 |
| 191 | | (Formed with 4th Bns. regiments of XXXVI Corps) **Rumanian Front** *9* summer 17 |
| 192 | | (Formed with 4th Bns. regiments of XLIV Corps) (probably) **Rumanian Front** *6* summer 17 |
| 193 | | (Formed with 4th Bns. regiments of II Corps) **Rumanian Front** *9* 3/17, summer 17 |
| 194 | | (Formation details unkown – possibly by XLV Corps[?]) **Rumanian Front** *9* 3/17, summer 17; to *S.W.Front* **E.Front** *S.W./11* summer 17 |

## (European/Russian) RIFLE BRIGADES/DIVISIONS

Brigades raised to Divisions in Autumn 1915.

| DIVISION | FORMED | COMBAT RECORD (where known) and formation details where appropriate |
|---|---|---|
| 1 | pre-war | **E.Front** *N.W./2* 8-9/14; *N.W./5* 1-2/15; *N./5* 10/15, winter 15/16; *N./1* 6/16 **Rumanian Front** *6* 3/17 |
| 2 | | **E.Front** *S.W./4* 8/14; *S.W./9* 9/14; *S.W./4* 1-2/15; *S.W./9* 5-6/15; *S.W./9* to *8* 10/15; *S.W./8* winter 15/16; *S.W./8* 6/16, 7/16; *S.W./9* 11/16 **Rumanian Front** *9* 3/17 |

## (European/Russian) RIFLE BRIGADES/DIVISIONS cont.

| DIVISION | FORMED | COMBAT RECORD (where known) and formation details where appropriate |
|---|---|---|
| 3 | pre-war | **E.Front** *S.W./8* 8-9/14; *S.W./11* 10/14; *S.W./8* 1-2/15; *S.W./3* 5-6/15; *S.W.* to *N.W.* 7-8/15; *N./5* 10/15, winter 15/16, 7/16; to *Army of Danube* late 7/16 **Rumanian Front** *Danube* (became *6 Army* 12/16) 11/16; *6* 3/17 |
| 4 | | **E.Front** *S.W./8* 8-9/14, 10/14, 1-2/15, 5-6/15, 9/15, 10/15, winter 15/16, 6/16, 7/16; *S.W./9* late 7/16 **Rumanian Front** *9* 3/17 |
| 5 | | **E.Front** *N.W./1* 8-9/14; *N.W./1* to *10* 10/14; *N.W./12* 1-2/15; *N./5* 10/15, winter 15/16, 6/16; *S.W./3* 7/16, 3/17 |
| 6 | autumn 1916-1917 | (Formed with 4th Bns. regiments of XL Corps) **Rumanian Front** *9* summer 17 |
| 7 | | (Formed with 4th Bns. regiments of XXIX Corps) **Rumanian Front** *6* 3/17; *Front Reserve* summer 17 |
| 8 | | (Formed with 4th Bns. regiments of XLVII Corps) Noted as of particularly low combat/morale value **Rumanian Front** *6* summer 17 |

## FINNISH RIFLE BRIGADES/DIVISIONS

Brigades raised to Divisions in Autumn 1915.

| DIVISION | FORMED | COMBAT RECORD (where known) and formation details where appropriate |
|---|---|---|
| 1 | pre-war | **E.Front** *N.W./10* 8-9/14; *S.W./11* 5-6/15, 9/15, 10/15, winter 15/16; *S.W./7* 6/16, 7/16, 11/16, 3/17, summer 17 |
| 2 | | **E.Front** *N.W./10* 8-9/14; *S.W./11* 5-6/15; *S.W.* to *N.W.* 7-8/15; *W./Front Reserve* 10/15, winter 15/16; *S.W./Front Reserve* 6/16; *S.W./11* 7/16, 11/16, 3/17, summer 17 |
| 3 | | **E.Front** record as for 1 Finnish Rifle Div. |
| 4 | | **E.Front** *N.W./10* 8-9/14; *S.W./11* 5-6/15; *S.W.* to *N.W.* 7-8/15; *W./Front Reserve* 10/15, winter 15/16; *S.W./8* 6/16, 7/16; *S.W./3* late 7/16; *S.W./Special* 11/16; *S.W./11* 3/17, summer 17 |
| 5 | autumn 1916-1917 | (Formed with 4th Bns. regiments of XXII Corps) **E.Front** *S.W./7* summer 17 |
| 6 | | (Formed with 4th Bns. regiments of XLIX Corps) **E.Front** *S.W./11* summer 17 |

## CAUCASIAN RIFLE BRIGADES/DIVISIONS

Brigades raised to Divisions in Autumn 1915.

| DIVISION | FORMED | COMBAT RECORD (where known) and formation details where appropriate |
|---|---|---|
| 1 | pre-war | *Caucasus Mil. Dist.* 8-9/14; Transferred to main E.Front **E.Front** *N.W./10* 10/14; *N.W./1* 1-2/15; *N./5* 10/15, winter 15/16; 6/16 |
| 2 | | *Caucasus Mil. Dist.* 8-9/14 (in Persia) **Armenia/Kurdistan** *Army of the Caucasus* 10/14 through to summer 17 |
| 3 | late 1914 | *Caucasus Mil. Dist.* Independent role 10/14; to main E.Front 1/15 **E.Front** *S.W./8* 5-6/15; *N./5* 10/15, winter 15/16; *N./1* 6/16 **Rumanian Front** *6* 3/17 |
| 4 | 1915-1916 | **Armenia/Kurdistan** *Army of the Caucasus* 1-2/15 through to summer 17 |
| 5 | | **Armenia/Kurdistan** *Army of the Caucasus* 6/16 through to summer 17 |
| 6 | autumn 1916-1917 | (Formed with 4th Bns. regiments of I Caucasus Corps) **Armenia/Kurdistan** *Army of the Caucasus* 1917 |
| 7 | | (Formed with 4th Bns. regiments of VII Caucasus Corps) **Armenia/Kurdistan** *Army of the Caucasus* 1917 |

## TURKESTAN RIFLE BRIGADES/DIVISIONS

Brigades raised to Divisions in Autumn 1915.

| DIVISION | FORMED | COMBAT RECORD (where known) and formation details where appropriate |
|---|---|---|
| 1 | pre-war | **E.Front** *N.W./10* 8-9/14; *N.W./New 1* 10/14; *N.W./12* 1-2/15; *W./4* 10/15, winter 15/16; *W./10* 6/16; *S.W./8* 7/16; *S.W./3* late 7/16; *S.W./Special* 11/16, 3/17 |
| 2 | | **E.Front** *En route N.W./10* (from Turkestan Mil. Dist.) 8-9/14; *N.W./New 1* 10/14; *N.W./12* 1-2/15; *W./4* 10/15, winter 15/16; *W./10* 6/16; *S.W./8* 7/16; *S.W./3* late 7/16; *S.W./Special* 11/16, 3/17 |
| 3 | | **E.Front** *En route N.W./10* (from Turkestan Mil. Dist.) 8-9/14; *Independent role* 10/14; *N.W./1* 1-2/15; *S.W./7* or *W./10* 6/16; *S.W./7* 7/16; *S.W./9* 11/16 **Rumanian Front** *9* 3/17 |
| 4 | | *Turkestan Mil. Dist.* 8-9/14; sent to reinforce Army of the Caucasus **Armenia/Kurdistan** *Army of the Caucasus* 10/14 through to summer 17 |
| 5 | | *record as for 4 Turkestan Rifle Div.* |
| 6 | | *Turkestan Mil. Dist.* 8-9/14; *Independent role* 10/14 Merged with 3 Turkestan Rifle Div. in 1915 |
| 7 | 1915-1916 | No information. Probably retained in *Turkestan Mil. Dist.* on internal security/guard duties 1916/17 |
| 8 | autumn 1916-1917 | (Formed with 4th Bns. regiments of I Turkestan Corps) **E.Front** *S.W./Special* 3/17; *S.W./11* summer 17 |
| 9 | | (Formed in Turkestan Military District) Retained in *Turkestan Mil. Dist.* for local defence 1917 |
| 10 | | (Formed in Turkestan Military District) Retained in *Turkestan Mil. Dist.* for local defence 1917 |

## SIBERIAN RIFLE DIVISIONS

| DIVISION | FORMED | COMBAT RECORD (where known) and formation details where appropriate |
|---|---|---|
| 1 | pre-war | En route from *Aumur Mil. Dist.* to *E.Front* 8-9/14 **E.Front** *N.W./2* 10/14; *N.W./1* 1-2/15; *W./1* 10/15, winter 15/16; *G.H.Q.Reserve* to *W./2* 6/16; en route to *S.W.* 7/16 |
| 2 | | *record as for 1 Siberian Rifle Div.* |
| 3 | | *Aumur Mil. Dist.* 8-9/14; to *E.Front* **E.Front** *N.W./2(?)* 10/14; *N.W./2* 1-2/15; *W./1* 10/15, winter 15/16; *N./12* 6/16 |
| 4 | | *Irkutsk Mil. Dist.* 8-9/14; to *E.Front* **E.Front** *N.W./2* 10/14, 1-2/15; *N./12* 10/15, winter 15/16, *N./5* to 5/16; *N./1* 6/16 |
| 5 | | *record as for 4 Siberian Rifle Div.* |
| 6 | | *Aumur Mil. Dist.* 8-9/14, 10/14; to *E.Front* **E.Front** *N.W./1* 1-2/15; *W./4* 10/15, winter 15/16; *N.* to *S.W./8* then *S.W./9* 6/16; *S.W./8* 7/16; *S.W./11* late 7/16, 11/16, 3/17; *S.W./8* summer 17 |
| 7 | | **E.Front** *N.W./10* 8-9/14, 10/14, 1-2/15; *W./10* 10/15, winter 15/16; *W./4* 6/16 |
| 8 | | *record as for 7 Siberian Rifle Div.* |
| 9 | | *Aumur Mil. Dist.* 8-9/14, 10/14; to *E.Front* **E.Front** *N.W./12* 1-2/15; *W./2* 10/15, winter 15/16, 6/16; *S.W./3* 7/16 **Rumanian Front** *Danube* (became *6 Army* 12/16) 11/16; *6* 3/17 |
| 10 | | *Aumur Mil. Dist.* 8-9/14, 10/14; to *E.Front* **E.Front** *Independent role* 10/14; *N.W./12* 1-2/15; *W./2* 10/15, winter 15/16, 6/16; *S.W./3* 7/16 **Rumanian Front** *Danube* (became *6 Army* 12/16) 11/16; *6* 3/17 |
| 11 | | *Omsk Mil. Dist.* 8-9/14; to *E.Front* **E.Front** *N.W./12* 10/14; *W./4* 10/15, winter 15/16 |

## SIBERIAN RIFLE DIVISIONS continued

| DIVISION | FORMED | COMBAT RECORD (where known) and formation details where appropriate |
|---|---|---|
| 12 | on mobilisation | (Parent Division – 7 Siberian R.D.) (Irkutsk M.D.) *Irkutsk Mil. Dist.* 8-9/14; to *E.Front* **E.Front** *Independent role* to *S.W./8* 10/14; *S.W./8* 1-2/15; *S.W./3* 5-6/15; *N./12* 10/15, winter 15/16, 6/16; *S.W./7* 11/16, 3/17, summer 17 (see 13 Div. below) |
| 13 | | (Parent Division – 8 Siberian R.D.) (Irkutsk M.D.) *Irkutsk Mil. Dist.* 8-9/14; to *E.Front* **E.Front** *Independent role* to *N.W./2* 10/14; *N.W./2* to *New 1* 10/14; *N./12* 10/15, winter 15/16, 6/16; *S.W./7* 11/16, 3/17, summer 17 N.B. 12 & 13 Siberian Rifle Divs. formed a combined div. in summer 17 |
| 14 | | (Parent Division – 11 Siberian R.D.) (Omsk M.D.) *Tomsk/Novonikolaev/Omsk Areas Independent role* 8-9/14; to *E.Front* **E.Front** *Independent* to *N.W./New 1* 10/14; *N.W./2* 1-2/15; *W./1* 10/15, winter 15/16; *N./12* 6/16 |
| 15 | autumn 1916-1917 | (Formed with 4th Bns. regiments of III Siberian Corps) **E.Front** *W./2* summer 17 |
| 16 | | (Formed with 4th Bns. regiments of I Siberian Corps) (This division may not have been fully formed) **E.Front** *W./10* summer 17 |
| 17 | | (Formed with 4th Bns. regiments of III Siberian Corps) (This division may not have been fully formed) **E.Front** *W./2* summer 17 |
| 18 | | (Formed with 4th Bns. regiments of VI Siberian Corps) **E.Front** *N./12* summer 17 |
| 19 | | (Formed with 4th Bns. regiments of VII Siberian Corps) **E.Front** *S.W./7* summer 17 |
| 20 | | (Formed with 4th Bns. regiments of II Siberian Corps) **E.Front** *N./12* summer 17 |
| 21 | | (Formed with 4th Bns. regiments of IV Siberian Corps) (Noted as of particularly low combat/morale value) **Rumanian Front** *6* summer 17 |
| 22 | | Re-designated from 158 Inf. Division (Formed with 4th Bns. regiments of V Siberian Corps) **E.Front** *S.W./11* 3/17; *S.W./8* summer 17 |
| Composite | | (Formed with 4th Bns. regiments of VII Siberian Corps) **E.Front** *S.W./7* summer 17 |

## FRONTIER GUARD DIVISIONS

| DIVISION | FORMED | COMBAT RECORD (where known) and formation details where appropriate |
|---|---|---|
| **Combined** | by early 1917 | **E.Front** *S.W./3* 3/17 |
| Trans-Amur Frontier Guard Divisions | | |
| 1 | by 1.1916 | **E.Front** *S.W./9* 5-6/15, 9/15, 10/15, winter 15/16, 6/16, 7/16; *S.W./7* 11/16, 3/17; *S.W./8* summer 17 |
| 2 | | **E.Front** *S.W./9* 9/15, 10/15, winter 15/16, 6/16, 7/16; *S.W./7* 11/16, 3/17, summer 17; to *S.W./8* summer 17 |
| 3 | by 6.1916 (?) or earlier | **E.Front** *S.W./9* 6/16, 7/16; *S.W./7* 11/16, 3/17, summer 17 |
| 4 | autumn 1916-1917 | (Formed with 4th Bns. regiments of XXXIII Corps) **E.Front** *S.W./7* 3/17, summer 17; to *S.W./8* summer 17 |
| 5 | | (Formed with 4th Bns. regiments of XLI Corps) **E.Front** *S.W./7* 3/17, summer 17 |
| Caucasus Frontier Guard Divisions | | |
| 1 | by early 1917 | Presumably retained for local defence/border guard security in Trans-Caucasia. No other references known |
| 2 | | |

## MARINE/NAVAL INFANTRY DIVISIONS

| DIVISION | FORMED | COMBAT RECORD (where known) and formation details where appropriate |
|---|---|---|
| **1** | by 8.1916 | (Baltic Marine Division) Russian designation *Matrosskaia Divisia* (Sailors' Division) *Baltic* presumably coastal defence of Baltic ports 1916/early 1917 **Rumanian Front** *6* 3/17 (according to Austro-Hungarian sources) |
| **2** | post 8.1916 ? | (Black Sea Landing Division) *Black Sea* presumably coastal defence of Black Sea ports 1916/1917 (possibly) **Rumanian Front** *6* 3/17 (*if* Austro-Hungarian sources are incorrect in identifying 1st Div. Logic suggests Black Sea Division as more likely) |

## MISCELLANEOUS 'FOREIGN' VOLUNTEER DIVISIONS*

| DIVISION | FORMED | COMBAT RECORD (where known) and formation details where appropriate |
|---|---|---|
| **1 Serb Volunteer Inf. Div.** | by 1.1917 | (Possibly re-designated as *Yugoslav* in 1917) (Formed from Austro-Hungarian P.O.W.s) *Odessa* 7/16 **Rumanian Front** *Dobrudja Det.* 8/16; *Danube* (became *6 Army* 12/16) 11/16 onwards |
| **2 Serb Volunteer Inf. Div.** | | (Possibly re-designated as *Yugoslav* in 1917) (Formed from Austro-Hungarian P.O.W.s) *Odessa area* (?) 1917 |
| **Polish Rifle Division** | | (It was intended to form I-III Polish Corps [1-6 Polish Rifle Divisions] but it would appear only one division was actually formed) **E.Front** *S.W./7* summer 17, then to *S.W./11* summer 17 |
| **Czecho-Slovak Rifle Div.** | | (Created as Czecho-Slovak Volunteer Druzhina in 1914. Expanded to a brigade and, possibly, to a division by 1916/17) **E.Front** *S.W./3* 3/17; *S.W./11* summer 17 |
| **1 Latvian Rifle Brigade** | | Presumably retained on local defence duties on Baltic coast. |
| **2 Latvian Rifle Brigade** | | |

## INFANTRY BRIGADES

The following Independent Infantry Brigades should be noted:

| DIVISION | FORMED | COMBAT RECORD (where known) and formation details where appropriate |
|---|---|---|
| Special Infantry Brigades | | |
| **1 to 8** | 1917 | Formed from chosen soldiers. They were intended to show Allied solidarity by serving on the Western Front. In fact only 1 & 3 served in France, 2 & 4 served in Macedonia. 5, 6, 7 & 8 served in 1917 on the North-western Front (Army Group) on main Eastern Front. According to some reports these four formed 3rd and 4th Special Infantry Divisions. |
| Cossack Infantry Brigades (*Plastun* Brigades) | | |
| **Kuban Plastun Brigades 1 to 6** | 1-4: 1914 5-6: 1917 | **Armenia/Kurdistan** *Army of the Caucasus* 1914 through to summer 17 (1-4 Bdes.) (Except 1-2 Bdes. to **E.Front** *S.W.Front* briefly Autumn 1915 – early 1916). 5-6 Bdes. service not known, probably in *Army of the Caucasus* 1917 |

## INFANTRY BRIGADES continued

| DIVISION | FORMED | COMBAT RECORD (where known) and formation details where appropriate |
|---|---|---|
| Cossack Infantry Brigades (*Plastun* Brigades) continued | | |
| **Independent Don Cossack Inf. Bde. One** | by early 1915 | **Armenia/Kurdistan** *Army of the Caucasus* Early 1915, 1916, possibly through to summer 17 |

## CAVALRY DIVISIONS (total = 53)

### GUARD CAVALRY DIVISIONS

| DIVISION | FORMED | COMBAT RECORD (where known) and formation details where appropriate |
|---|---|---|
| **1** | pre-war | **E.Front** *N.W./1* 8-9/14; *N.W./1* to *N.W./10* 10/14; *S.W./4* to *N.W./10* 1-2/15; *W./1* 10/15, winter 15/16; *G.H.Q.Reserve* 6/16; *S.W./Special* 7/16, 11/16, 3/17 |
| **2** | ↓ | **E.Front** *N.W./1* 8-9/14; *N.W./1* to *N.W./10* 10/14; *S.W./4* to *N.W./10* 1-2/15; *W./3* to *S.W./8* 9/15; *W./3* 10/15, winter 15/16; *G.H.Q.Reserve* 6/16; *S.W./Special* 7/16, 11/16, 3/17 |
| **3** | summer-autumn 1915 | Formed from Independent Guard Cav. Bde. (Life Guard Lancers of the Tsar, Life Guard Grodno Hussars) and Life Guard Cossack regiments (3rd Brigade/1st Guards Cavalry Division) **E.Front** *W./3* to *S.W./8* 9/15; *G.H.Q.Reserve* 6/16; *S.W./Special* 7/16, 11/16, 3/17 |

### CAVALRY DIVISIONS (Regular Line)

| DIVISION | FORMED | COMBAT RECORD (where known) and formation details where appropriate |
|---|---|---|
| **1** | pre-war | **E.Front** *N.W./1* 8/14; *N.W./10* 9/14; *N.W./10* to *N.W./1*, back to *N.W./10* 10/14; *N.W./10* 1-2/15; *S.W.* to *N.W.* 7-8/15; *N./5* 10/15, winter 15/16 |
| **2** | | **E.Front** *N.W./1* 8-9/14; *N.W./1* to *N.W./10* 10/14; *N.W./2* 1-2/15; *N./5* 10/15, winter 15/16 |
| **3** | | **E.Front** *N.W./1* 8-9/14; *N.W./1* to *N.W./10* 10/14; *N.W./10* 1-2/15; *W./3* to *S.W./8* 9/15; *W./3* 10/15, winter 15/16; *S.W./3* 7/16; *S.W./3* to *Dobrudja Det.* 8/16 **Rumanian Front** *Dobrudja Det.* 8/16; *Danube* (became *6 Army* 12/16) 11/16; *6* 3/17 |
| **4** | | **E.Front** *N.W./2* 8-9/14; *N.W./10* 10/14; *N.W./12* 1-2/15; *N./12* 10/15, winter 15/16 |
| **5** | | **E.Front** *N.W./9* 8/14; *S.W./9* 9/14; *S.W./9* to *N.W.* 10/14; *N.W./2* 1-2/15; *W./1* 10/15, winter 15/16 |
| **6** | | **E.Front** *N.W./2* 8-9/14; *N.W./2* to *Narew Group* to *N.W./New 1* 10/14; *N.W./12* 1-2/15; *W./1* 10/15, winter 15/16; *S.W./11* 3/17 |
| **7** | | **E.Front** *S.W./5* 8-9/14; *S.W./3* 10/14, 1-2/15, 5-6/15; *S.W./8* 9/15, 6/16; *S.W./11* 7/16; *S.W./8* 11/16, 3/17, summer 17 |
| **8** | | **E.Front** *S.W./4* 8/14; *S.W./9* 9/14; *S.W./9* to *N.W.* 10/14; *N.W./12* 1-2/15; *W./1* 10/15, winter 15/16; *N./5* to *Danube* 7/16 **Rumanian Front** *Danube* (became *6 Army* 12/16) 11/16; *6* 3/17 |
| **9** | | **E.Front** *S.W./3* 8-9/14; *S.W./11* 10/14, 1-2/15; *S.W./8* 5-6/15; *S.W./9* 10/15, winter 15/16; *S.W./7* 6/16, 7/16, 11/16, 3/17; *S.W./7* to *S.W./8* summer 17 |
| **10** | | **E.Front** *S.W./3* 8-9/14; *S.W./8* 10/14, 1-2/15; *S.W./9* 5-6/15, 9/15, 10/15, winter 15/16, 6/16, 7/16, 11/16 **Rumanian Front** *4* 3/17 |
| **11** | ↓ | **E.Front** *S.W./3* 8-9/14; *S.W./11* to *S.W./3* 10/14; *S.W./8* 1-2/15; *S.W./3* 5-6/15; *S.W./8* 9/15, 6/16, 7/16; *S.W./9* 11/16; *S.W./7* summer 17; to *S.W./11* summer 17 **Rumanian Front** *9* 3/17; returned *S.W. Front* summer 17 |

* The Russian Army designated these as *Inorodets* units meaning non-Russian (i.e. *not* Russian, Ukrainian or Byelorussian) rather than 'foreign'.

## CAVALRY DIVISIONS (Regular Line) continued

| DIVISION | FORMED | COMBAT RECORD (where known) and formation details where appropriate |
|---|---|---|
| 12 | pre-war | E.Front *S.W./8* 8-9/14, 10/14, 1-2/15; *S.W./9* 5-6/15, 9/15, 10/15, winter 15/16; *S.W./7* then *8* 6/16; *S.W./8* 7/16; *S.W./11* 11/16<br>**Rumanian Front** *4* 3/17 |
| 13 | | E.Front *S.W./4* 8/14; *S.W./9* 9/14, 10/14; *S.W./4* 1-2/15, 5-6/15; *W./1* 10/15, winter 15/16; *W./11* 3/17 |
| 14 | | E.Front *S.W./4* 8/14; *S.W./9* 9/14, 10/14; to *N.W./12* 10/14; *N.W./12* 1-2/15; *W./1* 10/15, winter 15/16 |
| 15 | | E.Front *N.W./2* 8-9/14; *N.W./10* 10/14; *N.W./12* 1-2/15; *N./5* 10/15, winter 15/16 |
| 16 | late 1914 (?) | (Formed from 2 & 3 Independent Cavalry Bdes.)<br>E.Front *S.W./3* 1-2/15, 5-6/15; *W./3* 9/15; to *S.W./8* 9/15; *W./3* 10/15, winter 15/16; *S.W./8* 6/16; *S.W./3* 7/16, 3/17 |
| 17 | | (Formed by expanding 4 Indep. Cav. Bde. and adding 1 Baltic *Ostsee* Cav. Bde.)<br>E.Front *(As Indep. Bde.) N.W./10* 8-9/14, 10/14; *(As division) N.W./12* 1-2/15 |
| Caucasus | pre-war | E.Front *N.W./9* 8/14; *Warsaw Det.* 9/14; *Narew Group* 10/14; *N.W./2* 10/14; *N.W./1* 1-2/15; *S.W./9* 9/15; then returned to *Army of the Caucasus*<br>**Armenia/Kurdistan** *Army of the Caucasus* Autumn 15 through to summer 17 |
| Combined | 1914 | The composition of this division varies at different periods of the was and it is not easy to establish which units are in the division in the orders of battle. The following represents an attempt to rationalise this: |
| (a) | August 1914 | Formed from 2 & 3 Indep. Cav. Bdes.<br>E.Front *S.W./5* 8-9/14; *S.W./3* 10/14<br>Now re-designated as 16 Cav. Div. Subsequent record see 16 Cav. Div. above |
| (b)<br>(c) | autumn 1915 | Formed from Independent Guards Cav. Bde.* (Life Guard Lancers of the Tsar, Life Guard Grodno Hussars) and 1 & 2 Mounted regts. Trans-Amur Frontier Guard.<br>E.Front *S.W./9* 9/15; *S.W./7* 6/16; *S.W./11* 7/16, 3/17 |

* Independent Guards Cav. Bde. later replaced by (c)1 Independent Cav. Bde. at unknown date.

## GUARD COSSACK CAVALRY DIVISIONS

| DIVISION | FORMED | COMBAT RECORD (where known) and formation details where appropriate |
|---|---|---|
| **Guard Cossack** | 10/14 | Temporary "division", later used to form 3 Guards Cavalry Division.<br>E.Front *N.W./New 1* 10/14; *N.W./1* 1-2/15; *W./3* to *S.W./8* 9/15; then absorbed by 3 Guards Cav. Div. q.v. |

## DON COSSACK CAVALRY DIVISIONS

| DIVISION | FORMED | COMBAT RECORD (where known) and formation details where appropriate |
|---|---|---|
| 1<br>Don | pre-war | E.Front *S.W./5* 8-9/14, 10/14; *S.W./9* 1-2/15, 5-6/15, 9/15, 10/15, winter 15/16, 6/16, 7/16; *S.W./11* 11/16<br>**Rumanian Front** *4* 3/17 |
| 2<br>(Combined Cossack) | | (Formed from 2 Don, 1 Terek and 1 Kuban Cossack Regts.)<br>E.Front *S.W./8* 8-9/14, 10/14, 1-2/15; *S.W./3* 5-6/15; *W./3* to *S.W./8* 9/15; *W./3* 10/15, winter 15/16; *S.W./8* 6/16; *S.W./3* 7/16, 3/17; *S.W./7* summer 17 |
| 3<br>Don | on mobilisation | E.Front *S.W./4* 8-9/14; *S.W./5* to *S.W./3* 10/14; *S.W./3* 1-2/15, 5-6/15; *W./3* to *S.W./8* 9/15; *W./1* 10/15, winter 15/16<br>**Rumanian Front** *6* 3/17 |
| 4<br>Don | | E.Front *S.W./5* 8-9/14; *S.W./5* to *Narew Group* 10/14; then *N.W./New 1* 10/14; *N.W./1* 1-2/15; *W./1* 10/15, winter 15/16 |
| 5<br>Don | | E.Front *S.W./5* 8-9/14; *S.W./9* to *S.W./5* 10/14; *S.W./5* 1-2/15; *S.W./7* 7/16; *S.W./Special* 11/16; *S.W./3* 3/17 |

## DON COSSACK CAVALRY DIVISIONS continued

| DIVISION | FORMED | COMBAT RECORD (where known) and formation details where appropriate |
|---|---|---|
| 6<br>Don | by summer 1916 | E.Front *S.W./7* 6/16, 7/16, 11/16<br>**Rumanian Front** *9* 3/17 |

## CAUCASUS COSSACK CAVALRY DIVISIONS

| DIVISION | FORMED | COMBAT RECORD (where known) and formation details where appropriate |
|---|---|---|
| 1 | pre-war | **Armenia/Kurdistan** *Army of the Caucasus* 8-9/14 through to 10/15 (Not mentioned in Caucasus O.B. after these dates. May have remained in Trans-Caucasia or moved to<br>E.Front *Northern* or *Western Fronts* although we have no mention of them in this area. |
| 2 | | As for 1 Caucasus Cossack Div. |
| 3 | | E.Front *S.W./3* 8-9/14, 10/14, 1-2/15, 5-6/15; *W./3* to *S.W./8* 9/15; *W./3* 10/15, winter 15/16; *S.W./8* 6/16; *S.W./3* 7/16; to *S.W./9* late 7/16; *S.W./8* 11/16, 3/17, summer 17 |
| 4 | autumn 1914 | **Armenia/Kurdistan** *Army of the Caucasus* 10/14 through to summer 17 |
| 5 | by early 1915 | **Armenia/Kurdistan** *Army of the Caucasus* 1-2/15 through to summer 17 |

## ORENBURG COSSACK CAVALRY DIVISIONS

| DIVISION | FORMED | COMBAT RECORD (where known) and formation details where appropriate |
|---|---|---|
| 1<br>2 | | These divisions seem to have been formed, if at all, on "paper".<br>Regiments nominally assigned acted independently. |
| 3 | on mobilisation | (Often referred to simply as The Orenburg Cossack Division, without number).<br>E.Front *G.H.Q.Reserve/6* 8-9/14, 10/14; *S.W./8* and *11* 1-2/15; *S.W./8* 5-6/15, 9/15, 6/16, 7/16; *S.W./9* 11/16; *S.W./7* summer 17<br>**Rumanian Front** *9* 3/17; returned to *S.W.Front* summer 17 |

## KUBAN COSSACK CAVALRY DIVISIONS

| DIVISION | FORMED | COMBAT RECORD (where known) and formation details where appropriate |
|---|---|---|
| 1 | on mobilisation | E.Front *S.W./8* 8-9/14, 10/14, 1-2/15; *S.W./9* 5-6/15; *S.W./11* 9/15; *S.W./3* 7/16, 3/17 |
| 2 | | E.Front *S.W./8* 8-9/14, 10/14, 1-2/15 |
| 3<br>4 | by 1.1916 | These divisions seem to have been formed, if at all, on "paper".<br>Regiments nominally assigned acted independently. |
| Combined Kuban | by early 1917 | see 3 & 4 Divisions |

## TEREK COSSACK CAVALRY DIVISIONS

| DIVISION | FORMED | COMBAT RECORD (where known) and formation details where appropriate |
|---|---|---|
| 1 | on mobilisation | E.Front *S.W./8* 8-9/14, 10/14, 1-2/15; *S.W./9* 5-6/15, 9/15, 6/16, 7/16, 11/16<br>**Rumanian Front** *4* 3/17 |

## TEREK COSSACK CAVALRY DIVISIONS continued

| DIVISION | FORMED | COMBAT RECORD (where known) and formation details where appropriate |
|---|---|---|
| 2 | | Seems to have been formed, if at all, on "paper". Regiments nominally assigned acted independently. |

## URAL COSSACK CAVALRY DIVISION

| DIVISION | FORMED | COMBAT RECORD (where known) and formation details where appropriate |
|---|---|---|
| **Ural** Cossack Div. | on mobilisation | E.Front *S.W./4* 8-9/14, 10/14, 1-2/15, 5-6/15 |

## TURKESTAN COSSACK CAVALRY DIVISIONS

| DIVISION | FORMED | COMBAT RECORD (where known) and formation details where appropriate |
|---|---|---|
| 1 | pre-war | E.Front *S.W./1* (1 Bde.) 8-9/14; *unallocated* (1 Bde.) 8-9/14; *S.W./9* to *S.W./5* (1 Bde.) 10/14; *Independent* (1 Bde.) 10/14; *N.W./12* 1-2/15 (Division); *W./4* 10/15, winter 15/16 |
| 2 | ↓ | This division seems to have been formed, if at all, on "paper". Regiments nominally assigned acted independently. |

## SIBERIAN COSSACK CAVALRY DIVISION

| DIVISION | FORMED | COMBAT RECORD (where known) and formation details where appropriate |
|---|---|---|
| **Siberian** Coss. Div. | autumn 1914 | (Initially a Brigade, upgraded to Division early in war) **Armenia/Kurdistan** *Army of the Caucasus* 10/14 through to summer 17 |

## TRANS-BAIKAL COSSACK CAVALRY DIVISIONS

| DIVISION | FORMED | COMBAT RECORD (where known) and formation details where appropriate |
|---|---|---|
| 1 | by autumn 1914 | (Initially a Brigade, upgraded to Division early in war) *Irkutsk Mil. Dist.* 8-9/14 E.Front *Independent* to *S.W./4* 10/14, 1-2/15, 5-6/15; *W./4* 9/15, 10/15, winter 15/16; *S.W./3* 7/16; *S.W./Special* 11/16; *S.W./11* 3/17, summer17 |
| 2* | ↓ | *Turkestan Mil. Dist.* 8-9/14 **Armenia/Kurdistan** *Army of the Caucasus* 10/14 through to summer 17 |

## MOUNTED DIVISIONS (*Reiter* Divisions)

| DIVISION | FORMED | COMBAT RECORD (where known) and formation details where appropriate |
|---|---|---|
| **Trans-Amur Ftr. Gd. Mtd. Div.** | by 8.1916 | E.Front *S.W./11* 6/16, 7/16, 11/16 **Rumanian Front** *4* 3/17 (N.B. 2 additional Mtd. Regts. served in the Combined Cav. Div. q.v.) |
| **Caucasian Native Volunteer Div.** | on mobilisation | E.Front *Independent* 10/14; *S.W./8* 1-2/15; *S.W./9* 5-6/15, 10/15, winter 15/16, 6/16, 7/16; *S.W./7* 11/16; to *Rumanian Front*; *S.W./8* summer17 **Rumanian Front** *4* 3/17; returned to *S.W.Front* summer 17 |
| **Ussuri†** | ↓ | *Amur Mil. Dist.* 8-9/14; to *E.Front* E.Front *Independent* 10/14; *N.W./12* 1-2/15; *W./1* 10/15, winter 15/16; *S.W./9* 7/16; *S.W./8* 11/16 **Rumanian Front** *2 Rumanian* 3/17 |

## INDEPENDENT CAVALRY BRIGADES (Guard and Line)

The following should be noted:

| BRIGADE | FORMED | COMBAT RECORD (where known) and formation details where appropriate |
|---|---|---|
| **Guard** | pre-war | (1) Formed Combined Cavalry Division with the Trans-Amur Frontier Guard Mounted Regts. (2) In early 1916 Formed 3rd Guard Cavalry Division with 3rd Brigade (Guard Cossack Units) of 1st Guards Cavalry Division. |
| 1 | | Replaced Indep. Guards Cavalry Brigade in Combined Cavalry Division in 1916 (Now consists of 19 Dragoons, 16 Hussars, 1 & 2 Trans-Amur Ftr. Gd. Regts.) q.v. |
| 2<br>3 | ↓ | (17 & 18 Hussars) } Formed 16 Cavalry Division in<br>(16 & 17 Lancers) } autumn 1914 *q.v.* |
| 4 | on mobilisation | Formed 17 Cavalry Division, possibly with 1 Indep. Cav. Bde. initially until re-organisation of Combined Cavalry Division *q.v.* |
| **1 Baltic** | by 1.1916 | Added to 17 Cavalry Division in 1917 to complete division. |
| **2 Baltic** | 1917 | Service unknown. Remained Independent throughout |
| **Combined Militia (Reichswehr)** | by 1.1916 | as above |

## INDEPENDENT COSSACK CAVALRY BRIGADES

Excluding those raised to Divisional status in their own right.

| BRIGADE | FORMED | COMBAT RECORD (where known) and formation details where appropriate |
|---|---|---|
| **1 Don** | 1916-1917 | Remained Independent throughout Service unknown |
| **1 Trans-Caspian** | pre-war | Remained Independent throughout **Armenia/Kurdistan** *Army of the Caucasus* 8-9/14 throughout (?) |
| **1 Siberian** | pre-war | Remained Independent throughout Service possibly *Army of the Caucasus* or *Home Military District* |

## Serbia

The Serbs fought in three major campaigns; two against the Austrians, in September-December 1914 and October-November 1915, and one in Macedonia, from May 1916, fighting alongside the Western Allies against the Bulgarians. The first thirteen infantry divisions in the following list are those that fought in Serbia itself, where they were largely destroyed during the winter of 1915-16. The next seven infantry divisions are those that were reconstituted or formed from scratch after the retreat from Serbia and eventual transport to Corfu and then Salonika. The cavalry division was also reconstituted but has been given just a single entry.

## INFANTRY DIVISIONS (total = 13/7)

| DIVISION | FORMED | COMBAT RECORD |
|---|---|---|
| **1 Danube** | pre-war | **Serbia**: *2* on 12/8/14; *3* on 6/10/15; *3* on 14/10/15; *3* on 29/10/15; *3* on 11/11/15 |
| **1 Drina** | ↓ | **Serbia**: *3* on 12/8/14; *3* on 6/10/15; *3* on 14/10/15; *3* on 29/10/15; *3* on 11/11/15 |
| **1 Morava** | ↓ | **Serbia**: *2* on 12/8/14; *2* on 6/10/15; *2* on 14/10/15; *2* on 29/10/15; *unatt.* on 11/11/15 |

* Muratoff & Allen *Caucasian Battlefields* refer to this division as two Independent Brigades – 2nd and 3rd Trans-Caspian Cossack Bdes. throughout.

† Initially a Brigade, raised to a Division by 8.1916 if not earlier.

* Reformed at Salonika when they arrived from Corfu between April and May 1916. Corfu had been the first stop after the evacuation of Serbian survivors from Albania and Montenegro in January.

† From 4/18 the division included one brigade of non-Serbian Yugoslavs, formed from Austro-Hungarian P.O.W.s of the Russians who had earlier formed part of two ethnic divisions formed by the Russians to fight on the Rumanian front. Plans to transfer the entire two divisions to Macedonia fell into abeyance.

‡ Moreover, from October 1915 East African H.Q. were empowered to deal directly with the South African authorities regarding the conduct and administration of the campaign. The disbandment of the East African divisions in large part reflected the fact that South African units were being withdrawn from the theatre.

## INFANTRY DIVISIONS continued

| DIVISION | FORMED | COMBAT RECORD |
|---|---|---|
| 1 Sumadija | pre-war | **Serbia**: 2 on 12/8/14; 2 on 6/10/15; 3 on 14/10/15; 3 on 29/10/15; *Belgrade Gp.* on 11/11/15 |
| 1 Timok | ↓ | **Serbia**: 1 on 12/8/14; 2 on 6/10/15; 2 on 14/10/15; 2 on 29/10/15; 2 on 11/11/15 |
| 2 Danube | 8/14 | **Serbia**: 1 on 12/8/14; 1 on 6/10/15; 1 on 14/10/15; 1 on 29/10/15; 1 on 11/11/15 |
| 2 Drina | | **Serbia**: 3 on 12/8/14; 1 on 6/10/15; 1 on 14/10/15; 1 on 29/10/15; 1 on 11/11/15 |
| 2 Morava | | **Serbia**: 1 on 12/8/14; 1 on 6/10/15; *Belgrade Gp.* on 14/10/15; 3 on 29/10/15; 2 on 11/11/15 |
| 2 Sumadija | | **Serbia**: *Uzice Gp.* on 12/8/14; *Timok Gp.* on 6/10/15; *Timok Gp.* on 14/10/15; 2 on 29/10/15; 2 on 11/11/15 |
| 2 Timok | | **Serbia**: 1 on 12/8/14; *Belgrade Gp.* on 6/10/15; *Belgrade Gp.* on 14/10/15; *Belgrade Gp.* on 29/10/15; *Belgrade Gp.* on 11/11/15 |
| Combined | ↓ | **Serbia**: 2 on 12/8/14; *Timok Gp.* on 6/10/15; *Timok Gp.* on 14/10/15; *Timok Gp.* on 29/10/15; *Timok Gp.* on 11/11/15 |
| Bregainica | 10/15 | **Serbia**: always unatt. in south |
| Vardar | 11/15 | **Serbia**: always unatt. in south |
| Danube | ref. 5/16* | **Macedonia**: 8/16; *3* in 12/16; *1* in 5/17; *1* in 10/18 |
| Drina | ref. 5/16* | **Macedonia**: 8/16; *3* in 12/16; *1* in 5/17; *1* in 10/18 |
| Morava | ref. 5/16* | **Macedonia**: 8/16; *1* in 12/16; *1* in 5/17; *1* in 10/18 |
| Sumadija | ref. 5/16* | **Macedonia**: 8/16; *2* in 12/16; *2* in 5/17; *2* in 10/18 |
| Timok | ref. 5/16* | **Macedonia**: 8/16 (in reserve); *2* in 12/16; *2* in 5/17; *2* in 10/18 |
| Vardar | ref. 5/16* | **Macedonia**: 8/16 (in reserve); *1* in 12/16; *2* in 5/17; *c. 2/18* renamed Yugoslav Division†; *2* in 10/18 |
| Yugoslav | ref. 5/16* | **Macedonia**: see Vardar Division. |
| | | Some sources also refer to the existence in 1914 of the Ibar, Kosovo and Monastrir Infantry Divisions but none of these saw any combat. |

## CAVALRY DIVISIONS (total = 1/1)

| DIVISION | FORMED | COMBAT RECORD |
|---|---|---|
| Cavalry | pre-war | **Serbia**: *Uzice Gp.* on 12/8/14; 2 on 6/10/15; 2 on 14/10/15; 3 on 29/10/15; 2 on 11/11/15 <br> **Macedonia**: 8/16 to 10/18. (From 4/18 both of its brigades fought mounted, as opposed to only one hitherto). |

## South Africa

Unusually, the three 'East African' divisions were so-called after the theatre in which they served rather than their provenance. As they fought under a South African C-in-C. and as two of the divisions (2nd and 3rd) were mostly made up of South African battalions, and had South African commanders, we have included them in this entry‡. Contrary to our usual practice we have also included the South African Brigade, which served on the Western Front and indubitably punched well above its weight.

| DIVISION | FORMED | COMBAT RECORD |
|---|---|---|
| 1 East African (Magadi Div. to 1/16) | 12/15 | **German E.Africa**: 3/16 to 5/17 when redesignated Kilwa Force.(Mainly comprised of E.African and Indian battalions). |
| 2 East African | 1/16 | **German E.Africa**: 2/16 to 1/17 when disbanded |
| 3 East African | 3/16 | **German E.Africa**: 5/16 to 11/16 when disbanded |
| South African Brigade | 8/15 | **W.Desert**: 1/16-4/16 as part of *W.F.F.* <br> **W.Front**: 4/16-9/18 as part *9 Div.*; *66 Div.* to end |

Two other very short-lived divisions appeared during the latter stages of the South-West African campaign. These were simply known as 1 Division (ex-Central Force) and 2 Division (ex-Southern and Eastern Forces) and existed only from April to May 1915.

# Turkey*

### INFANTRY DIVISIONS (total = 73†)

| DIVISION | FORMED | COMBAT RECORD |
|---|---|---|
| **1** Constantinople | pre-war | **Thrace‡**: in 10/14; in 1/15; in 4/15; in 7/15 (5); in 8/15 (5); in 12/15 (5); in 2/16; see Armenia/Kurdistan below<br>**Armenia/Kurdistan◊**: in 5/16; in 7/16; in 10/16; in 3/17; in 10/17; in 11/17; see below<br>**Syria/Palestine•**: from 12/17 to end |
| **1** Caucasus | 3/18 | **Armenia**: A small, scratch formation that was not part of the regular Turkish army |
| **2** Hadem-Keny | pre-war | **Thrace**: in 10/14; in 1/15; in 4/15; in 5/15 (5); in 6/15 (5); in 8/15 (5); in 12/15 (5); see below<br>**Mesopotamia**: from 2/16 to end |
| **2** Caucasus | 3/18 | **Armenia**: as 1 Caucasus Div. above |
| **3** Scutari | pre-war | **Thrace**: in 10/14 (Scutari); in 1/15; in 4/15 (5); in 7/15 (5); in 8/15 (5); in 12/15 (5); see below<br>**Syria/Palestine**: in 2/16; in 7/16; in 1/17; in 3/17; in 7/17; in 10/17; in 12/17; in 3/18; disbanded (by 10/18)<br>(Some sources have this division in Armenia/Kurdistan from 11/14 and on the Egyptian Frontier in 2/15. This is remarkable agility from the usually tortoise-like Turkish Army) |
| **3** Caucasus | 3/18 | **Armenia/Kurdistan**: to end |
| **3** Composite△ | 1/15 | See 45 Div. below |
| **4** Adrianople | pre-war | **Thrace**: in 10/14; in 1/15; in 4/15; (5) from 7/15; in 8/15 (5); in 12/15 (5); in 2/16; see below<br>**Mesopotamia**: in 6/16; in 1/17; in 3/17; disbanded |
| **4** Caucasus | 3/18 | **Armenia**: as 1 Caucasus Div. above |
| **5** Adrianople | pre-war | **Thrace**: in 10/14; in 1/15; in 4/15 (5); in 8/15 (5); in 9/15 (5); in 12/15; in 2/16; see Armenia/Kurdistan below<br>**Armenia/Kurdistan**: from 4/16; in 7/16; in 10/16; in 3/17; in 7/17; in 12/17; in 3/18; in 8/18; see below<br>**Mesopotamia**: from 9/18 to end |
| **5** Caucasus | 9/16 | (Formed from 9, 10 and 13 Divisions, now downgraded to regiments)<br>**Armenia/Kurdistan**: to 11/18 |
| **5** Composite△ | 1/15 | See 52 Div. below |
| **6** Kirk-Killissa | pre-war | **Thrace**: in 10/14; in 1/15; see W.Anatolia below; in 5/15 (5); in 7/15 (5); in 8/15 (5); in 12/15 (5); see W.Anatolia below<br>**W.Anatolia**: in 4/15; see above; from 12/15; in 1/16; see below<br>**Mesopotamia**: from 2/16; in 4/16; in 7/16; in 3/17; in 7/17; in 9/17; in 12/17; in 3/18; disbanded (by 10/18) |
| **7** Rodosta | pre-war | **Thrace**: in 10/14; in 1/15; in 4/15 (5); in 6/15 (5); in 8/15 (5); in 12/15; in 3/16; see Armenia/Kurdistan below<br>**Armenia/Kurdistan**: from 7/16; in 10/16; dissolved; see below<br>**Syria/Palestine**: reformed by 3/17; in 10/17; in 12/17; in 3/18; in 9/18; disbanded |
| **8** Balikessar | pre-war | **Syria/Palestine**: in 10/14; in 1/15; in 4/15; see Thrace below<br>**Thrace**: from 5/15; (5) from 7/15; in 8/15 (5); in 12/15 (5); in 2/16; see below<br>**Armenia/Kurdistan**: from 5/16; in 7/16; in 10/16; in 3/17; in 7/17; in 12/17; in 3/18; in 9/18; disbanded |
| **9** Gallipoli | pre-war | **Thrace**: in 10/14; in 1/15; in 4/15 (5); in 6/15 (5); in 8/15 (5); in 12/15 (5); see below<br>**Armenia/Kurdistan**: in 2/16; in 7/16; reduced to regiment 9/16 (see 5 Caucasus Div. above) |
| **9** Caucasus | 9/16 | (Formed from 17, 28 and 29 Divisions, now downgraded to regiments)<br>**Armenia/Kurdistan**: to 11/18 |

| DIVISION | FORMED | COMBAT RECORD |
|---|---|---|
| **10** Izmir | pre-war | **W.Anatolia**: in 10/14; see Syria/Palestine below<br>**Syria/Palestine**: in 1/15; in 4/15; see Thrace below<br>**Thrace**: in 6/15; in 8/15 (5); in 12/15 (5); in 2/16; see below<br>**Armenia/Kurdistan**: from 3/16; in 7/16; reduced to regiment 9/16 (see 5 Caucasus Div. above) |
| **10** Caucasus | 9/16 | (Formed from 30, 31 and 32 Divisions, now downgraded to regiments)<br>**Armenia/Kurdistan**: to 10/18; disbanded (?) |
| **11** Denizli | pre-war | **W.Anatolia**: in 10/14; in 1/15; in 3/15; see Thrace below<br>**Thrace**: in 4/15 (5); in 6/15 (5); in 8/15 (5); in 12/15 (5); in 2/16; see Armenia/Kurdistan below<br>**Armenia/Kurdistan**: from 7/16; in 10/16; in 3/17; 7/17; in 12/17; see below<br>**Syria/Palestine**: from 1/18; in 3/18; in 9/18; in 11/18 |
| **11** Caucasus | 9/16 | (Formed from 18, 33 and 34 Divisions, now downgraded to regiments)<br>**Armenia/Kurdistan**: to 11/18 |
| **12** Burdur | pre-war | **W.Anatolia**: in 10/14; in 1/15; in 4/15; see Thrace below<br>**Thrace**: in 5/15 (5); in 6/15 (5); in 8/15 (5); in 12/15 (5); in 2/16; in 6/16; see below<br>**Armenia/Kurdistan**: from 7/16 to end |
| **13** Angora | | **Anatolia**: in 10/14; see Thrace below<br>**Thrace**: in 1/15; in 4/15; in 8/15 (5); in 12/15 (5); in 2/16; see below<br>**Armenia/Kurdistan**: from 4/16; in 7/16; reduced to regiment 9/16 (see 5 Caucasus Div. above) |
| **14** Kastamoni | | **Anatolia**: in 10/14; see Thrace below<br>**Thrace**: in 1/15; in 4/15; in 8/15 (5); in 12/15 (5); in 2/16; in 6/16; see Armenia/Kurdistan below<br>**Armenia/Kurdistan**: in 7/16; in 1/17; see Mesopotamia below<br>**Mesopotamia**: from 3/17; in 7/17; in 12/17; in 3/18; destroyed |
| **15** Yozgad | | **Anatolia**: in 10/14; see Thrace below<br>**Thrace**: in 1/15; in 4/15 (5); in 6/15 (5); in 8/15 (5); in 12/15 (5); in 2/16; in 7/16; see Rumania below; in 12/17; in 3/18; see Armenia/Kurdistan below<br>**Rumania**: from 8/16; in 3/17; in 7/17; in 10/18; see Thrace above<br>**Armenia/Kurdistan**: in 6/18; in 10/18; in 11/18 |
| **16** Adana | | **Syria/Palestine**: in 10/14; in 1/15; see Thrace below; from 2/17 to 10/18; disbanded<br>**Thrace**: in 4/15 (5); in 8/15 (5); in 12/15 (5); in 2/16; see W.Anatolia below<br>**W.Anatolia**: in 7/16; in 12/16; see Syria/Palestine above |
| **17** Baiburt | | **Armenia/Kurdistan**: to 9/16; reduced to regiment (see 9 Caucasus Div. above) |
| **18** Kharput | ↓ | **Armenia/Kurdistan**: to 9/16; reduced to regiment (see 11 Caucasus Div. above) |
| **19** | 1/15 | **Thrace**: in 3/15; in 4/15 (5); in 7/15 (5); in 8/15 (5); in 12/15 (5); in 2/16; in 7/16; see Galicia below<br>**Galicia**: in 10/16; in 3/17; in 7/17; see below<br>**Syria/Palestine**: in 9/17; to 10/18; disbanded |
| **20** | 1/15 | **W.Anatolia**: in 4/15; in 12/15; see Thrace below<br>**Thrace**: in 2/16; in 7/16; see Galicia below<br>**Galicia**: in 10/16; in 3/17; in 7/17; in 9/17; see below<br>**Syria/Palestine**: in 10/17; in 3/18; in 10/18; disbanded |
| **21** Assir | pre-war | **Arabia**: in 10/14; to 11/18 |
| **22** Hejaz | | **Arabia**: in 10/14; to 11/18 |
| **23\*\*** (Homs) | | **S.Anatolia/Syria/Palestine/Arabia**: 10/14 to 11/18 |
| **24\*\*** | ↓ | **Syria/Palestine**: in 10/14; in 1/15; in 4/15; in 12/15; in 2/16; see below; in 8/17; to 11/18<br>**Thrace**: in 7/16; in 3/17; in 6/17; see above |

* As Turkish Armies tended to remain in the same region, and rarely numbered more than one or two in a region, it has not been thought necessary to give Army allocations within the regional headings. For location of Armies see Section 1: Maps 29-32.

† However, two are simple renumberings and four are each amalgamations of three other divisions. Therefore net total = 67.

‡ Includes Dardanelles. Units known to have been allocated to Fifth Army, the H.Q. responsible for containing the Allied landings, have the relevant dates succeeded by the figure '5' in brackets.

◊ Often referred to, inaccurately, as the Caucasus Front.

• Also includes Arabia, notably the Hejaz.

△ Also sometimes referred to as 3*bis* and 5*bis* Division, or 3 and 5 Expeditionary Forces.

** Titles not known (if any). Name-plate divisions only in peacetime. Name in brackets denotes recruiting area.

## INFANTRY DIVISIONS continued

| DIVISION | FORMED | COMBAT RECORD |
|---|---|---|
| 25 Damascus | pre-war | **Syria/Palestine**: in 10/14; in 1/15; in 4/15; in 12/15; *see Thrace below* <br> **Thrace**: in 2/16; in 7/16; *see Rumania below*; in 12/17; *disbanded* <br> **Rumania**: from 8/16; in 3/17; in 7/17; *see Thrace above* |
| 26 Aleppo | | **Syria/Palestine**: in 10/14; in 1/15; in 4/15; in 12/15; in 2/16; *see Thrace below*; in 7/17; in 10/17; in 12/17; in 3/18; in 10/18; *disbanded* <br> **Thrace**: in 7/16; in 9/16; *see below* <br> **Rumania**: from 10/16; in 3/17; *see Syria/Palestine above* |
| 27 Haifa | | **Syria/Palestine**: in 10/14; to 12/17; *disbanded* |
| 28 Erzurum | | **Armenia/Kurdistan**: in 10/14; to 9/16; reduced to regiment (see 9 Caucasus Div. above) |
| 29 Erzurum | | **Armenia/Kurdistan**: as above |
| 30 Erzingan | | **Armenia/Kurdistan**: in 10/14; to 9/16; reduced to regiment (see 10 Caucasus Div. above) |
| 31 Erzingan | | **Armenia/Kurdistan**: as above |
| 32 Sivas | | **Armenia/Kurdistan**: as above |
| 33 Van | | **Armenia/Kurdistan**: in 10/14; to 9/16; reduced to regiment (see 11 Caucasus Div. above) |
| 34 Mush | | **Armenia/Kurdistan**: as above |
| 35 Mosul | | **Mesopotamia**: in 10/14; *see below*; in 1/15; in 4/15; in 12/15; in 2/16; in 4/16; *disbanded* <br> **Syria/Palestine**: in 11/14; *see above* |
| 36 Caucasus* | | **Armenia/Kurdistan**: to 10/18; *disbanded* |
| 37 Caucasus* | | **Armenia/Kurdistan**: to 11/18 <br> (some sources have this division in Syria/Palestine from mid-1918) |
| 38 Basra | | **Mesopotamia**: in 10/14; to 1/16; *destroyed* |
| 39 Sanaa | | **Arabia**: in 10/14; to 11/18 |
| 40 Hodeida | ↓ | **Arabia**: in 10/14; to 11/18 |
| 41 | 1/16 | **Thrace**: in 2/16; *see below* <br> **Syria/Palestine**: in 7/16; in 3/17; in 7/17; in 12/17; in 3/18; in 11/18 |
| 42 | | **Thrace**: in 2/16; *see below*; in 3/17; in 7/17; in 12/17; *see below* <br> **Syria/Palestine**: in 7/16; *see above*; in 3/18; *disbanded* (by 10/18) |
| 43 | | **Thrace**: in 2/16; *see below* <br> **Syria/Palestine**: in 7/16; in 3/17; in 7/17; in 12/17; in 3/18; in 10/18 *disbanded* |
| 44 | ↓ | **Syria/Palestine**: in 2/16; to 11/18 |
| 45 (as 3 Composite Div. to 12/15) | 1/15 | **Armenia/Kurdistan**: in 4/15; in 8/15; *see below* <br> **Mesopotamia**: in 10/15; in 2/16; in 4/16; in 7/16; in 12/16; in 3/17; *disbanded* <br> (see 51 Div. below) |

| DIVISION | FORMED | COMBAT RECORD |
|---|---|---|
| 46 | 1/16 | **W.Anatolia**: in 2/16; in 7/16; in 11/16; *see Macedonia below* <br> **Macedonia**: in 11/16; in 4/17; in 7/17; *see below* <br> **Syria/Palestine**: in 8/17; in 12/17; in 3/18; in 9/18; in 10/18; *disbanded* |
| 47 | | **W.Anatolia**: in 2/16; in 6/16; *see Armenia/Kurdistan below*; in 7/17; in 12/17; in 3/18; *see Syria/Palestine below* <br> **Armenia/Kurdistan**: in 7/16; in 3/17; *see above* <br> **Syria/Palestine**: in 10/18; *disbanded* |
| 48 | | **W.Anatolia**: in 2/16; in 6/16; *see Armenia/Kurdistan below* <br> **Armenia/Kurdistan**: in 7/16; in 3/17; in 7/17; *see below* <br> **Syria/Palestine/Arabia**: from 12/17; to 11/18 <br> (Possibly disbanded and reformed whilst in Armenia c.10/16) |
| 49 | | **Thrace**: in 2/16; *see Armenia/Kurdistan below*; in 3/18; in 10/18; in 11/18 <br> **Armenia/Kurdistan**: from 5/16; in 7/16; in 3/17; *see below* <br> **W.Anatolia**: in 7/17; *see Thrace above* <br> (Possibly disbanded and reformed whilst in Armenia c.10/16) |
| 50 | ↓ | **Thrace**: in 2/16; in 7/16; in 9/16; *see Macedonia below* <br> **Macedonia**: from 9/16; to 6/17; *see below* <br> **Mesopotamia**: in 7/17; in 12/17; in 3/18; *destroyed* |
| 51 | 1915 | **Mesopotamia**: in 10/15; in 2/16; in 4/16; in 7/16; in 12/16; in 3/17; in 7/17; in 12/17; in 3/18; *disbanded* (by 10/18) <br> (Other sources have 51 Div. as being the renumbered 3 Composite Div. see 45 Div. above) |
| 52 (as 5 Composite Div. to 12/15) | 1/15 | **Armenia/Kurdistan**: in 4/15; in 9/15; *see below* <br> **Mesopotamia**: from 11/15; in 2/16; in 5/16; in 7/16; in 12/16; in 3/17; in 7/17; in 12/17; in 2/18; *disbanded* |
| 53 | 1916 | **Armenia/Kurdistan**: in 7/16; (used as a replacement depot); *see below* <br> **Syria/Palestine**: in 3/17; in 7/17; in 12/17; in 3/18; in 9/18; in 10/18; *disbanded* |
| 54 | 1916/17 | **W.Anatolia**: in 3/17; *see below* <br> **Syria/Palestine**: in 5/17; to 10/18; *disbanded* |
| 55 | | **Thrace**: in 3/17 to end |
| 56 | | **W.Anatolia**: in 3/17 to end |
| 57 | | **W.Anatolia**: as above |
| 58 | | **Arabia**: in 3/17 to 1/19; (Medina garrison) |
| 59 | ↓ | **W.Anatolia**: in 3/17; in 7/17; *see below* <br> **Syria/Palestine**: in 8/17; in 12/17; *disbanded* (by 3/18) |
| 60 | 1917 | **Thrace**: in 12/17 to end |
| 61 | 1917 | **Thrace**: as above |
| 62 (as Amman Expeditionary Force to mid-1918) | 1918 | **Syria/Palestine**: in 3/18 to 10/18; *disbanded* |
| 63 | 1918 | **Syria/Palestine**: as above |

* Originally in Iraq as Kirkuk and Baghdad Divisions respectively. Sources disagree as to whether they moved before or after the Turkish declaration of war.

### CAVALRY DIVISIONS (total = 3)

| DIVISION | FORMED | COMBAT RECORD |
|---|---|---|
| **1**<br>**Mixed** | 8/14 | **Armenia/Kurdistan**: 1914-15 but later existence uncertain |
| **2** | 8/14 | **Armenia/Kurdistan**: 1914-16 but later existence uncertain |
| **3** | (?) | **Armenia/Kurdistan**: in 6/16; in 8/16; largely destroyed by end of year; *see below*<br>**Syria/Palestine**: (reformed) from 2/17; in 10/17; in 12/17; in 9/18<br>(Possibly reformed in Mesopotamia 1916/17) |

## Ukraine

### INFANTRY DIVISIONS (and others)

Following the February 1917 revolution in Russia, a wave of patriotic Ukranian sentiment affected many of its units. By July upwards of twenty divisions on all fronts had been 'Ukrainianised' and ten exclusively Ukranian regiments and two corps (I Ukrainian and II *Zaporozhian Sich*) had been formed. The two corps, based near Kiev, rallied to the Provisional Government established in October 1917, and two *Serdiuk* (Guards) *Divisions* were formed in November. In January 1918, the Government disbanded most of its regular formations in favour of a patriotic militia but soon began to reform them. A so-called *Zaporozhian Division* appeared in February but most useful of all were the two *Bluecoats Divisions*, formed by the Germans from Ukranian prisoners-of-war, that also arrived that same month. These were soon followed by an equivalent *Greycoats Division* formed by the Austrians. In April the Provisional Government succumbed to a *coup d'état* and was succeeded by a reactionary Hetmanate. The *Bluecoats Divisions* were disbanded immediately and the *Greycoats* in October. At the time of the Armistice efforts had only just begun to raise a regular army of eight infantry corps and four-and-a-half cavalry divisions.

## United Kingdom

### INFANTRY DIVISIONS (total = 68)

| DIVISION | FORMED | COMBAT RECORD |
|---|---|---|
| **Guards*** | 8/15 | **W.Front**: *BEF* to 10/15; *1* to 12/15; *3* to 2/16; *2* to ?/16; *4* to ?/17; *5* to 12/17; *3* |
| **1*** | pre-war | **W.Front**: *BEF* 8/14 to 9/14; *1* to 12/14; *1* to 6/16; *4* to ?/17; *5* to 7/17; *4* to 10/17; *2* to 12/17; *4* to 4/18; *1* to 9/18; *4* |
| **2*** | | **W.Front**: as above to 12/14; *1* to 7/16; *4* to 9/16; *Res.* to 11/16; *5* to 4/17; *1* to 10/17; *2* to 12/17; *3* |
| **3*** | | **W.Front**: *BEF* 8/14 to 9/14; *II* to 12/14; *2* to 6/16; *4* to ?/16; *1* to 10/16; *Res.* to 11/16; *5* to 2/17; *3* to 4/18; *1* to ?/18; *5* to 8/18; *3* |
| **4*** | | **W.Front**: *BEF* 8/14 to 9/14; *II* to 11/14; *III* to 12/14; *2* to 4/15; *BEF* to 5/15; *2* to 7/15; *3* to 5/16; *4* to 7/16; *Res.* to 8/16; *2* to 10/16; *4* to 2/17; *3* to 4/18; *1* to ?/18; *5* to 9/18; *1* |
| **5*** | | **W.Front**: *BEF* 8/14 to 9/14; *III* to 11/14; *II* to 12/14; *2* to 7/15; *3* to 6/16; *4* to 10/16; *1* to 10/17; *2* to 11/17; *see below*; *1* to 4/18 to 6/18; *5* to 8/18; *3*<br>**Italy**: 11/17 to 4/18 |
| **6*** | | **W.Front**: *BEF* 8/14 to 9/14; *III* to 12/14; *2* to 4/15; *BEF* to ?/15; *2* to ?/16; *4* to 11/16; *1* to 10/17; *3* to 4/18; *2* to 9/18; *4* |
| **7*** | 9/14 | **W.Front**: *IV* 10/14 to 12/14; *1* to ?/15; *3* to 3/16; *4* to 10/16; *2* to 11/16; *5* to ?/16; *3* to 9/17; *2* to 11/17; *see below*<br>**Italy**: 11/17 to end |

| DIVISION | FORMED | COMBAT RECORD |
|---|---|---|
| **8*** | 9/14 | **W.Front**: *BEF* 10/14 to 11/14; *IV* to 12/14; *1* to 6/15; *BEF* to 7/15; *1* to 4/16; *4* to ?/16; *1* to 10/16; *4* to ?/17; *5* to 9/17; *2* to 12/17; *4* to 8/18; *1* |
| **9†**<br>**(Scottish)** | 8/14 | **W.Front**: *BEF* from 6/15; *1* 6/15 to ?/15; *2* to 5/16; *4* to ?/16; *1* to 10/16; *4* to 11/16; *3* to 9/17; *5* to 10/17; *BEF* to 12/17; *5* to 4/18; *2* |
| **10†**<br>**(Irish)** | | **Gallipoli**: 8/15 to 10/15<br>**Macedonia**: 10/15 to 9/17<br>**Palestine**: 9/17 to end |
| **11†**<br>**(Northern)** | | **W.Front**: *3* 7/16 to 8/16; *Res.* to 11/16; *5* to 5/17; *4* to 6/17; *5* to 10/17; *1*<br>**Gallipoli**: 8/15 to 12/15<br>**Egypt**: 2/16 to 7/16 |
| **12†**<br>**(Eastern)** | | **W.Front**: *BEF* 6/15 to 7/15; *2* to 10/15; *1* to 6/16; *4* to 7/16; *Res.* to 8/16; *4* to 10/16; *3* to 10/16; *4* to 11/16; *3* to 11/17; *1* to 4/18; *3* to 8/18; *4* to 10/18; *1* |
| **13†**<br>**(Western)** | | **Gallipoli**: 7/15 to 12/15<br>**Egypt**: 1/16-2/16<br>**Mesopotamia**: 2/16 to end |
| **14†**<br>**(Light)** | | **W.Front**: *2* 6/15 to 2/16; *3* to ?/16; *4* to 10/16; *3* to 7/17; *2* to 12/17; *4* to 1/18; *5* to 3/18; *4* to 4/18; *1* to 6/18; *England* to 7/18; *2* |
| **15†**<br>**(Scottish)** | 9/14 | **W.Front**: *1* 6/15 to ?/16; *4* to 2/17; *3* to ?/17; *5* to 9/17; *3* to 4/18; *1* to 9/18; *5* |
| **16†**<br>**(Irish)** | | **W.Front**: *1* 12/15 to ?/16; *4* to 10/16; *2* to ?/17; *5* to 9/17; *3* to 12/17; *5* to 4/18; *1* to 6/18; *England* to 7/18; *BEF* to 8/18; *1* to ?/18; *5* |
| **17†**<br>**(Northern)** | | **W.Front**: *2* 7/15 to 5/16; *4* to 8/16; *3* to 11/16; *4* to 2/17; *5* to 4/17; *3* to 10/17; *5* to 12/17; *3* to 8/18; *4* in 8/18; *3* |
| **18†**<br>**(Eastern)** | | **W.Front**: *3* 7/15 to 3/16; *4* to ?/16; *Res.* to 11/16; *5* to 4/17; *1* to ?/17; *3* to 7/17; *5* to 12/17; *4* to 3/18; *5* to 4/18; *4* |
| **19†**<br>**(Western)** | | **W.Front**: *1* 7/15 to 5/16; *4* to 9/16; *2* to 10/16; *Res.* to 11/16; *5* to 4/17; *2* to 12/17; *3* to 4/18; *2* to ?/18; *5* to 10/18; *3* |
| **20†**<br>**(Light)** | | **W.Front**: *1* 7/15 to 2/16; *2* to ?/16; *4* to ?/17; *3* to 7/17; *5* to 10/17; *3* to 12/17; *4* to 3/18; *5* to 4/18; *1* to 10/18; *3* |
| **21†** | | **W.Front**: *BEF* 7/15 to ?/15; *2* to 4/16; *4* to 10/16; *1* to 4/17; *3* to 9/17; *2* to 12/17; *5* to 4/18; *2* to 6/18; *3* |
| **22†** | | **W.Front**: *3* 9/15 to 10/15<br>**Macedonia**: 11/15 to end |
| **23†** | | **W.Front**: *BEF* 7/15 to 9/15; *1* to 6/16; *4* to 9/16; *2* to 10/16; *4* to 11/16; *2* to 11/17<br>**Italy**: 11/17 to end |
| **24†** | | **W.Front**: *BEF* 7/15 to ?/15; *2* to 7/16; *4* to 10/16; *1* to ?/17; *2* to 7/17; *5* to 9/17; *4* to 12/17; *3* to 12/17; *5* to 4/18; *1* to 9/18; *3* |
| **25†** | | **W.Front**: *BEF* 7/15 to 9/15; *3* to ?/15; *2* to 3/16; *3* to 6/16; *4* to 7/16; *Res.* to 11/16; *2* to ?/16; *5* to 9/17; *1* to 12/17; *3* to 4/18; *1* in 4/18; *2* to 5/18; *6 Fr.* in 6/18; *BEF* to 9/18; *4* |
| **26†** | | **W.Front**: *3* 9/15 to 11/15<br>**Macedonia**: 11/15 to end |
| **27*** | 11/14 | **W.Front**: *2* 1/15 to 5/15; *BEF* to 7/15; *1* to 9/15; *3* to 11/15<br>**Macedonia**: 11/15 to end |
| **28*** | 12/14 | **W.Front**: *2* 1/15 to 10/15<br>**Egypt**: 11/15 to 1/16<br>**Macedonia**: 1/16 to end |
| **29*** | 1/15 | **Gallipoli**: 4/15 to 12/15<br>**Egypt**: 12/15 to 3/16<br>**W.Front**: *4* from 6/16 to 7/16; *Res.* to ?/16; *2* to 10/16; *4* to 4/17; *3* to ?/17; *5* to 10/17; *3* to 12/17; *4* to 3/18; *2* |
| **30†‡** | 1/15 | **W.Front**: *3* 11/15 to 5/16; *4* to ?/16; *1* to 10/16; *4* to 11/16; *3* to ?/17; *5* to 12/17; *4* to 1/18; *5* to 4/18; *2* |
| **31†‡** | 1/15 | **Egypt**: 12/15 to 3/16<br>**W.Front**: *4* 3/16 to 7/16; *Res.* to ?/16; *1* to 10/16; *Res.* to 11/16; *5* to 4/17; *1* to 4/18; *2* |

* Regular divisions.

† New Army Divisions.

‡ 30 to 35 Divisions were originally numbered 37 to 42 until April 1915 when the original 30 to 35 Divisions were broken up for reinforcements to replace casualties in the first New Army Divisions 9 to 26. Moreover, the original 43 and 44 Divisions were renumbered 38 and 37 respectively, also in April 1915.

Left margin notes:

† New Army Divisions.

‡ 30 to 35 Divisions were originally numbered 37 to 42until April 1915 when the original 30 to 35 Divisions were broken up for reinforcements to replace casualties in the first New Army Divisions 9 to 26. Moreover, the original 43 and 44 Divisions were renumbered 38 and 37 respectively, also in April 1915.

◊ Territorial Divisions. Numbered (from May 1915) in the order that they departed overseas.

• Second-line Territorial Divisions. Numbered from August 1915.

∆ Formation authorised.

** Originally Royal Naval Division, formed 9/14. See below.

†† Formed specially for home service.

‡‡ Total takes account of fact that some divisions listed below are merely renumberings of existing divisions.

## INFANTRY DIVISIONS continued

| DIVISION | FORMED | COMBAT RECORD |
|---|---|---|
| **32**†‡ | 1/15 | **W.Front:** *3* from 11/15 to 3/16; *4* to 7/16; *Res.* to ?/16; *1* to 10/16; *5* to 2/17; *4* to 4/17; *5* to 7/17; *4* to 10/17; *2* to 12/17; *4* to 3/18; *3* to 7/18; *4* |
| **33**†‡ | | **W.Front:** *1* from 11/15 to 6/16; *4* to ?/16; *3* to 11/16; *4* to 3/17; *3* to 8/17; *4* to 9/17; *2* to 12/17; *4* to ?/18; *2* to 9/18; *3* |
| **34**†‡ | | **W.Front:** *BEF* 12/15 to 2/16; *1* to 4/16; *2* to 2/17; *3* to ?/18; *2* |
| **35**†‡ | | **W.Front:** *1* from 2/16 to 6/16; *4* to 9/16; *3* to 2/17; *4* to 7/17; *3* to 10/17; *5* to 12/17; *4* to 3/18; *5* in 3/18; *3* to 6/18; *2* |
| **36**† (Ulster) | 9/14 | **W.Front:** *BEF* 10/15 to 11/15; *3* to 5/16; *4* to 7/16; *Res.* to ?/16; *2* to 7/17; *5* to 9/17; *3* to 1/18; *5* to ?/18; *2* |
| **37**†‡ | 4/15 | **W.Front:** *3* 8/15 to ?/16; *1* to 11/16; *5* to 1/17; *1* to 4/17; *3* to ?/17; *2* to 12/17; *4* to ?/18; *3* |
| **38**†‡ (Welsh) | 4/15 | **W.Front:** *BEF* 12/15 to 1/16; *1* to 6/16; *4* to ?/16; *2* to ?/17; *5* to 9/17; *1* to ?/18; *3* |
| **39**† | 8/15 | **W.Front:** *1* 2/16 to ?/16; *Res.* to 11/16; *5* in 11/16; *2* to ?/17; *5* to 9/17; *2* to 12/17; *4* to 1/18; *5* to ?/18; *2* to 7/18; *Lines of Comm.* to end |
| **40**† | 9/15 | **W.Front:** *1* from 6/16 to ?/16; *5* to 11/16; *4* to 7/17; *3* to ?/18; *2* |
| **41**† | 9/15 | **W.Front:** *2* from 6/16 to ?/16; *4* to 11/16; *2* to 11/17; *see below, 3* from 3/18 to ?/18; *2*<br>**Italy:** 11/17 to 3/18 |
| **42**◊ (East Lancashire) | pre-war | **Egypt:** 9/14 to 5/15; *see below,* 1/16 to 2/17; *see below*<br>**Gallipoli:** 5/15 to 12/15<br>**W.Front:** *4* from 3/17 to 7/17; *3* to 9/17; *5* in 9/17; *4* to 11/17; *BEF* to 12/17; *1* to 3/18; *3* |
| **43**◊ (Wessex) | | **India:** 10/14 to end (Brigades served piecemeal) |
| **44**◊ (Home Counties) | | **India:** as 43 Div. |
| **45**• (2 Wessex) | 9/14 | **India:** 12/14 to end (as 43 Div.) |
| **46**◊ (North Midland) | pre-war | **W.Front:** *BEF* 2/15 to 4/15; *2* to 10/15; *1* to 12/15; *BEF* to 2/16; *3* to 4/17; *1* to 6/18; *5* to 9/18; *4* |
| **47**◊ (2 London) | | **W.Front:** *1* from 8/15 to ?/16; *4* to 11/16; *2* to 10/17; *1* to 12/17; *3* to ?/18; *4* to 9/18; *5* |
| **48**◊ (South Midland) | | **W.Front:** *BEF* from 4/15 to 6/15; *1* to 7/15; *3* to 3/16; *4* to 7/16; *Res.* to 8/16; *4* to 9/16; *Res.* to 10/16; *3* to 11/16; *4* to ?/17; *3* to 7/17; *5* to 10/17; *1* to 11/17; *see below*<br>**Italy:** 11/17 to end |
| **49**◊ (West Riding) | | **W.Front:** *1* from 4/15 to 6/15; *2* to 2/16; *3* to 3/16; *4* to 7/16; *Res.* to 8/16; *3* to 4/17; *1* to 7/17; *4* to 9/17; *2* to 12/17; *4* to ?/18; *2* to 9/18; *1* |
| **50**◊ (North-Umbrian) | | **W.Front:** *BEF* from 4/15 to 5/15; *2* to ?/16; *4* to 4/17; *3* to 10/17; *5* to 12/17; *4* to 3/18; *5* to ?/18; *Res.* to 6/18; *4* to 8/18; *Lines of Comm.* to 9/18; *4* |
| **51**◊ (Highland) | | **W.Front:** *1* 6/15 to 7/15; *3* to 6/16; *4* to ?/16; *2* to 10/16; *Res.* to 11/16; *5* to 2/17; *3* to ?/17; *5* to 10/17; *3* to ?/18; *1* |
| **52**◊ (Lowland) | | **Gallipoli:** 5/15 to 12/15<br>**Egypt:** 1/16 to 4/18<br>**W.Front:** *1* 4/18 to 9/18; *3* to 10/18; *1* |
| **53**◊ (Welsh) | | **Gallipoli:** 7/15 to 12/15<br>**Egypt:** 12/15 to end |
| **54**◊ (E. Anglian) | | As 53 Div. |

| DIVISION | FORMED | COMBAT RECORD |
|---|---|---|
| **55**◊ (West Lancashire) | pre-war reformed 1/16 | **W.Front:** *3* 1/16 to ?/16; *4* to 10/16; *2* to ?/17; *5* to 10/17; *3* to 12/17; *1* to 9/18; *5* |
| **56**◊ (1 London) | 2/16 | **W.Front:** *BEF* 12/15 to 2/16; *3* to ?/16; *4* to 11/16; *1* to 4/17; *3* to 7/17; *5* to 9/17; *3* to 12/17; *1* |
| **57**• (2 West Lancashire) | 9/14∆ | **W.Front:** *2* 2/17 to ?/17; *1* to 10/17; *5* to 12/17; *4* to ?/18; *1* to ?/18; *3* to 8/18; *1* to 10/18; *5* |
| **58**• (2/1 London) | 9/14∆ | **W.Front:** *3* from 1/17 to 3/17; *5* to ?/17; *3* to 9/17; *5* to ?/17; *2* to 12/17; *4* to 1/18; *5* to ?/18; *4* to 9/18; *1* to 10/18; *5* |
| **59**• (2 North Midland) | 9/14∆ | **Ireland:** 4/16 to 12/16<br>**W.Front:** *4* 2/17 to 7/17; *3* to 9/17; *5* to 10/17; *1* to 12/17; *3* to ?/18; *2* to 6/18; *3* to 9/18; *5* |
| **60**• (2/2 London) | 9/14∆ | **Ireland:** (179 Brig. only) 4/16 to 5/16<br>**W.Front:** *3* 6/16 to ?/16; *1* to 11/16<br>**Macedonia:** 11/16 to 6/17<br>**Egypt/Palestine:** 6/17 to end |
| **61**• (2 South Midland) | 9/14∆ | **W.Front:** *1* 7/16 to 11/16; *5* to 2/17; *4* to ?/17; *3* to 6/17; *5* to 10/17; *3* to 1/18; *5* to ?/18; *1* to 6/18; *5* to 10/18; *3* |
| **62**• (2 West Riding) | 9/14∆ | **W.Front:** *5* 1/17 to ?/17; *3* to 12/17; *1* to ?/18; *3* |
| **63**** | 7/16 | **W.Front:** *1* 7/16 to ?/16; *Res.* to 11/16; *5* to 4/17; *1* to 10/17; *2* to 12/17; *3* to 10/18; *1* |
| **65**• (2 Lowland) | 9/14∆ | **Ireland:** 1/17 to 3/18; *disbanded* |
| **66**• (2 East Lancashire) | 9/14∆ | **W.Front:** *1* 3/17 to ?/17; *5* to 7/17; *4* to 10/17; *2* to 12/17; *4* to 3/18; *5* to ?/18; *2* to 7/18; *4* to 7/18; *Lines of Comm.* to 9/18; *1* to 10/18; *4* |
| **74** (Yeomanry) | 3/17 (Egypt) | **Egypt:** 3/17 to 6/18<br>**W.Front:** *5* 7/18 to end |
| **75** | 6/17 (Egypt) | **Egypt:** 6/17 to end |
| **Royal Naval Division** | 9/14 | **W.Front:** Not in BEF Order of Battle but in Belgium 10/14 to 11/14<br>**E Med & Egypt:** 2/15 to 4/15<br>**Gallipoli and Aegean:** 4/15 to 1/16 |

The following infantry divisions were also formed, none of which left England:

| Division | Disbanded |
|---|---|
| 63 (2 Northumbrian)◊ | 7/16 |
| 64 (2 Highland)◊ | — |
| 67 (2 Home Counties)◊ | — |
| 68 (2 Welsh)◊ | — |
| 69 (2 East Anglian)◊ | — |
| 71 †† | 3/18 |
| 72 †† | 3/18 |
| 73 †† | 3/18 |

## CAVALRY DIVISIONS (total = 5‡‡)

| DIVISION | FORMED | COMBAT RECORD |
|---|---|---|
| **1** | pre-war | **W.Front:** *BEF* 8/14 to 11/14; *Cav. Corps* to 3/16; *1* to ?/16; *4* to 10/16; *Cav. Corps* to 3/17; *3* to ?/17; *1* to ?/17; *3* to 12/17; *5* to ?/18; *1* to 6/18; *BEF* |

## CAVALRY DIVISIONS continued

| DIVISION | FORMED | COMBAT RECORD |
|---|---|---|
| **2** | pre-war | **W.Front**: as *1 Cav.* to 3/16; *2* to *?/16*; *3* to 10/16; *Cav. Corps* to 3/17; *3* to *?/17*; *4* to *?/17*; as *1 Cav.* |
| **3** | pre-war | **W.Front**: *Cav. Corps* 11/14 to 3/16; *BEF* to 5/16; *Res.* to 9/16; *Cav. Corps* to 3/17; *3* to *?/17*; *4* to *?/17*; as *1 Cav.* |
| **4** | 11/16 | **W.Front**: (Formed from renamed 1 Indian Cav. Div.) *Cav. Corps* 11/16 to 4/17; *5* to *?/17*; *4* to 7/17; *3* to 12/17; *5* to 2/18; *disbanded* <br> **Palestine**: Reformed 7/18 from 1 Mtd. Div. To end |
| **5** | 11/16 | **W.Front**: (Formed from renamed 2 Indian Cav. Div.) *Cav. Corps* to 4/17; *4* to *?/17*; *3* to 12/17; *5* to 2/18; *disbanded* <br> **Palestine**: Reformed 8/18 from 2 Mtd. Div. To end |
| **1 Mounted** | 8/14 | First formation never left England and was disbanded in 11/16 <br> **Palestine**: Second formation in 4/18 from renamed Yeomanry Mtd. Div. Became 4 Cav. Div. 7/18 *see above* |
| **2 Mounted** | 8/14 | **Egypt**: 4/15 to 8/15; *see below*; 12/15 to 1/16; *disbanded* <br> **Gallipoli**: 8/15 to 11/15 <br> **Palestine**: Reformed 5/18. To 8/18 when became 5 Cav. Div. *see above* |
| **Yeomanry Mounted** | 6/17 | **Palestine**: 6/17 to 4/18 when renamed 1 Mtd. Div. *see above* |

**N.B.** A complete list of British regiments and battalions, giving details of overseas service, can be found on pp. 149-157.

## United States

### INFANTRY DIVISIONS (total = 43*)

| DIVISION | FORMED | COMBAT RECORD |
|---|---|---|
| **1†** | 5/17 | **W.Front**: *G.H.Q.* 6/17 to 10/17; *8 Fr.* to 1/18; *1 Fr.* to 3/18; *8 Fr.* and *5 Fr.* to 4/18; *1 Fr.* to 7/18; *10 Fr.* in 7/18; *8 Fr.* to 8/18; *1 U.S.* to end |
| **2†‡** | 9/17 | **W.Front**: *G.H.Q.* 10/17 to 3/18; *2 Fr.* to 5/18; *6 Fr.* to 7/18; *10 Fr.* in 7/18; *8 Fr.* to 8/18; *1 U.S.* to 9/18; *4 Fr.* to 10/18; *1 U.S.* |
| **3†** | 11/17 | **W.Front**: *G.H.Q.* 5/18 to 6/18; *6 Fr.* to 8/18; *1 U.S.* |
| **4†** | 11/17 | **W.Front**: *G.H.Q.* 5/18; *1 Br.* to 6/18; *6 Fr.* to 8/18; *1 U.S.* to 10/18; *2 U.S.* |
| **5†** | 11/17 | **W.Front**: *7 Fr.* 6/18 to 8/18; *1 U.S.* |
| **6†** | 11/17 | **W.Front**: *G.H.Q.* 7/18-8/18; *7 Fr.* to 10/18; *1 U.S.* |
| **7†** | 12/17 | **W.Front**: *G.H.Q.* 8/18 to 9/18; *1 U.S.* to 10/18; *2 U.S.* |
| **8†** | 12/17 | **W.Front**: Landed Brest 9/11/18 |
| **9-20** | | Formed July to September 1918 but never went overseas. 10, 11 and 12 Divisions did have advance parties in France at the time of the Armistice |
| **21-25** | | **Not formed** |
| **26◊** | 7/17 | **W.Front**: *G.H.Q.* 11/17 to 2/18; *6 Fr.* to 3/18; *8 Fr.* to 6/18; *6 Fr.* to 8/18; *1 U.S.* |
| **27◊** | | **W.Front**: *4 Br.* 5/18 to 6/18; *3 Br.* in 6/18; *2 Br.* to 9/18; *4 Br.* |
| **28◊** | | **W.Front**: *2 Br.* 5/18 to 6/18; *1 Br.* and *10 Fr.* in 6/18; *6 Fr.* to 9/18; *2 Fr.* |
| **29◊** | | **W.Front**: *G.H.Q.* 6/18 to 7/18; *7 Fr.* to 9/18; *1 U.S.* |
| **30◊** | | **W.Front**: *2 Br.* 6/18 to 9/18; *4 Br.* |
| **31◊** | | **W.Front**: Service of Supply (*SOS*) 10/18 |

| DIVISION | FORMED | COMBAT RECORD |
|---|---|---|
| **32◊** | 7/17 | **W.Front**: *G.H.Q.* 2/18 to 5/18; *7 Fr.* to 7/18; *6 Fr.* to 8/18; *10 Fr.* to 9/18; *2 Fr.* in 9/18; *1 U.S.* |
| **33◊** | | **W.Front**: *4 Br.* 5/18 to 8/18; *2 Fr.* to 9/18; *1 U.S.* to 10/18; *2 U.S.* |
| **34◊** | | **W.Front**: *G.H.Q.* 9/18 to 10/18; *SOS* |
| **35◊** | | **W.Front**: *4 Br.* 5/18 to 6/18; *7 Fr.* to 9/18; *1 U.S.* to 11/18; *2 U.S.* |
| **36◊** | | **W.Front**: *G.H.Q.*, *2 Fr.* and *1 Fr.* 8/18 to 10/18; *4 Fr.* to 11/18; *1 U.S.* |
| **37◊** | | **W.Front**: *G.H.Q.* 6/18 to 7/18; *8 Fr.* to 9/18; *1 U.S.* and *2 U.S.* to 10/18; *6 Fr.* |
| **38◊** | | **W.Front**: *G.H.Q.* and *SOS* 10/18 to 11/18 |
| **39◊** | | **W.Front**: *SOS* 8/18 to end |
| **40◊** | | **W.Front**: *SOS* 8/18 to end |
| **41◊** | | **W.Front**: *G.H.Q.* 1/18 to 4/18; *SOS* |
| **42◊** | 8/17 | **W.Front**: *G.H.Q.* 11/17 to 2/18; *8 Fr.* to 6/18; *4 Fr.* to 7/18; *6 Fr.* to 8/18; *1 U.S.* |
| **43-75** | | **Not formed** |
| **76•** | 8/17 | **W.Front**: *SOS* 7/17 to end |
| **77•** | | **W.Front**: *2 Br.* 4/18 to 5/18; *3 Br.* to 6/18; *8 Fr.* to 8/18; *6 Fr.* to 9/18; *5 Fr.* and *2 Fr.* in 9/18; *1 U.S.* |
| **78•** | | **W.Front**: *2 Br.* 6/18 to 7/18; *1 Br.* to 8/18; *1 U.S.* |
| **79•** | | **W.Front**: *G.H.Q.* 7/18 to 8/18; *1 U.S.* to 9/18; *2 Fr.* in 9/18; *1 U.S.* to 10/18; *2 U.S.* in 10/18; *1 U.S.* |
| **80•** | | **W.Front**: *G.H.Q.* 5/18 to 6/18; *1 Br.* in 6/18; *3 Br.* to 8/18; *1 U.S.* |
| **81•** | | **W.Front**: *G.H.Q.* 8/18 to 9/18; *7 Fr.* to 10/18; *1 U.S.* |
| **82•** | | **W.Front**: *4 Br.* 5/18 to 6/18; *8 Fr.* to 8/18; *1 U.S.* to 11/18; *G.H.Q.* |
| **83•** | | **W.Front**: *G.H.Q.* 6/18 to 7/18; *SOS* <br> **Italy**: 332 Regt. detached |
| **84•** | | **W.Front**: *G.H.Q.* 9/18 to 10/18; *SOS* |
| **85•** | | **W.Front**: *SOS* 8/18 to 11/18; *2 U.S.* <br> **Russia**: 339 Regt. detached 8/18 |
| **86•** | | **W.Front**: *G.H.Q.* 9/18 to 10/18; *SOS* |
| **87•** | | **W.Front**: *G.H.Q.* 9/18; *SOS* |
| **88•** | | **W.Front**: *G.H.Q.* 9/18; *7 Fr.* to 11/18; *2 U.S.* |
| **89•** | | **W.Front**: *G.H.Q.* 6/18 to 8/18; *8 Fr.* to 9/18; *1 U.S.* |
| **90•** | | **W.Front**: *G.H.Q.* 6/18 to 8/18; *8 Fr.* in 8/18; *1 U.S.* |
| **91•** | | **W.Front**: *G.H.Q.* 7/18 to 8/18; *1 U.S.* to 9/18; *2 Fr.* in 9/18; *1 U.S.* to 10/18; *6 Fr.* |
| **92• (Colored)** | 10/17 | **W.Front**: *G.H.Q.* 6/18 to 8/18; *7 Fr.* to 9/18; *1 U.S.* to 10/18; *2 U.S.* |
| **93• (Colored)** | 11/17 | **W.Front**: *G.H.Q.* 3/18 to 5/18; disbanded into separate regiments fighting as part of, variously, 16, 34, 35, 36, 59, 63, 157 and 161 French Inf. Divs. |
| **94-97** | | Formed after the U.S. declaration of war (94 Div. had a paper existence only) but none went overseas |

\* Of which 30 reached the front line.

† Regular Army.

‡ Includes two U.S. Marine corps regiments (5 & 6).

◊ National Guard.

• National Army.

## Supplement: (a) Imperial sub-divisional units
### AFRICA

The contribution of the African colonies to the wider European war was considerable, yet because of the dispersed nature of operations forces were rarely grouped into divisions. The units listed below are mainly regiments and battalions and are listed under the individual colonies or regions, themselves grouped under the relevant metropolitan power. (South Africa, which did organise divisions, has its own entry in the main listings above.)

### Belgian

Belgian colonial presence in Africa was limited to the Congo where in August 1914 they maintained 32 companies of the *Force Publique*. Most were essentially armed police units except for six companies in diamond-rich Katanga which had a more overtly military character. On the declaration of war three battalion groupings were formed, two of which were dispatched to help protect the North Rhodesian frontier. These remained in place until November 1915. Between October 1914 and January 1916, three other companies served with the French during the campaign in German Cameroon. In the Belgian Congo itself companies were formed into *Groupes* and later *Régiments*, each of three battalions, or into the six independent battalions which were also deployed. Most of these 18 battalions took part in the Allied invasion of German East Africa in 1916 but after the capture of Taborah, in September, the Belgian presence was reduced to just eight battalions.

### British

| UNIT | FORMED | COMBAT RECORD |
|---|---|---|
| **East Africa** | | |
| King's African Rifles | pre-war | Three regiments existed pre-war, 1, 3 and 4, each of one battalion. During the war, 1 and 3 KAR were expanded to four battalions and 4 KAR to six. Also raised were 2 KAR (four bns.), 5 KAR (one bn.), 6 KAR (two bns.) and 7 KAR (one bn.), making a grand total of 22 battalions. All served in the East African campaign exclusively, at times as part of the South African-led East African Divisions (see that entry in the main listing). |
| **N.Rhodesia** | | |
| N.Rhodesia Police* | pre-war | Only a few small, dispersed companies to 11/17 when officially deemed a battalion. Fought in East African campaign. |
| N.Rhodesia Rifles | 11/14 | Remained at company strength until disbanded 5/16. Fought in East African campaign. |
| **Nyasaland** | | |
| Nyasaland Police | pre-war | Few details available. Saw service locally and in East Africa. |
| Nyasaland Volunteer Rifles | pre-war † | A volunteer company in 8/14 which reached battalion strength by the end of the war. Served in the East African campaign and along the Nyasaland border. |
| **S.Rhodesia** | | |
| British S.Africa Police | pre-war | Dispersed companies in 8/14 that reached battalion strength later, fighting in the S.W.African campaign in 1914-15 and patrolling N.Rhodesia thereafter. |
| Rhodesia Regiments | 1914/15 | White volunterrs in August 1914 who formed 1 Regiment on the outbreak of war and 2 Regiment a few months later. Both were single battalions, the former fighting in the S.W.African campaign, from 12/14, and the latter in the East African. They were disbanded in 1915 and 1916 respectively. |
| Rhodesian African Rifles | 1918 | See Rhodesian Native Regiment. |

\* Became N.Rhodesia Regiment in 1924.

† As Central Africa Rifles.

‡ *Not* part of the W.African Frontier Force.

### British continued

| UNIT | FORMED | COMBAT RECORD |
|---|---|---|
| **S.Rhodesia** continued | | |
| Rhodesia Native Regiment | 7/16 | Only one battalion was formed at first which performed garrison duty in S.W.Africa once the campaign was over. 2 Battalion was formed in 1917 and served in the East African campaign. It continued to do so until the end of hostilities but was amalgamated with 1 Battalion in 1918 to form the Rhodesian African Rifles. |
| **Uganda** | | |

The main Ugandan contribution to the Allied war effort was the maintenance of four active battalions of the King's African Rifles (see East Africa above) but there were also formed:

| UNIT | FORMED | COMBAT RECORD |
|---|---|---|
| Baganda Rifles | 1914 | Formed from 3,000 native levies supplied by their chiefs as volunteers. 555 of them served as a local defence battalion until disbanded in 11/16. |
| Uganda Police Service Battalion | 1914 | Formed for local defence and disbanded in 1/17. |
| **West Africa** | | |
| W.African Frontier Force | pre-war | A multi-regimental force like the King's African Rifles (see E.Africa above) but in which the various regiments had their own title. These were:<br>*Nigeria Regiment* which comprised four infantry and one mounted infantry battalion by the end of the war and which served in the Cameroons in 1914 and East Africa between 12/16 and 2/18.<br>*Gold Coast Regiment* which comprised one battalion only and fought in Togoland in 1914 and East Africa between 7/16 and 8/18.<br>*Sierra Leone Battalion* which fought in Cameroon in 1914 as a composite unit with part of the Gold Coast Regiment.<br>*Gambia Company* which fought in East Africa between 7/17 and 2/18. |
| W.African Regiment‡ | pre-war | A single battalion which remained dispersed in West Africa except for service in Togoland in 1914 and in the Cameroons between 1914 and 1916. |

### French

Most of the black, Arab and white soldiers that served with African units during the war fought in Europe, either on the Western Front or in Macedonia. In these theatres they were usually part of the distinct colonial divisions and details of these formations will be found in the divisional listings under France proper. However, some regiments and individual battalions spent at least some of their time in Africa itself and the list below provides a summary of the most important of these. The units are of two main types: the *Tirailleurs Algériens* and *Marocains* of the *Armée d'Afrique*, a wholly North African force, and the *Tirailleurs Sénégalais* of sub-Saharan Africa who formed a key component of *la Coloniale*, comprising all units recruited from the rest of the Empire or for its defence. In peacetime the two forces usually kept out of each other's 'patch' but the demands of the Western Front meant that several *Sénégalais* units ended up in North Africa. (Unless specified otherwise the units listed below are regiments, normally consisting of between two and four battalions).

### North Africa

(Comprising Algeria, Tunisia and Morocco). During the war 63 Algerian *Tirailleur* battalions served on the Western Front whereas only 8 battalions remained in North Africa in August 1914 and only 6 by the end of the war. These latter acted mainly as garrison troops with military operations, mainly against Moroccan insurgents, being conducted by a further four battalions of Moroccan *Tirailleurs*.

The demands of the Western Front forced the French to also employ Senegalese *Tirailleurs* in North Africa and three regiments (2, 3 and 7) were stationed there. But again they served mainly as garrison troops and as depots for the raising and training of so-called *bataillons de marche* to serve at the front. Most of these went to Europe but a number (15 in 1915, 12 in 1917, 27 by the Armistice) remained to assist in mobile operations. Three regiments of Moroccan and Algerian *Spahis* also campaigned in this theatre. Most white colonial units went to the European fronts but the counter-insurgency effort in Morocco did employ two battalions of the Foreign Legion and two battalions of the *Infanterie Légère d'Afrique*, a penal regiment. There were also 15 battalions of elderly Zouave reservists who were assigned to garrison duties.

## Sub-Saharan Africa

(Comprising French West Africa and French Equatorial Africa, further subdivided into Cameroun, Chad, Dahomey, Gabon, Gambia, Ivory Coast, Madagascar, Niger, Senegal, Soudan, Togo, Upper Volta). Roughly 150 battalions of Senegalese *Tirailleurs* were raised during the war and most of them served in Europe or in North Africa (see above). Some, however, were stationed south of the Sahara and at least one battalion was usually available in Dahomey, Guinea and the Ivory Coast and often several battalions in Senegal and Soudan. There were also three *Régiments de Tirailleurs Malgaches* in Madagascar which served as garrison troops but which also provided 18 *bataillons de marche* for service in Europe.

Other units were available for more mobile operations against the German colonies in Africa (see Maps 33(b) and (d)) and for garrison duties once they were conquered. These included the *Régiment du Gabon*, the *Régiment de Tirailleurs Sénégalais du Tchad*, the *Régiment de Marche de Tirailleurs Sénégalais du Cameroun* (formed October 1915), two battalions of *Tirailleurs Sénégalais du Moyen-Congo* and three battalions of *Tirailleurs Sénégalais de L'Oubangi-Chari*. All of these units, or at least companies therefrom, took part in the Cameroon campaign.

## German

German colonial troops, or *askaris*, were grouped into *Schutz-, Feld-* and *Ersatzkompagnien*, as well as *Polizeitruppen*, and the government kept one or more types of unit on hand in each of the four African colonies. *Schutzkompagnien* were originally composed of better trained troops than the others but, as more and more *Feldkompagnien* in particular were raised, this distinction was gradually eroded.

### Togoland

Garrisoned by 900 *Polizeitruppen* (including 200 Germans), the colony could put up only a token resistance to the Allied invasion in August 1914.

### Cameroon

Here the Germans held out longer (from August 1914 to February 1916), with an original deployment of twelve companies of *Schutztruppen* (1,700 men) and roughly the same number of *Polizeitruppen*. By April 1915 the *Schutztruppen* companies had risen to 34, although it was still the original dozen that provided the most dependable troops.

### South-West Africa

In August 1914, the authorities here deployed nine companies of *Schutztruppen* (1,900 men). A call-up of reservists permitted an increase in the strength of each company and the formation of three extra reserve companies. By July 1915, when the Germans surrendered, another four *Ersatzkompagnien* and three *Polizei* companies had been formed, but this had been more than offset by the disbandment of six of the original companies.

### East Africa

Here, under von Lettow-Vorbeck, the Germans fought their most successful colonial campaign and here they deployed by far the largest force. In August 1914 it comprised 14 *Feldkompagnien* (2,700 men) and 2,200 *Polizeitruppen*. By March 1915 the call-up of reservists had permitted an expansion to nine *Schutzkompagnien*, 29 *Feldkompagnien* and 2 reserve companies. By early 1916 the Germans had a peak strength of *c.*60

companies all told, comprising 3,000 whites and 12,000 Africans.* By November 1917, however, when von Lettow-Vorbeck crossed into Mozambique, the main force was much reduced. Only fifteen companies crossed with him and by the Armistice these had been reduced to twelve.

## Italian

Italian colonial units took little part in the fighting against either German or Turkish troops.

## Portugese

Unusually, the Portuguese relied heavily on white troops from the metropolitan army to police their African empire. Annual expeditionary forces were sent to Angola and Mozambique to replace units ravaged by disease and plummeting morale.† However, it seems that most of the serious fighting, be it internal repression or operations against the German colonies, was done by the *companhias indígenas*, composed of locally-raised Africans and each about 250 men strong.

### Angola

Here the Portuguese were concerned only with internal garrison and punitive duties, for which they had available 26 local companies in 1916, rising to 40 in 1918, and the expeditionary forces sent out in 1914 and 1915, consisting respectively of one infantry battalion and one cavalry regiment, and then four infantry battalions and four cavalry regiments.

### Mozambique

Once Germany declared war on Portugal, in March 1916, the Portugese in Mozambique commenced their own operations against von Lettow-Vorbeck's forces in East Africa. Expeditionary forces had been sent out in 1914 and 1915 and these continued throughout the war. The forces arriving were as follows:

1914 One infantry battalion and one cavalry regiment
1915 (the same)
1916 three infantry battalions
1917 (the same)
1918 one infantry battalion

The *companhias indígenas* totalled 12 in 1915 and by the end of the war 40 or so had been formed, mainly so-called Expeditionary Companies, numbered 17, 19-40 and 42-45. There were also six companies raised by the local Chartered Companies. However, none of these troops performed particularly well in the field and from June 1917 were mostly restricted to garrison duties in the coastal towns, leaving the actual pursuit of the *askaris* to the British.

## EGYPT

The strength of the Egyptian Army throughout the war was derived mainly from its 17 battalions of well-trained infantry (8 Egyptian battalions and 9 Sudanese). There were also several companies of the elite Egyptian Camel Corps (not to be confused with the E.E.F.'s Imperial Camel Corps), two squadrons of cavalry and three companies of mounted infantry. The occupation and garrisoning of Egypt was entirely the responsibility of the British Army and the Egyptian Army served almost exclusively in the Sudan, for whose security it was responsible. Its most important military operation was the Darfur Expedition of spring 1916, although some infantry and Camel Corps companies did fight alongside Sharifian units during the Arab Revolt.

* Almost all of these were deployed against the British and the Belgians. Only three were ever facing Portuese units.

† The infantry component of these expeditionary forces was only ever taken from the 3rd Battalion of the Regiment(s) employed, the latter coming up for service overseas according to numerical rotation.

## NEWFOUNDLAND

In August 1914 the island raised one battalion, dubbed 1 Royal Newfoundland Regiment, which was attached to British 29 Division to April 1918, to GHQ to September and finally to British 9 Division. The Battalion suffered grievously on the first day of the Somme.

## WEST INDIES

| UNIT | FORMED | COMBAT RECORD |
|---|---|---|
| **Bermuda Volunteer Rifle Corps** | 8/14 | A company of white volunteers that on arrival in England was attached to 1 Lincolnshire Regiment with whom it served on the Western Front from 6/15 to 11/18. |
| **British W.India Regiment** | 5/15 | By 12/17 twelve battalions of this regiment had been formed of which the first four were sent to Egypt to serve as the W.Indian Brigade. This was broken up in 7/16 with two battalions going to France and two remaining in the Middle East. Five further battalions were sent to France in 1917-18 and three to Italy. |
| **W.India Regiment** | pre-war | The two pre-war battalions were the only ones formed and were stationed in West Africa before taking part in East African operations from 7/16. |

## Supplement: (b) Regiments and Battalions of the British Army*

* Includes the Machine Gun Corps and the Tank Corps.

The reasons for this deviation from our usual 'divisions only' policy are given on p.109. However, the following points should also be noted:

a) Home service battalions are not listed in the entries below.

b) In the Western Front box of each regimental entry the first single-digit battalions (max. 4) are the regular ones, already in existence in August 1914; those with a 1/N or 2/N number are first and second wave Territorials, for which cadres already existed; those with a single-digit number, and listed after the Territorials, are the Service/'Kitchener'/New Army/'Pals' battalions formed from scratch in 1914 and 1915. Where no Territorial battalion is listed in the France & Belgium box there will be a gap in the numerical sequence indicating the break between regular and Service battalions.

c) In the Front boxes for each regiment the figure in italics denotes the battalion and the figure(s) in brackets the division(s) to which it was affiliated. (Some very brief divisional affiliations have been omitted). Where there is no figure in brackets after an italicised one, refer to the last bracketed figure given.

d) Unfortunately there is no space here to give any dates of service for each battalion and anyone wishing for such detail should consult Becke and James as listed in the Bibliography.

*Abbreviations*

| | | | | | |
|---|---|---|---|---|---|
| B. | Bantam | L. | Labour | WFF. | Western Frontier |
| G. | Garrison | MGC. | Machine Gun | | Force |
| Gds. | Guards | | Corps | Yeo. | Yeomanry |
| Gib. | Gibraltar | Mtd. | Mounted | | |
| Gr. | Graduated | P. | Pioneer | | |
| Ind. | Indian | RN. | Royal Naval | | |
| | | | Division | | |

## Battalions that served in:

† Includes N.Persia Force.

| REGIMENT | France & Belgium | Italy | Gallipoli | Macedonia | Egypt & Palestine | Mesopotamia† | Ireland, India & other |
|---|---|---|---|---|---|---|---|
| **INFANTRY** | | | | | | | |
| Argyll & Sutherland Highlanders (Princess Louise's) | *1* (27); *2* (6, 27, 2, 33); *1/5* (52, 34); *1/6* (51); *1/7* (4, 7, 51); *1/8* (51, 61, 15); *1/9* (27, 4); *10* (9, 32); *11* (15); *14* (39, 30, 14) | *1/6* (P)(5) | *1/5* (52) | *1* (27); *12* (26) | *1/5* (52) | | Ire; *3* |
| Bedfordshire Regt. | *1* (5); *2* (7, 30, 18); *4* (63); *6* (37); *7* (18); *8* (24, 6) | | *1/5* (54) | | *1/5* (54) | | Ind; *1* (G); *2* (G); *3* (G) |
| Berkshire Regt. (Princess Charlotte of Wales's Royal) | *1* (2); *2* (8); *1/4* (48); *2/4* (61); *5* (12); *6* (18); *8* (1, 18); *10* (L); *11* (L); *12* (L); *13* (L) | *1/4* (48) | | *7* (26) | | | Ire; *3* |
| Black Watch (Royal Highlanders) | *1* (1); *1/4* (7 Ind., 46, 15, 51, 39, 15); *1/5* (8, 51, 39, 15); *1/6* (51); *1/7*; *8* (9); *9* (15, 39, 16); *10* (26, 66); *12* (L); *13* (27, 50); *14* (74) | | | *10* (26); *13* (27) | *2* (7 Ind.); see also Scottish Horse & Fife & Forfar Yeo. | *2* (7 Ind.) | Ire; *3* |
| Border Regt. | *1* (29); *2* (7); *1/5* (50, 66, 32); *6* (11); *7* (17); *8* (25, 50); *11* (32) | *2* (7) | *1* (29); *6* (11) | *9* (P) (22) | | | Ind; *1/4* ; *2/4* |
| Buffs (E.Kent Regt.) | *1* (6); *6* (12); *7* (18); *8* (24); *10* (74) | | | *2* (28) | see E.Kent & W.Kent Yeo. | *1/5* (7 Ind. & 14 Ind.) | Ind; *1/4* |
| Cambridgeshire Regt. | *1/1* (27, 39, 12) | | | | | | |

## Battalions that served in: (continued)

| REGIMENT | France & Belgium | Italy | Gallipoli | Macedonia | Egypt & Palestine | Mesopotamia | Ireland, India & other |
|---|---|---|---|---|---|---|---|
| **INFANTRY continued** | | | | | | | |
| Cameronians (Scottish Rifles) | 1 (6, 27, 2, 33); 2 (8, 20); 1/5 (6, 27, 2, 33); 1/6 (8, 51, 33); 1/7 (52); 1/8 (52, 34); 9 (9); 10 (15); 14 (L) (–); 18 (16) | | 1/7 (52); 1/8 (52) | 11 (26) | | | Ire; 2/5; 2/6; 2/7; 2/8 Ind.; 1 (G) |
| Cameron Highlanders (Queen's Own) | 1 (1); 2 (27); 1/4 (8, 7, 51); 5 (9); 6 (15); 7 (15); 9 (L) (–); 11 (40) | | | 2 (27); see also Lovat's Scouts | | | Ire; 3 |
| Cheshire Regt. | 1 (5); 2 (28); 1/4 (34); 1/5 (P)(5, 56); 1/6 (5, 7, 39, 25, 30); 1/7 (34); 9 (19); 10 (25); 11; 13; 15 (35); 16; 18 (L)(–); 19 (L); 20 (L); 21 (L); 22 (L); 23 (59, 40) | 1 (5) | 1/4 (53); 1/7 (53); 8 (13) | 2 (28); 12 (22) | 1/4 (53); 1/7 (53); 2 (G) | 8 (13) | Ire; 51 (Gr.); 52 (Gr.) Gib.; 1 (G) |
| Coldstream Guards | 1 (1, Gds.); 2; 3 (Gds., 31); 4 (P) (Gds.) | | | | | | |
| Connaught Rangers | 1 (3 Ind.); 2 (3 Ind.); 5 (14, 66); 6 (16, 34, 39) | | 5 (10, Anzac Corps) | 5 (10) | 1 (3 Ind.); 5 (10) | 1 (3 Ind.) | Ire; 3; 4 |
| Devonshire Regt. | 1 (3, 5); 2 (8); 1/5 (75, 62); 9 (7, 25); 12 (L)(–); 14 (L); 16 (74) | | | 10 (26) | 1/5 (75); 2/4 (75); 2/5 (–); 1 (G)(–); see also Devon & Royal N.Devon Yeo. | 1/4 (14 Ind.); 1/6; 2/6 (–) | Ire; 3/4; 3/5; 3/6 Ind.; 1/4; 1/5; 1/6 |
| Dorsetshire Regt. | 1 (5, 32); 5 (11); 6 (17) | | 5 (11) | | 2 (3 Ind.); 2/4 (75) | 2 (6 Ind. & 3 Ind.); 1/4 (15 Ind.) | Ire; 3/4 Ind.; 1/4, 2/4 |
| Dublin Fusiliers (Royal) | 1 (29, 16, 29); 2 (4, 16, 50); 6 (10, 66); 7 (10); 8 (16); 9, 10 | | 1 (29); 6 (10); 7 | 6 (10); 7 | 6 (10); 7 | | Ire; 4; 5; 11 |
| Duke of Cornwall's Light Infantry | 1 (5); 1/5 (P)(61); 6 (14); 7 (20); 10 (P)(66, 2); 12 (L)(–) | 1 (5) | | 2 (27); 8 (26) | 1/4 (75) | | Ire; 3/4 Ind.; 1/4, 2/4 |
| Durham Light Infantry | 2 (6); 1/5 (50, 39); 1/6; 1/7 (P) (50, 8); 1/8 (50, 39); 1/9 (50, 39, 62); 2/6 (59); 10 (14); 11 (20); 12 (23); 13 (23, 25); 14 (6); 15 (21); 18 (31); 19 (B)(35); 20 (41); 22 (P)(19, 8); 29 (14) | 12 (23); 13 (23); 20 (41) | | 2/5 (P)(28, Crete‡); 2/9 (–) | | | Ire; 1 (G) Ind.; 1 Russia; 2/7 |
| E.Lancashire Regt. | 1 (34, 61); 2 (8, 23, 8); 1/4 [became 4] (66, 39); 2/4 (66); 2/5; 7 (19); 8 (37); 11 (31); 13 (40) | | 1/4 (42); 6 (13) | 9 (22) | 1/4 (42) | 6 (13) | |
| E.Surrey Regt. | 1 (5); 2 (28); 7 (12); 8 (18); 9 (24); 12 (41); 13 (41, 40) | 1 (5); 12 (41) | | 2 (28) | | 1/5 (18 Ind.) | Ind.; 1/5; 1/6 |
| E.Yorkshire Regt. | 1 (6, 21); 1/4 (50, 39); 6 (P)(11); 7 (17); 8 (3); 10 (31); 11; 12; 13 | | 6 (P)(11) | 2 (28) | | | Ind.; 1 (G) Bermuda; 2/4 |
| Essex Regt. | 1 (29, 37); 2 (4, 36, 4); 9 (12); 10 (18); 11 (6); 13 (2); 15 (59) | | 1 (29); 1/4 (54); 1/5; 1/6; 1/7; 1 (G)(–) | | 1/4 (54); 1/5; 1/6; 1/7; 1 (G) (–) | | Ire; 1/8 Ind.; 2 (G) |
| Gloucestershire Regt. | 1 (1); 2 (27); 1/4 (48); 1/5 (48, 25); 2/4 (61); 2/5; 2/6; 8 (19); 9 (26, 66); 10 (1); 12 (5); 13 (P)(39, 66); 14 (35); 18 (16) | 1/4 (48); 1/5; 12 (5) | 7 (13) | 2 (27); 9 (26) | | 7 (13) | |
| Gordon Highlanders | 1 (3); 2 (7); 1/4 (3, 51); 1/5 (51, 61, 15); 1/6 (7, 51); 1/7 (51); 8 (15); 9 (P); 10 | 2 (7) | | | | | Ind.; 1 (G) |
| Grenadier Guards | 1 (7, Gds.); 2 (2, Gds.); 3 (Gds); 4 (Gds.) | | | | | | |
| Hampshire Regt. | 1 (4); 2 (29); 2/4 (62); 11 (16); 14 (39); 15 (41); 1 (G)(–) | 15 (41) | 2 (29); 1/8 (54); 10 (10) | 10 (27); 12 (26) | 1/8 (54); 2/4 (75); 2/5 | 1/4 (12 Ind. & 14 Ind.); 1/6 (17 Ind.); 2/7 (13) | Ind.; 1/5; 1/7; 1/9, 2/4; 2/5; 2/7 Ire; 3/4 Aden; 1/7 Russia; 1/9 |
| Herefordshire Regt. | 1/1 (34); | | 1/1 (53) | | 1/1 (53) | | |
| Hertfordshire Regt. | 1/1 (2, 39, 37) | | | | | | |
| Highland Light Infantry | 1 (3 Ind.); 2 (2); 1/5 (52); 1/6; 1/7; 1/9 (2, 33); 10 (9, 15, 40, 34, 14); 11 (15); 12 (15, 35); 14 (B)(40, 34, 39, 66); 15 (32); 16; 17; 18 (B)(35) | | 1/5 (52); 1/6; 1/7 | | 1/5 (52); 1/6; 1/7 | 1 (3 Ind. & 17 Ind.) | Ire; 2/5; 2/6; 2/7; 2/9 |

‡ The Crete Division was a Greek formation.

## Battalions that served in: (continued)

| REGIMENT | France & Belgium | Italy | Gallipoli | Macedonia | Egypt & Palestine | Mesopotamia | Ireland, India & other |
|---|---|---|---|---|---|---|---|
| **INFANTRY continued** | | | | | | | |
| Honourable Artillery Company | 1/1 (3, 63); 2/1 (7) | 2/1 (7) | | | | | |
| Inniskilling Fusiliers (Royal) | 1 (36); 2 (2, 5, 32, 36); 5 (66); 6 (14, 34, 50); 7 (16, 34, 30); 8; 9 (36); 10; 11; 13 (40) | | 1 (29); 5 (10); 6 | | 5 (10); 6 | 5 (10); 6 | Ire; 3; 4; 12 |
| Irish Guards | 1 (2, Gds.); 2 (7, Gds.) | | | | | | |
| King's Regt. (Liverpool Regt.) | 1 (2); 4 (3 Ind., 46, 19, 33); 1/5 (2, 55); 1/6 (5, 55); 1/7 (2, 7, 55); 1/8 (51, 55, 57); 1/9 (1, 55, 57); 1/10 (3, 55); 2/5 (57); 2/6; 2/7; 2/8; 2/9, 2/10, 11 (P)(14); 12 (20); 13 (3); 14 (66); 17 (30, 66); 18 (30, 66); 19; 20 (30); 25 (59) | | | 7 (28); 14 (22); 2 (G)(−) | 1 (G)(−) | | Ire; 3 Russia; 17 |
| King's Own (Royal Lancaster Regt.) | 1 (36, 4); 1/4 (51,55); 1/5 (28, 1, 55); 2/5 (57); 7 (19); 8 (25, 3); 11 (40) | | 6 (13) | 2 (28); 9 (22) | | 6 (13) | Ire; 2/4 |
| King's Own Scottish Borderers | 1 (29); 2 (5); 1/4 (52); 1/5 (52, 34); 6 (9); 7 (15); 8; 10 (40) | 2 (5) | 1 (29); 1/4 (52); 1/5 | | 1/4 (52); 1/5 | | |
| King's Own Yorkshire Light Infantry | 1 (28, 50); 2 (32); 1/4 (49); 2/4 (62); 2/5; 6 (14); 7 (20); 8 (23, 8, 23); 9 (21); 10; 12 (P)(31); 15 (40); 2 (G)(−) | 8 (23) | | 1 (28) | | | Ire; 1 (G) |
| King's Royal Rifle Corps | 1 (2); 2 (1); 3 (27); 4 (27, 50); 7 (14); 8 (14, 34, 39); 9, 10 (20); 11; 12; 13 (37); 16 (33); 17 (39, 66); 18 (41); 20 (P)(3); 21 (41); 25 (P)(59) | 18 (41); 21 | | 3 (27); 4 | | | |
| Lancashire Fusiliers | 1 (29); 2 (4, 36, 4); 1/5 (42); 1/6 (42, 66); 1/7 (42); 1/8; 2/5 (51, 55); 2/6 (66); 2/7; 2/8; 3/5; 9 (11); 10 (17); 11 (25); 12 (66); 15 (32); 16; 17 (B)(35); 18 (B); 19 (P)(32, 49); 20 (35); 23 (59, 40) | | 1 (29); 1/5 (42); 1/6; 1/7; 1/8; 9 (11) | 12 (22) | 1/5 (42); 1/6; 1/7; 1/8 | | |
| Leicestershire Regt. | 1 (6); 1/4 (46); 1/5; 2/4 (59); 2/5; 6 (37, 21); 7; 8; 9; 11 (P)(6); 13 (L)(−); 14 (16) | | | | 2 (7 Ind.) | 2 (7 Ind.) | Ire; 2/4 (59); 2/5 |
| Leinster Regt. (Prince of Wales's [Royal Canadians]) | 1 (27, 10); 2 (24, 16, 29); 6 (66); 7 (16) | | 6 (Anzac) | 1 (27); 6 (10) | 1 (27); 6 (10) | | Ire; 4; 5 |
| Lincolnshire Regt. | 1 (3, 21); 2 (8, 21); 1/4 (46, 59, 39); 1/5 (46, 59, 46); 2/4 (59); 2/5 (59, 21, 30, 66); 6 (11); 7 (17); 8 (21, 37); 10 (34, 39, 66); 12 (L)(−) | | 6 (11) | | | | Ire; 2/4 (59); 2/5; 3 Ind.; 1 (G) |
| London Regt. | 1/1 (8, 56); 1/2 (6, 24, 56); 1/3 (7 ind., 47, 56, 58); 1/4 (3 Ind., 47, 56); 1/5 (4, 56); 1/6 (47, 58); 1/7; 1/8; 1/9 (5, 56, 58); 1/10 (54); 1/11; 1/12 (28. 56, 58); 1/13 (8, 56); 1/14 (1, 56); 1/15 (47); 1/16 (6, 56); 1/17 (47); 1/18; 1/19; 1/20; 1/21; 1/22; 1/23; 1/24; 1/28 (63); 2/1 (53); 2/2, 3/3; 2/4; 2/5 (58); 2/6; 2/7; 2/8; 2/9, 2/10, 2/11; 2/12, 2/13 (60); 2/14 (60, 30); 2/15; 2/16; 2/17; 2/18 (60); 2/19 (60); 2/20 (60, 66, 62); 2/21 (60); 2/22; 2/23 (60, 30); 2/24 (60, 66, 58); 3/1 (58); 3/2; 3/3; 3/4; 33 (14); 34 (16) | | 1/10 (54); 1/11; 2/1 (29); 2/2 (RN); 2/3 (29); 2/4 (RN) | 2/13 (60); 2/14; 2/15; 2/16; 2/17; 2/18; 2/19; 2/21; 2/22; 2/23; 2/24 | 1/10 (54); 1/11; 2/13 (60); 2/18; 2/19, 2/21; 2/22, 2/23; 2/24 | | Ire; 2/13 (60); 2/14; 2/15; 2/16 Ind.; 1/25 Malta; 1/1; 1/2; 1/3; 1/4; 2/2; 2/3; 2/4 |
| Loyal North Lancashire Regt. | 1 (1); 2 (31, 34); 1/4 (54, 55); 1/5 (46, 50, 9, 55, 57); 2/4 (57); 2/5; 4/5; 7 (19); 8 (25); 9 (25); 10 (37); 1/12 (P)(32, 74); 15 (P)(14) | | 6 (13) | | 2 (75); 1/12 (P)(60) | 6 (13); 1/12 (P)(60) | Ire; 3/4; 3/5 E.Africa; 2 |

## Battalions that served in: (continued)

| REGIMENT | France & Belgium | Italy | Gallipoli | Macedonia | Egypt & Palestine | Mesopotamia | Ireland, India & other |
|---|---|---|---|---|---|---|---|
| **INFANTRY continued** | | | | | | | |
| Manchester Regt. | 1 (3 Ind.); 2 (5, 32); 1/5 (42); 1/6; 1/7; 1/8; 1/9 (42, 66); 1/10 (42); 2/5 (66); 2/6; 2/7; 2/8; 2/9; 2/10, 11 (11); 12 (17); 13 (22, 66); 16 (30, 14); 17 (30, 66); 18 (30); 19 (30); 20 (30, 7, 25); 21; 22 (30, 7); 23 (35); 24 (30, 7) | 20 (7); 21; 22, 24 | 1/5 (42); 1/6; 1/7; 1/8; 1/9, 1/10, 11 (11) | 13 (22) | 1 (3 Ind.); 1/5 (42); 1/6; 1/7; 1/8; 1/9, 1/10; 11 (11) | 1 (3 Ind.) | Ind.; 1 (G) |
| Middlesex Regt. (Duke of Cambridge's Own) | 1 (6, 27, 2, 33); 2 (8); 3 (28); 4 (21, 37); 1/7 (8, 56); 1/8; 3/10 (9, 4); 11 (12); 12 (18); 13 (24); 16 (33, 29); 17 (33, 2); 18 (P)(33); 19 (P)(41); 20 (40, 16, 14); 21 (40, 39, 25); 23 (41) | 19 (P)(41); 23 | 2/10 (53) | 3 (28); 26 (P)(27) | 2/7 (WFF); 2/8; 2/10 (53) | 1/9 (18 Ind.) | Ind.; 1/9, 1/10 Gib.; 1/7; 1/8; 2/7; 3/7 Hong Kong; 25 Russia; 25 |
| Monmouthshire Regt. | 1/1 (28, 46); 1/2 (4, 28, 4, 29); 1/3 (28) | | | | | | |
| Munster Fusilier (Royal) | 1 (16, 57); 2 (1, 31, 50); 6 (39); 7, 8 (16); 9 | 1 (G)(–) | 1 (29); 6 (10); 7 | 6 (10); 7 | 6 (10); 7 | | Ire; 3; 4; 5 |
| Norfolk Regt. | 1 (5); 7 (12); 8 (18); 9 (24, 6); 12 (31) | 1 (5) | 1/4 (54); 1/5 | | 1/4 (54); 1/5; see also Norfolk Yeo. | 2 (6 Ind., 14 Ind.) | Ire; 1/6 Ind.; 1 (G) |
| North Staffordshire Regt. (Prince of Wales's) | 1 (6, 24); 4 (56, 35); 1/5 (46, 59, 16, 39); 1/6 (46); 2/5 (59); 2/6; 8 (19); 9 (P)(37); 12 (40); 1 (G)(–) | | 7 (13) | | 7 (13) | | Ire; 2/5; 2/6 Ind.; 2 |
| Northamptonshire Regt. | 1 (1); 2 (8, 23, 8); 5 (P)(12); 6 (18); 7 (24, 18) | | 1/4 (54) | | 1/4 (54); 1 (G)(–) | | |
| Northumberland Fusiliers | 1 (3); 2 (28, 50); 1/4 (50, 39); 1/5; 1/6; 1/7 (50, 42); 8 (11); 9 (17, 34, 61); 10 (23); 11; 12 (21); 13; 14 (P)(21); 16 (32); 17 (P)(32, 52); 18 (P)(34, 39, 66); 19 (P)(35); 20 (34); 21; 22 (34, 16); 23 (34, 39, 66); 24 (34); 25; 26; 27; 36 (59) | 10 (23); 11 | 8 (11) | | 2/7 (G)(–) | 2 (28) | Ire; 3 (G) Ind.; 2 (G) Malta; 1 (G) |
| Oxfordshire and Buckinghamshire Light Infantry | 2 (2); 1/4 (48); 1/1; 2/4 (61); 2/1; 5 (14); 6 (20); 2 (G)(–) | 1/4 (48); 1/1 | | 7 (26); 8 (P)(26) | | 1 (6 Ind., 7 Ind., 15 Ind.) | Ind.; 1 (G) |
| Rifle Brigade (Prince Consort's Own) | 1 (4); 2 (8); 3 (24); 4 (27); 7 (14); 8 (14, 34); 9 (14, 39); 10 (20); 11; 12; 13 (37); 16 (39, 66) | | | 4 (27); 22 (G) | 19 (G); 20 (G); 21 (G) | | Ind.; 18 (G); 23 (G); 24 (G) |
| Royal Fusiliers (City of London Regt.) | 1 (6, 24); 2 (29); 3 (50); 4 (3); 7 (63); 8 (12); 9, 10 (18, 37); 11 (18); 12 (24); 13 (37); 17 (2); 18 (33); 19, 20, 21; 22 (33, 2); 23 (33); 24 (2); 26 (41); 32 (41); 33 (L)(–); 34 (L); 35 (L); 36 (L); 37 (L); 43 (G)(–); 44 (G) | 26 (41); 32 | 2 (29) | 3 (28, Anzac Mtd.) | 38 (10); 39 (Anzac Mtd.); 40 (–) | | E.Africa; 25 |
| Royal Guernsey Light Infantry | 1 [Service] (29, GHQ) | | | | | | |
| Royal Irish Fusiliers (Princess Victoria's) | 1 (36); 2 (27); 5 (66, 16); 6; 7 (16); 8; 9 (36); 11 (16) | | 5 (10); 6 | 2 (27); 2 (G)(28) | 6 (10) | | Ire; 3; 4; 10; 3 (G) Ind.; 1 (G) |
| Royal Irish Regt. | 1 (27); 2 (3, 4, 7, 16, 63); 5 (P)(52, 50); 6 (16); see S.Irish Horse; 8 (59, 40); 2 (G)(59) | | 5 (P)(10); 1 (G) | 1 (27); 5 (P)(10) | 1 (10); 1 (G) | | Ire; 3; 4; 2 (G) |
| Royal Irish Rifles | 1 (8, 36); 2 (25, 36); 7 (16, 36); 8 (36, 4, 36); 9, 10, 11 (36); 12; 13; 14; 15 (36, 4, 36); 16 (P)(36) | | 6 (10) | 6 (10) | 6 (10) | | Ire; 3; 4; 5; 17; 18; 19, 20 Ind.; 1 (G) |
| Royal Scots (Lothian Regt.) | 1 (27); 2 (3); 1/4 (52); 1/5 (32); 1/7 (52); 1/8 (7, 51[as P]); 1/9 (27, 5, 51, 61, 15); 11 (9); 12; 13 (15); 15 (34, 39); 16; 17 (B)(35); 19 (L)(–) | | 1/4 (52); 1/5 (29); 1/7 (52) | 1 (27) | 1/4 (52); 1/6 (WFF); 1/7 (52); 1 (G) | | Ire; 3; 1/10, 2/4; 2/7; 2/8 (65); 2/9 (65); 2/10 Russia; 2/10 |
| Royal Scots Fusiliers | 1 (3); 2 (7, 30, 40, 9); 1/4 (52); 1/5; 6 (9, 15); 7 (15); 11 (59); 12 (31) | | 1/4 (52); 1/5 | 8 (26) | 1/4 (52); 1/5: see Ayr & Lanark Yeo. | | Ire; 2/4 (65); Ind.; 1 (G) |

## Battalions that served in: (continued)

| REGIMENT | France & Belgium | Italy | Gallipoli | Macedonia | Egypt & Palestine | Mesopotamia | Ireland, India & other |
|---|---|---|---|---|---|---|---|
| **INFANTRY continued** | | | | | | | |
| Royal Welsh Fusiliers | 1 (7); 2 (6, 2, 33, 38); 1/4 (P)(1, 47); 9 (19); 10 (25, 3); 13 (38); 14; 15; 16; 17 (43); 19 (B)(40); 24 (31); 25 (74); 26 (59) | 1 (7) | 1/5 (53); 1/6; 1/7; 8 (13) | | 1/5 (53); 1/6; 1/7; see Denbigh Yeo.; see Mont. & Welsh Yeo. | 8 (13); 11 (22) | Ire; 3 |
| Scots Guards | 1 (1, Gds.); 2 (Gds.) | | | | | | |
| Seaforth Highlanders (The Duke of Albany's Ross-shire Buffs) | 1 (7 Ind.); 2 (4); 1/4 (7 Ind., 46, 15, 51); 1/5 (51); 1/6; 7 (9); 8 (15); 9 (P)(9) | | | 1 (G)(28, Crete) | 1 (7 Ind.) | 1 (7 Ind.) | |
| Sherwood Foresters (Nottinghamshire and Derbyshire Regt.) | 1 (8, 23, 8); 2 (6); 1/5 (46); 1/6; 1/7 (46, 30, 66, 39); 1/8 (46); 2/5 (59, 39); 2/6 (59); 2/7; 2/8; 9 (11); 10 (17); 11 (23, 8, 23, 25); 12 (P)(24); 15 (35); 16 (39, 66); 17 (39); 20 (L)(–) | 11 (23) | 9 (11) | | 9 (11); 1 (G) | | Ire; 2/5 (59); 2/6; 2/7; 2/8 |
| Shropshire Light Infantry (The King's) | 1 (6); 2 (27); 1/4 (63, 19); 5 (14); 6 (20); 7 (25, 3); 10 (17) | | | 2 (27); 8 (22) | see Shropshire and Cheshire Yeo. | | Ire; 3 Singapore; 1/4 Hong Kong; 1/4 (part) |
| Somerset Light Infantry (Prince Albert's) | 1 (4); 2/4 (P)(34); 6 (14, 16); 7 (20); 8 (21, 37); 11 (59); 12 (74) | | | | 1/5 (75); 2/4 (75); see W.Somerset Yeo. | 1/4 (3 Ind., 14 Ind.) | Ire.; 3 Ind.; 2, 1/4; 1/5; 2/4; 2/5; 1 (G) Andaman Is.; 2/4 |
| South Lancashire Regt. (The Prince of Wales's Volunteers) | 2 (3, 25, 30); 1/4 (P)(3, 55); 1/5 (4, 36, 55); 2/4 (57); 2/5; 7 (19); 8 (25); 11 (P)(30, 25) | | 6 (13) | 9 (22) | | 6 (13) | Ind.; 1 |
| South Staffordshire Regt. | 1 (7); 2 (2); 4 (25, 50, 39); 1/5 (46); 1/6; 2/5 (59); 2/6 (59, 66); 7 (11); 8 (17); 9 (P)(23); 12 (L)(–) | 1 (7); 9 (P)(23) | 7 (11) | | 7 (11) | | Ire; 2/5 (59); 2/6 Ind.; 1 (G) |
| South Wales Borderers | 1 (1); 2 (29); 5 (P)(19); 6 (P)(25, 30); 10 (38); 11; 12 (40) | | 2 (29); 4 (13) | 7 (22); 8 | | 4 (13) | Ire; 1/1 Aden; 1/1 Tsingtao; 2 |
| Suffolk Regt. | 1 (28); 2 (5, 3); 1/4 (3 Ind., 15, 33, 58 [as P]); 7 (12, 66); 8 (18); 9 (24, 6); 11 (34, 61); 12 (40, 14); 15 (74) | | 1/5 (54) | 1 (28) | 1/5 (54); see Suffolk Yeo. | | |
| Sussex Regt. | 2 (1); 1/4 (34); 1/5 (1, 48 [as P]); 7 (12); 8 (P)(18); 9 (24); 11 (39); 12, 13; 16 (74); 17 (59) | 1/5 (P)(48) | 1/4 (53) | | 1/4 (53); see Sussex Yeo. | | Ire; 1/6 Ind.; 1 Russia; 11 |
| Warwickshire Regt. (Royal) | 1 (4); 2 (7); 1/5 (48); 1/6; 1/7; 1/8 (48, 25); 2/5 (61); 2/6; 2/7; 2/8; 10 (19); 11 (37); 14 (32, 5); 15; 16 | 2 (7); 1/5 (48); 1/6; 1/7; 1/8, 14 (5); 15; 16 | 9 (13) | | 1 (G) | 9 (13) | |
| Welsh Guards | 1 (Gds.) | | | | | | |
| Welsh Regt. | 2 (1); 1/6 (28, 1); 9 (19); 10 (38); 13; 14; 15; 16; 17 (B)(40); 18 (B)(40, 16); 19 (P)(38); 24 (74) | | 1/4 (53); 1/5; 8 (P)(13) | 1 (28); 11 (22); 23 (69, 28 [as P]) | 1/4 (53); 1/5; see Pembroke & Glamorgan Yeo. | 8 (P)(13) | |
| West Kent Regt. (The Queen's Own Royal) | 1 (5); 3/4 (9, 17); 6 (12); 7 (18); 8 (24); 10 (41); 11 | 1 (5); 10 (41); 11 | 2/4 (53) | | 2/4 (53) | 2 (6 Ind., 15 Ind., 17 Ind.); 1/5 (18 Ind.) | Ind.; 1/4; 1/5 |
| West Riding Regt. (Duke of Wellington's) | 2 (5, 4); 1/4 (49); 1/5 (49, 62); 1/6 (49); 1/7; 2/4 (62); 2/5; 2/6; 2/7; 8 (11); 9 (17); 10 (23); 12 (L)(–); 13 (59) | 10 (23) | 8 (11) | | 8 (11) | | Ind.; 1 |
| West Surrey Regt. (The Queen's Royal) | 1 (1, 2, 33); 2 (7); 2/4 (34); 3/4 (21); 6 (12); 7 (18); 8 (24); 10 (41); 11; 13 (L)(–); 14 (L); 15 (L) | 2 (7); 10 (41); 11 | 2/4 (53) | | 2/4 (53) | 1/5 (12 Ind., 15 Ind.) | Ind.; 1/4; 1/5 |
| West Yorkshire Regt. (The Prince of Wales's Own) | 1 (6); 2 (8); 1/5 (49); 1/6; 1/7; 1/8 (49, 62); 2/6; 2/7; 2/8; 9 (11); 10 (17); 11 (23); 12 (21); 15 (31); 16; 17 (35); 18 (31); 21 (P)(4); 22 (L)(–) | 11 (23) | 9 (11) | | 9 (11); 15 (31); 16; 18 | | Ire; 3/7; 3/8 Malta; 1 (G) |
| Wiltshire Regt. (The Duke of Edinburgh's) | 1 (3, 25, 21); 2 (7, 30, 19); 6 (19, 14); 7 (50) | | 5 (13) | 7 (26) | 1/4 (75) | 5 (13) | Ire; 3/4 Ind.; 1/4; 2/4 |

## Battalions that served in: (continued)

| REGIMENT | France & Belgium | Italy | Gallipoli | Macedonia | Egypt & Palestine | Mesopotamia | Ireland, India & other |
|---|---|---|---|---|---|---|---|
| **INFANTRY continued** | | | | | | | |
| Worcestershire Regt. | 1 (8, 23, 8); 2 (2, 33); 3 (3, 25, 19); 4 (29); 1/7 (48); 1/8 (48, 25); 2/7 (61); 2/8; 10 (19, 40); 14 (P)(63); 17 (P)(40) | 1/7 (48); 1/8 | 4 (29); 9 (13) | 11 (26) | | 9 (13) | Ire; 1 (G) |
| Yorkshire Regt. (Princess of Wales's Own) | 2 (30, 11); 1/4 (50, 39); 1/5; 6 (11); 7 (17); 8 (23); 9 (23, 25); 10 (21); 12 (P)(40); 13 (B)(40); 16 (L)(–) | 8 (23); 9 | 6 (11) | | 6 (11) | | Ind.; 1; 1 (G) Russia; 6 |
| York and Lancaster Regt. | 1 (28); 2 (16); 1/4 (49); 1/5; 2/4 (62); 2/5; 6 (11); 7 (P)(17); 8 (23, 8, 23); 9, 10 (21, 37); 12 (31); 13; 14; 17 (L)(–); 18 (14) | 8 (23); 9 | 6 (11) | 1 (28) | 6 (11); 12 (31); 13; 14 | | |
| **CAVALRY** | | | | | | | |
| Ayrshire Yeo. | 1/1 (as 12 Royal Scots Fus. [74, 31]) | | 1/1* (52) | | 1/1 (became 12 Royal Scots Fus. [74]) | | Ire; 2/1† |
| Bedfordshire Yeo. | 1/1 (1 Cav.) | | | | | | |
| Berkshire Yeo. | 1/1 (as 101 MGC) | | 1/1 (2 Mtd.) | | 1/1 (Imp. Mtd., Yeo. Mtd.) then to MGC | | Ire; 2/1 |
| Buckinghamshire Yeo. | 1/1 (as 101 MGC) | | 1/1 (2 Mtd.) | | 1/1 (as 1/1 Berks.) | | |
| Cheshire Yeo. | 1/1 (as 10 Shropshire Light Inf. [74, 17]) | | | | 1/1 (became 10 Shropshire L. I. [74]) | | Ire; 2/1 |
| City of London Yeo. | 1/1 (as 103 MGC) | | 1/1 (2 Mtd.) | 1/1 | 1/1 (Yeo. Mtd.) later became E Bn. MGC | | |
| County of London Yeo. | 1/2 (as 104 MGC); 1/3 (as 103 MGC) | | 1/1; 1/2; 1/3; (all 2 Mtd.) | 1/1; 1/3 | 1/1; 1/2; 1/3 | | Ire; 2/1; 2/2; 2/3 |
| 1 (King's) Dragoon Guards | (1 Ind. Cav., 4 Cav.) | | | | | | Ind.; yes |
| 2 (Queen's Bays) Dragoon Guards | (Cav., 1 Cav.) | | | | | | |
| 3 (Prince of Wales's) Dragoon Guards | (3 Cav.) | | | | | | |
| 4 (Royal Irish) Dragoon Guards | (Cav., 1 Cav.) | | | | | | |
| 5 (Princess Charlotte's) Dragoon Guards | (Cav., 1 Cav.) | | | | | | |
| 6 (Carabiniers) Dragoon Guards | (Cav., 1 Cav., 2 Cav.) | | | | | | |
| 7 (Princess Royal's) Dragoon Guards | (2 Ind. Cav., 5 Cav., 3 Cav.) | | | | | | |
| 1 (Royal) Dragoons | (3 Cav.) | | | | | | |
| 2 (Royal Scots Greys) Dragoons | (2 Cav.) | | | | | | |
| 6 (Inniskilling) Dragoons | (2 Ind. Cav., 1 Ind. Cav., 4 Cav., 3 Cav.) | | | | | | |
| Denbighshire Yeo. | 1/1 (as 24 Royal Welsh Fusiliers [74, 31]) | | | | 1/1 (became 24 Royal Welsh Fusiliers [74]) | | |
| Derbyshire Yeo. | | | 1/1 (2 Mtd.) | 1/1 | 1/1 | | |
| 1 Devon Yeo. (Royal) | 1/1 (as 16 Devons [74]) | | 1/1 | | 1/1 (became 16 Devonshire Regt. [74]) | | Ire; 2/1 |
| Dorset Yeo. | | | 1/1 (2 Mtd.) | 1/1 | 1/1 (2 Mtd., Imp. Mtd., Yeo. Mtd., 4 Cav.) | | Ire; 2/1 |

\* Cavalry regiments at Gallipoli all arrived dismounted and remained thus, despite mostly belonging to 2 Mtd. Div.

† Most Yeomanry regiments went to Ireland as cyclist battalions.

## Battalions that served in: (continued)

* Roman numerals in brackets indicate that the regiment became Corps Cavalry Regt. for that particular Corps.

† The Household Battalion was formed in 1916 from Household Cavalry reserve regiments.

| REGIMENT | France & Belgium | Italy | Gallipoli | Macedonia | Egypt & Palestine | Mesopotamia | Ireland, India & other |
|---|---|---|---|---|---|---|---|
| **CAVALRY continued** | | | | | | | |
| Duke of Lancaster's Own Yeo. | 1/1 (III*) later became 12 Manchester Regt. (17) | | | | | | Ire; 2/1 |
| E.Kent Yeo. (Royal) | 1/1 (as 10 Buffs [74]) | | 1/1 (42) | | 1/1 (became 10 Buffs [74]) | | Ire; 2/1 |
| E.Riding of Yorkshire Yeo. | 1/1 (as 102 MGC) | | | | 1/1 (Anzac Mtd., Yeo. Mtd.) Later became 'D' Bn. MGC. | | Ire; 2/1 |
| Essex Yeo. | 1/1 (3 Cav., 1 Cav.) | | | | | | Ire; 2/1 |
| Fife and Forfar Yeo. | 1/1 (as 14 Black Watch [74]) | | 1/1 | | 1/1 (became 14 Black Watch [74]) | | Ire; 2/1 |
| Glamorgan Yeo. | 1/1 (as 24 Welsh Regt. [74]) | | | | 1/1 (became 24 Welsh Regt. [74]) | | |
| Glasgow Yeo. (Queen's Own Royal) | 1/1 (V) Later as part 18 Highland L.I. (35) | | 1/1 (part)(52) | | 1/1 (part)(52) | | Ire; 2/1 (65) |
| Gloucestershire Yeo. | | | 1/1 (2 Mtd.) | | 1/1 | | Ire; 2/1 |
| Hampshire Yeo. | 1/1 (later as 15 Hampshire Regt. [41]) | 1/1 (as 15 Hants.) | | | | | Ire; 2/1 |
| Hertfordshire Yeo. | 1/1 (part) (VI) | | 1/1 (2 Mtd.) | | 1/1 (part) (XXI) | 1/1 (part) | |
| Horse Guards (Royal) | (3 Cav.) Later as 3 Gds. MG Bn. | | | | | | |
| Household Cavalry (see also Life Guards and Royal Horse Guards) | H.C.Comp. Regt.(Cav. Div., 1 Cav.) H/hold Batt. (4)† | | | | | | |
| 3 (King's Own) Hussars | (Cav. Div., 1 Cav., 2 Cav.) | | | | | | |
| 4 (Queen's Own) Hussars | (Cav., 2 Cav.) | | | | | | |
| 7 (Queen's Own) Hussars | | | | | | (Ind. Cav.) | Ind; yes |
| 8 (King's Royal Irish) Hussars | (1 Ind. Cav., 2 Ind. Cav., 5 Cav.) | | | | | | |
| 10 (Prince of Wales's Own) Hussars | (3 Cav.) | | | | | | |
| 11 (Prince Albert's) Hussars | (Cav., 1 Cav.) | | | | | | |
| 13 Hussars | (2 Ind. Cav.) | | | | | (Ind. Cav.) | Ind; yes |
| 14 (King's) Hussars | | | | | | (Ind. Cav.) | |
| 15 (King's) Hussars | (1 Cav.) | | | | | | |
| 18 (Queen Mary's Own) Hussars | (Cav., 1 Cav.) | | | | | | |
| 19 (Queen Alexandra's Own Royal) Hussars | (1 Cav.) | | | | | | |
| 20 Hussars | (2 Cav.) | | | | | | |
| King Edward's Horse | (IV, XVIII, XI) | (XI) | | | | | |
| Lanarkshire Yeo. | 1/1 (as 12 Royal Scots Fusiliers [74, 31]) | | 1/1 (52) | | 1/1 (became 12 Royal Scots Fusiliers [74]) | | Ire; 2/1 |
| Lancashire Hussars Yeo. | 1/1 (VIII) later became 18 King's Regt. (30, 66) | | | | | | Ire; 2/1 |
| 5 (Royal Irish) Lancers | (Cav., 2 Cav.) | | | | | | |
| 9 (Queen's Royal) Lancers | (Cav., 1 Cav.) | | | | | | |
| 12 (Prince of Wales's Royal) Lancers | (2 Cav.) | | | | | | |

## Battalions that served in: (continued)

| REGIMENT | France & Belgium | Italy | Gallipoli | Macedonia | Egypt & Palestine | Mesopotamia | Ireland, India & other |
|---|---|---|---|---|---|---|---|
| **CAVALRY continued** | | | | | | | |
| 16 (Queen's) Lancers | (Cav., 2 Cav.) | | | | | | |
| 17 (Duke of Cambridge's Own) Lancers | (1 Ind. Cav., 4 Cav., 3 Cav.) | | | | | | |
| 21 (Empress of India's) Lancers | | | | | | | India; *yes* |
| Leicestershire Yeo. | *1/1* (3 Cav.) | | | | | | |
| 1 Life Guards | (3 Cav.) Later as 1 Gds. MG Bn. | | | | | | |
| 2 Life Guards | (3 Cav.) Later as 2 Gds. MG Bn. | | | | | | |
| Lincolnshire Yeo. | *1/1* (as *102* MGC) | | | | *1/1* (Anzac Mtd., Yeo. Mtd.) later became 'D' Bn. MGC | | |
| Lothians and Border Horse Yeo. | *1/1* (split as divisional cavalry) | | | *1/1* (XII) | | | Ire; *2/1* |
| 1 Lovat's Scouts Yeo. } 2 Lovat's Scouts Yeo. } | *1/1* (as *10* Cameron High. [–]) | | *1/1* | *1/1* (as *10* Cameron High. [27]) | *1/1* | | |
| Montgomeryshire Yeo. | *1/1* (as *25* Royal Welsh Fusiliers [74]) | | | *1/1* (became *25* Royal Welsh Fusiliers [74]) | | | |
| Norfolk Yeo. | *1/1* (as *12* Norfolk Regt. [74, 31]) | | *1/1* (54) | *1/1* (became *12* Norfolk Regt. [74]) | | | Ire; *2/1* |
| Northamptonshire Yeo. | *1/1* (VI, XV, (?) | *1/1* (XIV) | | | | | |
| North Devon Yeo. | *1/1* (as *16* Devon Regt. [74]) | | *1/1* | *1/1* (became *16* Devon Regt. [74]) | | | Ire; *2/1* |
| North Irish Horse | 1st (VII, XIX, V) 2nd (X) | | | | | | |
| N. Somerset Yeo. | *1/1* (3 Cav.) | | | | | | Ire; *2/1* |
| Northumberland Yeo. | *1/1* (7, XIII, VIII, III, XII); *2/1* (XIX) Later as *9* Northumberland Fus. [34, 61]) | | | | | | |
| Nottinghamshire Yeo. (Sherwood Rangers) | . | | *1/1* (2 Mtd.) | *1/1* | *1/1* (2 Mtd.) | | |
| Nottinghamshire Yeo. (S. Notts. Hussars) | *1/1* (as *100* MGC) | | *1/1* (2 Mtd.) | *1/1* | *1/1* (Became 'B' Bn. MGC) | | |
| Oxfordshire Yeo. | *1/1* (1 Cav., 2 Cav.) | | | | | | Ire; *2/1* |
| Pembroke Yeo. | *1/1* (as *24* Welsh Regt. [74]) | | | | *1/1* (Became *24* Welsh Regt. [74]) | | |
| Scottish Horse | *1/1* (as *13* Black Watch [50]); *1/2* | | *1/1*; *1/2* (2 Mtd.) | *1/1* (as *13* Black Watch [27]); *1/2* | *1/1*; *1/2*; *1/3* (as *26* MGC) | | Ire; *2/1*; *2/2*; *2/3* |
| Shropshire Yeo | *1/1* (as *10* K.S.L.I. [74]) | | | | *1/1* (became *10* K.S.L.I. [74]) | | Ire; *2/1* |
| Staffordshire Yeo | | | | | *1/1* (Anzac Mtd,. Yeo. Mtd., 1 Mtd., 4 Cav.) | | |
| South Irish Horse | 1st (I)* 2nd (IX, XVIII)* | | | | | | |
| Suffolk Yeo | *1/1* (as *15* Suffolk Regt. [74]) | | *1/1* (54) | | *1/1* (became *15* Suffolk Regt. [74]) | | Ire; *2/1* |
| Surrey Yeo | *1/1* (part) Became *10* W.Surrey Regt. [74] | | | *1/1* (part)(XVI) | *1/1* (part) | | Ire; *2/1* |
| Sussex Yeo | *1/1* (as *16* Sussex Regt. [74]) | | *1/1* (42) | | *1/1* (became *16* Sussex Regt. [74]) | | Ire; *2/1* |
| Warwickshire Yeo | *1/1* (as *100* MGC) | | *1/1* (2 Mtd.) | | *1/1* (2 Mtd., Imp. Mtd., Australian Mtd.) Later became 'B' Bn. MGC | | |

\* !917 both regiments amalgamated as 7 Royal Irish.

## Battalions that served in: (continued)

| REGIMENT | France & Belgium | Italy | Gallipoli | Macedonia | Egypt & Palestine | Mesopotamia | Ireland, India & other |
|---|---|---|---|---|---|---|---|
| **CAVALRY continued** Welsh Horse Yeo. | 1/1 (as 25 Welsh Fus. [74]) | | 1/1 (54) | | 1/1 (became 25 Welsh Fusiliers [74]) | | |
| West Kent Yeo. | 1/1 (as 10 Buffs [74]) | | 1/1 (42) | | 1/1 (became 10 Buffs [74]) | | Ire; 2/1 |
| West Somerset Yeo. | 1/1 (as 12 S.L.I. [74]) | | 1/1 (11, 2 Mtd., 53) | | 1/1 (WFF); became 12 S.L.I. (74) | | Ire; 2/1 |
| Westmoreland and Cumberland Yeo. | 1/1 (XI) later as 7 Border Regt. (17) | | | | | | Ire; 2/1 |
| Wiltshire Yeo. (Royal) | 1/1 (XV) later as 6 Wiltshire Regt. (19, 14) | | | | | | Ire; 2/1 |
| Worcestershire Yeo. | | | 1/1 (2 Mtd.) | | 1/1 (2 Mtd., Imp. Mtd., Australian Mtd., XX) | | Ire; 2/1 |
| Yorkshire Dragoons | 1/1 (II, Cav. Corps, 4 Cav., II) | | | | | | Ire; 2/1 |
| Yorkshire Hussars Yeo. | 1/1 (XVII) Later as 9 W.Yorkshire Regt. (11) | | | | | | Ire; 2/1 |
| **MACHINE GUN CORPS*** | 1, 2, 3 [x 2], 4, 5, 6, 7 [x 3], 8, 9, 11, 12, 14 thru' 21, 23 [x 2], 24, 25, 29 thru' 42, 46, 47, 48 [x 2], 49 thru' 52, 55 thru' 58, 61, 62, 63, 74, 100 thru' 104, 200 | 7, 23, 48 | | | 3, 7, 10, 53, 54, 75 | | |
| **TANK CORPS†** | 'A' thru' 'M' Bns. in France were numbered 1 thru' 13 Bns. Jan 1918. Subsequently 14 thru' 18 Bns. also arrived in France. (19 thru' 26 Bns. in England never went overseas). | | | | 'E' Coy. Machine Gun Corps (Heavy Branch)† arrived in Egypt 1/17. It never became a battalion and was disbanded in early 1918 | | |

* Organised into battalions 6/18.

† Originally Machine Gun Corps (Heavy Section) f. 4/16. From 11/16 was M.G.C. (Heavy Branch) when tank companies 'A' throug 'D' were expanded into battalions. In 7/17 became the Tank Corps.

# Supplement: (c) Summary of Corps-Level Headquarters

Frequent references to the Corps level of Command will be found in the following Order of Battle section. The constrictions of space mean these cannot be fully listed in the same way as Armies and Divisions.

Therefore a brief listing is given here of all numbered Corps headquarters, by country.

A number of 'named' Corps will be found in the Orders of Battle. Named after their Commanders they were usually of a temporary and provisional nature. Some were later formally constituted as numbered Corps in the regular numerical sequence. Their temporary Staffs have not been listed individually.

| SUMMARY OF CORPS | |
|---|---|
| **AUSTRIA-HUNGARY** On Mobilisation | I-XVII |
| Raised post-Mobilisation | XVIII-XXVI |
| Named Corps level Commands | 23 of which 4 were Cavalry commands. 8 were later formally numbered in the sequence above. |
| **BELGIUM** | None as such, but the 6 Belgium 'Army Divisions' in existence up to 1.1918 were, in effect, small corps rather than divisions. |
| **BULGARIA** | None. |
| **FRANCE** On Mobilisation | I-XVIII, XX, XXI, I Colonial (XIX was the permanent garrison of North Africa) |
| Raised post-Mobilisation | XXX-XL, II Colonial, I-III Cavalry |
| Named Corps level Commands | 4 Cavalry commands |
| **GERMANY** On Mobilisation | Guard, I-XXI, I-III Bavarian Guard Reserve, I, III-X, XII, XIV, XVIII Reserve I Bavarian Reserve, Landwehr |
| Post-Mobilisation | XV, XVII, XXII-XXVII, XXXVIII-XLI Reserve II Bavarian Reserve, Marine I-VI Higher Cavalry Commands (H.K.K.) General Commands 51-68 |

**NB1** The General Commands (Gen.Kommando z.b.v.) were designated by Arabic numbers to indicate that they were not formally established as Corps Staffs, but were more provisional in status.
**NB2** The German Alpenkorps was a division not a corps. See German Divisional lists.

| | |
|---|---|
| **GREECE** | I-V, National Defence |
| **ITALY** On Mobilisation | I-XIII |
| Formed post-Mobilisation | XIV, XVI, XVIII, XX, XXII-XXX, Special Assault, Czech, Cavalry |
| **PORTUGAL** | A Corps H.Q. was formed to control the two Portuguese divisions on the Western Front |
| **RUMANIA** Peacetime | I-V |
| War formed | VI-VII |
| **RUSSIA** On Mobilisation | Guard (later I Guard), Grenadier, I-XXV, I-III Caucasus, I-V Siberian, I-II Turkestan |
| Formed post-Mobilisation | II Guard, XXVI-L, IV-VI Caucasus, VI-VII Siberian, Serbian, Guard Cavalry, I-VII Cavalry, I-II Caucasus Cavalry |
| **SERBIA** | None |

| SUMMARY OF CORPS continued | |
|---|---|
| **TURKEY** On Mobilisation | I-XIII |
| Formed post-Mobilisation | XIV-XVI, XVIII, XX, XXII XVII, XIX, XXI – It is not certain as to whether or not these Corps were formed. |
| **UNITED KINGDOM (including British Empire)** On Mobilisation | I-III |
| Formed post-Mobilisation | IV-XXIV (XXIII Home service only), Cavalry, Desert Mounted, I-II Anzac, Canadian, I-III Indian, Indian Cavalry |
| **UNITED STATES** | I-IX |

# PART II CAMPAIGNS

## Introduction

In this section we have made a conscious decision to try and give a broad overview of each front rather than give Orders of Battle for specific actions/ campaigns. We have tried to provide Orders of Battle at least once a year for the whole length of the front. We believe that anyone seeking,say, an Order of Battle for the Somme or Third Ypres will find them covered in specialised works and the official histories.

An exception to this is the Eastern Front where we found no detailed Russian Orders of Battle for the northern part of the front (the Russian Northern and Western Fronts/Army Groups) after the early part of 1915. We have therefore given fullest possible details of the Russian South Western Front/ Army Group in 1916/17 during the Brusilov and Kerensky offensives.

Constrictions of space have caused us to delete much of the information we had available. In order to concentrate on the main European fronts we had to drastically cut back on peripheral campaigns (e.g. Gallipoli, Palestine, Mesopotamia, Armenia-Kurdistan). Most regrettably space has led us to omit entirely the minor campaigns in Africa and the Far East. We had assembled details down to battalion and even company level in these minor theatres. We hope that the Supplement on Imperial/Colonial Forces in PART I – DIVISIONS will go some way to compensate for this.

## General Note

We have usually taken the Orders of Battle down to individual divisions but have mentioned brigades/regiments in summary rather than detail. Where the expression 'minor units' is used it means battalion size units or less. The arrangement of the Campaign Section is as follows:–

1. Survey of Military Resources of the European States as at August 1914
2. Western Front
3. Eastern Front
4. Balkan Front
5. Italian Front
6. Gallipoli
7. Egypt/Palestine
8. Mesopotamia
9. Armenia-Kurdistan (the Caucasus Front) – we have used the term Armenia-Kurdistan as being more geographically correct

## Abbreviations and Conventions used

**1** Nationality Indicators

**A**  Used at all times

| | | |
|---|---|---|
| Aust. | – | Australian |
| Bav. | – | Bavarian |
| Bulg. | – | Bulgarian |
| Cdn. | – | Canadian |
| Cau. | – | Caucasus/Caucasian (Russian Army only) |
| Finn. | – | Finnish (Russian Army only) |
| Ind. | – | Indian |
| N.Z. | – | New Zealand |
| Pol. | – | Polish |
| Port. | – | Portuguese |
| Rum. | – | Rumanian |
| Sib. | – | Siberian (Russian Army only) |
| S.A. | – | South African |
| T-A. | – | Trans-Amur (Russian Army only) |
| T-B. | – | Trans-Biakal (Russian Army only) |
| T-C. | – | Trans-Caspian (Russian Army only) |
| Turk. | – | Turkestan (Russian Army only) |

**B** Used to indicate nationality where divisions/corps etc. were serving under another national command. Usually shown in brackets.

| | | |
|---|---|---|
| (A-H) | – | Austro-Hungarian |
| (Br.) | – | British |
| (Fr.) | – | French |
| (G.) | – | German |
| (It.) | – | Italian |
| (Russ.) | – | Russian |
| (T.) | – | Turkish |
| (U.S.) | – | United States |

**2** Formations/Units

| | | |
|---|---|---|
| Abt. | – | Abteilung (Detachment) |
| Bde. | – | Brigade |
| Bn. | – | Battalion |
| Bty. | – | Battery |
| Coy. | – | Company |
| Div. | – | Division |
| Rgt. | – | Regiment |
| Sqn. | – | Squadron (*Sotnia* is Cossack equivalent of a squadron) |

3 Division/Briagde Types

| | | |
|---|---|---|
| Cav. Div.<br>CD | } – | Cavalry Division |
| Cav. à P. | – | *Cavalerie à Pied* (Dismounted Cavalry) (French only) |
| Col. ID | – | Colonial Infantry Division (French only), see also DIC. |
| Comb. | – | Combined. A composite formation drawn from different divisions. |
| Coss. | – | Cossack<br>Usually used in conjunction with the various Cossack hosts e.g. Don, Kuban, Orenburg, Terek, Ural, Ussuri etc. |
| Div. | – | Division: in British and American armies infantry divisions were simply designated as . . . Division |
| Div. de M. | – | *Division de Marche* (French only). A temporary formation, usually had only brief existence |
| DI | – | *Division d'Infanterie* (French only) |
| DIC | – | *Division d'Infanterie Colonial* (French only), see also Col. ID |
| DIT | – | *Division d'Infanterie Territoriale* (French only) Territorial Infantry Division. Some were upgraded to line Inf. Divs. during the war, most were of short duration |
| Dismtd. CD | – | Dismounted Cavalry Division |
| Ers. | – | *Ersatz* (German Army only) |
| Ftr. Gd. | – | Frontier Guard, as in Trans-Amur Frontier Guard divisions (Russian Army only) |
| GDR | – | *Groupe de Divisions de Réserve* |
| Gren. | – | Grenadier |
| Gd. | – | Guard |
| HCD | – | *Honved* Cavalry Division } Hungarian equivalent of |
| HID | – | *Honved* Infantry Division   *Landwehr* type divisions |
| ID | – | Infantry Division |
| Indep. | – | Independent. Usually used in conjunction with Brigades/Divisions outside normal Divisional/Corps organisations |
| Kav. Sch. Div. | | |
| | – | *Kavallerie Schützen Division* (literally Cavalry Rifle division) Austrian and German designation for dismounted cavalry formations |

Lst.(Div/Bde) – *Landsturm* (Central Powers only)
LW(Div/Bde) – *Landwehr* (Central Powers only)
Mtn. – Mountain (German *Gebirgs*)
Plastun – (Given in full) Cossack infantry units, usually brigade strength. *Druzhina* is battalion size Cossack infantry unit
Prov. – Provisional/*Provisoire* (French). A temporary formation usually of short duration.
Res. (Div.) – Reserve (Division)
1) Sch. Div. – *Schützen* Division. Austrian *Landwehr* division

2) Sch.Bde/Div – *Schützen* Brigade/Division. Russian Army where European rifle units were eventually raised to division status

Many of these symbols will be found in combination e.g.

Gd. Res. ID – Guard Reserve Infantry Division
Bav. Ers. Div. – Bavarian *Ersatz* Division
Kuban Coss. Div. – Kuban Cossack Division
Sib. Sch. Div. – Siberian *Schützen* (Rifle) Division

# European Armies at the outbreak of war 1914

## *Table 3.1* British Army Organisation 8.1914

**DISTRIBUTION OF UNITS**

| | CAVALRY RGTS | ARTILLERY BTYS/COYS HORSE | FIELD | GARRISON | INFANTRY BNs | COLONIAL & INDIAN INFANTRY BNs* |
|---|---|---|---|---|---|---|
| **HOME** | 19 | 13 | 87+ 12 Depot Bdes | 43 | 83 | |
| **SOUTH AFRICA** | 2 | | 3 | 2 | 4 | |
| **MAURITIUS** | | | | 1 | 1 | |
| **WEST AFRICA** | | | | 1 | | 2* |
| **EAST AFRICA** | | | | | | 3* |
| **BERMUDA** | | | | 2 | 1 | |
| **JAMAICA** | | | | 1 | | 1* |
| **CEYLON** | | | | 1 | | 1 |
| **STRAITS SETTLEMENTS** | | | | 2 | 1 | 1 |
| **HONG KONG** | | | | 3 | 1 | 5 |
| **NORTH CHINA** | | | | | 2 | 1 |
| **GIBRALTAR** | | | | 7 | 2 | |
| **MALTA** | | | | 8 | 5 | |
| **CYPRUS** | | | | | 1 Coy. | |
| **EGYPT (inc. SUDAN)** | 1 | 1 | | 1 (Mountain) | 5 (-1 Coy. Cyprus) | |
| **INDIA British Troops** | 9 | 11 | 45 | 35 (inc 8 Mtn.) | 52 inc 3 in Burma & 1 in Aden | |
| **INDIA Indian Troops** | 39 + 4 Escort Sqns. | | | 12 Mountain 1 Fortress | 136† inc 20 Gurkhas | |
| **TOTAL BRITISH** | **31** | **25** | **147** | **107** | **157** | |
| **INDIAN** | **39 + 4 Sqns.** | **–** | **–** | **13** | **136** | |
| **NATIVE COLONIAL** | | | | | **6** | |

\* Asterisk denotes colonial battalions.

† 8 serving in Colonial Garrisons 6 in Burma 1 in Aden 1 in Muscat (Gulf)

‡ 2 W.Indian 1 W.African 3 E.African

**REGULARS**

| COMMAND | DIVISION | INF. BRIGADES | CAVALRY BDE. | ADDITIONAL REGULAR UNITS CAVALRY RGTS | INF. BNS. |
|---|---|---|---|---|---|
| **ALDERSHOT** | 1 | 1, 2, 3 | 1 | 1 | |
| | 2 | 5, 6 | | | |
| **EASTERN** | 4 | 10, 11, 12 | 4 (part) | 1 | 2 |
| | | | 5 (part) | | |

**REGULARS continued**

| COMMAND | DIVISION | INF. BRIGADES | CAVALRY BDE. | ADDITIONAL REGULAR UNITS CAVALRY RGTS | INF. BNS. |
|---|---|---|---|---|---|
| **IRELAND** | 5 | 13, 14, 15 | 3 | | |
| | 6 | 16, 17 | | | |
| **LONDON DISTRICT** | 2 (part) | 4 | 4 (part) | 3 | 2 |
| **NORTHERN** | 6 (part) | 18 | 5 (part) | | |
| **SCOTTISH** | | | | | 3 |
| **SOUTHERN** | 3 | 7, 8, 9 | 2 | | 1 |
| **WESTERN** | | | | | 1 |
| **CHANNEL ISLANDS** | | | | | 2 |

**OVERSEAS COMMANDS**

* Includes 3 in Burma 1 in Aden.

† Includes 1 in Sudan & 1 Coy. in Cyprus.

| COMMAND | CAVALRY RGTS | INF. BNS. | NATIVE INF. BNS. |
|---|---|---|---|
| **INDIA** | 9 | 52* | (See Note on Indian Army) |
| **STRAITS SETTLEMENTS** | | 1 | 1 (Indian) |
| **NORTH CHINA** | | 2 | 1 (Indian) |
| **HONG KONG** | | 1 | 5 (Indian) |
| **CEYLON** | | | 1 (Indian) |
| **EGYPT** | 1 | 5† | |
| **GIBRALTAR** | | 2 | |
| **MALTA** | | 5 | |
| **SOUTH AFRICA** | 2 | 4 | |
| **MAURITIUS** | | 1 | |
| **WEST AFRICA** | | | 2 (1 W.African, 1 W.Indian) |
| **WEST INDIES** | | 1 | 1 (W.Indian) |

On mobilisation the B.E.F. absorbed most of the regular units in the United Kingdom.

**B.E.F.**

| | | | |
|---|---|---|---|
| I Corps | 1 Inf. Div. | 1 (Gd.), 2, 3, Inf. Bdes. | 12 Bns. each |
| | 2 Inf. Div. | 4 (Gd.), 5, 6 Inf. Bdes. | |
| II Corps | 3 Inf. Div. | 7, 8, 9 Inf. Bdes. | |
| | 5 Inf. Div. | 13, 14, 15 Inf. Bdes. | |
| III Corps | 4 Inf. Div. | 10, 11, 12 Inf. Bdes. | |
| | 6 Inf. Div. | 16, 17, 18 Inf. Bdes | |
| | 1 Cav. Div. | 1, 2, 3, 4 Cav. Bdes. | 3 Regts. each |
| Independent | 5 Cav. Bde. | | 3 Regts. |
| | 19 Inf. Bde.(formed from LofC units) | | 4 Inf. Bns. |

**Summary B.E.F.**

| | BNs. | CAV REGTs. | NOTES |
|---|---|---|---|
| INF. DIVs. | 72 | | |
| CAV. DIV. | | 12 | (including 1 Composite Rgt. drawn from Household Cavalry) |
| L of C/19 INF. BDE. | 5 | | (4 went to form 19 INF. BDE.) |
| 5 CAV. BDE. | | 3 | |
| ARMY TROOPS | 1 | | |
| DIVISIONAL CAVALRY | | 2 | |
| **TOTALS** | **78** | **16** | **+ 1 Composite Unit** |
| Remaining in U.K. & Channel Islands | 5 | 3 | |
| Of these To 7 DIV. by 10.14 | 4* | | * Including 1 in Channel Islands |
| In U.K. until 7.15 | 1† | | † Then to Guards Division |
| To 3 CAV. DIV. by 9.14 | | 3 | |
| Regular Units in U.K 1914 | 83 | 19 | All but 1 Inf. Bn. in France by Oct. 1914 |

## DISPOSAL OF OVERSEAS GARRISONS IN 1914/15

### Infantry

| ALLOCATED TO NEW REGULAR DIVISIONS | U.K. | INDIA | GIBRALTAR | MALTA | EGYPT | S.AFRICA | MAURITIUS | CHINA | STRAITS SETT. | W.INDIES |
|---|---|---|---|---|---|---|---|---|---|---|
| 7 Div. | 4 | | 2 | 2 | 1 | 3 | | | | |
| 8 Div. | | 3+1 Aden | | 3 | 3 | 1 | | | | 1 |
| 27 Div. | | 10 | | | | | | 2 | | |
| 28 Div. | | 10 | | | 1 | | | | 1 | |
| 29 Div. | 1* | 6+3 Burma | | | | | 1 | 1 | | |
| Indian Corps to France | | 6 | | | | | | | | |
| Indian Corps to E.Africa | | 1 | | | | | | | | |
| Ind. Cps. to Mesopotamia | | 4 | | | | | | | | |
| Remained India throughout the war | | 8 | | | | | | | | |
| **TOTALS** | 4 | 52 | 2 | 5 | 5 | 4 | 1 | 3 | 1 | 1 |

\* A Territorial Force Bn.

### Cavalry

| | INDIA | EGYPT | S.AFRICA |
|---|---|---|---|
| 3 Cav. Division† | | 1 | 2 |
| 1 & 2 Indian Cav. Divs. | 6 | | |
| To Mesopotamia | 2 (1 in 1917) | | |
| Remained in India | 1 | | |
| **TOTALS** | 9 | 1 | 2 |

† Completed with 3 Household Cavalry and 3 Yeomanry Regts. in U.K.

### Reserve Forces (Territorial Force‡)

| COMMAND | MOUNTED BDEs. (14) | DIVISIONS (14) (of 3 Bdes. each) | NON-DIVISIONAL INF. BDEs. (3) |
|---|---|---|---|
| **ALDERSHOT** | Nil | Nil | |
| **EASTERN** | Eastern, South Eastern | East Anglian, Home Counties | |
| **LONDON DISTRICT** | London | 1st London, 2nd London | |
| **NORTHERN** | Yorkshire, North Midland, Notts. & Derby | Northumbrian, West Riding, N. Midland | |
| **SCOTTISH** | Highland, Lowland | Highland, Lowland | Black Watch, Lothian (Scottish Coast Defences) |
| **SOUTHERN** | 1st South Midland | South Midland | |
| | 2nd South Midland | Wessex | |
| | 1st South Western | | |
| | 2nd South Western | | |
| **WESTERN** | Welsh Border | Welsh | South Wales (Attached to Welsh Div.) |
| | South Wales | West Lancashire | |
| | | East Lancashire | |

‡ Territorial Force divisions were not allocated numbers until they began to go overseas.

---

### *Table 3.2* Indian Army Organisation 8.1914

| SUMMARY | CAV. RGTs. | INF. BNs. | ARTILLERY BTYs./COYs. | | | GARRISON/ FORTRESS |
|---|---|---|---|---|---|---|
| | | | HORSE | FIELD | MOUNTAIN | |
| BRITISH TROOPS | 9 | 52 | 11 | 45 | 8 | 27 |
| INDIAN TROOPS | 39 + 4 Sqns. | 136 | | | 12 | 1 |

These units were organised as follows in 10 Divisions and 4 Brigades.

**NORTHERN ARMY**
1 (Peshawar) Div.
2 (Rawalpindi) Div.
3 (Lahore) Div.
7 (Meerut) Div.
8 (Lucknow) Div.
Kohat Bde.
Bannu Bde.
Derajat Div.

**SOUTHERN ARMY**
4 (Quetta) Div.
5 (Mhow) Div.
6 (Poona) Div.
9 (Secunderabad) Div.
Burma Div.
Aden Bde.

* The 3 missing battalions must have been amongst the 9 serving in Colonial Garrisons and the Gulf in 8.1914. The other 6 must be "double counted" in the Northern and Southern Army totals.

As Indian forces were sent abroad they were organised into 7 lettered Expeditionary Forces. These varied in size from full Corps to a few battalions. They may be briefly summarised as below:

**Indian Expeditionary Force**

**A** Troops forming Corps sent to France 3 (Lahore), 7 (Meerut), 1st and 2nd Indian Cavalry Divisions.

**B** 27 (Bangalore) and Imperial Service Brigades sent to East Africa.

**C** 5 Battalions to defend East Africa – Zanzibar and Uganda.

**D** 6 (Poona) Div. sent to Mesopotamia and subsequent forces sent there (6 Div, was originally mobilised for I.E.F. 'A').

**E** 22 (Lucknow) Bde. sent to Egypt. Designation retained for subsequent Indian forces sent there.

**F** 28,29 and 30 Indian Bdes. and other troops sent to Egypt.

**G** 29 Indian Bde. sent from Egypt to Gallipoli.

Units were assigned as follows:

| | NORTHERN ARMY | SOUTHERN ARMY | TOTAL |
|---|---|---|---|
| BRITISH CAV. REGTs. | 6 | 3 | 9 |
| INDIAN CAV. REGTs. | 22 | 17 | 39 |
| BRITISH INF. BNs. | 28 | 24 | 52 |
| INDIAN INF. BNs. | 73 | 60 | 133* |
| Artillery BRITISH HORSE ARTY. BTYs. | 7 | 4 | 11 |
| BRITISH FIELD ARTY. BTYs. | 22 | 23 | 45 |
| BRITISH MOUNTAIN BTYs. | 5 | 3 | 8 |
| BRITISH GARRISON COYs. | 14 | 13 | 27 |
| INDIAN MOUNTAIN BTYs. | 10 | 2 | 12 |
| INDIAN FORTRESS COY. | 1 | – | 1 |

**Other Indian Forces**
Indian States Forces
These forces of the princely states provided a number of units for Imperial Service. A number of them served in overseas theatres.
Cavalry Rgts.  6½ of which 4 served overseas.
Infantry Bns.  13 of which 12 served overseas.
Camel Corps  2 of which 1 served overseas.
Sapper Coys.  4 of which 4 served overseas.

Total strength was about 22,500 of which 18,000 saw overseas service.

**European Volunteers**
10  Lt. Horse or Mtd. Rifle Corps.
45  Infantry type units (varying size from Coy. to Rgt.)
Mainly used to provide officer reinforcements as the Indian Army expanded in W.W.I.

---

**Table 3.3 French Army Organisation 1.8.1914**

**Metropolitan France and North Africa only.**

Cavalry Regiments  4 Sqns. each except *Spahis*  Total 365 Sqns
12 *Cuirassier*
32 Dragoons
21 *Chasseur a Chéval*
14 Hussars
6 *Chasseurs d'Afrique*
4 *Spahis* 5, 6 and 9 Sqns. (25 Sqns.)
(5th *Spahis* created on 1.8.14 by dedoubling 2nd *Spahis*.

Infantry Regiments  (No. of Bns.)
173  Line Regts. (164 of 3 Bns., 9 of 4 Bns.)  (528)
31  *Bataillons de Chasseur à Pied* + 10 groups of cyclists (Attached to 10 Cav. Divs.)  (31)
4  *Régts. de Zouaves* of 6 Bns. (A 7th Bn. was forming for 4th *Zouaves*)  (29)
9  *Régts. de Tirailleurs Algériens* of 2 to 6 Bns. (40 Bns in total)  (40)
2  *Régts. de Étrangers* (Foreign Legion) of 6 Bns.†  (12)
5  *Bataillons d'Infanterie Légère d'Afrique*  (5)
12  *Régiments d'Infanterie Coloniale* of 3 Bns.  (36)
7  *Bataillons de Marche Coloniaux‡*  (7)
5  *Bataillons de Troupes Auxiliares Marocaines*  (5)

*Zouaves*, Rgts. of Colonial Infantry and *Chasseurs d'Afrique* were European recruited. *Spahis* and *Tirailleurs* were native units.

† 3 Foreign Legion battalions were serving in Tonkin.

‡ 6 of these battalions were formed into 6 *Régiments de Marche Coloniaux du Maroc* by adding 2 battalions of *Tirailleurs Sénégalais* to each of the six.

Artillery
62  Regts. of Field Artillery
42 Divisional Regiments of 9 batteries each
20 Corps Artillery Regts. of 12 batteries each
10  Groups Horse Artillery of 3 batteries each
2  Regts. of Mountain Artillery
11  Regts. of Foot Artillery
5  Regts. of Heavy Field Artillery
10  Groups of *Artillerie d'Afrique* (of which 2 were Foot Artillery)
3  Regts. of *Artillerie Coloniale*

**Artillery Batteries by Type**

| | Btys. Montée 75mm. | Horse Btys. | Mountain Btys. | Foot Btys. | Heavy Btys. |
|---|---|---|---|---|---|
| Rgts. Field Artillery | 618 | 30 | | | |
| Rgts. Mountain Artillery | | | 14 | | |
| Rgts. Foot Artillery | | | | 68 | |
| Rgts. Heavy Artillery | | | | | 55 |
| *Groupes d'Afrique* | 17 | | 4 | 7 | |
| Rgts. Artillery Colonial | 24 | | 4 | 14 | |
| **TOTALS** | **659** | **30** | **22** | **89** | **55** |

## DISTRIBUTION Cavalry

| | Sqns. Metropolitan France | Sqns. North Africa | |
| --- | --- | --- | --- |
| | | Morocco | Algeria-Tunisia |
| *Cuirassiers* | 48 | | |
| *Dragoons* | 128 | | |
| *Chasseur à Cheval* | 84 | | |
| Hussars | 56 | | |
| *Chasseurs d'Afrique* | | 9 | 15 |
| *Spahis* | | 13 | 12 |
| **TOTALS** | **316** | **22** | **27** |
| **GENERAL TOTAL** | **365 Sqns.** | | |

## DISTRIBUTION Artillery

| | Btys. Metropolitan France | Btys. North Africa | |
| --- | --- | --- | --- |
| | | Morocco | Algeria-Tunisia |
| **Field & Horse Btys.** | 648 (75mm.) | | |
| **Colonial Artillery** | 21 (75mm.) | 3 (75mm.) | |
| **Mountain Btys.** | 10 | 4 | |
| **Foot Btys.** (Met. & Col.) | 82 | | |
| **Heavy Batteries** | 55 | | |
| **African Artillery** (75mm.) | | 8 | 9 |
| **African Artillery** (Mountain) | | 3 | 1 |
| **African Artillery** (Foot) | | | 7 |
| **Colonial Artillery** (Mountain) | | 4 | |
| **TOTALS** | **816** | **22** | **17** |
| **GENERAL TOTAL** | **855 Btys.** | | |

## DISTRIBUTION Infantry

| | Bns. Metropolitan France | Bns. North Africa | |
| --- | --- | --- | --- |
| | | Morocco | Algeria-Tunisia |
| Line | 528 | | |
| *Chasseur a Pied* | 30 | | |
| *Zouaves* | 4 | | |
| **Colonial Infantry** | 36 | | |
| *Chasseurs Alpins* | | 1 | |
| *Zouaves* | | 9 | 12 |
| *Tirailleur Algériens* | | 19 | 21 |
| **Foreign Legion** | | 5 | 4 |
| *Bns. d'Afrique* | | 3 | 2 |
| *Bns. de Marche Coloniaux* | | 7 | |
| *Bns. de Troupes Auxiliaires Marocaines* | | 5 | |
| **TOTALS** | **598** | **49** | **39** |
| **GENERAL TOTAL** | **686 Bns.** | | |
| *Bns. Sénégalais* | | 12 | 2 |
| *Goumiers* (1 Coy & 14 Goums Mikte) (Para Military Gendarmerie) | Equal to | 4 | |

## COLONIAL ARMY *(TROUPES COLONIALES)*

The Colonial Army had two main elements:–

**1** *La Coloniale Blanche* – French European recruited units *Régiments d'Infanterie Coloniale* (R.I.C.) and *Régiments d'Artillerie Coloniale* (R.A.C.).

**2** Non-European units – mainly *Tiralleurs Sénégalais* (T.S.).

Distribution of *Troupes Coloniales*

**France**

1 Army Corps, 3 Divisions, 12 Rgts. (CAC, 1e-3e DIC, 1-8, 21-24 RIC)*

**Morocco**

6 *Rgts. de Marche d'Inf. Coloniale*† (1e-6e RMx IC Maroc), 1 Sqn. *Spahis Sénégalais*, 2 mixed groups *Artillerie Coloniale*

**Algeria**

1e and 2e *BTS. d'Algérie*

* These units are also included under Metropolitan France.

† Each comprise one battalion of IC (Europeans) and two battalions TS (Africans).

## Overseas Colonies

| | REGIMENTS (BATTALIONS) | SQNs. | ARTILLERY(BTYs.) |
|---|---|---|---|
| **WEST AFRICA** | 1er-4e RTS (11) 1er-3e BTS (3) | 1 Sqn. *Spahis Sénégalais* | 6e RAC (6) |
| **EQUATORIAL AFRICA** | RTS d'Tchad, RTS Gabon (5) | | |
| | BTS 2 du Moyen Congo (1) | | |
| | BTS 3 de l'Oubangui-Chari (1) | 1 Sqn. *Spahis Sénégalais* | (1) |
| **MADAGASCAR** | 1er-3e RTMal* (10) | | 7e RAC (6) |
| | BIC Diego Suarez, BIC Tananarive (2) | | |
| | BTS de Madagascar (1) | | |
| **DJIBOUTI** | 1 Coy – *Cie de Garde Somalis* | | |
| **INDOCHINA** | 3 Bns. Foreign Legion† | | |
| | 3 Colonial Rgts. 9e-10e-11e RIC (10 Bns.) | | |
| | 4 Tonkinese Tir. Rgts. 1er-4e RTTon (12 Bns.) | | |
| | 1 Annamite Tir. Rgt. 1er RTAn (4 Bns.) | | |
| | 2 Colonial Artillery Rgts. | | 4e, 5e RAC (19) |
| **CHINA** | 1 Colonial Rgts. 16e RIC (2 Bns.) | | (1) |
| **NEW CALEDONIA** | 1 Colonial Inf. Btn. of 2 Coys | | |
| **WEST INDIES** | 2 Colonial Inf. Coys | | (1) |

*\* Régiments Tirailleurs de Malgache.*

*† IV/1er RE, VI/2e RE plus 1 For. Legion in I/China.*

## SUMMARY *Troupes Coloniales* ‡

*‡ Regiments d'Infanterie Coloniale (R.I.C.) Missing regiments in numerical sequence were disbanded in the 1900's viz 12, 14, 15 (1903), 13, 17 (1908), 18 (1902).*

| COLONIES | Bns. | Coys. | Sqns. | Btys. |
|---|---|---|---|---|
| WEST AFRICA | 14 | | 1 | 6 |
| EQUATORIAL AFRICA | 7 | | 1 | 1 |
| MADAGASCAR | 13 | | | 6 |
| DJIBOUTI | | 1 | | |
| INDOCHINA | 29 | | | 19 |
| CHINA | 2 | | | 1 |
| NEW CALEDONIA | 1 | | | |
| WEST INDIES | | 2 | | 1 |
| **TOTAL** | **66** | **3** | **2** | **34** |
| To which should be added | | | | |
| In Metropolitan France | 36 | | | 33 |
| In North Africa | 20 | | 1 | 14 |

## Strength after Mobilisation of Reserves

| UNITS | Bns. | Sqns. | Btys. |
|---|---|---|---|
| 21 Corps (inc. Colonial Corps.) (42 Inf. Divs.) | 612 | 128 | 642 |
| 3 Ind. Divs. (2 Algeria-Tunisia, 1 S.E.France) | 45 | 12 | 30 |
| 25 Reserve Divisions | 314 | 50 | 222 |
| 8 Territorial Divisions (Field) | 96 | 16 | 48 |
| 4 Territ. Divs. + 1 Bde. Inf. (Fort, Camp of Paris) | 54 | 8 | 12 |
| 10 Divisions of Cavalry | 10 | 232 | 30 |
| Miscellaneous units, army level | 53 | 50 | 67 |
| Garrisons of Fortresses | 341 | 49 | 417 |
| **TOTALS** | **1,525** | **545** | **1,468** |

## Numbering of Formations

| 21 Army Corps | 1-18, 20, 21, Colonial (19 was in (Algeria-Tunisia) |
|---|---|
| 3 Independent Divisions | 37-38 (Algeria-Tunisia) 44 (S.E.France) |
| 25 Reserve Divisions | 51-75 |
| 12 Territorial Divisions | 81-92 |
| 1 Territorial Inf. Bde. | 185 |
| 10 Cavalry Divisions | 1-10 |

## Final Summary (after Mobilisation of Reserves in North Africa and Transfer of Reserve units from France)

| | Bns. | Sqns. | Btys. |
|---|---|---|---|
| METROPOLITAN FRANCE | 1,525 | 549 | 1,468 |
| ALGERIA-TUNISA | 47 | 31 | 37 |
| MOROCCO | 64 | 24 | 22 |
| **TOTAL** | **1,636** | **600** | **1,527** |
| Of these Peacetime Army | 686 | 365 | 855 |
| Created by Mobilisation | 950 | 235 | 672 |

## French O.O.B. 5.8.1914

| ARMY | CORPS | DIVISIONS |
|---|---|---|
| 1st ARMY | VII | 14 ID 41 ID |
| | VIII | 15 ID 16 ID |
| | XIII | 25 ID 26 ID |
| | XIV | 27 ID 28 ID |
| | XXI | 13 ID 43 ID |
| | | 6 CD 8 CD |
| 2nd ARMY | IX | 17 ID 18 ID |
| | XV | 29 ID 30 ID |
| | XVI | 31 ID 32 ID |
| | XVIII | 35 ID 36 ID |
| | XX | 11 ID 39 ID |
| | 2 GDR | 59 ID 68 ID 70 ID |
| | | 2 CD 10 CD |
| 3rd ARMY | IV | 7 ID 8 ID |
| | V | 9 ID 10 ID |
| | VI | 12 ID 40 ID 42 ID |
| | 3 GDR | 54 ID 55 ID 56 ID |
| | | 7 CD |
| 4th ARMY | XII | 23 ID 24 ID |
| | XVII | 33 ID 34 ID |
| | CAC | 2 DIC 3 DIC |
| | | 9 CD |
| 5th ARMY | I | 1 ID 2 ID |
| | II | 3 ID 4 ID |
| | III | 5 ID 6 ID |
| | X | 19 ID 20 ID |
| | XI | 21 ID 22 ID |
| | | 52 ID 60 ID |
| | | 4 CD |
| 1st CAVALRY CORPS | | 1 CD 3 CD 5 CD |
| Disposal Ministry of War | | 61 ID 62 ID 67 ID |
| Disposal C-in-C | | 37 ID 38 ID |
| Unattached | | 44 ID |
| 1 GDR | | 58 ID 63 ID 66 ID |
| 4 GDR | | 51 ID 53 ID 69 ID |
| Défence Mobile du Nord Est | | 57 ID 71 ID 72 ID 73 ID |
| Reserve of 14th and 15th Regions | | 64 ID 65 ID 74 ID 75 ID |
| En route from N.Africa | | Div. de Marche du Maroc |

### *Table 3.4* Russian Army Organisation 28.6.1914

Peacetime Army was established in 1910 as follows:

| | | |
|---|---|---|
| Corps H.Q. | 37 | Guards, Grenadier, I-XXV, I-III Caucasus, I-V Siberian, I-II Turkestan |
| Infantry Divisions | 70 | 1-3 Guards, 1-3 and Caucusus Grenadier, 1-52 Infantry, I-II Siberian Rifle |
| Rifle Brigades (*Schutzen* Brigades) | 18 | Guard, 1-5 (Line), 1-4 Finnish, 1-2 Caucasus, 1-6 Turkestan |
| Other Inf. Bdes. | 4 | 1-3 Transamur Border (or Frontier Guard), 1 *Plastun* (Cossack Infantry) |
| Cavalry Divisions | 24 | 1-2 Guards, 1-15, Caucasus, 1 Don Cossack, 2 Composite Cossack, 1-3 Caucasus Cossack, Turkestan Cossack |

Independent Cavalry Brigades
(4 Guard/Line, 4 Cossack)

| | | |
|---|---|---|
| | 8 | Guards, 1-3, Ussuri, Siberian, Trans-Baikal, Transcaspian Cossack |
| Artillery | 70 | Brigades (1 per Inf. Div) |
| | 18 | Battalions (1 per Rifle Bde.) |
| | 17 | Horse Artillery Battalions |
| | 6 | Cossack Horse Artillery Battalions |
| | 37 | Mortar Battalions |
| | 8 | Heavy Artillery Battalions |

On mobilisation on 18 July 1914 following units were formed:

| | | |
|---|---|---|
| Higher Level H.Q. | 2 | North Western and South Western Fronts |
| | 7+1 | 1-7 Armies (+ 8th very shortly afterwards) |
| Corps H.Q. | 2 | VI Siberian, Cavalry |
| Infantry Divisions | 35 | 53-84, 12-14 Siberian Rifle |
| Artillery Brigades | 32 | 53-84 |
| Siberian Art. Bdes. | 3 | 12-14 |
| Transamur Art. Bdes. | 2 | 1-2 |
| Finnish Art. Btn. | 1 | Finnish |

### Russian O.O.B. 28.6.1914

| ARMY GROUP/ARMY | CORPS | DIVISIONS |
|---|---|---|
| GHQ RESERVE (Warsaw area) | Guards | 1 GD ID 2 GD ID GD Sch. Bde. |
| | I | 22 ID 24 ID |
| | XVIII | 23 ID 37 ID |
| | – | 1 Sch. Bde. Cau. Coss. D |
| 6 INDEPENDENT ARMY (Finland) | XXII | 50 ID 1, 2, 3, 4 Finnish Sch. Bdes. 55, 67, 68, 74 ID (Not yet in place) |
| NORTH WESTERN FRONT | | |
| 1 ARMY | XX | 28 ID 29 ID |
| | III | 25 ID 27 ID |
| | IV | 30 ID 40 ID 5 Sch. Bde. |
| | Army Cavalry | 1 GD ID, 2 GD ID 1, 2, 3 CD 1 Indep. Cav. Bde. |
| 2 ARMY | II | 26 ID 43 ID |
| | VI | 4 ID 16 ID |
| | XIII | 1 ID 36 ID |
| | XV | 6 ID 8 ID |
| | XXXIII | 3 GD ID 2 ID |
| | Army Cavalry | 4, 6, 15 CD |

**Russian O.O.B. 28.6.1914 continued**

| ARMY GROUP/ARMY | CORPS | DIVISIONS |
|---|---|---|
| **SOUTH WESTERN FRONT** | | |
| En route from Caucasus | III Cau. | 21 ID 52 ID |
| | | 8 CD |
| **4 ARMY** | XIV | 18 ID 2 Sch. Bde. |
| | XVI | 41 ID 45 ID 47 ID |
| | Grenad. | 1 Grenadier D 2 Grenadier D |
| | Army Cavalry | 5, 13, 14 CD Ural Coss. Bde. Indep. GD Cav. Bde. |
| **5 ARMY** | XXV | 3 Gren. D 46 ID 70 ID |
| | XIX | 17 ID 38 ID |
| | V | 7 ID 10 ID |
| | XVII | 3 ID 35 ID 61 ID |
| | Army Cavalry | 7 CD 1 Don Coss. D 2, 3 Indep. Cav. Bdes. (formed Composite Cav. Div.) 3, 4, 5 Don Coss. D |
| **3 ARMY** | XXI | 33 ID 44 ID 69 ID |
| | XI | 11 ID 32 ID 78 ID |
| | IX | 5 ID 42 ID 58 ID |
| | X | 9 ID 31 ID 60 ID |
| | Army Cavalry | 9, 10, 11 CD 3 Cau. Coss. D |
| **8 ARMY** | VII | 13 ID 34 ID |
| | XII | 12 ID 19 ID 65 ID 3 Sch. Bde. |
| | VIII | 14 ID 15 ID 4 Sch. Bde. |
| | XXIV | 48 ID 49 ID |
| | Army Cavalry | 12 CD 2 Comp. Coss. D (Later) 1 Kuban Coss. D, 2 Kuban Coss. CD, Terek Coss. D |
| **7 INDEPENDENT ARMY** | | 62, 63, 64, 71 ID (Not yet in place) |

| | | Inf. Divs. | Cav. Divs. |
|---|---|---|---|
| **TOTAL** | N.W.Front | 16$\frac{1}{2}$ | 8$\frac{1}{2}$ |
| | S.W.Front | 38$\frac{1}{2}$ | 20$\frac{1}{2}$ |
| | Reserve & Indep. Armies | 16 | 2 |

N.B. *Schutzen* (Rifle) Brigades counted as $\frac{1}{2}$ Div. They were later expanded into Divisions by adding necessary Artillery.

**CAUCASUS ARMY** (*circa* 10.1914)

| CORPS. | DIVISIONS |
|---|---|
| I Cau. | 20 ID 39 ID 66 ID |
| II Turk | 4, 5 Turk Sch. Bdes. |
| (in Persia) | 2 Cau. Sch. Bde. |
| Army Reserve | 3 CD 5 CD |

The following formations are not included in the Mobilisation O.O.B., *viz.*

| II Caucasus Corps | Cav. Gren. Div., 51 ID, 2 Cau. Coss. Div. 1 Cau. Sch. Bde. (presumably in the Caucasus region) |
|---|---|
| Reserve Inf. Divisions | 53, 54, 56, 57, 59, 65, 72, 73, 75, 76, 77, 79-84 still organising |
| Turkestan Rifle Divisions | 1, 2, 3, 6 ⎫ |
| Siberian Rifle Divisions | 1-11 ⎭ At home stations |

Most had joined the Field Armies by the battles of 9.1914. See Russian O.O.B. for 8/9.1914.

---

**Table 3.5** Belgian Army Organisation 1.8.1914

| ARMY DIVISION | MIXED BDE. | ACTIVE INF. REGT. | Add on Mobilisation RESERVE INF. REGT. | CAVALRY | ARTILLERY REGT. |
|---|---|---|---|---|---|
| **1** | 2 | 2 | 22 | | |
| | 3 | 3 | 23 | | |
| | 4 | 4 | 24 | | |
| | | | | 3 Lancers | 1 |
| **2** | 5 | 5 | 25 | | |
| | 6 | 6 | 26 | | |
| | 7 | 7 | 27 | | |
| | | | | 4 *Chasseur à Cheval* | 2 |
| **3** | 9 | 9 | 29 | | |
| | 11 | 11 | 31 | | |
| | 12 | 12 | 32 | | |
| | 14 | 14 | 34 | | |
| | | | | 2 Lancers | 3 |
| **4** | 8 | 8 | 28 | | |
| | 10 | 10 | 30 | | |

**Belgian O.O.B. 1.8.1914 continued**

| ARMY DIVISION | MIXED BDE. | ACTIVE INF. REGT. | Add on Mobilisation RESERVE INF. REGT. | CAVALRY | ARTILLERY REGT. |
|---|---|---|---|---|---|
| **4 continued** | 13 | 13 | 33 | | |
| | 15 | 1 *Chasseur à Pied* | 4 *Chasseur à Pied* | | |
| | | | | 1 Lancers | 4 |
| **5** | 1 | 1 | 21 | | |
| | 16 | 2 *Chasseur à Pied* | 5 *Chasseur à Pied* | | |
| | 17 | 3 *Chasseur à Pied* | 6 *Chasseur à Pied* | | |
| | | | | 2 *Chasseur à Cheval* | 5 |
| **6** | 18 | 1 Grenadiers | 2 Grenadiers | | |
| | 19 | 1 Carabiniers | 3 Carabiniers | | |
| | 20 | 2 Carabiniers | 4 Carabiniers | | |
| | | | | 1 *Chasseur à Cheval* | 6 |

| CAVALRY DIVISION | CAVALRY BDE. | | |
|---|---|---|---|
| | **1** | 1 Guides | |
| | | 2 Guides | |
| | **2** | 4 Lancers | |
| | | 5 Lancers | (New regiment) |
| Projected, not formed | **3** | 4 *Chasseur à Cheval* | (Actually with 2 Army Division |
| | | 5 *Chasseur à Cheval* | (Not raised) |

**NOTES**

1  When mobilised the 6 Army Divisions had 3 or 4 brigades of 2 regiments of 3 battalions. This gave a total of 18 battalions or 24 battalions (3 & 4 Divs,). In effect they were more akin to small army corps than divisions.

2  Each brigade's Reserve Infantry regiment was numbered by adding 20 to the regular regiment of that brigade except in the case of the Grenadier, Carabinier and *Chasseur à Pied* regiments where the number was doubled.

3  The projected 3rd Cav. Bde. seems not to have been formed.

4  Summary of Division Strengths

| DIVISIONS | BATTALIONS | SQUADRONS | GUNS |
|---|---|---|---|
| 1, 2, 5, 6 | 18 | 4 | 18 |
| 3, 4 | 24 | 4 | 21 |
| Cavalry | 1 Cyclist | 16 | 3 |
| | | (24 projected) | |

---

**Table 3.6 Serbian Army Organisation 1914**

| | | Peacetime Structure (I BAN) | Wartime, formed on Mobilisation (II BAN) |
|---|---|---|---|
| **DIVISION ARGAS** | | I BAN | II BAN |
| **Infantry** | **1 MORAVA** | I BAN | II BAN |
| | **2 DRINA** | I BAN | II BAN |
| | **3 DANUBE** | I BAN | II BAN |
| | **4 SHUMADIA** | I BAN | II BAN |
| | **5 TIMOK** | I BAN | II BAN |
| | *Forming in New Territories – Not completed before Mobilisation on outbreak of war* | | |
| | **6 IBAR** | I BAN | |
| | **7 KOSSOVO** | I BAN | |
| | **8 VARDAR** | I BAN | |
| | **9 BREGALNICA** | I BAN | |
| | **10 MONASTIR** | I BAN | |
| | *Formed on Mobilisation (from supernumerary regiments)* | | |
| | **COMPOSITE DIV.** | | |
| **Cavalry** | **CAVALRY DIV.** (4 Rgts. at 4 Sqns. each) | | |
| | **I BAN DIVISION** | 4 Inf. Regts. of 4 Bns. & M.G. Det. | |
| | | 3 Sqn. Divisional Cavalry | |
| | | 1 Fd. Artillery Regts. of 9 batteries of 4 guns | |

**Serbian O.O.B. 1914 continued**

| Cavalry continued | | Peacetime Structure (I BAN) | Wartime, formed on Mobilisation (II BAN) |
|---|---|---|---|
| **II BAN DIVISION** | | 3 Inf. Regts. of 4 Bns. & M.G. Det. | |
| (Landwehr-type units) | | 2 Sqn. Divisional Cavalry | |
| | | 1 Fd. Artillery Regts. of 6 batteries of 4 guns | |
| **III BAN FORMATIONS** | | Landsturm-type units | |

### Table 3.7 Montenegrin Army Organisation 1914

| DIVISION | BRIGADE | | No. of Bns. | Reserve Bn. |
|---|---|---|---|---|
| I | 1 | KATUSHKA | 6 | 1 |
| | 2 | RIJEKA CRMNIK* | 4 | 1 |
| | 3 | PRIMORSKA-CRMNIKA | 6 | 1 |
| II | 4 | ZETSKA | 6 | 1 |
| | 5 | SPUZKA | 3† | 1 |
| | 6 | BRDSKA | 4 | 1 |
| III | 7 | NIKSICKA | 5 | 1 |
| | 8 | VUCEDOLSKA | 4 | 1 |
| | 9 | DURMITORSKA | 5 | 1 |
| IV | 10 | KOLASIUSKA | 6 | 1 |
| | 11 | VASOJEVICKA | 6 | 1 |

* or RIJECKO-LJEBANSKA.

† Later 4 Bns.

Each Brigade had 1 Mtn. Battery, 1 M.G.Det., & Pioneer and Reconnaissance Platoons additionally.
Each Division had a further Mtn. Battery & 1 Field Artillery Battery.
Mountain Batteries had 4 guns.

### Table 3.8 Italian Army Organisation 1.9. 1914

| ARMY | CORPS | DIVISIONS |
|---|---|---|
| **1 ARMY** | III | 5, 6, 35 |
| | I | 1, 2, 9 |
| **2 ARMY** | II | 3, 4, 32 |
| | IV | 7, 8, 33 |
| | X | 19, 20 |
| | Army Troops | 1 CD, 2 Alpine Groups (A & B), Provisional Div. Bersaglieri |
| **3 ARMY** | VI | 11, 12 |
| | VII | 13, 14 |
| | XI | 21, 22 |
| | Army Troops | 2 CD, 3 CD, 4 CD |
| **4 ARMY** | V | 10, 34 |
| | VIII | 15, 16 |
| | IX | 17, 18 |
| **At Disposition of Supreme Command** | | |
| | **ZONA CARNA** | **Sub-Divisional Units** |
| | XII | 23, 24 |
| | XIII | 25, 30, 31 |
| | XIV | 26, 27, 28, 29 |

### Table 3.9 Rumanian Army Organisation 1914

| CORPS | DIVISIONS | BRIGADES |
|---|---|---|
| **I (Crajova)** | 1 (Turnu-Severin) | 1, 2 |
| | 2 (Crajova) | 3, 4 |
| **II (Bucharest)** | 3 (Tirgoviste) | 5, 6 |
| | 4 (Bucharest) | 7, 8 |
| | 9 Dobrudja (Constantza) | 17 |
| **III (Galatz)** | 5 (Buzau) | 9, 10 |
| | 6 (Focsani) | 11, 12 |
| **IV (Jassy)** | 7 (Roman) | 13, 14 |
| | 8 (Botosani) | 15, 16 |
| **CORPS TROOPS** **I** | | 1 Cav. Bde. (3 Regts.) |
| | | 1 Artillery Bde. (3 Regts.) |
| **II** | | 2 Cav. Bde., 5 Cav. Bde, (3 Regts. each) |
| | | 3 Artillery Bde. (3 Regts.) |
| **ARMY TROOPS** | | |
| | Cavalry Div. | 3, 4 Cav. Bdes. |

### Table 3.10 Greek Army Organisation 1914

| DIVISION | TITLE & BASE | BRIGADES | DIVISIONAL TROOPS |
|---|---|---|---|
| 1 | Larissa | 1 Larissa 2 Lamia | 1 Cav. Regt., 1 Artillery Regt, 1 Engineer Bn. etc |
| 2 | Athens | 3 Athens 4 Napulia | 1 Cav. Regt., 1 Artillery Regt, 1 Engineer Bn. etc |
| 3 | Missolonghi | 5 Missolonghi 6 Patras | 1 Cav. Regt., 1 Artillery Regt, 1 Engineer Bn. etc |

Each Brigade had 2 Inf. Regts. of 2 Bns. + Cadre of 3rd Bn. and 1 Rifle (Evzone) Bn.

| | Peace | War |
|---|---|---|
| Inf. Bns. | 30 | 48, eventually 60 |
| Squadrons | 12 | 18 |
| Artillery Batts. | 27 | 33 |
| Technical Companies | 13 | 19 |

## Table 3.11 German Army Organisation 8.1914

On completion of mobilisation the German Army fielded the following formations:–

| | | |
|---|---|---|
| Army H.Q. (8) | 1-8 ( A 9th was added in 9.1914) | |
| Corps H.Q. (40) | | |
| Active (25) | Guard, I-XXI, I Bavarian - III Bavarian | |
| Reserve (14) | Guards Reserve, I, III-X, XII, XIV, XVIII, Bavarian Reserve | |
| Landwehr (1) | Landwehr | |
| Infantry Divs. (92) | | |
| Active (51) | 1-3 Guard, 1-42, 1-6 Bavarian | |
| Reserve (31) | 1-2 Guards Reserve, 1, 3, 5-7, 9-19, 21-26, 28, 30, 33, 35, 36, 1, 5 Bavarian Reserve | |
| Landwehr (4) | 1-4 | |
| Ersatz (6) | Guard, 4, 8, 10, 19, Bavarian Ersatz | |
| Cavalry Divs. (11) | Guard, 1-9 Bavarian | |
| Infantry Regts. (218) | | |
| Guard (5) | 1-5 | |
| Grenadier (5) | 1-5 | |
| Guard Fusilier (1) | 1 | |
| Lehr Inf. Regt. (1) | 1 (expanded from Lehr Inf. Bn. on mobilisation) | |
| Infantry Regts.* (182) | 1-182 (includes 17 Saxon and 10 Württemberg) | |
| Bavrian (24) | Leib, 1-23 | |
| Reserve Infantry Regts. (113) | | |
| Guard Reserve (2) | 1-2 | |
| Reserve I.R.(97) | 1-3, 5-13, 15-32, 34-40, 46, 48, 49, 51-53, 55-57, 59-61, 64-84, 86-88, 90-94, 98-104, 106, 107, 109-111, 116, 118-121, 130, 133 (100-104, 106, 107, 133 were Saxon, 119-121 were Württemberg) | |
| Bavarian Reserve I.R. (14) | 1-8, 10-15 | |
| Landwehr I.R. (96) | (Includes 10 Bavarian, 7 Saxon, 7 Württemberg) | |
| Reserve I.R. Metz (1) | | |
| Jäger Battalions (18) | Guard, Guard Schützen, 1-14, 1-2 Bavarian | |
| Reserve Jäger Btns. (18) | Reserve Btns. of those above | |

### Summary of Infantry on Mobilisation

| | Regiments | Battalions |
|---|---|---|
| Active Infantry | 218 | 654 |
| Reserve Infantry | 113 | 332 |
| Landwehr | 96 | 294 |
| Reserve I.R. Metz | 1 | 2 |
| Active Jäger Battalions | | 18 |
| Reserve Jäger Battalions | | 18 |
| Other Reserve/Ersatz elements: | | |
| Brigade Ersatz Battalions | | 86 |
| Reserve Brigade Ersatz Battalions | | 12 |
| Landwehr Brigade Ersatz Battalions | | 21 |
| Excess Landwehr Bns. IV Corps | | 6 |
| Westphalian Landwehr Bns. Breslau | | 4 |
| Mobile Esratz Bns. | | 58 |
| **TOTALS** | **428** | **1,505** of which |
| | | Regimental 1, 282 |
| | | Independent 223 |

| | | |
|---|---|---|
| Cavalry Regts. - **Active** (110) | | |
| Heavy/Cuirassier type (12) | Garde du Corps, Garde, Leib, 2-8 Cuirassiers, Saxon Guard Reiter, Saxon Karabinier | |
| Dragoons (28) | 1, 2, Guard, 1-26 | |
| Hussars (21) | Guard, 1, 2 Leib, 3-20 | |
| Uhlans (24) | 1-3, Guard, 1-21 | |
| Jäger zu Pferd (13) | 1-13 | |
| Bavarian (12) | 1, 2 Schwere Reiter, 1-8 Chevauleger, 1-2 Uhlans (literally "heavy riders") | |
| **Reserve** (33) | + (1) | |
| Heavy (3) | 1-3 Schwere Reserve Reiter | |
| Dragoons (10) | Garde Reserve, 1-8 Reserve, Württemberg Reserve | |
| Hussars (9) | 1-2, 4-9 Reserve, Saxon Reserve | |
| Uhlans (8) | Garde Reserve, 1-6 Reserve, Saxon Reserve | |
| Jäger zu Pferd (1) | 1 Reserve | |
| Bavarian (2)+(1) | 1 and 5 Bavarian Reserve Cavalry + 6 Bavarian Res. Cav. formed shortly after | |
| **Landwehr (2) & Ersatz (1)** | 1-2 Landwehr Cavalry (later numbered 10-11) VI Army Corps Ersatz Cavalry Regt. | |

### Summary of Cavalry Regiments

| | Squadrons |
|---|---|
| 110 Active (104 of 4 and 6 of 6 Sqns.) | 452 |
| 33 Reserve (of 3 Sqns.) | 99 |
| 2 Landwehr (of 3 Sqns.) | 6 |
| 1 Ersatz (of 3 Sqns.) | 3 |
| **TOTAL** | **560** |

* Some designated as Grenadier or Fusilier Regiments for historical/ traditional reasons.

### Artillery on Mobilisation 2.8.1914

| | |
|---|---|
| Field Artillery Regts. (102) | 1-6 Guard, 1-84, 1-12 Bavarian |
| Reitende Abteilungen† (11) | III Abteilungen of 1 Guard, 1, 3, 5, 8, 10, 11, 12, 15, 35 and 5 Bavarian FD. Regts. |
| Reserve Fld. Aty. Regts. (29) | 1 and 3 Guard, 1, 3, 5-7, 9-26, 29, 36 1, 5 and 6 Bavarian |
| Ersatz Abteilungen (40) | 1 and 2 Guard, 6, 14, 18, 20, 22-23, 25, 27-29, 31-32, 38-41, 43-48, 53, 55, 57, 60, 62, 65, 67, 75-77 1, 2, 4, 8, 10, 12 Bavarian |
| Landwehr Abteilungen (3) | Numbers not known |

† Horse Artillery Battalions.

Heavy Artillery:

| | |
|---|---|
| Foot Artillery Regts. (25) | 1-2 Guard, 1-20, 1-3 Bavarian |
| Reserve Ft. Aty. Regts. (23) | 1-2 Guard, 1-11, 13-18, 20 1-3 Bavarian Reserve |
| Landwehr Ft. Aty. Regtl. Staffs (12) | 1, 3-5, 7, 8, 10, 11, 14-16 3 Bavarian Landwehr |

Reserve:

| | |
|---|---|
| Foot Artillery Battalions (3) | 12, 19, 6 Bavarian Reserve |
| Landwehr Ft. Aty. Btns. (24) | 1-2 Guard, 1-11, 13-18, 20 1-3 Bavarian Reserve |
| Mobile Landsturm Ft. Aty. Btns. (23) | I-XV, XVII-XX; I, II Bavarian; 1, 2/III Bavarian |
| Mobile Ft. Aty. Ersatz Btns. (6) | 21, 26-28, 2 and 3 Bavarian |

Organisation:

| | |
|---|---|
| Field Artillery Regiments | 2 Bns. of 6 Btys. each. Each Bty. had 6 guns (11 FD. Artillery Regts. had a third Bn. of Horse Artillery, these battalions had 3 4-gun batteries). |
| Foot Artillery Regiments | 2 Bns. of 4 Btys. each of 4 guns. |
| *Except* Mortar Bns. | 2 Bns. of 2 Btys. each of 4 pieces. |

### German O.O.B. Western Front 18.8.1914

| ARMY GROUP/ ARMY | CORPS | DIVISIONS |
|---|---|---|
| **1 ARMY** | II | 3 ID 4 ID |
| | III | 5 ID 6 ID |
| | IV | 7 ID 8 ID |
| | IX | 17 ID 18 ID |
| | III Res. | 5 Res.D 6 Res.D |
| | IV Res. | 7 Res.D 22 Res.D |
| | | 3 Landwehr Bdes. |
| **2 ARMY** | Guard | 1 GD ID 2 GD ID |
| | VII | 13 ID 14 ID |
| | X | 19 ID 20 ID |
| | Guard Res.* | 3 GD ID 1 GD Res.D |
| | VII Res. | 13 Res.D 14 Res.D |
| | X Res. | 2 GD Res.D 19 Res.D |
| | | 2 Landwehr Bdes. |
| **3 ARMY** | XI* | 22 ID 38 ID |
| | XII | 23 ID 32 ID |
| | XIX | 24 ID 40 ID |
| | XII Res. | 23 Res.D 24 Res.D |
| | | 1 Landwehr Bde. |
| **4 ARMY** | VI† | 11 ID 12 ID |
| | VIII | 15 ID 16 ID |
| | XVIII | 21 ID 25 ID |
| | VIII Res. | 15 Res.D 16 Res.D |
| | XVIII Res. | 21 Res.D 25 Res.D |
| | | 1 Landwehr Bde. |
| **5 ARMY** | V | 9 ID 10 ID |
| | XIII | 26 ID 27 ID |
| | XVI | 33 ID 34 ID |
| | V Res. | 9 Res.D 10 Res.D |
| | VI Res. | 11 Res.D 12 Res.D |
| | Higher LW CD II | 5 Landwehr Bdes. |
| **6 ARMY** | XXI | 31 ID 42 ID |
| | I Bav. | 1 Bav. ID 2 Bav. ID |
| | II Bav. | 3 Bav. ID 4 Bav. ID |
| | III Bav. | 5 Bav.D 6 Bav.D |
| | I Bav. Res. | 1 Bav. Res.D 5 Bav. Res.D |
| | | 1 Landwehr Bde. |
| **7 ARMY** | XIV | 28 ID 29 ID |
| | XV | 30 ID 39 ID |

* To Russian Front 26.8.14.

† To 5 Army 28.8.14.

| ARMY GROUP/ ARMY | CORPS | DIVISIONS |
|---|---|---|
| **7 ARMY continued** | XIV Res. | 26 Res. ID 28 Res. ID |
| | | 1 Landwehr Bde. |
| **Covering Force, Upper Rhine** | | 3 Landwehr Bdes., 1 Landwehr IR |
| **At Disposal Grand H.Q.** | Higher Cav. CD 1 | GD CD 5 CD (To support 3 Army) |
| | Higher Cav. CD 2 | 2 CD 4 CD 9 CD (To support 1 & 2 Armies) |
| | Higher Cav. CD 3 | 7 CD 8 CD Bav. CD (To support 6 Army) |
| | Higher Cav. CD 4 | 3 CD 6 CD (To support 4 & 5 Armies) |
| **NORTH ARMY** | IX Res. | 17 Res. D 18 Res. D (Added to 1 Army 8.1914) |
| | Higher LW CD | 4 Landwehr Bdes. |
| **Mobile Ersatz Formations** | | GD, 4, 8, 10, 19, Bav. Ersatz Divs. |
| **Fortress Metz** | | 33 Res. D |
| **Ftress. Strasbourg** | | 30 Res. D |

### German O.O.B. Eastern Front 18.8.1914

| ARMY GROUP/ ARMY | CORPS | DIVISIONS |
|---|---|---|
| **8 ARMY** | I | 1 ID 2 ID |
| | XVII | 35 ID 36 ID |
| | XX | 37 ID 41 ID |
| | I Res. | 1 Res. D 36 Res. D |
| | | 1 CD |
| | | 3 Res. D |
| | Landwehr | Higher LW Commands 3, 4 |
| | | 3 Landwehr Bdes. |
| **Fortress Thorn** | | 35 Res. D |
| **Ftess. Königsberg** | | 11 Bns. 6 Sqns. 6 Btys. (Field Artillery) |
| **Fortress Posen** | | 9 Bns. 1 Sqn. 4 Btys. (Field Artillery) |
| **Fortress Graudenz** | | 6 Bns. 1 Sqn. 3 Btys. (Field Artillery) |

### Summary

| | Bns. | Sqns. | Btys. | (Guns) |
|---|---|---|---|---|
| **WEST** **1 Army** | 164 | 41 | 138 | (796) |
| **2 Army** | 159 | 40 | 152 | (848) |
| **3 Army** | 104 | 30 | 105 | (602) |
| **4 Army** | 123 | 39 | 113 | (646) |
| **5 Army** | 147 | 41 | 123 | (698) |
| **6 Army** | 131 | 39 | 133 | (746) |
| **7 Army** | 108 | 28 | 81 | (468) |
| **North Army** | 57 | 12 | 20 | (112) |
| **Cav. Command 1** | 5 | 48 | 6 | (24) |

**Summary continued**

|  | Bns. | Sqns. | Btys. | (Guns) |
|---|---|---|---|---|
| **WEST continued** Cav. Command 2 | 5 | 72 | 9 | (36) |
| Cav. Command 3 | 2 | 72 | 9 | (36) |
| Cav. Command 4 | 2 | 48 | 6 | (24) |
| **EAST** 8 Army (26.8.14) | 158 | 78 | 140 | (774) |
| 8 Army (1.9.14)* | 229 | 119 | 219 | (1,194) |

---

### *Table 3.12* Austro-Hungarian Army Organisation 8.1914

On completion of mobilisation the Austro-Hungarian Army could field the following formations:–

| | |
|---|---|
| Army H.Q. (6) | 1-6 |
| Army Corps (18) | I-XVII and Armee Gruppe Kummer |
| Infantry Divisions† (50) | 1-48, 95 Landsturm, 106 Landsturm (see N.B. 1) |
| Independent Inf. Bdes. (19) | Numbered in same sequence as Divisional Brigades |
| Mountain Inf. Bdes. (5) | Numbered in same sequence as Divisional Brigades |
| Marsch Brigades (14) | 1-14 all disbanded in 9.1914 (see N.B. 2) |
| Landsturm Inf. Bdes. (5) | 1-5 |
| Landsturm Territorial Bdes. (17) | 1-17 |
| Cavalry Divisions (11) | 1-11 (see N.B. 3) |
| Field Artillery Bdes. (44) | Carry divisional number (1, 18, 47, 48, 95 and 106. Inf. Divs./Landsturm Divs. had no field artillery brigade). |
| Fortress Artillery Bdes. (5) | 1-5 |

N.B. 1   Of the infantry divisions 16 were designated as *Schützen* or *Honved* divisions, viz   *Schützen*   Nos. 13, 21, 22, 26, 43, 44, 45, 46 (8)
  *Honved*   Nos. 20, 23, 37-42 (8)

N.B. 2   'Marsch' Brigades were temporary formations conducting reinforcements to units at the front.

N.B. 3   Of the 11 Cavalry Divisions Nos. 5 and 11 were designated as *Honved* Cavalry Divisions.

N.B. 4   *Schützen* and *Honved* divisions were Austrian and Hungarian Landwehr respectively.

These higher formations contained the following regiments;

| Infantry: | No. of Regts. | No. of Bns. | |
|---|---|---|---|
| k-u-k‡ Infantry Regiments | 102 | 408 | |
| Tiroler Kaiserjäger | 4 | 13 | (No.2 had 4 Bns.) |
| Bosnia-Herzegovina Inf. Regts. | 4 | 15 | (No.4 had only 3 Bns.) |
| Feldjäger Battalions ◊ | | 29 | |
| Bosnia-Herzegovina Feldjäger Bn. | | 1 | |
| Bosnia-Herzegovina Reserve Bn. | | 1 | |
| Grenzjäger Companies (6) | | = 1½ | |
| Schützen Regiments | 37 | 113 | |
| Kaiser Schützen Regiments | 3 | 16 | (No.1 had 6 Bns.) |
| Honved Infantry Regts. | 32 | 97 | (No.19 had 4 Bns.) |
| Austrian Landsturm Inf. Regts. | 40 | 136 | |
| Hungarian Landsturm Inf. Regts. | 32 | 97 | |
| Volunteer Formations– | | | |
| Polish Battalions | | 3 | |
| **Total Battalions Mobilised** | | **930½** | |

By 9.1914 Landsturm Territorial and *Etappen* (L of C) battalions could be added to this total      227
**Total**      **1,157½**

| Cavalry: | No. of Regts. | No. of Sqns. |
|---|---|---|
| Dragoons | 15 | 90 |
| Hussars | 16 | 96 |
| Uhlans | 11 | 66 |
| Mounted Schützen | 6 | 36 |
| Mounted Tiroler Landeschützen Divisions | – | 3 |
| Mounted Dalmatiner Landeschützen Divisions | – | 2 |
| Honved Hussars | 10 | 60 |
| Landsturm Hussar Divisions | – | 30 |
| **Total** | | **383** |
| + Kavallerie Machine Gun Abteilungen | | 22 |

* Following reinforcement by 4 ID/Res. D, 1½ LW Divs., 1 CD.

| Field & Mountain Artillery: | No. of Regts. | No. of Btys. | No. of Guns |
|---|---|---|---|
| Field Artillery Regts. | 42 | 222 | |
| Field Artillery Divisions | 8 | 16 | 1,614 |
| Honved Field Artillery Regts. | 8 | 31 | (6 per Bty.) |
| Horse Artillery Divisions | 9 | 27 | 120 |
| Honved Horse Artillery Division | 1 | 3 | (4 per Bty.) |
| Field Howitzer Regts. | 14 | 54 | 420 |
| Field Howitzer Divisions | 8 | 16 | (6 per Bty.) |
| Mountain Artillery Regts. | 10 | Gun 50 | 200 |
| | | Howitzer 22 | 88 (4 per. Bty.) |
| Dalmatiner Mountain Artillery Div. | – | Gun 2 | 8 |
| Heavy Howitzer Divisions (14) | – | 28 | 112 (4 per. Bty.) |
| Improvised Units: | | | |
| 3 Landsturm Field Artillery Regts. | 3 | 12 | 48 (4 per. Bty.) |

† Containing 93 Inf. Bdes. and 9 Mountain Inf. Bdes.

**Summary**

| | No. of Btys. | No. of Guns |
|---|---|---|
| Field Artillery Btys. | 299 | 1,734 |
| Field Howitzer Btys. | 70 | 420 |
| Mountain Gun Btys. | 52 | 208 |
| Mountain Howitzer Btys. | 22 | 88 |
| Heavy Howitzer Btys. | 28 | 112 |
| Improvised Btys. | 12 | 48 |
| **Total** | **483** | **2,610** |

Fortress Artillery (only mobile Btys. listed)

| | No. of Btys. | No. of Guns |
|---|---|---|
| 30.5 cm. Mortar Btys. (2 pieces) | 12 | 24 |
| 24 cm. Mortar Btys. (4 pieces) | 12 | 48 |
| 15 cm. Howitzer Btys. (4 guns) | 32 | 128 |
| 12 cm. Gun Btys. (4 guns) | 20 | 80 |
| **Total** | **76** | **280** |

‡ k-u-k: Kaiserlich und Königlich.

◊ 1-32 excluding 3, 15, 18.

### Austro-Hungarian O.O.B. Northern Front August 1914

| ARMY/ ARMY GROUP | CORPS | DIVISIONS |
|---|---|---|
| **1 Army** | I | 5 ID 46 Sch. D |
| | V | 14 ID 33 ID 37 HID |
| | X | 2 ID 24 ID 45 Sch. D |
| | Army Disposal | 12 ID 3 CD 9 CD |
| | | 4 Landsturm Inf. Bdes., 3 Marsch Bdes., Polish Legion (3 Bns.) |
| **2 Army** | XII | 16 ID 35 ID 38 HID |
| | III | 6 ID 28 ID 22 Sch. D |

| ARMY/ ARMY GROUP | CORPS | DIVISIONS |
|---|---|---|
| **2 Army continued** | Army Disposal | 11 ID 43 Sch. D 20 HID 1 CD 5 HCD 8 CD |
| | | 5 Landsturm Inf. Bdes, 3 Marsch Bdes./Formations |
| | To transfer from Balkans: | |
| | VII | 17 ID 34 ID |
| | IV | 31 ID 32 ID |
| **3 Army** | XI | 30 ID |
| | XIV | 3 ID 8 ID 44 Sch. D |
| | Army Disposal | 41 HID 23 HID 4 CD 2 CD 11 HCD |
| | | 2 Landsturm Inf. Bdes., 5 Marsch Bdes./formations |
| **4 Army** | II | 4 ID 25 ID 13 Sch.D |
| | VI | 15 ID 27 ID 39 HID |
| | IX | 10 ID 26 Sch. D |
| | XVII | 19 ID |
| | Army Disposal | 6 CD 10 CD |
| | | 1 Marsch Bde. |
| **Army Group Kummer v. Falkenfehd** | | 7 CD 95 L St. ID 106 L St. ID |
| | Army Group Disposal | German LW Corps (3 & 4 LW Divs) |
| **Fortress Security Units** | | 21 Bns. Landsturm 7 Sqns. 1 Bty 83 Fortress Arty. Coys. |

## Summary

| | Bns. | Sqns. | Btys. (Guns) | Machine Guns |
|---|---|---|---|---|
| Field Army | 798½ | 377 | 379 (2,076) | 1,234 |
| Fortress Security | 21 | 7 | 1 (6) | — |
| **Total** | **819½** | **384** | **380(2,082)** | **1, 234** |

## Austro-Hungarian O.O.B. Balkan Front August 1914

| ARMY/ ARMY GROUP | CORPS | DIVISIONS |
|---|---|---|
| **5 Army** | VIII | 9 ID 21 Sch. D |
| | XIII | 36 ID 42 HID |
| | Under Army Cd. | 11 Mtn. Bde. 104 L St. I Bde. 13 Marsch Bde. |
| **6 Army** | XV | 1 ID 48 ID |
| | XVI | 18 ID 1, 2, 13 Mtn. Bdes. |
| | Under Army Cd. | 3 Mtn. Bde. 47 ID 48 HID |
| **2 Army & Rayon Banat** | IV | 31 ID 32 ID |
| | VII | 17 ID 34 ID |
| | IX | 29 ID |
| | Under Army Cd. | 23 HID ½7 ID 10 Cav. D |
| | Rayon Banat | Minor Units |
| **Fortress Garrisons** | | Total of 36 L St. I Bns. 4 Sqns. 2 Btys. |

2 Army and its component corps were transferred to Galicia in late August 1914.

## Summary

| | Bns. | Sqns. | Btys. (Guns) | Machine Guns |
|---|---|---|---|---|
| Field Army (5, 6 and 2 Armies) | 319½ | 60 | 142 (744) | 486 |
| After transfer of 2 Army | 239½ | 37 | 101 (516) | 342 |
| Garrison Units | 36 | 4 | 2 (12) | 6 |
| **Total (late August)** | **275½** | **41** | **103 (528)** | **348** |

### *Table 3.13* Turkish Army Organisation 5.8.1914

| ARMY CORPS | DIVISIONS | (LOCATION) |
|---|---|---|
| **Inspectorate I (Constantinople)** | | Area: Constantinople, Thrace, Anatolia |
| **I (Constantinople)** | 1 | (Constantinople) |
| | 2 | (Constantinople) |
| | 3 | (Constantinople) |
| **II (Adrianople)** | 4 | (Adrianople) |
| | 5 | (Adrianople) |
| | 6 | (Kirk Kilisse) |
| **III (Rodesto)** | 7 | (Gallipoli) |
| | 8 | (Rodesto) |
| | 9 | (Paderma) |
| **IV (Smyrna)** | 10 | (Smyrna) |
| | 11 | (Balikessar) |
| | 12 | (Egardir) |
| **V (Angoria)** | 13 | (Angoria) |
| | 14 | (Angoria) |
| | 15 | (Yozgat) |
| **Inspectorate II (Erzindjan, Kurdistan)** | | Area: Kurdistan |
| **IX (Erzerum)** | 17 | (Sivas) |
| | 28 | (Erzerum) |
| | 29 | (Baihurt) |
| **X (Erzindjan)** | 30 | (Erzindjan) |
| | 31 | (Erzindjan) |
| | 32 | (Kharput) |
| **XI (Van)** | 18 | (Mezra) |
| | 33 | (Van) |
| | 34 | (Mush) |
| **Inspectorate III (Damascus)** | | Area: Syria |
| **VI (Aleppo)** | 16 | (Adana) |
| | 24 | (Aintab) |
| | 26 | (Aleppo) |
| **VIII (Damascus)** | 23 | (Homa) |
| | 25 | (Damascus) |
| | 27 | (Haifa) |
| **Inspectorate IV (Baghdad)** | | Area: Mesopotamia |
| **XII (Mosul)** | 35 | (Mosul) |
| | 36 | (Kirkuk) |
| **XIII (Baghdad)** | 37 | (Baghdad) |
| | 38 | (Basra) |

**Turkish O.O.B. 5.8.1914 continued**

| ARMY CORPS | DIVISIONS | (LOCATION) |
|---|---|---|
| **Independent formations** | | Area: Arabia/Yemen |
| **VII (Yemen)** | 39 | (Sanar) |
| | 40 | (Hodeida) |
| **(Arabia)** (No Corps level H.Q.) | 21 | (Assir) |
| | 22 | (Hedjaz) |

Divisions not activated in peacetime    19
20
23 } But shown in
24 } Inspectorate OB for Syria

Nominally each division had 3 Infantry Regts. of 3 Bns. each, 1 Artillery Regiment of 4 Batteries (16 guns) and, usually, 1 Cavalry Squadron. However there were frequent variations to this.

Higher Cavalry formations were very loose with, nominally at any rate, 1 Division each in the Caucasus, Syria and Mesopotamia. The latter two were certainly more akin to Brigades than Divisions.

**Table 3.14 Bulgarian Army Organisation 1914**

| ARMY INSPECTION | DIVISION/TITLE | BASED |
|---|---|---|
| **I (Sofia)** | 1 Sofia | Sofia |
| | 6 Vidin | Vraca |
| | 7 Rilo | Rilo-Dupnica |
| **II (Philip-Popel)** | 2 Trakia | Philip-Popel |
| | 3 Sliven | Slivna |
| | 8 Tundza | Stara Zagora |
| | 10 Gumulozina | Gumulozina (formed 1915?) |
| **III (Ruscuk)** | 4 Preslaw | Sumla |
| | 5 Danube | Ruscuk |
| | 9 Plevna | Plevna |
| **Army Troops** | Cavalry Division | Sofia |

**Summary**

| | |
|---|---|
| 120 | Inf.Bns. |
| 40 | Machine Gun Dets. |
| 44 | Squadrons |
| 11 | Cavalry Machine Gun Dets. |
| 92 | Field Batteries |
| 20 | Mtn. Batteries |
| 12 | Howitzer Batteries |
| 12 | Fortress Artillery Batteries |
| 5 | Pioneer Battalions |

## WESTERN FRONT

**Table 3.15 Allied O.O.B. Western Front 8.1914/9.1914**

| ARMY GROUP/ ARMY | CORPS | DIVISIONS |
|---|---|---|
| **BELGIAN** | | 1, 2, 3, 4, 5, 6 ID, CD |
| **B.E.F.** | I | 1 Div, 2 Div |
| | II | 3 Div, 5 Div |
| *(formed 31.8.14)* | III | 4 Div, 6 Div |
| | | Cav. Div. |
| **FRENCH ARMY 5 ARMY** | I | 1 ID 2 ID |
| | II | 3 ID 4 ID |
| | III | 5 ID 6 ID |
| | X | 19 ID 20 ID |
| | XI | 21 ID 22 ID |
| | | 52 ID 60 ID |
| | | 4 CD |
| **4 ARMY** | XII | 23 ID 24 ID |
| | XVII | 33 ID 34 ID |
| | CAC | 2 DIC 3 DIC |
| | | 9 CD |
| **3 ARMY** | IV | 7 ID 8 ID |
| | V | 9 ID 10 ID |
| | VI | 12 ID 40 ID 42 ID |
| | 3 GDR | 54 ID 55 ID 56 ID |
| | | 7 CD |
| **2 ARMY** | IX | 17 ID 18 ID |
| | XV | 29 ID 30 ID |
| | XVI | 31 ID 32 ID |
| | XVIII | 35 ID 36 ID |
| | XX | 11 ID 39 ID |
| | 2 GDR | 59 ID 68 ID 70 ID |
| | | 2 CD 10 CD |
| **1 ARMY** | VII | 14 ID 41 ID |
| | VIII | 15 ID 16 ID |
| | XIII | 25 ID 26 ID |
| | XIV | 27 ID 28 ID |
| | XXI | 13 ID 43 ID |
| | | 6 CD 8 CD |
| | I CC | 1 CD 3 CD 5 CD |
| **Disposal M of W** | | 61 ID 62 ID 67 ID |
| **Disposal C-in-C** | | 37 ID 38 ID |
| **Unattached** | | 44 ID |
| | 1 GDR | 58 ID 63 ID 66 ID |
| | 4 GDR | 51 ID 53 ID 69 ID |
| **Défence Mobile du Nord Est** | | 57 ID 71 ID 72 ID 73 ID |
| **Reserve of 14e and 15e Regions** | | 64 ID 65 ID 74 ID 75 ID |

**Western Front Allied O.O.B. continued**

| ARMY GROUP/ ARMY | CORPS | DIVISIONS |
|---|---|---|
| FRENCH ARMY continued En Route from N.Africa | | D de M du Maroc |
| Modification 8/9.1914 ADD: | | |
| 1 ARMY | | 44 ID 1 GDR (58, 63, 66 ID) |
| 4 ARMY | | 1 DIC |
| | | II, XI, 52 ID, 60 ID, 4 CD (from 5 Army) |
| 5 ARMY | | XVIII (from 2 Army) 4 GDR 37, 38 ID Conneau CC (2, 8, 10 CD) I CC (1, 3, 5 CD) |
| | | Deduct II, XI, 52 ID, 60 ID, 4 CD (to 4 Army) |
| Formation of 6 Army 9.1914 | IV | 7 ID 8 ID |
| | VII | 14 ID 63 ID |
| | XIII | 25 ID 26 ID |
| | 5 GDR | 55 ID 56 ID |
| | 6 GDR | 61 ID 62 ID |
| | I CC | 1 CD 3 CD 5 CD |
| Formation of 9 Army 9.1914 | IX | 17 ID 18 ID |
| | XI | 21 ID 22 ID |
| | XXI | 13 ID 43 ID |
| | | 42 ID Maroc Div. |
| | | 52 ID 60 ID |
| | | 6 CD 9 CD |

### Table 3.16 Allied O.O.B. Western Front 15.9.1914

| ARMY GROUP/ ARMY | CORPS | DIVISIONS |
|---|---|---|
| BELGIAN | | 1, 2, 3, 4, 5, 6 ID, CD |
| B.E.F. | I | 1 ID 2 ID |
| | II | 3 ID 5 ID |
| (formed 31.8.14) | III | 4 ID 6 ID |
| | | Cav. Div. (- 2 Bdes.) |
| FRENCH ARMY 6 ARMY (on left of B.E.F.) | IV | 7 ID 8 ID |
| | VII | 14 ID 63 ID |
| | XII | 25 ID 26 ID |
| | 5 GDR | 55 ID 56 ID |
| | 6 GDR | 61 ID 62 ID |
| | CC Bridoux | 1 CD 5 CD |
| | | 37 ID 45 ID |
| | | 3 CD |
| 5 ARMY | I | 1 ID 2 ID |
| | III | 5 ID 6 ID |
| | X | 19 ID 20 ID |
| | XVIII | 35 ID 36 ID |

| ARMY GROUP/ ARMY | CORPS | DIVISIONS |
|---|---|---|
| 5 ARMY continued | 4 GDR | 53 ID 69 ID |
| | | 38 ID 51 ID |
| | CC Conneau | 4 CD 8 CD 10 CD |
| 9 ARMY | IX | 17 ID 18 ID |
| | XI | 21 ID 22 ID |
| | XXI | 13 ID 43 ID |
| | | 42 ID Moroccan Div. 52 ID 60 ID |
| | | 6 CD 9 CD |
| 4 ARMY | II | 3 ID 4 ID |
| | XII | 23 ID 24 ID |
| | XVII | 33 ID 34 ID |
| | CAC | 2 Col ID 3 Col ID |
| 3 ARMY | V | 9 ID 10 ID |
| | VI | 12 ID 40 ID |
| | XV | 29 ID 30 ID |
| | 3 GDR | 65 ID 67 ID 75 ID |
| | | 7 CD |
| | Fortress Verdun | 72 ID |
| 2 ARMY | XVI | 31 ID 32 ID |
| | XX | 11 ID 39 ID |
| | 2 GDR | 59 ID 64 ID 68 ID |
| | | 70 ID 73 ID 74 ID |
| | | 2 CD |
| 1 ARMY | Vosges Group | 58 ID 66 ID |
| | XIV | 27 ID 28 ID |
| | Delétoille | Div. Barbot Div. de Vassart |
| | | 41 ID 71 ID |
| | Fortress Belfort | 57 ID |
| ARMY RESERVES | Group of Territorial Divs. | 81, 82, 84, 88 ID CD Beaudemoulin |
| | VIII | 15 ID 16 ID |

### Table 3.17 German O.O.B. Western Front 15.9.1914

| ARMY GROUP/ ARMY | CORPS | DIVISIONS |
|---|---|---|
| 1 ARMY | II | 3 ID 4 ID |
| | III | 5 ID 6 ID |
| | IV | 7 ID 8 ID |
| | IX | 17 ID 18 ID |
| | IV Res. | 7 Res.D 22 Res.D |
| | Cav. Cmd. 2 | 4 CD 9 CD |
| | | 3 Landwehr Bdes. |
| 7 ARMY | XV | 30 ID 39 ID |
| | VIII Res. | 13 Res.D 14 Res.D |
| | IX Res. | 17 Res.D 18 Res.D |
| | | 7 CD |
| | | 1 Landwehr Bde. |

**Western Front German O.O.B. 15.9.1914 continued**

| ARMY GROUP/ ARMY | CORPS | DIVISIONS |
|---|---|---|
| **2 ARMY** | Guard | 1 Gd ID 2 GD ID |
| | VII | 13 ID 14 ID |
| | X | 19 ID 20 ID |
| | XII | 23 ID 32 ID |
| | XVII | 21 ID 25 ID |
| | X Res. | 2 Gd Res.D 19 Res.D |
| | Cav. Cmd. 1 | Gd CD 2 CD |
| | | 1 Landwehr Bde. |
| **3 ARMY** | XIX | 24 ID 40 ID |
| | XII Res. | 23 Res.D 24 Res.D |
| | | 5 CD |
| | | 1 Landwehr Bde. |
| **4 ARMY** | VI | 11 ID 12 ID |
| | VIII | 15 ID 16 ID |
| | XVIII Res. | 21 Res.D 25 Res.D |
| | VIII Res. | 15 Res.D 16 Res.D |
| | Cav. Cmd. 4 | 3 CD 6 CD |
| | | 1 Landwehr Bde. |
| **5 ARMY** | XIII | 26 ID 27 ID |
| | XVI | 33 ID 34 ID |
| | V Res. | 9 Res.D 10 Res.D |
| | VI Res. | 11 Res.D 12 Res.D |
| | | 2 LW Div. 2 Landwehr Bdes. |
| **Army Det. Strantz** | V | 9 ID 10 ID |
| | III Bav. | 5 Bav.ID 6 Bav.ID |
| | | 33 Res.D (Metz) |
| | | Bav.CD |
| **6 ARMY** | XIV | 28 ID 29 ID |
| | XXI | 31 ID 42 ID |
| | I Bav. | 1 Bav.ID 2 Bav.ID |
| | II Bav. | 3 Bav.ID 4 Bav.ID |
| | XIV Res. | 26 Res.D 28 Res.D |
| | I Bav. Res. | 1 Bav.Res.D 5 Bav.Res.D Bav. LW Div. |
| | Ersatz | 4 Ers.D 8 Ers.D 10 Ers.D verst. Gd Ers.D 19 Ers. D |
| | Eberhardt | 30 Res.D Bav.Ers.D |
| **Covering Force Upper Rhine** | | 4 Landwehr Bdes. |
| **Gen. Govt. Belgium** | III Res | 5 Res.D 6 Res.D |
| | | Marine Div. |
| | | 4 Landwehr & 2 Ersatz Bdes. |

***Table 3.18* Allied O.O.B. Western Front 10.12.1914**

| ARMY GROUP/ ARMY | CORPS | DIVISIONS |
|---|---|---|
| **BELGIAN** | | 1, 2, 3, 4, 5, 6 ID 1, 2 CD |
| **B.E.F.** | I | 1 Div, 2 Div |
| | II | 3 Div, 5 Div |
| | III | 4 Div, 6 Div |
| | IV | 7 Div, 8 Div |
| | Indian | 3 Ind.Div. 7 Ind.Div. 19 Inf.Bde. (from III Corps) |
| | Cavalry | 1 CD 2 CD 3 CD |
| N.B. On 26.12.14 B.E.F. was re-organised into two Armies | Indian Cavalry | 1 Ind.CD 2 Ind.CD (not fully arrived as yet) |
| | En route | 27 Div. |
| **1 ARMY** | I, IV, Indian | |
| **2 ARMY** | II, III + 27 Div. | |
| **G.H.Q.** | Cavalry | |
| **FRENCH ARMIES Army Det. Vosges** (u/c 1 Army) | – | 41 ID 66 Res.D 71 Res.D 10 CD Fortress of Belfort (57 Res.D) & Epinal |
| **1 ARMY** | VIII | 15 ID 16 ID Attached Bde. Belfort |
| | XXXI | 64 Res.D 76 Res.D 1 Bde./59 Res.D |
| | 2.Gp.Res.Divs. | 59 Res.D (-1 Bde.) 68 Res.D 74 Res.D |
| | Army Reserves | 65 Res.D 73 Res.D 2 CD Fortress Toul |
| **3 ARMY** | V | 9 ID One Res.Bde. (10 ID transferred to 4 Army) |
| | VI | 12 ID 40 ID 67 Res.D One Res.Bde. |
| | XV | 29 ID 30 ID One Res.Bde. |
| | Army Reserves | 72 Res.D One Res.Bde. |
| | Fortress Verdun | 1 Div. du Marche (Div. de Morlaincourt)* |
| **4 ARMY†** | II | 3 ID 4 ID 10 ID (from 3 Army) |
| | XII | 23 ID 24 ID 60 Res.D 91 DIT 96 DIT |
| | XVII | 33 ID 34 ID |
| | Colonial | 2 DIC 3 DIC |
| **5 ARMY** | I | 1 ID (2 ID in Army Reserve) |
| | III | 5 ID 6 ID Provisional Div. Vassin |
| | XVIII | 35 ID 36 ID 69 Res.D |
| | Army Reserve | 2 ID |
| | Reims Sector | Div. Marocain 51 Res.D 52 Res.D |
| | VII | 14 ID 63 Res.D |
| **6 ARMY** | 5.Gp.Res.Divs. | 55 Res.D Bde. Klein |
| | 6.Gp.Res.Divs.‡ | 37 ID 61 Res.D |
| | Army Reserve | 6 CD |

\* Reserve Brigades were drawn from the disbanded 54 and 75 Reserve Divisions.

† I and IV Corps were scheduled to join 4 Army in late 12.14.

‡ Became XXXV Corps 15.12.14.

**Western Front Allied O.O.B. 10.12.1914 continued**

| ARMY GROUP/ ARMY | CORPS | DIVISIONS |
|---|---|---|
| **2 ARMY** | IV | 7 ID 8 ID |
| | XI | 21 ID 22 ID |
| | XIII | 25 ID 1 Bde. Marocain |
| | XIV | 27 ID 28 ID |
| | Army Reserve | 26 ID (from 8 Army) 53, 56, 62 Res.D 82 DIT 8 CD |
| **Provisional Army Group North** *Groupe Provisoire du Nord* **(GPN)** **10 ARMY** | | |
| | X | 19 ID 20 ID 88 DIT |
| | XXI | 13 ID 58 Res.D 92 DIT Bde./43 ID |
| | XXXIII | 45 ID 70 Res.D 77 Res.D 84 DIT |
| | I Cavalry | 1 CD 3 CD 9 CD |
| | Army Reserve | Bde./43 ID |
| **8 ARMY** (Army Det. Belgium – D.A.B until 16.11.14) | IX | 17 ID 18 ID |
| | XVI | 31 ID 32 ID 12 Bns. Chasseur à pied |
| | XX | 11 ID 39 ID |
| | XXXII | 38 ID 42 ID Bde. Foreign Legion (*Légion Etrangère*) |
| | Group Hely d'Oisel | 87 DIT 89 DIT Marine Fusilier Bde. |
| | II Cavalry | 4 CD 5 CD |
| | Army Reserve | 7 CD |
| **Independent** | Detachment Furnes 81 DIT (- 1 Bde.) | |
| **Independent** | Fortress Dunkirk 1 Bde./81 DIT | |

## SUMMARY

| Army | Inf. Divs. | Cav. Divs. |
|---|---|---|
| **BELGIAN** | 6 | 2 |
| **B.E.F.** | 12 | 5 |
| **FRENCH ARMIES** Army Det. VOSGES | 4 | 1 |
| **1 ARMY** | 9½ | 1 |
| **3 ARMY** | 10 | |
| **4 ARMY** | 12½ | |
| **5 ARMY** | 11 | |
| **6 ARMY** | 5½ | 1 |
| **2 ARMY** | 12½ | 1 |
| **ARMY GROUP NORTH** **10 ARMY** | 11 | 3 |
| **8 ARMY** | 12 | 3 |
| **Furnes/Dunkirk** | 1 | |
| **FRENCH TOTAL** | 89 | 10 |
| **ALLIED TOTAL** | 117 | 17 |

*Table 3.19* **German O.O.B. Western Front 10.12.1914**

| ARMY GROUP/ ARMY | CORPS | DIVISIONS |
|---|---|---|
| **Right flank Army Group** (Crown Prince Rupert) **4 ARMY** | XV | 30 ID 39 ID Composite Gd D Winckler |
| | XXII Reserve | 43 Res.D 44 Res.D |
| | XXIII Reserve | 45 Res.D 46 Res.D |
| | XXVI Reserve | 51 Res.D 52 Res.D One mixed LW Bde. |
| | XXVII Reserve | 53 Res.D 54 Res.D One mixed LW Bde. |
| | — | 4 Ers.D |
| | Marine | 1 Marine Div. 2 Marine Div. |
| | Cavalry | Gd CD |
| **6 ARMY** | Guard | 1 Gd ID 3 Gd Inf.Bde. |
| | IV | 7 ID 8 ID |
| | VII | 13 ID 14 ID |
| | XIV | 28 ID 29 ID |
| | XIX | 24 ID 40 ID One mixed LW Bde. |
| | II Bavarian | 3 Bav.ID 4 Bav.ID |
| | I Bavarian Res. | 1 Bav.Res.D 5 Bav.Res.D |
| | — | 6 Bav.Res.D |
| **2 ARMY** | XVIII | 21 ID 25 ID One mixed LW Bde. |
| | XXI | 31 ID 42 ID One mixed LW Bde. |
| | I Bavarian | 1 Bav.ID 2 Bav.ID |
| | XIV Reserve | 26 Res.D 28 Res.D |
| **Central Army Group** (v. Heeringen) **1 ARMY** | III | 5 ID 6 ID |
| | IX | 17 ID 18 ID |
| | IV Reserve | 7 Res.D 22 Res.D |
| | IX Reserve | 17 Res.D 18 Res.D |
| | | Two mixed LW Bdes. |
| **7 ARMY** | X | 19 ID 20 ID |
| | XII | 23 ID 32 ID |
| | VII Reserve | 13 Res.D 14 Res.D |
| | X Reserve | 2 Gd Res.D 19 Res.D |
| | | One mixed LW Bde. |
| **3 ARMY** | VI | 12 ID strengthened 22 Inf. Bde. |
| | VIII | 15 ID 16 ID (Each less 1 Bde.) |
| | VIII Reserve | 15 Res.D 16 Res.D |
| | XII Reserve | 23 Res.D 24 Res.D |
| | | Elements: Two mixed LW Bdes. |
| **Left flank Army Group** (German Crown Prince) **5 ARMY** | Army Gp. Res. | Div. Fuchs (Staff 16 ID + 29, 31 Inf. Bdes.) 7 CD |
| | XVI | 27 ID 34 ID One mixed LW Bde. |
| | V Reserve | 9 Res.D 10 Res.D One mixed LW Bde. |
| | VI Reserve | 11 Res.D 12 Res.D 2 LW Div. |
| | XVIII Reserve | 11 ID (-1 Bde.) One mixed LW Bde. |
| **Army Det. Strantz** | V | 9 ID 10 ID 33 Res.D |
| | III Bavarian | 5 Bav.Res.D 6 Bav.Res.D Bav.Ers.D |
| | — | 5 LW Div. |

**Western Front German O.O.B. 10.12.1914 continued**

| ARMY GROUP/ ARMY | CORPS | DIVISIONS |
|---|---|---|
| Army Det. Falkenhausen | – | 10 Ers.D Gd.Ers.D 8 Ers.D 61 Res.Inf.Bde. 1 Bav.LW Div. 19 Ers.D |
| | XV Reserve (ex Corps Eberhardt) | 30 Res.D 39 Res.D (ex Div. Rekowski) |
| | | Two LW Bdes. |
| Army Det. Gaede | – | Four Mixed LW Bdes. |
| GEN. GOVT. BELGIUM | – | 3 CD Bav.CD 2 Mixed LW Bdes. 1 Mixed Ers.Bde. |

### SUMMARY

| | Inf. Divs. Equivalents | Cav. Divs. |
|---|---|---|
| **R.F.ARMY GROUP** **4 ARMY** | 15 | 1 |
| **6 ARMY** | 15½ | – |
| **2 ARMY** | 8½ | – |
| **ARMY GROUP TOTAL** | **39** | **1** |
| **CENTRAL ARMY GROUP** **1 ARMY** | 9 | |
| **7 ARMY** | 8½ | |
| **3 ARMY** | 7 | |
| **ARMY GROUP TOTAL** | **24½** | |
| **L.F.ARMY GROUP** **5 ARMY** | 11½ | |
| Army Det. Strantz | 7 | |
| Army Det. Falkenhausen | 9 | |
| Army Det. Gaede | 2 | |
| **ARMY GROUP RESERVE** | 1 | 1 |
| **ARMY GROUP TOTAL** | **30½** | **1** |
| **GEN. GOVT. BELGIUM** | 1½ | 2 |

---

**Table 3.20 Allied O.O.B. Western Front 4.1915**

| ARMY GROUP/ ARMY | CORPS | DIVISIONS |
|---|---|---|
| **D.A.B.** *Dét. d'Armée de Belgique* (formerly 8 Army) | IX | 17 ID 18 ID |
| | XX | 89 DIT 87 DIT 11 ID 39 ID |
| | Army Reserves | 45 ID |
| **B.E.F.*** **1 ARMY** | I | 1 Div. 2 Div. 1/2 London Div. (47 Div. 5.15) |
| | IV | 7 Div. 8 Div. 1/1 W.Riding Div. (49 Div. 5.15) |
| | Indian | 3 Ind.Div. 7 Ind.Div. |
| **2 ARMY** | II | 3 Div. 5 Div. 1/1 W.Midland Div. (46 Div. 5.15) |
| | V | 27 Div. 28 Div. 1 Cdn.Div. |
| **–** | III | 4 Div. 6 Div. 19 Inf.Bde. 1/1 S.Midland Div. (48 Div. 5.15) |
| | General Reserve | 1/1 Northumberland Div. (50 Div. 5.15) |
| **G.H.Q. Disposal** | Cavalry | 1, 2, 3 CD |
| | Indian Cavalry | 1, 2 Ind.CD |

| ARMY GROUP/ ARMY | CORPS | DIVISIONS |
|---|---|---|
| **FRENCH ARMIES 10 ARMY†** | XXXIII | 70 ID 77 ID 84 DIT |
| | XXI | 92 DIT 58 ID 13 ID |
| | X | 19 ID 20 ID 88 DIT |
| | Army Reserve | 43 ID |
| | II Cavalry | 5 CD 7 CD |
| **6 ARMY** | VII | 14 ID |
| | 5 Gp.Res.Divs. (5 GDR)‡ | 63 ID 55 ID |
| | XXXV | 37 ID 61 ID |
| | Army Reserve | 85 DIT 89 DIT 9 CD |
| **5 ARMY** | III | 5 ID 6 ID Div.d'Inf.Provisoire Tassin |
| | XVIII | 36 ID 35 ID 69 ID |
| | Reims Group | 51 ID 52 ID |
| | I | 1 ID 5 ID◊ Div.d'Inf.Provisoire Guérin |
| **4 ARMY** | 1 Colonial | 5 DIC 2 DIC |
| | IV | 7 ID 8 ID 91 DIT 96 DIT 8 CD |
| | XVI | 31 ID 32 ID |
| | Army Reserves | 60 ID 48 ID 154 ID |
| **2 ARMY** | XIV | 27 ID 28 ID |
| | XIII | 25 ID 86 DIT |
| | XI | 22 ID 21 ID 82 DIT+151 ID |
| | XVII | 33 ID 45 ID Div. Marocain |
| | Army Reserves | 53 ID 56 ID 62 ID 26 ID 4 CD |
| **G.P.E.** *Groupement Provisoire de L'Est* | V | 9 ID 10 ID |
| | XV | 30 ID 29 ID |
| | XXXII | 42 ID 40 ID |
| **3 ARMY** | Army Reserves | 2 ID (from VIII Corps/1 Army) |
| **1 ARMY** | VIII | 15 ID 16 ID |
| | XXXI | 64 ID 76 ID |
| | VI | 12 ID 67 ID 65 ID |
| | XII | 24 ID 23 ID |
| | Army Reserves | 73 ID 3 CD |
| **Dét. d'Armée de Lorraine (D.A.L.)** formerly 2 Gp. Res. Divs. | – | 59 ID 68 ID 74 ID 71 ID |
| | – | 2 CD 3 CD (See also 1 Army) |
| **7 ARMY** formerly *Dét. d'Armée des Vosges* | Group Contades | 57 ID 10 CD *Groupement Mobile* Belfort Fortress |
| | Army Reserves | 66 ID 41 ID 47 ID |
| | – | 6CD |
| **Dét. d'Armée de Gérard** | (I) | See 5 Army. Date of allocation of this Corps uncertain. |
| | II | 3 ID |
| | Army Reserves | Div.Inf.de Marche Verdun |
| | 1 Cavalry | 1 CD |
| Independent Command **Gouvt. Militaire de Paris** | – | 83, 97, 99 100 DIT |

* British Territorial Divisions were not numbered until 11/12/14.5.1915.

◊ It is not clear if 5 ID was in I or III Corps.

N.B. The organisation for the B.E.F. is that for 21.4.1915. The organisation for the French Armies has been reconstructed from the O.O.B. Volumes of the French Official History. The format of these volumes and the day to day transfer of divisions within Corps and Armies makes it difficult to establish a complete O.O.B. for a specific date. This can lead to duplication of units within the various Armies and Corps. However it gives a broad overview of the entire French Army on the Western Front during April 1915.

† The D.A.B. and 10 French Army formed *Groupe Provisoire du Nord* (G.P.N.).

‡ 5 GDR became XXXVII Corps 10.6.15.

**Table 3.21** Allied O.O.B. Western Front June/July 1916

*Temporary formation.

† As at 17.6.1916.

‡ To 5 Army 7.7.16.

◊ Left Corps in early 7.16.

● Early July.

| ARMY GROUP/ ARMY | CORPS | DIVISIONS |
|---|---|---|
| BELGIAN | | 1, 2, 3, 4, 5, 6 ID 1 CD 2 CD* |
| B.E.F.† | I | 1, 12, 15, 16, 40 Divs. |
| 1 ARMY | IV | 2, 23, 47, R.N. Divs. |
| | XI | 33, 35, 38, 38, 61 Divs. |
| | Army Reserve | 1 Cav. Div. |
| 2 ARMY | II | 41 Div. |
| | V | 3, 24, 50 Divs. |
| | XIV | Gds, 6, 20 Divs. |
| | I Anzac | 1 Aust., 2 Aust., NZ Divs. |
| | II Anzac | 4 Aust., 5 Aust. Divs. |
| | Canadian | 1, 2, 3 Cdn. Divs. |
| | Army Reserve | 2 Cav. Div. |
| 3 ARMY | VI | 5, 14, 55 Divs. |
| | VII | 37, 46, 56 Divs. |
| | XVII | 25, 51, 60 Divs. |
| | Army Reserve | 1 Ind.Cav.Div. Cdn.Cav.Bde. |
| 4 ARMY | III | 8, 19, 34 Divs. |
| | VIII | 4, 29, 31, 48 Divs. |
| | X | 32, 36, 49 Divs. |
| | XIII | 9, 18, 30 Divs. |
| | XV | 7, 17, 21 Divs. |
| | Army Reserve | 2 Ind.Cav.Div. |
| RESERVE ARMY | – | 3 Cav.Div. |

**SUPPLEMENTARY NOTE**
**Formations serving on the Somme 1.7.1916-18.11.1916**

| | |
|---|---|
| **Armies** | 3rd, 4th, Reserve (formed 23.5.1916, became 5th Army 30.10.1916) |
| **Corps** | II, III, V, VII, VIII, X, XIII, XIV, XV, Canadian, I Anzac |
| **Divisions** | |
| Regular | Guards, 1, 2, 3, 4, 5, 6, 7, 8, 29 (10) |
| Territorial | 46 (N.Midland), 47 (2nd London), 48 (S.Midland), 49 (W.Riding), 50 (Northumbrian), 51 (Highland), 55 (W.Lancashire), 56 (1st London) (8) |
| New Army | 9 (Scottish), 11 (Northern), 12 (Eastern), 14 (Light), 15 (Scottish), 16 (Irish), 17 (Northern), 18 (Eastern),19 (Western), 20 (Light), 21, 23, 24, 25, 30, 31, 32, 33, 34, 35, 36 (Ulster), 37, 38 (Welsh), 39, 40, 41 (26) |
| Naval | 63 (Royal Navy) (2 Bdes. Royal Naval/Royal Marine personnel, 1 Bde. Army personnel) (1) |
| Commonwealth | 1, 2, 4, 5 Australian, New Zealand, 1, 2, 3, 4 Canadian (9) |
| Cavalry | 1 Cavalry, 2 Indian Cavalry (2) |

| ARMY GROUP/ ARMY | CORPS | DIVISIONS |
|---|---|---|
| G.A.N. Gp. d'Armées du Nord | X | 20 ID + 26 ID (14.7.16) |
| | II | 3 ID 4 ID |
| 6 ARMY | XXXV | 121 ID (to 5.7.16) 61 ID 51 ID + 53 ID (4.7.16) 132 ID (10.7.16) |
| | XX | 39 ID 11 ID 153 ID 72 ID ( to 3.7.16) + 47 ID (9.7.16) |
| | I Colonial | 3 DIC 2 DIC 99 ID 16 DIC Div. Marocain + 72 ID (3.7.16) |
| | I Cavalry | 1 CD 3 CD |
| | Army Reserve | 47 ID 121 ID |
| 10 ARMY | XXX | 58 ID 62 ID |
| | Army Reserve | 158 ID 41 ID 132 ID 104 ID |
| 3 ARMY | XIII | 25 ID 120 ID 81 ID |
| | II Colonial | 10 DIC 15 DIC 87 ID |
| | Army Reserve | 26 ID (to 1.7.16) |
| Dunkirk Fortress/ Region | XXXVI | 29 ID |
| G.A.C. Gp. d'Armées du Centre | XIV | 154 ID 28 ID 27 ID 16 ID |
| | III | 6 ID 5 ID |
| 2 ARMY | VII‡ | 48 ID + 41 ID (16.7.16) |
| | XV | 123 ID 126 ID |
| | XXXI | 64 ID 19 ID 65 ID |
| | VI | 12 ID 52 ID◊ 130 ID◊ 127 ID 131 ID 71 ID 128 ID |
| | XI | 21 ID 30 ID 129 ID 151 ID 60 ID |
| | V | 9 ID 10 ID 125 ID |
| | Army Reserve● | 37 ID 55 ID 8 ID |
| 4 ARMY | IV | 7 ID 124 ID + 34 ID (7.7.16) |
| | XXI | 43 ID 13 ID |
| | XVII | 33 ID 34 ID + (from 7.7.16) 100 ID 152 ID 5 CD |
| | IX | 18 ID 17 ID |
| | XVIII | 36 ID 35 ID |
| | Army Reserve● | 8 ID 152 ID 33 ID |
| | II Cavalry | 5 CD 7 CD 100 ID |
| 5 ARMY | XXXVIII | 97 ID 67 ID 56 ID |
| | XXXVII | 22 ID 69 ID |
| | XVI | 32 ID 89 ID 31 ID + 23 ID (5.7.16) |
| | I | 1 ID 2 ID |
| | XII | 23 ID 24 ID |
| | Army Reserves | 48 ID 24 ID |
| G.A.E. Gp. d'Armées de L'Est | VIII | 101 ID 40 ID |
| | XXXIII | 70 ID 77 ID |
| 1 ARMY | Army Reserves | 73 ID + 129 ID (10.7.16) |
| 7 ARMY | XXXIV | 157 ID 133 ID |
| | Army Reserves | 66 ID 46 ID 14 ID 76 ID 63 ID 52 ID |
| D.A.L. Dét. d'Armée de Lorraine | XXXIX | 74 ID 59 ID |
| | XXXII | 42 ID 45 ID |

**Western Front French Army O.O.B. 7.1916 continued**

| ARMY GROUP/ ARMY | CORPS | DIVISIONS |
|---|---|---|
| **D.A.L.continued** | Army Reserves | 88 ID 15 ID |
| | III Cavalry | 8 CD 6 CD |
| *Gouvt. Militaire de Paris* | – | 83 ID 158 ID |
| Divisions Overseas (4) *Armée d'Orient* | – | 156 ID 57 ID 122 ID 17 DIC |

**Note**

This order of battle has been reconstituted from the O.O.B. Volumes of the French Official Histories. The organisation of these volumes makes it difficult to do this for a specific date because of the frequent movement of divisions between Corps and Armies. It should be taken as representing the position in the first seven to ten days in July and there may be some duplication of divisions as a result.

---

### *Table 3.22* German O.O.B. Western Front 30.8.1916

| ARMY GROUP/ ARMY | CORPS | DIVISIONS |
|---|---|---|
| **Coastal Defence Sector** | Marine | 1 Marine Div. 2 Marine Div. |
| **4 ARMY** | – | 3 Gd.ID (being replaced by 206 ID) 204 ID |
| | XXVI Reserve | 52 Res.ID 51 Res.ID 207 ID |
| | – | 4 Ers.D 5 Ers.D |
| | XXIII Reserve | 46 Res.D 45 Res.D (being replaced by XIII Corps below) |
| | XIII | 27 ID 26 ID |
| **Army Group Crown Prince Rupert** | VI Reserve | 12 Res.D 11 Res.D |
| | – | 50 Res.D 6 Bav.Res.D |
| **6 ARMY** | XXVII Reserve | 54 Res.D 53 Res.D (being replaced by XIX Corps below) |
| | XIX | 24 ID 40 ID |
| | IX Reserve | 17 Res.D 18 Res.D |
| | III Bavarian | 5 Bav.ID 23 Res.D 183 ID |
| | IV | 7 ID 8 ID |
| | – | 12 ID + 1 LW Bde. |
| **1 ARMY** | XIV Reserve | 2 Gd.Res.D (replaced by 24 Res.D) 52 ID 26 Res.D |
| Group Marschall | Gd Reserve | 4 Gd.ID 1 Gd.Res.D |
| | II Bavarian | 3 Bav.ID 4 Bav.ID |
| | XII Reserve | 56 ID 111 ID } 1 Bav.Res.D |
| | I Bav. Reserve | 2 Gd.ID 1 Gd.ID } 5 Bav.Res.D |
| **2 ARMY** | IX | 28 ID 17 ID 18 ID Div. Francke 8 Bav.Res.D |
| | XVII | 35 ID 36 ID One strengthened Res.Bde. |
| | Guard | 11 ID 44 Res.D 15 LW D |
| **7 ARMY** | XI | 113 ID 16 Res.D 15 Res.D 208 ID |
| | VIII | 15 ID Div. Dumrath |
| | XVIII | One LW Bde. 25 ID 21 ID 23 ID |
| | Group Kühne | 16 ID 32 ID 47 Res.D |

| ARMY GROUP/ ARMY | CORPS | DIVISIONS |
|---|---|---|
| **Army Group German Crown Prince** | VIII | 58 ID 22 Res.D |
| | III | 5 ID 6 ID 185 ID |
| **3 ARMY** | V Reserve | 9 Res.D 10 Res.D |
| | XIV | 29 ID 28 Res.D |
| **5 ARMY** | X Reserve | 9 LW Div. 7 Res.D 19 Res.D |
| | XVI | 6 Bav.ID + Unidentified Div. |
| | Group Francke | 24 LW Div. 4 ID |
| | Group Höhe | 54 ID 38 ID 304 ID 10 Ers.D |
| | VII | 13 ID 14 ID |
| | VII Reserve | 14 Res.D 13 Res.D 25 Res.D |
| | Alpine | 34 ID 33 ID |
| | XVIII Reserve | 14 Bav.ID 21 Res.D |
| | XV | 50 ID 30 ID 39 ID 192 ID 33 Res.D |
| **Army Detachment Strantz** | – | Bav.Ers.D |
| | V | 10 ID 9 ID 103 ID |
| | I Bavarian | 1 Bav.D 2 Bav.D 5 LW Div. |
| | – | Gd.Ers.D 8 Ers.D |
| **Battle Sector Metz** | – | One LW Bde. |
| **Army Detachment A** | – | 13 LW Div. 1 Bav.LW Div. 19 Ers.D |
| | XV Reserve | One LW Bde. 30 Res.D 39 Bav.Res.D One LW Bde. |
| **Army Detachment B** | – | 6 Bav.LW Div. 12 Bav.ID 12 LW Div. 7 LW Div. 8 LW Div. |
| | | In reserve 187 ID |

---

### *Table 3.23* Allied O.O.B. Western Front 19.3.1917

| ARMY GROUP/ ARMY | CORPS | DIVISIONS |
|---|---|---|
| *Détachment G.A.N. Groupe d'Armées du Nord* | XXXVI | 29 ID 174 Terr.Bde. |
| **BELGIAN ARMY** | | 1, 2, 3, 4, 5, 6 Army Divs. |
| **B.E.F.*** | | |
| **2 ARMY** | VIII | 38, 39, 55 Divs. |
| | X | 23, 41, 47 Divs. |
| | IX | 16, 25, 36 Divs. |
| | II Anzac | 57 (Br.), NZ, 3 Aust.Divs. |
| **1 ARMY** | XI | 5, 56, Port.Div. |
| | I | 6, 21, 24, 37 Divs. |
| | Canadian | 1, 2, 3, 4 Cdn.Divs. |
| | Army Reserve | 1 CD |
| **3 ARMY** | XVII | 9, 34, 51 Divs. |
| | VII | 14, 30, 46 Divs. |
| | VI | 3, 12, 15 Divs. |
| | XVIII | 49, 58 Divs. |
| | XIX (in Reserve) | Corps Troops only |
| | Army Reserve | 3 CD 2 CD |

* Divisional Allocation: The German source this O.B. was taken from did not include divisions allocated to Corps. The divisions we have given are believed to be valid in early March 1917.

| ARMY GROUP/ARMY | CORPS | DIVISIONS |
|---|---|---|
| **B.E.F. (continued)** **5 ARMY** | V | 7, 11, 19, 62 Divs. |
| | II | 2, 17, 18, 63 Divs. |
| | I Anzac | 1, 2, 4, 5 Aust.Divs. |
| | Reserve XIII | 31 Div. |
| | Army Reserve | 5 CD |
| **4 ARMY** | XIV | Gds. 20, 29 Divs. |
| | XV | 4, 8, 33, 40 Divs. |
| | III | 1, 48, 50, 59 Divs. |
| | IV | 32, 35, 61 Divs. |
| | H.Q. Cavalry | Divs. allocated to various Armies |
| | Army Reserve | 4 CD |
| **FRENCH ARMIES** **G.A.N.** *Groupe d'Armées du Nord* | X | 28, 19, 20 ID |
| | I Colonial | 3 Col.ID 2 Col.ID 45, 154 ID |
| | (in reserve) XIV | 62, 27 ID |
| **3 ARMY** | (in reserve) XVIII | 35, 36 ID |
| | Army Reserve | Moroccan Div. |
| | Direct Control Army | 1 Cav.D |
| **1 ARMY** | XXXV | 120, 61, 121 ID |
| | XXXIII | 81 DIT 70, 77 ID |
| | (in reserve) XIII | 25, 26, 53 ID, 87 DIT |
| | Army Reserve | 56 ID |
| | Direct Control Army | 3 Cav.D |
| **G.A.R.** *Groupe d'Armées du Réserve* | XXXVII | 127, 158 ID |
| | VI | 12, 166 ID |
| **6 ARMY** | II Colonial | 15 Col.ID, 10 Col.ID |
| | (in reserve) XX | 39, 153 ID |
| | (in reserve) XI | 22 ID |
| | Army Reserve | 21, 38 ID, 97 DIT |
| **5 ARMY** | I | 51, 2, 1 ID |
| | V | 10, 125 ID |
| | XXXII | 69, 42, 165 ID |
| | VII | 14, 41 ID, Russian Bde. |
| | XXXVIII | 37, 151 ID |
| | Group Baquet | 89 DIT |
| | Army Reserve | 162, 9, 40 ID |
| **10 ARMY** Organising | | 2, 4, 7 Cav.Divs. |
| **G.A.C.** *Groupe D'Armees du Centre* | XVII | 34, 33, 15 ID |
| | XII | 23, 60, 24 ID |
| **4 ARMY** | VIII | 169, 16 ID |
| | (in reserve) IX | 18, 17, 152 ID |
| | Army Reserve | 133, 71 ID |
| **2 ARMY** | XXXI | 65, 64 ID |
| | XVI | 132, 31 ID |
| | XV | 55, 126, 123 ID |
| | XXX | 72, 128, 163 ID |
| | IV | 59, 8, 63 ID |
| | Army Reserve | 124, 32, 74 ID |

| ARMY GROUP/ARMY | CORPS | DIVISIONS |
|---|---|---|
| **G.A.E.** *Groupe d'Armées de L'Est* | Unattached | 130 ID |
| | XXXIX | 67, 48, 88 ID |
| **8 ARMY** | Unattached | 68, 167, 6 ID |
| | XXXX | 73, 5, 7 ID |
| | (in reserve) II | 3, 4 ID |
| | Army Reserve | 131, 168, 11 ID |
| **7 ARMY** | Unattached | 129, 161, 52, 157 ID |
| | XXXIV | 134, 47, 13, 43, 58 ID |
| | (in reserve) XXI | 170 ID |
| | Army Reserve | 66, 164, 46 ID, 5, 6 Cav.Div. |

### *Table 3.24* German O.O.B. Western Front 19.3.1917

| ARMY GROUP/ARMY | SECTOR/CORPS | DIVISIONS |
|---|---|---|
| **Army Group Kronprinz Rupprecht** **4 ARMY** | Gr.North/Marine | 1 Mar. 2 Mar.Divs 20 LW Div. |
| | Gr.Ypres/IX Reserve | 19 LW 21 LW 17 Res. 207, 18 Res.Divs. |
| | Gr.Wytschaete/XIX | 204, 24, 40 Divs. |
| | Army Reserve | 185, 208, 2 Divs.$^2/_3$ 2 Cav.Div |
| **6 ARMY** | II Bavarian | 4 Bav. 3 Bav.Divs. 38 LW Bde. |
| | III Bavarian | 5 Bav. 6 Bav. 6 Bav.Res.Divs. |
| | IV | 7, 8 Divs. |
| | VI Reserve | 11 Res., 16 Bav.Divs. |
| | I Bav. Reserve | 79 Res., 1 Bav.Res.Divs. |
| | XII | 24 Res., 23 Res., 220 Divs. |
| | Army Reserve | 49 Res., 80 Res.Divs. |
| **1 ARMY** | A/XIV Reserve | 26 Res., 2 Gd.Res.Divs. |
| | B/Guard Reserve | 38, 4 Ersatz, 4 Gd., 50 Res.Divs. |
| | | 1 Gd.Res.Div. – moving to 6 Army |
| | C/XIII | 9 Res., 22 Res., 199, 26 Divs. |
| | Army Reserve | 27 Div. |
| **2 ARMY** | O/VIII Reserve | 29, 111 Divs. |
| | P/XVIII | 221, 25 Divs. |
| | Q/XVII | 11, 35, 36 Divs. 15 Res.Div. |
| | R/Guard | 44 Res., 47 LW Divs. |
| | | 23 Div. – moving to 3 Army; 15 LW Div. – moving to E.Front |
| | Army Reserve | 2 Gd.Div., 56 Div. – moving to 6 Army |
| **Army Group Reserves** | In Belgium | 233 (new) Div., 7, 6 Cav.Divs. |
| | | 12 Res.Div. – moving to VI Reserve |
| | IX | 18, 17 Divs. |
| | | 14 Bav.Div. – moving to XII Reserve |
| | | 32 Div. – moving to 3 Army |
| | | 2 Cyclist Bde., $^1/_3$ 2 Cav.Div. |
| **Army Group Deutsche Kronprinz** | Gp K/XXIII Reserve | 46 Res., 13 LW Divs. |
| | Gp P/XI | 211, 222, 25 LW, 183 Divs. |
| **7 ARMY** | Gp L/GKDO 54 | 16 Res., 19 Res.Divs., 5 Gd.Divs. |

**Western Front German O.O.B. 19.3.1917 continued**

| ARMY GROUP/ ARMY | SECTOR/CORPS | DIVISIONS |
|---|---|---|
| 7 ARMY continued | Gp H/XV Bav. Res. | Bav.Ersatz, 9 Bav.Res.Divs. |
| | Gp E/X Reserve | 10 Res., 21, 43 Res.Divs. |
| | Army Reserve | 213, 20, 235(new), 4 Divs. |
| | | 235(new)Div. – moving to 2 Army |
| 3 ARMY | VII Reserve | 19, 223 Divs., 13 Res.Div. |
| | XIV | 14 Res., 214, 212 Divs. |
| | XII | 30, Gd.Ers.Divs., 54 Res.Div. |
| | XXVI Reserve | 52 Res., 51 Res., 39 Divs. |
| | XVI | 9 LW, 227, 33 Divs. |
| | Army Reserve | 34 Div. |
| 5 ARMY | VII | 2 LW, 28 Res., 13, 14 Divs. |
| | V Reserve | 103, 7 Res., 28 Divs. |
| | Vaux/XVIII Reserve | 10 Ers., 192, 19 Ers.Divs. |
| Army Det. C | V | 8 LW, 9, 10 Divs. |
| | I Bavarian | 2 Bav., 1 Bav., 5 LW Divs. |
| | – | 54 Div. |
| | – | 8 Ers.Div., 44 LW Bde. |
| Army Group Reserves (North-to-South) | 4 Army Area | 1 Gd, 45 Res., 5 Bav.Res.Divs. |
| | 3 Army Area | 239(new), 15 Bav.(new), 50 Divs. |
| | 5 Army Area | 58 Div. – moving to 3 Army, 25 Res.Div. |
| | Army Det.C Area | 41 Div. |
| Army Group Herzog Albrecht v. Württemberg | Abschnitt III/Metz | } Div.Kdo. 255 with 31 LW Bde. |
| | Abschnitt IV/Metz | |
| | Gen.Kdo. 65 | 21 Res., 206 Divs. |
| Army Det. A | Gen.Kdo. 63 Bav. | 1 Bav.LW, 3 Gd.Divs. |
| | Gen.Kdo. 59 | 219, 7 LW Divs. |
| | Army Reserve | 242(new) Div. |
| Army Det. B | XV | 84 LW Bde., 30 Bav.Res., 39 Bav.Res.Divs., 61 LW Bde. |
| | Gen.Kdo. 64 | 6 Bav. LW, 12 LW Divs. |
| | X | 26 LW, 113 Divs. |
| | III | 52, 37 Divs. |
| | Army Reserve | Div. Staff 301 |
| Army Group Reserves | Army Det. A Area | 187, 33 Res.Divs. |
| | Army Det. B Area | 11 Bav., 6, 5 Divs. |

## Table 3.25 Allied O.O.B. Western Front 20.6.1917

| ARMY GROUP/ ARMY | CORPS | DIVISIONS |
|---|---|---|
| 1 (French) ARMY | XV(British) | 1 Br.Div., 32 Br.Div., 66 Br.Div |
| | XXXVI | 29 ID 133 ID |
| | I | No Divisions assigned |
| BELGIAN ARMY | | 1, 2, 3, 4, 5, 6 Divs. 1, 2 Cav.Divs. |
| B.E.F. | XIV | Gd.Div., 38 Div. |
| 5 ARMY | XVIII | 39 Div. 51 Div. |
| | XIX | 55 Div. ½ 15 Div. |

| ARMY GROUP/ ARMY | CORPS | DIVISIONS |
|---|---|---|
| 5 ARMY continued | II | 8 Div. 30 Div. |
| | Army Reserve | H.Q. VIII + 11 Div. 16 Div. |
| 2 ARMY | X | 24 Div. 41 Div. |
| | IX | 36 Div. |
| | II Australian | 2 Aust.Div. N.Z.Div. |
| | Army Reserves | 19, 23, 37, 47 Divs., 4 Aust.Div. |
| 1 ARMY | XI | 57 Div. 49 Div. Port.Div. 2 Div. |
| | I | 6 Div. 46 Div. |
| | Canadian | 4 Cdn., 3 Cdn., 1 Cdn.Divs. |
| | XIII | 5 Div. 31 Div. |
| | Army Reserves | 25 Div. 63 Div. 1 CD 2 Cdn.Div. Port.Div. + En route to 5 Army ½ 15 Div. |
| 3 ARMY | XVII | 17 Div. 4 Div. |
| | VI | 12 Div. 56 Div. |
| | VII | 50 Div. 33 Div. |
| | V | 7 Div. |
| | IV | 20 Div. 48 Div. |
| | Army Reserves | 3, 9, 14, 18, 21, 29, 34, 58, 61, 62 Divs. |
| 4 ARMY | III | 42 Div. 59 Div. 40 Div. 35 Div. |
| | Cavalry | 3, 2, 4, 5 Cav.Divs. |
| | Army Reserves | I Aust.Corps – 1, 2, 5 Aust.Divs. |
| G.A.N. *Groupe d'Armées du Nord* | XIII | 120 ID 26 ID 25 ID |
| | XXXV | 121 ID 61 ID 53 ID |
| 3 ARMY | I Cavalry | 8 CD 3 CD 5 CD 70 ID |
| | Army Res. XI | 21 ID 22 ID |
| 6 ARMY | XXXVII | 62 ID |
| | XXI | 13 ID 170 ID 43 ID |
| | XXXIII | 129 ID 77 ID |
| | III | 5 ID |
| | XIV | 28 ID 27 ID 87 ID 38 ID |
| | Army Reserve | 6 ID 81 ID 158 ID 166 ID |
| 10 ARMY | IX | 164 ID 154 ID 18 ID |
| | V | 47 ID 10 ID 125 ID |
| | Army Res. XVIII | No Divisions assigned |
| | Army Reserve | 1, 2, 9, 17, 51, 66, 162 ID |
| G.A.C. *Groupe d'Armées du Centre* | XXXVIII | Div. Marocain 46 ID 152 ID |
| | VII | 45 ID 6 CD 14 ID |
| 5 ARMY | II Cavalry | 151 ID 2 CD 4 CD 7 CD |
| | Army Res. XXXIV | 157 ID |
| | Army Reserve | 167 ID |
| 4 ARMY | X | 59 ID 132 ID |
| | XVII | 55 ID 134 ID |
| | XII | 60 ID 23 ID 41 ID |
| | VIII | 15 ID 48 ID 169 ID |
| | XXXII | 40 ID 42 ID 69 ID 165 ID |
| Army Reserves: { | II | 3 ID 4 ID |
| | – | 8, 24, 71, 72, 74, 124, 128 ID |

* Territorial units.

| ARMY GROUP/ ARMY | CORPS | DIVISIONS |
|---|---|---|
| G.A.C. continued 2 ARMY | XXXI | 65 ID 64 ID |
| | XVI | 97 ID 32 ID 31 ID |
| | XV | 126 ID 123 ID 20 ID |
| | XXX | 19 ID 131 ID |
| | IV | 34 ID Gp. Balagny* 33 ID |
| | Army Reserves | 16 ID 163 ID 73 ID |
| G.A.E. *Groupe d'Armées de L'Est* | – | 130 ID |
| | XXXIX | 67 ID 88 ID 2 Territorial Bdes. |
| 8 ARMY | – | 37 ID |
| | II Colonial | 15 DIC 10 DIC |
| Army Reserves: { | XX | 11 ID 39 ID 153 ID |
| | – | 7 ID 68 ID 168 ID |
| 7 ARMY | – | 12 ID |
| | – | 63 ID |
| | – | 161 ID |
| | – | 52 ID |
| | I Colonial | 2 DIC 3 DIC 1 Territorial Bde. 1 Colonial Bde. |
| Army Reserves: { | VI | 56 ID 127 ID |
| | – | 35 ID 36 ID 58 ID |
| | H.Q.XXXX | No Divisions assigned |

### Table 3.26 German O.O.B. Western Front 20.6.1917

| ARMY GROUP/ ARMY | GROUP/CORPS | DIVISIONS |
|---|---|---|
| Army Group Crown Prince Rupert | North/Marine | 1, 3, 2 Marine Divs. |
| | Dixmude/XIV | 20 LW Div. 19 LW Div. 49 Res.D. |
| 4 ARMY | Ypres/III Bavarian | 80 Res.D. 233 ID 17 ID |
| | Wytschaete/IX Res. | 119 ID 195 ID 24 ID 11 ID 207 ID |
| | Lille/II Bavarian | 22 Res.D 16 Bav.ID 9 Res.D |
| G.H.Q. Reserves: { | | 199 ID 23 Res.D 50 Res.D 221 ID 38 ID 12 ID 18 Res.D |
| | | 16 ID 2 Gd.Res.D 4 Bav.ID |
| | | 2 CD |
| | Group Ghent/ XII Reserve | 40 ID 10 Bav.ID |
| 6 ARMY | Aubers/XIX | 38 Res.D 79 Res.D 1 Bav.Res.D |
| | Loos/IV | 185 ID 8 ID |
| | Gouchez/VI Reserve | 56 ID 11 Res.D 4 Gd.ID |
| | Vimy/I Bav. Res. | 6 Bav.ID 5 Bav.ID 238 ID |
| | Arras/XIV Reserve | 26 ID 17 Res.D 236 ID 220 ID |
| | Quéant/Gd. Reserve | 26 Res.D 3 Gd.ID |
| | G.H.Q. Reserves | 36 ID 6 Bav.Res.D 1 Gd.Res.D |
| 2 ARMY | Cambrai/IX | 121 ID 18 ID |
| | Caudry/XIII | 27 ID 3 Res.D 111 ID |
| | Quentin/XVIII | 234 ID 12 Res.D 235 ID |
| | Oise/XVII | 208 ID 13 LW Div. |
| | G.H.Q. Reserves | 35 ID 25 ID |

| ARMY GROUP/ ARMY | GROUP/CORPS | DIVISIONS |
|---|---|---|
| Army Group German Crown Prince 7 ARMY | Trépy/Gen.Kdo.54 | 113 CD 211 ID 78 Res.D |
| | Bailly/XI | 50 ID 103 ID 46 Res.D 10 ID rep. by 47 Res.D |
| | Liesse/XXXIX Res. | 37 ID 13 ID 1 Bav.ID rep. by 14 ID |
| | Sissonne/Gen.Kd.65 | 15 ID 41 ID 15 Bav.ID 9 ID |
| 1 ARMY | Aisne/Guard | 243 CD 227 ID |
| | Brimont/X Reserve | 39 ID 34 ID 239 ID |
| | Reims/VII Reserve | 242 ID 13 Res.D 14 Res.D 4 ID |
| | Prosnes/III | 231 ID 19 ID 7 Res.D 23 ID |
| | G.H.Q. Reserves | 32 ID 21 Res.D 187 ID 43 Res.D 2 Bav.ID |
| | | Leaving the front – 52 Res.D |
| 3 ARMY | Pu/XII | 30 CD 54 ID 54 Res.D |
| | Dormoise/XXVI Reserve | 51 Res.D 20 ID 214 ID |
| | Argonne/XVI | 9 LW Div. 2 Gd.ID 1 Gd.ID 33 ID |
| | G.H.Q. Reserve | 29 ID |
| 5 ARMY | VII | 2 LW Div. 10 Res.D 6 Res.D |
| | V Reserve | 28 Res.D 228 ID 28 ID |
| | Vaux Sector/ XVIII Reserve | 192 ID 19 Ers.D |
| | G.H.Q. Reserves | 25 Res.D 213 ID 48 Res.D 3 Bav.ID |
| Army Group Duke Albert Army Det.C | V | 8 LW Div. 45 Res.D 44 Res.D |
| | I Bavarian | 5 Bav.Res.D Bav.Ers.D 5 LW Div. |
| | XXIII Reserve | Gd.Ers.D 10 Ers.D |
| | G.H.Q. Reserve | 5 ID 36 Res.D |
| Army Det.A | Metz Govt. | 44 LW Div. 31 LW Bde. 255 ID |
| | XV Bavarian Res. | 30 Bav.Res.D 9 Bav.Res.D |
| | Gen.Kdo.63 | 1 Bav.LW Div. 33 Res.D |
| | Gen.Kdo.59 | 219 ID 6 CD |
| | G.H.Q. Reserve | 206 ID 204 ID 7 ID |
| Army Det.B | XV | 84 LW Bde. 301 ID 39 Bav.Res.D 61 LW Bde. |
| | Gen.Kdo.64 | 6 Bav.LW Div. 7 CD |
| | X | 26 LW Div. Alpenkorps |
| | VIII Reserve | 240 ID 25 LW Div. |
| | G.H.Q. Reserve | 183 ID 6 ID 16 Res.D |

## Table 3.27 Schematic O.O.B. Allied Armies Western Front 21.3.1918**

| ARMY GROUP/ARMY | DIVISIONS AT FRONT & IMMEDIATE RESERVE | ARMY RESERVES | TOTAL |
|---|---|---|---|
| BELGIAN | 10 | 2 + 1 Cavalry | 12 + 1 Cavalry |
| B.E.F.<br>2 ARMY (4 ARMY redesignated 17.3.18) | 12 | 2 | 14 |
| 1 ARMY | 12 + 2 Portuguese | 2 | 16 |
| 3 ARMY | 14 | 2 | 16 |
| 5 ARMY | 12 + 3 Cavalry | 2 | 14 + 3 Cavalry |
| TOTAL B.E.F. | 50 + 2 Port. + 3 Cavalry | 8 | 60 + 3 Cavalry |
| FRENCH ARMIES<br>G.A.N. Groupe d'Armées du Nord<br>6 ARMY | 10 | 4 | 14 |
| 5 ARMY | 9 | – | 9 |
| 4 ARMY | 18 | 1 | 19 |
| TOTAL G.A.N. | 37 | 5 | 42 |
| G.A.E. Groupe d'Armées de L'Est<br>2 ARMY | 18 + 1 American | – | 19 |
| 1 ARMY | 8 + 1 American | – | 9 |
| 8 ARMY | 7 + 1 American | 4 | 12 |
| 7 ARMY | 12 | 4 | 16 |
| TOTAL G.A.E. | 45 + 3 American | 8 | 56 |
| G.H.Q. RESERVES | | 5 + 1 American | 6 |
| | | 6 Cavalry | 6 Cavalry |
| TOTAL FRENCH ARMIES | 82 + 3 American | 18 + 1 American + 6 Cavalry | 104 + 6 Cavalry |

**
1. American Army. The 4 Divisions available at this date were allocated to French Commands.
2. Two French Dismounted Cavalry Divisions are included in the Infantry totals.
3. A further 10 French and 5 British Divisions were on the Italian Front.

## Table 3.28 German O.O.B. Western Front Offensive 21.3.1918

| ARMY GROUP/ARMY | CORPS | DIVISIONS/OPERATION NAME | | |
|---|---|---|---|---|
| | | 1st LINE | 2nd LINE | 3rd LINE |
| ARMY Gp. CROWN PRINCE RUPERT | | "MARS" | | |
| 17 ARMY | I Bavarian Reserve | 240 ID | | |
| | | 5 Bav.Res.D | 187 ID | |
| | III Bavarian | 185 ID | | 2 Gd.ID* 12 ID* |
| | IX Reserve | 236 ID | 26 Res.D | 26 ID* |
| | | "MICHAEL I" | | |
| | XVIII | 234 ID | | |
| | | 221 ID | 6 Bav.ID | |
| | | 111 ID | 2 Gd.Res.D | 239 ID† |
| | VI Reserve | 17 ID | 1 Gd.Res.D | 24 ID† |
| | | 195 ID | 5 Bav.ID | |
| | XIV Reserve | 16 Bav.ID | | |
| | | 20 ID | 39 ID | |
| | | 3 Gd.ID | | |
| | XI | 119 ID | | |
| | | 24 Res.D | | |
| | | 53 Res.D | | |
| | No. of Divisions | 15 | 7 | 5 |
| | Summary | 27 Divs.   2,234 guns   1,197 mortars   c. 380 aircraft | | |
| | | "SCHEIN-ANGRIFF" | | |
| 2 ARMY | XXXIX Reserve | 16 Res.D | | |
| | | 21 Res.D | | |

* Division in G.H.Q. Reserve.

† Division in Army Reserve.

† Division in Army Reserve.

* Division in G.H.Q. Reserve.

| ARMY GROUP/ARMY | CORPS | DIVISIONS/OPERATION NAME | | |
|---|---|---|---|---|
| | | 1st LINE | 2nd LINE | 3rd LINE |
| **ARMY Gp. CROWN PRINCE RUPERT** continued | | "MICHAEL II" | | |
| **2 ARMY** continued | XIII | 107 ID | 54 Res.D† | 3 Marine Div.† |
| | | 27 ID | | |
| | | 183 ID | | |
| | XXIII Reserve | 79 Res.D | 9 Res.D† | 199 ID† |
| | | 50 Res.D | 13 ID | |
| | | 18 ID | | |
| | | (9 Bav.Res.D withdrawn) | | |
| | XIV | 25 ID | 1 ID | 228 ID† |
| | | 4 Gd.ID | | 243 ID* |
| | 51 Gen.Kdo. | 208 ID | 19 ID | Gd.Ers.D† |
| | **No. of Divisions** | **11** | **5** | **5** |
| | **Summary** | 21 Divs. | 1,751 guns     1,080 Mortars | c. 340 aircraft |
| **ARMY Gp. GERMAN CROWN PRINCE** | | "MICHAEL III" | | |
| **18 ARMY** | III | 113 ID | 6 ID | |
| | | 88 ID | 206 ID | 23 ID† |
| | | 28 ID | 5 ID | 51 Res.D* |
| | IX | 50 ID | 231 ID | 1 Gd.ID† |
| | | 45 Res.D | 5 Gd.ID | |
| | XVII | 238 ID | 9 ID | 10 Res.D† |
| | | 36 ID | 10 ID | 7 Res.D† |
| | | 1 Bav.ID | | |
| | IV Reserve | 34 ID | | |
| | | 37 ID | 33 ID | |
| | | 103 ID | | |
| | H.Q. 13 LW Div. | 13 LW Div. | | |
| | | 47 Res.D | 211 ID | |
| | **No.of Divisions** | **13** | **9** | **5** |
| | **Summary** | 27 Divs. | 2,623 guns     1,257 Mortars | c. 350 aircraft |
| | **SUMMARY 17, 2, 18 ARMIES** | **76 Divs.** | **6,608 guns     3,354 Mortars** | **c. 1,070 aircraft** |

### Table 3.29 Allied O.O.B. Western Front 11.11.1918

| ARMY GROUP/ARMY | CORPS | DIVISIONS |
|---|---|---|
| *G.A. de Flandres* BELGIAN ARMY | | 1-12 ID (The former 1-6 Army Divisions reorganised in 12 smaller divisions.) |
| *Armée Francais de Belgique* (6 FRENCH ARMY) | XXXIV | 11 ID 5 ID 1(U.S.)ID |
| | VII | 41 ID 164 ID |
| | XXX | 12 ID 132 ID |
| | Attached | 70 ID 77 ID 128 ID |
| **2 (BRITISH) ARMY** | II | 9 Div. 34 Div. |
| | X | 29 Div. 30 Div. |
| | XV | 14 Div. 36 Div. 40 Div. |
| | XIX | 31 Div. 35 Div. 41 Div. |
| **B.E.F.** **5 ARMY** | I | 15, 16, 58 Divs. |
| | III | 55, 74 Divs. |
| | XI | 47, 57, 59 Divs. |
| | Portuguese | 1 Port.Div. 2 Port.Div. |
| **1 ARMY** | VII | No Divs. assigned |
| | VIII | 8, 12, 49, 52 Divs. |
| | XXII | 4, 11, 51, 56, 63 (R.N.) Divs. |

| ARMY GROUP/ARMY | CORPS | DIVISIONS |
|---|---|---|
| **1 ARMY** continued | Canadian | 1, 2, 3, 4 Cdn.Divs. |
| **3 ARMY** | IV | 5, 37, 42, N.Z. Divs. |
| | V | 17, 21, 33, 38 Divs. |
| | VI | Gds., 2, 3, 62 Divs. |
| | XVII | 19, 20, 24, 61 Divs. |
| **4 ARMY** | IX | 1, 6, 32, 46 Divs. |
| | XIII | 18, 25, 50, 66 Divs. |
| | Australian | 1, 2, 3, 4, 5 Aust.Divs. |
| **Unattached** L of C | Cavalry | 1, 2, 3 Cav.Divs. |
| | | 39 Div. |
| | Tk Corps | H.Q. and 6 Bdes. |
| **FRENCH ARMIES** G.A.R. *Groupe d'Armées de Réserve* | XXXI | 33 ID 166 ID |
| | XXXVI | 133 ID 166 ID |
| | XV | 123 ID 51 ID |
| **1 ARMY** | VIII | 58 ID 37 ID |
| | XX | 153 ID 47 ID 168 ID |
| | Attached | 169, 126, 15, 35, 66, 34, 64, 46, 33, 152, 67 IDs. |
| **3 ARMY** | XVI | 32 ID 17 ID 59 ID |
| | XVIII | 59 ID |

**Western Front Allied O.O.B. 11.11.1918 continued**

| ARMY GROUP/ ARMY | CORPS | DIVISIONS |
|---|---|---|
| G.A.R. 3 ARMY continued | XXXV | 121 ID 72 ID 25 ID |
| | Attached | 36, 19, 31, 29 ID |
| G.A.C. Groupe d'Armées du Centre | V | 10 ID 52 ID |
| | XIII | 151 ID 13 ID |
| 5 ARMY | IV | 8 ID |
| | XXI | 62 ID 9 ID 43 ID |
| | Attached | 170, 125, 16, 45, 28, 124, 6, 167 ID 2 Col.ID |
| 4 ARMY | XXXVIII | 71 ID 74 ID 87 ID 42 ID |
| | XI | 62 ID 2 Dismtd.CD |
| | IX | 40 ID 120 ID 48 ID 7 ID |
| | XIV | 22 ID 163 ID |
| | Attached | 134, 53, 21, 14 ID 1 Dismtd.CD |
| AMERICAN EXPEDITIONARY FORCE | V U.S. | 77, 2, 89 U.S.Divs. |
| | III U.S. | 90, 5, 32 U.S.Divs. |
| 1 U.S. ARMY | II(French) Col. | 15(Fr.)Col.ID 79 U.S., 26 U.S., 10(Fr.)Col.ID 81 U.S. |
| | Assigned | 36 U.S., 42 U.S. Divs. |
| | Army Reserve | 1, 3, 6, 29, 80 U.S. Divs. |
| 2 U.S. ARMY | XVII(French) | 33 U.S.Div., 15 Col.ID(Fr.), 10 Col.ID(Fr.) |
| | IV | 28, 7 U.S.Divs., Res.½ 4 U.S.Div. |
| | VI | 92 U.S.Div. |
| | Assigned | ½ 4 U.S.Div., 35 U.S.Div. |
| | Army Reserve | 88 U.S.Div. |
| G.A.E. Groupe d'Armées de L'Est | XXXIII | 10 Col.ID (?) |
| | XXXII | 165 ID 1 Div. Maroc 69 ID |
| 10 ARMY | I CAC | 3 Col.ID |
| | III | 6 ID (?) |
| | Attached | 39, 2, 26, 56, 127, 1, 18, 27, 20 ID |
| 7 ARMY | XL | 68 ID 154 ID 2 Div. Maroc |
| | X | 157 ID 60 ID |
| | I | 162 ID 161 ID |
| | Attached | 38 ID |
| 8 ARMY | VI | 3 ID 73 ID |
| | II | 129 ID 4 ID |
| | Attached | 131 ID |
| At Disposal G.Q.G. | I CC | 3 CD 1 CD 5 CD |
| | II CC | 4 CD 6 CD 2 CD |
| H.Q. 2 ARMY | | No units assigned |
| Military Govt. of Paris | | 15 ID 31 ID |

**Note**

See note at foot of Table 3.21. The same caveat applies to this Table.

*Table 3.30* **Administrative Organisation of American Expeditionary Force at the Armistice 11.11.1918**

| ARMY ALLOCATED | CORPS | DIVISIONS | | | |
|---|---|---|---|---|---|
| 1 ARMY | I | 36 Div. | 78 Div. | 80 Div. | 88 Div. |
| 2 ARMY | II | 27 Div. | 30 Div. | 37 Div. | 91 Div. |
| 3 ARMY | III | 2 Div. | 32 Div. | 42 Div. | |
| 3 ARMY | IV | 1 Div. | 3 Div. | 4 Div. | |
| 1 ARMY | V | 26 Div. | 29 Div. | 82 Div. | |
| 2 ARMY | VI | 7 Div. | 28 Div. | 92 Div. | |
| 3 ARMY | VII | 5 Div. | 89 Div. | 90 Div. | |
| 1 ARMY | VIII | 6 Div. | 77 Div. | 81 Div. | |
| 2 ARMY | IX | 33 Div. | 35 Div. | | |
| Not Assigned to Corps | | 79 Div. | | | |
| With Belgian Army | | 39 Div. | 91 Div. | | |
| Divisions arriving in France | | 8 Div. | 10 Div. | 11 Div. | 12 Div. |
| Depot Divisions (used for Replacements) | | 41 Div. | 83 Div. | | |
| Regional Replacement Depot Divisions | | 40 Div. | 85 Div. | | |
| 7 Cadre Divisions | | 31, 34, 38, 39, 76, 84, 86 Divs. | | | |
| Divisions assigned to Service of Supply Duties | | 87 Div. + 5 Bde.U.S.Marine Corps | | | |
| Coloured Inf. Regts. serving with French | | 369 IR 370 IR | | | |
| With Murmansk Expedition | | 339 IR (from 85 Div.) | | | |
| With Italian Army | | 332 IR (from 83 Div.) | | | |

**NB1** There are marked differences between this organisation and that quoted in the Western Front O.O.B. for 11.11.1918 where the American section is drawn from the official American O.O.B. Volumes for 1 & 2 Armies.
**NB2** 2 Div. includes 4 Bde. U.S.Marine Corps (5 & 6 Marine Regts.)

*Table 3.31* **German O.O.B. Western Front as at 30.10.1918***

| ARMY GROUP/ ARMY | CORPS | DIVISIONS |
|---|---|---|
| Army Group Kronprinz Ruprecht | Marine | 1 Marine, 2 Marine, 38 LW(-), ⅓ 3, 85 LW Divs. |
| 4 ARMY | Guard Reserve | 3 Res.(+⅔ 3), 13 Res., 16 Bav., 36 Res., 11 Bav., 4(+⅓ 31 LW), 16 Res., 23, 3 LW Divs. |
| | Guard | 26, 19, Gd.Ers., 207, 1 Bav.Res., 21, 52 Res.Divs., 6 CDiv. |
| | X Reserve | 49, 23 Res., 11 Res., 56, 6 Bav.Res., 39, 40 Divs. |
| 6 ARMY | LV | 38, 12 Bav., 5 Bav., 4 Ers.(-), 9 Res Divs. |
| | IV | 2 Gd.Res., ⅓ 4 Ers., 36 Divs. |
| | XL Reserve | 16, 8 Divs. |
| | H.Q. XI | No units assigned |
| 17 ARMY | I Bavarian Reserve | 187, 26 Res., 10 Ers., 208 Divs. |
| | II Bavarian | 234, 25 Divs. |
| | XVIII | 220, 35, 6 Divs. |

* This is the last O.B. from German sources we could trace. We have used this in preference to one dated for 11.11.1918 based on Allied Intelligence sources rather than official German records.

| ARMY GROUP/ ARMY | CORPS | DIVISIONS |
|---|---|---|
| **17 ARMY** continued | XIV Reserve | 214, 111, 48 Res., 206, 12, 28 Res.Divs. |
| **2 ARMY** | LIV | 21 Res., 22, 4, 113, 239, 12 Res., Jäger, 185 Divs. |
| | IV Reserve | 14, 58, 18 Res., 30, 44 Res.Divs. |
| | LI | 2 Cyclist Bde., 243, 121, 54, 1 Gd.Res., 22 Res.Divs. |
| | – | 17 Res.Div. |
| **Army Group of Deutscher Kronprinz** | I Bavarian | 19 Res., 29, 15 Res., 200, 204, 34 Divs. |
| | XXVI | 75 Res., 9, 18, 6 Bav.Divs. |
| **18 ARMY** | XVIII Reserve | 231, 238, 81, 2, 1 Res., ²/₃ 82 Res., 5 Res.Divs. |
| | XIV | 232, 237, 11, 221, 105, 87 Divs. |
| | – | 5 Ers.Div. |
| **7 ARMY** | XVII | 24 Res., 86, ¹/₃ 10 Res.Divs. |
| | III | ¹/₃ 10 Res., 26, 227, 3 Marine Divs. |
| | VIII Reserve | 84, 19, 2 Bav., ¹/₃ 10 Res.Divs. |
| | LXV | 5, 4 Gd., 216, 50 Divs. |
| | H.Q. VII | No units assigned |
| | – | 24 Div. – moving to Army Det.A |
| **1 ARMY** | VII Reserve | 1, 50 Res., 8 Bav.Res., 17, parts Gd.Cav. |
| | VI Reserve | 80 Res., Gd.Cav.Divs. |
| | XXIV Reserve | 51 Res., 7 Divs. |
| **3 ARMY** | XXV Reserve | 9 LW, 199, 3 Gd., 1 Gd.Divs. |
| | XVI | 213, 242, 1 Bav.Divs. |
| | I Reserve | 202, 14 Res., 203, 195, 76 Res., 42, 103 Divs. |
| | H.Q. XXXVIII Res. | no units assigned |
| | – | 4 Bav.D moving to Bavaria |
| **Army Group Gallwitz** | LVIII | 240, 15 Bav., 52, 31 Divs. |
| **5 ARMY** | XXI | 13, 28, 107, 5 Bav.Res., 88, 115 Divs. |
| | V Reserve | 123, 1 A-H, parts106 A-H, 228, 192, 41, 27, 117 Divs. |
| | IX Reserve | 1 LW, 15 Divs. |
| | XVIII (A-H) | 33, 32, 106 A-H, 37, 236, 20 Divs. |
| | – | 45 Res.Div. moving to Army Det. C |
| **Army Det. C** | XIII | 5 Gd., 3 Bav., 241 Divs. |
| | V | 13 LW, 94, 35 A-H Divs. |
| | XII Reserve | 5 LW, 224 |
| | LVII | 8 LW, 255 |
| | Group Metz | 31 LW Bde., 10, 18 LW, 2 LW Divs. |
| **Army Group Herzog Albrecht v. Württemberg** | XIX | 84 LW Bde., 48 LW Div. |
| | LXVI | 2 Bav.LW, 19 Ers., 17 Res.Divs. |
| **19 ARMY** | XV | 1 Bav.LW, 83 Divs. |

| ARMY GROUP/ ARMY | CORPS | DIVISIONS |
|---|---|---|
| **Army Det. A** | LIX | 96, 21 LW, 75 Res.Divs. |
| | VII | 82 Comp.Res.Inf.Bde., 301 Div. |
| | XV Bavarian Res. | 39 Bav.Div., 61 LW Bde. |
| | IX (A-H) | 37 A-H, 4 LW Divs. |
| **Army Det. B** | LXIV | 6 Bav.LW, 4 Cav., 7 Cav.Divs. |
| | X | 26 LW, 30 Bav.Res., 31 Divs. |
| | XII | 44 LW, 25 LW Divs. |

## EASTERN FRONT

### Table 3.32 Russian Army O.O.B. 8.1914/9.1914

| ARMY GROUP/ ARMY | CORPS | DIVISIONS |
|---|---|---|
| **Northwest Front** **1 ARMY** | II | 26 ID 43 ID |
| | III | 25 ID 27 ID |
| | IV | 30 ID 40 ID |
| | XX | 28 ID 29 ID |
| | Army Tps | 5 Sch.B 56 Res.ID |
| | Cavalry | 1 Gd.CD 2 Gd.CD 1 CD 2 CD 3 CD |
| *Added by 10.9.1914* | XXVI Reserve | 53, 54, 57, 68, 72, 73, 76 Res.ID |
| **2 ARMY** | I | 22 ID 24 ID |
| | VI | 4 ID 16 ID |
| | XIII | 1 ID 36 ID |
| | XV | 6 ID 8 ID |
| | XXIII | 3 Gd.ID 2 ID |
| | | 1 Sch.Bde. |
| | | 4 CD 6 CD 15 CD |
| *Added by 10.9.1914* | | 59, 77, 79 Res.ID |
| **9 ARMY** | Guard | 1 Gd.ID 2 Gd.ID |
| | I | To 2 Army except 2 Regts. |
| | XVIII | To S.W.Front 25.8.14 |
| | | 5 CD Caucasian CD 3 Bde./1 Gd.CD |
| **10 ARMY** | XXII | 1, 2, 3, 4 Finland Sch.Bdes. |
| | III Siberia | 7, 8 Sib.Sch.Divs. |
| | II Caucasus | Absent |
| | | (1 CD – To 1 Army) |
| **Warsaw Detachment** | XXVII | 59, 77 Res.ID |
| | | (Caucasian CD – To 9 Army) |
| **Southwest Front** **3 ARMY** | IX | 5 ID 42 ID |
| | X | 9 ID 31 ID |
| | XI | 11 ID 32 ID |
| | XXI | 33 ID 44 ID |
| | III Caucasus | To 4 Army |
| | | 58, 69, 78 Res.ID |
| | | 9, 10, 11 CD, 3 Cau.Cossack Div. |

**Russian/Rumanian Fronts Russian Army O.O.B. 8/9.1914 continued**

| ARMY GROUP/ ARMY | CORPS | DIVISIONS |
|---|---|---|
| **4 ARMY** | Guard | 1, 2 Gd.ID (from 9 Army) |
| | Grenadier | 1, 2 Gren.D |
| | (XIV) | Only to 3.9.14, then to 9 Army |
| | XVI | 41 ID 47 ID |
| | III Cauc. | 21 ID 52 ID |
| | | (2 Sch.Bde. only to 3.9.14, then to 9 Army |
| | | (80*), 82, 83 Res.ID |
| | | (8*, 13*, 14* CD), Indep.Gd.Cav. Bdes., 3 Don Coss.Div., Ural Coss.Div. |
| **5 ARMY** | V | 7, 10 ID |
| | XVII | 3, 35 ID |
| | XIX | 17, 38 ID |
| | XXV | 3 Gren.D, 46 ID |
| | | 61, 70, 81† Res.ID |
| | | 55 Res.ID (Probably to I.S. Duties Moscow or Brest-Litovsk, later to N.W.Front) |
| | | 7 CD, Comb.CD (2 & 3 Indep. Cav.Bdes.) |
| **8 ARMY** | VII | 13 ID 34 ID |
| | VIII | 14 ID 15 ID |
| | XII | 12 ID 19 ID |
| | XXIV | 48 ID 49 ID |
| | | 3 & 4 Sch.Bdes. |
| | | 60, 65, 71 Res.ID |
| | | 12 CD, 2 Comb.Cossack Div., 1 Kuban, 2 Kuban, 1 Terek Cossack Divs. |
| **9 ARMY** | XIV | 18 ID 45 ID (4 Army until 3.9.14) |
| | XVIII | 23, 37 ID |
| | | Guard Sch.Bde., 2 Sch.Bde. (4 Army until 3.9.14) |
| | | 75 Res.ID (Fortress of Ivangorod) 80 Res.ID (4 Army until 3.9.14) |
| | | 5 CD 8 CD 13 CD 14 CD (last 3 with 4 Army until 3.9.14) |
| **Other Forces** | | |
| **Rest 6 ARMY (St. Petersburg)** | (XVIII) | To 9 Army |
| | (XXII) | To 10 Army |
| | | 50 ID |
| | | 67, 74, 84 Res.ID |
| | | Orenburg Cossack Div. |
| **Rest 7 ARMY (Odessa)** | | 62, 63, 64 Res.ID |
| | | 2 Cossack Regts. |
| **Not included in Army Organisation** | I Cauc. II Turk I Sib II Sib IV Sib V Sib | 11, 12, 13, 14 Sib.Sch.Divs. 1, 2 Cauc.Sch.Bdes. 6 Turk Sch.Bdes. 55 (see 5 Army) & 66 Res.ID 1, 2 Cauc. Cossack Divs. ½ Turk Cossack Div |

---

### *Table 3.33* German O.O.B. Eastern Front 1.10.1914

| ARMY | CORPS | DIVISIONS |
|---|---|---|
| **8 ARMY** | I | 1 ID 2 ID |
| | I Reserve | 1 Res.D 36 Res.D |
| | | 3 Res.D |
| | | LW Div. Goltz, LW Div. Königsberg |
| | | 3 LW Bdes. 1 Mixed Ers.Bde. |
| | | 1 CD |
| | | Fortresses of Königsberg, Pillau, Lötzen, Thorn, Kurm, Graudenz. Marienburg |
| *Added 12.10.14* | XXV Reserve | 49 Res.D 50 Res.D |
| **9 ARMY** | Gd. Reserve | 3 Gd.ID 1 Gd.Res.D |
| | XI | 22 ID 38 ID |
| | XVII | 35 ID 36 ID |
| | XX | 37 ID 41 ID |
| | Landwehr | 3 LW Div. 4 LW Div. |
| | | 35 Res.D (Thorn) |
| | | LW Div. Bredow (Posen) |
| | | 1 LW Bde. |
| | Higher Cav.Kdo.3 | 8 CD |
| | – | Three LW Bdes. |
| | Fortresses of Posen, Breslau, Glogau | |

\* Only to 3.9.14, then to 9 Army.

† 81 Det. to Fortress of Brest-Litovsk.

---

### *Table 3.34* Russian O.O.B. Eastern Front (Southwest *Front*) 23.1.15‡

| ARMY/ARMY GROUP | CORPS | DIVISIONS |
|---|---|---|
| **Southwest Front** | | |
| **4 ARMY** | (½) XVI | 47 ID |
| | XIV | 45 ID 2 Sch.Bde. 18 ID |
| | III Caucasus | 21 ID 52 ID |
| | Grenadier | 1 Gren.ID 2 Gren.ID |
| | (½) XVI | 41 ID |
| | Army Control | 13 CD Ural Coss. D 1 Transbaikal Coss.Bde. |
| | In Army Group Reserve | 1 Gd.CD 2 Gd.CD |
| **9 ARMY** | XXV | 3 Gren.ID 46 ID 80 ID |
| | XVIII | 23 ID 37 ID |
| | XVII | 83 ID 3 ID 35 ID 75 ID |
| | Army Control | 1 Don Coss.D Indep.Gd.C.Bde. |
| **3 ARMY** | (½) XI | 11 ID |
| | IX | 5 ID 74 ID 42 ID |
| | XXI | 33 ID 44 ID |
| | X | 70 ID 31 ID 61 ID |
| | (½) XI | 32 ID |
| | Army Control | 7 CD 16 CD 3 Don CD 3 Cau.Coss.D |
| **8 ARMY** | XXIV | 49 ID 48 ID |
| | XII | 12 Sib.Sch.D 12 ID 19 ID |

N.B. Please note that in all Russian O.O.B.s the term 'Eastern Front' is used geographically to describe the whole front north of Rumania. The terms North-West, Northern, Western and South-West Fronts refer to indiviual Army Groups, known in Russian as *Fronts*.

‡ This O.B. excludes Russian Militia *Opolchenie* formations. Corps numbered above XXV, Inf. Divs, numbered above 52 and Siberian *Schützen* Divs. numbered above II are Russian units.

| ARMY/ARMY GROUP | CORPS | DIVISIONS |
|---|---|---|
| Southwest Front 8 ARMY continued | VIII | 3 Sch.Bde. 4 Sch.Bde. 14 ID 15 ID |
| | VII | 13 ID 65 ID 34 ID |
| | XXIX | 69 ID 60 ID |
| | Unattached | 78 ID 71 ID |
| | XXX | (Only Landwehr Bdes.) |
| | II Cav. | 12 CD Caucasian Native CD |
| | Army Control | 10 CD 11 CD 2 Comb.Coss.D ½ Orenburg Coss.D 1 Kuban Coss.D |
| | | 2 Kuban Coss.D 1 Terek Coss.D |
| 11 ARMY | XXVIII | 58 ID 81 ID 82 ID |
| | Army Control | 9 CD ½ Orenburg Coss.D |

| ARMY/ARMY GROUP | CORPS | DIVISIONS |
|---|---|---|
| 5 ARMY | I | 22 ID 24 ID |
| | IV | 40 ID 30 ID |
| | XXIII | 3 Gd.ID ½ 2 ID 62 ID 1 Sch.Bde. |
| | XIX | 17 ID 38 ID |
| | V | 7 ID 10 ID |
| | Army Control | 5 Don Coss.D |

* 5 Divisions from 1 Army, 2 Divisions from 5 Army, 2 Divisions from Army Group Reserve *viz*
  from 1 Army   VI Siberian, 55 ID, 14 Sib.Sch.D, 3 Sib.Sch.D, 13 Sib.Sch.D, 67 ID
  from 5 Army   Comb.ID of I & IV Corps
  from Army Group Reserve
      XXVII, 63 ID, 76 ID

### Table 3.35 Russian O.O.B. Eastern Front (Northwest *Front*) 8.2.1915

| ARMY/ARMY GROUP | CORPS | DIVISIONS |
|---|---|---|
| Northwest Front 10 ARMY | III | 56 ID 73 ID |
| | XX | 27 ID 29 ID 53 ID 28 ID |
| | XXVI | 84 ID 64 ID |
| | III Siberian | 8 Sib.Sch.D 7 Sib.Sch.D 57 ID |
| | Army Control | 1 CD 3 CD 1 Indep.C.Bde. |
| | Independent | ½ 68 ID (the other ½ 68 ID was u/c Mil.Dist.Dunaberg |
| 12 ARMY | I Turkestan | 11 Sib.Sch.D 1, 2 Turk.Sch.Bdes. |
| | – | 5 Sch.Bde. |
| | IV Siberian | 9 Sib.Sch.D 10 Sib.Sch.D |
| | – | 77 ID ½ 2 ID |
| | I Cavalry | 6, 8, 15 CD |
| | Cav.Corps Erdeli | 14 CD 4 Don Coss.D |
| | – | 4 CD 4 Indep.C.Bde. Ussuri Mtd. Bde. Turk Coss.Bde. |
| 1 ARMY | V Siberian | 50 ID 79 ID 6 Sib.Sch.D |
| | II | 26 ID 43 ID |
| | II Caucasus | Cauc.Gren.Div. 51 ID 1 Cauc.Sch. Bde. |
| | – | 3 Turk.Sch.Bde. |
| | I Siberian | 1 Sib.Sch.D 2 Sib.Sch.D |
| | Army Control | Cauc.CD Comb.Gd.Coss.D |
| 2 ARMY* | VI | 55 ID 59 ID 14 Sib.Sch.D 25 ID 3 Sib.Sch.D 4 ID 13 Sib.Sch.D |
| | VI Siberian | 16 ID 67 ID |
| | II Siberian | 5 Sib.Sch.D 4 Sib.Sch.D |
| *from Army Group Reserve* | XXVII | 63 ID 76 ID |
| | – | 1 Comb.ID of I Corps, 1 Comb.ID of IV Corps (both from 5 Army) |
| *in Army Group Reserve* | Guard | 1 Gd.ID 2 Gd.ID Gd.Sch.Bde. |
| | Army Control | 2 CD 5 CD |

### Table 3.36 German O.O.B. Eastern Front 8.2.1915

| ARMY GROUP/ ARMY | CORPS | DIVISIONS |
|---|---|---|
| Supreme Command East *Oberbefehlshabers Ost* | Tilsit Command | Minor Units (4Bns.3Sqns.4½Btys.) |
| | At Army Disposal | 5 Gd.Inf.Bde. (reinf.) 1 CD (reinf.) 16 LW Div. |
| 10 ARMY | XXI | 31 ID 42 ID |
| | XXXIX Reserve | 78 Res.D 77 Res.D |
| | XXXVIII Reserve | 76 Res.D 75 Res.D |
| 8 ARMY | At Army Disposal | 10 LW Div. 3 Res.D 1 LW Div. |
| | I | 2 ID 11 LW Div. |
| | XL Reserve | 79 Res.D 80 Res.D |
| | – | 3 Cav.Bde. L St.Ftr.Gd.Detachment (3½ Bn. 1 Sqn.) |
| Army Det. Gallwitz | Gp. Scholz | 37 ID L St.Gp. Goslich |
| | | Corps Zastrow (Div. Wernitz, Div. Breugel, Bde. Pfeil) |
| | | 2 CD |
| | | 41 ID |
| | | 1 Gd.Res.Div. |
| | | Corps Dickhuth (Thorn) (17 Bn. 3 Sqns. 11 Btys.) |
| 9 ARMY | Gp. Beseler | 21 mixed LW Bde. 3 CD (A-H) Tp. Abteilung Westernhagen III Reserve (5, 6 Res.D) |
| | Corps Fabeck (Gen.Kdo. XIII) | 26 ID 25 Res.D |
| | XVII | 35 ID 36 ID |
| | Corps Morgen (Gen.Kdo. I Res.) | 4 ID 49 Res.D 1 Res.D 36 Res.D |
| Gp. Scheffer | XI | 22 ID 38 ID |
| | XXV Reserve | 50 Res.D 8 CD |
| Gp. Frommel | Corps Posen | 23 Bns. 5 Sqn. 12 Btys. (Brigade size formation) |
| | | Div. Menges (Landwehr & Ersatz units) |
| | | 3 ID |
| | Higher Cav. Kdo. 1 | 6 CD 9 CD |

**Table 3.37** Austro-Hungarian O.O.B. Eastern Front 23.1.1915

| ARMY/ARMY GROUP | CORPS | DIVISIONS |
|---|---|---|
| ARMY WOYRSCH (G) | Gallwitz | 35 ID 27 ID |
| 2 ARMY | IV | 32 ID 31 ID |
| | XII | 16 ID 35 Res.D(G) |
| | Army Tps. | 3 CD 7 CD 9 CD |
| Army Detachment Woyrsch (G) | Landwehr (G) | 4 LW Div.(G) 3 LW Div.(G) |
| | Unattached | LW Div. Bredow(G) |
| 1 ARMY | II | 25 ID 4 ID |
| | I | 5 ID 46 Sch.D |
| | Group Martiny | 14 ID 106 L St.ID 91 Sch.Bde. 2 CD |
| 4 ARMY | XVII | 121 I.Bde. 41 HID |
| | XIV | 47 Res.D(G) 8 ID 3 ID L St.Group Grzeficki (3 Bns.) |
| | XI | 11 ID 15 ID 30 ID 6 CD |
| | VI (Gp Arz) | 39 HID 12 ID 45 Sch.D |
| | Gp Bartheldy | 38 HID Comb.HID |
| | IX | 13 Sch.D 10 ID 26 Sch.D 11 HCD 5 C.Bde. |
| 3 ARMY | III | 28 ID 22 Sch.D 4 CD |
| | VII | 17 ID 20 HID 1 CD |
| | X | 2 ID 24 ID 34 ID 43 Sch.D |
| | (Group Puhallo) XVIII | 122 Sch.D 101 L St.I.Bde. |
| | V | 37 HID 33 ID |
| | Group Szurmay | 128 L St.I.Bde. 8 CD 7 ID 75 HI.Bde 40 HID 1 L St.Hussar Bde. |
| Army Reserve | XIX | 29 ID |
| SOUTH ARMY (G) | Hofmann | 55 ID 131 I.Bde. 1 ID(G) |
| | XXIV Reserve(G) | 12 L St.Terr.Bde. 48 Res.D(G) 19 ID |
| | Army Control | 3 Gd.ID(G) 5 CD(G) 10 CD |
| Armeegruppe Pflanzer-Baltin | – | Polish Legion 123 L St.I.Bde. Group Bekesi 6 ID 54 ID Group Schreitter |
| En route | XIII | 42 HID 36 ID |
| | | 5 HCD |
| Fortress of Przemysl | | 23 HID 85 Sch.Bde. 93, 97, 108, 111 L St.I.Bdes. |

**Table 3.38** Russian O.O.B. Eastern Front (Southwest Front) 1.5.1915

| ARMY/ARMY GROUP | CORPS | DIVISIONS |
|---|---|---|
| Southwest Front 4 ARMY | XIV | 45 ID 18 ID |
| | XVI | 41 ID 47 ID |
| | Grenadier | 1 Gren.D 2 Gren.D |
| | XXV | 46 ID 3 Gren.D |
| | XXXI | 83 ID 75 ID |

| ARMY/ARMY GROUP | CORPS | DIVISIONS |
|---|---|---|
| 4 ARMY continued | Army Control | 13 CD Ural Coss.D 1 Trans-Baikal Coss.Bde. |
| | (Also) | (4 LW-type Bdes.) |
| 3 ARMY | IX | 5 ID 42 ID 70 ID |
| | X | 31 ID 61 ID 9 ID |
| | XXIV | 49 ID 48 ID |
| | XII | 12 Sib.Sch.D 12 ID 19 ID |
| | XXI | 33 ID 44 ID |
| | XXIX | 3 Sch.Bde. 81 ID (1 Bde. in Army Reserve) |
| | Army Reserve | 63 ID |
| | Army Control | 7, 11, 16 CD 2 Comb.Coss.D 3 Don Coss.D 3 Cauc.Coss.D |
| | (Also) | (5 LW-type Bdes.) |
| In Army Group Reserve | En Route III Caucasus | 21 ID 52 ID |
| 8 ARMY | VIII | 15 ID 35 ID 13 ID |
| | XVII | 14 ID 3 ID |
| | XXVIII | 23 ID 60 ID |
| | VII | 65 ID 34 ID 69 ID 4 Sch.Bde. |
| | Army Control | 9 CD Orenburg Coss.D |
| | (Also) | (1 LW-type Bde.) |
| 11 ARMY | XXII | 1, 2, 3, 4 Finnish Sch.Bdes. |
| | XVIII | 37 ID 80 ID 58 ID |
| 9 ARMY | XI | 74 ID 11 ID 32 ID |
| | XXX | 71 ID 2 Sch.Bde. |
| | XXXIII | 82 ID Transamur Bdr.Gd.Div. |
| | XXXII | 78 ID Several LW Bdes. |
| | II Cavalry | 12 CD Caucasus Native Mtd.D |
| | III Cavalry | 10 CD 1 Don Coss.D Indep.Gd.C.Bde. |
| | Army Control | 1 Kuban Coss.D 1 Terek Coss.D |

**Table 3.39** Austro-Hungarian O.O.B. Eastern Front 1.5.1915

| ARMY/ARMY GROUP | CORPS | DIVISIONS |
|---|---|---|
| ARMY WOYRSCH (G) | | |
| Armeegruppe Kövess (XII Corps) | | 35 ID 16 ID 9 CD Bde. Goldbach 7 CD |
| Army Detachment Woyrsch (G) | Landwehr(G) | 4 LW Div.(G) 3 LW Div.(G) |
| | | LW Div. Bredow(G) |
| 1 ARMY | II | 25 ID 4 ID 1 Bde. Polish Legion |
| | I | 92 Sch.Bde. 2 CD 46 Sch.D |
| 4 ARMY | – | Div. Stöger-Steiner (23½ Bns. 7 Sqns.) |
| | XIV | 47 Res.D(G) Gp. Morgenstern (8 Bns.) 8 ID 3 ID |
| | IX | 106 L St.Div. 10 ID |
| | – | 31 I.Bde. 11 HCD |

| ARMY/ARMY GROUP | CORPS | DIVISIONS |
|---|---|---|
| **11 ARMY (G)** | Guard(G) | 1 Gd.ID(G) 2 Gd.ID(G) |
| | VI | 39 HID 12 ID |
| | XLI Res.(G) | 81 Res.D(G) 82 Res.D(G) |
| | Kneutzl(G) | 119 ID(G) 11 Bay ID(G) |
| | X(G) | 19 ID (G) 20 ID (G) |
| **3 ARMY** | X | 21 Sch.D 45 Sch.D 2 ID 24 ID |
| | III | 28 ID 26 Sch.D 22 Sch.D |
| | XVII | 11 ID 4 CD 1 Lst.Hussar Bde. |
| | VII | 1 CD 17 ID 20 HID |
| | Beskiden Corps (G) | 4 ID(G) 35 Res.D(G) 35 Res.D(G) |
| **2 ARMY** | XIX | 34 ID 29 ID |
| | VIII | 51 HID 14 ID 41 HID |
| | IV | 13 Sch.D 32 ID 31 ID 43 Sch.D 54 I.Bde. |
| | XVIII | 44 Sch.D 9 ID 53 I.Bde. |
| | V | 37 HID 33 ID |
| **SOUTH ARMY (G)** | Gp Szurmay | 128 I.Bde. 7 ID 40 HID |
| | Bothmer(G) | 38 HID 3 Gd.ID(G) 1 ID(G) |
| | Hofmann | 55 ID 12 Lst.Terr.Bde. 131 I.Bde. |
| | XXIV Res.(G) | 48 Res.D(G) 19 ID |
| ***Armeegruppe Pflanzer-Baltin*** became 7 Army 8.5.1915. | XIII | Gp Ljubicic (3 Bdes. 21 Bns. 1 Sqn.) 6 ID 5 ID |
| | Czibulka | 36 ID 15 ID |
| | Gp Marschall | 5 CD(G) 30 ID 10 CD |
| | XI | 41 HID 5 HCD 2 Bde./Polish Legion 6 CD Bde.Papp (9 Bns.) Bde. Schnitzler (3 Bns.) |
| | Army Reserve | 8 CD |

| ARMY/ARMY GROUP | CORPS | DIVISIONS |
|---|---|---|
| **3 ARMY continued** | XXXI (part) | Main Body 83 Res.D One Militia Bde. |
| **11 ARMY** | VI | 4 ID 16 ID |
| | XVIII | 23 ID 37 ID |
| | XXII | 1 Finn.Sch.D 3 Finn.Sch.D |
| | – | One Militia Bde. TransAmur Coss. Bde. Kuban Coss.Bde. |
| **9 ARMY** | XI | 11 ID 32 ID |
| | XXX | 2 Sch.D 71 Res.D 80 Res.D – To 8 Army 9/10.15 |
| | XXXIII | 1 TransAmur D 2 TransAmur D 1 Kub.Plastun Bde. 2 Kub.Plastun Bde. 74 Res.D |
| | – | 82 Res.D – To 8 Army 9/10.15 |
| | XXXII | 101 Res.D 103 Res.D |
| | II Cav. Corps | 9 CD 12 CD Caucasus CD |
| | III Cav. Corps | 1 Don Coss.D 10 CD |
| | – | Comb.CD Comb.C.Bde. Terek Coss.D |
| **Reserve to Southwest Front** | | 125 Res.D – To 8 Army 9/10.15 |
| **Leaving Southwest Front to Northwest Front July/August 1915** | XXVIII | 3 Sch.D 60 Res.D |
| | V Caucasus | 2 Finn.Sch.D 4 Finn.Sch.D (Returned in 11.1915) |
| | – | 58 Res.D 65 Res.D 69 Res.D 78 Res.D |
| | – | 3 Don Coss.D(?) |
| **Added in November 1915** | XXIV | 48 ID 49 ID from 3 Army to 8 Army |
| | V Caucasus | 2 Finn.Sch.D 4 Finn.Sch.D from 10 Army (formed XXXXI Corps) |
| | II | 26 ID 43 ID (from 10 Army) |
| | XVI | 41 ID 47 ID (from 4 Army) |
| | | 1 Coss.Bde. from West Front for new 7 Army |

---

***Table 3.40* O.O.B. Russian Eastern Front (Southwest *Front*) Autumn 1915**

| ARMY/ARMY GROUP | CORPS | DIVISIONS |
|---|---|---|
| **Southwest Front** **8 ARMY** | XXXIX | 102 Res.D 105 Res.D |
| | – | 4 Sch.D |
| | XII | 12 ID 19 ID |
| | VIII | 14 ID 15 ID |
| | XVII | 3 ID 35 ID |
| | VII | 13 ID 34 ID |
| | CC Veljassiev | 3 Orenburg Coss.D 3 Don Coss.D(?) 11 CD |
| | CC Rerberg | 7 CD 2 Indep.Don Coss.Bde. – To new 7 Army 11.15 |
| **3 ARMY (part)** | IV Cav. Corps | 2 Gd.Coss.D 3 Gd.Coss.D(?) 3 Caucasus Coss.D 2 Comb.Coss.D |
| | | 3 CD(?) 16 CD 3 Don Coss.D(?) 77 Res.D |

***Table 3.41* Austro-Hungarian O.O.B. Eastern Front Autumn 1915**

| ARMY/ARMY GROUP | CORPS | DIVISIONS |
|---|---|---|
| **Army Gp. Erzherzog Josef Ferdinand** | | |
| **4 ARMY** | – | 4 CD 7 CD |
| | XIV | 2 ID 3 ID 21 Sch.D |
| | X | 24 ID 62 ID |
| | IX | 10 ID 26 Sch.D |
| **1 ARMY** | – | 13 Sch.D |
| | Szurmay | 7 ID 40 HID |
| | I | 9 ID 46 Sch.D |
| | II | 25 ID |
| **Army Group Reserve** | Gr. Smekal | 45 Sch.D 4 ID |
| **2 ARMY** | XVIII | 31 ID 32 ID 1 Lst.I.Bde. 1 Lst.Hussar Bde. 1 CD |

**Austro-Hungarian O.O.B. Eastern Front Autumn 1915 continued**

| ARMY/ARMY GROUP | CORPS | DIVISIONS |
|---|---|---|
| **2 ARMY continued** | IV | 27 ID 51 HID |
| | XIX | 29 ID |
| | V | 33 ID 34 ID 14 ID 43 Sch.D |
| **South Army (G)** | Marschall | 38 HID 19 ID 3 Gd.ID(G) |
| | Hofmann | 55 ID Comb.Inf.Bde. 131 I.Bde. |
| | – | 48 Res.D(G) |
| **7 ARMY** | XIII | 36 ID 15 ID |
| | Gr. Henriquez | 8 CD 30 ID |
| | Gr. Benigni | 6 CD 3 CD 6 ID 5 HCD 5 ID |
| | XI | 42 HCD 2 Bde./Polish Legion Bde. Papp |
| | – | 10 CD |
| **Army Reserve** | VI | 12 ID 39 HID |
| | VIII | 37 HID 106 Lst.ID 1, 3 Bdes./ Polish Legion |
| | XVII | 11 ID 41 HID |
| **Austrian Units in German Army Commands in East** | | |
| **9 ARMY (G)** | | 2 CD 9 CD |
| **Army Woyrsch (G)** | XII | 35 ID 16 ID |
| **Bug Army (G)** | | 11 HCD |
| **German Units transferred from Bug Army to Austro-Hungarian Command** | | |
| | – | 5 CD(G) |
| | XXIV Res.(G) | 1 ID(G) 22 ID(G) |

---

**Table 3.42 Russian O.O.B. Eastern Front May/June 1916**

(Outline only for Northern and Western Fronts. Full details for Southwest Front).

| ARMY GROUP/ ARMY | CORPS |
|---|---|
| **Stavka Reserve** (behind 2 & 4 Armies) | I Guard II Guard I Siberian Guard Cavalry |
| **Northern Front** | |
| **In Finland** | XLII Independent |
| **Front Reserve** | I, III |
| **12 ARMY** | VII Siberian, XLIII, VI Siberian, XXXVIII |
| **1 ARMY** | XXIX, XXI, IV, XIV, I Cavalry |
| **Western Front** | |
| **Front Reserve** | XLIII (behind 2 & 4 Armies) |
| **2 ARMY** | XXVII, XXXIV, XV, I Siberian, XXXVI |
| **4 ARMY** | XX, XXIV, III Siberian, II Caucasus, XXXV |
| **10 ARMY** | XXIV, III Cauc., I Turk., XXXVIII, XLIV, VII Cav. |
| **3 ARMY** | XX, Grenadier, IX, XXXI, VI Cavalry |

| | CORPS | DIVISIONS |
|---|---|---|
| **South Western Front (4.6.1916)** | | |
| **Front Reserve** | XLV | |
| **8 ARMY** | IV Cavalry | 16 CD 2 Comb.Coss.Div. 7 CD 3 Cauc.Coss.Div. |

| ARMY GROUP/ ARMY | CORPS | DIVISIONS |
|---|---|---|
| **8 ARMY continued** | XLVI | 77 ID 100 ID |
| | V Cavalry | 11 CD 3 Orenburg Coss.Div. |
| | XXX | 71 ID 80 ID |
| | XXXIX | 102 ID 125 ID |
| | XL | 2 Sch.D 4 Sch.D |
| | VIII | 14 ID 15 ID |
| | XXXII | 101 ID 105 ID |
| | Army Reserve | 4 Finn.Sch.D 12 CD |
| **11 ARMY** | XVII | 3 ID 35 ID |
| | VII | 13 ID 14 ID Saratov Inf.Bde. |
| | VI | 4 ID 16 ID |
| | XVIII | 23 ID 37 ID |
| | Army Reserve | TransAmur Ftr.Gd.Mtd.Div. |
| **7 ARMY** | XXII Finnish | 1, 3 Finn.Sch.D |
| | XVI | 41 ID 47 ID |
| | II | 26 ID 43 ID 3 Turk.Sch.D |
| | II Cavalry | 9 CD Comb.Coss.Div. 6 Don Coss.Div. |
| **9 ARMY** | XXXIII | 1, 2 TransAmur Ftr.Gd.Divs. |
| | XLI | 74 ID 3 TransAmur Ftr.Gd.Div. |
| | XI | 11 ID 32 ID |
| | XII | 12 ID 19 ID |
| | Combined | 82 ID 103 ID |
| | III Cavalry | 10 CD 1 Terek Coss.Div. 1 Don Coss.Div. Caucasus Native Cav.Div. |
| **FRONT RESERVE** | | 2 Finn.Sch.D 126 ID |

**TOTALS**
**SOUTH WEST FRONT** 40½ ID 15 CD
**NORTHERN & WESTERN FRONT** 106 ID 19 CD
Reinforcements En Route from NORTHERN Front
         V Siberian       6 Sib.Sch.D 50 ID

**Location Remaining Corps**
Caucasus Army      V Caucasus II Turkestan I Caucasus
                 IV Caucasus Caucasus Cavalry

---

**Table 3.43 Russian O.O.B. Eastern Front (Southwest Front) 3.7.1916 (Brusilov Offensive)**

| ARMY GROUP/ ARMY | CORPS | DIVISIONS |
|---|---|---|
| **Southwest Front** **3 ARMY** | XXXI | 75 ID 83 ID |
| | Bulatov* | 27 ID 78 ID |
| | XLVI | 77 ID 100 Res.D |
| | IV Cavalry | 16 CD 2 Comb.Coss.D 3 Cauc.Coss.D |
| | Unattached | 5 Don Coss.D 1 Kuban Coss.D 1 Transbaikal Coss.D 3 CD |
| **8 ARMY** | V Cavalry | 11 CD 3 Orenburg Coss.D |
| | I Turk | 1 Turk.Sch.D 2 Turk.Sch.D |
| | XXX | 71 ID 80 ID |
| | I | 22 ID 24 ID |

\* Also called 'Combined Corps'.

| ARMY GROUP/ARMY | CORPS | DIVISIONS |
|---|---|---|
| 3 ARMY continued | XXXIX | 102 Res.D 125 Res.D |
| | XXIII | 20 ID 53 ID |
| | XL | 2 Sch.D 4 Sch.D |
| | Unattached | 4 Finn.Sch.D 12 CD |
| | V Siberian | 50 ID 6 Sib.Sch.D |
| 11 ARMY | VIII | 14 ID 15 ID |
| | XLV | 2 Finn.Sch.D 126 Res.D |
| | XXXII | 101 Res.D 105 Res.D |
| | XVII | 3 ID 35 ID |
| | VII | 13 ID 34 ID Saratov I.Bde. |
| | V | 7 ID 10 ID |
| | Wadbolski Cav. | Comb.CD TransAmur Bdr.Gd.Mtd.Div. |
| | Unattached | 7 CD |
| 7 ARMY | VI | 4 ID 16 ID |
| | XVIII | 23 ID 37 ID |
| | XXII Finnish | 1 Finn.Sch.D 3 Finn.Sch.D |
| | XVI | 41 ID 47 ID |
| | II | 26 ID 43 ID |
| | II Cavalry | 9 CD 6 Don Coss.D |
| | Unattached | 3 Turk.Sch.D 108 Res.D* 113 Res.D |
| 9 ARMY | XXXIII | 1 & 2 TransAmur Bdr.Gd.D |
| | XLI | 74 ID 3 TransAmur Bdr.Gd.D |
| | XII | 12 ID 19 ID |
| | XI | 11 ID 32 ID |
| | | 82 ID† 103 Res.D† 117 Res.D‡ |
| | III Cavalry | 10 CD 1 Don.Coss.D 1 Terek Coss.D |
| | | Cauc.Native Coss.D Ussuri Coss.D◊ |
| TOTAL (57½ ID 20 CD) | | |

* From North Front 5.7.16.

† Comb. Korps dissolved.

‡ From Bessarabia 5.7.16.

◊ From North Front 8.7.16.

### Table 3.44 Central Powers O.O.B. Eastern Front 3.7.1916

| ARMY GROUP/ARMY | CORPS | DIVISIONS |
|---|---|---|
| 7 ARMY | XI | 51 HID• 40 HID 10 I.Bde. |
| | CC Brudermann | 3 CD 8 CD |
| | Gr Benigni (VIII) | 24 ID 59 ID 44 Sch.D |
| | Gr Hadfy | 30 ID 42 HID 5 HCD 21 Sch.D |
| | Gr Kraewel(G) | 6 CD 119 ID(G) 105 ID(G) Gr Leide (Pts. 30 ID, 39 HID) |
| SOUTH ARMY (G) | XIII | 15 ID 2 CD 36 ID |
| | VI | 12 ID 39 HID |
| | Hofmann | 54 ID 55 ID |
| | IX | 38 ID 19 ID 32 ID |
| | Army Reserve | 1 Res.(G) |
| 2 ARMY | IV | 14 ID 33 ID |
| | V | 31 ID |

• HID, HCD – Honved Infantry and Cavalry Divisions.

∆ Formed from Austro-Hungarian P.O.W.s.

| ARMY GROUP/ARMY | CORPS | DIVISIONS |
|---|---|---|
| 2 ARMY continued | Gr Kosak | 27 ID |
| Army Gp. Linsingen (G) | | |
| 1 ARMY | XVIII | 1 Lst.I.Bde. 25 ID 46 Sch.D |
| Armeegruppe Marwitz (G) | – | 7 ID 108 ID(G) 22 ID(G) 48 ID |
| | Gr Falkenhayn | 61 ID 7 CD 4 CD 43 Res.D(G) 9 CD(G) |
| 4 ARMY | Army Kdo. | 10 CD |
| | Szurmay | 70 HID 11 ID |
| | X | 13 Sch.D 2 ID 37 HID |
| Direct Cd. Army Group Linsingen | X(G) | 20 ID(G) 19 ID(G) 29 ID |
| | Gr. Bernhardi(G) | Comb.ID(G) 11 Bav.ID(G) 107 ID(G) |
| | II | 41 HID 4 ID |
| | Fath | 45 Sch.D 26 Sch.D 53 ID |
| | CC Hauer | Polish Legion (1, 3 Bdes.) 11 HCD 1 CD 9 CD |
| Army Group Reserve | | Polish Legion (2 Bde.) |
| Units of German Army Woyrsch | XII | 16 ID 35 CD |

### Table 3.45 Rumanian Army O.O.B. 27.8.1916

| ARMY/ARMY GROUP | CORPS | DIVISIONS |
|---|---|---|
| North West Front | | |
| NORTH (4) ARMY | | 14 ID 4 Mixed Bde. 4 Cav.Bde. |
| | IV | 7 ID 8 ID |
| | | 2 Cav.D |
| 2 ARMY | III | 6 ID 5 ID 3 Cav.Bde. + 7.9.16 22 ID |
| | II | 4 ID 3 ID 2 Cav.Bde. + 7.9.16 21 ID |
| | | 1 Cav.D |
| 1 ARMY | | Gp. Alt Lotru (1.9.16 became 23 ID) 13 ID |
| | I | 2 ID 11 ID 1 Cav.Bde. |
| | | 1 ID 12 ID |
| South Front | | |
| 3 ARMY | | 20 ID |
| | VI | 16 ID 18 ID |
| | VII | 17 ID 9ID 19 ID 5 Cav.Bde. |
| Strategic Reserve | V | 10 ID 15 ID |
| | | Rumanian Danube Flotilla |
| Russian Auxiliary Corps in the Dobrudja (attached to 3 Rumanian Army) | | |
| | XLVII | 61 ID Serbian Volunteer Div.∆ 3 Cav.D (Russian units) |

**Summary**

| | Bns. | Sqns. | Batteries |
|---|---|---|---|
| 4 ARMY | 70 | 25 | 48 |
| 2 ARMY | 78 | 43 | 63 |
| 1 ARMY | 88 | 11 | 67 |

O.O.B. Rumanian Army 27 August 1916 continued

**Summary continued**

| | Bns. | Sqns. | Batteries |
|---|---|---|---|
| **Total N.W.Front.** | **236** | **89** | **178** |
| 3 ARMY | 104 | 15 | 107 |
| Strategic Reserve | 26 | 2 | 40 |
| **TOTAL** | **366** | **106** | **325 + 2 Heavy Art Bdes** |

**Russian Auxiliary Corps** *c.* 30,000 Inf. 3,600 Cav. 100 Guns

---

***Table 3.46*** **Summary Russian O.O.B. Eastern Front 31.8.1916**

| ARMY GROUP/ARMY | INF.DIVS. | CAV.DIVS |
|---|---|---|
| **Northern Front** | | |
| 6 ARMY | 4 | $\frac{1}{2}$ |
| 12 ARMY | 16$\frac{1}{2}$ | 4$\frac{1}{2}$ |
| 5 ARMY | 9$\frac{1}{2}$ | 4 |
| 1 ARMY | 6 | 1 |
| **TOTAL** | **36** | **10** |
| **Western Front** | | |
| 10 ARMY | 14 | 1 |
| 4 ARMY | 8 | 1 |
| 2 ARMY | 9$\frac{1}{2}$ | 4 |
| 3 ARMY | 15 | 5 |
| SPECIAL ARMY | 10 | 3 |
| **TOTAL** | **56$\frac{1}{2}$** | **14** |
| **South Western Front** | | |
| 8 ARMY | 12 | 3 |
| 11 ARMY | 13$\frac{1}{2}$ | 3 |
| 7 ARMY | 13 | 3 |
| 9 ARMY | 11$\frac{1}{2}$ | 5 |
| **TOTAL** | **50** | **14** |

---

***Table 3.47*** **Summary Allied O.O.B. Eastern and Rumanian Fronts 31.10.1916**

| ARMY GROUP/ARMY | ARMIES | TOTAL DIVS. |
|---|---|---|
| **Northern** | 6, 12, 5, 1 | 29$\frac{1}{2}$ |
| **Western** | 10, 4, 2, 3 | 32$\frac{1}{2}$ |
| **South Western** | Special | 23 |
| | 11 | 12$\frac{1}{2}$ |
| | 7 | 15 |
| | 8 | 10 |
| | 9 | 13 |
| **TOTAL** | | **73$\frac{1}{2}$** |
| **Rumanian Army** | | 23$\frac{1}{2}$ |
| **Danube-Dobrudja-New 6 Army** | | 7 |
| **OVERALL TOTAL** | **142$\frac{1}{2}$ Russian + 23$\frac{1}{2}$ Rumanian** | |

---

***Table 3.48*** **Austro-Hungarian O.O.B. Rumanian Front September 1916**

| ARMY/ARMY GROUP | CORPS | DIVISIONS |
|---|---|---|
| **A. Siebenburg Sector** | XXXIX Res.(G) | Gp. v.Szivo - Danube Gp. 145 IB |
| **German 9 ARMY** | | Gp. Sunkel - 187 ID(G) 144 IB pt. Alpenkorps(G)(part) |
| | Gp. Krafft | Alpenkorps(G)(part) |
| | Schmettow Cav. | 51 HID 3 Cav.D(G) 1 Cav.D |
| | *En Route* | 76 Res.D(G) |
| **1 ARMY** | I Reserve(G) | 71 ID 1 Lst.Hussar Bde. 39 HID 89 ID(G) |
| | VI | 61 ID 37 HID 72 ID |
| **B. North Bulgarian Sector** | – | Mobile Garrison Varna, Bde./6 ID, 1 Cav.D, 1 ID, 4 ID (all Bulgarian) |
| **Heeresgruppe Mackensen** | | German/Bulgarian Det.Kauffmann |
| **Bulgarian 3 ARMY** | (Security duties on Danube) | 12 Bulg.ID pt.Det.Kauffmann |
| | A.H.Gp. Gaugl | Minor Units |
| **Austro-Hungarian Danube Flotilla** | | 1 Monitor Div. 2 Monitor Div. |

**Summary**

| | Bns. | Sqns. | Btys. | (Guns) | Machine Guns |
|---|---|---|---|---|---|
| 9 ARMY (German) | 51$\frac{1}{4}$ | 32 | 70 | (281) | 486 |
| | + 4 Cav.Sch.Divs. | | | | |
| 1 ARMY (A-H) | 61$\frac{1}{2}$ | 24$\frac{1}{4}$ | 63 | (234) | 217 |
| | + 1$\frac{1}{3}$ Cav.Sch.Div. | | | | |
| **Total Siebenburg** | **115** | **56$\frac{1}{4}$** | **133** | **(515)** | **550** |
| | + 5$\frac{1}{3}$ | | | | |
| **Heeresgr. Mackensen** | **71** | **39** | **66**(not known) | | not known |

---

***Table 3.49*** **Allied O.O.B. Russian-Rumanian Front March 1917**

| ARMY GROUP/ARMY | CORPS | DIVISIONS |
|---|---|---|
| **South Western Front** | | |
| **8 ARMY** | XVIII | 37, 43, 64, 166 ID |
| | XXIII | 59, 79, 82, 167 ID |
| | XI | 11, 12, 32, 165 ID |
| | – | 7 CD 3 Cau.Coss.D |
| **7 ARMY** | XVI | 41, 47, 160 ID |
| | XII | 19, 117 ID |
| | XXXIII | 1, 2, 4 Trans-Amur Ftr.Gd.Divs. |
| | XXII Finnish | 1, 3 Finn.Sch.D |
| | VI Siberian | 12, 13 Sib.Sch.D 23 ID |
| | XLI | 74, 108, 113 ID 3, 5 Trans-Amur Ftr.Gd.Divs. |
| | III Caucasus | 21, 52 ID |
| | II Cavalry | 9 CD Combined CD |

| ARMY GROUP/ ARMY | CORPS | DIVISIONS |
|---|---|---|
| South Western Front continued 11 ARMY | VI | 4, 16 ID |
| | XVII | 3, 35, 156 ID |
| | V Siberian | 6 Sib.Sch.D 50, 158 ID* |
| | XXXII | 101, 105, 157 ID |
| | VII Cavalry | 6, 13 CD 20 ID |
| | – | 2, 4 Finn.Sch.D Transbaikal Coss.D |
| SPECIAL ARMY | V | 7, 10, 151 ID |
| | II Guard | 3 Gd.ID Gd.Sch.D |
| | I Guard | 1, 2 Gd.ID |
| | XXV | 3 Gren.D 46, 152 ID† |
| | XXXIX | 53, 102, 125, 154 ID |
| | I Turkestan | 1, 2, 8 Turk.Sch.Divs. |
| | XXXIV | 56, 104, 153 ID |
| | Guard Cavalry | 1, 2, 3 Gd.Cav.Divs. |
| (Belonging to West Front) 3 ARMY | XLVI | 5 Don Coss.D 77, 100 ID Comb.Ftr.Gd.Div. |
| | III | 73 ID 5 Sch.D |
| | IV Cavalry | 27 ID 16 CD 2 Comb.Coss.D 1 Kuban Coss.D |
| | XXXI | 75, 83, 130 ID |
| | – | Czech.Sch.Bde. |
| Rumanian Front 6 ARMY | XLVII | 1 Marine Div. 115 ID |
| | IV Siberian | 9 Sib.Sch.Div. 10 Sib.Sch.Div. 61 ID |
| | XXIX | 1 Sch.Div. 7 Sch.Div. 3 Cau.Sch.D |
| | IV | 30 ID 40 ID 124 ID 3 Sch.Div. |
| | – | 57 ID 111 ID |
| | VI Cavalry | 3 CD 8 CD |
| | – | 3 Don Coss.Div. |
| 4 ARMY | XXX | 71 ID 80 ID 190 ID |
| | VII | 13 ID 34 ID 179 ID |
| | VIII | 2 ID 14 ID 15 ID |
| | III Cavalry | 10 CD 1 Don Coss.D 1 Terek Coss.D |
| | – | 12 CD Caucasus Native Coss.D. Trans-Amur Ftr.Gd.Mtd.Div. |
| 2 RUMANIAN ARMY | II (Rum) | 1, 3, 12 Rum.ID |
| | IV (Rum) | 6, 7, 8 Rum.ID |
| | Army Reserve | Ussuri Coss.D.(Russian) |
| 9 ARMY | XXXX | 2 Sch.D 4 Sch.D 3 Turk.Sch.D |
| | XXIV | 48 ID 49 ID 126 ID 188 ID |
| | – | 103 ID |
| | XXXVI | 25 ID 68 ID |
| | II | 26 ID 84 ID 193 ID |
| | XXVI | 65 ID 78 ID |
| | XLV | 122 ID 194 ID |
| | V Cavalry | 11 CD 3 Orenburg Coss.D |

* 158 ID was redesignated as 22 Siberian Sch.Div.

† 152 ID was redesignated as 6 Gren.Div.

‡ H.Q. LII Gen.Kdo. seems to have had a command function at a level above Corps but lower than an Army.

◊ The alpha-numeric subdivisions in the later Austro-Hungarian O.O.B.s are from offical Austrian sources and represent their attempt to clarify the complex command arrangement on the Central Powers fronts (see also Balkans and Italy O.O.B.s).

| ARMY GROUP/ ARMY | CORPS | DIVISIONS |
|---|---|---|
| Rumanian Front continued 9 ARMY continued | – | 6 Don Coss.D |
| Newly organised:– 1 RUMANIAN ARMY | I (Rum) | 2, 4, 11 Rum.ID |
| | III (Rum) | 5, 13, 14 Rum.ID |
| | V (Rum) | 9, 10, 15 Rum.ID |
| | – | 1, 2 Rum.CD |

### Table 3.50 Central Powers O.O.B. Russian-Rumanian Front 1.3.1917

| ARMY/ARMY GROUP | CORPS | DIVISIONS |
|---|---|---|
| **A. Army Group Mackensen (Heeresgruppe)** | | |
| 3 (BULGARIAN) ARMY | – | 4 Bulg.ID 12 Bulg.ID 1 Bulg.CD (reinforced) |
| 9 (GERMAN) (1)◊ ARMY | LII (Danube Army)‡ | Inf.Rgt. 217 ID(G) Turkish VI Corps (15, 25, 26 Turkish ID) 145 Inf.Bde.(A-H) 1 Bulg.ID Combined (6) Bulg.ID |
| (2) | – | 115 ID(G) |
| (3) | Group Schaer | 109 ID(G) 7 CD(A-H) |
| (4) | I Reserve(G) | 216 ID(G) 12 Bav.ID(G) 76 Res.D(G) 89 ID(G) |
| (5) | Group Sontag | 73 ID(A-H) Alpenkorps(G) |
| | Army Reserve | Bulk of 217 ID(G) 11 Cav.Bde.(A-H) |
| **B. Army Group Archduke Joseph (Heeresfront)** | | |
| 1 (AUST-HUNG.) (1)◊ ARMY | Group Gerok (XXIV Res.(G)) | Gp. Ruiz – 1 CD(A-H) 218 ID(G) Gp. Sursich – 71 ID(A-H) 70 HID(A-H) |
| En Route | H.Q.VIII (A-H) | |
| (2) | Group Litzmann (XXXX Res.(G)) | |
| | VI (A-H) | 39 HID(A-H) 24 ID(A-H) 225 ID(G) |
| | Gp. Seekirchner | 8 Bav.Res.D(G) 10 CD(A-H) 47 Inf.Bde.(A-H) 16 Lst.Inf.Bde.(A-H) |
| (3) | XXI (A-H) | 72 ID(A-H) 31 ID(A-H) 37 HID(A-H) 3 CD(A-H) |
| 7 (AUST-HUNG.) ARMY | XI (A-H) | 51 HID(A-H) 5 HCD(A-H) Gp. Paschen (6 CD(A-H) 23 Inf.Bde.(A-H)) Part 1 ID(G) |
| | I (A-H) | 8 CD 11 HCD 59 ID 40 HID (all A-H) |
| | Karpathen (G) | 12 ID(A-H) 200 ID(G) |
| | XXV Reserve (G) | 34 ID(A-H) 30 ID(A-H) 117 ID(G) |
| | Army Reserve | 16 Inf.Bde.(A-H) |
| **C. Southern Wing, Army Group Prince Leopold of Bavaria (Heeresfront)** | | |
| Army Gp. Böhm-Ermolli (Heeresgruppe) | – | 5 ID(A-H) |
| | XIII (A-H) | 42 HID(A-H) 36 ID(A-H) |
| 3 (AUST-HUNG.) ARMY | Gp. Hadfy (A-H) | 21 Sch.D(A-H) 15 ID(A-H) 2 CD(A-H) 48 Res.D(G) |
| SOUTH ARMY (G) | XXVII Res. (G) | 119 ID(G) 53 Res.D(G) 75 Res.D(G) |
| | XV (Turkish) | 20 ID(T) 19 ID(T) 36 Res.D(G) |

**Central Powers O.O.B. Russian-Rumanian Front 1.3.1917 continued**

| ARMY/ARMY GROUP | CORPS | DIVISIONS |
|---|---|---|
| **C. Southern Wing continued** | | |
| **SOUTH ARMY** continued | XXV(A-H) | 54 ID(A-H) 51 ID(A-H) |
| | Army Reserve | 38 HID(A-H) |
| **2 (AUST.-HUNG.) ARMY** | **(a)** Abschnitt Zloczow (Commanding [1] to [4]) (Gen Kdo. I[G]) | |
| | [1] IX(A-H) | 19 ID(A-H)  32 ID(A-H) |
| | [2] | 197 ID(G) |
| | [3] | 195 ID(G) |
| | [4] IV(A-H) | 33 ID(A-H) Leibhusaren Bde.(G) |
| | **(b)** V(A-H) | 27 ID(A-H) 10 Bav.Res.D(G) 4 CD(A-H) |
| | **(c)** XVIII(A-H) | 106 Lst.ID(A-H) 25 ID(A-H) |
| **Army Group Linsingen (Heeresgruppe)** | | |
| **A. Abschnitt Lipa** | (Gen Kdo. XXII Res.(G)) | 46 Sch.D(A-H) 22 ID(G) 20 HCD(A-H) 215 ID(G) |
| **B. 4 (AUST.-HUNG.) ARMY** | [1] Abschnitt Luga (Gen Kdo. VI(G)) | |
| | **(a)** Abschnitt Raczyn (Kdo. 108 ID(G)) | 108 ID(G) 2 Gd.Cav.Bde.(G) (reinforced) 224 ID(G) |
| | **(b)** XXIV(A-H) | 11 ID(A-H) 10 LW D(G) |
| | [2] X(A-H) | 13 Sch.D(A-H) 2 ID(A-H) |
| | [3] VIII(G) (reinforced) | 15 ID(G) 16 ID(G) 29 ID(A-H) |
| **C. Abschnitt Kowel** (Gen Kdo. LV(G)) | [1] | 92 ID(G) |
| | [2] II(A-H) | 107 ID(G) 4 ID(A-H) |
| | [3] XXII(A-H) | Gp.Wernitz (26 Sch.D 45 Sch.D)(A-H) Gp.Clausius (53 ID(A-H) 91 ID(G)) |
| | [4] | 45 LW Div.(G) |
| **D.** | Cav.Corps Hauer | 9 CD(A-H) 1 LW Div.(G) Bav.CD(G) |
| Other forces in Theatre **Austro-Hungarian formations in Army Gp. (Heeresgruppe) Woyrsch** | | |
| | XII(A-H) | 35 ID(A-H) 26 Sch.Bde.(A-H) |
| **Military Govt. Lublin** | | 21 Lst.Bns. 1 Lst.Sqn.(A-H) |

---

**Table 3.51 Outline Russian O.O.B. Eastern Front June 1917**

| ARMY GROUP/ARMY | CORPS |
|---|---|
| **Northern Front** | |
| **In Finland** | XLII |
| **1 ARMY** (Baltic Coast) | I |
| | XXXVII |
| **12 ARMY** (Riga Area) | VI Siberian |
| | II Siberian |
| | XLIII |
| | XXI |
| **6 ARMY** (Dvinsk Sector) | XIII |
| | XXVIII |
| | XIX |

| ARMY GROUP/ARMY | CORPS |
|---|---|
| **6 ARMY continued** | XXVII |
| | XIV |
| | I Cavalry |
| **Western Front** | |
| **Front Reserve** | XLVIII |
| **3 ARMY** (Polotsk Sector) | XV |
| | XXXV |
| | X |
| | XX |
| **10 ARMY** (Smorgon-Krevo Sector) | II Caucasus |
| | I Siberian |
| | XXXVIII |
| | III |
| **2 ARMY** (Baranovichi Sector) | III Siberian |
| | Grenadier |
| | IX |
| | L |
| | Composite |
| **South Western Front** | |
| **Front Reserves** | I Guard |
| | II Guard |
| | V |
| | XXV |
| | XLV |
| | V Cavalry |
| **SPECIAL ARMY** (Polesi) | XXXI |
| | IV Cavalry |
| | XLVI |
| | XXXIX |
| **11 ARMY** (Dubno-Brody Sector) | I Turkestan |
| | VII Cavalry |
| | XXXII |
| | V Siberian |
| | XVII |
| | XLIX |
| | VI |
| **7 ARMY** (Gnilaya Lipa Valley) | XLI |
| | VII Siberian |
| | XXXIV |
| | XXII |
| | III Caucasus |
| **8 ARMY** (Around Dnestr River) | XXXIII |
| | XII |
| | XVI |
| (In Bucovina) | XI |
| | XXIII |
| | XVIII |
| **Rumanian Front** | |
| **9 ARMY** | II Cavalry |

| ARMY GROUP/ARMY | CORPS |
|---|---|
| **9 ARMY continued** | XXVI |
| | II |
| | XXXVI |
| | XL |
| **2 Rumanian ARMY** (Subordinated to 4 ARMY) | IV Rumanian |
| | II Rumanian |
| **4 ARMY** (Sushitsa Valley) | VIII |
| | VII |
| | XXX |
| **6 ARMY** (Seret and Danube Rivers) | IV |
| | IV Siberian |
| | XLVII |
| | VI Cavalry |
| **1 Rumanian ARMY** (Probably subordinated to 6 ARMY) | III Rumanian |
| | V Rumanian |
| | VI Rumanian |
| **Caucasus ARMY** | V Caucasus |
| | II Turkestan |
| | I Caucasus |

| ARMY GROUP/ARMY | CORPS |
|---|---|
| **Caucasus ARMY continued** | VI Caucasus |
| | IV Caucasus |
| | VII Caucasus |
| | Caucasus Cavalry |

**Total – Northern, Western and South Western Fronts**

| | |
|---|---|
| | 216 Inf.Divs. (72 without divisional artillery- see below) |
| | 42 Cav.Divs. |
| + | 6 Inf.Divs. on Baltic Coast |
| | 6 Inf.Divs. in Finland and Petroland Area |
| + | Unknown no. of Divs. in Caucasus Army |

Divisions lacking artillery
All those formed in Autumn 1916 from 4th Bns. of existing regiments and new 'March' Battalions of new recruits. They were numbered in the following sequence:–

| | |
|---|---|
| 5, 6 Grenadier, 2 Caucasus Grenadier Divs. | (3) |
| 128-193 Inf.Divs. (but no 139-150 Divs.) | (54) |
| 6-8 Rifle Divs. | (3) |
| 5-6 Finnish Rifle Divs. | (2) |
| 15-22 Composite Siberian Rifle Divs. | (9) |
| 6-7 Caucasus Rifle Divs. | (2) |
| 8-10 Turkestan Rifle Divs. | (3) |
| 4-5 Transamur Frontier Guard Divs. | (2) |

**Total 78**

Presumably 6 of the 78 were in minor theatres as 72 were at the main front.

---

**Table 3.52** Russian O.O.B. Eastern Front – The Kerensky Offensive July 1917

| | ARMY GROUP/ARMY | CORPS | DIVISIONS | IN RESERVE |
|---|---|---|---|---|
| **South West Front** | | | | |
| 1/3.7.17 (see also 19/21.7.17) | **11 ARMY** | XVII | 3 ID 35 ID | |
| | | XLIX | 4 Finn.Sch.D 82 ID Czech Bde. 6 Finn.Sch.D | I Gd.Corps 1, 2 CD ID |
| | | VI | 2 Finn.Sch.D 4 ID 16 ID 155 ID 151 ID | I Trans Baikal Coss.Div. |
| | | V | 7 ID 10 ID | |
| | Add from 9 ARMY | XLV | 122 ID 126 ID 194 ID | |
| 1/3.7.17 | **7 ARMY** | XLI | 113 ID 3, 5 Trans-Amur Ftr.Gd.D 74 ID | |
| | | VII Siberian | Comb.Sib.Sch.D (from 12, 13 Sib.Sch.D) 108 ID | Polish Sch.D |
| | | XXXIV | 19 Sib.Sch.D 23 ID 104 ID 153 ID (from XXII Corps) | |
| | | XXII Finnish | 5, 1, 3 Finn.Sch.D 159 ID | II Gd.Corps 3 Gd.ID Gd.Sch.D |
| | | III Caucasus | 52 ID 162 ID 21 ID | II Cav.Corps 9 CD Comb.Coss.Div. |
| | | XXXIII | 2, 4 Trans-Amur Ftr.Gd.D | V Cav.Corps (3 Orenburg Coss.Div. 11 CD) |
| 8/13.7.17 | **8 ARMY** | XXXIII | as above | |
| | | XII | 1 Trans-Amur Ftr.Gd.D 19 ID 56 ID | 3 Cau.Coss.Div |
| | | | 11 ID 117 ID 164 ID | Cau.Native Coss.Div |
| | | XVI | 47 ID 160 ID 41 ID 9 CD | 7 CD |
| | | V Siberian | 50 ID 6 Sib.Sch.D 22 Sib.Sch.D | |
| 19/21.7.17 | **11 ARMY** (reorganised) | XXV | 6 Gren.D 156 ID 46 ID 3 Gren.D | |
| | | XVII | 3 ID 35 ID | |
| | | XLIX | 2, 4, 6 Finn.Sch.D | |
| | | | 82 ID Czech Bde. | |
| | | I Guard | 1 Gd.ID 2 Gd.ID | Trans Baikal Coss.Div. |

**Russian O.O.B. Eastern Front/Kerensky Offensive July 1917 continued**

| | ARMY GROUP/ARMY | CORPS | DIVISIONS | IN RESERVE |
|---|---|---|---|---|
| 19/21.7.17 continued | **11 ARMY** | V | 10 ID 7 ID | |
| | | VI | 151 ID 155 ID 16 ID Polish Sch.D | 4 CD 11 CD |

**Outline O.O.B. in East Galicia and the Bukovina North-South**

| 21.7.17 - 8.8.17 | **11 ARMY (part)** | I Gd, V, XXXXV | III Cav. V Cav. |
|---|---|---|---|
| | **7 ARMY** | XXXIV, XXXXI, VII Sib., II Gd. | VI Finn. XXII |
| | **8 ARMY** | XII, III Cauc.Cav.Corps Wrangel XXXIII XVI | |
| | **1 ARMY** | XI, XXIII XVIII | II Cav. |
| | **9 ARMY (part)** | 12 CD, XXVI, II | VI Cav. XXXX |

### *Table 3.53* Austro-German O.O.B. Eastern Front 1.7.1917 (Battles of Konichy-Zborow and Brzezany)

| ARMY GROUP/ ARMY | DIVISIONS AT FRONT | IN RESERVE |
|---|---|---|
| **Heeresgruppe Böhm-Erolli** | | |
| **3 ARMY (A-H)** | 5 A-H Divs. – (5, 42, 36, 15 ID 2 CD) | 16 ID(A-H) 83 ID(G) |
| **SOUTH ARMY (G)** | 4 German Divs. – (53, 75, 15, 24 Res.D) | 2 German Divs. 4 Ers.D, 241 ID |
| | 3 A-H Divs. – (38 HID, 55 ID, 54 ID) | |
| | 1 Turkish Div. – (20 ID) | |
| **2 ARMY (A-H)** | 3 German Divs. – (197 ID, 12 LW Div., 15 LW Div.) | 2 German Divs. 223, 96 ID |
| | 6 A-H Divs. – (19, 32, 33, 27, 25 ID, 4 CD) | |
| Lemberg-Zloczow | 237 ID(G) | |
| In Lemberg | 12 Mtd.Sch.D(A-H) | |

### *Table 3.54* Austro-German O.O.B. Eastern Front 19-21.7.1917 (Battle of Zborow)

| ARMY GROUP/ ARMY | CORPS | DIVISIONS |
|---|---|---|
| **Abschnitt Zloczow** | German Beskiden Corps | 223 ID(G) 96 (Saxon) ID(G) |
| | Gruppe Wilhelmi | 197 ID(G) 63 Inf.Bde.of 32 ID(A-H) 237 ID(G) |
| | XXIII Reserve (G) | 1 Gd.ID(G) 2 Gd.ID(G) 6 ID(G) (all from Western Front) 33 ID(A-H) |
| | Gen.Kdo. LI (G) | 5 ID(G) (from Western Front) 22 ID(G)(from Army Group Linsingen) |
| | Abschnitt Reserve | 42 ID(G) (from German Ost Front) 92 ID(G)(from Army Group Linsingen) (Reinf. Leibhusaren Bde.(G)(from Army Group Linsingen) |

**Summary**

| | Bns. | Sqns. | Btys. | (Guns) |
|---|---|---|---|---|
| Beskiden Corps | 18 | 2 | 22 | (87) |
| Gp. Wilhelmi | 27 | 2 | 60 | (309) |
| XXIII Res.Corps | 27 | 3 | 42 | (164) |
| Gen.Kdo.LI | 18 | 2 | 24 | (96) |
| Reserve | 18 | 14 | 25 | (179) |
| **Totals** | **108** | **23** | **173** | **(835)** |
| **Totals Inc. Units outside Corps Organisation:** | **124¹/₄** | **24** | **219** | **(935)** |

### *Table 3.55* Central Powers O.O.B. Russian-Rumanian Front 23.7.1917

| ARMY/ARMY GROUP | INTERMEDIATE COMMAND LEVEL | CORPS | DIVISIONS |
|---|---|---|---|
| **A. Army Group Mackensen (Heeresgruppe)** | | | |
| **3 BULGARIAN ARMY** | – | – | 4, 12 Bulg.ID 1 Bulg.CD (reinforced) |
| **9 GERMAN ARMY** (a)* | Gen.KDO LII(G) | – | Abschnitt Goltz (1 German Lst.Inf.Rgt.) |
| | (Danube Army) | VI(Turkish) | 15, 25 ID(Turk.) |
| | | – | 212 ID(G) |
| | | – | 145 Inf.Bde.(A-H) |
| | | – | Bulg.Comb.(6) ID |
| | (b) | | 115 ID(G) |
| | (c) | | 76 Res.D(G) |
| | (d) | Gp. Behr | 109 ID(G) 92 ID(A-H) |
| | (e) | I Res.(G) | 216 ID(G) 12 Bav.ID(G) 89 ID(G) |
| | (f) | Gp. Gallwitz | 62 ID(A-H) 217 ID(G) |
| **B. Heeresfront Archduke Joseph** | | | |
| **1 (AUSTRO-HUNG.) ARMY** (a) | Gp. Gerok(G) Gen.Kdo. XXIV Res.(G) | [1] Gp.Ruiz (A-H) | 218 ID(G) 1 CD(A-H) |
| | | [2] VIII(A-H) | 71 ID 70 HID(A-H) |
| | | Reserve | 7 CD(A-H) |
| | (b) | VI(A-H) | 225 ID(G) 39 HID(A-H) |
| | (c) | Gp.Liposcak (A-H) | 7 ID, 16 Lst.Inf.Bde., 10 CD (all A-H) |
| | (d) | XXI(A-H) | 72 ID 31 ID 37 ID 3 CD(all A-H) |
| | *En route from 3 ARMY* | | 15 ID(A-H) |
| **7 (AUSTRO-HUNG.) ARMY** (a) | Gp. Krauss (Kdo. I(A-H)) | [1] XI(A-H) | 51 HID 74 HID(A-H) |
| | Gp.Apur (A-H) | | 5 HID 6 CD(A-H) |
| | | [2] Gp. Pichler(A-H) | 11 HCD 59 ID(A-H) |
| | (b) | Karpathen Korps(G) | 40 HID(A-H) 1 ID(G) 200 ID(G) |
| | (c) | XVII(A-H) | 68 Inf.Bde. 8 CD 34 ID 30 ID (all A-H) |

* See note ◊ on page 195.

| ARMY/ARMY GROUP | INTERMEDIATE COMMAND LEVEL | CORPS | DIVISIONS |
|---|---|---|---|
| **B. Heeresfront Archduke Joseph continued** | | | |
| (d) | | | 16 Inf.Bde. (30 ID)(A-H) |
| *En route to Gp. Krauss* | | 117 ID(G) | |
| **C. Army Group Böhm-Ermolli** | | | |
| I.3 AUST-HUNG. ARMY | | – | 5 ID(A-H) |
| | | XIII(A-H) | 42 HID 36 ID(A-H) |
| | | XXVI(A-H) | 15 ID 2 CD(A-H) |
| | | Army Res. | 16 ID(A-H) + (assembling) 83 ID(G) |
| In July added to 3 ARMY | | XXXX Res.(G) (Gp. Litzmann) | 8 Bav.Res.D. 16 Res.D 20 ID Bav.CD (reinf. by 1 Prussian Cav.Bde.)(all G) |
| II.GERMAN SOUTH ARMY | XXVII | Res.(G) 36 HID(A-H) | 53(Saxon) Res.D (G) 75 Res.D(G) |
| | | XV (Turkish) | 20 ID(Turk.) + A-H & G Artillery units |
| | | XXV Res.(G) | 15 Res.D(G) 24(Saxon) Res.D (G) |
| | | XXV(A-H) | 35 ID 54 ID(A-H) |
| | | Army Res. | 241 ID(G) 4 Ers.D(G) |
| III.2 AUST-HUNG. ARMY (a) | Abschnitt Zloczow (Gen Kdo. I(G)) | [1] IX(A-H) | 19 ID 32 ID(A-H) |
| | | [2] | 197 ID(G) |
| | | [3] | 33 ID(A-H) |
| | | Abschnitt Reserve | 223 ID(G) 96 ID(G) + En route 237 ID(G) |
| (b) | | V(A-H) | 12 LW Div.(G) 27 ID(A-H) 4 CD(A-H) |
| (c) | | XVIII(A-H) | 15 LW Div.(G) 25 ID(A-H) Leibhusaren Bde.(G) 12 Mtd.Sch.Div.(A-H) |
| **(1.7.1917) Army Group Linsingen** | | | |
| I. | Abschnitt Lipa (Gen Kdo. XXII Res,(G)) | [1] | 46 Sch.D |
| | | [2] Abschnitt Buzany | 22 ID 20 HID |
| | | [3] | 215 ID(G)(reinforced) |
| II.4 AUST.-HUNG. ARMY | | [1] Abschnitt Luga (Gen Kdo VI(G)) | 108 ID(G) 2 Gd.Cav.Bde. (reinf.)(G) 224 ID(G) 11 ID(A-H) |
| | | [2] Abschnitt Mitte (Centre) (X(A-H)) | 10 LW Div.(G) 13 Sch.D(A-H) 2 ID(A-H) |
| | | [3] VIII(Reinf.)(G) | 86 ID(G) 7 LW Div.(G) 29 ID(A-H) |
| III. | Abschnitt Kowel (Gen Kdo. LV(G)) | [1] | 45 LW Div.(G) |
| | | [2] II(A-H) | 107 ID(G) 4 ID(A-H) |
| | | [3] XXII(A-H) | 26 Sch.D 45 Sch.D(A-H) Gp. Clausius(G) (53 ID(A-H) 91 ID(G)) |
| IV. | | Cav.Corps Hauer(A-H) | 9 CD(A-H) 1 LW Div.(G) 4 Bav.Cav.Bde.(G) |
| V. | | Army Group Reserve | 92 ID(G) |

| ARMY/ARMY GROUP | INTERMEDIATE COMMAND LEVEL | CORPS | DIVISIONS |
|---|---|---|---|
| **Belonging to Heeresgruppe Woyrsch** | | | |
| | | XII(A-H) | Two German Divs. and I Regt. 18(A-H) |

**Summary** (Army Group Mackensen not given)

| | Inf.Bns. | Sqns. | Btys. (Guns) | Dismtd.Cav.Units |
|---|---|---|---|---|
| 1 ARMY | 111 | 13 | 183 (829) | 32 |
| 7 ARMY | 108 | 14½ | 155 (779) | 29 |
| **Total Army Group Archduke Joseph** | **219** | **27½** | **338 (1,608)** | **61** |
| 3 ARMY | 77 | 7 | 92 (441) | 8 |
| SOUTH ARMY (G) | 108 | 10 | 150 (708) | – |
| 2 ARMY | 122¼ | 21 | 198 (976) | 16 |
| **Total Army Group Böhm-Ermolli** | **307¼** | **38** | **440 (2,125)** | **24** |
| Abschnitt Lipa | 55¾ | 4 | 61 (282) | – |
| 4 ARMY | 88½ | 9 | 140 (658) | 3 |
| Abschnitt Kowel | 73 | 7 | 105 (499) | – |
| Cav.Corps Hauer | 10 | 2 | 15 (75) | 10 |
| Army Group Reserve | 9½ | 1 | 9 (27) | – |
| **Total Army Group Linsingen** | **236¾** | **23** | **330 (1,514)** | **13** |

### *Table 3.56* Central Powers O.O.B. Russian-Rumanian Front 15.10.1918

| ARMY/ARMY GROUP | CORPS | DIVISIONS |
|---|---|---|
| OST ARMEE (Eastern Army) | XXV(A-H) | 155 HID 54 Sch.D(A-H) |
| | XVII(A-H) | 7 CD 11 ID(A-H) |
| | XII(A-H) | 5 HCD 15 ID(A-H) |
| Under direct (a) command Army H.Q. (b) | Govt. of Odessa | 145 I.Bde.(A-H) |
| (b) | | 2 CD(A-H) |
| (c) | | 2 Inf.Bns.(VI, VII/103) |
| (d) Forming part of | Army Gp.Kiev(G) | 1 Inf.Bn.(II/93) |
| (e) In transfer to | Army Gp.Kövess (A-H) (Balkan Front) | 59 ID 4 CD(A-H) IR 93 (of 34 ID)(A-H) |
| **4 General Command(A-H)** | Bessarabia Cmd | 187 Lst.Inf.Bde. |
| | Frontier Security Troops | 3 Inf.Bns + Ukranian Legion |
| L of C Command | Wladimir-Volynski | 3 Bns. |
| | Command Schilling | 2 Sqns. |
| **General Govt. Poland(A-H)** | | 33 Bns. 1 Sqn. (All L of C units) |
| **Group Command Siebenbürgen (A-H)** | | 1 CD (reinf.) 216 HI.Bde. |
| Assigned to Army Group Mackensen **16 General Command(A-H)** | | 62 ID(A-H) 143 Inf.Bde.(A-H) |

| Summary | Bns. | Sqns. | Btys. (Guns) | Dismtd.Cav.Units |
|---|---|---|---|---|
| OST ARMEE | 66¾ | 8¾ | 54 (300) | 27 |
| 4 General Command | 13¼ | 2 | 1 (6) | – |

**Central Powers O.O.B. Russian-Rumanian Front 15.10.1918 continued**

| Summary | Bns. | Sqns. | Btys. | (Guns) | Dismtd.Cav.Units |
|---|---|---|---|---|---|
| Gen.Govt.Poland Gp.Command | 33 | 1 | – | | – |
| Siebenburgen | 19 | 2 | 6 | (36) | 7¹/₄ |
| Austrian Units assigned to Army Mackensen | | | | | |
| | 20 | 1¹/₄ | 9 | (54) | – |

## Austro-Hungarian Units Assigned to Western Front 15 October 1918

| ARMY/ARMY GROUP | CORPS | DIVISIONS | ASSIGNED TO GERMAN COMMAND |
|---|---|---|---|
| (In Army Gp. Gallwitz (G)) | XVIII | 106 ID | Abschnitt Ornes |
| | | 1 ID | V Reserve Corps |
| | | 35 ID | Army Detachment C |
| | | 37 HID | Army of Duke Albert of Wurttenberg |

In organisation H.Q. IX

In addition a number of Austrian artillery units were assigned to German formations and a number of minor units were assigned to German LofC Command West.

**Total Units Assigned to Western Front**

| | Bns. | Sqns. | Btys. | (Guns) |
|---|---|---|---|---|
| | 45³/₄ | 4 | 96 | (360) |

## Austro-Hungarian Units in Turkey 15 October 1918

5 Artillery Regts. and 5 Motor Columns.

## Austro-Hungarian Units in the Interior 15 October 1918

32 ID (13 Bns.) In transfer to Balkans, Army Gp. Kövess.

Feldjäger Bns. (2)

Landsturm Bns. (2)

Field Training Bns. (19)

**Total 36 Bns.**

NB. As this is the last O.B. for the Austro-Hungarian Army on the Eastern Front we have appended a summary of Austro-Hungarian Units allocated to other fronts. For Austro-Hungarian Units on the South West Front see the Italian Front O.B. Section for October 1918.

# BALKAN FRONT

## Table 3.57 Serbian O.O.B. November 1914

| ARMY | DIVISION |
|---|---|
| 1 ARMY | Timok I Ban |
| | Timok II Ban |
| | Morava II Ban |
| 2 ARMY | Composite Div. I Ban |
| | Shumadia I Ban |
| | Morava I Ban |
| | Danube I Ban |
| 3 ARMY | Drina I Ban |
| | Drina II Ban |
| UZICE ARMY | Shumadia II Ban |
| | Uzice Bde. |
| BRANITCHEVO DETACHMENT | Danube II Ban |

| ARMY | DIVISION |
|---|---|
| OBRENOVATZ DETACHMENT | Regimental level units only |
| BELGRADE DETACHMENT | Regimental level units only |
| G.H.Q. Troops | Cavalry Division |
| FRONTIER UNITS | Regimental level units only |
| In Macedonia | Supernumerary Regiments, I Ban |

| Strenths | Inf.Bns. | Cav.Sqns. | Artillery (No. of Guns) |
|---|---|---|---|
| 1 ARMY | 40 | 8 | 90 |
| 2 ARMY | 64 | 13 | 134 |
| 3 ARMY | 28 | 6 | 72 |
| UZICE ARMY | 24 | 2 | 54 |
| BRANITCEVO DET. | 12 | 4 | 12 |
| OBRENOVATZ DET. | 18 | – | 26 |
| BELGRADE DET. | 9 | – | 43 |
| CAVALRY DIVISION | – | 16 | 9 |
| FRONTIER TROOPS | 25 | – | 78 |
| Troops in Macedonia | 52 | – | 66 |
| **Grand Total** | **272** | **49** | **583** |

## Table 3.58 Serbian O.O.B. 5.10.1915

| ARMY/ARMY GROUP | DIVISIONS |
|---|---|
| **Western & Northern Front** | |
| 1 ARMY | Uzice Gp. Sokol Bde. Don Div.II Drin Div.II Mor Div.II |
| Belgrade Defences | 20 Bns.* 2 Sqns. 79 guns |
| 3 ARMY | Branicevo Det. Don Div.I Drin Div.I Krajina Det. |
| – | Tim Div.II |
| **Eastern Front (Serbian-Bulgarian Border)** | |
| Timok Army Group | Negotinee Gp. Comb.Div. Sum Div.II + 3rd Line Troops in Fortresses |
| 2 ARMY | Tumba Gp. Mor Div.I Tim Div.I Sum Div.I Cav.Div. |
| **In New Districts (Macedonia)** | |
| Against Bulgaria | 31 Bns. 54 guns |
| Against Albania | Prizren Gp. Podrim Gp. Ochrida Gp. 13 Bns. 24 guns |
| **Montenegrin Army (End 9.1915)** | |
| Lovcen Group | 12¹/₂ Bns. 42 guns |
| Herzegovina Group | 2 Div. 3 Div. 15 Bns. 19 guns |
| Sandzak Group | 1, 2 & 3 Sandzak Divs. Kolasin Bde. 40 Bns. 54 guns |
| Old Serbia Group | 15¹/₄ Bns. 20 guns |

\* 3rd Line Units.

## Table 3.59 Austro-Hungarian O.O.B. Balkan Front Autumn 1915

| ARMY/ARMY GROUP | CORPS | DIVISIONS |
|---|---|---|
| **Army Group Mackensen (G)** | | |
| 3 ARMY | – | 62 ID Gpe. Streith Gpe. Sorsich |
| | XIX | 53 ID 205, 206, Lst.I.Bdes. Lst.I.Bde. Schwarz |
| | XXII Reserve(G) | 43 Res.D(G) 44 Res.D(G) 26(Wurt.) ID(G) |
| | VIII | 57 ID 59 ID Lst.I.Bdes. Haustein, Mrazek |

| ARMY/ARMY GROUP | CORPS | DIVISIONS |
|---|---|---|
| **Army Group Mackensen (G) continued** | | |
| **11 ARMY(G)** | III(G) | 6 ID(G) 25 Res.D(G) |
| | IV Reserve(G) | 11 Bav.ID(G) 105 ID(G) 107 ID(G) |
| | X Reserve(G) | 103 ID(G) 101 ID(G) |
| | Lst.Gruppe Fulopp(A-H) | 6½ Bns. ¼ Sqn. 6 Btys. |
| **1 Bulgarian Army** | – | 6 Bulg.ID 8 Bulg.ID 9 Bulg.ID 1 Bulg.ID Bulg. Gr. Stoikoff |
| *Added later* | (For 3 ARMY) | 10 Mtn.Bde.(A-H) |
| | – | Det.Alpenkorps(G) |
| **Troops in Dalmatia, Bosnia & Herzegovina** | Fortress & Garrison units(A-H) 47½ Bns. (of which only 11¾ were mobile units) 36½ Btys. (148 guns) | |
| **2 Bulgarian Army** | | 3 Bulg.ID 7 Bulg.ID |
| **Distribution Other Bulgarian Forces** | | |
| Greek Frontier | | 2 Bulg.ID 10 Bulg.ID |
| Rumanian Frontier | | 4 Bulg.ID 5 Bulg.ID |
| Army Reserve | | 11 Bulg.ID |

---

### Table 3.60 Allied O.O.B. Macedonian Front 31.8.1916

| ARMY | CORPS | DIVISIONS |
|---|---|---|
| **A. French Army of Orient** | – | 17 Col.ID 57 ID 122 ID 156 ID Cav.Bde. Frotiée |
| | Army Reserve | 2 Zouave Regt. 1 Ch.d'Afrique Regt. |
| **British Salonika Army** | XII | 22 ID 26 ID 28 ID |
| | XVI | 27 ID 10 ID Marine Bde. |
| | Army Reserve | 7 Mtd.Bde. 1 Cyclist Bn. |
| **Serbian Army** | | |
| **1 ARMY** | – | Morava Div. Vardar Div. |
| **2 ARMY** | – | Timok Div. Sumadija Div. |
| **3 ARMY** | – | Danube Div. Drina Div. |
| **Popovic Volunteer Gp.** | – | 3 Bns. + 1 Volunteer Bn. |
| **Army Reserve** | – | Cav.Div. |
| **Italian Contingent** | | 35 ID |
| **Russian Contingent** | | Brigade Diterichs |
| **Albanian Contingent** | | Abteilung (Bn.) Essad Pasha |

| Summary | Strength Circa |
|---|---|
| French Army of Orient | 115,400 |
| British Salonika Army | 119,100 |
| Serbian Army | 122,600 |
| Italian Contingent | 16,000 |
| Russian Contingent | 95,500 |
| Albanian Contingent | 800 |
| **Total Circa** | **383,400** |

| ARMY | CORPS | DIVISIONS |
|---|---|---|
| **B. Italian Troops in Albania** | XVI | 38 ID 10 Bersaglieri Regt. 6 Militia Rgts. 2 Cavalry Rgts. |
| | | 30 Bns. 12 Sqns. 56 Btys. (26 FD & Mtn. 30 Fortress) |

---

### Table 3.61 Austro-Hungarian O.O.B. Balkan Front 31.8.1916

| ARMY/ARMY GROUP | CORPS | DIVISIONS |
|---|---|---|
| **Field Troops** | XIX | 47 ID 211 LSt.Inf.Bde. |

**Troops of General Cmding Bosnia-Herzegovina**

| | Bns. | Btys. | (Guns) | M.G.Abteilungen |
|---|---|---|---|---|
| Coastal Defences | | | | |
| Wucherer | 6 | 3 | (24) | 2 |
| Andrian | 4 | 6½ | (32) | 3 |
| Cattaro Harbour Cmd. | 6 | 6½ | | 7 |
| | | & 27 Fortress Coys.(227) | | |
| Fortress Garrisons | 5 | 4½ | | 2 |
| | | & 11 Fortress Coys.(291) | | |
| Misc. Formations | 5 LSt.Bns. | ¾ Sqn. | | |

| | Bns. | Sqns. | Btys. | | |
|---|---|---|---|---|---|
| Mil.Govt. Serbia | 27 | 2¾ | 11 | | |
| Mil.Govt. Montenegro | 23 | 2½ | 13 | | |

| Summary | Inf.Bns. | Sqns. | Btys. | (Guns) | M.G.Abteilungen |
|---|---|---|---|---|---|
| XIX | 37 | ¾ | 31 | (119) | – |
| Bosnia-Herzegovina Command | 25 | ¾ | 20½ | (574) | 14 |
| | | & 38 Fortress Coys | | | |
| Mil.Govt. Serbia | 27 | 2¾ | 11 | | |
| Mil.Govt. Montenegro | 23 | 2½ | 13 | | |

---

### Table 3.62 German and Bulgarian O.O.B. Macedonian Front 31.8.1916

| ARMY GROUP/ ARMY | CORPS | DIVISIONS |
|---|---|---|
| **German Army Gp. von Below** | | |
| **1 Bulgarian Army** | – | 8 ID 3 ID Bde. Popoff 3 Cav.Bde. |
| **11 German Army** | – | Pt. 101 ID(G) 5 Bulg.ID Comb.Bulg. ID ⅓ 9 Bulg.ID ⅓ 2 Bulg.ID |
| **2 Bulgarian Army** | – | 11 ID 7 ID 10 ID ⅙ 6 ID |

| Summary | Bns. | Sqns. | Btys. |
|---|---|---|---|
| 1 Bulgarian Army | 57½ | 11 | 51 |
| 11 German Army | 63 | 4 | 64 |
| 2 Bulgarian Army | 63 | 3 | 52 |
| **Totals** | **183½** | **18** | **167** |
| | | | *(c.* **800 Guns)** |

## Table 3.63 Allied O.O.B. Balkans May 1917

| ARMY GROUP/ ARMY | CORPS | DIVISIONS |
|---|---|---|
| **A. Macedonian Front** | | |
| **French Army of Orient** | – | Nine* ID One Cav.Bde. |
| **British Salonika Army** | XII | Six and a half ID 1 Marine Bde. 1 Cav.Bde. |
| | XVI | |
| **Serbian Army 2 Army H.Q.** | | Six ID One Cav.Div. |
| **Italian Contingent** | | One Inf.Div. |
| **Russian Contingent** | | Two Inf.Bdes. |
| **Greek Venizelist Contingent** | | One Inf.Div. |

Divisions are not identified in this outline O.O.B. but the following is probably an accurate summary of the Divisions present:

| | |
|---|---|
| French | 30, 57, 76, 122, 156 ID 11, 16, 17 DIC(Colonial Inf.Divs.) (eight not nine as given) |
| British | 10, 22, 26, 27, 28, 60 Divs. |
| Serbian | Morava, Vardar, Sumadija, Timok, Drina, Danube Divs. |
| Italian | 35 ID |
| Russian | 2nd & 4th Bdes. |
| Greek Venizelist | Seres Div. |

| | | |
|---|---|---|
| **B. Albania** | | |
| **Italian Forces in Albania** | XVI | Two and a half Divs.† One Cav.Bde. |

## Table 3.64 Central Powers O.O.B. Balkan Front 31.5.1917

| ARMY/ARMY GROUP | CORPS | DIVISIONS |
|---|---|---|
| **Field Troops** | XIX | 47 ID Gp. Gerhauser (20 Mtn.Bde. Albanian Volunteer Gp.) |

| | Bns. | Sqns. | Btys. | (Guns) |
|---|---|---|---|---|
| Mil.Govt. Serbia | 13 | 3¼ | 3 | (54) |
| Mil.Govt. Montenegro | | | | |
| Garrison Troops | 11 | 1½ | – | (4) |
| Coast Defence | 5½ | – | 3½ | (37) |
| General Command Bosnia Herzegovina | | | | |
| Coast Def. N.Dalmatia | 5 | | 3 | (24) |
| Coast Def. S.Dalmatia | 3 | | 2½ | (42) |
| Cattaro Harbour Command | 8 | | 4 | (293) |
| Miscellaneous Garrison Troops | 8 | | 2½ | (297) |

**German-Bulgarian Front in Macedonia Army Group Scholtz**

| | | |
|---|---|---|
| **11 German Army** | Gen.Kdo.LXII | 1, 6, 8 Bulg.ID |
| | Gen.Kdo.LXI | 302(G)ID 2, 3 Bulg.ID |
| | Army Reserve | Bulg.-Macedonian Mtn.Div. |
| **1 Bulgarian Army** | – | 5, 9 Bulg.ID 101(G)ID |
| **2 Bulgarian Army** | – | 7, 10, 11 Bulg.ID 3 Bulg.Cav.Bde. 50(Turk)ID |

## Table 3.65 Allied O.O.B. Macedonian Front 14.9.1918

| ARMY/ARMY GROUP | CORPS | DIVISIONS |
|---|---|---|
| **Allied Armies in East *Armées Alliés en Orient*** | | |
| **A.F.O. *Armée Française d'Orient*** | 2 Gp. of Divs. | 30 DI 76 DI 11 DIC 156 DI(- 1 Rgt.) 1 Rgt/3(Greek)Div. |
| | 3 Gp. of Divs. | 57 DI 1 Rgt./156 DI 2 Serbian Bns. 1 Albanian Bn. 1 Algerian Bn. |
| | | 1 Indo-Chinese Bn. Tasor of Essad Pasha |
| | | 35(Italian)Div. 3(Greek)Div.(- 1 Rgt.) |
| | Army Troops | Gpment de Cav.(2 Regts. Ch d'Afrique 1 Regt. de Marche Moroccan Spahis) |
| **C.A.A. *Commandement des Armées Alliées en Orient*** | 1 Gp. of Divs. | 16 DIC(French) 4 Div.& Archipelago Div.(Greek) |
| **Serbian Armies** | | |
| **1 Serbian Army** | | Morava, Drina & Danube Divs. |
| **2 Serbian Army** | | Sumadija, Timok & Yugoslav Divs. |
| | | 17 DIC 126 DI(French) |
| **Army Group Troops** | | Serbian Cav.Div. |
| **British Salonika Army** | XII | 22, 26, 27 Divs. 83 Bde.(- 2 Bns.) (British) |
| | | Greek Seres Div. One Rgt. Zouaves (French) |
| | XVI | 28 Div.(- 83 Bde.H.Q.) Greek Crete Div. |
| | I Greek | 1, 2 & 13 Greek Divs. |
| **French G.H.Q. Troops** | | 9 & 14 Greek Divs. |
| **Greek Army‡** | National Defence | Archipelago Div.– Attached 1 Gp. of Divs.(French) |
| | | Seres Div.– Attached XII(British) Corps |
| | | Crete Div.– Attached XVI(British) Corps |
| | I Greek | 1, 2 & 13 Greek Divs.– Attached British Salonika Army |
| | II Greek | 3 Greek Div.– Attached A.F.O. |
| | | 4 Greek Div.– Attached 1 Gp. of Divs. |
| | | 14 Greek Div.– French G.H.Q. Troops |
| | Unattached | 9 Greek Div.– French G.H.Q. Troops |

*\* Actually only eight Divs. present.*

*† The Divisions will be 38, 43 and 44 ID.*

*‡ Administrative O.B.*

## Table 3.66 Bulgarian and German O.O.B. Macedonian Front September 1918

| ARMY/ARMY GROUP | CORPS/Gen.Kdos. | DIVISIONS |
|---|---|---|
| **Bulgarian G.H.Q.** | | |
| **Macedonian Army Group von Scholtz** | | |
| **11 German Army** | LXI(61)(G) | 2 Bulg.Div.(6 Regts.) Attached 4 LofC Regts. 1 German(Saxon)Jäger Bn. |

| ARMY/ARMY GROUP | CORPS/Gen.Kdos. | DIVISIONS |
|---|---|---|
| **Bulgarian G.H.Q. continued**<br>**Macedonian Army Group von Scholtz** | | |
| **11 German Army continued** | | 4 Bulg.Div.(4 Regts.) |
| | | 302(G)Div.(4 Regts. + 1 Saxon Reserve Jäger Bn.) |
| | LXII(62)(G) | 1 Bulg.Div.(5 Regts.) 6 Bulg.Div.(4 Regts.) |
| | | Composite (Ohrid)Div.(5 Regts. + 1 Austro-Hungarian Bn.) |
| | | Lakes Det.(2 Regts. + 1 Bn.) |
| | u/c 11 Army | 3 Bulg.Div.(6 Regts.) Attached 4 Regts. + 1 Bn. + 2 Landwehr Bns.(G) |
| **1 Bulgarian Army** | | 5 Bulg.Div.(6 Regts.) Attached 2 Regts. 9 Bulg.Div.(5 Regts.) |
| | | Bulg.Mtn.Div.(2 Regts.) Attached 1 Regt. & 1 Bn. |
| | | 1 Macedonian Bde.(11 Bulg.Div.)(2 Regts.) |
| | Army Troops | 2 Regts. |
| | Army Group Troops | 1 Bulgarian Bn. 3 German Bns. |
| **Under Direct Command Bulgarian H.Q.**<br>**2 Bulgarian Army** | | 7 Bulg.Div.(4 Regts.) Attached 1 Disciplinary Regt. |
| | | 8 Bulg.Div.(3 Regts.) Attached 1 Regt.& 2 Cav.Regts. |
| | | 11 Bulg.Div.(4 Regts.) Attached 1 Cav.Regt. |
| **4 Bulgarian Army** | | 10 Bulg.Div.(3 Regts.) Attached 1 Regt.& 1 Bn.Landwehr |
| | | Aegean Def.Force (2 Bulgarian Landwehr Regts.) |
| | | 1 Bulg.Cav.Div.(3 Cav.Regts.) |
| | | 2 Bulg.Cav.Div.(2 Cav.Regts. 1 Landwehr Regt. 1 Landwehr Bn.) |
| | Army Troops | 1 Regt. 1 Frontier Bn. |
| **Not located** | German Units | 2 Landwehr Bns. 3 Landsturm Bns. 1 Depot/LofC Bn. |

**NB** H.Q. of Macedonian Army Group, 11 Army, LXI 'Corps', LXII 'Corps' and 302 Div. were German. We have followed the convention in the British Official History of using Roman numerals for the two German 'Corps' H.Q. for the sake of clarity. However, they were officially 'General Kommandos' – temporary formations equating to French 'Groupements de Divisions' rather than true Corps H.Q. As such they are officially designated by the Germans in Arabic numerals (61 & 62).

**Allocation of Regiments to Bulgarian Divisions**

<table>
<tr><td>* The semi-colons divide the regiments (one, two or three) which were brigaded together.</td><td>

Division | Regiments* | Attached Regiments
---|---|---
1 | 1 6; 25 ; 41 42 | Nil
2 | 10 30; 28 44; 21 43 | 16 53 81 9 LofC
3 | 11 24; 29 32; 45 46 | 14 49 80 87 1 Bn.,/18
4 | 7 31; 47 48; | Nil
5 | 2 5; 18 20; 50 83 | 54 65
6 | 3 15; 51 52 | Nil
7 | 83 84; 22 26 | Disciplinary Regt.
8 | 12 23; 56 | 85 8 Cav. 10 Cav.
9 | 17 ;33 34; 57 58 | Nil
10 | 37 38; 86 | 88 1 Bn./11 Landwehr
11 | 60 61; 59 62; 63 64 | 4 Cav.
Mountain | 67 68; | 39 1 Bn./4
1 Cavalry | 1 Cav. 5 Cav. 7 Cav. |
2 Cavalry | Gd.Cav. 11 Cav. | 8 Landwehr 1 Bn./11 LW

</td></tr>
</table>

**Allocation of Regiments to Bulgarian Divisions continued**
Provisional Divs/Groupings
| | | |
|---|---|---|
| Composite (Ohrid) | 19 82; 36 71 72; | 2 Storm Bn. |
| Lakes Det. | 35 70 1 Bn./36 | |
| Aegean Defence Force | 1 Landwehr 10 Landwehr | |

Not forming part of Divisions
| | |
|---|---|
| (1 Army Troops) | 4 66 |
| (Army Gp. Troops) | 75 |
| (4 Army Troops) | 40 12 Frontier Bn. |

## ITALIAN FRONT

### *Table 3.67* Italian O.O.B. Autumn 1915

| ARMY/ARMY GROUP | CORPS | DIVISIONS |
|---|---|---|
| **1 ARMY**<br>(Trento Front) | III | 5, 6 ID |
| | V | 9, 34, 35 ID |
| | Army Reserve | Bde. Mantua/15 ID |
| **4 ARMY**<br>(Cadore sector) | IX | 1, 17, 18 ID |
| | I | 2, 10 ID |
| **Carnia Group**<br>(Carnia Zone) | XII | 24, 26 ID |
| **2 ARMY**<br>(Upper & Central Isonzo Front) | IV | 7, 8, 33 ID Bersaglieri Div. (strengthened) Alpine Groups A & B |
| | VIII | 27 ID 1 Bde./13 ID |
| | II | 3, 4, 32 ID |
| | VI | 11, 12 ID |
| **3 ARMY**<br>(Lower Isonzo Front) | XIV | 28, 29, 30 ID ½ 23 ID |
| | X | 19, 20 ID |
| | VII | 14 ID (strengthened) 16 ID Bde. Tritpani |
| **Supreme Command Reserve**[1] | XI | 21, 22 ID |
| | XIII | 25, 31 ID |
| | Cavalry | 1, 2, 3, 4 CD |
| **Reinforcements to Isonzo Front** | | |
| 10/11.1915 | | 9 ID (from 1 Army) 10 ID (from 4 Army) |
| Mid 11.1915 | | Bde. Novara/35 ID (from 1 Army) |
| **[1] In Libya, Dodecanese & Albania** | | 65 Bns. 6 Sqns.Cav. & unspecified No. of Art.Btys. |

| Summary | Bns. | Sqns. | Btys. |
|---|---|---|---|
| 1 ARMY | 114 | 16 | 70 |
| 4 ARMY | 74 | 10 | 73 |
| Carnia Group | 37 | 6 | 49 |
| 2 ARMY | 163 | 24 | 164 |
| 3 ARMY | 125 | 20 | 136 |
| Supreme Command Reserve | 49 | 92 | 50 |
| | + 4 Cycle | | |
| **Grand Total (Mid-October)** | *c.*566 | **170** | **500** |
| (Excludes reinforcements & troops in Libya etc.) | | | |

## Table 3.68 Austro-Hungarian O.O.B. Italian Front Autumn 1915

| ARMY/ARMY GROUP | CORPS | DIVISIONS |
|---|---|---|
| **South West Front** | | |
| **A.Tyrol Defence Command Tyrol** | Rayon I | 53 half Bde. + Independent Units |
| | Rayon II | 88 Cav.Sch.Bde. + Independent Units |
| | Rayon III | 91 ID 8 ID 52 half Bde. + Independent Units |
| | XIV – Rayon IV | 90 ID |
| | – Rayon V | Comb.Div. Pustertal |
| **B.Carinthia Army Group Rohr** | Sector I† | 48 ID |
| | Sector II | 94 ID |
| | Sector III | 92 ID |
| | Sector IV | 44 Sch.ID |
| **C.Coastal Area 5 ARMY** | Sector I (XV) | 50 ID 1 ID |
| | Sector II (XVI) | 18 ID 58 ID |
| | | 61 ID |
| | Sector IIIa (VII) | 20 HID 17 ID 106 LSt.ID |
| | Sector IIIb (III) | 28 ID 22 Sch.D + 2 Bdes. |
| | Sector IV – Trieste | Cav.Gp. City a Trieste Gp. Vogelhuber |
| | Sector V – Fiume | Independent Units |
| | Pola District | Independent Units |
| Reinforcements during 3 Isonzo Battle | | Total of 27 Bns. 1 Sqn. 5 Btys. inc. 6 ID(from Russian Front 27.10.15) To 5 Army 206 LSt.I.Bde.(from Syrmna 28.10.15) To Trieste Independent Units |
| Reinforcements during 4 Isonzo Battle | | Total of 23 Bns. 1 Sqn. 6 Btys. inc. 9 ID(from Russian Front 21.11.15) 9 Inf.Bde.(from Russian Front 21.11.15) |

| Summary | Bns. | Sqns. | Btys. | Independent M.G.Dets. | St.Sch.Abt. |
|---|---|---|---|---|---|
| A. Tyrol | 62½ | 4 | 58½ | 54 | 51 |
| B. Carinthia | 46½ | 5¼ | 58½ | | |
| C. Coastal Area | 135½ | 20 | 142½ | | |
| **Total (Mid-October)** | **245** | **30** | **256** | **54** | **51** |
| (Prior to reinforcement) | | | | | |

## Table 3.69 Italian O.O.B. 1.8.1916

| ARMY/ARMY GROUP | CORPS | DIVISIONS |
|---|---|---|
| **1 ARMY** (Trento Front) | III | 5*, 6* ID |
| | Unattached | 37 ID |
| | V | 44*, 27 ID Alp.Gp.6 |
| | X | 9, 20, 32 ID |
| **Mambretti Cd.** | XXIV | 30, 33 ID |
| | XXII | 25, 28, 29 ID |

| ARMY/ARMY GROUP | CORPS | DIVISIONS |
|---|---|---|
| **Mambretti Cd. continued** | XX | 4, 13 ID Alp.Gps. 4, 8, 9 |
| | XVIII | 10, 15*ID |
| | Unattached | 2, 3 CD |
| *Added* [1] 7/8.1916 | To Isonzo Front | 24 ID |
| [2] 7.8.1916 | XIV | 10*, 34 ID |
| [3] 17.8.1916 | XXIV | 4, 33 ID |
| *From 5 Army* | | 3 CD |
| [4] 27.7.1916 | | 19 ID |
| [5] 7.8.1916 | VIII | 43, 48 ID |
| | XXVI· | 23, 46 ID |
| **4 ARMY** (Cadore sector) | | Gp. Ferrari |
| | IX | 17, 18 ID |
| | | Alp.Gp.5 |
| | I | 1, 2 ID |
| **Carnia Group** (Carnia Zone) | XII | 26 Comb.ID 36 Comb.ID |
| **2 ARMY** (Upper & Central Isonzo Front) | IV | 1 Comb.ID 1, 2 Alp.Cps. 8*ID 7*ID |
| | II | 3 Comb.ID 4(Dismtd.) CD |
| **3 ARMY** (Gorizia bridgehead & Upper Isonzo Front) | VI | 45, 24, 11, 12, 43 ID |
| | XI | 22*, 21 ID |
| | XIII | Comb.Gp. 31 ID |
| | VII | 16*ID 14*ID 1(Dismtd.) CD |
| *Added* [1] 1.8.1916 | | 19, 49 ID |
| [2] 31.7.1916 | VIII | 48 ID |
| *En route* | XXVI | 23, 46 ID |
| **Reserve of Supreme Command** | XIV | 10(3 Bdes.) 34 ID |
| | XXIV | 4, 33 ID Bde. Benevento |
| | | 3 CD |

| Summary | Bns. | Sqns. | Lt.Guns | Med.& Heavy Guns |
|---|---|---|---|---|
| 1 ARMY & Mambretti Cd. | c. 288 | 48 | 640 | 530 |
| 4 ARMY | c. 63 | – | 252 | 153 |
| Carnia Group | c. 38 | – | 80 | 100 |
| Isonzo { 2 ARMY | c. 62 | 24 | 344 | 229 |
| 3 ARMY | c. 220 | 40 | 728 | 467 & 56 |
| From Supreme Cd. Reserve (during 6 Isonzo Battle) | c. 60 | 24 | 150 Guns | |

## Table 3.70 Austro-Hungarian O.O.B. Italian Front 1.8.1916

| ARMY/ARMY GROUP | CORPS | DIVISIONS |
|---|---|---|
| **A. Army Group Archduke Eugen (Heeresgruppe)** | | |
| | Rayon I | 53 half Bde. + Independent Units |
| | Rayon II | Independent Units |
| **11 ARMY** | Rayon III | 50 half Bde. + Independent Units |
| | XXI | Gr.v.Guseck Cav.Sch.D |
| | XX | 3 ID 8 ID(KJD) |

† We have used 'sector' as the equivalent of the German word *Abschnitt*.

\* Indicates Inf. Div.(reinforced).

| ARMY/ARMY GROUP | CORPS | DIVISIONS |
|---|---|---|
| **A. Army Group Archduke Eugen (Heeresgruppe) continued** | | |
| **11 ARMY** continued | III | 6 ID 22 Sch.D 28 ID 10 ID |
| | XVII | 18 ID 181 I.Bde. 2, 8 Mtn.Bdes. |
| **(East Tyrol Front)** | Roth – Rayon IV | 90 ID 57 ID |
| | Rayon V | Comb.D Pustertal, 56 Mtn.Bde. |
| **B. 10 ARMY** | Sector I | 94 ID |
| | Sector II | 92 ID |
| | Sector III | 59 Mtn.Bde. |
| | Sector IV | 27 Mtn.Bde. |
| **C. 5 ARMY** | Sector I (XV) | 50 ID 1 ID |
| | Sector II (XVI) | 62 ID 58 ID |
| | Sector IIIa (VII) | 20 HID 17 ID |
| | Sector IIIb | 9 ID 24 LSt.Mtn.Bde. 59 I.Bde. |
| | Army Reserve | 43 Sch.D |
| **(Trieste Coastal Dist.)** | Sector IV | Minor Units |
| **(Fiume Coastal Dist.)** | Sector V | Minor Units |
| **(Pola Dist.)** | | Minor Units |

| | | |
|---|---|---|
| **5 ARMY** Reinforcements during 6 Isonzo Battle. Total of 28 Bns. 1¼ Sqns. 8 Btys. inc: | | |
| | From A.G. AD Eugen | Comb.ID Hrozny + Minor Units |
| | From 10 Army | Minor Units |
| | From Russian Front | Minor Units |
| **5 ARMY** Reinforcements during 6 Isonzo Battle to end of 8.1916. Total of 37½ Bns. 2½ Sqns. 45 Btys. inc: | | |
| | From A.G. AD Eugen | 28 ID |
| | From Russian Front | 44 Sch.D 16 ID |
| | From Balkan Front | Minor Units |

**Summary**

| | Bns. | Sqns. | Btys. | St.Sch.Abt. | Indep.M.G.Dets. |
|---|---|---|---|---|---|
| A.11 ARMY | 144³/₄ | 11 | 136½ | 24 | 28 |
| **Total HGR Archduke (Including 11 Army & Other Commands)** | | | | | |
| **Eugen** | **195½** | **14³/₄** | **168½** | **53†** | **78** |
| B.10 ARMY | 42 | 3 | 46 | | |
| C. 5 ARMY | 110 | 7¼ | 120½ | | |
| **Total Italian Front at 1.8.1916** | | | | | |
| | **357** | **25** | **355** | **51†** | **78** |

† As given. Clearly, one is incorrect.

| ARMY/ARMY GROUP | CORPS | DIVISIONS |
|---|---|---|
| **4 ARMY** (Cadore sector) | XVIII | 15, 51, 56 ID |
| | IX | 17*, 18 ID |
| | Val Costenna Sector | Alp.Gp.6 |
| | I | 1*ID |
| **Carnia Group** (Carnia zone) | XII | 26*, 36 ID |
| **2 ARMY** Isonzo Front | IV | 50*, 43*, 46*, 34 ID |
| | XXVII | 19*ID Alp.Gp.10, 65, 22, 64 ID |
| | XXIV | 10, 49, 68 ID |
| | II | 8, 44, 67 ID |
| | VI | 24, 66 ID |
| | VIII | 48, 59, 7 ID |
| | VII | 3*, 62 ID |
| | XIV | 25, 30 ID |
| | XXVIII | 23*, 47* ID |
| **3 ARMY** Isonzo Front | XI | 31, 58 ID |
| | XIII | 14*, 54 ID |
| | XXIII | 61, 28, 45 ID |
| | XXV | 4, 33 ID |
| **At Disposal of Supreme Command** | | |
| **4 ARMY Sector** | | 5 Bersaglieri Cycle Bns. |
| **2 ARMY Sector** | | 13*, 53*, 60 ID |
| **3 ARMY Sector** | XXX | 16, 21 ID |
| | | 20*, 63*ID 1, 2, 3, 4 CD |

**Summary**

| | Bns. | Sqns. | Btys. |
|---|---|---|---|
| III Corps | 32 | | 84 |
| 1 ARMY | 122 | 9 | 293 |
| 4 ARMY | 91 | 3 | 129 |
| Carnia Group | 31 | 2 | 98 |
| 2 ARMY | 346 | 11 | 604 |
| 3 ARMY | 108 | 8 | 247 |
| G.H.Q. Reserve | 114 | 102 | |
| **Grand Total** | **891** | **135** | **1,455** |

**(6,918 guns – 3,828 Lt. 2,933 Med. 157 Hvy.)**

* See note for Table 3.69.

---

**Table 3.71 Italian O.O.B. 24.10.1917**

| ARMY/ARMY GROUP | CORPS | DIVISIONS |
|---|---|---|
| Stilfrerjoch-Gardasee | III | 5*, 6*ID |
| **1 ARMY** (Gardasee-Val Sugane) | XXIX | 27, 37 ID |
| | V | 55*, 69 ID |
| | X | 9, 32 ID |
| | XXVI | 11, 12 ID |
| | XXII | 2, 57 ID |
| | XX | 29, 52 ID |
| | Army Reserve | One Bde. |

**Table 3.72 Austro-Hungarian O.O.B. Italian Front October 1917**

| ARMY/ARMY GROUP | CORPS | DIVISIONS |
|---|---|---|
| **A. Army Group Conrad (Heeresgruppe)** | | |
| **[1] Gp. Archduke Peter Ferdinand** | Rayon I | Minor Units only |
| | Rayon II | Minor Units only |
| **[2] 11 ARMY (I)** | Rayon III | Minor Units only |
| (II) | | 56 Sch.D |
| (III) | XIV | 8 CD(KJD) 15 I.Bde. |
| (IV) | III | Gp.Vidossich 19 ID 6 ID |
| (V) | | 18 ID |

Austro-Hungarian O.O.B. Italian Front October 1917 continued

| ARMY/ARMY GROUP | CORPS | | DIVISIONS |
|---|---|---|---|
| **A. Army Group Conrad (Heeresgruppe) continued** | | | |
| [3] | XX | Rayon IV | 52 ID |
| | | Rayon V | 49 ID |
| *Added 1-4.11.17* | | | 106 LSt.D 21 Sch.D |
| **B. (To Army Group Archduke Eugen 31.10.17)** | | | |
| 10 ARMY | | | 94 ID Gp.Hordt |
| **C. Heeresfront Archduke Eugen** | | | |
| [1] 14 ARMY (G) (a) | Gp.Krauss(I) | | 3 ID 22 Sch.D 55 ID Jäger Div.(G) |
| (b) | Gp.Stein (II Bavarian) | | 50 ID 12 ID(G) Alpine Corps(G) 117 ID(G) |
| (c) | Gp.Berrer (Gen.Kdo.LI(G)) | | 26 ID(G) 200 ID(G) |
| (d) | Gp.Scotti(XV) | | 1 ID 5 ID(G) |
| **[2] Heeresgruppe Boroevic** | | | |
| 2 Isonzo ARMY | Gp.Kosak | | 60 ID 35 ID 57 ID |
| | XXIV | | 24 ID 53 ID |
| | IV | | 43 Sch.D 20 HID |
| | II (Army Reserve) | | 28 ID 29 ID 9 ID |
| 1 Isonzo ARMY | XVI | | 58 ID 63 ID 14 ID |
| | VII | | 44 Sch.D 17 ID 48 ID |
| | XXIII | | 41 HID 10 ID 12 ID |
| | Trieste Sector | | Minor Units |
| | (Army Reserve) | | 21 Sch.D |
| | Army Group Res. | | 106 LSt.ID Fiume Sector |
| **D. Army Reserves** | | | 4 ID 13 Sch.D 33 ID |

| Summary | Bns. | Sqns. | Batteries | St.Sch.Abt. |
|---|---|---|---|---|
| A. 11 ARMY | 69¹/₂ | 1³/₄ | 96³/₄ | 23 |
| Heeresgruppe Conrad* | 120¹/₄ | 1³/₄ | 141²/₃ | 49 |
| B. 10 ARMY | 29¹/₄ | ³/₄ | 41¹/₃ | |
| C. 14 ARMY | 123 | 7³/₄ | 334¹/₂ | |
| Heeresgruppe Boroevic | 260¹/₂ | 16¹/₂ | 338 | |
| **Total Heeresfront Archduke Eugen** | **383¹/₂** | **24³/₄** | **672¹/₂** | |
| D. G.H.Q. Reserves | 41 | 2 | – | |
| **Grand Total** | **574** | **28³/₄** | **855¹/₂** | **49** |

**Table 3.73** Italian O.O.B. 15.6.1918

| ARMY GROUP/ ARMY | CORPS | DIVISIONS |
|---|---|---|
| **3 ARMY** | XXIII | 4 ID 61 ID Marine Regt. 12 Bns. Cyclists |
| | XI | 45 ID 31 ID 23 ID |
| | XXVII | 25 ID 53 ID |
| | Army Reserve | 2 CD |
| **8 ARMY** | VIII | 48 ID 58 ID |
| | XXX | 47 ID 50 ID |

| ARMY GROUP/ ARMY | CORPS | DIVISIONS |
|---|---|---|
| **8 ARMY** continued | XXVII | 51 ID 66 ID |
| **4 ARMY** | I | 70 ID 24 ID |
| | VI | 59 ID 15 ID |
| | XVIII | 1 ID 56 ID |
| | IX | 17 ID 18 ID |
| **6 ARMY** | XX | 2 ID 10 ID |
| | XIV (British) | 23 Div. 48 Div. 7 Div. (All British) |
| | XIII | 28 ID 14 ID |
| | XII (French) | 23 ID(French) 24 ID(French) 52 ID(Italian) |
| **1 ARMY** | X | 12 ID 9 ID 32 ID |
| | XXIX | 34 ID 26 ID 54 ID |
| | V | 69 ID 55 ID 29 ID |
| **7 ARMY** | XIV | 20 ID 22 ID 6 ID 21 ID |
| | III | 5 ID 75 ID |
| **9 ARMY** | XXV | 7 ID 33 ID |
| | XXVI | 11 ID 13 ID |
| | XXII | 57 ID 60 ID |
| | Assault | Assault Div. Czech Div. |
| | XII | 27 ID 37 ID |
| | Army Reserve | 4 CD |
| **G.H.Q. Direct Control** | | 1 CD 3 CD |

**Summary**
725 Bns. *c.*100 Sqns. 7,550 guns.

**Table 3.74** Austro-Hungarian O.O.B. Italian Front 15.6.1918 (South-West Front)

| ARMY GROUP/ ARMY | CORPS | DIVISIONS |
|---|---|---|
| **A. Army Group Conrad** | | |
| **10 ARMY** Gp. Erzherzog Peter Ferdinand | Rayon I | 164 Inf.Bde. |
| | Rayon II | 1 ID 22 Sch.D |
| | XX | 49 ID, Abschnitt Riva (Artillery units only) |
| | XXI | 19 ID 56 Sch.D |
| | XIV(Edelweiss) | KJD 159 Inf.Bde. |
| **11 ARMY** | III | 6 KD 6 ID 52 ID 28 ID |
| | XIII | 38 HID 16 ID 42 HID 74 HID 5 ID |
| | VI | 18 ID Edelweiss Div. 26 Sch.D |
| | XXVI | 27 ID 32 ID 4 ID |
| | I | 60 ID 55 ID |
| | XV | 50 ID 20 HID 48 ID |
| | Army Reserve | 36 ID 53 ID 3 CD 10 CD |
| **B. Army Group Boroevic** | | |
| **6 ARMY** | II | 8 CD |
| | XXIV | 31 ID 13 Sch.D 17 ID |
| | Army Reserve | 11 HCD |

\* As a whole, i.e. 11 Army + other Commands.

| ARMY GROUP/ ARMY | CORPS | DIVISIONS |
|---|---|---|
| **B. Army Group Boroevic continued** Isonzo Army | XVI | 33 ID 58 ID 46 Sch.D |
| | IV | 64 HID 70 HID 29 ID |
| | VII | 14 ID 24 ID 9 CD 44 Sch.D |
| | XXIII | 12 ID 10 ID 1 CD |
| | Army Reserve | 57 ID 201 LSt.Inf.Bde. |
| | Army Group Res. | 9 ID 35 ID 41 HID 51 HID 12 Mtd.Sch.D |

**Summary**

| | Bns. | Sqns. | Guns | Dismtd.Cav.Regts |
|---|---|---|---|---|
| 10 ARMY | 108 | 5³/₄ | 1,360 | 1 |
| 11 ARMY | 274 | 23 | 2,935 | 28 |
| 6 ARMY | 42 | 5 | 768 | 17 |
| Isonzo Army | 166¹/₂ | 14¹/₄ | 1,770 | 19 |
| Army Group Reserve | 52 | 5 | – | 8¹/₂ |
| | **642¹/₂** | **53** | **6,833** | **73¹/₂** |

### Table 3.75 Italian O.O.B. 4.11.1918

| ARMY/ARMY GROUP | CORPS | DIVISIONS |
|---|---|---|
| **1 ARMY** | V | 55, 69 ID |
| | X | 6, 32 ID |
| | XXIX | 26 ID Other non-divisional units |
| **3 ARMY** | XXVI | 45, 54 ID |
| | XXVIII | 25, 53 ID |
| | Army Disposal | 23 ID |
| **4 ARMY** | VI | 15, 59 ID |
| | IX | 18, 21 ID |
| | XXX | 47, 50 ID |
| | Army Disposal | 17, 22 ID 80 Alp.D |
| **6 ARMY** | XII | 20, 27 ID |
| | XIII | 14 ID Other non-divisional units |
| | XX | 7, 29 ID |
| | Army Disposal | 24(French)ID 48(British)ID |
| **7 ARMY** | II | 5, 75 ID |
| | XXV | 4, 11 ID |
| **8 ARMY** | VIII | 48, 58 ID |
| | XXII | 57, 60 ID |
| | XXVII | 51, 66 ID |
| | Assault | 1, 2 Assault Divs.(Divisioni d'Assalto) |
| | Army Disposal | 1, 2, 10, 12 ID |
| **9 ARMY** | XIV | 9, 34 ID |
| | XXIII | 28, 61 ID 6 Czech D |
| **10 ARMY** | XI | 31, 37 ID |
| | XVIII | 33, 56 ID |
| | XIV(British) | 7(Brit.), 23(Brit.)ID |
| | Army Disposal | 332 US IR |

| ARMY/ARMY GROUP | CORPS | DIVISIONS |
|---|---|---|
| **12 ARMY** | I | 24, 70 ID |
| | Army Disposal | 52 Alp.D, 23(French)ID |
| | Unattached | 1, 2, 3, 4 CD |
| **Detached on other Fronts** | | |
| France | II | 3, 8 ID |
| Albania | XVI | 13, 36, 38 ID |
| Macedonia | | 35 ID (= Corps in strength) |
| Near East | CSI | Corpo di Spedizione Italiani (c.8,000 men) |

### Table 3.76 Austro-Hungarian O.O.B. Italian Front October 1918

| ARMY GROUP/ ARMY | CORPS | DIVISIONS |
|---|---|---|
| **Heeresgruppe Archduke Joseph** | | |
| **10 ARMY** | V | 164 IB 22 Sch.D |
| | XX | 49 ID, Riva Sector |
| | XXI | 3 Cav.D 56 Sch.D |
| | XIV | KJD 19 ID |
| | Army Reserve | 159 IB |
| | Army Gp.Reserve | 3 ID |
| **11 ARMY** | III | 6 Cav.D 6 ID 52 ID |
| | XIII | 27 ID 38 HID 10 Cav.D |
| | VI | 53 ID 18 ID 39 HID |
| | Army Reserve | 5 ID 16 ID |
| | Army Gp.Reserve | 36 ID 74 HID |
| **Heeresgruppe Boroevic** | | |
| **Armeegruppe Belluno** | XXVI | 40 HID 28 ID 42 HID 4 ID |
| | I | 48 ID 13 Sch.D 17 ID |
| | XV | 50 ID 20 HID |
| | Army Reserve | 60 ID 55 ID 21 Sch.D |
| **6 ARMY** | II | 31 ID 25 ID 11 H.Cav.D 12 Mtd.Sch.D |
| | XXIV | 41 HID 51 HID |
| | Army Reserve | 10 ID 43 Sch.D 34 ID |
| **Isonzo Army** | XVI | 29 ID 7 ID 201 LSt.IB |
| | IV | 64 HID 70 HID 8 Cav.D |
| | VII | 33 ID 12 ID 24 ID |
| | XXIII | 46 Sch.D 58 ID |
| | XXII | 14 ID 2 ID |
| | Army Reserve | 57 ID 26 Sch.D |
| | Army Gp.Reserve | 44 Sch.D |
| **Under Heeresgruppe Control** | Trieste Sector | Minor Units |
| | Fiume Sector | Minor Units |
| | Coastal Sector Pola | Minor Units |
| | LofC Gp.Commands | |
| | Gorizia | Minor Units |
| | Belluno | Minor Units |

**Austro-Hungarian O.O.B. Italian Front October 1918 continued**

| Summary | Bns. | Sqns. | Btys. | Vol.Sch.Bns./Halb.Rgt.zu Fuss. St.Sch.Bns. | |
|---|---|---|---|---|---|
| **Hgr. Archduke Joseph** | | | | | |
| 10 ARMY | 88 | 6¹/₄ | 370⁵/₂ | 6/9 | 10 |
| HGr. Reserve | 7 | 1 | 3¹/₂ | | |
| 11 ARMY | 108 | 11 | 284²/₂ | | 20 |
| HGr. Reserve | 17 | 2 | | | |
| **Total** | **220** | **20¹/₄** | **654⁷/₂** | **6/9** | **30** |
| | | | | | |
| **Hgr. Boroevic** | | | | | |
| Armee Gp.Belluno | 144³/₄ | 11¹/₂ | 300 | | |
| 6 ARMY | 83 | 9 | 206¹/₂ | | 20 |
| Isonzo Army | 113³/₄ | 14¹/₄ | 325²/₂ | | 12 |
| HGr. Reserve | 13 | 1 | 18 | | |
| **Total*** | **338³/₄** | **35³/₄** | **867³/₂** | | **32** |

# TURKISH FRONT
## Gallipoli

**Table 3.77** Allied Order of Battle Gallipoli 1915

| H.Q. | CORPS | DIVISIONS |
|---|---|---|
| **April 1915** British & Imperial **Mediterranean Expeditionary Force** | – | 29 Div. R.Naval Div.(2 Naval & 1 R.Marine Bde.) |
| | A.&N.Z. | 1 Aust.Div. N.Z. & Aust.Div. |
| French *Corps Expéditionnaire d'Orient* | | 1 Div.CEO (1 Metropolitan Bde.) † |
| | | (2 Colonial Bde.) ‡ |
| **Corps Troops** | | 7 Indian Mtn. Artillery Bde. |
| **August 1915** British & Imperial **Mediterranean Expeditionary Force** | VIII | 29 Div. 42(E.Lancs.)Div. 52(Lowland)Div. R.Naval Div.(1 Naval & 1 R.Marine Bde.) |
| | IX | 10(Irish)Div. 11(Northern)Div. 13(Western)Div. |
| | Attached IX | 53(Welsh)Div. 54(E.Anglian)Div. 2 Mounted Div.(dismounted) |
| | A.&N.Z. | 1 Aust.Div. N.Z.& Aust.Div. 2 Aust.Div.◊ |
| | | Corps Troops – 2 & 3 Aust.Lt.Horse Bdes.(dismounted) |
| | Attached A.&N.Z. | 29 Indian Inf.Bde. |
| | G.H.Q. Troops | 2 Bdes. R.G.A.● Armoured Cav.Div. R.N.A.S.Δ |
| French *Corps Expéditionnaire d'Orient* | | 1 Div.CEO (1 Metropolitan Bde. 2 Colonial Bde.) |
| | | 2 Div.CEO (3 Metropolitan Bde. 4 Colonial Bde.)** |
| | Corps Artillery | 4 Heavy Btys. Naval Bty. 2 Siege guns |

**Table 3.78** Turkish Order of Battle Gallipoli 1915

| ARMY | CORPS | DIVISIONS |
|---|---|---|
| **April 1915** **5 ARMY** | III | 5 Div. 7 Div. 9 Div. (Gallipoli Peninsula) |
| | XV | 3 Div. 11 Div. (Asiatic Shore) |
| **Winter 1915** **5 ARMY** | Anarfarta Group XVI | (Covers Suvla Bay) 9 Div. 11 Div. 12 Div. |
| | XV | 4 Div. 6 Div. 8 Div. |
| | Northern Group – | Combined Div. 16 Div. 19 Div. |
| | Southern Group XIV | 1 Div. 10 Div. |
| | V | 13 Div. 14 Div. |
| | Army Reserve | 3 Div. 26 Div. |

\* Including Sector Commands and Coastal Defences.

## Egypt/Palestine

**Table 3.79** Egyptian Expeditionary Force Order of Battle October 1917

| ARMY/G.H.Q. | CORPS | DIVISIONS |
|---|---|---|
| **G.H.Q.** | Desert Mtd.Corps | A.&N.Z.Mtd.Div. (1, 2 ALH NZMR Bdes.) Aust.Mtd.Div. (3, 4 ALH 5 Mtd. Bdes.) Yeomanry Mtd.Div.(6, 8, 22 Mtd.Bdes.) |
| | XX | 53(Welsh)Div. 60(London)Div. 74(Yeomanry)Div. |
| | XXI | 52(Lowland)Div. 54(E.Anglian)Div. 75 Div. |
| | G.H.Q. Troops | Palestine Bde.RFC 7 Mtd.Bde., Imp.C.C.Bde.(Attached Desert Mtd. Corps) |
| | | 10(Irish)Div.(Attached XX Corps) |

† Formed of 1 Metropolitan Line IR (175th) & *RdM. d'Afrique* (Zouave & Foreign Legion).

‡ Formed of European Colonial Bns. & Senegalese Bns.

◊ 2 Aust.Div. 1 Bde. only in August, 2 Bdes. arrived September. A.&N.Z.Div. N.Z. Mtd.Rifle Bde. and 1 Aust.Lt.Horse Bdes. were serving in a dismounted role.

● Royal Garrison Artillery.

Δ Royal Naval Air Service.

** Formed of 3rd Metropolitan Bde.(1 Line Regt.–176th, 1 *RdM. d'Afrique* (Zouave)) and 4th Colonial Bde.(2 Regts. of Infanterie Coloniale – Mixed European and Senegalese.

**Table 3.80** Egyptian Expeditionary Force Order of Battle September 1918

| ARMY/G.H.Q. | CORPS | DIVISIONS |
|---|---|---|
| **G.H.Q.** | Desert Mtd.Corps | (Mixed British-Indian Divs.) 4 Cav.Div. (10, 11, 12 Cav.Bdes.) 5 Cav.Div. (13, 14, 15 [Imp.Serv.] Cav.Bdes.) A.&N.Z. Mtd.Div. – Part of Chaytor's Force Aust.Mtd.Div. (3, 4, 5 ALH Bdes.) |
| | XX | 10(Irish)Div. 53(Welsh)Div. |

| ARMY/G.H.Q. | CORPS | DIVISIONS |
|---|---|---|
| | XXI | 3(Lahore)Ind.Div. 7(Meerut)Ind.Div. 54(E.Anglian)Div. 60(London)Div. 75 Div. *Détachement Français de Palestine et Syrie* (u/c 54 Div.) (*R de M de Tirailleurs,R de M de la L.E.*) |
| | Chaytor's Force | A.&N.Z.Mtd.Div.(1, 2 ALH NZMR Bdes.) 20 Indian Inf.Bde. + 4 unattached Bns.(of which 2 West Indian) |
| | G.H.Q.Troops | Palestine Bde. R.A.F. |

### Table 3.81 Ottoman and German Order of Battle October 1917*

| ARMY/ARMY GROUP | ARMY | CORPS | DIVISIONS |
|---|---|---|---|
| **G.H.Q. Yilderim** | | | |
| | 7 ARMY | III | 3 Cav. 27 Div. 2, 48 Regts. |
| | | – | 24 Div.(-2 Regt.) |
| | 8 ARMY | XX | 16 Div.(-48 Regt.) 26 Div. 54 Div. |
| | | XIII | 3 Div. 53 Div. |
| | | – | 7 Div. |
| | G.H.Q. Troops | | 19 Div. 10 Depot Regt. |
| | | | German Flying Corps (301-304 Flight Dets. |

### Table 3.82 Ottoman and German Order of Battle September 1918

| ARMY/ARMY GROUP | ARMY | CORPS | DIVISIONS |
|---|---|---|---|
| **G.H.Q. Yilderim** | | | |
| | 4 ARMY | II | Hauran Det. Amman Div. Ma'an Det. |
| | | VIII | Caucasus Cav.Bde. 48 Div. Composite Div. Mule Mtd.Inf.Rgt. + various battalion size units |
| | | Army Troops | 3 Cav.Div. 63 Regt. 146(G)Regt. |
| | 7 ARMY | III | 1 Div. 11 Div. |
| | | XX | 24 Div. 26 Div. 53 Div. |
| | 8 ARMY | XXII | 7 Div. 20 Div. |
| | | Asia | 16 Div. 19 Div. Pasha II(G)Bde. |
| | | Army Troops | 46 Div. |
| | G.H.Q. Troops | | 109 Regt.(Att. 7 ARMY) 110 Regt. 13 & 17 Depot Regts. |
| | | | Yilderim Flying Command (1 Pursuit, 302-304 Recce.Dets.) |
| **German Formations with Yilderim** | | | |
| | Asia Corps (Pasha II) | | 701, 702, 703 Bns.(strengthened with M.G. Cav., Artillery Dets.) 701 Artillery Det.(2 x 77 mm.Btys. 1 x 105 mm.Bty.) M.G.Det. Hentig. |
| | Pasha II Reinforcements | | 146 Inf.Regt. 11 Res.Jäger.Bn. Mountain Artillery Det. Mountain M.G. Det. |

*Left margin notes:*

* All Units are Turkish unless otherwise stated.

† According to Intelligence Summary WO 106/1475.

‡ Ex 3 Composite.

◊ Ex 5 Composite.

## Mesopotamia

### Table 3.83 Anglo-Indian Divisions in Mesopotamia 1914-1918

**Build Up of Anglo-Indian Forces in Theatre**

| Date of Arrival | Formation | Final Disposal |
|---|---|---|
| 11.1914 | Indian Expeditionary Force 'D' 6(Poona) Division arrives in theatre | 4.1916 P.O.W. Kut-al-Amara |
| 3-4.1915 | 12 Indian Division | 3.1916 Broken up |
| 1.1916 | 3(Lahore), 7(Meerut) Divisions (from France via Egypt) | 3.1918 (3 Div.) to Egypt 1.1918 (7 Div.) to Egypt |
| 2/3.1916 | 13(British)Div. (from Egypt) | Remained in theatre to end of war |
| 5.1916 | 14 Indian Division (from Bdes. in Mesopotamia) | Remained in theatre to end of war |
| | 15 Indian Division (from Bdes. in Mesopotamia) Replaced 12 Indian Division – see above. | Remained in theatre to end of war |
| 12.1916 | Cavalry Division (from Bdes. in Mesopotamia) The Division was never allocated a number. | 4.1918 Broken up |
| 8.1917 | 17 Indian Division (maintly from units in Mesopotamia) | Remained in theatre to end of war |
| 11/12.1917 | 18 Indian Division (from units in Mesopotamia and newly arriving units from India) | Remained in theatre to end of war |

### Table 3.84 Turkish Divisions in Mesopotamia 1914-18†

| DIVISION | FIRST MENTION | LAST MENTION | FROM | TO |
|---|---|---|---|---|
| •35 | 5.8.14 | 6.11.14 | 6.1.15 | 16.2.16 |
| •36 | 5.8.14 | } To Caucasus | | |
| •37 | 5.8.14 | | | |
| •38 | 5.8.14 | 20.12.15 | | |
| •45 | 20.12.15 | 11.3.17 | | |
| •51‡ | 20.12.15 | 1.3.18 | | |
| •52◊ | 20.12.15 | 9.12.17 | | |
| •2 | 16.2.16 | 11.11.18 | | |
| •6 | 7.16 | 1.3.18 | | |
| •4 | 11.3.17 | only date listed | | |
| •14 | 7.17 | 1.3.18 | | |
| 50 | 9.12.17 | 1.3.18 | | |
| 5 | 10.18 | 11.11.18 | | |

The Return lists Turkish Divisions by Theatre/Area at Specific dates. The dates quoted above are those at which Division is first and last listed.
•These divisions have been confirmed in O.B.s not all of which are reproduced here. 50 and 5 Divs, arrived late in war. 26 or 44, 13, 23 Divs. (see O.B. 2.1916) are not mentioned in the above Summary as serving in Mesopotamia.

### Table 3.85 Anglo-Indian O.O.B.s Mesopotamia 1915-1918

| ARMY | CORPS | DIVISIONS |
|---|---|---|
| **Anglo-Indian O.O.B. Mesopotamia 2.1916** | | |
| **Besieged in Kut-al-Amara** | | 6(Poona)Div. (16, 17, 18, 30 Bdes.) + Detachments of 2 British Bns. |
| **Relief Force on Tigris Front** | Tigris Corps | 3 Indian Div. (7, 9 Bdes.) (-Dets.) |
| | | 7 Indian Div. (19, 21, 35 Bdes.) |
| | Corps Troops | 28 Inf.Bde. 6 Cav.Bde. 1 RHA Bty. 1 Fd.Bde.RFA 3 Howitzer Btys. |
| | | 1 Mtn.Bty. 1 Fd.Bty.(Indep.) |
| | L of C & Garrisons | Detached Coys. & Troops/Sqns. of various Indian Inf.Bns. & Cav.Regts. but, principally, at Nasiriyeh, Botaniya 12 Inf.Bde. 34 Inf.Bde. |
| *Ordered to move to* | Tigris Front | 2 RFA Bdes. & 1 Bty.RFA |
| **Anglo-Indian O.O.B. Mesopotamia May-November 1917** | | |
| **Mesopotamia E.F.** | I Indian | 3(Lahore)Div.(7, 8, 9 Bdes.) 7(Meerut)Div.(19, 21, 28 Bdes.) |
| | | 1 Cav.Rgt.(32 Lancers) |
| | III Indian | 13(British)Div.(38, 39, 40 Bdes.) 14 Indian Div.(35, 36, 37 Bdes.) |
| | | 1 Cav.Rgt.(12 Cavalry) |
| | Indian Cav.Div. | (6, 7 Cav.Bdes.) |
| | Independent | 15 Indian Div.(12, 34, 42 Bdes.) |
| | LofC etc. | 5 British Bns. 22 Indian Bns. 3 Indian Cav.Rgts |
| *By 11.1917 modified as follows:* | 15 Division | 50 Bde. replaces 34 Bde., transferred to new 17 Indian Div. |
| | 17 Indian Division | (34, 51, 52 Bdes.) |
| | 18 Indian Division | Forming |
| | 11 Cav.Bde. | (1 British 2 Indian Rgts.) Remained Independent |
| **Anglo-Indian O.O.B. Mesopotamia October 1918** | | |
| **Mesopotamia E.F.** | I Indian | 17, 18 Indian Divs. |
| | | 32 Lancers 7, 11 Cav.Bdes. |
| | III Indian | 13(British)Div.(38, 40 Bdes.)(39 Bde. attached) |
| | | 14 Indian Div.(35, 37 Bdes.)(56 Bde. attached to I Corps) |
| | | 12 Cavalry 6 Cav.Bde. |
| | Independent | 15 Indian Div.(12, 42, 50 Bdes.) |
| | North Persia Force | 36, 39 Inf.Bdes. one Cavalry Rgt. 4 Indian Bns. for L of C duties |
| | L of C, Garrisons | 4 Indian Cav.Rgts. 3 British Bns. 18 Indian Bns. |
| | South Persia Rifles | Kerman & Fars Bdes.(7 Inf.Bns. 3 Cav.Rgts. 2 Btys. L of C Sqns.) |

### Table 3.86 Turkish O.O.B.s in Mesopotamia 1915-1918

| ARMY | CORPS | DIVISIONS |
|---|---|---|
| **Original Organisation as at February 1915** | | |
| **IV Inspectorate** | XII | 35(Mosul) 36(Kirkuk)Divs. 13 Cav.Bde. |
| | XIII | 37(Baghdad) 38(Basra)Divs. 31 Cav.Rgt. |

**Turkish O.O.B. in Mesopotamia 1915-1918 continued**

These so-called 'Irak' Divisions were composed of locally recruited Arabs and were held in very low regard by the Ottoman High Command.

Shortly after the outbreak of war both Corps were broken up –

      35 Div. was sent to Syria, but then returned to Mesopotamia
      36 Div. went to the Caucasus
      37 Div. appears to have been disbanded or transferred to Caucasus
      38 Div. joined 35 Div. on its return to form a new XIII Corps
      Muratteb Div. Formed in part from Constantinople Fire Brigade, sent
      to Mesopotamia 12.1914, merged in re-organised Mesopotamian
      Army

**August 1915**

Mesopotamia Army now appears to be composed of 5 Divisions (35, 38, 45, 51[ex-3 Composite] and 52[ex-5 Composite]) under two Corps H.Q. (XIII, [new] XVIII)

**February 1916**

| ARMY | CORPS | DIVISIONS |
|---|---|---|
| **IV ARMY** *or* **VI ARMY** | XIII | 35, 38, 52 Divs. |
| | XVIII | 45, 51Divs. |
| | (from I) | 2 Div. |
| *Reported as en route* | from Aleppo | 26 Div. or, more probably, 44 Div. |
| | (3 Divs. from 2 ARMY Syria) | 13 Div. 23 Div. plus one unidentified |
| | Cavalry | A Cavalry Bde. 2 Camel Mounted Bns. Mule mounted infantry |
| **August 1917** **6 ARMY** | XVIII | 14, 51, 52 Divs.; 31 Cav. Regt |
| | XIII | 6,2, Divs. Cav. Brigade (two regts.); unattached inf.regt. |
| | Mosul Group | 22 Inf.Regt. |
| | Army Reserve | 46 Div. |

## Armenia and Kurdistan

### Table 3.87 Summary of Russian Divisions in Armenia-Kurdistan 1914-1917

| INFANTRY DIVISIONS | REMAINED IN CAUCASUS | TRANSFERRED TO EUROPEAN FRONT |
|---|---|---|
| **20** | | 2.1915 |
| **21** | | 8/9.1914 |
| **39** | Yes | |
| **51** | | 8/9.1914 |
| **52** | | 8/9.1914 |
| **66** | Yes | |
| **123** | Yes(?) | |
| **127** | Yes(?) | |
| **Caucasus Grenadier** | | 8/9.1914 |
| **1 Caucasus Rifle Bde./Div.*** | | 8/9.1914 |

\* Upgraded to Divisions in Autumn 1915.

| INFANTRY DIVISIONS | REMAINED IN CAUCASUS | TRANSFERRED TO EUROPEAN FRONT |
|---|---|---|
| 2 Caucasus Rifle Bde./Div.* | Yes (Initially in Persia) | |
| 3 Caucasus Rifle Div. | | 1.1915 |
| 4 Caucasus Rifle Div. | Yes | |
| 5 Caucasus Rifle Div. | Yes | |
| 6 Caucasus Rifle Div. | Yes | |
| 7 Caucasus Rifle Div. | Yes | |
| 4 Turkestan Rifle Bde./Div.* | Yes (After tfr. from Turkestan Mil.Dist.) | |
| 5 Turkestan Rifle Bde./Div.* | Yes (After tfr. from Turkestan Mil.Dist.) | |
| CAVALRY DIVISIONS | REMAINED IN CAUCASUS | TRANSFERRED TO EUROPEAN FRONT |
| Caucasus | (Returned to Caucasus Army Spring 1915) | 8/9.1914 |
| 1 Caucasus Coss.Div. | Yes | |
| 2 Caucasus Coss.Div. | Yes | |
| 3 Caucasus Coss.Div. | | 8/9.1914 |
| 4 Caucasus Coss.Div. | Yes | |
| 5 Caucasus Coss.Div. | Yes | |

**Movements between Caucasus and European Fronts**

| DATE | TO MAIN FRONT/ OTHER FRONTS | REINF. TO CAUCASUS/ NEW UNITS |
|---|---|---|
| 8/9.1914 | II Caucasus(Cav.Gren.Div., 51 ID) III Caucasus(21, 52 ID) 1 Cav.Rifle Bde. Caucasus Cav.Div. 3 Caucasus Coss.Div. I Turkestan(1, 2, 3 Turk RB) | II Turkestan(4, 5 Turk RB) Siberian Coss.Bde. Transcaspian Coss.Bde. |
| Early 1915 | V Caucasus(3 Cav.RD, 1, 2 Plastun Bdes.)(To Crimea & Odessa) 20 ID (To Main Front) 43 Bns. lost | 4 Cav.RD/3rd Bns. for 2 Cav.RB= 17 Bns. 4 Kuban Plastun Bde.(6 Bns.) Don Foot Bde.(4 Bns.) 27 Bns. gained + 1 Armenian Druzhina, Militia Bns. 8 Cossak Rgts. 17 Cossak Sotnia Returned from Western Front Caucasian Cav.Div. 2, 3 Transbaikal Coss.Bdes. |

**Table 3.88** Russian Army of the Caucasus O.O.B.s 1914-1917

| AREA | DIVISIONS |
|---|---|
| **10.1914** Erzurum-Kars† | 39 ID One Bde./20 ID 1 Kuban Plastun Bde.(5 Bns.) 1 Cau.Coss.Div. |
| Erzurum-Oltu† | One Bde./20 ID 1 Coss.Rgt. |
| Erevan-Bayazit | One Bde./66 ID 2 Kuban Plastun Bde. 2 Cau.Coss.Div. Transcaspian Coss.Bde. |
| Batum Region | 264 IR/66 ID 1 Bn./1 Kuban Plastun Bde. 1½ Bns. Frontier Guards |
| Black Sea Coast | 3 Kuban Plastun Bde. |
| Persian Azerbaijan | 2 Cau.RB 4 Cau.Coss.Div. |
| Garrison of Kars | 263 IR/66 ID |
| Gen. Reserve | II Turkestan Army Corps Siberian Coss.Bde. |

*Left margin notes:*

* Upgraded to Divisions in Autumn 1915.

‡ Divisions as in 6.1916 except where Noted.

† Both Groups u/c I Caucasian Corps Cdr. Bergmann.

**O.O.B. Russian Army of the Caucasus 1914-1917 continued**

| Summary | Bns. | Sotnia | Guns |
|---|---|---|---|
| Erzurum-Kars | 29 | 30 | 96 |
| Erzurum-Oltu | 8 | 6 | 24 |
| Erzurum-Bayazit | 14 | 36 | 52 |
| Batum Region | 6½ | | 8 |
| Black Sea Coast | 6 | | |
| Persian Azerbaijan | 8 | 24 | 24 |
| Grn. of Kars | 4 | | |
| General Reserve | 21 | 12 | 46 |
| **Total** | **96½** | **108** | **250** |

| CORPS/SECTOR | DIVISIONS |
|---|---|
| **Autumn 1915** Black Sea Coast & Coruh Valley | Minor units inc. 19 Turk.RR |
| II Turkestan (Right-Centre) | 15-18, 20 Turk.IR, 264 IR(66 ID), Siberian Coss.Bde. |
| I Caucasian (Centre) | Don Coss.Foot Bde. 11 Militia Druzhiny 154, 155, 156 IR (39 ID) 1 Cav.Coss.Div. |
| IV Caucasian (Left) | 5 Cau.Cav.Div. 261, 262, 263 IR(66 ID) Reserve – 2 Cav.RD Caucasian CD |
| Strategic Reserve of C-in-C | 153 IR(39 ID) 4 Cau.RD 4 Plastun Bde.(26 Bns. in all) 2 Cau.Cav.Civ. |
| Azerbaijan-Van Force | 4 Armenian Druzhiny 1 Opolcheniye (Militia) Bde. (8 Druzhiny) 4 Cau.Coss.Div. 2 Bdes. Transbaikal Coss. |
| **June 1916** V Caucasus | 1, 2 Plastun Bdes. 123, 127 ID Coast Detachment (10 Bns.) |
| II Turkestan | 4, 5 Turk.RD 3 Plastun Bde.(4 Bns.) Siberian Coss.Bde. |
| I Caucasus | 39 ID Don Ft,Bde. 1, 2 Transcaucasian RB (ex-Militia) 5 Cau.Coss.Div. |
| Strategic Reserve | 4 Cau.RD 5 Cau.RD(Newly formed) 1, 2 Kars Regts.(Kars Fortess Troops) 4 Plastun Bde.(re-called from Armenia) |
| IV Caucasus | 2 Cau.RD 66 ID 3 Armenian Rifle Bns. 6 Cossack Regts. 1 Mtd.Border Regt. |
| Azerbaijan-Van Force | 3 Border Rgt. Georgian RR 1 Armenian Rifle Bn. 12 Militia Druzhiny 2, 3 Transbaikal Coss.Bdes. 4 Cau.Coss.Div. |
| SECTOR | CORPS‡ |
| **Winter 1916-1917** Coast-Pir Ahmet | V Caucasus (- 1 Plastun Bde.)(To Gen.Reserve) |
| Pir Ahmet-Kelkit-Erzincan Plain | II Turkestan + 3 Plastun Bde. (-2 Turk.RR to Gen.Reserve) |
| Erzincan Plain-Seytan Dag | I Caucasus + 6 Cau.RR(?) or 6 Cau.RD(?), 4 Plastun Bde. |
| Seytan Dag-Boglan Pass | VI Caucasus (Newly constituted) - 4, 5 Cau.RD 2 Plastun Bde. |
| Boglan Pass-Mus-Bitlis | IV Caucasus |
| Newly created formation | 7 Cau.RD (from Militia units) |
| **Summer 1917 – Russian Offensive against Mosul-Diyarbekir** IV Caucasus | 66 ID 2 Cau.RD 4 Cav.Coss.Div. |
| VI Caucasus | 4 Cau.RD 5 Cau.RD(reinf. from Gen.Reserve with – 1, 2 Plastun Bdes. Siberian Coss.Bde.) |

**Table 3.89** Turkish O.O.B.s Armenia-Kurdistan-Persia 1914-1918

| ARMY | CORPS | DIVISIONS |
|---|---|---|
| **10/11.1914**<br>**3 ARMY** | IX | 17, 28, 29 Divs. |
| | X | 30, 31, 32 Divs. |
| | XI | 18, 33, 34 Divs. |
| | *En route from Iraq* | 37 Div. |
| **January 1916 (Battle of Köprüköy)**<br>**3 ARMY** | IX | 17, 28, 29 Divs. |
| | X | 30, 31, 32 Divs. |
| | XI | 18, 33, 34 Divs. |
| | | 36, 37 Divs. |
| | | 15-20 Auxiliary Bns. (Gendarmes & Frontier Guards) |
| | | 2 Cav.Div. |
| | | Several thousand Kurds |

**Winter 1916-1917**
**Reorganisation of 3 Army**

V, IX, X, XI Corps de-activated. Equivalent of 8 Inf.Divs. lost, half through desertion.
Replaced by 2 new Corps of 3 Divs. of 6,000 men

| | |
|---|---|
| I Caucasian | 9, 10, 36* Caucasian Divs. |
| II Caucasian | 5, 11, 37* Caucasian Divs. |

**Reorganisation of 2 ARMY** 3 Corps of 2 Divs.

| | |
|---|---|
| XVI | 5, 8 |
| II | 1, 47 |
| IV | 11, 12 |
| Disbanded | 7, 48, 49, H.Q. III Corps |
| Transferred to Iraq | 14, 3 Cavalry Divs. |

**Further Reorganisation of 3 ARMY 1917-1918**

| | |
|---|---|
| II Caucasian | 5, 11, 37 Caucasian Divs. |
| I Caucasian | 9, 10, 36 Caucasian Divs. |
| From disbanded 2 ARMY | 5, 12 Inf.Divs.(embodying remnants of 8 Div.) |
| At Mus | 5 ID |
| At Palu | 12 ID |

**Disbandment of 2 ARMY**

| | |
|---|---|
| To 3 ARMY | 5, 12 ID |
| To other areas | 1, 11, 47 Divs. |
| Incorporated in 5 & 12 ID | 8 Div. |

* Also shown as Independent.

# PART III NAVIES

## CRUISER WARFARE 1914-1915

After the years of Anglo-German naval rivalry expectation in 1914 was of fleet actions between the British Grand Fleet and Germany's High Seas Fleet. In fact the only such action, and that in many ways inconclusive, was at Jutland in May 1916. Of far greater immediate consequence for the Allies in August 1914 was the threat posed by Germany's overseas squadrons and cruisers, particularly to Allied commerce and trade. These overseas German forces were distributed as follows at the outbreak of war.

The following abbreviations are used in this sub-section:

| | | | |
|---|---|---|---|
| AC | Armoured Cruiser | PBB | Pre-dreadnought Battleship |
| AMC | Armoured Merchant Cruiser | RAN | Royal Australian Navy |
| BC | Battle Cruiser | RCN | Royal Canadian Navy |
| BB | Battleship | RN | Royal Navy |
| C | Cruiser | RNZN | Royal New Zealand Navy |
| CES | Commissioned Escort Ship | S | Sloop |
| GB | Gunboat | SNO | Senior Naval Officer |
| LC | Light Cruiser | TGB | Torpedo Gunboat |
| PC | Protected Cruiser | (F) | Flagship |

### Table 3.90 German Overseas Forces August 1914

| | |
|---|---|
| **Mediterranean Division** R.Adm. *Souchon* | BC *Goeben* LC *Breslau* |
| **East Asia Squadron** V.Adm. *Graf von Spee* | AC *Scharnhorst, Gneisenau* |
| | LC *Emden* LC *Leipzig, Nürnberg* (detached to West Coast of America) 5 Gunboats, 3 River Gunboats, 2 Destroyers (These smaller vessels were scuttled, interned or destroyed very quickly) |
| **Australian Waters** | 1 Gunboat, 1 Survey vessel (interned) |
| **East Africa** | LC *Königsberg* |
| **West Africa** | GB *Eber* (scuttled) |
| **East Coast of America and West Indies Area** | LC *Karlsruhe* |
| | LC *Dresden* (just relieved by *Karlsruhe*) |

### Allied Countermoves

The danger the German cruisers posed to Allied shipping was clear and the British quickly instituted a series of interlocking force areas to guard against the German raiders including any additional ships which might break out from German ports. Whilst it is true that all modern vessels were concentrated in the Grand Fleet these forces absorbed much of the Royal Navy's secondary forces. Each area was allocated a cruiser squadron to which were soon added a considerable number of requisitioned armed merchant cruisers and a number of pre-dreadnought battleships. These Areas/Forces were as follows:

### Table 3.91 Royal Navy Area Forces/Squadrons August 1914

| AREA/ FORCE | CRUISER SQN. | AREA OF OPERATIONS |
|---|---|---|
| **A** | – | The battle cruiser force of the Grand Fleet (not allocated to the hunt for the German overseas forces) |
| **B†** | 10th | Northern Patrol (Northern trade routes to Germany) |
| **C†** | 7th | North Sea (Disbanded 10.1914) |
| **D\*** | 5th | Canaries-Cape Verde Sounds-Sierra Leone-Ascension Island |

\* Most closely involved with operations against Spee and German raiders.

† Mainly associated with Grand Fleet.

### Royal Navy Area Forces/Squadrons August 1914 continued

| AREA/ FORCE | CRUISER SQN. | AREA OF OPERATIONS |
|---|---|---|
| **E** | 11th | Atlantic approaches West of Ireland |
| **F** | – | Not formed – intended to cover Southern approaches to Irish Channel |
| **G** | 12th | Western approach to English Channel |
| **H\*** | 4th | North America and West Indies Station |
| **I\*** | 9th | Finistere-Azores-Madeira |
| **Overseas Stations** | | Ships already on station at outbreak of war: |
| **S.E.Coast America\*** | | 1 Lt.cruiser, but reinforced from Force D |
| **Cape Station\*** | | 2 Lt.cruisers |
| **China and E.Indies Station** (+ Australian Fleet & N.Z.Sqn.) | | 2 Pre-dreadnought battleships, 2 Armoured cruisers, 3 Lt. cruisers, 4 Sloops + Gunboats, Destroyers etc. (+ 1 battle cruiser 7 Lt. cruisers) |
| **Pacific Coast of America\*** | | 2 Lt.cruisers, 2 Sloops |
| **Mediterranean Fleet** | | 3 Battle cruisers, 4 Armoured cruisers, 4 Lt. cruisers, 16 Destroyers |

## France

Main French fleet was based on Toulon. It had 19 battleships (of which 4 of Dreadnought type), 7 armoured cruisers, 6 flotillas of destroyers, and 2 of submarines.

The French Atlantic squadron had a further 9 armoured cruisers and 7 protected and light cruisers, of these two were detached in West Indian waters. Additionally there were 4 destroyer and 2 submarine flotillas.

In the Far East the French had 2 armoured cruisers and a number of smaller vessels.

## Japan

The Japanese navy provided a powerful addition to Allied forces in the Far East. Its reputation was justifiably high after its performance in the Russo-Japanese War of 1904-05. The Anglo-Japanese treaty of 1902 had enabled Britain to reduce its commitments in the Far East and begin to concentrate its major naval effort in home waters.

According to Japanese classifications the Japanese navy had a strength in 1914 of 10 battleships (2 Dreadnought type), 6 battle cruisers (2 Dreadnought type), 6 1st Class coast defence ships (mainly ex-Russian battleships captured in 1904-05), 9 1st Class armoured cruisers, 13 2nd Class cruisers and 8 2nd Class coast defence ships. A further battleship and two more battlecruisers of the Dreadnought type were nearing completion.

A number of Japanese ships were allocated to operations on Pacific coast of S.America, support for Adm. Jerran's China station and the *Emden* hunt. Three South Sea squadrons were constituted to participate in the hunt for von Spee's squadron operating from the Marshall Islands, Rabaul and in the Indian Ocean.

## Fate of the German Overseas Squadrons
### Mediterranean

*Goeben* and *Breslau* evaded the combined attempts of the French and British Mediterranean fleets to intercept them, arriving in Turkish waters on 10.8.1914. They were transferred to Turkey (16.8.14) and saw service against the Russian Black Sea Fleet once Turkey entered the war. *Breslau* was mined in 1918 but *Goeben* remained in Turkish service until she was de-commissioned in 1960, the last survivor of the High Seas Fleet.

## Caribbean

*Dresden* sank 76,000 tons of Allied shipping before rounding Cape Horn to join Spee's squadron in the Pacific. Surviving the Battle of the Falklands she was eventually scuttled in March 1915, after action with British cruisers *Kent* and *Glasgow*.

*Karlsruhe*, the most modern of the German cruisers overseas, was destroyed by an internal explosion on 4.11.1914 some 200 miles east of Trinidad. The Allies were unaware of her loss for several months. A study of the tables describing Allied cruiser deployment on pages 215-217 will show that not inconsiderable forces were devoted to countering what, in fact, was a non-existent threat.

## East Africa

The activities of the *Königsberg* in East African and Indian Ocean waters necessitated the creation of a squadron of light cruisers drawn from the Mediterranean and East Indies stations. She was blockaded in the Rufiji delta by the end of October 1914, but not finally destroyed until July 1915 by the R.N. monitors *Severn* and *Mersey*. Her crew and guns provided a useful reinforcement to von Lettow-Vorbeck's forces in the East African land campaign.

## *Emden*

Detached on independent service by von Spee, *Emden* enjoyed a spectacular three months cruise before being destroyed by H.M.A.S. *Sydney* at Cocos-Keeling Islands on 9.11.1914. Sinking 18 British ships with a displacement of 80,000 tons, capturing 5 others and sinking a Russian light cruiser and a French destroyer, Captain von Muller and his crew created havoc in the Far East. Indeed they showed such dash, gallantry and chivalry that his eventual defeat was marked with generous and complimentary leading articles in a wide cross section of a British press usually more inclined to the 'beastly Hun' genre of journalism. The scale of the problems caused by the *Emden* may be appreciated from the list of Allied ships engaged in hunting down the single German cruiser, exclusive of smaller destroyers and ships.

**Table 3.92 Allied Ships Involved in the Pursuit of the Emden August to November 1914**

| BRITISH SHIPS | | JAPANESE SHIPS | |
|---|---|---|---|
| AC | *Hampshire* | BC | *Ibuki* |
| AC | *Minotaur* | LC | *Chikuma* |
| LC | *Sydney* (R.A.N.) | LC | *Yahagi* |
| LC | *Melbourne* (R.A.N.) | AC | *Nisshin* |
| LC | *Yarmouth* | AC | *Tokiwa* |
| LC | *Psyche* | AC | *Yakumo* |
| LC | *Pyramus* | | |
| LC | *Philomel* (R.N.Z.N.) | **BRITISH ARMED MERCHANT** | |
| | | **CRUISERS** | |
| **FRENCH SHIPS** | | AMC *Empress of Asia* | |
| AC | *Montcalm* | AMC *Empress of Russia* | |
| AC | *Dupleix* | AMC *Himalaya* | |
| **RUSSIAN SHIPS** | | | |
| PC | *Askold* | | |
| PC | *Zhemchug* (Sunk by *Emden*) | | |

## Von Spee's Squadron – Coronel and the Falklands

Von Spee united his armoured cruisers with his detached cruisers and was joined by *Dresden* following her West Indies cruise. His united squadron met Rear Admiral Sir Christopher Cradock's weak squadron off the Chilean coast at Coronel on 1.11.1914. Cradock's elderly armoured cruisers, largely crewed by hastily mobilized reservists, were overwhelmed by von Spee's squadron. The Royal Navy suffered its first defeat in a fleet action for over a hundred years in a shattering blow to British prestige.

Churchill and Fisher reacted with great speed and ruthlessness within days of the news of Coronel. In conditions of the utmost secrecy two of

Jellicoe's precious battle cruisers were ordered to the South Atlantic. Even the Admiralty's movement books, themselves classified secret, did not name the ships referring to them simply as 'K' or Force K. Within days a third battle cruiser, *Princess Royal*, was ordered to North America to guard against any possibility of Spee moving through the Panama Canal to the Caribbean and Atlantic. The Pacific coast was strengthened by an Australian battle cruiser, a Japanese Battleship and a further Japanese armoured cruiser. In the interim Stoddart was ordered to concentrate a powerful squadron of armoured cruisers including the modern *Defence* at the Falklands to await the arrival of Sturdee's battle cruisers.

Just over a month after Coronel the combined squadrons of Sturdee and Stoddart inflicted a crushing defeat on Spee's squadron at the Falkland Islands. Spee himself was among the 2,000 German dead. Only the *Dresden* survived the action troubling the British for a further three months before she was cornered at Juan Fernandez Island in March 1915. It is worth noting that this single vessel necessitated retaining an average of 6 British cruisers on station until her demise.

A study of the Tables on pages 215-217 will indicate clearly the huge effort required to hunt down the German cruisers based overseas. Had the Germans succeeded in breaking out such ships as *von der Tann* and *Moltke* in 1914 the problem would have been even greater.

## German Armed Merchant Cruisers

As with the British the Germans also commissioned a number of armed merchant cruisers/raiders from converted liners and cargo vessels early in the war. They added to the problems faced by Allied cruiser forces in the early months of the war. The principal German armed merchant cruisers were as follows:

**Table 3.93 German Armed Merchant Cruisers 1914-17**

| SHIP | FATE |
|---|---|
| **First Wave** | |
| *Cap Trafalgar* | Sunk 14.9.14 S.Atlantic by AMC *Carmania* |
| *Kaiser Wilhelm der Grosse* | Disabled 27.8.14 by *H.M.S. Highflyer* and scuttled Rio de Oro |
| *Kronprinz Wilhelm* | 11.4.15 Interned U.S.A. |
| *Prinz Eitel Friedrich* | 9.3.15 Interned U.S.A. |
| *Yorck* | 12.14 Interned Valparaiso |
| *Kormoran* (Ex-Russian prize) | 13.12.14 Interned Guam |
| **Second Wave** | |
| *Möwe* | 2 cruisers 1915-16, 1916-1917 |
| *Wolf* (II) | 11.1916 - 2.1918 Survived the war |
| *Leopard* | 3.1917 - sunk 16.3.17 by R.N. vessels |
| *Greif* | 2.1916 - sunk 27.2.16 by R.N. vessels |
| *Iltis* | 1917 - scuttled 15.3.17 to avoid capture |

The ships most closely involved in the operations outside home waters were those listed in the table opposite, for the most part consisting of squadrons and lesser forces not attached to the Grand Fleet.

* Special service.

† En route.

‡ Detached.

◊ Sunk 20.9.14 by *Königsberg*.

**Table 3.94 Composition of Allied Cruiser Squadrons and Overseas Stations at Various Dates 1914-15**

| DATE | FORCE B (10th Cru.Sqn.) | FORCE C (7th Cru.Sqn.) | FORCE D (5th Cru.Sqn.) | FORCE E (11th Cru.Sqn.) | FORCE G (12th Cru.Sqn.) | FORCE H (4th Cru.Sqn.) | FORCE I (9th Cru.Sqn.) | S.ATLANTIC S.AMERICA | PACIFIC COAST AMERICA | CAPE STATION | WEST COAST AFRICA | EAST COAST AFRICA |
|---|---|---|---|---|---|---|---|---|---|---|---|---|
| 5.8.1914 | C *Crescent* (F)<br>C *Edgar*<br>C *Grafton*<br>C *Endymion*<br>C *Gibraltar*<br>C *Theseus*<br>C *Royal Arthur*<br>C *Hawke* | AC *Bacchante* (F)<br>AC *Cressy*<br>AC *Aboukir*<br>AC *Euryalus* | AC *Carnarvon* (F)<br>AC *Cornwall*<br>AC *Cumberland*<br>AC *Monmouth* | LC *Doris* (F)<br>LC *Juno*<br>LC *Isis*<br>LC *Venus*<br>LC *Minerva* | LC *Charybdis* (F)<br>LC *Eclipse*<br>LC *Diana*<br>LC *Talbot* | AC *Suffolk* (F)<br>AC *Lancaster*<br>AC *Berwick*<br>AC *Essex*<br>LC *Bristol* | C *Amphitrite* (F)<br>C *Argonaut*<br>C *Europa*<br>LC *Vindictive*<br>LC *Highflyer*<br>LC *Challenger* | LC *Glasgow* | S *Algerine*<br>S *Shearwater* | LC *Hyacinth* (F)<br>LC *Astraea*<br>LC *Pegasus* | GB *Dwarf* | Nil |
| 28.8.1914 | C *Crescent* (F)<br>C *Edgar*<br>C *Grafton*<br>C *Endymion*<br>C *Gibraltar*<br>C *Theseus*<br>C *Royal Arthur*<br>C *Hawke*<br>AMC *Alsatian*<br>AMC *Oceanic*<br>AMC *Mantua* | AC *Bacchante* (F)<br>AC *Cressy*<br>AC *Aboukir*<br>AC *Hogue*<br>AC *Euryalus**<br>LC *Sapphire*<br>LC *Amethyst* | AC *Carnarvon* (F)<br>AC *Cornwall*<br>AC *Cumberland*<br>LC *Highflyer*<br>BB *Canopus*<br>AMC *Macedonia*<br>AMC *Marmora* | LC *Doris* (F)<br>LC *Juno*<br>LC *Isis*<br>LC *Venus*<br>LC *Pelorus*<br>BB *Ocean*<br>AMC *Aquitania*<br>AMC *Caronia* | LC *Charybdis* (F)<br>LC *Eclipse*<br>LC *Diana*<br>LC *Talbot* | North Atlantic Area<br>AC *Suffolk* (SNO)<br>AC *Lancaster*<br>C *Niobe* (RCN)<br>AC *Essex*<br>BB *Glory*<br>West Indies<br>AC *Good Hope* (F)<br>AC *Berwick*<br>LC *Bristol*<br>AMC *Carmania* | C *Amphitrite* (F)<br>C *Argonaut*<br>C *Europa*<br>LC *Vindictive*<br>AC *Sutlej*<br>LC *Challenger*<br>LC *Minerva* | LC *Glasgow*<br>AC *Monmouth*<br>AMC *Otranto*<br>AMC *Empress of Britain*<br>AMC *Victorian* | LC *Newcastle*†<br>LC *Rainbow* (RCN)<br>S *Algerine*<br>S *Shearwater* | LC *Hyacinth* (F)<br>LC *Astraea*<br>LC *Pegasus*<br>AMC *Kinfauns Castle*<br>AMC *Armadale Castle*<br>AC *Leviathan* | GB *Dwarf* | Nil |
| 15.9.1914 | C *Crescent* (F)<br>C *Edgar*<br>C *Grafton*<br>C *Endymion*<br>C *Gibraltar*<br>C *Theseus*‡<br>C *Royal Arthur*<br>C *Hawke*<br>TGB *Dryad*<br>AMC *Alsatian*<br>AMC *Mantua* | Disbanded during 10.1914 | AC *Carnarvon* (F)<br>LC *Highflyer*<br>BB *Albion*<br>AMC *Victorian*<br>AMC *Marmora*<br>AMC *Empress of Britain* | AC *Sutlej* (F)<br>LC *Doris*<br>LC *Juno*<br>LC *Isis*<br>LC *Venus*<br>LC *Pelorus* | LC *Charybdis* (F)<br>LC *Eclipse*<br>LC *Diana*<br>LC *Talbot* | North Atlantic Area<br>AC *Suffolk*<br>AC *Lancaster*<br>C *Niobe* (RCN)<br>BB *Glory*<br>West Indies<br>AMC *Caronia*<br>AC *Berwick*<br>AC *Essex* | C *Amphitrite* (F)<br>C *Argonaut*<br>C *Europa*<br>LC *Vindictive*<br>AC *Leviathan*<br>BB *Ocean*<br>LC *Minerva* | AC *Good Hope* (F)<br>AC *Monmouth*<br>LC *Glasgow*<br>AMC *Otranto*<br>LC *Bristol*<br>AC *Cornwall*<br>BB *Canopus*<br>AMC *Macedonia*<br>AMC *Carmania* | LC *Newcastle*<br>LC *Rainbow* (RCN)<br>S *Algerine*<br>S *Shearwater* | LC *Hyacinth* (F)<br>LC *Astraea*<br>LC *Pegasus*◊<br>AMC *Kinfauns Castle*<br>AMC *Armadale Castle* | AC *Cumberland*<br>LC *Challenger*<br>GB *Dwarf* | Nil |
| 16.10.1914 | C *Crescent* (F)<br>C *Edgar*<br>C *Grafton*<br>C *Endymion*<br>C *Gibraltar*<br>C *Theseus*<br>C *Royal Arthur*<br>C *Hawke*<br>TGB *Dryad*<br>AMC *Alsatian*<br>AMC *Mantua*<br>AMC *Teutonic* | | AC *Carnarvon* (F)<br>LC *Highflyer*<br>BB *Albion*<br>AMC *Victorian*<br>AMC *Marmora*<br>AMC *Empress of Britain* | AC *Sutlej* (F)<br>LC *Doris*<br>LC *Juno*<br>LC *Isis*<br>LC *Venus*<br>LC *Pelorus* | LC *Charybdis* (F)<br>LC *Eclipse*<br>LC *Diana*<br>LC *Talbot*<br>AC *Bacchante*<br>AC *Euryalus* | North Atlantic Area<br>AC *Suffolk*<br>AC *Lancaster* (F)<br>C *Niobe* (RCN)<br>BB *Glory*<br>West Indies<br>AMC *Caronia* (F)<br>AC *Berwick*<br>AC *Essex* | C *Argonaut* (F)<br>C *Amphitrite*<br>C *Europa*<br>LC *Vindictive*<br>AC *Leviathan*<br>AMC *Calgarian* | AC *Good Hope* (F)<br>AC *Monmouth*<br>LC *Glasgow*<br>AMC *Otranto*<br>LC *Bristol*<br>AC *Cornwall*<br>BB *Canopus*<br>AC *Kent*<br>AMC *Macedonia*<br>AMC *Carmania*<br>AMC *Orama* | LC *Newcastle*<br>LC *Rainbow* (RCN)<br>S *Algerine*<br>S *Shearwater* | LC *Hyacinth* (F)<br>LC *Astraea*<br>AMC *Kinfauns Castle*<br>AMC *Armadale Castle*<br>Castle | AC *Cumberland*<br>LC *Challenger*<br>GB *Dwarf* | Nil |

## Composition of Allied Cruiser Squadrons and Overseas Stations at Various Dates 1914-15 continued

| DATE | FORCE B (10th Cru.Sqn.) | FORCE C (7th Cru.Sqn.) | FORCE D (5th Cru.Sqn.) | FORCE E (11th Cru.Sq.) | FORCE G (12th Cru.Sqn.) | FORCE H (4th Cru.Sqn.) | FORCE I (9th Cru.Sqn.) | S.ATLANTIC S.AMERICA | PACIFIC COAST AMERICA | CAPE STATION | WEST COAST AFRICA | EAST COAST AFRICA |
|---|---|---|---|---|---|---|---|---|---|---|---|---|
| **1.11.1914** (at time of Battle of Coronel) | C Crescent (F)<br>C Edgar<br>C Grafton<br>C Endymion<br>C Gibraltar<br>C Theseus<br>C Royal Arthur<br>C Hawke<br>TGB Dryad<br>AMC Alsatian<br>AMC Mantua<br>AMC Teutonic | Disbanded | LC Highflyer (SNO)<br>AC Kent •<br>AMC Victorian<br>AMC Marmora<br>AMC Empress of Britain | AC Sutlej (F)<br>LC Doris<br>LC Juno<br>LC Isis<br>LC Venus<br>LC Pelorus | AC Euryalus<br>LC Charybdis<br>LC Eclipse (F)<br>LC Diana<br>LC Talbot<br>AC Bacchante | North Atlantic Area<br>AMC Caronia (F)<br>BB Glory<br>AC Suffolk<br>C Niobe (RCN)<br>West Indies<br>AC Berwick<br>AC Lancaster<br>AC Essex<br>French ships<br>AC Condé<br>C Descartes Δ | C Amphitrite (F)<br>C Argonaut<br>C Europa<br>LC Vindictive<br>AMC Calgarian<br>To be added<br>AC Donegal | With CRADOCK<br>AC Good Hope (F)<br>AC Monmouth<br>LC Glasgow<br>AMC Otranto<br>At Falkland Islands<br>BB Canopus<br>En route with STODDART<br>AC Carnarvon (F)<br>AC Cornwall<br>LC Bristol<br>AMC Macedonia<br>AMC Orama<br>To be added<br>AC Defence<br>AMC Edinburgh Castle<br>Ordered to S.American Station<br>4.11.14. Dep. U.K.<br>11.11.14<br>**FORCE K**<br>BC Invincible<br>BC Inflexible | LC Newcastle<br>LC Rainbow (RCN)<br>S Shearwater<br>Japanese ship<br>AC Itzumo | BB Albion<br>LC Astraea<br>LC Hyacinth<br>AMC Kinfauns Castle<br>AMC Armadale Castle | AC Cumberland<br>LC Challenger<br>GB Dwarf<br>12.11.14<br>Proposed Squadron for W.Africa<br>AC Warrior<br>AC Black Prince<br>AC Donegal<br>LC Highflyer<br>Cancelled.<br>The 3 AC were sent to the Grand Fleet | LC Chatham (SNO)<br>LC Dartmouth<br>LC Weymouth<br>BB Fox<br>BB Goliath |
| **18.12.1914** (at time of Battle of Falklands) | C Crescent ** (F)<br>C Grafton **<br>C Royal Arthur **<br>C Edgar<br>TGB Dryad<br>AMC Alsatian<br>AMC Mantua<br>AMC Teutonic<br>AMC Otway<br>Deactivated 12.14/1.15 | Disbanded | LC Highflyer (F)<br>AMC Marmora<br>AMC Empress of Britain<br>AMC Victorian | AC Sutlej (F)<br>LC Juno<br>LC Isis<br>LC Venus | AC Bacchante (F)<br>AC Euryalus<br>LC Charybdis<br>LC Eclipse<br>LC Diana<br>LC Talbot | North American Group<br>BB Glory<br>AC Essex<br>AMC Caronia<br>AC Suffolk (unserv.)<br>C Niobe (RCN) (refit)<br>from N.America Station to W.Indies Group<br>West Indies Group<br>BC Princess Royal<br>AC Berwick<br>AC Lancaster<br>AMC Edinburgh Castle<br>French ships<br>AC Condé<br>C Descartes | C Amphitrite<br>C Argonaut (To Gibraltar)<br>C Europa<br>AMC Carmania (Gibraltar)<br>BB Vengeance (Gibraltar)<br>At Ascension Is. on W/T link<br>LC Vindictive | BC Invincible (F)<br>BC Inflexible<br>AC Carnarvon<br>AC Cornwall<br>AC Kent<br>LC Bristol<br>LC Glasgow<br>AMC Orama<br>Guard Ships<br>Falklands<br>BB Canopus<br>Detached<br>AC Defence ††<br>AMC Macedonia (Repairs)<br>AMC Otranto (Repairs) | BC Australia<br>LC Newcastle<br>Japanese Sqn.<br>BB Hizen<br>AC Asama<br>AC Itzumo | BB Albion<br>LC Astraea<br>LC Hyacinth<br>AC Minotaur<br>LC Weymouth +<br>AC Defence (En route from S.American Stn.) | AC Cumberland<br>LC Challenger<br>GB Dwarf<br>French ship<br>AC Pothuau | BB Goliath<br>LC Chatham<br>LC Fox<br>AMC Kinfauns Castle |

• To join S.American Station.

Δ Relieved by *Essex*.

** Paid off 12.1914.

†† To Cape Station.

## Composition of Allied Cruiser Squadrons and Overseas Stations at Various Dates 1914-15 continued

‡‡ Present at sinking of *Dresden*, Juan Fernandez Island, 14.3.15.

* Not in main action.

| DATE | FORCE B (10th Cru.Sqn.) | FORCE C (7th Cru.Sqn.) | FORCE D (5th Cru.Sqn.) | FORCE E (11th Cru.Sqn.) | FORCE G (12th Cru.Sqn.) | FORCE H (4th Cru.Sqn.) | FORCE I (9th Cru.Sqn.) | S.ATLANTIC S.AMERICA | PACIFIC COAST AMERICA | CAPE STATION | WEST COAST AFRICA | EAST COAST AFRICA |
|---|---|---|---|---|---|---|---|---|---|---|---|---|
| 14.3.1915 (at time of sinking of *Dresden* and blockade of *Königsberg*) | Deactivated | Disbanded | LC *Highflyer* (SNO) AMC *Empress of Britain* AMC *Marmora* | AC *Sutlej* (F) LC *Juno* LC *Isis* LC *Venus* + 4 Armed Boarding vessels | LC *Diana* (SNO) LC *Talbot* + 4 Armed Boarding vessels | North America & W.Indies AC *Leviathan* (F) BB *Glory* (F.2) AC *Suffolk* AC *Berwick* C *Niobe* (RCN) LC *Melbourne* (RAN) LC *Charybdis* (Paid off, Bermuda) AMC *Caronia* Returned to U.K. AC *Essex* | Azores-Madeira-Gibraltar C *Europa* C *Amphitrite* C *Argonaut* AMC *Calgarian* AMC *Carmania* AMC *Victorian* AMC *Edinburgh Castle* AMC *Ophir* | LC *Sydney* (F) (RAN) AC *Carnarvon* AC *Kent* ‡‡ LC *Bristol* LC *Glasgow* ‡‡ LC *Orama* ‡‡ AMC *Otranto* AMC *Macedonia* AMC *Celtic* | LC *Newcastle* (SNO) LC *Rainbow* (RCN) S *Shearwater* | LC *Astraea* AMC *Armadale Castle* AMC *Laconia* Detached to E.African Coast BB *Goliath* (F) | LC *Challenger* GB *Dwarf* AMC *Laurentic* | BB *Goliath* (F) LC *Weymouth* LC *Hyacinth* LC *Pyramus* LC *Pioneer* (RAN) AMC *Kinfauns Castle* + 4 Armed Whalers |

The next ten tables give details of ships engaged in the major naval battles of the war, half of them involving the Grand Fleet and German High Seas Fleet, the others including more *ad hoc* formations in remote or subsidiary locations.

---

### *Table 3.95* Ships involved in the Battle of Coronel 1.11.1914

| BRITISH SQUADRON *Cradock* | | GERMAN SQUADRON *von Spee* | |
|---|---|---|---|
| AC | *Good Hope* | AC | *Scharnhorst* |
| AC | *Monmouth* | AC | *Gneisenau* |
| LC | *Glasgow* | | |
| | | LC | *Leipzig* |
| AMC | *Otranto*　　Not engaged | LC | *Dresden* |
| | | | |
| Absent, at Falkland Islands | | Joined later, not engaged | |
| PBB | *Canopus* | LC | *Nürnberg* |

| Ships en route to join Cradock's Command to form a second squadron under Stoddart | |
|---|---|
| AC | *Cornwall* |
| AC | *Defence* (from Mediterranean) |
| LC | *Bristol* |
| | |
| AC | *Carnarvon* |
| AMC | *Macedonia* |
| AMC | *Orama* |
| | |
| LC | *Kent* |
| LC | *Highflyer* |

| Ships lost | Ships lost |
|---|---|
| *Good Hope* | None |
| *Monmouth* | |

| Main Armament | | Main Armament | |
|---|---|---|---|
| *Good Hope* | 2 x 9.2" 16 x 6" | *Scharnhorst, Gneisenau* 8 x 8.2" 6 x 5.9" | |
| *Monmouth* | 14 x 6" | | |
| *Glasgow* | 2 x 6" 10 x 4" | *Leipzig* | |
| *Otranto* | 8 x 4.7" | *Dresden* } 10 x 4.1" | |
| | | *Nurnberg* | |

---

### *Table 3.96* Ships involved in the Battle of the Falkland Islands 8.12.1914

| BRITISH SQUADRON *Sturdee* | | GERMAN SQUADRON *von Spee* | |
|---|---|---|---|
| BC | *Invincible* | AC | *Scharnhorst* |
| BC | *Inflexible* | AC | *Gneisenau* |
| | | | |
| AC | *Kent* | LC | *Dresden* |
| AC | *Cornwall* | LC | *Nürnberg* |
| AC | *Carnarvon* | LC | *Leipzig* |
| | | | |
| LC | *Bristol** | | Supply ships |
| LC | *Glasgow* | | *Santa Isabel* |
| | | | *Baden* |
| AMC | *Macedonia** | | *Seydlitz* |
| | | | |
| In Port Stanley — not engaged | | | |
| PBB | *Canopus* | | |

| Ships lost | Ships lost |
|---|---|
| None | *Scharnhorst, Gneisenau* |
| | *Nürnberg, Leipzig* |
| | *Santa Isabel, Baden* |

## Ships involved in the Battle of the Falkland Islands 8.12.1914 continued

| BRITISH SQUADRON *Sturdee* | GERMAN SQUADRON *von Spee* |
|---|---|
| **Main Armament** | **Main Armament** |
| *Invincible, Inflexible* 8 x 12" 16 x 4" | See Coronel |
| *Kent, Cornwall* 14 x 6" | |
| *Carnarvon* 4 x 7.5" 6 x 6" | |
| *Bristol, Glasgow* 2 x 6" 10 x 4" | |
| *Macedonia* 8 x 4.7" | |
| *Canopus* 4 x 12" 12 x 6" | |

**Details of Formation of Sturdee's Squadron**

| | |
|---|---|
| *Invincible, Inflexible* | Detached from Grand Fleet. The movements of these ships were so secret that the contemporary Admiralty "Movements of H.M. Ships" books do not name them, simply referring to 'K' or Force 'K' |
| *Carnarvon* | From Force D (5th Cruiser Squadron, Stoddart) via West Africa Squadron. |
| *Cornwall* | From Force D (5th Cruiser Squadron) via Canary Islands |
| *Kent* | From U.K. via Sierra Leone & Cape Verde Islands (Force D) |
| *Defence* | From Mediterranean, departed Gibraltar 15.10.14 but ordered to Cape Sqn. prior to battle (26.11.14) |
| *Bristol* | From Cruiser Force H in the West Indies, ordered south to join Stoddart's Sqn. (Force D) |
| *Glasgow* | On S.American Station at outbreak of war. Survivor of Cradock's Sqn. |
| *Canopus* | From 8th Battle Sqn. U.K. waters. Ordered to reinforce Cradock. Guardship at Falklands. |
| *Macedonia* (AMC) *Orama* (AMC) | Part of Cruiser Force D (Stoddart's Sqn.) (*Orama* detached to escort colliers prior to battle) |
| *Vindictive* | From U.K. to Ascension Island to act as wireless link |
| *Highflyer* *Cumberland* | Originally part of Force D (Stoddart) *Highflyer* remained at Cape Verde Islands. *Cumberland* detached to strengthen forces on West coast of Africa |

### Table 3.97 Ships involved in the Battle of Heligoland Bight 28.8.1914

| BRITISH | GERMAN |
|---|---|
| 1st Battle Cruiser Sqn. | 2nd Submarine Flotilla Leader |
| *Lion* (F) | *Stettin* |
| *Queen Mary* | |
| *Princess Royal* | 2nd Scouting Group (3 ships absent) |
| | *Coln* |
| Cruiser Force K | *Mainz* |
| *Invincible* (F) | *Stralsund* |
| *New Zealand* | *Strassburg* |
| | |
| 1st Lt. Cruiser Sqn. | 3rd Scouting Group (4 ships absent) |
| *Southampton* | *Frauenlob* |
| *Birmingham* | |
| *Nottingham* | 3rd Harbour Flotilla (Jade/Weser) |
| *Lowestoft* | *Ariadne* |
| *Falmouth* | |
| *Liverpool* | 1st T.B.Flotilla |
| | *V 187* (Ldr.) |
| 4th Div./1st Destroyer Flotilla (Attached Force K) | 1st ½ Flotilla |
| | *V 188, V 189, V 190, V 191, G 197* |
| *Badger, Beaver, Jackal, Sandfly* | 2nd ½ Flotilla |
| | *G 192, G 193, G 194, G 195, G 196* |
| Cruiser Force C (In reserve) | |
| Subdivided into – | 5th T.B.Flotilla |
| Force A (1) | *G 12* (Ldr.) |
| Southern Force (2) | 9th ½ Flotilla |
| (2) *Eurythmus* (F) | *V 2, V 3, V 4, V 5, V 6* |
| (1) *Bacchante* (F) | 10th ½ Flotilla |
| (1) *Adoukir* | *G 7, G 8, G 9, G 10, G 11* |
| (1) *Cressy* | |
| (1) *Hogue* | 3rd Minesweeping Div. |
| (2) *Amethyst* | *D 8* (Ldr.) |
| | *T 28, T 29, T 31, T 33, T 34, T 35* |
| 3rd Destroyer Flotilla | *T 36, T 37, T 40, T 71, T 72, T 73* |
| *Arethusa* | |
| 1st Div. | En route from Jade, arriving after end of action: |
| *Lookout, Leonidas, Legion, Lennox* | 1st Scouting Group (Battle Cruisers) |
| 2nd Div. | *Moltke* |
| *Lark, Lance, Linnet, Landrail* | *von der Tann* |
| 3rd Div. | *Seydlitz* |
| *Laforey, Lawford, Louis, Lydiard* | |
| 4th Div. | |
| *Laurel, Liberty, Lysander, Laertes* | |
| | |
| 1st Destroyer Flotilla | |
| *Fearless* | |
| 1st Div. | |
| *Acheron, Attack, Hind, Archer* | |
| 2nd Div. | |
| *Ariel, Lucifer, Llewellyn* | |
| 3rd Div. | |
| *Ferret, Forester, Druid, Defender* | |
| 4th Div. | |
| (Detached to Force K) | |
| 5th Div. | |
| *Goshawk, Lizard, Lapwing, Phoenix* | |
| | |
| Submarines | |
| By Heligoland *E4, E5, E9* | |
| Outer line *E6, E7, E8* | |
| Off the 'Ems' *D2, D8* | |
| | |
| Tenders | |
| *Lurcher* | |
| *Firedrake* | |

| Ships lost | | | Ships lost | | |
|---|---|---|---|---|---|
| Sunk – | None | | Sunk – | *Mainz* | |
| Damaged – | *Arethusa* | | | *Coln* | |
| | *Laurel* | | | *Ariadne* | |
| | *Liberty* | | | *V 187* | |
| | *Laertes* | | Damaged – | *Frauenlob* | |
| | | | | *V 1* | |
| | | | | *T 33* | |
| | | | | *D 8* | |

**Table 3.98** Ships involved in North East Coast Raid 16.12.1914

| GERMAN | BRITISH FORCES RESPONDING |
|---|---|
| **Reconnaissance 10.12.1914** | **From Cromarty** |
| Lt. Cruisers — *Graudenz, Kolberg, Stralsund, Strassburg, Rostock* | 1st Battle Cruiser Sqn. |
| Destroyers — 6th and 7th Flotillas |     *Lion* |
| |     *Queen Mary* |
| **Raiding Force 15/16.12.1914** |     *Tiger* |
| 1st Scouting Group — *Seydlitz* (F) |     *New Zealand* |
| (5 Battle Cruisers) — *Blucher* } Attacked Hartlepools | Att. Lt. Cruiser — *Blonde* |
|     *Moltke* | |
|     *Derfflinger* } Attacked Scarborough & Whitby | 2 Divs. 4th Destroyer Flotilla |
|     *von der Tann* |     *Lynx, Ambuscade, Unity, Hardy, Shark, Acasta, Spitfire* |
| 2nd Scouting Group — *Strassburg* | **From Scapa Flow** |
| (4 Lt. Cruisers) — *Stralsund* } Joint Support Force (High Seas Fleet) | 2nd Battle Sqn. — *King George V* |
|     *Graudenz* |     *Ajax* |
|     *Kolberg* — In Scarborough & Whitby force |     *Centurion* |
|     (*Rostock* - Absent)(With High Seas Fleet Destroyer Flotilla) |     *Orion* |
| |     *Monarch* |
| Two TBD Flotillas |     *Conqueror* |
| 1st Destroyer Flotilla *V 191* (S.O.)† | Att. Lt. Cruiser — *Boadicea* (returned to port) |
|   1st Half Flotilla — *V 186, V 188, G 197, V 189‡, V 190* | |
|   2nd Half Flotilla — *G 196, G 192, G 194, G 193, G 195* | 1st Light Cruiser Sqn. *Southampton* |
| |     *Birmingham* |
| 9th Destroyer Flotilla *V 28* (S.O.) |     *Nottingham* |
|   17th Half Flotilla — *V 25, V 26, V 27, S 31◊* |     *Falmouth* |
|   18th Half Flotilla — *V 29◊, S 35◊* |     *Blanche* (Attached from 3rd Battle Sqn.) In lieu of *Liverpool* |
| |     [refitting], *Lowestoft* [unavailable] but returned to port with |
| **Support Force – HIGH SEAS FLEET** |     *Boadicea*) |
| 14 Dreadnought Battleships, 8 Pre-dreadnought Battleships, 2 Armoured Cruisers, | |
| 7 Lt. Cruisers, 54 Destroyers | **From Rosyth** |
| 1st Battle Sqn. — 4 Westfalen Class, 4 Helgoland Class (Dreadnoughts) | 3rd Cruiser Sqn. (Armoured cruisers) |
| 2nd Battle Sqn. — 8 Pre-dreadnoughts |     *Antrim* |
| 3rd Battle Sqn. — 4 Kaiser Class, 1 König Class● (*Grosser Kurfurst*) |     *Devonshire* |
|     (Dreadnoughts) |     *Argyll* |
| Fleet Flagship — *Friedrich der Grusse* (Kaiser Class) (Dreadnought) |     *Roxburgh* |
| | **From Hartlepool** |
| 3rd & 4th Scouting Groups | Local Patrol Forces |
|     Armoured and Lt. Cruisers** | Scouts — *Patrol, Forward* |
| 5 Destroyer Flotillas | 9th Destroyer Flotilla *Duon, Waveney, Test, Moy* |
| | Submarine — *C 9* |
| | **From Harwich** |
| | 4 Lt. Cruisers — *Aurora, Undaunted, Fearless, Arethusa* |
| | 2 Flotillas Destroyers — Returned to port |

† (S.O.) - Senior Officer Ship (of Flotilla/Squadron).

‡ Utilized as Despatch Vessel.

◊ Detached or lost touch on 15/16.12.1914 for varying reasons (low on fuel, unserviceable etc.).

● *König* was under repair, *Mark Graf, Kronprinz* - absent on trials.

** Including *Roon Prinz Heinrich, Stuttgart, Hamburg, München, Stettin, Rostock.*

**Table 3.99 Ships involved in the Battle of Dogger Bank 24.1.1915**

| BRITISH FORCES | | | | | GERMAN FORCES | | |
|---|---|---|---|---|---|---|---|

**BRITISH FORCES**

**1st Battle Cruiser Sqn.**
*Lion* (F)
*Tiger*
*Princess Royal*

**2nd Battle Cruiser Sqn.**
*New Zealand* (F)
*Indomitable*

**1st Light Cruiser Sqn.**
*Southampton* (F)
*Birmingham*
*Nottingham*
*Lowestoft*

**Destroyer Flotillas**
*Arethusa* (F)
**10th Flotilla**
'M' Division
*Meteor*
*Miranda*
*Milne*
*Mentor*
*Mastiff*
*Minos*
*Morris*

**1st Flotilla**
Lt. Cruiser
*Aurora* (Capt. D.1)‡

| 1st Division | 3rd Division | 4th Division | 5th Division |
|---|---|---|---|
| *Acheron* | *Ferret* | *Hornet* | *Goshawk* |
| *Attack* | *Forester* | *Tigress* | *Phoenix* |
| *Hydra* | *Defender* | *Sandfly* | *Lapwing* |
| *Ariel* | *Druid* | *Jackal* | |

**3rd Flotilla**
*Undaunted* (Capt. D.3)

| 1st Division | 2nd Division | 3rd Division | 4th Division |
|---|---|---|---|
| *Lookout* | *Laurel* | *Laforey* | *Legion* |
| *Lysander* | *Liberty* | *Lawford* | *Lark* |
| *Landrail* | *Laertes* | *Lydiard* | |
| | *Lucifer* | *Louis* | |

**GERMAN FORCES**

**1st Scouting Group*** (Battle Cruisers)
*Seydwitz*
*Moltke*
*Derfflinger*
*Blücher*

**2nd Scouting Group†** (Light Cruisers)
*Stralsund*
*Graudenz*
*Rostock* (1st Leader, Torpedo Boats)
*Kolberg* (2nd Leader, Torpedo Boats)

**Destroyer Flotillas**
5th Destroyer Flotilla
*G 12*

| 9th Half Flotilla | 18th Half Flotilla | 15th Half Flotilla |
|---|---|---|
| *V1* | *V 30* | *V 181* |
| *V 4* | *V 33* | *V 182* |
| *V 5* | *S 34* | *V 185* |
| | *S 29* | |
| | *S 35* | |

10th Half Flotilla
*G 11*
*G 9*
*G 7*
*G 8*
*V 2*

Leader 8th Destroyer Flotilla
*S 178*

U Boats at sea
*U 19*   *U 32*
*U 21*   *U 33*

**Ships Lost**
Sunk      *Blücher*

* 1st Scouting Group – *von der Tann* absent, unserviceable in dockyard hands.

† 2nd Scouting Group – *Strassburg* absent, unserviceable in dockyard harbour. Replaced by *Rostock* (1st Leader, Torpedo Boats). *Regensburg* absent, working up after completion.

‡ Capt. D.1 - Captain commanding 1st Destroyer Flotilla etc.

**Table 3.100 Allied Ships involved in the Dardanelles Campaign 1915**

**Build up of Allied Forces 1.1915 - 4.1915**
Arriving
1.1915   *Inflexible* (fm Gibraltar, via Falklands) to relieve *Indefatigable* (to U.K.)
*Queen Elizabeth* (fm Gibraltar, gunnery trials)
2.1915   *Albion* (fm Cape)
*Triumph* (fm China)
*Vengeance* (fm Cape Verde Is. - Gibraltar)
*Canopus* (fm S.America Station)
*Ocean* (fm Gulf)      } in Egyptian waters
*Swiftsure* (fm East Indies) }
During 2.1915 from U.K.
*Cornwallis, Majestic, Prince George, Irresistible, Agamemnon, Lord Nelson* (to replace *Queen Elizabeth*)

From French Fleet
*Suffren, Bouvet, Gaulois, Charlemagne*

3.1915 From U.K.
*Queen, Implacable, Prince of Wales, London*
From Egypt & East Africa later in March:
*Goliath*

3.1915 From France
*Henri IV* replaced *Bouvet, Gaulois; Jaureguiberry* replaced *Charlemagne*
4.1915   *Inflexible* ordered home 6.4.15
5.1915   *Queen Elizabeth* ordered home◊, replaced by *Venerable, Exmouth*

**Naval O.O.B. 1st Bombardment of Dardanelles 18.2.1915**

| 1st Division | 2nd Division | 3rd Division (French) |
|---|---|---|
| *Inflexible* | *Vengeance* | *Suffren* |
| *Agamemnon* | *Albion* | *Bouvet* |
| *Queen Elizabeth* | *Cornwallis* | *Charlemagne* |
| | *Irresistible* | *Gaulois* |
| | *Triumph* | |

**2nd Bombardment of Dardanelles 25.2.1915**

| | Assault Force | Support Force | Spotting Duties |
|---|---|---|---|
| 1 | *Vengeance* | *Agamemnon* | LC  *Dublin* |
| | *Cornwallis* | *Queen Elizabeth* | |
| 2 | *Suffren* | *Irresistible* | |
| | *Bouvet* | *Gauolois* | |
| 3 | *Triumph* | | |
| | *Albion* | | |

**Attempt to force passage of Dardanelles 18.3.1915**

| 1st Division | 2nd Division | 3rd Division |
|---|---|---|
| 1st Sub-Division | 3rd Sub-Division | 6th Sub-Division |
| *Queen Elizabeth* | *Ocean* | *Suffren* |
| *Inflexible* | *Irresistible* | *Bouvert* |
| | *Albion* | *Gaulois* |
| 2nd Sub-Division | *Vengeance* | *Charlemagne* |
| *Agamemnon* | | |
| *Lord Nelson* | 4th Sub-Division | 7th Sub-Division |
| | *Swiftsure* | *Triumph* |
| | *Majestic* | *Prince George* |
| 5th Sub-Division | | |
| *Canopus* | | |
| *Cornwall* | | |

◊ 12.5.1915.

## Allied Ships involved in the Dardanelles Campaign 1915 continued

**Naval Forces in Support of Gallipoli Landings**
By 19.4.1915 losses of 18.3.1915 (see right) had been replaced and the Allied naval forces in the Eastern Mediterranean, organised in seven squadrons consisted of:—

|  | | BRITISH | FRENCH | RUSSIAN |
|---|---|---|---|---|
| 19 Battleships | of which | 16 | 3 | |
| 13 Cruisers | | 9 | 3 | 1 |
| 29 Destroyers | | 24 | 5 | |
| 12 Submarines | | 8 | 4 | |
| 9 Minesweepers | | 6 | 3 | |
| 5 Torpedo Boats | | | 5 | |
| 1 Seaplane Carrier | | 1 | | |

**Losses during Dardanelles Campaign**

| Sunk | Date | Seriously Damaged | Date |
|---|---|---|---|
| Ocean | 18.3.15 | Suffren | 18.3.15 (French) |
| Irresistible | 18.3.15 | Gaulois | 18.3.15 (French) |
| Bouvet | 18.3.15 (French) | Inflexible | 18.3.15 |
| Goliath | 15.5.15 | | |
| Triumph | 25.5.15 | | |
| Majestic | 27.5.15 | | |

**Table 3.101** Ships involved in the Battle of Jutland 3.5.1916

| BRITISH GRAND FLEET | | | GERMAN HIGH SEAS FLEET | | |
|---|---|---|---|---|---|

**BRITISH GRAND FLEET**

**BATTLE FLEET**
*Iron Duke* (F)

Attached
  *Active* (Lt. Cru.)      *Oak* (Destroyer)

| 2nd Battle Sqn. | 4th Battle Sqn. | 1st Battle Sqn. |
|---|---|---|
| *King George V* | *Iron Duke* | *Marlborough* |
| *Ajax* | *Royal Oak* | *Revenge* |
| *Centurion* | *Superb* | *Hercules* |
| *Erin* | *Canada* | *Agincourt* |
| *Orion* | *Benbow* | *Colossus* |
| *Monarch* | *Bellerophon* | *Collingwood* |
| *Conqueror* | *Temeraire* | *Neptune* |
| *Thunderer* | *Vanguard* | *St. Vincent* |

Attached
  *Boadicea* (Lt. Cru.)    *Blanche* (Lt. Cru.)    *Bellona* (Lt. Cru.)
Absent in dockyard hands or remained in harbour:
  *Emperor of India*    *Royal Sovereign*

| 3rd Battle Cruiser Sqn. | 1st Cruiser Sqn. | 2nd Cruiser Sqn. |
|---|---|---|
| *Invincible* | *Defence* | *Minotaur* |
| *Inflexible* | *Warrior* | *Hampshire* |
| *Indomitable* | *Duke of Edinburgh* | *Cochrane* |
| | *Black Prince* | *Shannon* |

Absent on detached service
  *Achilles, Donegal*

**4th Lt. Cruiser Sqn.**    Lt. Cruisers attached 3rd Battle Cruiser Sqn.
*Calliope*          *Chester* (from 3rd Lt. Cruiser Sqn.)
*Caroline*         *Canterbury* (from 5th Lt. Cruiser Sqn. Harwich)
*Constance*
*Royalist*        Seaplane Carrier
*Comus*         *Campania* (returned to Scapa u/svc.)

**BATTLE CRUISER FLEET**
**Battle Cruisers**          **Battleships**
  *Lion* (F)

| 1st Battle Cruiser Sqn. | 2nd Battle Cruiser Sqn. | 5th Battle Sqn. |
|---|---|---|
| *Princess Royal* | *New Zealand* | *Barham* |
| *Queen Mary* | *Indefatigable* | *Valiant* |
| *Tiger* | In dockyard hands: | *Warspite* |
| | *Australia* | *Malaya* |
| | | In dockyard hands: |
| | | *Queen Elizabeth* |

**Light Cruisers**

| 1st Lt. Cruiser Sqn. | 2nd Lt. Cruiser Sqn. | 3rd Lt. Cruiser Sqn. |
|---|---|---|
| *Galatea* | *Southampton* | *Falmouth* |
| *Phaeton* | *Birmingham* | *Yarmouth* |
| *Inconstant* | *Nottingham* | *Birkenhead* |
| *Cordelia* | *Dublin* | *Gloucester* |
| | | *Chester* |
| | | under repair |
| | | *Chatham* |

**Destroyer Flotillas see over**

**GERMAN HIGH SEAS FLEET**

*Friedrich der Grosse* (Fleet F)

| 1st Battle Sqn. | 2nd Battle Sqn. | 3rd Battle Sqn. |
|---|---|---|
| *Ostfriesland* (F) | *Deutschland* (F) | *König* (F) |
| *Posen* | *Hannover* | *Kaiser* |
| *Thuringen* | *Pommern* | *Grosser Kurfürst* |
| *Helgoland* | *Schlesien* | *Markgraf* |
| *Oldenburg* | *Schleswig Holstein* | *Kronprinz* |
| *Rheinland* | *Hessen* | *Prinzregent Luitpold* |
| *Nassau* | | *Kaiserin* |
| *Westfalen* | | |

**Scouting Forces**

| 1st Scouting Group | 2nd Scouting Group | 4th Scouting Group |
|---|---|---|
| (Battle Cruisers) | (Lt. Cruisers) | (Lt. Cruisers) |
| *Lützow* (F) | *Frankfurt* (F) | *Stettin* (F) |
| *Seydlitz* | *Pillau* | *München* |
| *Moltke* | *Elbing* | *Frauenlob* |
| *Derfflinger* | *Wiesbaden* | *Stuttgart* |
| *von der Tann* | *Rostock*  } See Destroyer | *Hamburg* |
| | *Regensburg* } Flotillas | |

**Destroyer Flotillas see over**

## Ships involved in the Battle of Jutland 3.5.1916 continued

| BRITISH GRAND FLEET | | | GERMAN HIGH SEAS FLEET | | | |
|---|---|---|---|---|---|---|

**Destroyer Flotillas**

| 1st Flotilla | 13th Flotilla | 9th & 10th Flotillas |
|---|---|---|
| *Fearless* (LC) | *Champion* (LC) | *Lydiard* |
| *Acheron* | *Nestor* | *Liberty* |
| *Ariel* | *Nomad* | *Landrail* |
| *Attack* | *Narborough* | *Laurel* |
| *Hydra* | *Obdurate* | *Moorsom* |
| *Badger* | *Petard* | *Morris* |
| *Goshawk* | *Pelican* | *Turbulent* |
| *Defender* | *Nerissa* | *Termagant* |
| *Lizard* | *Onslow* | |
| *Lapwing* | *Moresby* | |
| | *Nicator* | |

| 12th Flotilla | 11th Flotilla | 4th Flotilla |
|---|---|---|
| *Faulkner* (F.Ldr.)* | *Castor* (LC) | *Tipperary* (F.Ldr.) |
| *Marksman* (F.Ldr.) | *Kempenfelt* (F.Ldr.) | *Broke* (F.Ldr.) |
| *Obedient* | *Ossory* | *Achates* |
| *Maenad* | *Mystic* | *Porpoise* |
| *Opal* | *Moon* | *Spitfire* |
| *Mary Rose* | *Morning Star* | *Unity* |
| *Marvel* | *Magic* | *Garland* |
| *Menace* | *Mounsey* | *Ambuscade* |
| *Nessus* | *Mandate* | *Ardent* |
| *Narwhal* | *Marne* | *Fortune* |
| *Mindful* | *Minion* | *Sparrowhawk* |
| *Onslaught* | *Manners* | *Contest* |
| *Munster* | *Michael* | *Shark* |
| *Nonsuch* | *Mons* | *Acasta* |
| *Noble* | *Martial* | *Ophelia* |
| *Mischief* | *Milbrook* | *Christopher* |
| | | *Owl* |
| | | *Hardy* |
| | | *Midge* |

**Seaplane Carrier**
*Engadine*

Absent, in dockyard hands or remaining in harbour:
*Botha, Jackal, Archer, Tigress, Phoenix, Negro, Nereus, Paladin, Penn, Pigeon, Nepean, Napier, Mameluke, Marmion, Musketeer, Cockatrice, Paragon, Victor*

**Destroyer Flotillas**

Lt. Cruisers     *Rostock* (F)
       *Regensburg* (F. 2nd in Cd.)

| 1st Flotilla | 2nd Flotilla | 3rd Flotilla | 5th Flotilla |
|---|---|---|---|
| 1st Half Flotilla | *B 98* | *S 53* | *G 11* |
| *G 39* | 3rd Half Flotilla | 5th Half Flotilla | 9th Half Flotilla |
| *G 40* | *G 101* | *V 91* | *V 2* |
| | *G 102* | *V 73* | *V 4* |
| | *B 112* | *G 88* | *V 6* |
| | *B 97* | | *V 1* |
| | | | *V 3* |
| | 4th Half Flotilla | 6th Half Flotilla | 10th Half Flotilla |
| | *B 109* | *S 94* | *G 8* |
| | *B 110* | *V 48* | *G 7* |
| | *B 111* | *G 42* | *V 5* |
| | *G 103* | | *G 9* |
| | *G 104* | | *G 10* |

| 6th Flotilla | 7th Flotilla | 9th Flotilla |
|---|---|---|
| *G 41* | *S 24* | *V 28* |
| 11th Half Flotilla | 13th Half Flotilla | 17th Half Flotilla |
| *V 44* | *S 15* | *V 27* |
| *G 87* | *S 17* | *V 26* |
| *G 86* | *S 20* | *S 36* |
| | *S 16* | *S 51* |
| | *S 18* | *S 52* |
| 12th Half Flotilla | 14th Half Flotilla | 18th Half Flotilla |
| *V 69* | *S 19* | *V 30* |
| *V 45* | *S 23* | *S 34* |
| *V 46* | *V 189* | *S 33* |
| *S 50* | | *V 29* |
| *G 37* | | *S 35* |

Absent in dockyard hands
*V 190, G 197, G 192, G 195, G 196, G 193, S 165, V 74, G 85, V 70, S 55, S 49, V 43.* (*V 186* sent to Heligoland u/svc)

Absent
*V 189*

| U Boats | | | Air Ships | | |
|---|---|---|---|---|---|
| *U 24* | *U 44* | *UB 22* | *L 11* | *L 23* | *L 22* |
| *U 32* | *U 52* | *UB 21* | *L 17* | *L 16* | *L 24* |
| *U 63* | *U 47* | *U 53* | *L 14* | *L 13* | |
| *U 66* | *U 46* | *U 64* | *L 21* | *L 9* | |
| *U 70* | *U 22* | | | | |
| *U 43* | *U 19* | | | | |

* F.Ldr. - Flotilla Leader.

---

**Ships lost**

Battleships

---

Battle Cruisers
   *Indefatigable*
   *Invincible*
   *Queen Mary*

Armoured Cruisers
   *Black Prince*
   *Defence*
   *Warrior*

Light Cruisers

Destroyers
   *Ardent*
   *Fortune*
   *Nester*
   *Nomad*
   *Shark*
   *Sparrowhawk*
   *Tipperary*
   *Turbulent*

**Ships lost**

Battleships
   *Pommern*

Battle Cruisers
   *Lützow*

Armoured Cruisers

Light Cruisers
   *Elbing*
   *Frauenlob*
   *Rostock*
   *Wiesbaden*

Destroyers
   *S 35*
   *V 4*
   *V 27*
   *V 29*
   *V 48*

**Table 3.102 Ships involved in the 2nd Battle of Heligoland Bight 16/17.11.1917**

| BRITISH FORCES | | | GERMAN FORCES | |
|---|---|---|---|---|
| **1st Cruiser Sqn.**<br>*Courageous*<br>*Glorious* | **6th Lt. Cruiser Sqn.**<br>*Cardiff*<br>*Ceres*<br>*Calypso*<br>*Caradoc* | **1st Lt. Cruiser Sqn.**<br>*Caledon*<br>*Galatea*<br>*Royalist*<br>*Inconstant* | **II Scouting Group** (Lt.Cruisers)<br>*Königsberg*<br>*Nürnberg*<br>*Frankfurt*<br>*Pillau* | **Part IV Battle Sqn.**<br>*Kaiser*<br>*Kaiserin* |
| **Attached Destroyers**<br>*Ursa*<br>*Nerissa*<br>*Urchin*<br>*Vampire* | **Attached Destroyers**<br>*Valentine*<br>*Vimiera*<br>*Vanquisher*<br>*Vehement* | **Attached Destroyers**<br>*Vendetta*<br>*Medway* | **Attached**<br>*S 62*<br>*V 43* | **Attached**<br>*S 24*<br>*S 18* (fm. Flanders<br>Destroyer Flotilla) |
| **1st Battle Cruiser Sqn.**<br>*Lion*<br>*Princess Royal*<br>*Tiger*<br>*New Zealand* (Attached)<br>*Repulse* | **1st Battle Sqn.**<br>*Revenge*<br>*Royal Oak*<br>*Resolution*<br>*Canada*<br>*Benbow*<br>*Emperor of India* | | **IV Sperrbrecher Group**<br>2 *Sperrbrecher* (unidentified)<br>**Attached** (fm. 14th Destroyer Half Flotilla)<br>*V 83*<br>*G 93* | |
| **Attached Destroyers**<br>*Champion*<br>*Verdun*<br>*Telemachus*<br>*Oriana*<br>*Nepean*<br>*Obdurate*<br>*Tristram*<br>*Petard*<br>*Tower* | **Attached Destroyers**<br>*Noble*<br>*Nonsuch*<br>*Napier*<br>*Penn*<br>*Paladin*<br>*Saumarez*<br>*Valhalla*<br>*Prince*<br>*Mischief*<br>*Munster*<br>*Narborough* | | **VI Minesweeping Flotilla**  **IV Aux. M/Swpr. Flotilla**  **II & VI Aux. M/S. Flots.**<br>*M 66*  *A 63*  (Requisitioned fishing<br>*M 7*  *A 68*  vessels)<br>*A 36*  *A 69*<br>*T 74*  *A 74*<br>*M 53*  *A 41*<br>*M 4*  *A 52*<br>*M 3*<br>*M 1* | |
| | | | **Nordsee Vorposten Flotilla**<br>*Kehdinger*<br>*Fritz Reuter* | |
| | | | **Destroyers**<br>12th Half Flotilla  13th Half Flotilla  14th Half Flotilla  Leader, 7th Flotilla<br>*V 43* (Att. II  *V 83* (Att. IV  *G 87*  *S 62* (Att. II<br>Sct.Gp.)  Sp/B.Gp.)  *G 92*  Sct.Gp.)<br>*V 44*  *G 93* (Att. IV Sp/B.Gp.)<br>*V 45*  *G 94* | |
| | | | **Added to German Forces later**<br>1  *Stralsbund* (Lt. Cruiser) *S 42 G 94*<br>2  4 Boats II Destroyer Flotilla<br>3  *Graudenz* (Lt. Cruiser)<br>4  2nd Half Flotilla + *G 193*<br>5  *Hindenburg, Moltke* (Battle Cruisers); *Friedrich der Grosse, König Albert*<br>   (Battleships); 1st Half Flotilla; part Flanders Destroyer Flotilla | |

**Table 3.103 British Forces involved in the Zeebrugge and Ostend Raids 22/23.4.1918**

| **Zeebrugge** | | **Ostend** | |
|---|---|---|---|
| (a) Special Service Duties | *61 Wing R.A.F.* (Aerial Escort)<br>Special Service Vessel *Lingfield* (M/Swpr.) *ML 555, 557* | (a) Bombarding Forces | |
| (b) Offshore Forces | | Monitors | *Marshall Soult, Lord Clive, Prince Eugene, General Crauford*<br>*M 24, M 26, M 21* |
| Outer Patrol | *Attentive* (Scout), *Scott, Ulleswater, Teazer, Stork* (Destroyers) | Destroyers | *Mentor, Lightfoot, Zubian* |
| Long Range<br>Bombardment | *Erebus, Terror* (Monitors), *Termagant, Truculent,*<br>*Manly* (Destroyers) | Motor Launches | *ML 249, 448, 538* + 3 others |
| | | French Destroyers &<br>Torpedo Boats | *Lestin, Roux, Bouclier*<br>T.B. Nos. *1, 2, 3, 34* |
| (c) Inshore Forces | | French Motor Launches | Nos. *1, 2, 33, 34* |
| Flagship | *Warwick* (Destroyer)(Flag of V.Adm. R.Keyes) | + British Seige Guns in Flanders | |
| Blockships | *Thetis, Intrepid, Iphigenia* (Obsolete Light Cruisers) | (b) Inshore Forces | |
| Storming vessels | *Vindictive* (Obsolete Lt. Cruiser), *Iris II, Daffodil* (Special<br>vessels – Liverpool Ferries) | Blockships | *Sirius, Brilliant* (Obsolete Light Cruisers) |
| Attack on viaduct | *C 1, C 3* (Submarines) 1 Picket Boat | Destroyers | *Swift, Faulknor, Matchless, Mastiff, Afridi, Tempest, Tetrarch* |
| Aerial Attack | *65 Wing R.A.F.* | Motor Launches | *ML 11, 16, 17, 22, 23, 30, 60, 105, 254, 274, 276, 279, 283,* |
| Other operations | *Phoebe, North Star* (Unit L), *Trident, Mansfield* (Unit M),<br>*Whirlwind, Myngs* (Unit F), *Velox, Morris, Moorsum,*<br>*Melpomene* (Unit R) (Units L, M, F, R were all Destroyers) | | *429, 512, 532, 551, 556* |
| | | Coastal Motor Boats | Nos. *2, 4, 10, 12, 19, 20, 29A, 34A* |
| Motor Launches | *79, 110, 121, 128, 223, 239, 241, 252, 258, 262, 272, 280,*<br>*282, 308, 314, 345, 397, 416, 420, 422, 424, 513, 525, 526,*<br>*533, 549, 552, 558, 560, 561, 562* | **Covering Squadron for Both Enterprises** – Drawn from Harwich Force<br>7 Light Cruisers<br>2 Leaders | |
| Coastal Motor Boats | *5, 7, 15, 16A, 17A, 21B, 22B, 24A, 25BD, 26B, 27A, 30B,*<br>*32A, 35A* | 14 Destroyers | |

## Table 3.104 Allied Ocean Convoys

| NO. OF CONVOYS | DIRECTION | SHIPS ESCORTED SAFELY | SHIPS LOST | | |
| --- | --- | --- | --- | --- | --- |
| | | | TORPEDOED IN CONVOY | MARINE ACCIDENT | NOT IN CONVOY |
| | **HOMEWARDS** | | | | |
| 56 | Halifax | 556 | 2 | 1 | 1 |
| 63 | Sydney | 1,432 | 4 | 3 | 7 |
| 89 | New York | 1,619 | 7 | 4 | 5 |
| 24 | Halifax-Channel | 307 | 1 | – | – |
| 78 | Hampton Roads | 1,596 | 13 | – | 5 |
| 56 | Sierra Leone | 421 | 2 | 1 | 1 |
| 57 | Dakar | 596 | 3 | – | 2 |
| 119 | Gibraltar | 1,732 | 16 | 2 | 9 |
| 23 | Med. Through | 344 | 7 | – | 1 |
| 22 | Rio de Janeiro | 305 | 2 | – | – |
| 20 | Bay | 342 | 4 | 1 | – |
| **607** | **TOTALS** | **9,250** | **61** | **12** | **13** |
| | **OUTWARDS** | | | | |
| 57 | Falmouth | 791 | 5 | – | – |
| 136 | Devonport | 1,715 | 6 | – | 3 |
| 113 | Milford | 2,652 | 8 | 2 | 2 |
| 29 | Queenstown | 209 | – | – | – |
| 85 | Lamlash | 954 | 8 | 1 | – |
| 8 | Liverpool Special | 22 | 1 | – | – |
| 39 | Liverpool | 319 | 7 | – | – |
| 25 | Med. Through | 304 | 5 | 1 | – |
| 10 | Channel | 93 | – | – | – |
| 12 | L'pool-Buncrana | 103 | – | – | – |
| 13 | Liverpool Fast | 127 | 1 | – | – |
| **527** | **TOTALS** | **7,289** | **41** | **4** | **5** |

Notes to Ocean Convoy Table
1. Includes all convoys arrived or departed to 23 November 1918.
2. Losses include 1 or 2 armed merchant cruisers or commissioned escort vessels.
3. Losses 'NOT IN CONVOY' includes ships sunk after:
   (a) Dispersal
   (b) Being detached
   (c) Dropping out of convoy for lack of speed or as a result of adverse weather.

## Table 3.105 Allied Short Sea Convoys

| | TOTAL SAILINGS | LOSSES IN CONVOY |
| --- | --- | --- |
| **SCANDANAVIA** | | |
| 28.4.1917 – 1.1918 | 3,423 | 40 |
| 19.1.1918 – 25.11.1918 | 4,230 | 15 |
| **COASTAL SYSTEM** | | |
| 1.4.1917 – 31.12.1917 (Then amalgamated with East Coast Series) | 3,304 | 2 |
| **EAST COAST** | | |
| 28.4.1917 – 15.1.1918 | 3,654 | 34 |
| 16.1.1918 – 25.11.1918 | 16,102 | 35 |
| **U.K.– FRANCE COAL TRADE** | 39,352 | 53 |
| **DUTCH CONVOYS** | 1,861 | 6 |
| **MEDITERRANEAN LOCAL** | 10,464 | 127 |
| **TOTAL** | **82,390** | **312** |

## Table 3.106 Allied Escort Forces to Ocean Convoys at Selected Periods*

**A. CRUISERS**

| JUNE-JULY 1917 | NUMBER | LOSSES | DECEMBER 1917 | NUMBER | LOSSES |
| --- | --- | --- | --- | --- | --- |
| Cruisers | 7 | 2 | | 13 | 2 |
| A.M.C.† | 3 | – | | 22 | 3 |
| C.E.S.‡ | 4 | 1 | | 7 | 1 |
| **TOTAL** | **14** | **3** | | **42** | **6** |

| JUNE 1918 | | | NOVEMBER 1918 | | |
| --- | --- | --- | --- | --- | --- |
| Cruisers | 14 | 2 | | 14◊ | – |
| A.M.C. | 28 | 2 | | 26 | – |
| C.E.S. | 8 | 2 | | 10 | – |
| **TOTAL** | **50** | **6** | | **50** | **–** |

**B. DESTROYERS, SLOOPS and PATROL BOATS**
Flotillas based on Buncrana, Queenstown, Devonport, Portsmouth. Includes U.S. Destroyers based at Queenstown.

| | TOTAL AVAILABLE | TOTAL EMPLOYED ON ESCORT DUTY | ATLANTIC CONVOYS ESCORTED | |
| --- | --- | --- | --- | --- |
| | | | INWARD | OUTWARD |
| **JULY 1917** | 91 | 48 | 9 | – |
| **NOV. 1917** | 170 | 116 | 34 | 36 |
| **APRIL 1918** | 193 | 125 | 37 | 34 |
| **SEPT. 1918** | 150 | 114 | 35 | 38 |

\* These figures do not include Grand Fleet destroyers which were involved from time to time.

† A.M.C. – Armed Merchant Cruiser.

‡ C.E.S. – Commissioned Escort Ship.

◊ Includes 1 Battleship.

# SECTION 4

# TABLES OF ORGANISATION AND EQUIPMENT

When consulting the following divisional T.O.&E.s it should be constantly borne in mind that these are *theoretical* tables, often merely counsels of perfection for armies that had no real chance, especially as the war dragged on from months into years, of maintaining the requisite scales of manpower and, above all, munitions. This consideration applies especially to the armies of the Central Powers which were increasingly troubled by blockade and embargo and the subsequent shortages of raw materials as well as growing industrial unrest.

For reasons of space, and relative military importance, we have omitted any T.O.&E.s for Japan, Montenegro and Portugal. It should also be borne in mind that the sources consulted have not allowed us to draw up full T.O.&E.s for all the different infantry and cavalry divisions, or to chart all the changes in organisation and scales of equipment over the course of the war.

## AUSTRALIA

These divisions and air squadrons were organised according to the same T.O.&E.s as the British. See United Kingdom for further details.

## AUSTRIA-HUNGARY
### Army

The 1918 British War Office Handbook on Austro-Hungarian forces observed that "two important points must be borne in mind regarding the establishment of . . . [the] infantry divisions: (1) No two divisions necessarily have a similar establishment even in their number of . . . battalions. (2) All divisions are in practice below strength." In short, treat Austro-Hungarian T.O.&E.s with particular scepticism. .

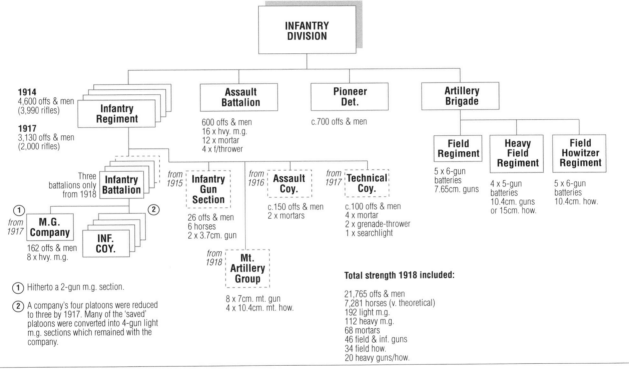

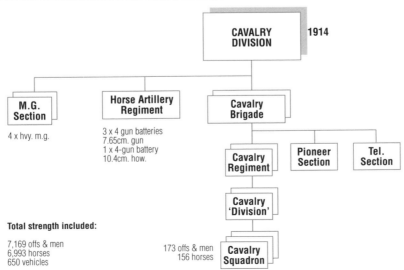

Because of a chronic shortage of remounts and fodder, from late 1915 the cavalry regiments were progressively dismounted until by the end of 1917 the new T.O.&E. included hardly any riding animals at all.

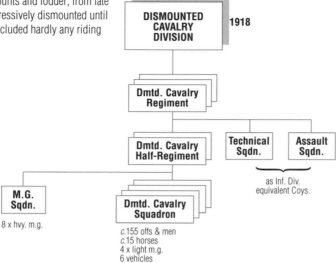

### Air Force

Airplanes were organised into flying companies (*fliegerkompagnien*). Originally these were of six aircraft each, almost all reconnaissance types, and were individually attached to the various divisions. From late 1917 the companies began to assume more specialised roles (See Section Five

[Strengths]: Air Forces) and differing T.O.&E.s were established. The various types of reconnaissance companies now contained between 8 and 10 airplanes plus 3 to 4 escorts; the fighter companies had 16 to 20 airplanes and the bomber companies 10 specialised planes plus 4 escort.

### BELGIUM
### Army

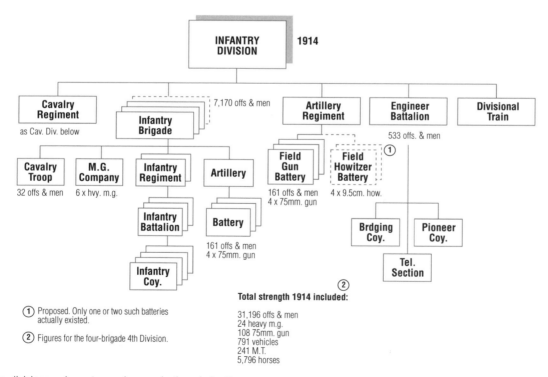

Belgian infantry divisions underwent several reorganisations during the war. In 1915, after the gruelling retreat to the River Yser, they contracted to just three regiments, each of four (in actuality often three) battalions, and four artillery groups. By early 1917 the divisions were back to their 1914 infantry establishment except that each battalion now had only three infantry companies and one of machine guns. The artillery complement of the division was now a two-regiment brigade. By the time of the great Allied counter-offensive of 1918, the divisions had become mini-corps, each with a doubled-up infantry establishment.

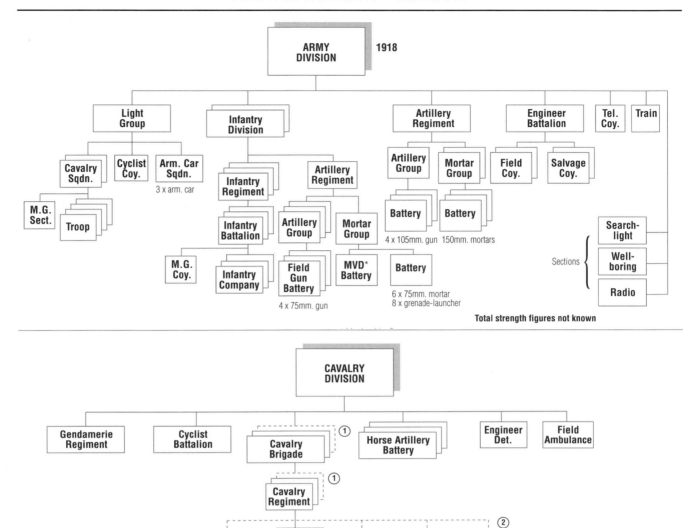

**1918**

Total strength figures not known

(1) Reduced to two two-regiment brigades in 1915.

(2) All dotted-line units from 1917.

Total strength figures not known

## Air Force

Airplanes were organised into squadrons (*escadrilles*) from the beginning of the war. By the Armistice squadron establishment had increased from four to fifteen aircraft. In March 1918 the three dedicated fighter squadrons were formed into a *group de chasse*.

**BULGARIA**
**Army**

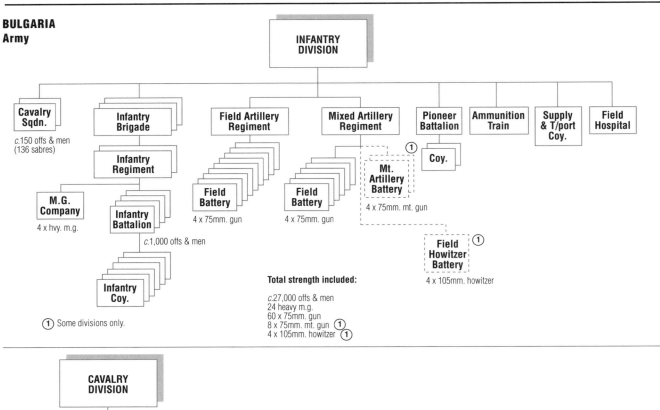

INFANTRY DIVISION

Cavalry Sqdn.
c.150 offs & men (136 sabres)

Infantry Brigade
Infantry Regiment
M.G. Company
4 x hvy. m.g.
Infantry Battalion
c.1,000 offs & men
Infantry Coy.

Field Artillery Regiment
Field Battery
4 x 75mm. gun

Mixed Artillery Regiment
Field Battery
4 x 75mm. gun
Mt. Artillery Battery ①
4 x 75mm. mt. gun
Field Howitzer Battery ①
4 x 105mm. howitzer

Pioneer Battalion
Coy. ①

Ammunition Train

Supply & T/port Coy.

Field Hospital

① Some divisions only.

**Total strength included:**

c.27,000 offs & men
24 heavy m.g.
60 x 75mm. gun
8 x 75mm. mt. gun ①
4 x 105mm. howitzer ①

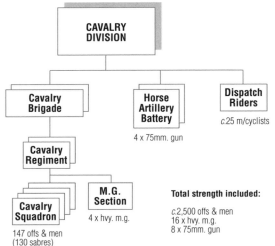

CAVALRY DIVISION

Cavalry Brigade
Cavalry Regiment
Cavalry Squadron
147 offs & men (130 sabres)
M.G. Section
4 x hvy. m.g.

Horse Artillery Battery
4 x 75mm. gun

Dispatch Riders
c.25 m/cyclists

**Total strength included:**

c.2,500 offs & men
16 x hvy. m.g.
8 x 75mm. gun

## Air Force

With German help the meagre Bulgarian air assets when she first declared war were expanded into an Aviation Battalion (f.4/16) which attained a maximum strength of 82 airplanes. It seems to have been mainly sub-divided into two or three Aviation Sections.

## CANADA

These divisions and air squadrons were organised according to British T.O.&E.s. See United Kingdom below for further details.

**FRANCE**
**Army**

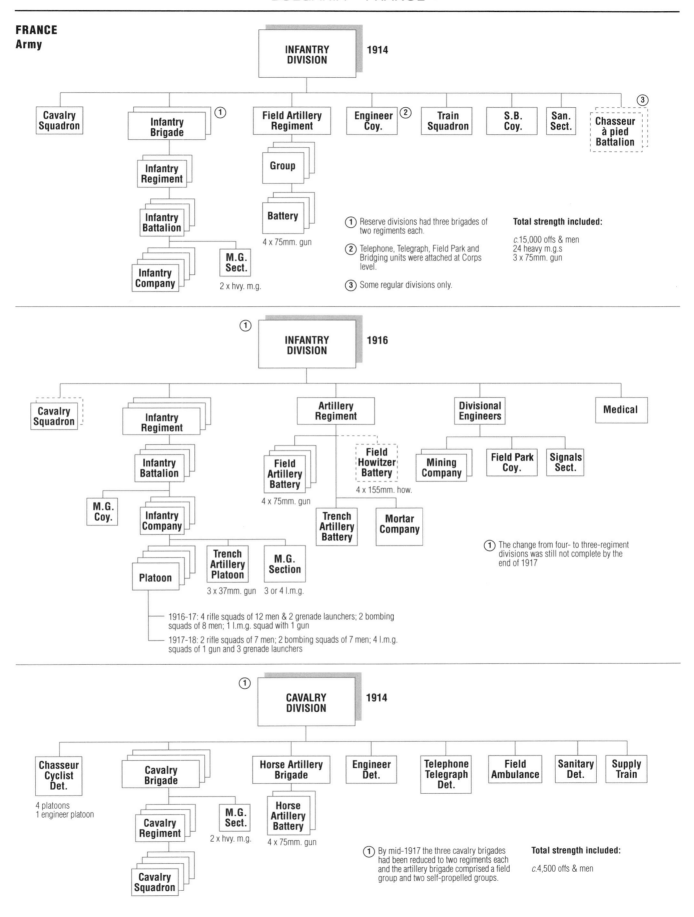

**INFANTRY DIVISION** — 1914

- Cavalry Squadron
- Infantry Brigade ①
  - Infantry Regiment
    - Infantry Battalion
      - Infantry Company
      - M.G. Sect. — 2 x hvy. m.g.
- Field Artillery Regiment
  - Group
    - Battery — 4 x 75mm. gun
- Engineer Coy. ②
- Train Squadron
- S.B. Coy.
- San. Sect.
- Chasseur à pied Battalion ③

① Reserve divisions had three brigades of two regiments each.

② Telephone, Telegraph, Field Park and Bridging units were attached at Corps level.

③ Some regular divisions only.

**Total strength included:**

c.15,000 offs & men
24 heavy m.g.s
3 x 75mm. gun

---

① **INFANTRY DIVISION** — 1916

- Cavalry Squadron
- Infantry Regiment
  - Infantry Battalion
    - M.G. Coy.
    - Infantry Company
      - Platoon
      - Trench Artillery Platoon — 3 x 37mm. gun
      - M.G. Section — 3 or 4 l.m.g.
- Artillery Regiment
  - Field Artillery Battery — 4 x 75mm. gun
  - Field Howitzer Battery — 4 x 155mm. how.
  - Trench Artillery Battery
  - Mortar Company
- Divisional Engineers
  - Mining Company
  - Field Park Coy.
  - Signals Sect.
- Medical

1916-17: 4 rifle squads of 12 men & 2 grenade launchers; 2 bombing squads of 8 men; 1 l.m.g. squad with 1 gun

1917-18: 2 rifle squads of 7 men; 2 bombing squads of 7 men; 4 l.m.g. squads of 1 gun and 3 grenade launchers

① The change from four- to three-regiment divisions was still not complete by the end of 1917

---

① **CAVALRY DIVISION** — 1914

- Chasseur Cyclist Det. — 4 platoons / 1 engineer platoon
- Cavalry Brigade
  - Cavalry Regiment
    - Cavalry Squadron
  - M.G. Sect. — 2 x hvy. m.g.
- Horse Artillery Brigade
  - Horse Artillery Battery — 4 x 75mm. gun
- Engineer Det.
- Telephone Telegraph Det.
- Field Ambulance
- Sanitary Det.
- Supply Train

① By mid-1917 the three cavalry brigades had been reduced to two regiments each and the artillery brigade comprised a field group and two self-propelled groups.

**Total strength included:**

c.4,500 offs & men

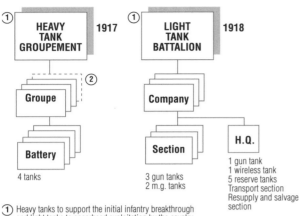

① **HEAVY TANK GROUPEMENT** 1917
② Groupe
Battery
4 tanks

① **LIGHT TANK BATTALION** 1918
Company
Section
H.Q.
3 gun tanks
2 m.g. tanks

1 gun tank
1 wireless tank
5 reserve tanks
Transport section
Resupply and salvage section

① Heavy tanks to support the initial infantry breakthrough and light tanks to spearhead exploitation by the cavalry.

② Four Schneider tank *groupes* per *groupement* or three St. Chamond. (See Section 8: Tanks).

### Air Force

French squadrons (*escadrilles*) began the war with a strength of six airplanes. In 1915 this was increased to fifteen and this remained the official establishment throughout the rest of the war (except for a brief flirtation with ten-airplane squadrons in early 1917). *Escadrilles* were the building blocks of a hierarchy of formations that tapered through *groupes* to *escadres*, to *groupements* and, in one instance, to *division aérienne*.

## GERMANY
### Army

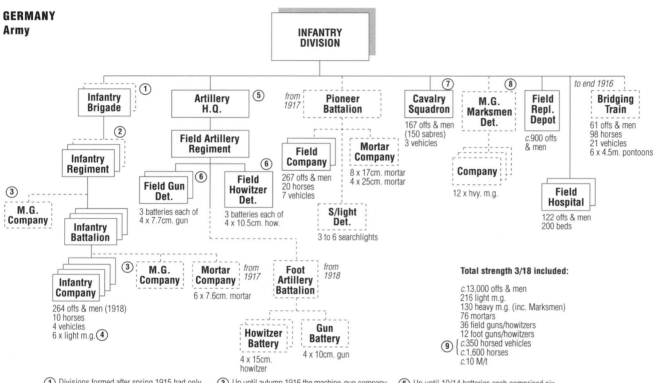

**INFANTRY DIVISION**

① **Infantry Brigade**
⑤ **Artillery H.Q.**
*from 1917* **Pioneer Battalion**
⑦ **Cavalry Squadron**
167 offs & men (150 sabres)
3 vehicles
⑧ **M.G. Marksmen Det.**
**Field Repl. Depot**
*c.*900 offs & men
*to end 1916* **Bridging Train**
61 offs & men
98 horses
21 vehicles
6 x 4.5m. pontoons

② **Infantry Regiment**
**Field Artillery Regiment**
⑥ **Field Company**
267 offs & men
20 horses
7 vehicles
**Mortar Company**
8 x 17cm. mortar
4 x 25cm. mortar
**Company**
12 x hvy. m.g.

③ **M.G. Company**
⑥ **Field Gun Det.**
3 batteries each of 4 x 7.7cm. gun
**Field Howitzer Det.**
3 batteries each of 4 x 10.5cm. how.
**S/light Det.**
3 to 6 searchlights
**Field Hospital**
122 offs & men
200 beds

**Infantry Battalion**

③ **Infantry Company**
264 offs & men (1918)
10 horses
4 vehicles
6 x light m.g. ④

③ **M.G. Company**
**Mortar Company** *from 1917*
6 x 7.6cm. mortar
**Foot Artillery Battalion** *from 1918*

**Howitzer Battery**
4 x 15cm. howitzer
**Gun Battery**
4 x 10cm. gun

**Total strength 3/18 included:**

*c.*13,000 offs & men
216 light m.g.
130 heavy m.g. (inc. Marksmen)
76 mortars
36 field guns/howitzers
12 foot guns/howitzers
⑨ { *c.*350 horsed vehicles
*c.*1,600 horses
*c.*10 M/t

① Divisions formed after spring 1915 had only one infantry brigade and existing divisions were progressively reduced to one only, a process not completed until mid-1917.

② When single-brigade divisions were introduced the number of regiments in the brigade was increased from two to three.

③ Up until autumn 1916 the machine-gun company was allocated at regimental level, during which time it was increased from 6 to 12 heavy machine guns. It was then split between the three infantry battalions as three new companies, who were each progressively increased from 4 to 6, to 8, to 10 and finally to 12 machine guns – a sixfold increase since the beginning of the war.

④ The stripped-down 08/15 machine gun. Actual allocation was rarely more than three guns per company. A number of light machine-gun sections, each armed with nine Bergmann guns, were formed in autumn 1916. They appeared only on the Eastern Front and had been mostly disbanded by early 1918.

⑤ In command of all artillery within the divisional sector, including foot artillery deployed by corps and armies.

⑥ Up until 10/14 batteries each comprised six guns/howitzers.

⑦ Each division had two to three squadrons at the beginning of the war. Reduced to one during 1915 when it began to take its turn in the trenches, often manning the observation posts.

⑧ Specialist machine-gunners. Not an official part of the divisional T.O.&E. but between autumn 1916 and early 1918 most divisions, at least on the Western Front, seem to have acquired such a unit.

⑨ In early 1917 the divisional infantry and artillery ammunition columns were regrouped as sector units, no longer under divisional control. This reduced the transport establishment by roughly 120 vehicles and 500 horses.

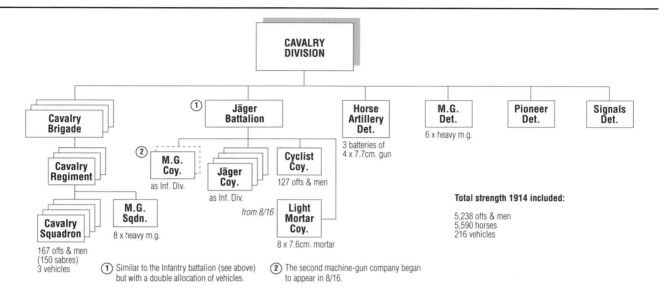

**CAVALRY DIVISION**

- **Cavalry Brigade**
  - **Cavalry Regiment**
    - **Cavalry Squadron**
      167 offs & men
      (150 sabres)
      3 vehicles
    - **M.G. Sqdn.**
      8 x heavy m.g.
- ① **Jäger Battalion**
  - ② **M.G. Coy.**
    as Inf. Div.
  - **Jäger Coy.**
    as Inf. Div.
    *from 8/16*
  - **Cyclist Coy.**
    127 offs & men
  - **Light Mortar Coy.**
    8 x 7.6cm. mortar
- **Horse Artillery Det.**
  3 batteries of
  4 x 7.7cm. gun
- **M.G. Det.**
  6 x heavy m.g.
- **Pioneer Det.**
- **Signals Det.**

**Total strength 1914 included:**

5,238 offs & men
5,590 horses
216 vehicles

① Similar to the Infantry battalion (see above) but with a double allocation of vehicles.

② The second machine-gun company began to appear in 8/16.

The static nature of much of the fighting, even on the Eastern Front, and the chronic shortage of horses, meant that there was only a limited role for large cavalry formations. Between October 1916 and March 1918, in fact, seven of the existing eleven cavalry divisions were disbanded with many of the component regiments being transformed into dismounted Cavalry Marksmen Commands. These were attached to infantry divisions to speed up the rotation of units in the trenches. However, in 1918 some of these Commands were formed into three Cavalry Marksmen Divisions, organised as follows:

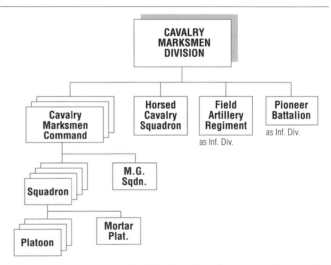

**CAVALRY MARKSMEN DIVISION**

- **Cavalry Marksmen Command**
  - **Squadron**
    - **Platoon**
    - **Mortar Plat.**
  - **M.G. Sqdn.**
- **Horsed Cavalry Squadron**
- **Field Artillery Regiment**
  as Inf. Div.
- **Pioneer Battalion**
  as Inf. Div.

**A7V Assault Tank Detachment**

178 offs & men
5 heavy tanks (A7V)
8 light tanks*
3 armoured cars*

**Captured Assault Tank Detachment**

142 offs & men
5 heavy tanks (British Mk.IV/V)
8 light tanks*
3 armoured cars*

\* captured

**Air Force**

***Abteilung:***
Festungsflieger – 4 airplanes
Feldflieger – 6 airplanes
Artillerieflieger – 4 airplanes
Feldflieger (A) – 6 airplanes (9 from mid-1917).

***Staffel:***
Kampf – 6 airplanes
Jagd – 18 airplanes (often half this in 1918)
Schutz- and Schlacht – 6 airplanes

***Geschwader:***
Kampf – 6 Staffeln
Bomben – 3 Staffeln
Jagd – 4 Staffeln

## GREECE
### Army

The following organigrams refer to the Greek Royal Army only. We have been unable to find details on the organisation of the Venizelist divisions of the National Army although it might be assumed that by late 1918, as both Greek forces were being re-equipped by the Allies, that the latter had insisted on similar T.O.&E.s.

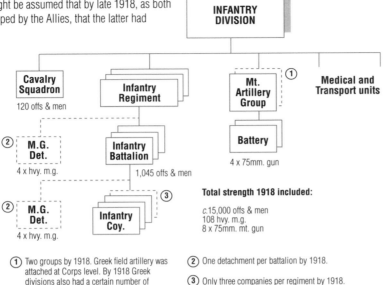

**Total strength 1918 included:**

c.15,000 offs & men
108 hvy. m.g.
8 x 75mm. mt. gun

(1) Two groups by 1918. Greek field artillery was attached at Corps level. By 1918 Greek divisions also had a certain number of 58mm. mortars attached.

(2) One detachment per battalion by 1918.

(3) Only three companies per regiment by 1918.

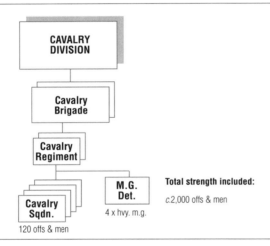

**Total strength included:**

c.2,000 offs & men

### Air Force

By 1918, when the air force saw its only real action, squadrons had been trained and re-equipped by the French and were organised according tp their T.O.&E.s.

## INDIA
### Army

Indian T.O.&E.s were largely identical to the British (see United Kingdom below). However, the following differences between infantry divisions should be noted. At the beginning of the war all Indian divisions possessed two mountain batteries of 10-pdr. guns in addition to their field-gun batteries. Indian divisions never acquired a trench mortar brigade. Until late 1916 a full cavalry regiment served with each division.

**ITALY**
**Army**

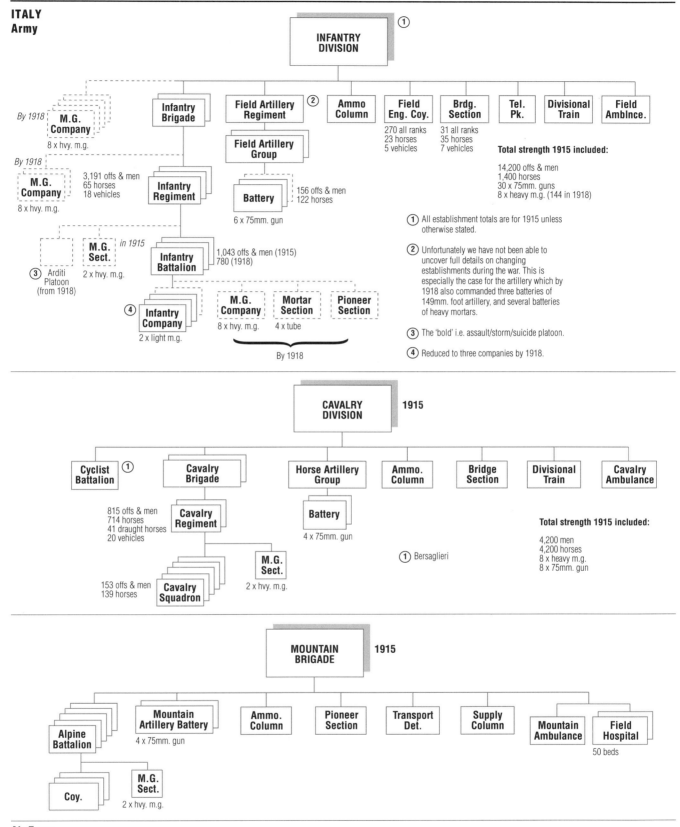

INFANTRY
DIVISION
①

By 1918 — M.G. Company — 8 x hvy. m.g.

By 1918 — M.G. Company — 8 x hvy. m.g.

Infantry Brigade

3,191 offs & men
65 horses
18 vehicles

Infantry Regiment

M.G. Sect. — *in 1915* — 2 x hvy. m.g.

③ Arditi Platoon (from 1918)

Infantry Battalion

1,043 offs & men (1915)
780 (1918)

④ Infantry Company — 2 x light m.g.

M.G. Company — 8 x hvy. m.g.
Mortar Section — 4 x tube
Pioneer Section

By 1918

Field Artillery Regiment ②

Field Artillery Group

156 offs & men
122 horses

Battery — 6 x 75mm. gun

Ammo Column

Field Eng. Coy. — 270 all ranks / 23 horses / 5 vehicles

Brdg. Section — 31 all ranks / 35 horses / 7 vehicles

Tel. Pk.

Divisional Train

Field Amblnce.

**Total strength 1915 included:**

14,200 offs & men
1,400 horses
30 x 75mm. guns
8 x heavy m.g. (144 in 1918)

① All establishment totals are for 1915 unless otherwise stated.

② Unfortunately we have not been able to uncover full details on changing establishments during the war. This is especially the case for the artillery which by 1918 also commanded three batteries of 149mm. foot artillery, and several batteries of heavy mortars.

③ The 'bold' i.e. assault/storm/suicide platoon.

④ Reduced to three companies by 1918.

---

CAVALRY DIVISION — 1915

Cyclist Battalion ①

Cavalry Brigade

815 offs & men
714 horses
41 draught horses
20 vehicles

Cavalry Regiment

Cavalry Squadron — 153 offs & men / 139 horses

M.G. Sect. — 2 x hvy. m.g.

Horse Artillery Group

Battery — 4 x 75mm. gun

Ammo. Column

Bridge Section

Divisional Train

Cavalry Ambulance

① Bersaglieri

**Total strength 1915 included:**

4,200 men
4,200 horses
8 x heavy m.g.
8 x 75mm. gun

---

MOUNTAIN BRIGADE — 1915

Alpine Battalion

Coy.

M.G. Sect. — 2 x hvy. m.g.

Mountain Artillery Battery — 4 x 75mm. gun

Ammo. Column

Pioneer Section

Transport Det.

Supply Column

Mountain Ambulance

Field Hospital — 50 beds

---

**Air Force**

Italian airplanes were organised in squadrons, by type, and the squadrons were formed into groups (*gruppi*) of one, two or three squadrons, which were in turn attached to the various army headquarters. There were usually two or three groups with each army.

## NEW ZEALAND

The New Zealand Division (f.2/16) was organised according to the same
T.O.&E. as a British Infantry division (see United Kingdom below).

## RUMANIA
**Army**

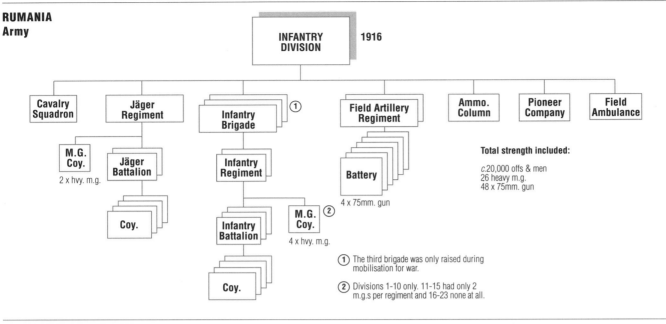

① The third brigade was only raised during mobilisation for war.

② Divisions 1-10 only. 11-15 had only 2 m.g.s per regiment and 16-23 none at all.

Total strength included:

*c.*20,000 offs & men
26 heavy m.g.
48 x 75mm. gun

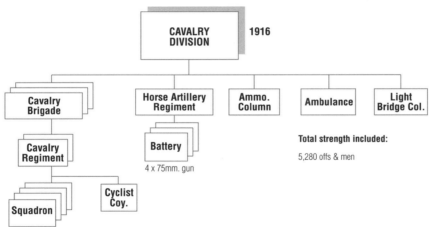

Total strength included:

5,280 offs & men

### Air Force

Throughout the war most Rumanian squadrons (*grupuls*) flew
reconnaissance types; usually with two or three airplanes each. The fighter
squadrons had eight airplanes each and the two bomber squadrons eight
and ten.

**RUSSIA**
**Army**

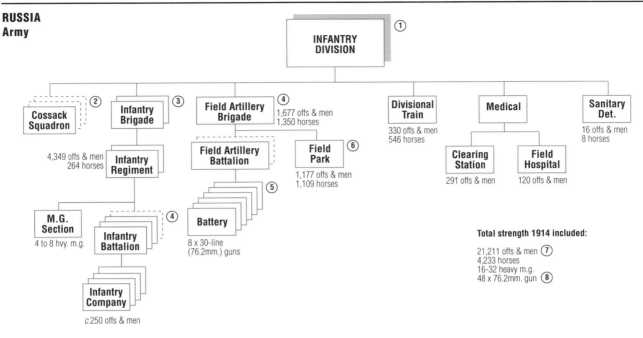

A pioneer battalion, two 122mm. howitzer batteries, one 107mm. (42-line) gun battery, a radio station, an airplane detachment, train and vetinary detachment were all allocated at corps level. Corps were supposed to comprise two infantry and one cavalry division.

(1)

Not part of the official establishment in 1914. Between one and three squadrons thereafter.

(2)

In 1914 there also existed 18 independent brigades each comprising four regiments of two battalions each, plus one battalion of field artillery.

(3)

In autumn 1916 the infantry regiments began reducing to three battalions each. The extra battalions helped form fourth wave divisions which had no artillery allotment at all.

(4)

Third wave divisions, which began forming in spring 1915, had only one battalion of artillery, though some of these were upgraded to brigades later in the war.

(5)

Artillery field park establishment is in addition to that for the brigade.

(6)

Of whom 2,026 were theoretically 'non-line' soldiers who were not to serve in the front line.

(7)

By 1917 batteries were down to 6 guns apiece but, according to contemporary German sources, divisions also deployed some 40 or so mortars and grenade launchers.

(8)

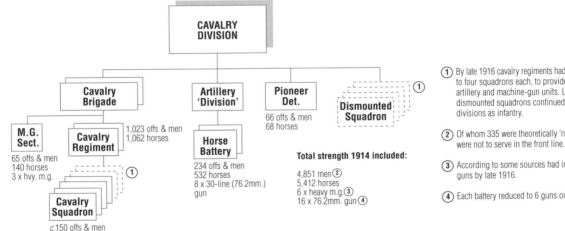

By late 1916 cavalry regiments had mostly been reduced to four squadrons each, to provide horses for the artillery and machine-gun units. Up to four of the dismounted squadrons continued to serve with the divisions as infantry.

(1)

Of whom 335 were theoretically 'non-line' troopers who were not to serve in the front line.

(2)

According to some sources had increased to up to 24 guns by late 1916.

(3)

Each battery reduced to 6 guns only by late 1916.

(4)

**Air Force**

The basic unit was the *otryad* (detachment) which comprised six airplanes at the beginning of the war and by late 1916 had increased, theoretically at least, to ten planes plus two in reserve. The famous squadron of Flying Ships — the huge Ilya Mourometz bombers — comprised all of these airplanes available at any given time. Its maximum strength never exceeded 15 planes.

## SERBIA
### Army

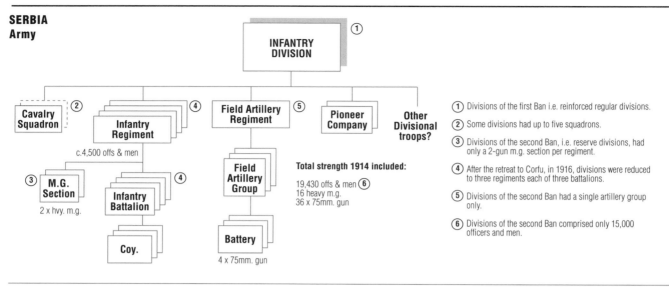

1. Divisions of the first Ban i.e. reinforced regular divisions.

2. Some divisions had up to five squadrons.

3. Divisions of the second Ban, i.e. reserve divisions, had only a 2-gun m.g. section per regiment.

4. After the retreat to Corfu, in 1916, divisions were reduced to three regiments each of three battalions.

5. Divisions of the second Ban had a single artillery group only.

6. Divisions of the second Ban comprised only 15,000 officers and men.

**Infantry Division**

Cavalry Squadron (2)

Infantry Regiment (4) — c.4,500 offs & men

M.G. Section (3) — 2 x hvy. m.g.

Infantry Battalion (4)

Coy.

Field Artillery Regiment (5)

Field Artillery Group

Battery — 4 x 75mm. gun

Pioneer Company

Other Divisional troops?

Total strength 1914 included:

19,430 offs & men (6)
16 heavy m.g.
36 x 75mm. gun

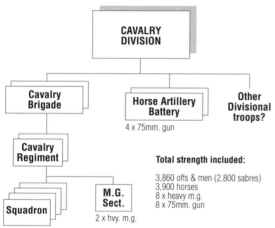

**Cavalry Division**

Cavalry Brigade

Cavalry Regiment

Squadron

M.G. Sect. — 2 x hvy. m.g.

Horse Artillery Battery — 4 x 75mm. gun

Other Divisional troops?

Total strength included:

3,860 offs & men (2,800 sabres)
3,900 horses
8 x heavy m.g.
8 x 75mm. gun

### Air Force
The small Serbian air force was largely destroyed during the 1914 campaigns and was not reformed until spring 1916. The new squadrons were organised, equipped and partially manned by the French and adopted that air force's nomenclature and T.O.&E.s.

## SOUTH AFRICA

The smaller South African units, including the South African Brigade in France, were organised according to British T.O.&E.s (see United Kingdom below). However, the three short-lived divisional formations in East Africa were very much *ad hoc* agglomerations, with 1 Division comprising two infantry brigades, a field artillery brigade and a machine-gun company; and 2 and 3 Divisions comprising an infantry, cavalry and field artillery brigade and a machine-gun company.

## TURKEY
### Army

Of all the major belligerents the Turks' actual establishments were the ones most at variance with the theoretical T.O.&E.s. Even on mobilisation some divisions, particularly those destined for a secondary theatre, might be as much as two-thirds under-strength. Allocations of artillery were especially problematic. The figures below, therefore, should be treated with particular caution.

**Infantry Division**

Infantry Regiment — 1,081 offs & men / 122 animals / 29 vehicles

Infantry Battalion

M.G. Coy. — 116 offs & men / 53 animals / 5 vehicles / 4 x m.g.

Infantry Company

Artillery Regiment — six to nine batteries each of: 4 x field or mt. gun / 158 offs & men / 134 animals / 16 vehicles

Field Hospital — 200 beds / 105 offs & men

Pontoon Section — 25 metres bridging

Field Engineer Coy. — 236 offs & men

Transport Coy. — 137 offs & men / 123 animals / c.50 vehicles

Theoretically part of the Field Engineer and Transport Battalions attached to each corps.

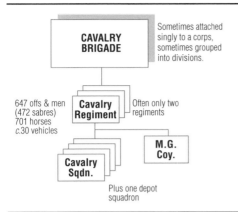

**CAVALRY BRIGADE**

Sometimes attached singly to a corps, sometimes grouped into divisions.

647 offs & men
(472 sabres)
701 horses
*c.*30 vehicles

**Cavalry Regiment**

Often only two regiments

**M.G. Coy.**

**Cavalry Sqdn.**

Plus one depot squadron

## Air Force

Turkish squadrons (*tayyare bölük* = airplane company) were usually very small, two to three aircraft and casualties or unserviceability often meant that they had no airplanes at all for extended periods. Occasionally, in critical sectors, squadrons were built up to as many as twenty airplanes.

# UNITED KINGDOM
## Army

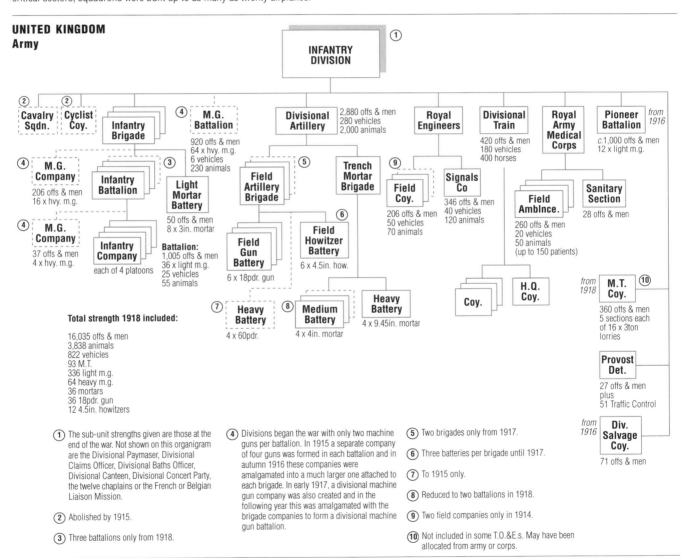

**INFANTRY DIVISION** (1)

**Cavalry Sqdn.** (2)  **Cyclist Coy.** (2)

**Infantry Brigade**

**M.G. Battalion** (4)
920 offs & men
64 x hvy. m.g.
6 vehicles
230 animals

**Divisional Artillery**
2,880 offs & men
280 vehicles
2,000 animals

**Royal Engineers**

**Divisional Train**
420 offs & men
180 vehicles
400 horses

**Royal Army Medical Corps**

**Pioneer Battalion** *from 1916*
*c.*1,000 offs & men
12 x light m.g.

**M.G. Company** (4)
206 offs & men
16 x hvy. m.g.

**Infantry Battalion** (3)

**Light Mortar Battery**
50 offs & men
8 x 3in. mortar

**Field Artillery Brigade** (5)

**Trench Mortar Brigade** (9)

**Field Coy.**
206 offs & men
50 vehicles
70 animals

**Signals Co**
346 offs & men
40 vehicles
120 animals

**Field Amblnce.**
260 offs & men
20 vehicles
50 animals
(up to 150 patients)

**Sanitary Section**
28 offs & men

**M.G. Company** (4)
37 offs & men
4 x hvy. m.g.

**Infantry Company**
each of 4 platoons

Battalion:
1,005 offs & men
36 x light m.g.
25 vehicles
55 animals

**Field Gun Battery** (6)
6 x 18pdr. gun

**Field Howitzer Battery**
6 x 4.5in. how.

**Heavy Battery**
4 x 9.45in. mortar

**Coy.**

**H.Q. Coy.**

**M.T. Coy.** (10) *from 1918*
360 offs & men
5 sections each of 16 x 3ton lorries

**Heavy Battery** (7)
4 x 60pdr.

**Medium Battery** (8)
4 x 4in. mortar

**Provost Det.**
27 offs & men
plus
51 Traffic Control

**Total strength 1918 included:**

16,035 offs & men
3,838 animals
822 vehicles
93 M.T.
336 light m.g.
64 heavy m.g.
36 mortars
36 18pdr. gun
12 4.5in. howitzers

**Div. Salvage Coy.** *from 1916*
71 offs & men

(1) The sub-unit strengths given are those at the end of the war. Not shown on this organigram are the Divisional Paymaster, Divisional Claims Officer, Divisional Baths Officer, Divisional Canteen, Divisional Concert Party, the twelve chaplains or the French or Belgian Liaison Mission.

(2) Abolished by 1915.

(3) Three battalions only from 1918.

(4) Divisions began the war with only two machine guns per battalion. In 1915 a separate company of four guns was formed in each battalion and in autumn 1916 these companies were amalgamated into a much larger one attached to each brigade. In early 1917, a divisional machine gun company was also created and in the following year this was amalgamated with the brigade companies to form a divisional machine gun battalion.

(5) Two brigades only from 1917.

(6) Three batteries per brigade until 1917.

(7) To 1915 only.

(8) Reduced to two battalions in 1918.

(9) Two field companies only in 1914.

(10) Not included in some T.O.&E.s. May have been allocated from army or corps.

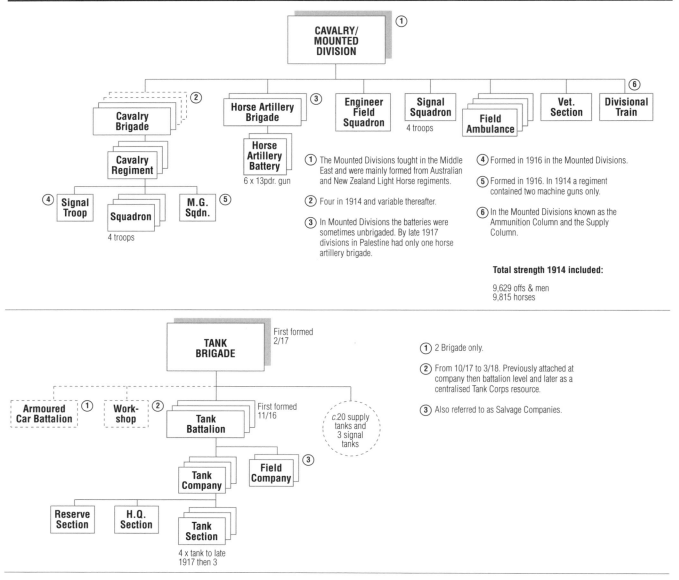

① The Mounted Divisions fought in the Middle East and were mainly formed from Australian and New Zealand Light Horse regiments.

② Four in 1914 and variable thereafter.

③ In Mounted Divisions the batteries were sometimes unbrigaded. By late 1917 divisions in Palestine had only one horse artillery brigade.

④ Formed in 1916 in the Mounted Divisions.

⑤ Formed in 1916. In 1914 a regiment contained two machine guns only.

⑥ In the Mounted Divisions known as the Ammunition Column and the Supply Column.

**Total strength 1914 included:**

9,629 offs & men
9,815 horses

① 2 Brigade only.

② From 10/17 to 3/18. Previously attached at company then battalion level and later as a centralised Tank Corps resource.

③ Also referred to as Salvage Companies.

## Air Force

At the beginning of the war squadrons each contained twelve miscellaneous reconnaissance airplanes. By the time of the Armistice all kinds of specialised squadrons had evolved, with varying numbers of aircraft allotted to each. The official establishment for each type of squadron is listed below:

| | |
|---|---|
| Fighter | 25 |
| Army Cooperation | 24 |
| Reconnaissance | 18 |
| Day-Bomber | 18 |
| Naval Cooperation | 18 |
| Flying Boat | 10 |
| Night-bomber | 10 |

By this time, also, squadrons had been grouped into larger formations, with two making up a wing, and two or more wings a brigade.

**UNITED STATES**
**Army**

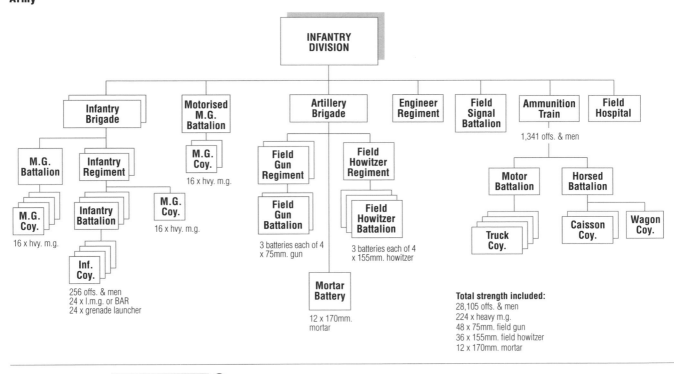

INFANTRY DIVISION

Infantry Brigade — Motorised M.G. Battalion — Artillery Brigade — Engineer Regiment — Field Signal Battalion — Ammunition Train — Field Hospital

1,341 offs. & men

**Infantry Brigade:**
M.G. Battalion — Infantry Regiment

M.G. Battalion:
M.G. Coy.

16 x hvy. m.g.

Infantry Regiment:
Infantry Battalion — M.G. Coy.

16 x hvy. m.g.

Infantry Battalion:
Inf. Coy.

256 offs. & men
24 x l.m.g. or BAR
24 x grenade launcher

**Motorised M.G. Battalion:**
M.G. Coy.

16 x hvy. m.g.

**Artillery Brigade:**
Field Gun Regiment — Field Howitzer Regiment — Mortar Battery

Field Gun Regiment:
Field Gun Battalion

3 batteries each of 4 x 75mm. gun

Field Howitzer Regiment:
Field Howitzer Battalion

3 batteries each of 4 x 155mm. howitzer

Mortar Battery:
12 x 170mm. mortar

**Ammunition Train:**
Motor Battalion — Horsed Battalion

Motor Battalion:
Truck Coy.

Horsed Battalion:
Caisson Coy. — Wagon Coy.

**Total strength included:**
28,105 offs. & men
224 x heavy m.g.
48 x 75mm. field gun
36 x 155mm. field howitzer
12 x 170mm. mortar

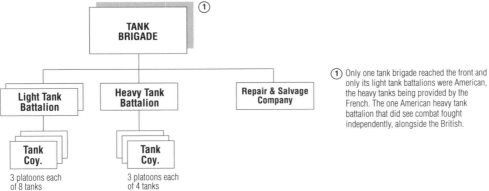

TANK BRIGADE ①

Light Tank Battalion — Heavy Tank Battalion — Repair & Salvage Company

Light Tank Battalion:
Tank Coy.

3 platoons each of 8 tanks

Heavy Tank Battalion:
Tank Coy.

3 platoons each of 4 tanks

① Only one tank brigade reached the front and only its light tank battalions were American, the heavy tanks being provided by the French. The one American heavy tank battalion that did see combat fought independently, alongside the British.

**Air Force**

All American types of squadron (pursuit, observation, day bombing and night bombing) consisted of twelve airplanes. Many of these squadrons were formed into Groups (4 squadrons per pursuit and day bomber group and two per observation group, the last being attached one per army corps). By the end of the war one wing had been formed comprising a pursuit and day bombing group and a single night bombing squadron.

# SECTION 5

# STRENGTHS

# PART I MILITARY MANPOWER AND ARMIES

*Table 5.1* Military Manpower of the Belligerents 1914-18

| COUNTRY | POPULATION | STRENGTH ON ENTERING WAR | | STRENGTH 11/18 | TOTAL MOBILISED | NOTES |
|---|---|---|---|---|---|---|
| | | PEACE | AFTER MOBILISATION | | | |
| Australia | 4,872,000 | ? | 65,000* | 298,000† | 416,800 | * 20,000 in first wave of AIF volunteers and 45,000 militia not liable for overseas service.<br>† including 185,000 overseas. |
| Austria-Hungary | 49,900,000 | 450,000 | 3,350,000* | 2,229,500† | 7,800,000 | * Of whom 2m. went to the front.<br>† Field Army. Also 1,722,000 (1/10/18) serving at home. |
| Belgium | 7,517,000 | 47,500 | 177,000* | 145,000 | 267,000 | * Of whom about 35 per cent were fortress troops. |
| Bulgaria | 5,500,000 | 66,000 | 850,000* | 425,000 | 1,200,000† | * Of whom 70,000 were home guard. Of the rest about 1/2m. were combat troops.<br>† A staggering 22 per cent of total population. |
| Canada | 7,400,000 | 3,000 | 32,000* | 364,000† | 620,000 | * First Canadian Division left Canada 10/14.<br>† Of whom 276,000 were overseas, including 154,000 in France. |
| France | 39,600,000 | 739,000 | 3,781,000 | 2,794,000* | 8,660,000† | * Of whom 2,562,000 in W.Front.<br>† Of whom 569,000 N.African and Colonial troops. |
| Germany | 67,000,000 | 880,000 | 4,500,000 | 4,200,000* | 13,400,000 | * Of whom 3,400,000 in W.Front. |
| Greece | 4,800,000 | ? | c.150,000* | c.250,000† | 280,000 | * Army partially demobilised 6/16 and then remobilised the following year.<br>† Of whom c.160,000 in Macedonia. |
| India | 316,000,000 | 223,700* | – | 654,000† | 1,680,000 | * Of whom 74,600 British.<br>† Of whom 260,000 overseas. |
| Italy | 35,000,000 | 310,000 | 875,000 | 2,274,000* | 5,903,000 | * Of whom 2,075,000 in Italy. |
| Japan | 67,200,000* | c.240,000† | – | 272,000‡ | 800,000 | * Empire.<br>† Of whom 23,000 in Tsingtao expedition.<br>‡ Of whom 70,000 at Vladivostock. |
| New Zealand | 1,050,000 | 30,000* | 8,430† | 30,000‡ | 128,525 | * Including the Territorials.<br>† Sailed with NZEF 10/14.<br>‡ Overseas. |
| Portugal | 6,000,000 | 32,000 | 150,000 | 35,000* | 200,000+ | * W.Front. |
| Rumania | 7,510,000 | 100,000 | 564,000 | – | ?* | * Figures given vary from 3/4 m. to 11/4 m. |
| Russia | 167,000,000 | 1,400,000 | 5,000,000* | –† | 12,000,000 | * Only 40% intended for front-line service.<br>† Peak strength at front c.11/4 m. spring 1916. |
| Serbia | 5,000,000 | 30,000 | 460,000 | 110,500 | 707,000 | |
| S.Africa | 6,000,000 | 57,000* | 50,000 | 9,000† | 231,000‡ | * Inc. 7,000 British. South African ACF were part-timers.<br>† Overseas. Includes 3,000 blacks in France. Does not include unspecified number blacks in E.Africa.<br>‡ Of whom 85,000 black. |
| Turkey | 21,300,000 | 235,000 | ? | 930,000* | 2,600,000 | * Total on army rolls. |
| United Kingdom | 46,400,000 | 247,500 | 733,500 | 3,196,000* | 5,704,400 | * Of whom 1,561,000 on W.Front. |
| United States | 92,000,000 | 208,000* | – | 1,982,000† | 4,355,000 | * In 4/17.<br>† In France. |

**Table 5.2** Comparative Totals Allied and Central Powers Front-Line Divisions at the Beginning and End of the War

| BRITISH EMPIRE | | |
|---|---|---|
| COUNTRY | No. DIVISIONS* | |
| | 8/14 | 11/18 |
| U.K. | 8(2) | 69(5) |
| Australia | – | 7(2) |
| Canada | – | 4 |
| India | 5(2) | 6 |
| New Zealand | – | 1 |
| S.Africa | – | – |
| TOTAL | 13(4) | 87(7) |

| OTHER ALLIES | | |
|---|---|---|
| COUNTRY | No. DIVISIONS* | |
| | 8/14 | 11/18 |
| Belgium | 7(1) | 7(1) |
| France | 96(10) | 221(6) |
| Greece | – | 11 |
| Italy | – | 61(4) |
| Japan | 1 | 1 |
| Portugal | – | 2 |
| Rumania | – | – |
| Russia | 94(24) | – |
| Serbia | 12(1) | 7(1) |
| U.S.A. | – | 42 |
| TOTAL | ? | 352(12) |

| CENTRAL POWERS | | |
|---|---|---|
| COUNTRY | No. DIVISIONS* | |
| | 8/14 | 10/18 |
| Austria-Hungary | 64(11) | 78(12) |
| Bulgaria | – | 16(2) |
| Germany | 113(11) | 220(7) |
| Turkey | – | 28(1) |
| TOTAL | 177(22) | 342(22) |

* First figure is total number divisions. Figure in brackets is number cavalry divisions.

**Table 5.3** Number of Troops who Served Overseas (Selected Countries)

| COUNTRY | NUMBER SENT OVERSEAS | % OF TOTAL MOBILISED | MAIN THEATRES† |
|---|---|---|---|
| Australia | 381,800 | 91 | F&B; D; E&P |
| Canada | 442,400 | 71 | F&B |
| India | 1,096,000 | 65 | F&B; E.Af; Mesp; E&P |
| Japan | c.100,000 | 12 | Tsingtao; Vladivostock |
| New Zealand | 98,900 | 77 | F&B; D; E&P |
| S.Africa | 213,000‡ | 92 | F&B; S.W.Afr; E.Afr |
| U.K. | c.4,500,000 | 79 | F&B; D; E&P; Mesp; Mac; I |
| U.S.A. | 2,086,000 | 48 | F&B |

**Table 5.4** Arrival of U.S. Divisions in France (Cumulative Total)

| DATE | No. DIVS | DATE | No. DIVS | DATE | No. DIVS |
|---|---|---|---|---|---|
| 6/17 | 1 | 12/17 | 5 | 6/18 | 25 |
| 7/17 | 1 | 1/18 | 5 | 7/18 | 29 |
| 8/17 | 2 | 2/18 | 6 | 8/18 | 35 |
| 9/17 | 3 | 3/18 | 8 | 9/18 | 39 |
| 10/17 | 3 | 4/18 | 9 | 10/18 | 42 |
| 11/17 | 4 | 5/18 | 18 | 11/18 | 42 |

† Abbreviations denote:
D= Dardanelles
E.Af= E.Africa
E&P= Egypt & Palestine
F&B= France & Belgium
I= Italy
Mesp= Mesopotamia
Mac= Macedonia

‡ Of whom 77,000 black. 'Overseas' includes S.W.Africa and E.Africa.

**Table 5.5** Location of British, Indian & Commonwealth Divisions by Theatre 1914-18

| DATE | DIVISIONS SERVING IN: ◊ | | | | | | | |
|---|---|---|---|---|---|---|---|---|
| | FRANCE & BELGIUM | EGYPT & PALESTINE | MESOPOTAMIA | DARDANELLES | MACEDONIA | ITALY | EAST AFRICA• | TOTAL |
| 8/14 | 11(0) | 1(0) | – | – | – | – | – | 12(0) |
| 1/15 | 19(4) | 3(2) | 1(1) | – | – | – | – | 23(7) |
| 9/15 | 42(6) | – | 2(2) | 10(1) | – | – | – | 54(9) |
| 1/16 | 46(5) | 8(0) | 4(4) | – | 5(0) | – | – | 63(9) |
| 1/17 | 63(10) | 5(1) | 7(6) | – | 6(0) | – | 2(2) | 83(19) |
| 1/18 | 62(10) | 11(3) | 7(6) | – | 4(0) | 5(0) | – | 89(19) |
| 11/18 | 63(10) | 12(4) | 5(4) | – | 4(0) | 3(0) | – | 87(18) |

◊ First figure is total. Figure in brackets denotes number divisions from Empire & Commonwealth.

• Troops in E.Africa throughout but only briefly organised in divisions.

*Table 5.6* Location of German Divisions by Theatre 1914-18

* First figure is total. Figure in brackets denotes number of cavalry divisions.

| DATE | DIVISIONS SERVING IN: * | | | | | | | |
| | FRANCE & BELGIUM | RUSSIA | SERBIA | RUMANIA | MACEDONIA | ITALY | FINLAND | TOTAL |
|---|---|---|---|---|---|---|---|---|
| **8/14** | 92(10) | 21(1) | – | – | – | – | – | **113(11)** |
| **1/15** | 91(4) | 41(7) | – | – | – | – | – | **132(11)** |
| **1/16** | 113(1) | 55(9) | 3 | – | – | – | – | **171(10)** |
| **1/17** | 123(1) | 53(7) | – | 19(2) | 2 | – | – | **197(10)** |
| **1/18** | 178(2) | 49(8) | – | 9(1) | 1 | 7 | – | **244(11)** |
| **11/18** | 185(4) | 27(3) | 3 | 3 | 1 | – | 1 | **220(7)** |

*Table 5.7* Location of Austro-Hungarian Divisions by Theatre 1914-18

† As above.

| DATE | DIVISIONS SERVING IN: † | | | | | | | |
| | RUSSIA | ITALY | SERBIA | RUMANIA | MACEDONIA | ALBANIA | W.FRONT | TOTAL |
|---|---|---|---|---|---|---|---|---|
| **8/14** | 50(11) | – | 14 | – | – | – | – | **64(11)** |
| **1/15** | 57(11) | – | 7 | – | – | – | – | **64(11)** |
| **1/16** | 49(11) | 20 | 4 | 1 | – | 1 | – | **75(11)** |
| **1/17** | 40(7) | 25 | – | 12(4) | – | 1 | – | **78(11)** |
| **1/18** | 33(10) | 38 | – | 9(2) | – | 1 | – | **81(12)** |
| **10/18** | 7(4) | 55(5) | 1 | 1 | 7(2)‡ | 3(1) | 4 | **78(12)** |

‡ Cavalry divisions en route.

*Table 5.8* Location of Turkish Divisions by Theatre 1914-18

◊ Infantry divisions only.

| DATE | DIVISIONS SERVING IN: ◊ | | | | | | | |
| | CONSTANTINOPLE & DARDANELLES | SMYRNA | SYRIA & PALESTINE | ARABIA | MESOPOTAMIA | ARMENIA | EUROPE | TOTAL |
|---|---|---|---|---|---|---|---|---|
| **10/14** | 12 | 3 | 7 | 4 | 1 | 11 | – | **38** |
| **1/15** | 11 | 2 | 8 | 4 | 2 | 13 | – | **40** |
| **1/16** | 16 | 2 | 5 | 4 | 5 | 11 | – | **43** |
| **3/17** | 3 | 4 | 9 | 4 | 7 | 14 | 7 | **48** |
| **1/18** | 7 | 3 | 18 | 4 | 6 | 9 | – | **47** |
| **11/18** | 4 | 2 | 7 | 4 | 2 | 7 | – | **26** |

## Table 5.9 Opposing Strengths in Selected Battles and Campaigns 1914-18

Because of the variable nature of the sources it has not been possible to provide directly comparable data in each entry in this table, with some strengths being expressed as numbers of men, some as divisions and some as battalions. Where possible alternative sets of figures are provided. Readers can also use the T.O.&E. figures provided in Section 4 to translate figures into comparable totals but it should be borne in mind that actual battlefield totals for battalions per division or, above all, men per battalion were often dramatically below the official table of organisation. Total strengths given for individual battles refer to the first day or so of that battle and do not include reserves or formations used in minor diversions. However, as some battles lasted several months, an attempt has been made in the footnotes to indicate how many divisions were employed overall in such a battle.

| W.FRONT | E.FRONT | BALKANS | ITALY | TURKEY | AFRICA | |
|---|---|---|---|---|---|---|
| **1914** | | | | | | NB: All notes in this table are to be found in the individual columns |
| | **Poland/Galicia 8/14**<br>Russia 1,250,000<br>Austria-H. 800,000 | **Serbia 8/14**<br>Serbia 215,000*<br>Austria-H. 200,000 | | | **Togoland 8/14**<br>Allies 1,750<br>Germany 1,500 | |
| | **East Prussia 8/14**<br>Russia 380,000<br>Germany 200,000 | | | | **Cameroons 8/14***<br>Allies 15,700<br>Germany 3,200 | |
| **The Marne 9/14***<br>Allies 56 divs.†<br>Germany 44 divs. | | | | | **S.W.Africa 9/14***<br>S.Africa 50,000<br>Germany 10,000 | |
| | **Lodz 11/14**<br>Russia 550,000<br>Germany 250,000 | | | **Armenia 11/14**<br>Russia 100,000<br>Turkey 190,000 | **E.Africa 10/14**<br>British 10,400†<br>Germany 5,000 | |
| * Paris-Verdun front.<br>† Of which 51 French. | | * Front-line troops. | | | * Max. strength during whole campaign.<br>† Including 8,000 Indian troops. | |
| **1915** | | | | | | |
| | **Masuria 2/15**<br>Russia 250,000<br>Germany 250,000 | | | **Gallipoli 2/15***<br>Allies 78,000/134,000<br>Turks 1 div./16 divs. | **Cameroons**<br>**S.W.Africa** } see above | |
| **2ⁿᵈ Artois 5/15**<br>France 225 bns.<br>Germany c.55 bns. | **Gorlice/Tarnow 5/15**<br>Russia 220,000<br>C.Powers 215,000 | | **Second Isonzo 7/15**<br>Italy 260 bns.<br>Austria-H. 129 bns. | | | |
| **2ⁿᵈ Champagne 9/15**<br>France 20 divs.<br>Germany 7 divs. | | | | | | |
| **3ʳᵈ Artois/Loos 9/15**<br>Allies 22 divs.*<br>Germany 7 divs. | | **Serbia 10/15**<br>Serbia 220,000*<br>C.Powers 300,000 | **Third Isonzo 10/15**<br>Italy 338 bns.<br>Austria-H. 125 bns.* | **Ctesiphon 11/15†**<br>British 14,000<br>Turkey 21,000 | | |
| * Of which 16 French divisions against 6 German. | | * 45,000 French and British troops landed in Macedonia in 11/15 but were unable to do much to help the Serbs. | * Total Austro-Hungarian manpower was 120,000 men. | * Totals given for 2/15 and 11/15.<br>† Mesopotamia | | |
| **1916** | | | | **Erzerum 2/16**<br>Russia 80,000<br>Turkey 72,000 | **Cameroons to 2/16**<br>see 1914 | |
| **Verdun 2/16***<br>France 150,000†/300,000<br>Germany 140,000/300,000 | | | **Trentino 5/16**<br>Italy 176 bns.*<br>Austria-H. 192 bns.† | | **E.Africa 4/16**<br>Britain 44,500<br>Germany c.4,000 | |
| **Somme 7/16**<br>Allies 29 divs.‡<br>Germany 8 divs. | **Brusilov Offensive 6/16**<br>Russia 600,000<br>C.Powers 500,000 | | **Asiago Plateau 6/16**<br>Italy 177 bns.<br>Austria-H. 168 bns. | | | |
| | **Rumania 8/16**<br>Russia 440,000*<br>C.Powers 200,000 | | **Sixth Isonzo 8/16**<br>Italy 140 bns.<br>Austria-H. 67 bns. | | | |
| | * Effectives (out of 600,000+) inc. 366 bns. | | * Of which 45 low-grade.<br>† 157,000 rifles. | | | |
| * Totals given for 2/16 and 6/16. By late 6/16 the French had employed 66 divisions on the Verdun Front and the Germans 44.<br>† Mainly fortress troops. Only 6 divs.<br>‡ Of which 18 British. Total British force was 420,000. During the whole battle, to 11/16, 56 British and 48 | | | | **Mesopotamia 12/16**<br>British 130,000<br>Turkey 20,000*<br><br>* Rifle strength. | | |

NB: All notes in this table are to be found in the individual columns

| W.FRONT | E.FRONT | BALKANS | ITALY | TURKEY | AFRICA |
|---|---|---|---|---|---|
| **1917** | | | | | |
| **The Nivelle Offensive 4/17***<br>France 19 divs.<br>Germany 17 divs. | | **Macedonia 5/17**<br>Allies 274 bns.*<br>C.Powers 255 bns. | **Tenth Isonzo 5/17**<br>Italy 28 divs.*<br>Austria-H. 11 divs.* | | |
| **3rd Ypres 7/17†**<br>Britain 16 divs.‡<br>Germany 11 divs. | **Kerensky Offensive 7/17***<br>Russia 37 divs.<br>C.Powers 23 divs. | | **Trentino 6/17**<br>Italy 98 bns.<br>Austria-H. 42 bns. | **Mesopotamia 8/17**<br>Britain 194,000<br>Turkey 35,000* | |
| | **Maraseti (Rumania) 10/17†**<br>Rumania 4 divs.<br>C.Powers 2 divs. | | **Caporello<br>(Twelfth Isonzo) 10/17**<br>Italy 224 bns.<br>C.Powers 168 bns. | **Gaza/Beersheba 11/17**<br>Britain 82,000<br>Turkey 40,000 | **E.Africa 9/17**<br>Britain 58,300 (peak)<br>Germany c.2,500 |
| * The failure of the initial attacks prevented Nivelle from taking advantage of his overall superiority in this sector – 56 divs. opposing 31 German.<br>† Includes 2 French divs.<br>‡ During the battle as a whole, to 11/17, 54 British and 83 German divs. took part. | * In terms of rifle strength, 225,000 Russians vs. 199,500 C.Powers troops. The latters' battalions totalled 253.<br>† The Rumanian front as a whole was manned by 58 Rumanian and Russian divs. opposing 36 C.Powers. | * Total ration-strength in theatre was 619,000. | * Comprising roughly 280,000 Italian and 165,000 Austro-Hungarian front-line combat troops. | * Rifle strength. | |
| **1918** | | | | | |
| **2nd Somme<br>(Op. Michael) 3/18**<br>Britain 26 divs.(inf.)<br>Germany 65 divs. | | | | | |
| **Lys (Op. Georgette) 4/18**<br>Britain 11 divs.<br>Germany 26 divs. | | | | | |
| **3rd Aisne<br>(Blücher/Yorck) 5/18**<br>France 16 divs.*<br>Germany 37 divs. | | | | | |
| **2nd Marne 7/18**<br>France 49 divs.<br>Germany 50 divs.† | | | **Piave 6/18**<br>Allies 29 divs.<br>Austria-H. 43 divs.* | | |
| **Amiens 8/18**<br>Allies 21 divs.<br>Germany 14 divs. | | | | **Mesopotamia 8/18**<br>Britain 217,000<br>Turkey 22,000* | |
| **The Last Offensive 9/18‡**<br>France 91(41) divs.<br>Britain 61(34) divs.<br>U.S.A. 25(10) divs.<br>Belgium 7(5) divs.<br>Portugal 2(2) divs.<br>Germany 171(97) divs.<br>Austria-H. 3(2) divs. | | **Macedonia 9/18**<br>Allies 28 divs.*<br>C.Powers 16 divs.* | **Vittorio Veneto 10/18**<br>Allies 61(51) divs.†<br>Austria-H. 60(45) divs.† | **Megiddo 9/18**<br>Britain 67,000†<br>Turkey 35,000 | **E.Africa 11/18**<br>Britain 33,700<br>Germany 1,300 |
| * Of which 5 British.<br>† 2,350,000 men.<br>‡ First figure is total number of divs. in France & Belgium (north-west of Nancy) and figure in brackets denotes number of these divisions at the front. | | * 550,000 Allies (291 bns.) 450,000 enemy (302 bns.) | * 382 battalions. The average strength of an infantry division at this time was roughly 6,500 men.<br>† First figure is that for the whole front, the one in brackets denotes the number of divisions in the main offensive sector. Respective strengths were 2.2 and 1.8m. and respective numbers of battalions were 725 and 757. | * Rifle strength.<br>† Of whom 11,000 cavalry. | |

We have, unfortunately, been unable to find sufficient data to permit a comparative table of artillery strengths during the war, whether by country, by year or by battle. Some idea of comparative strengths can be derived from Table 7.7, in the section on Production.

To provide some further insight into the phenomenal growth of the artillery arm during the war we have included the following table giving details of British expansion.

It is interesting to note that whilst British artillery on the Western Front constituted just over 80% of total guns overseas, it used up 97% of all ammunition (4,959,000 tons out of 5,130,000) sent overseas.

### *Table 5.10* Allocation of British Artillery on Western and Other Fronts 1914-18

| DATE | FIELD GUNS & HOWITZERS | | | HEAVY GUNS & HOWITZERS | | | W.FRONT TOTAL | GRAND TOTAL |
|------|---------|-------|-------|---------|-------|-------|---------|---------|
|      | W.FRONT | OTHER | TOTAL | W.FRONT | OTHER | TOTAL |         |         |
| 8/14 | 462 | – | 462 | 24 | – | 24 | **486** | **486** |
| 1/15 | 833 | – | 833 | 33 | – | 33 | **866** | **866** |
| 7/15 | 1,215 | 198 | 1,413 | 310 | 72 | 382 | **1,525** | **1,795** |
| 1/16 | 2,533 | 660 | 3,193 | 203 | 72 | 275 | **2,736** | **3,468** |
| 7/16 | 3,567 | 696 | 4,263 | 470 | 48 | 518 | **4,037** | **4,781** |
| 1/17 | 4,212 | 854 | 5,066 | 609 | 52 | 661 | **4,821** | **5,727** |
| 7/17 | 5,106 | 994 | 6,100 | 1,051 | 110 | 1,161 | **6,157** | **7,261** |
| 1/18 | 4,895 | 1,036 | 5,931 | 1,564 | 162 | 1,726 | **6,459** | **7,657** |
| 6/18 | 5,482 | 1,398 | 6,880 | 1,227 | 164 | 1,391 | **6,709** | **8,271** |
| 11/18 | ? | ? | ? | ? | ? | ? | **6,488** | **?** |

# PART II NAVIES AND MERCHANT MARINE

This subsection contains only three summary tables on naval strengths as much more detailed breakdowns on ships involved in various naval campaigns and battles are provided in Section 3: Orders of Battle.

---

**Table 5.11 Comparative Naval Strengths of the Major Powers in August 1914**

| | FRANCE | ITALY | JAPAN | RUSSIA | U.K. | U.S.A | TOTAL* | AUST-H. | GERMANY | TURKEY | TOTAL† |
|---|---|---|---|---|---|---|---|---|---|---|---|
| **Dreadnought** | 8 | 3 | 2 | – | 22 | 10 | 30 | 6 | 15 | – | 21 |
| **Pre-dreadnought** | 14 | 7 | 10 | 10 | 40 | 23 | 54 | 6 | 22 | 2 | 28 |
| **Battle-cruiser** | – | – | 1 | – | 9 | – | 9 | – | 5 | – | 5 |
| **Armoured Cruiser** | 19 | 7 | 12 | 6 | 34 | 12 | 53 | 2 | 7 | – | 9 |
| **Protected Cruiser** | 9 | 11 | 15 | 6 | 52 | 22 | 61 | 3 | 17 | 2 | 20 |
| **Other Cruiser** | – | 3 | 6 | – | 35 | – | 35 | 2 | 16 | – | 18 |
| **Destroyer** | 81 | 33 | 50 | 25 | 221 | 50 | 302 | 18 | 90 | 8 | 108 |
| **Torpedo Boat** | 187 | c.80 | – | 72 | 109 | 23 | 296 | c.65 | 115 | 9 | c.180 |
| **Submarine** | c.70 | 23 | 12 | 22 | 73 | 18 | c.143 | 5 | 31 | – | 36 |

*\* U.K. and France only.*

*† Austria-Hungary and Germany only.*

It has not been possible to compile accurate strength figures for each year of the war but the reader is advised that combining the figures above with the shipbuilding figures in Table 7.11 and the naval losses figures in Table 6.6 will give an approximate picture of naval strength at the time of the Armistice.

---

**Table 5.12 Comparative Strengths in Major Naval Engagements 1914-18**

| BATTLE AND DATE | | D/n. | B/Cr. | A/Cr. | Cr. | Dest. |
|---|---|---|---|---|---|---|
| **Heligoland Bight 28/8/14** | | | | | | |
| | U.K. | – | 5 | – | 8 | 31 |
| | Germany | – | (3) | – | 10 | 22 |
| **Coronel 1/11/14** | | | | | | |
| | U.K. | – | – | 2 | 2 | – |
| | Germany | – | – | 2 | 3 | – |
| **Falkland Islands 8/12/14** | | | | | | |
| | U.K. | – | 2 | 3 | 3 | – |
| | Germany | – | – | 2 | 3 | – |
| **Dogger Bank 24/1/15** | | | | | | |
| | U.K. | – | 5 | – | 7 | 33 |
| | Germany | – | 3 | 1 | 4 | 18 |

| BATTLE AND DATE | | D/n. | B/Cr. | A/Cr. | Cr. | Dest. |
|---|---|---|---|---|---|---|
| **Jutland 31/5/16** | | | | | | |
| | U.K. | 28 | 9 | 8 | 26 | 77 |
| | Germany | 22‡ | 5 | – | 11 | 61 |
| **Straits of Otranto 15/5/17◊** | | | | | | |
| | Allies | – | – | – | 4 | 9 |
| | Austria-Hungary | – | – | – | 3 | 2 |
| **Ösel and Dragö Landings 11-19/10/17** | | | | | | |
| | Russia | 2• | – | 2 | 1 | 26 |
| | Germany | 10 | 1 | – | 9 | 55 |
| **Heligoland Bight 17/11/17** | | | | | | |
| | U.K. | 6∆ | 7 | – | 8 | 30** |
| | Germany | 2 | – | – | 4 | 8 |

‡ Inc. 6 pre-dreadnoughts.

◊ Pursuit only.

• Pre-dreadnoughts.

∆ In distant covering force.

** Of which 11 in distant covering force.

---

**Table 5.13 Monthly Total German U-Boat Strength 1914-18††**

†† Commissioned boats.

‡‡ Figures are for the end of the month.

| MONTH‡‡ | | TOTAL STRENGTH | MONTH | TOTAL STRENGTH | MONTH | | TOTAL STRENGTH | MONTH | TOTAL STRENGTH |
|---|---|---|---|---|---|---|---|---|---|
| 1914 | Aug | 29 | March | 41 | | Oct | 58 | May | 89 |
| | Sept | 32 | April | 46 | | Nov | 58 | June | 97 |
| | Oct | 33 | May | 53 | | Dec | 64 | July | 103 |
| | Nov | 34 | June | 56 | 1916 | Jan | 67 | Aug | 111 |
| | Dec | 34 | July | 58 | | Feb | 72 | Sept | 120 |
| 1915 | Jan | 33 | Aug | 57 | | March | 79 | Oct | 132 |
| | Feb | 37 | Sept | 57 | | April | 84 | Nov | 140 |

**Monthly Total German U-Boat Strength 1914-18** *continued*

| MONTH | | TOTAL STRENGTH | MONTH | TOTAL STRENGTH | MONTH | | TOTAL STRENGTH | MONTH | TOTAL STRENGTH |
|---|---|---|---|---|---|---|---|---|---|
| **1916** | Dec | 149 | June | 160 | | Dec | 169 | June | 172 |
| **1917** | Jan | 153 | July | 162 | **1918** | Jan | 162 | July | 175 |
| | Feb | 152 | Aug | 169 | | Feb | 166 | Aug | 176 |
| | March | 152 | Sept | 166 | | March | 168 | Sept | 177 |
| | April | 156 | Oct | 174 | | April | 171 | Oct | 170 |
| | May | 154 | Nov | 171 | | May | 166 | Nov | 171 |

**Table 5.14** Size of the World's Major National Merchant Fleets in 1914 and 1919 (gross tonnage)

| | DATE | |
|---|---|---|
| | **6/14** | **6/19** |
| **British Empire** | | |
| U.K. | 18,892,000 | 16,345,000 |
| Dominions & Colonies* | 1,632,000 | 1,863,000 |
| **TOTAL** | **20,524,000** | **18,208,000** |
| **Allies** | | |
| Belgium | 341,000 | 306,000 |
| Brazil | 308,000 | 493,000 |
| France | 1,922,000 | 1,962,000 |
| Greece | 821,000 | 291,000 |
| Italy | 1,430,000 | 1,238,000 |
| Japan | 1,708,000 | 2,325,000 |
| Russia | 852,000 | 514,000 |
| U.S.A. | 2,070,000 | 9,824,000 |
| **TOTAL** | **9,452,000** | **16,953,000** |

| | DATE | |
|---|---|---|
| | **6/14** | **6/19** |
| **Central Powers** | | |
| Austria-Hungary | 1,052,000 | 713,000* |
| Germany | 5,135,000 | 3,247,000* |
| Turkey | 116,000 | 99,000 |
| **TOTAL** | **6,303,000** | **4,059,000** |
| **Neutrals** | | |
| Denmark | 770,000 | 631,000 |
| Holland | 1,472,000 | 1,574,000 |
| Norway | 1,957,000 | 1,597,000 |
| Spain | 884,000 | 709,000 |
| Sweden | 1,015,000 | 917,000 |
| **TOTAL** | **6,098,000** | **5,428,000** |
| **WORLD TOTAL** | **43,144,000†** | **45,737,000†** |

* Figures are for 11/18.

† Includes other countries.

# PART III AIR FORCES

Unfortunately, we have not had the space, as originally hoped, to chronicle the remarkable growth of First World War air power squadron by squadron. Except for the very smallest air forces we have had to limit national entries to tables of aggregate figures, though it should be emphasised that these have usually been compiled from the detailed squadron lists that are now available for most of the belligerents. Moreover, at the end of each major power entry there will be found a list, by aircraft type, of the squadron number sequences current in November 1918.

## AUSTRALIA

At the end of the war the Australian Flying Corps comprised four squadrons. All had been formed in Australia but on going overseas were numbered as British Royal Flying Corps (RFC) squadrons. On 19/1/18, however, they took on their national identity as detailed in the table below. All but one served on the Western Front only.

| SQUADRON | | ARRIVED UK | ARRIVED FRANCE | AIRPLANE TYPE |
|---|---|---|---|---|
| AFC | ex-RFC | | | |
| 1 | 67 | (Arrived Egypt 4/16) | | F.2B |
| 2 | 68 | 1/17 | 9/17 | S.E.5A |
| 3 | 69 | 12/16 | 8/17 | R.E.8 |
| 4 | 71 | 3/17 | 12/17 | Snipe |

A fifth RFC squadron, no.30, in Mesopotamia, was also based around an original Australian contingent that had arrived there in May 1915. This, however, remained an RFC, later RAF, squadron. Four Australian training squadrons were also formed in September and October 1917 and later grouped within 1 Wing, AFC. These were numbers 5, 6, 7, 8 (ex-RFC 29, 30, 32, 33).

## AUSTRIA-HUNGARY

In July 1914 the Austro-Hungarian air service, the *Luftfahrtruppen*, had at its disposal 114 pilots, 48 front-line airplanes, 27 training planes, 1 airship and 10 balloons. These were distributed amongst the ten static *Flugparken* run by the Airship Section, but immediately upon mobilisation the airplanes began reorganising into fifteen *Fliegerkompagnien* (Fliks), each of six airplanes plus two in reserve. By the end of the war, 77 such companies had been formed. Most were known as *Divisions-Fliegerkompagnien*, or D-Fliks, although later in the war four other types of company were also formed. These were

F-Fliks which undertook *Fernaufklärung* (long-distance reconnaissance) missions
G-Fliks which undertook *Grossflugzeug* (bomber) missions
J-Fliks which undertook *Jagd* (fighter) missions
Rb-Fliks which undertook *Reihenbild* (strip photography) missions.

During the war the following Fliks were formed each year

| | D-Fliks | F-Fliks | J-Fliks | G-Fliks | Rb-Fliks | TOTAL |
|---|---|---|---|---|---|---|
| 1914 | 15 | 1 | — | — | — | 16 |
| 1915 | 3 | — | — | — | — | 3 |
| 1916 | 17 | — | — | — | 1 | 18 |
| 1917 | 15 | 4 | 7 | — | — | 26 |
| 1918 | 6 | 1 | 4 | 3 | — | 14 |
| TOTAL | 56 | 6 | 11 | 3 | 1 | 77 |

Towards the end of the war, however, all the D-Fliks were recategorised in

more specialised roles, including three extra types of Flik. These were
K-Fliks which undertook *Korps* (corps observation) missions
P-Fliks which undertook *Photoaufklärung* (photo-reconnaissance) missions
S- or DS-Fliks which undertook *Schlacht* (ground-support) missions.

By the end of the war, therefore, the 56 D-Fliks had been recategorised as follows

In 1917: 1 became an F-Flik
1 became an Rb-Flik

In 1918: 14 became K-Fliks
13 became S/DS-Fliks
10 became F-Fliks
9 became J-Fliks
7 became P-Fliks
2 became G-Fliks
1 became an Rb-Flik

In fact, several of these redesignated Fliks changed role yet again before the end of the war, although they usually remained within their basic reconnaissance or photography function. At the end of 1918, therefore, the *Luftfahrtruppen* comprised

| | | |
|---|---|---|
| 20 J-Fliks | 14 S-Fliks | 1 F-Flik |
| 18 P-Fliks | 5 G-Fliks | 0 S-Fliks |
| 17 K-Fliks | 2 Rb-Fliks | **77 Fliks TOTAL** |

The geographical distribution of the Fliks at various dates was as follows

| DATE | 31/1/14 | 1/1/15 | 1/1/16 | 1/1/17 | 1/1/18 | 31/10/18 |
|---|---|---|---|---|---|---|
| RUSSIAN FRONT | 7 | 10 | 8 | 18 | 22 | 3 |
| RUMANIA | — | — | — | 5 | 6 | — |
| SERBIA/ MONTENEGRO/ ALBANIA | 3 | 4 | 3 | 1 | 1 | 3 |
| MACEDONIA | — | — | — | — | — | 2 |
| ISONZO/ PIAVE | — | — | 4 | 8 | 21 | 44 |
| TIROL | — | — | 2 | 4 | 11 | 16 |
| OTHER ITALY | — | — | 1 | 1 | 3 | 9 |
| TOTAL | 10 | 14 | 18 | 37 | 64 | 77 |

### Unit Numbering

The Fliks were numbered in a roughly chronological sequence 1 to 74 and 101 to 103. Numbering had nothing to do with type except for the 100-series which were all bomber units. In April 1918 Fliks 29 and 33 were renumbered 104 and 105 to reflect their conversion to bombing.

### Naval Aviation

In July 1914, the *Marineluftwaffe* comprised 64 aircraft of which only five were front-line planes. There were 25 pilots. By September 1918 there were 131 planes but only 48 pilots (plus 31 observers). During the war 591 planes entered service, including 319 front-line flying-boats, 53 reconnaissance aircraft and 147 fighters. The latter two categories included land- and seaplanes.

## BELGIUM

At the outbreak of war the *Aviation Militaire Belge/Belgian Militar Vliegwezen* comprised four *escadrilles*, although nos. 3 and 4 were not fully mobilised for several days. Each *escadrille* consisted of four Henry Farman airplanes. By the end of the war the following *escadrilles* were in existence *(see over)*

| ESCADRILLE | FORMED | TYPE | NOTES |
|---|---|---|---|
| 1(i) | pre-war | Obs. to 2/16 Chasse | In 31/18 was renumbered 9ᵉᵐᵉ de Chasse |
| 1(ii) | 3/18 | Maintenance | No aircraft |
| 2 | pre-war | Observation | |
| 3 | pre-war | Observation | |
| 4 | pre-war | Observation | |
| 5(i) | 8/14 | Obs.to 8/16 Chasse | In 3/18 was renumbered 10ᵉᵐᵉ de Chasse |
| 5(ii) | 3/18 | Observation | |
| 6 | Between 6/15 – 2/16 | Observation | |
| 7 | Between 2/16 – 3/18 | Observation Photos | |
| 8 | Between 2/16 – 3/18 | Bombing/ Night obs | |
| 9 | 3/18 | Chasse | ex- 1ᵉᵐᵉ de Chasse |
| 10 | 3/18 | Chasse | ex- 5ᵉᵐᵉ de Chasse |
| 11 | 3/18 | Chasse | Not operational until 6/18 |

The number of operational aircraft available at any one time remained fairly modest, even in the last two years of the war. Thus there were on hand

in February 1917 44 front-line airplanes
in August 1917 81 front-line airplanes
in October 1918 140 front-line airplanes.

## Naval Aviation

A single *Escadrille Navale* was formed at Calais in 1915. Equipped with flying-boats the squadron soon left for Africa where it patrolled Lake Tanganyika until 1917 when it returned to Calais. The squadron moved to Ostend at the end of the year but continued its main duties of patrolling the Channel and the North Sea.

## BULGARIA

The Army Aviation Corps had figured prominently in the last Balkan War but had been forcibly disbanded under the harsh terms. It was not reformed until October 1915, just a few days before Bulgaria threw in her lot with the Central Powers.

## CANADA

The Canadians' major contribution to the Allied air war was in the provision of aircrew. For not only did 22,000 Canadians serve with the RFC and the Royal Naval Air Service (RNAS), but they also provided the personnel and facilities to raise 16 Canadian Training Squadrons (RFC) which between them turned out over 3,300 pilots, 75 per cent of whom served at the front. These figures do not include US aircrew trained by the Canadians when their squadrons were transferred to Texas in late 1917.

A Canadian Air Force proper hardly existed during the war. In August 1914, a single plane and two officers were sent to England and dubbed the Canadian Aviation Corps but this was soon moribund. In late 1918, two newly forming RAF squadrons (81 and 123) were renamed 1 and 2 Canadian Squadrons. They were equipped with Sopwith Dolphin fighter/ ground attack aircraft but did not reach France before the Armistice.

## FRANCE

In April 1914, the *Aviation Militaire* became an independent service with its own department within the Ministry of War. But it was still very much subordinate to the Army and in August 1914 its 25 *escadrilles* were attached either to the 21 infantry corps or to the 4 cavalry corps. The total number of front-line planes was 150, with a further 126 modern types in general reserve as well as 300 others of dubious utility. There were 4,342 officers and men in the air service, of whom 220 were pilots. The squadrons were organised according to aircraft type, there being 9 with Farmans, 8 Blériot, 3 Voisin, 2 Deperdussin, and one each with Breguets, Caudrons and REPs.

Over the next four years the *Aviation Militaire* grew prodigiously. with the following totals of airplanes available at the front at certain dates

| DATE | No. AIRPLANES | OF WHICH: | |
|---|---|---|---|
| | | FIGHTER | BOMBER |
| 8/14 | 150 | — | — |
| 4/15 | 390 | ? | ? |
| 2/16 | 1,150 | 135 | 138 |
| 6/16 | 1,120 | ? | ? |
| 12/16 | 1,420 | 328 | 253 |
| 6/17 | 2,170 | 690 | 296 |
| 8/17 | 2,335 | ? | ? |
| 4/18 | 2,750 | 797 | 413 |
| 7/18 | 3,260 | 1,090 | 438 |
| 11/18 | 3,222* | 1,152 | 485 |

The parallel growth of French squadrons is summarised in the next table *(opposite)*. Throughout the war squadrons continued to be named after the make of aircraft they flew but implicitly they were divided into five main types: general reconnaissance, army cooperation (which involved much tactical bombing and ground attack), artillery cooperation, fighters, and bombers. There were also a few dedicated ground attack squadrons.

* W. Front only. The total front-line and reserve holdings at the end of the war were some 6,000 airplanes.

‡ These totals take account of the numerous squadron renumberings and re-formations that took place in the first two years of the war. Squadrons that were renumbered are only counted on the date of their original formation.

| PERIOD | | RECCE. | ARMY COOP. | GROUND ATTACK | ARTILLERY COOP. | FIGHTER | BOMBER | TOTAL‡ |
|---|---|---|---|---|---|---|---|---|
| | To August 1914 | 22 | 3 | — | — | — | — | 25 |
| | August–December 1914 | 9 | 2 | — | 1 | — | 3 | 15 |
| **1915** | January–June | 15 | 10 | 1 | — | 4 | 10 | 40 |
| | July–December | 4 | 9 | — | — | 5 | 10 | 28 |
| **1916** | January–June | — | 1 | 1 | 22 | 3 | 3 | 30 |
| | July–December | — | 1 | — | 3 | 8 | — | 12 |
| **1917** | January–June | 2 | — | — | 4 | 23 | 9 | 38 |
| | July–December | 12 | 2 | — | 4 | 10 | 4 | 32 |
| **1918** | January–June | 15 | 3 | — | 26 | 11 | — | 55 |
| | July–December | 6 | — | — | 2 | 18 | 1 | 27 |
| **TOTAL** | | **85** | **31** | **2** | **62** | **82** | **40** | **302** |

*N.B.* This grand total does not take account of 21 other squadrons, in the 500- series, for which we have been unable to establish a formation date (though all were created in the last 18 months of the war). They comprised 8 reconnaissance squadrons, 1 artillery cooperation, 1 fighter and 11 bomber. Adding these to the totals at the bottom of the table gives us the following revised totals

| RECCE. | ARMY COOP. | GROUND ATTACK | ARTILLERY COOP. | FIGHTER | BOMBER | TOTAL |
|---|---|---|---|---|---|---|
| 93 | 31 | 2 | 63 | 83 | 51 | 323 |

However, as the role of individual squadrons frequently changed during the war (especially between the reconnaissance, army and artillery cooperation roles) neither of these sets of totals gives an accurate picture of the actual structure of the *Aviation Militaire* at the end of the war. Thus in November 1918 the existing squadrons were assigned the following duties

| RECCE. | ARMY COOP. | GROUND ATTACK | ARTILLERY COOP. | FIGHTER | BOMBER | TOTAL |
|---|---|---|---|---|---|---|
| 43† | 77 | — | 49 | 107 | 45 | 321 |

† Includes 5 night-reconnaissance and 11 coastal squadrons attached to the *Aviation Maritime.*

Most squadrons fought exclusively on the Western Front but an appreciable number were posted to support peripheral theatres or to provide imperial policing. During the war

- 2 squadrons (both reconnaissance) served in the Dardanelles in 1915.
- 34 squadrons (10 reconnaissance, 6 army cooperation, 2 artillery cooperation, 11 fighter, 5 bomber) served in Serbia, Macedonia and Greece from 1915 to the Armistice.
- 1 reconnaissance squadron served in Albania from late 1915.
- 3 squadrons (2 fighter and 1 bomber) served in Russia and Rumania.
- 13 squadrons (3 reconnaissance, 4 army cooperation, 3 artillery cooperation, 3 fighter) served in Italy from late 1917, although most had returned to France by spring of the following year.
- 24 squadrons (9 reconnaissance, 12 bomber and 3 convoy escort) served in North Africa.

### Unit Numbering

By November 1918 the following squadron assignments were in force

**Reconnaissance** (including coastal)

1, 7, 9, 11, 35, 43–45, 104, 141, 290–294, 481–491, 504, 505, 521, 522, 524, 525, 532–534, 544, 545, 549, 553, 554, 571, 575.

**Army Cooperation**

2, 4–6, 8–10, 13, 14, 16–22, 24, 27, 28, 30, 32–34, 36, 39–42, 47, 50–56, 58–61, 63, 64, 70–72, 74, 105, 106, 122, 140, 212, 215, 251–256, 258–266, 268, 270, 276–280, 284–286, 288, 289.

**Artillery Cooperation**

141, 201–211, 213, 214, 216–238, 243–245, 250, 257, 267, 269, 271–275, 508.

**Fighter**

3, 12, 15, 23, 26, 31, 37, 38, 46, 48, 49, 57, 62, 65–69, 73, 75–100, 102, 103, 112, 124, 150–176. 239, 240, 242, 246, 313–315, 387, 390, 391, 412, 441, 442, 461–471, 506, 507, 523, 531, 561, 562.

**Bomber**

25, 101, 107–111, 113–121, 123, 125–137, 501–503, 509, 510, 541, 542, 543, 547, 551, 552, 555–558.

### Naval Aviation

The *Aviation Maritime* also grew enormously during the war. The number of operational aircraft available at six-monthly intervals and the number of missions flown in that six months are shown in the following table:

| DATE | No. OPERATIONAL AIRCRAFT | MISSIONS FLOWN |
|---|---|---|
| 8/14 | 8 | — |
| 1/15 | 20 | ? |
| 7/15 | 54 | ? |
| 1/16 | 64 | ? |
| 7/16 | 96 | 2,860 |
| 1/17 | 159 | 3,660 |
| 7/17 | 277 | 11,080 |
| 1/18 | 691 | 20,814 |
| 7/18 | 1,119 | 16,505 |
| 11/18 | 1,264 | 14,600 |

*Aviation Maritime* personnel grew from 208 in August 1914 to 11,059 (including 702 pilots and 693 observers) by the end of the war.

The building blocks of the service were the naval aviation bases from which it waged its primary campaign against enemy submarines. These were of two types: the *Centres d'Aviation Maritime* (CAM), at key points along the coast, and the interspersed *Postes de Combat* (PC) which provided support. Some of these bases had full *escadrilles* whilst others had only half-a-dozen aircraft or less. The table following shows the growth of these bases during the war and is divided according to the Navy's main regional groupings. (Some formations were created from scratch and some involve the upgrading/downgrading of an existing PC or CAM.)

| REGION | BASE | No. BASES FORMED BY | | | | | | | | | |
|---|---|---|---|---|---|---|---|---|---|---|---|
| | | 8/14 | 1/15 | 7/15 | 1/16 | 7/16 | 1/17 | 7/17 | 1/18 | 7/18 | 11/18 |
| North Atlantic and English Channel | CAM | — | 1 | 1 | 1 | 1 | 1 | 4 | 5 | 5 | 5 |
| | PC | — | — | 1 | 2 | 2 | 2 | 2 | 3 | 4 | 3 |
| Atlantic | CAM | — | — | 1 | 1 | 1 | 3 | 4 | 6 | 9 | 9 |
| | PC | — | — | — | — | — | — | 4 | 3 | 3 | 2 |
| Mediterranean/Aegean | CAM | } 2* | 1 | 2 | 3 | 5 | 7 | 11 | 14 | 19 | 20 |
| | PC | | — | — | 1 | — | 3 | 8 | 6 | 11 | 10 |
| Total | CAM | } 2* | 2 | 4 | 5 | 7 | 11 | 19 | 25 | 33 | 34 |
| | PC | | — | 1 | 3 | 2 | 5 | 14 | 12 | 18 | 15 |
| **GRAND TOTAL** | | 2* | 2 | 5 | 8 | 9 | 16 | 33 | 37 | 51 | 49 |

\* Bases plain and simple. Not counted in later columns until finally defined as PC/CAM.

The only full squadrons to serve with the *Aviation Maritime* were eleven coastal squadrons (Nos. 481–491) formed between March 1917 and June 1918 and seconded from their parent *Aviation Militaire*. They were equipped mainly with Voisin bombers or Caudron reconnaissance planes. Two of the squadrons were stationed in the Channel sector, four in the Atlantic and five in the Mediterreanean and Aegean.

## GERMANY

In October 1912, the airship and airplane sections of the *Verkehrstruppen* (Transport Troops) were combined as the *Fliegertruppen*, now attached to the Guards Corps. (Bavaria maintained its own Military Flying Section). By August 1914 the *Fliegertruppen* possessed 450 aircraft of all types, flown by 250 pilots and a score of observers. The growth in the number of front-line planes during the war is shown in the table below. (In October 1916 the Flying Troops were renamed the *Luftstreitkräfte*, or Air Combat Forces).

| DATE | FRONT-LINE AIRPLANES | PERSONNEL |
|---|---|---|
| 8/14 | 250 | 520 † |
| 10/15 | 800 | ? |
| 10/16 | 1,550 | ? |
| 3/17 | 2,270 | 2,550 ‡ |
| 3/18 | 3,970 | 80,000 total |
| 8/18 | 2,470 | ? |
| 11/18 | 2,710 | 4,500 ◊ |

The history of the air force's component units is a complex one involving a whole series of role reallocations and renumberings. It can only be dealt with here in the barest detail. During the war twelve types of air unit were formed.

17 *Festungs-Fliegerabteilungen* (Fortress Flying Sections) existed in August 1914. These were located at Boyen (2), Graudenz (2), Königsberg (2), Metz (2), Posen (2), Strassburg (2), Breslau, Cologne, Germersheim, Glogau and Lüttich (all the duplicate sections were formed immediately after the initial mobilisation). The sections were designated as reconnaissance assets for fortress commanders but as none of these places were really threatened in the first months the sections were all soon transformed into Field Flying Sections (see below). By May 1915 only two remained.

89 *Feldflieger-Abteilungen* (Field Flying Sections) were formed in the war, of which 39 were created in the initial mobilisation. These were attached to individual Armies and (for the first two years of the war) Corps and tactically were entirely at their behest. Their main duties were reconnaissance and artillery liaison although they became increasingly involved in infantry support and ground attack. In October 1916, 35 of these sections were converted into *Flieger-Abteilungen (Artillerie)* (see below) and the remainder were redesignated simply as *Flieger-Abteilungen* (see below). Nine of the original *Feldflieger-Abteilungen* were Bavarian.•

57 *Flieger-Abteilungen* were formed from those *Feldflieger-Abteilungen* left after 35 of them had been converted into Artillery Sections. The role of these new Flying Sections was to be long-range reconnaissance on behalf of Army and Army Group commanders. Ten of these sections were designated *Leichtbild* (Lb), or photographic units. In early 1918 seven Flying Sections were converted to *Schutzstaffeln* (see below). Δ

43 *Artillerie-Fliegerabteilungen* were formed in 1915 and 1916 to take over the artillery liaison role from the over-worked *Feldflieger-Abteilungen*. Three of these Artillery Sections were Bavarian.

101 *Flieger-Abteilungen (Artillerie)* or *(A)* were formed in late 1916 from 43 sections immediately above, from the conversion of 35 *Feldflieger-Abteilungen* (see above), and from the creation of 23 new *(A)* Sections. Three of these were designated as *Leichtbild* units (see above). In early 1918, one *(A)* Section was converted to a *Schutzstaffel* (see below).

38 *Schutzstaffeln* (Protection Squadrons) were formed in 1917 and 1918 to provide cover for the low-flying, dawdling *(A)* Sections described immediately above. The first 24 *Schutzstaffeln* were formed from squadrons made available when the *Kampfgeschwadern* (see below) were drastically slimmed down.

38 *Schlachtstaffeln* (Battle Squadrons) were formed in late March 1918 by simply redesignating the *Schutzstaffeln* immediately above. Their new role was to provide close ground support for the infantry. It had been decided that the *(A)* Sections, many of them having had their complement of aircraft increased, were now capable of fending for themselves over enemy lines. The *Schlachtstaffeln* retained their old numbers.

91 *Jagdstaffeln* (Pursuit or Fighter Squadrons) were formed between August 1916 and the end of the war, five of them from *Kampfstaffeln* (see below) and the rest from scratch. Dates of formation (unfortunately not available for other unit types) were as in the table below.

67 *Kampfstaffeln* †† were formed in 1915 and 1916. Thirteen of these were at the disposal of Army and Corps headquarters and nine were dedicated

• During this reorganisation almost every *Abteilung* was renumbered. For example, 32 *Feldflieger-Abteilungen* became 263 *Flieger-Abteilung (A)*, and the number 32 was taken over by 64 *Feldflieger-Abteilungen*, now designated as a long-range reconnaissance *Flieger-Abteilung*.

† Pilots and observers.

‡ Pilots only.

◊ All aircrew (inc. mechanics).

Δ These were sections withdrawn from the now quiescent Russian Front.

†† Literally 'fighter' squadron. Possibly 'interceptor' squadron might best reflect their role.

| MONTH | 1916 | | | | | 1917 | | | | | | | | | | | | 1918 | | | | | | | | | | |
|---|---|---|---|---|---|---|---|---|---|---|---|---|---|---|---|---|---|---|---|---|---|---|---|---|---|---|---|---|
| | A | S | O | N | D | J | F | M | A | M | J | J | A | S | O | N | D | J | F | M | A | M | J | J | A | S | O | N |
| No. *JAGDSTAFFELN* FORMED | 7 | 7 | 9 | 2 | 6 | 2 | 4 | — | — | — | 5 | — | 1 | 1 | 1 | 1 | 13 | 15 | 8 | — | — | — | — | — | — | — | — | 9 |

to home defence against Allied bombers. The former were often referred to as 'Fokkerstaffeln' and the latter were dubbed Kampf-Einsitzer-Staffeln or single-seater squadrons. A further 45 Staffeln were formed as the building blocks of the Kampfgeschwadern (see below). Most Kampfstaffeln had disappeared by the end of the war, 27 becoming Schutzstaffeln, 12 Jagdstaffeln*, and 6 being dissolved.

8 Kampfgeschwadern (renamed Bombengeschwadern in January 1917) were formed between December 1915 and March 1918. The first two of these were the renamed Brieftauben-Abteilung Ostend and Brieftauben-Abteilung Metz, formed in November 1914 and August 1915†. All were intended as dedicated bombing formations at the disposal of the OHL, the Supreme Command‡. Kampfgeschwadern 5, 6 and 7 were temporarily dissolved for much of 1917 and all except Kampfgeschwader 3 were reduced from six to three Staffeln in December 1917. This latter was exempted because it had been equipped with Gotha bombers, and as the so-called 'Englandgeschwader', was assigned to cross-channel bombing operations.

4 Reisenflugzueg-Abteilungen (Long-Distance Aircraft Sections) were formed in 1916, equipped with four-engined aircraft and dedicated to long-range bombing. Two of the sections were dissolved in September 1917 and the surviving pair merged in October 1918.

6 Reihenbildzüge were formed, usually within a Flieger-Abteilungen (see above). These were equipped with 'mosaic' automatic cameras to take multiple photo-sequences for mapping purposes.

Because of the shortage of precise formation dates for sections and squadrons, it has not been possible to draw up a table showing the numbers of different types of unit at regular intervals. The short table below, however, showing a breakdown of unit types at the beginning and end of the war, does give some impression of the increasing unit specialisation during the war.

| DATE | FELDFLIEGER or FLIEGER ABTS. | ARTILLERIE or (A) ABTS. | FESTUNG ABTS. | SCHUTZ-STAFFELN | SCHLACHT-STAFFELN | JAGD-STAFFELN | KAMPF-STAFFELN | RIESEN-FAHRZUEG ABTs. | REIHEN-BILD ZÜGE |
|---|---|---|---|---|---|---|---|---|---|
| August 1914 | 39 | — | 8 | — | — | — | — | — | — |
| November 1918 | 41◊ | 99● | — | — | 38 | 91 | 37 | 1 | 6 |

Most Luftstreikräfte units served only on the Western Front. A few, however, did serve on each of the other front and these are itemised below.
RUSSIAN/RUMANIAN FRONT:
At least seven Feldflieger- or Flieger-Abteilungen, one Kampfgeschwader and one Jagdstaffel.
SERBIAN/MACEDONIAN FRONT:
At least one Kampfgeschwader and one Jagdstaffel.
BULGARIAN FRONT:
At least one Feldflieger-Abteilung and one Jagdstaffel.
ITALIAN FRONT:
At least one Bombengeschwader and three Jagdstaffeln.
GALLIPOLI FRONT:
Two Feldflieger-Abteilungen.
PALESTINIAN FRONT:
Six Feldflieger-Abteilungen (specially formed for service with the Turks)∆ and one Jagdstaffel.

### Unit Numbering
#### Festungs-Fliegerabteilungen
1 to 10, representing one for each fortress except Lüttich. The latter referred to by fortress name only, as were the six duplicate sections e.g. Abteilung Posen 2.
#### Feldflieger-Abteilungen
1 to 74; 300 to 305 (the 'Paschas'); 1 to 9 Bavarian.
#### Flieger-Abteilungen
Redesignated from 1 to 48 above plus 1 to 9 Bavarian.

#### Artillerie-Fliegerabteilungen
201 to 245; 101 to 103 Bavarian.
#### Flieger-Abteilungen (Artillerie)
As above plus 246 to 298.
#### Schutzstaffeln
1 to 38.
#### Schlachtstaffeln
As above redesignated.
#### Jagdstaffeln
1 to 90 plus Jagdfliegerstaffel Süd (Galicia). Nos. 16, 23, 32, 35, 76 to 80 were Bavarian.
#### Kampfstaffeln
Those within the Kampfgeschwadern were numbered 1 to 45; the Kampf-Einsitzer-Staffeln were numbered 1 to 9; the rest were known by a bewildering array of Arabic and Roman numbers and proper names.
#### Kampfgeschwadern/Bombengeschwadern
1 to 7; 8 Bavarian.
#### Riesenflugzeug-Abteilungen
500 to 503.
#### Reihenbildzüge
1 to 6 (?).

### Naval Aviation
At the beginning of the war Imperial German Navy warplanes were organised within the Marinerflieger-Abteilung. There were 24 serviceable planes in all, based at three Seeflugstationen along the coast. By November 1918 there were 32 seaplane bases organised under I Marine-Flieger-Abteilung on the North Sea coast and II Abteilung in the Baltic. By this time there were also 17 Landflugplätze for land-based planes. The entire naval air service comprised 1,478 land- and seaplanes and 16,212 personnel of whom 2,116 were aircrew. Like the Luftstreitkräfte the naval planes had become much more specialised and the land-based units in Flanders at the end of the war comprised††

3 Marine-Feldflieger-Abteilungen (reconnaissance). Formed December 1914 to May 1915.
2 Küstenstaffeln (coastal artillery cooperation). Formed 1917.
2 Marine-Schutzstaffeln (to escort the above). Formed 1917 (?).
5 Marine-Jagdstaffeln (mainland fighters). Concentrated in one Geschwader. Formed between February 1917 and September 1918.
1 Seefrontstaffeln (seaplane fighters over the North Sea). Formed August 1914.
1 Stabsbildabteilung (photo-reconnaissance).
3 Fliegermeldung (intelligence flight).

### GREECE
The first Greek aircraft squadron (Mira Aeroplani) was formed in September 1912 and in November was renamed as the Epirus Naval Detachment. Naval aircraft remained a priority up to the outbreak of war but in August 1914 a batch of aircraft on order from Britain were commandeered by the British Royal Naval Air Service. Converted to land-planes these were then flown to Greece by the British Naval Mission there and flown on the Greeks' 'behalf', In September 1916, such properly indigenous aviation units as there were in Greece declared for the Provisional Government in Salonika and thereafter four land-based and four coastal squadrons were formed. The Royal Hellenic Army Air Force operated the former which comprised one fighter squadron (Mira Dioxcos), two bombing and reconnaissance squadrons (Mira Vomvarthismou ke Anagnorisseos) and one unspecified

### Side notes (left margin)

* The nine Jagdstaffeln formed in 1918 were the renamed Kampf-Einsitzer-Staffeln.

† "Carrier-pigeon Sections".

‡ They were thus usually referred to as Kagohl 1–8 i.e. Kampfgeschwader der O.H.L. and later Bogohl 1–8.

◊ Including 10 Luftbild Abts.

● Including 5 Luftbild Abts.

∆ Known as 'Paschas', one was formed in January 1916 and the rest in 1917. The latter were intended for Mesopotamia but in the event had to be diverted to Palestine.

†† There were a further 15 land-based units scattered around the other fronts but we have been unable to find details of their nomenclature and deployment.

squadron. These fought with the French in Macedonia and were formed between December 1917 and September 1918. The squadrons of the Royal Hellenic Naval Air Service fought with the British in the Aegean and one of them, known as Z Squadron, was attached to the RNAS's 2 Wing.

## INDIA
No Indian Air Force was formed until 1932. Responsibility for aerial defence rested solely with the Royal Flying Corps/RAF, specifically 31 and 114 Squadrons.

## ITALY
An Italian military aviation inspectorate had been established in 1911 and aircraft were first used offensively in Libya in 1911–12. In January 1915, the Army formed a *Corpo Aeronautica Militare* and by May 1915, when Italy declared war, this had grown to 15 *squadriglie*, comprising 150 front-line airplanes, 91 pilots and 20 observers. A naval unit, the *Sezione Idroplani della Marina*, formed in October 1912, contained only 19 seaplanes, split between three stations and used mainly for training. By the end of the war the *Corpo Aeronautica* had 1,055 front-line army airplanes available whilst its naval component had 109 land- and 381 seaplanes, deployed at ten main stations∆. (Army and Navy units are being treated together because their parent services cooperated somewhat better than in other countries and a government decree of 17 September 1917 combined them into a single air arm). The growth of Army and Navy squadrons is detailed in the table below which lists the number of new squadrons formed at six-monthly intervals.

The distribution of Italian squadrons during the war, both at home and overseas, is given in the table at the bottom of this page. With two exceptions, both clearly indicated, the seaplane squadrons are not included in these totals.

### Unit Numbering
In November 1918 the following squadrons were operational
**Reconnaissance**
21–23, 26–28. 31–33, 35–39, 48, 56–59, 61, 89, 90, 104, 106, 111–116, 118, 120, 121, 131, 136, 139.
**Fighter**
70–85, 91.
**Home Defence**
101, 102, 105, 107, 110, 242, 301–303, 306.
**Bomber**
1–15.
**Coastal**
87, 103, 181, 182, 201, 241, 251–286, 1–3 Seaplane, 1 Naval (Torp.).

## JAPAN
Aviation in Japan was from the very beginning under military control. The first official body set up was the Provisional Committee for Military Balloon Research, in 1909††. This was a combined Army and Navy body but, as was their wont, both soon fell out and the Navy formed its own Naval Committee for Aeronautical Research, in 1912. By August 1914 the Army had acquired 16 airplanes and the Navy 12 and both services participated in

∆ about 70 per cent of the naval planes were involved in anti-submarine warfare and other maritime support operations in the Adriatic, whilst the remainder were responsible for defending the lines of communication between Italy's scattered islands.

†† Despite the title the main interest was in heavier-than-air aircraft.

* Formed and Dissolved.

† Does not include six squadrons formed but never up to strength.

‡ Two of which were deemed Fighter units.

◊ Includes one special ops, and one advanced training squadron.

• Including six squadrons which never saw active service.

** The figure in brackets is the number of seaplane squadrons.

| PERIOD | | SQUADRONS | | | | | | | | | | | | | | TOTAL | | NET TOTAL |
|---|---|---|---|---|---|---|---|---|---|---|---|---|---|---|---|---|---|---|
| | | ALL-PURPOSE 2-Seater | | FIGHTER | | BOMBER | | GROUND-ATTACK | | SEAPLANE | | TORPEDO | | | | | | |
| | | F.* | Diss.* | F. | Diss. | F. | Diss. | F. | Diss. | F. | Diss. | F. | Diss. | | | F. | Diss. | |
| | To May 1915 | 15 | 1 | — | — | 1 | — | — | — | — | — | — | — | | | 16 | 1 | 15 |
| | To April 1916 | 15 | 8 | 5 | — | 7 | 1 | — | — | 1 | — | — | — | | | 28 | 9 | 19 |
| | To December 1916 | 11 | — | 6 | — | 8 | — | — | — | 1 | — | — | — | | | 26 | — | 26 |
| **1917** | January to June | 8 | 1 | 5 | — | — | — | 1 | — | 7 | — | — | — | | | 21 | 1 | 20 |
| | July to December | 12† | 13 | 1 | 1 | 1 | 1 | — | — | 6‡ | — | — | — | | | 20 | 15 | 5 |
| **1918** | January to June | 7 | 1 | 2 | — | 3 | 1 | — | — | 18 | — | 1 | — | | | 31 | 2 | 29 |
| | July to December | 10◊ | 8 | — | — | 2 | — | — | 1 | 10• | — | — | — | | | 22 | 9 | 13 |
| | **TOTAL** | 78 | 32 | 19 | 1 | 22 | 3 | 1 | 1 | 43 | — | 1 | — | | | 164 | 37 | 127 |
| | **NET TOTAL** | 46 | | 18 | | 19 | | — | | 43 | | 1 | | | | 127 | | |

| | NUMBER SQUADRONS AT FRONT | | | | | | | | | |
|---|---|---|---|---|---|---|---|---|---|---|
| | | | ITALY | | | ALBANIA | MACEDONIA | FRANCE | LIBYA | TOTAL |
| DATE | ISONZO/ PIAVE | TIROL | CARNIA | SUPREME COMMAND | HOME DEFENCE | | | | | |
| 12/15 | 12 | 6 | — | 5 | — | — | — | — | 1 | **24** |
| 4/16 | 13 | 6 | — | 10 | — | 1 | — | — | 1 | **31** |
| 9/16 | 16 | 10 | — | 15 | — | 1 | — | — | 1 | **43** |
| 1/17 | 15 | 9 | — | 16 | 10 | 2 | 1 | — | 2 | **55** |
| 5/17 | 20 | 11 | 3 | 16 | 4 | 2 | 1 | — | 2 | **59** |
| 8/17 | 28 | 6 | 2 | 15 | — | 3(1)** | 1 | — | 2 | **57** |
| 10/17 | 24 | 15 | 3 | 16 | — | 4(1) | 1 | — | 3 | **66** |
| 3/18 | 24 | 17 | — | 16 | — | 4(1) | 2 | 3 | 3 | **69** |
| 6/18 | 25 | 19 | — | 15 | — | 4(1) | 2 | 2 | 4(1)** | **71** |
| 11/18 | 30 | 16 | — | 15 | — | 4(1) | 2 | 2 | 3(1) | **72** |

the Tsingtao campaign, between September and November, to eliminate the German toehold in China. The Army's five planes made 86 sorties, the Navy's four made 49, and between them they dropped 243 bombs, all to little effect. By the end of the war the Army had formed two Air Battalions (of six airplanes each) and the Navy two Air Corps, or *Kokutai*. The only offensive activity before the Armistice, however, was limited Army air support for the Japanese intervention in the Russian Civil War, in summer 1918.

## NEW ZEALAND
No national air force, nor even any specifically New Zealand squadrons within the RFC, were created during the war. An RE.8 shipped out to the New Zealand authorities was handed back to serve with 7 Squadron RFC. The country's main contribution to the Allied air effort was in the training of pilots in domestic flying schools, though sources differ as to whether the number of graduates was around 200 or 300.

## POLAND
Poland did not exist as a national entity during the war but towards the end, as Allied recognition of a Polish state seemed increasingly likely, several attempts were made to form its own fledgling air force. The most significant of these was between August 1917 and June 1918 when Poles in Russian service formed 1 Polish Aviation Unit, at Minsk. In April this became the Aviation of the First Polish Corps at Bobruysk, and its fifteen or so airplanes undertook several combat missions before the base was overrun by the Germans. Another squadron, the Polish Aviation Unit, at Odessa, was a more putative affair. Formed in October 1917, it had to dismantle its planes and keep them hidden in crates until it, too, was overrun, this time by the Austro-Hungarians, in April 1918.

A Polish II Corps came into existence on the Rumanian front, in December 1917, and this too created its own air support, 1 Polish Combat Aviation Unit, recruited from Polish fliers with Russian 19 Fighter Squadron. Once again this unit was overrun by the advancing Germans, in May 1918, as was its sister 2 Polish Combat Aviation Unit, formed at Jassy in December 1917 and partly drawing upon Polish pilots from Russia's 14 Aviation Section. The last squadron to be formed in the east prior to November 1918 contained Poles caught up in the Russian Civil War battles fought along the Black Sea coast. Formed in October 1918, 1 Aviation Unit of the Polish Forces was based in Odessa in November at the time of the German surrender.

Efforts were also made to provide an aviation component for General Hallr's Polish Army, forming in France in 1918. The so-called 'Polish Aviation' received its colours in June 1918 but no actual squadrons had been formed prior to the Armistice.

## PORTUGAL
In 1912, an Institute of Portuguese Military Aviation was formed consisting of three airplanes. With the outbreak of war Portuguese volunteers went off to flying schools in France, England and the USA and in 1917 the Army established an *Arma de Aeronautica* and the Navy its own *Aviação Maritima*. By the end of the war the former comprised a fighter and a bomber squadron and the latter was operating from two naval stations at Lisbon and Aveiro. None of these played much part in combat operations, although three Portuguese pilots were assigned to the French fighter squadron SPAD 124, on the Western Front.

## RUMANIA
In late 1911 an Aviation Group had been formed and in 1913 this became the *Corp al Aeronautilor Permanenti* and in September 1915 the *Corpui Aerian Romana*. This was soon expanded to ten squadrons but by the time Rumania declared war, in the following August, most of the airplanes had become unserviceable. By November 1916 the airforce had been largely destroyed and its bases abandoned, despite the flying in of Allied replacement aircraft from Macedonia. In the first half of 1917 the squadrons were rebuilt but by the time of the Armistice between Rumania and the Central Powers, in December, they had been largely destroyed once again. The table at the bottom of this page shows the squadron and aircraft strength of the CAR at certain dates.

### Unit Numbering
In early 1917 the Rumanians fielded the following operational squadrons

**Reconnaissance**
2, 4, 5, 6, 7, 9.
**Fighter**
1, 3, 11, 14.
**Bomber**
8, 12.

## RUSSIA
In early 1910, the Russian Defence Ministry created a Department of the Air Fleet which soon became the Russian Imperial Air Service. The first airplane, as opposed to airship, was purchased in 1911. In that same year the Russians began forming *otryady*, or air sections, of which there were eight in 1913 and 39 when war broke out. By this time the Air Fleet included 224 airplanes, 200 pilots and 100 observers. The table directly below gives some idea of the growth in aircraft strengths during the war. (Whenever possible the figures are for front-line strengths only, although even here it remains problematic just how many of these planes were actually serviceable. No air force was ever able to get more than a fraction of its total air strength into the air at any one time, but Russian serviceability represented an even smaller tip of the iceberg than usual. This is made clear in an atypically detailed inventory for November 1917 which lists 579 airplanes at the front, 237 snarled up in the railway system, 400 in reserve parks, and roughly 1,000 scattered around various military and industrial sites, many uncompleted).

| DATE | FRONT-LINE AIRPLANES | DATE | FRONT-LINE AIRPLANES |
|---|---|---|---|
| 8/14 | 224 | 12/16 | 724 |
| 1/9/14 | 145 | 2/17 | 1,040† |
| 6/15 | 350 | 7/17 | 461 |
| 10/15 | 553 | 11/17 | 579 |
| 6/16 | 383* | 3/18 | 125 |
| 9/16 | 716 | 10/18 | 260 |

The next table (below) shows the growth of the Imperial Air Service in terms of the number of *otryady*, by type, that had been created by certain dates.

*Side notes (left margin):*

\* Of which 250 serviceable.

† Of which 545 serviceable.

‡ Groups of anything between one and four squadrons.

◊ Includes three artillery observation squadrons.

| | SQUADRONS | | | | | AIRCRAFT | | | |
|---|---|---|---|---|---|---|---|---|---|
| DATE | GRUPULS‡ | RECCE. | FIGHTER | BOMBER | TOTAL | RECCE. | FIGHTER | BOMBER | TOTAL |
| 9/15 | 3 | 6◊ | 3 | 1 | **10** | 30 | 6 | 8 | **44** |
| 8/16 | 3 | Only five of the above squadrons were still at all effective | | | | 11 | 4 | — | **15** |
| 10/16 | 4 | 5 | 1 | 1 | **7** | 20 | 8 | 2 | **30** |
| 8/17 | 3 | 6 | 4 | 2 | **12** | 15 | 24 | 18 | **57** |

| DATE | AIR SERVICE SECTIONS | | | | | | | |
|---|---|---|---|---|---|---|---|---|
| | ARMY | CORPS | ARTILLERY | FIGHTER | GUARDS | SIBERIA | TURKESTAN | TOTAL |
| 8/14 | — | — | — | — | — | — | — | **39*** |
| 10/15 | 13 | 37 | — | — | 2 | 5 | 1 | **58** |
| 9/16 | 13 | 37 | 4 | 12 | 2 | 5 | 1 | **74** |
| 11/17 | 13 | 37 | ? | 24 | ? | ? | ? | **91** |
| 3/18 | ? | ? | ? | ? | ? | ? | ? | **33** |

*\* Grouped in 8 Fortress Companies and 6 Aviation Companies.*

The Air Service also included the so-called Squadron of Flying Ships, a dedicated long-range bombing unit equipped with huge Sikorski Ilya Mourometz bombers. This unit was usually about 25 aircraft strong although almost 40 were on hand in February 1917. It operated exclusively under Supreme Headquarters control.

Despite the relative paucity of figures on aircraft strengths and the types of section operational, there does exist a very detailed breakdown of the missions flown per month by Russian pilots, at least up until August 1916. The following table presents these figures aggregated into quarterly totals.

| QUARTER | | MISSIONS FLOWN | QUARTER | | MISSIONS FLOWN |
|---|---|---|---|---|---|
| **1914** | 3 | 1,531 | **1916** | 1 | 2,902 |
| | 4 | 1,698 | | 2 | 5,129 |
| **1915** | 1 | 2,713 | | 3† | 3,463 |
| | 2 | 4,842 | | | |
| | 3 | 4,669 | | | |
| | 4 | 2,614 | | | |

### Unit Numbering

*Otryady* were not numbered in a single sequence, each with its unique number, but within sequences for each unit type, e.g. 1 to 37 Corps *otryady* or 1 to 24 fighter.

### Naval Aviation

In August 1914, the Imperial Navy possessed about 25 seaplanes split between the Baltic and the Black Sea. Maximum strength in the Baltic reached around 70 airplanes, organised into five flights at various stations. In the Black Sea peak strength was roughly 150 airplanes, mainly seaplanes, some of which were attached to the six seaplane tenders that operated in this region.

### SERBIA

Serbian airplanes had been used extensively during the Balkan Wars and in July 1914 some ten planes were available for operations. By mid-August, however, all but three had been lost in crashes and the air force remained moribund until the arrival of a French *escadrille*, in February 1915, to form the basis of a new air force in exile. By the end of the year, four French reconnaissance squadrons were permanently assigned to the Serbs and in 1916 these were joined by a further three French fighter squadrons. Some of these *escadrilles* had all-French personnel and some were Franco-Serbian. In January 1918, one of the reconnaissance squadrons became 1 Serbian *Escadrille* and a second national squadron was formed later that year. The Serb armies on the Macedonian front also had some support from normal French and British squadrons stationed in this theatre.

### Unit Numbering

Most of the seconded French squadrons retained their national numbering although this was twice changed during the war. Thus 82 *Escadrille*, a reconnaissance unit, became 382 in 1916 and 521 in 1917. Similarly, the other reconnaissance squadrons, 84, 98 and 99 became 384, 398 and 399 and later 522, 524 and 525. The fighter squadrons arrived as 387, 391 and one other. The first two became 523 and 507 but we have been unable to identify the third.

### SOUTH AFRICA

The first steps toward forming a South African air arm were taken in 1913 when five putative pilots were chosen for training in England. In August 1914 they were already enrolled on an advanced flying course with the RFC and were immediately enlisted. In November they were seconded back home and became the nucleus of the South African Aviation Corps, formed in January 1915. This became operational in May, with ten or so Farmans and B.E.2s, and took part in the SW Africa campaign (see Map 33c). Once German forces there had surrendered, however, the Corps was immediately dissolved. But volunteers were allowed to travel to England and there they were absorbed into what became known as 26 (South African) Squadron RFC. In January 1916, this unit returned to Africa to take part in the campaign against von Lettow Vorbeck in 'German East' (see Map 34). Other South Africans made independent arrangements to participate in the war in the air and in all some 3,000 of them served in the RFC/RAF as air- and ground-crew.

### TURKEY

The tiny pre-war Turkish air arm was very much under French tutelage and was equipped with French airplanes. This connection was severed once war broke out and the Turks soon turned to the Germans for planes and for technical expertise. By the end of the war the Germans had provided 265 planes, the Turks' sole source of supply except for a handful of captured Allied planes. There also came from Germany 390 aviators and 1,740 mechanics and ground-crew. Air units had originally been subordinated to the Corps of Engineers but in early 1916 an independent Air Service (*Osmanli Havakuvvetleri*) was formed, with a German commander and a Turkish chief-of-staff. During the war fifteen flying sections, or *boluks*, were formed, of which three were equipped with fighters and the rest with a mixture of general-purpose two-seaters and one or two fighters. By 1918, the flying sections were deployed as shown in the table below.

| NUMBER OF FLYING SECTIONS IN | | | | | | |
|---|---|---|---|---|---|---|
| THRACE | DARDANELLES/ BOSPHORUS | W ANATOLIA | SE ANATOLIA/ SYRIA | JORDAN/ SAUDI ARABIA | MESOPOTAMIA | NE ANATOLIA/ CAUCASUS |
| 1‡ | 3◊ | 1 | 1 | 2 | 2• | 5△ |

The Turks were also supported by six German *Flieger-Abteilungen* formed specially for service in this theatre. The first of these was dispatched in 1916, the rest in the following year. They served exclusively in Syria and Palestine. So, too, did the one *Jagdstaffel* sent to fight with Turkish forces, in March 1918. The peak combined strength of these units was some 40 two-seater machines and 16 fighters.

### Unit Numbering

The Turkish flying sections were numbered in a single sequence 1–10, 12 and 14–17. However, No. 12 was redesignated 13 in 1917. The German sections, known as 'Pascha' (Pasa) *Abteilungen*, were numbered 300–305, whilst the *Jagdstaffel*, formed in Germany as No. 55, was usually known in its new theatre as 1F, or the first *Jasta* attached to *Heeresgruppe* F.

### Naval Aviation

Three naval flying sections were formed, one of which was based on the

*† July and August only.*

*‡ Fighter section.*

*◊ Two of which were fighter sections.*

*• One of which had recently been transferred from Western Anatolia.*

*△ One of which had no aircraft or pilots.*

Black Sea and two in the Dardanalles and Aegean. There was also a German *Wasserflieger-Abteilung*, dispatched to the Dardanalles in June 1915.

## UNITED KINGDOM
### Royal Flying Corps and Royal Air Force

As in many other countries, aviation for the Army was originally under the command of the engineers, but in 1912 the Royal Flying Corps was formed which took over the Royal Engineers Air Battalion as well as all naval air assets. These became, respectively, the RFC's Military Wing and Naval Wing. From July 1914 the Naval Wing went its own way (see below) but by then the Military Wing had expanded into seven squadrons, one of which was equipped with balloons. Once war was declared military aviation began to mushroom, as is evidenced in the table below showing the growth of front-line airplane strength in France and Flanders during the war.

| DATE | FRONT-LINE AIRPLANES | DATE | FRONT-LINE AIRPLANES |
|------|------|------|------|
| 8/14 | 50 | 1/17 | 717 |
| 1/15 | 61 | 6/17 | 794 |
| 3/15 | 90 | 11/17 | 997 |
| 6/15 | 106 | 3/18 | 1,232 |
| 9/15 | 153 | 6/18 | 1,736 |
| 7/16 | 410 | 11/18 | 1,799 |

Aircraft strength figures for other theatres have proved elusive but the following ones show front-line planes available on different fronts in June 1918.

| FRANCE & FLANDERS | ITALY | MACEDONIA | MIDDLE EAST | MEDITERRANEAN | HOME DEFENCE |
|------|------|------|------|------|------|
| 1,736 | 104 | 41 | 269 | 144 | 336 |

The total personnel of the RFC (renamed the Royal Air Force in April 1918 when it once again took over all naval aviation) grew from 1,844 all ranks in August 1914 to a little under 300,000 in November 1918. Of the latter figure, 54,075 were stationed in France and Flanders and 31,419 in other overseas theatres.

The next two tables chart the expansion in the number of squadrons during the war. The first gives a month-by-month tally of squadrons formed at home and overseas. As most of these were equipped with obsolescent two-seater types until just prior to being sent overseas, it has not been thought necessary to distinguish squadrons by type.

* Figures in brackets denote number of total which were formed overseas

† These seeming explosions in squadron formations were mainly accounted for by the redesignation of sixteen RNAS squadrons on the Western Front to the RAF and by the grouping and redesignation of RNAS coastal flights as RAF squadrons.

‡ Mainly putative bomber squadrons never equipped with combat airplanes. Also includes four squadrons assigned to the newly-created Australian Flying Corps. (*See Australia*).

◊ In November 1918 there were also 199 training squadrons.

| YEAR | J | F | M | A | M | J | J | A | S | O | N | D | TOTAL | DISBANDED | NET TOTAL |
|------|---|---|---|---|---|---|---|---|---|---|---|---|------|------|------|
| 1914 | | | | | | | | — | — | — | — | 1 | **8** | — | **8** |
| 1915 | 3 | 5 | 2(1)* | — | 1 | — | 1 | — | 6 | 2 | 3 | — | **23** | — | **23** |
| 1916 | 3 | 4 | 2 | 6 | 6 | 6 | 4 | 2 | 3(1)* | 2 | 1 | 1 | **40** | — | **40** |
| 1917 | 5 | 1 | 1 | — | — | 2 | 8 | 8(2)* | 10(1)* | 4 | 3 | 3 | **45** | — | **45** |
| 1918 | 7 | 9(1)* | 8(1)* | 31(5)*† | 5(1)* | 4 | 7(1)* | 27(1)*† | 8(5)* | 4(1)* | 1 | — | **111** | 27† | **84** |
| | | | | | | | | | | | | | **227** | 27 | **200◊** |

The next table does distinguish squadrons by type and shows the build-up of RFC squadrons in various theatres. (The six-monthly totals are net, which is to say that they take account of disbandments and, most importantly, of conversions from one type of aircraft to another, most commonly from two-seater to fighter).

| PERIOD | | FRANCE & FLANDERS | | | ITALY | | | | MACEDONIA | | | AEGEAN & MEDITERRANEAN | | | | EGYPT & PALESTINE | | |
|---|---|---|---|---|---|---|---|---|---|---|---|---|---|---|---|---|---|---|
| | | R* | F* | B* | R | F | B | C* | R | F | B | R | F | B | C | R | F | B |
| 1914 | Aug–Dec | 5 | — | — | — | — | — | — | — | — | — | — | — | — | — | — | — | — |
| 1915 | Jan–June | 3 | 1 | — | — | — | — | — | — | — | — | — | — | — | — | — | — | — |
| | July–Dec | 7 | 1 | — | — | — | — | — | — | — | — | — | — | — | — | 1 | — | — |
| 1916 | Jan–June | 6 | 4 | 2 | — | — | — | — | — | — | — | — | — | — | — | — | — | — |
| | July–Dec | 5 | 5 | — | — | — | — | — | 1 | 1 | — | — | — | — | — | — | — | — |
| 1917 | Jan–June | -1 | 7 | 2 | — | — | — | — | — | — | — | — | — | — | — | — | — | — |
| | July–Dec | 1 | 8 | 2 | 2 | 2 | — | — | — | — | — | — | — | — | — | 1 | 1 | — |
| 1918 | Jan–June | 5 | 15† | 15† | -1 | 1 | — | 3 | — | 1 | — | — | — | — | 4 | 1 | 2 | — |
| | July–Dec | -1 | 4 | 4 | — | — | — | 2 | — | — | — | — | — | — | 5 | — | — | — |
| TOTAL Nov 1918 | | 30‡ | 45‡ | 25° | 1 | 3 | — | 5 | 1 | 2 | — | | | | 9◊ | 3• | 3 | — |
| GRAND TOTAL | | 100 | | | 9 | | | | 3 | | | 9 | | | | 6 | | |

| PERIOD | | MESOPOTAMIA | | | INDIA | | | E AFRICA | | | HOME (OPERATIONAL) | | | | TOTAL | | | |
|---|---|---|---|---|---|---|---|---|---|---|---|---|---|---|---|---|---|---|
| | | R | F | B | R | F | B | R | F | B | R | F | B | C | R | F | B | C |
| 1914 | Aug–Dec | — | — | — | — | — | — | — | — | — | — | — | — | — | 5 | — | — | — |
| 1915 | Jan–June | — | — | — | — | — | — | — | — | — | — | — | — | — | 3 | 1 | — | — |
| | July–Dec | 1 | — | — | 1 | — | — | — | — | — | — | — | — | — | 9 | 2 | — | — |
| 1916 | Jan–June | — | — | — | — | — | — | 1 | — | — | 5 | — | — | — | 12 | 4 | 2 | — |
| | July–Dec | — | — | — | — | — | — | — | — | — | 5 | 1 | — | — | 11 | 7 | — | — |
| 1917 | Jan–June | — | — | — | — | — | — | — | — | — | -1 | 2 | — | — | -2 | 9 | 2 | — |
| | July–Dec | 1 | — | — | 1 | — | — | — | — | — | 1 | 3 | — | — | 7 | 14 | 2 | — |
| 1918 | Jan–June | 1 | — | — | — | — | — | -1 | — | — | -2 | 3 | 1 | 11◊ | 3 | 22 | 16 | 18 |
| | July–Dec | — | — | — | — | — | — | — | — | — | — | — | 2 | 32◊ | -1 | 4 | 6 | 39 |
| TOTAL Nov 1918 | | 3 | — | — | 2 | — | — | — | — | — | 8△ | 9 | 3 | 43 | 47 | 63 | 28 | 57 |
| GRAND TOTAL | | 3 | | | 2 | | | — | | | 63 | | | | 195 | | | |

*NB* With regard to France and Flanders, it should be remembered that the figures in the table above are for RFC postings only and do not therefore include eleven Royal Naval Air Service squadrons which were officially attached to the RFC on the Western Front at various dates between October 1916 and March 1918. Two of these were bomber squadrons with the Independent Force, two were other bomber squadrons briefly attached in March 1918, and the remainder were fighter squadrons which were mainly attached between March and August 1917 (*see below for further details on RNAS squadrons*).

## Unit Numbering
By November 1918 the following RAF squadrons were operational. Role designations are as at that date and may well have been changed since the squadron's formation.
### Reconnaissance
2, 4–10, 12–16, 20–23, 26, 30, 31, 33–36, 38, 39, 42, 52, 53, 59, 63, 67, 69, 72, 75–78, 82, 83, 102, 105, 106, 114, 142, 144, 148–150.
### Fighter
1, 3, 11, 17, 19, 24, 28, 29, 32, 37, 40, 41, 43, 44–46, 48, 50, 51, 54, 56, 60–62, 64–66, 68, 70, 71, 73, 74, 79, 80, 84, 85, 87–89, 94, 101, 139, 141, 142, 145, 151–153.
### Bomber
18, 25, 27, 47, 49, 55, 57, 58, 97–100, 103, 104, 107, 108, 110, 115.
### Ex-RNAS (all types)
201–260, 263, 264, 226–269, 271–273.

## Royal Naval Air Service
The War Office had originally intended that the RFC should control both Army and Navy aviation but the latter, pleading their own specialised demands, soon began to operate as a separate service. In July 1914, this was made official and the RFC Naval Wing, already usually referred to as the Eastchurch Wing, after its HQ, became the Royal Naval Air Service. In April 1918, Army and Navy aviation was reunited within the Royal Air Force, but prior to that date the Navy's independent arm had enjoyed a remarkable growth, as the figures below indicate.

*August 1914* 830 personnel with 39 land- and 52 seaplanes.
*December 1915* 606 land- and 319 seaplanes.
*October 1916* 655 land-planes, 283 float-planes, 50 flying-boats and 1 ship's airplane.
*April 1918* 994 landplanes, 646 float-planes, 152 flying-boats and 231 ship's airplanes, as well as 67,000 personnel.
(*November 1918* Even after the reabsorption into the RAF, a number of airplanes, referred to as 'Air Force contingents', continued to serve on board Royal Navy ships. These were mainly assigned to the battleships, battle-cruisers and 22 of the light cruisers, which between them could embark approximately 120 airplanes on specially constructed turret-decks, as well as to the 10 float-plane and 3 land-plane carriers **. These latter had a lift capacity of 51 and 48 planes respectively.).
The story of RNAS expansion is a complex one and is best dealt with in a chronological narrative rather than the usual tables.
*1914* At the start of the war the RNAS comprised just one squadron, the so-called Eastchurch 'Wing', and six seaplane stations on the British Coast.

* Denoting Reconnaissance (2-seater), Fighter, Bomber and Coastal.

† Mainly RNAS squadrons being amalgamated into the newly constituted RAF.

‡ Includes two fighter and one reconnaissance squadron transferred to the newly constituted Australian Flying Corps in January 1918.

° Of which 4 day- and 5 night-bomber squadrons formed the Independent Force, RAF, undertaking long-range, 'strategic' bombing.

◊ All renumbered RNAS flights and squadrons (except one torpedo-bomber squadron f. 10/18).

• Includes one reconnaissance squadron transferred to the Australian Flying Corps.

△ Includes two squadrons sent to Ireland in May 1916.

** One of the float-plane carriers, in fact, was sunk in collision just before the Armistice.

* Five squadrons
equipped with
Sopwith Pups and
Camels but
normally
employed on
reconnaissance,
maritime patrol
and bombing
missions.

† Some sources
state that in
addition two of 6
Wing's contingents
in the Adriatic had
attained squadron
status.

‡ Even when
including a further
20 administrative/
training stations
and 18 airship/kite
balloon stations
we have been
unable to fully
account for the
126 stations cited
in some sources
as the April 1918
total.

◊ Shortly after
this, however, a
further two RAF
squadrons were
formed in this
theatre, both from
ex-RNAS flights.

● Although two of
these squadrons
flew Sopwith
Camels they rarely
performed in the
fighter role.

Δ This squadron
appears in the
main RFC/RAF
table (column
**France and
Flanders:
Jan–June 1918**)
as a reconn.
squadron.

** No US
squadrons served
in either theatres
although 65 pilots
flew with the Allies
in Italy.

†† Known to the
Americans as
Observation and
Pursuit
respectively

The squadron immediately left for Belgium and in October two more squadrons were formed there. One squadron was also sent to German East Africa.

**1915** In March one of the Western Front squadrons was sent to the Dardanelles to assist naval operations there and in September was joined by a second contingent from France. By this time, in fact, all three RNAS squadrons had been expanded into Wings (since June), with the one remaining on the Western Front having been subdivided into squadrons A, B, and C.

**1916** Following the evacuation from Gallipoli, one of the Wings there was disbanded whilst the other remained in the Aegean, subdivided into flights based on the islands of Lemnos, Imbros, Mitylene, Stavros and Thassos. The RNAS also extended its reach into the Red Sea with aircraft aboard four seaplane carriers. In France and Flanders two more Wings were formed, each divided into squadrons A and B. In November the RNAS began once more creating squadrons individually, attaching them to Wings but if necessary moving them from one to another. These squadrons were numbered and to achieve conformity the seven A, B, and C squadrons in the west were also given individual numbers. The RNAS also took the lead in long-range bombing operations and 3 Wing, disbanded in the Dardanelles, was reformed in France for this purpose, in September.

**1917** The formation of individual squadrons gathered pace, with six being established in France and Flanders. In the Aegean, the island-based flights were also expanded into squadrons, although for some reason these were given letter designations, A to G, plus a Z Squadron formed from Greek naval fliers. In the Adriatic, an entire new Wing was formed, based at Otranto, though this was subdivided into flights rather than squadrons. In June, 3 Wing was disbanded once more, relinquishing its 'strategic' bombing role to 41 Wing RFC.

**1918** Prior to the reabsorption into the RAF in April 1918, four more squadrons were formed in the west. On 1 April 1918, therefore, the number of RNAS squadrons was as follows

| SQUADRON TYPE | NUMBER OF SQUADRONS IN: | | | TOTAL |
|---|---|---|---|---|
| | UK | FRANCE & FLANDERS | AEGEAN | |
| FIGHTER | — | 8 | — | 8 |
| RECONNAISSANCE & BOMBER | — | 7 | 8* | 15 |
| LONG-RANGE BOMBER | — | 2 | — | 2 |
| TOTAL | — | 17 | 8 | 25† |

By April also, the original six coastal stations had grown to 46 which operated combat airplanes. These were located as follows

| AIRCRAFT TYPE | NUMBER OF STATIONS IN: | | | | | TOTAL |
|---|---|---|---|---|---|---|
| | UK | FRANCE | ITALY | AEGEAN & MED | MESO-POTAMIA | |
| SEAPLANE | 23 | 1 | 1 | — | 1 | 26 |
| LANDPLANE | 8 | — | 1 | 6 | — | 15 |
| BOTH | 6 | — | 1 | — | — | 7 |
| TOTAL | 37 | 1 | 3 | 6 | 1 | 48‡ |

After the merging with the RAF all naval squadrons adopted a number in the 200 series, with those that already had a numerical designation simply adding 200 to their existing one. It was some months before the Aegean squadrons followed suit and by then the original eight squadrons in this theatre had been merged into just four RAF and one Greek◊. The Adriatic Wing was divided into four squadrons, with a further three being created before the Armistice. The consolidation of the air service also meant that airplanes serving on the coastal stations were grouped into squadrons and

by the end of the war, a further 52 squadrons had been created in this way. By November 1918, then, the total ex-RNAS component of the RAF accounted for 69 of its squadrons, distributed as follows

| AIRCRAFT TYPE | NUMBER OF SQUADRONS IN: | | | | TOTAL |
|---|---|---|---|---|---|
| | UK | FRANCE | ITALY | AEGEAN & MED | |
| FIGHTER | 2 | 7 | 1 | — | 10 |
| RECONN. & BOMBER | 1 | 7 | 3 | 4● | 15 |
| LONG-RANGE BOMBER | — | 2 | — | — | 2 |
| **MARITIME PATROL** | | | | | |
| Seaplane | 5 | 1Δ | 1 | 3 | 10 |
| Flying-boat | 6 | — | — | — | 6 |
| Land-plane | 10 | — | — | — | 10 |
| Mixed | 12 | — | 1 | 3 | 16 |
| TOTAL PATROL | 33 | 1 | 2 | 6 | 42 |
| GRAND TOTAL | 36 | 17 | 6 | 10 | 69 |

**Unit Numbering**

In March 1918, RNAS squadrons were numbered 1–17, and A–G and Z. For renumberings when absorbed into the RAF, including the large number of maritime patrol flights formed into squadrons, see the RFC/RAF section preceding.

**UNITED STATES**

Not until July 1914 did America get around to setting up an Aviation Section within the Army Signal Corps, and even when it entered the war, in April 1917, US air assets were still a mere 55 airplanes, to which 1,165 personnel were assigned. Of the planes, 51 were obsolete. From June 1917 almost all Army planes, air- and ground-crew were concentrated within the newly-formed Air Service, American Expeditionary Corps, and its front-line air strength grew as follows

*26 September 1918:* 646.

*15 October 1918:* 579.

*11 November 1918:* 740 (of which 457 serviceable).

Flight personnel had grown from 26, in April 1917, to 767 pilots, 481 observers and 23 aerial gunners with front-line squadrons, at the time of the Armistice. Total personnel had grown to 78,507, of whom 58,090 were in France. The expansion in the number of squadrons in France, showing the number of new squadrons assigned each month, is charted in the table below.**

| DATE | NUMBER SQUADRONS ASSIGNED TO FRONT | | | TOTAL |
|---|---|---|---|---|
| | RECONN.†† | FIGHTER†† | BOMBER | |
| 4/18 | 2 | 1 | — | 3 |
| 5/18 | 2 | 3 | 1 | 6 |
| 6/18 | 2 | 3 | — | 5 |
| 7/18 | 1 | — | — | 1 |
| 8/18 | 5 | 5 | — | 10 |
| 9/18 | 2 | — | 3 | 5 |
| 10/18 | 4 | 6 | 2 | 12 |
| 11/18 | — | 2 | 1 | 3 |
| TOTAL | 18 | 20 | 7 | 45 |

**Unit Numbering**

In November 1918 the following US squadrons were assigned to the front in France.

***Observation***

1, 8, 9, 12, 24, 50, 85, 88, 90, 91, 99, 104, 135, 168, 186, 258, 278, 354.

*Pursuit*

13, 17, 22, 25, 27, 28, 41, 49, 93–95, 103, 138, 139, 141, 147, 148, 185, 213, 638.

*Bomber*

11, 20, 96, 100, 155, 163, 166.

## Naval Aviation

In 1910 the US Navy appointed an officer in charge of aviation matters, in 1911 it took delivery of its first three airplanes, and in July 1914 it set up the Office of Naval Aeronautics. By April 1917, however, when the United States entered the war, what was now known as the Naval Flying Corps still possessed only 6 flying-boats and 45 float-planes. Yet by the end of the war fully 2,705 planes had been procured, of which 1,600 were combat types. In November 1918, 2,107 of these were still on hand, although only about 400 were overseas.* In this same period total personnel grew from 300 to almost 40,000, of whom just over 50 per cent were posted overseas.

The planes were divided between 41 naval air stations, whose locations were as set out below

| USA | | | | |
|---|---|---|---|---|
| ATLANTIC COAST | PACIFIC COAST | GULF COAST | CANAL ZONE | TOTAL |
| 10 | 1 | 3 | 1 | 15 |

| EUROPE | | | | | |
|---|---|---|---|---|---|
| ENGLAND | IRELAND | FRANCE | ITALY | PORTUGAL | TOTAL |
| 2 | 5 | 16 | 2 | 1 | 26 |

By the time America entered the war, the US Marine Corps had also succeeded in forming its own naval service. This comprised a mere 50 personnel in April 1917, with hardly any aircraft. By the end of the year it had been expanded into 1st Maritime Aeronautic Company, with 18 flying-boats and float-planes, and 1st Aviation Squadron, with 260 personnel but awaiting delivery of DH.4 land-planes. In January 1918, the Aeronautic Company sailed for the Azores to take part in anti-U-boat operations. The Aviation Squadron did not embark for overseas until July, by which time it had become 1st Marine Aviation Force, subdivided into squadrons A to D, soon to be redesignated 7 to 10.† These became the Day Wing of the Northern Bombing Group, formed to attack German U-boat pens at Bruges, Ostend and Zeebrugge. It only mounted its first raid in mid-October and little was accomplished by the Marine fliers or by the Navy crews of the smaller Night Wing in their Caproni bombers.

### APPENDIX: INTER-ALLIED INDEPENDENT AIR FORCE

Not formed until 26 October 1918, this was a combined 'strategic' bombing force built around the block of British squadrons that made up the RAF's own Independent Force, formed in June 1918. The IAIAF was to have comprised the nine British bomber squadrons of the IF, three Italian Caproni squadrons already in France, and an uncertain number of French and American squadrons. It conducted no operations as an inter-Allied force.

*  Of the 2,107 only 242 were land-based, the rest being flying-boats and float-planes.

†  10 Squadron did not in fact join the other three until October.

## Table 5.15 German Bombing Raids on England 1914-18

| | AIRSHIPS | | | BOMBERS | | | | | |
|---|---|---|---|---|---|---|---|---|---|
| | No. RAIDS | No. SORTIES | TONS BOMBS | No. RAIDS | | No. SORTIES | | TONS BOMBS | |
| 1914 | – | 3 | – | 1‡ | –◊ | 1‡ | –◊ | ? | |
| 1915 | 18 | 46 | ? | 7 | 1 | 13 | 1 | ? | |
| 1916 | 21 | 146 | ? | 14 | 3 | 25 | 9 | ? | |
| 1917 | 7 | 46 | ? | 8 | 14 | 167 | 174 | ? | |
| 1918 | 4 | 18 | ? | – | 6 | – | 72 | ? | |
| TOTAL | 51 | 259 | 196 | 30 | 24 | 206 | 256 | c.200 | |

‡ Daylight raids.

◊ Night raids.

## Table 5.16 RAF 'Strategic' Bombing Raids Nov. 1917-Nov. 1918•

| DATE | No. MISSIONS | | BOMBS DROPPED | | INCEND-IARIES DROPPED |
|---|---|---|---|---|---|
| | DAY | NIGHT | No. | TONS | |
| 11/17-5/18 | 55 | 87 | 2,370 | 107 | - |
| 1915 June△ | - | - | - | 57 | - |
| July | - | - | - | 88 | - |
| Aug | - | - | - | 101 | - |
| Sept | - | - | - | 179 | - |
| Oct | - | - | - | 98 | - |
| Nov | - | - | - | 20 | - |
| Total | 205 | 373 | 12,514 | 543** | - |
| TOTAL | 260 | 460 | 14,884 | 650 | 816,019 |

• Whilst 99 of the pre-June 1918 were against industrial targets the later effort became very tied up with the tactical support of the armies.

△ Formation of the Independent Air Force.

** Of which 390 tons at night.

*Table 5.17* German Bombing of Paris Jan-Sept 1918

* Except for January these figures are speculative, and are based on average weight per bomb figures derived from the partial statistics available.

| | No. Airplanes Took Off | Bombs Dropped | |
|---|---|---|---|
| | | No. | Weight*(tons) |
| Jan | 30 | 267 | 14.0 |
| Feb | – | – | – |
| March | 131 | c.200 | 9.8 |
| April | 8 | c.35 | 1.7 |
| May | 29 | c.110 | 5.4 |
| June | 9 | 55 | 2.7 |
| July | – | – | – |
| Aug | – | – | – |
| Sept | 50 | 85 | 4.2 |
| **TOTAL** | **257** | **c.762** | **37.8** |

*Table 5.18* Austro-Hungarian Bombing of Venice 1915-18

| | No. Airplanes | No. Bombs Dropped |
|---|---|---|
| **1915** | 24 | 141 |
| **1916** | 93+ | 402 |
| **1917** | 61 | 106 |
| **1918** | 73+ | 392 |
| **TOTAL** | **251+** | **1,041** |

# SECTION 6

# CASUALTIES AND LOSSES

# PART I OVERALL AND ARMY CASUALTIES

The following points should be borne in mind when consulting the table below.

(i) We have been unable to find front-by-front breakdowns of casualty figures for France, Germany and Italy.

(ii) Even where figures are available it is often impossible to strip out those for soldiers missing, which are, therefore, sometimes included under soldiers killed and sometimes under prisoner-of-war.

(iii) In the Austro-Hungarian entries below the figures do not include casualties for October and November 1918. Moreover, the aggregate number of soldiers killed in these entries is far below that given in Table 6.2. We assume that this is because the totals do not include men who died of wounds or disease, or men missing, but have included the figures anyway as they give some idea of the relative fatalities on the various fronts.

### Table 6.1 Aggregate Military Casualties and Civilian Deaths of the Belligerents 1914-18

| COUNTRY | POPULATION (millions) | NUMBER SERVED IN FORCES (millions) | FORCES CASUALTIES | | | | TOTAL CIVILIAN DEATHS | NOTES |
|---|---|---|---|---|---|---|---|---|
| | | | KILLED & MISSING | WOUNDED | P.O.W. | TOTAL KILLED, WOUNDED & MISSING | | |
| AUSTRALIA | 4.87 | 0.42 | 53,560* | 155,130 | 3,650 | 208,690 | – | * Also 6,300 non-battle deaths. |
| AUSTRIA-HUNGARY | 49.90 | 7.80 | 1,016,200* | ?† | 1,691,000‡ | ? | ? | * Both sets of figures come from two different tables in the Austrian Official History (V.7). In the lower set the P.O.W. figure includes the missing. † Some sources give up to 3.6m. wounded. ‡ Includes 478,000 P.O.W.s who died who are not included in no. killed |
| | | | 539,630* | 1,943,240* | 2,118,190* | 2,482,870 | ? | |
| BELGIUM | 7.52 | 0.27 | 38,170 | 44,690 | 10,200 | 82,860 | c.30,000 | |
| BULGARIA | 5.50 | 1.20 | 77,450* | 152,400 | 10,620† | 229,850 | c.275,000 | * Does not include 24,500 died of disease to 9/18 plus thousands more in the subsequent retreat. † To 12/17 only. 150,000 by Armistice. |
| CANADA | 7.40 | 0.62 | 58,990* | 149,710 | 2,820 | 208,700 | – | * Also 3,830 died other causes. |
| FRANCE | 39.60 | 8.66 | 1,385,300* | 4,329,200† | 446,300 | 5,714,500 | c.40,000 | * Includes 58,000 colonial troops, mostly in Europe. † Including 690,000 permanently disabled. |
| GERMANY | 67.00 | 13.40 | 2,037,000*† | 5,687,000 | 993,800 | 6,400,000 | c.700,000 | * Including 14,000 black troops. † Regimental rolls of honour compiled after the war aggregate almost 4m. |
| GREECE | 4.80 | 0.28 | c.5,000 | c.20,000 | c.1,000 | c.25,000 | c.130,000 | |
| INDIA | 316.00 | 1.68 | 62,060 | 66,690* | 11,070 | 128,750 | – | * It remains unclear why the ratio of killed to wounded should, most unusually, be almost 1:1. |
| ITALY | 35.00 | 5.90 | 462,400* | 955,000† | 530,000 | 1,417,400 | ? | * Austrian sources give a figure of 497,000. † 416,000 discharged to 7/18. |
| JAPAN | 67.20 | 0.80 | ? | ? | – | 1,970* | – | * Casualties at Tsingtao 1914. |
| NEW ZEALAND | 1.05 | 0.13 | 16,710 | 41,320 | 500 | 58,030 | – | |
| PORTUGAL* | 6.00 | 0.20 | 7,220† | 13,751‡ | 6,680‡ | c.40,000? | – | * White and black troops. † Of whom 5,550 in Africa. There were probably a further 5,000 missing in Africa. ‡ W.Front only. |
| RUMANIA | 7.51 | ? | 219,800* | c.120,000* | c.60,000 | 455,700 | 265,000 to 500,000 | * Dead include 70,500 who died as P.O.W.s. The ratio of dead to wounded is still, however, unusual. |
| RUSSIA | 167.00 | 12.00 | c.1,800,000* | c.4,950,000* | c.2.5m.* / 3.91m.† | c.6.75m.* / 5.31m.† | c.2,000,000* | * Figures usually given. † Recent Russian figures. |
| SERBIA | 5.00 | 0.71 | 127,500* | 133,150 | 70,000† / 200,000‡ | 160,400 | c.600,000 | * Of whom 65% died of sickness. † Allied figure. ‡ Austrian figure |
| SOUTH AFRICA* | 6.00 | 0.23 | 7,120 | 12,030 | 1,540 | 19,150 | ? | * Figures for whites only. A total of 38,723 Africans generally are known to have died in hospital in 1917-18, in East Africa, whilst serving as labourers and porters. |

*Table 6.1* **Aggregate Military Casualties and Civilian Deaths of the Belligerents 1914-18 (continued)**

| COUNTRY | POPULATION (millions) | NUMBER SERVED IN FORCES (millions) | FORCES CASUALTIES | | | | TOTAL CIVILIAN DEATHS | NOTES |
|---------|----|----|----|----|----|----|----|----|
| | | | KILLED & MISSING | WOUNDED | P.O.W. | TOTAL KILLED, WOUNDED & MISSING | | |
| TURKEY | 21.30 | 0.99 | 236,000 | 770,000* | 145,000 | 1,006,000 | c.2,000,000† | * Also c.500,000 invalided out, mostly through sickness. † Mainly Armenian. |
| UNITED KINGDOM | 46.40 | 5.70 | 702,410 | 1,662,625* | 170,389 | 2,365,035 | 1,386† | * Of whom 600,000 discharged as disabled. † In air-raids. |
| UNITED STATES | 92.00 | 4.35 | 51,822 | 230,074 | 4,434 | 255,896 | – | |

*Table 6.2* **Aggregate Casualties by Nationality on the Various Fronts 1914-18**

**France and Belgium 1914-18**

| | KILLED | WOUNDED | P.O.W. |
|---|---|---|---|
| France | 1,300,000 | c.3,000,000 | 508,000 |
| U.K. | 512,600 | 1,528,500 | 223,600 |
| Belgium | 38,200 | 44,700 | 10,200 |
| Australia | 48,900 | 130,900 | ? |
| Canada | 56,400 | 149,700 | ? |
| New Zealand | 12,900 | 34,800 | ? |
| South Africa | 3,250 | 8,720 | 2,220 |
| India | 6,670 | 15,750 | 1,090 |
| Portugal | 1,690 | 13,750 | 6,680 |
| U.S.A. | 51,800 | 230,100 | 4,430 |
| Italy | ← 20,870 → | | |
| TOTAL | 2,032,410+ | 5,156,920+ | ? |
| Germany | 1,493,000 | 2,579,000 | 774,000 |
| Austria-Hungary | 3,200 | c.10,000 | 4,100 |
| TOTAL | 1,496,200 | 2,589,000 | 778,100 |
| GRAND TOTAL | 3,258,610 | 7,745,920 | ? |

**Eastern Front 1914-18**

| | KILLED | WOUNDED | P.O.W. |
|---|---|---|---|
| Russia* | 4.78m. | | ? |
| Germany | c.500,000 | c.1,000,000 | ? |
| Austria-Hungary† | 311,300 | 1,212,800 | 1,246,700 |
| Turkey | c.10,000 | ? | ? |

**Serbia 1914-15**

| | KILLED | WOUNDED | P.O.W. |
|---|---|---|---|
| Serbia‡ | ? | ? | ? |
| Austria-Hungary◊ | 39,600 | 146,300 | 87,700 |
| Germany | ← c.8,000 → | | |
| Bulgaria | ? | ? | ? |

**Armenia 1914-17**

| | KILLED | WOUNDED | P.O.W. |
|---|---|---|---|
| Russia* | 0.53m. | | ? |
| Turkey | ? | ? | ? |

**Dardanelles 4/15-1/16**

| | KILLED | WOUNDED | P.O.W. |
|---|---|---|---|
| U.K. | 18,800 | 46,700 | 7,500 |
| France | ← 27,000 → | | |
| Australia | 8,100 | 17,900 | ? |
| New Zealand | 2,700 | 4,650 | ? |
| India | 1,360 | 3,420 | 110 |
| Turkey | 86,700 | 164,600 | ? |

**Mesopotamia 1914-18**

| | KILLED | WOUNDED | P.O.W. |
|---|---|---|---|
| U.K. | 15,600 | 20,300 | 3,500 |
| India | 24,000 | 52,900 | 3,800 |
| TOTAL | 39,600 | 53,200 | 7,300 |
| Turkey | ← 200,000 → | | 45,000 |

* Estimated *pro rata* given that Russians maintained an average of 10 per cent of total combat troops on Armenia-Azerbaijan Front.

† See note (iii) in preamble to this table.

‡ Probably at least 80% of total casualties (see Table 6.1).

◊ Balkans total for whole war. Serbia share probably c.90%.

*Table 6.2* Aggregate Casualties by Nationality on the Various Fronts 1914-18 (continued)

**Egypt and Palestine 1914-18**

|  | KILLED | WOUNDED | P.O.W. |
|---|---|---|---|
| **U.K.** | 14,600 | 29,100 | 3,200 |
| **Australia** | 1,370 | 3,550 | ? |
| **New Zealand** | 540 | 1,150 | ? |
| **India** | 3,400 | 6,300 | 270 |
| **TOTAL** | **19,910** | **40,100** | **?** |
| **Turkey** | ? | ? | 80,000 |

**Macedonia 1915-18**

|  | KILLED | WOUNDED | P.O.W. |
|---|---|---|---|
| **U.K.** | 9,700 | 16,300 | 2,600 |
| **France** | ← 30,500 → | | |
| **Serbia** | ← 19,400 → | | |
| **Greece** | ← 26,000 → | | |
| **Italy** | ← 8,400 → | | ? |
| **Russia** | ← 3,100 → | | |
| **TOTAL** | ← **77,200** → | | |
| **Central Powers** | ? | ? | ? |

**Rumania 1916-18***

|  | KILLED | WOUNDED | P.O.W. |
|---|---|---|---|
| **Rumania** | 219,800 | 120,000 | 60,000 |
| **Germany** | ? | ? | ? |
| **Austria-Hungary** | ? | ? | ? |
| **Bulgaria** | ? | ? | ? |
| **Turkey** | ? | ? | ? |
| **C.POWERS TOTAL** | ← c,60,000 → | | |

**Italy 1915-18**

|  | KILLED | WOUNDED | P.O.W. |
|---|---|---|---|
| **Italy** | c.450,000 | c.930,000 | c.520,000 |
| **U.K.** | 2,100 | 4,700 | 200 |
| **France** | ← 2,900 → | | |
| **Austria-Hungary** | 145,200 | 591,900 | 226,400 |
| **Germany** | ← 12,000 → | | |

**South-West Africa 1914-15**

|  | KILLED | WOUNDED | P.O.W. |
|---|---|---|---|
| **S.Africa** | 427 | 560 | 782 |
| **Germany** | ← 583 → | | 4,000 |

**Cameroons 1914-16**

|  | KILLED | WOUNDED | P.O.W. |
|---|---|---|---|
| **U.K.** | ← 2,300 → | | |
| **France** | ← 3,900 → | | |
| **Germany** | ← 6,575 → | | |

**East Africa 1914-18**

|  | KILLED† | WOUNDED | P.O.W. |
|---|---|---|---|
| **U.K.** | 1,200 | 600 | 200 |
| **India (Troops)** | 2,100 | 1,800 | 500 |
| **S.Africa (Troops)** | 1,700 | 1,100 | 100 |
| **Africa (Troops)** | 4,300 | 4,000 | 500 |
| **Africa (Other)** | 42,300 | 1,300 | 600 |
| **TOTAL** | **51,600** | **8,800** | **1,900** |
| **Germany** | ? | ? | ? |

* Russian figures included in E.Front total.

† Of whom the following percentages died from disease:
U.K. = 72%
India = 46%
S.Africa = 72%
Africa (Troops) = 68%
Africa (Other) = 99%
TOTAL = 71%

*Table 6.3* Casualties in Major Battles (France & Belgium, E.Front, Italy and Middle East) 1914-18

| BATTLE | DATE | TOTAL CASUALTIES* |
|---|---|---|
| **FRANCE & BELGIUM** | | |
| **Frontiers** | 8/14 | |
| France | | 211,000 |
| B.E.F | | 14,000 |
| Belgium | | 12,300 |
| Germany | | *c.*220,000 |
| **Marne** | 9/14 | |
| France | | 80,000 |
| U.K. | | 1,700 |
| Germany | | ? (15,200 p.o.w.s) |
| **1ˢᵗ Ypres** | 10-11/14 | |
| British | | 58,200 |
| French | | *c.*50,000 |
| German | | 134,300 |
| **2ⁿᵈ Artois** | 5-6/15 | |
| France | | 102,500 (35,000) |
| B.E.F. | | 28,200 |
| Germany | | 49,500 |
| **2ⁿᵈ Champagne** | 9-10/15 | |
| France | | 143,600 |
| Germany | | 85,000 |
| **3ʳᵈ Artois/Loos** | 9-10/15 | |
| France | | 48,200 |
| B.E.F. | | 61,700 |
| Germany | | 56,000 |
| **Verdun** | 2-12/16 | |
| France | | 362,000 |
| Germany | | 336,000 |
| **Somme** | 7-11/16 | |
| B.E.F. | | 498,000 (108,700) |
| France | | 195,000 |
| Germany | | 420,000 |
| **2ⁿᵈ Aisne** | 4-5/17 | |
| France | | 182,000 |
| Germany | | 163,000 |
| **3ʳᵈ Ypres** | 7-11/17 | |
| B.E.F. | | 396,800 (60,300) |
| France | | 112,000 |
| Germany | | 348,300 |
| **2ⁿᵈ Somme/Lys** | 3-4/18 | |
| B.E.F. | | 343,800 (31,400) |
| France | | 112,000 |
| Germany | | 348,300 |

| BATTLE | DATE | TOTAL CASUALTIES* |
|---|---|---|
| **FRANCE & BELGIUM continued** | | |
| **3ʳᵈ Aisne** | 5-6/18 | |
| France | | 96,200 |
| B.E.F. | | 28,700 |
| Germany | | 130,400 |
| **(TOTAL)** | **(3-7/18)** | |
| France | | (220,000 killed) |
| B.E.F. | | (61,600 killed) |
| Germany | | (124,000 killed) |
| **2ⁿᵈ Marne** | 7-8/18 | |
| France | | 95,200 |
| B.E.F | | 16,000 |
| U.S. | | 40,000 |
| Germany | | 168,000 |
| **Amiens** | 8/18 | |
| France | | 24,200 |
| B.E.F. | | 27,000 |
| Germany | | 75,000 |
| **(GERMANY)** | **(3-9/18)** | (536,000 k.& m., 808,300 w.) |
| **Meuse-Argonne** | 9-11/18 | |
| U.S. | | 117,000 |
| Germany | | 100,000 |
| **EASTERN FRONT** | | |
| **Tannenburg & Masurian Lakes** | 8-9/14 | |
| Russia | | 267,000 (137,000 p.o.w.) |
| Germany | | *c.*80,000 |
| **Lemberg** | 8-9/14 | |
| Russia | | 255,000 (45,000 p.o.w.) |
| Austria-Hungary | | 400,000 (100,000 p.o.w.) |
| **Lodz** | 11/14 | |
| Russia | | 95,000 |
| Germany | | 35,000 |
| **Gorlice/Tarnow** | 5/15 | |
| Russia | | *c.*1,000,000 |
| Austria-Hungary | | ? |
| Germany | | 87,000 |
| **Brusilov Offensive** | 6-10/16 | |
| Russia | | *c.*1,400,000 |
| Austria-Hungary | | 750,000 (380,000 p.o.w.) |
| Germany | | 150,000 |
| Turkey | | 17,800 |
| **Kerensky Offensive** | 7/17 | |
| Russia | | 40,000 killed |
| Central Powers | | 12,500 killed |

* Figure in brackets denotes number killed, unless otherwise stated.

*Table 6.3* Casualties in Major Battles (France & Belgium, E.Front, Italy and Middle East) 1914-18 (continued)

* Figure in brackets denotes number killed, unless otherwise stated.

† Number killed usually too low as missing almost always included in combined total with P.O.W.s. Even so, usually a higher proportion of wounded than on other fronts.

| BATTLE | DATE | TOTAL CASUALTIES* |
|---|---|---|
| **ITALY†** | | |
| **1st Isonzo** | 5-7/15 | |
| Italy | | 14,900 (1,900) |
| Austria-Hungary | | 9,950 |
| **2nd Isonzo** | 7-8/15 | |
| Italy | | 41,900 |
| Austria-Hungary | | 46,600 (7,700) |
| **3rd Isonzo** | 10-11/15 | |
| Italy | | 65,500 (20,400) |
| Austria-Hungary | | 41,800 (8,200) |
| **4th Isonzo** | 10-11/15 | |
| Italy | | 49,000 (7,500) |
| Austria-Hungary | | 25,400 (3,900) |
| **5th Isonzo** | 3/16 | |
| Italy | | 1,900 |
| Austria-Hungary | | 2,000 |
| **Trentino** | 5-6/16 | |
| Italy | | 52,000 (40,000 p.o.w..) |
| Austria-Hungary | | c.30,000 (5,000) |
| **6th Isonzo** | 8/16 | |
| Italy | | 51,200 |
| Austria-Hungary | | 37,500 (3,700) |
| **7th Isonzo** | 9/16 | |
| Italy | | 17,500 |
| Austria-Hungary | | c.15,000 |
| **8th Isonzo** | 10/16 | |
| Italy | | 21,100 |
| Austria-Hungary | | c.20,000 |
| **9th Isonzo** | 11/16 | |
| Italy | | 28,900 |
| Austria-Hungary | | 28,000 |
| **10th Isonzo** | 5-6/17 | |
| Italy | | 159,000 (36,000) |
| Austria-Hungary | | 65,700 (7,300) |
| **Asiago** | 6/17 | |
| Italy | | 23,700 |
| Austria-Hungary | | 8,800 |
| **11th Isonzo** | 8-9/17 | |
| Italy | | 166,000 (40,000) |
| Austria-Hungary | | 85,000 (10,000) |
| **Caporetto** | 10-11/17 | |
| Italy | | c.330,000‡ |
| Austria-Hungary | | 20,400 (2,400) |
| Germany | | c.15,000 |
| **Piave** | 6/18 | |
| Italy/Allies | | 84,800 (8,000) |
| Austria-Hungary | | 152,100 (11,600) |

‡ Of whom 10,000 killed and 293,000 P.O.W.

| BATTLE | DATE | TOTAL CASUALTIES* |
|---|---|---|
| **ITALY continued** | | |
| **Vittorio Veneto** | 10/18 | |
| Italy/Allies | | 37,000 |
| Austria-Hungary | | Include: 30,000 killed 427,000 p.o.w. |
| **MIDDLE EAST** | | |
| **Armenia** | 11/14-1/15 | |
| Russia | | inc. 16,000 k. |
| Turkey | | c.130,000 |
| **Ctesiphon** | 11/15 | |
| British/Indian | | 6,500 |
| Turkey | | 9,600 |
| **Erzerum** | 1-2/16 | |
| Russia | | c.14,000 |
| Turkey | | c. 38,000 (inc. 15,000 p.o.w.) |
| **Kut** | 4/16 | |
| British/Indian | | 17,000 (inc.10,000 mil. p.o.w.) |
| Turkey | | ? |
| **Erzincan** | 7/16 | |
| Russia | | ? |
| Turkey | | 34,000 (inc. 17,000 p.o.w.) |
| **Gaza/Beersheba/ Jerusalem** | 11-12/17 | |
| Br. Empire | | c.18,000 |
| Turkey | | c.25,000 (inc. 12,000 p.o.w.) |
| **Megiddo** | 9-10/18 | |
| Br. Empire | | 5,600 |
| Turkey | | inc. 75,000 p.o.w. |

The following two tables relate to the British Empire but are included to make clear just how great a drain on military manpower was sickness and disease. The figures for East Africa, for example, make it clear that the Germans imposed an enormous military burden on their enemy simply by keeping their own tiny force in existence.

**Table 6.4 Proportions of Battle to Non-Battle Casualties Among British and Imperial Troops on the Major Fronts 1914-18**

| FRONT | PERIOD | FORCE | BATTLE CAS. (a) | NON-BATTLE CAS. (b) | RATIO a:b |
|---|---|---|---|---|---|
| **France and Belgium** | 1914-18 | B.E.F. | 2,690,100 | 3,528,500 | 1:1.31 |
| **Dardanelles** | 1915-16 | British | 68,800 | 145,200 | 1:2.11 |
| **Mesopotamia** | 1914-18 | Empire | 85,200 | 820,100 | 1:9.63 |
| **Egypt and Palestine** | 1915-18 | Empire | 51,500 | 503,400 | 1:7.98 |
| **Macedonia** | 1915-18 | Empire | 23,800 | 481,300 | 1:20.25 |
| **Italy** | 1917-18 | British | 6,300 | 51,300 | 1:8.12 |
| **S.W.Africa** | 1914-15 | S.Africa | 1,600 | 24,700 | 1:15.58 |
| **E.Africa** | 1916-18 | Empire &S.Africa | 10,700 | 336,600 | 1:31.40 |

**Table 6.5 Aggregate British Army Battle Deaths and Deaths from Sickness on the Major Fronts 1914-18**

| | FRANCE & BELGIUM | DARDANELLES | MESOPOTAMIA | EGYPT & PALESTINE | MACEDONIA | ITALY | EAST AFRICA |
|---|---|---|---|---|---|---|---|
| **Killed and Died of wounds** | 467,000 | 15,600 | 7,400 | 8,900 | 4,300 | 1,300 | 350 |
| **Died of sickness** | 45,500 | 3,100 | 8,200 | 5,600 | 5,400 | 800 | 890 |

# PART II NAVIES

**Table 6.6** Aggregate Naval Losses of the Major Powers, by Type of Ship, and aggregate Personnel Losses 1914-18

| | U.K. | FRANCE‡ | RUSSIA | ITALY | JAPAN | U.S.A. | TOTAL | GERMANY | AUSTRIA-HUNGARY | TURKEY | TOTAL |
|---|---|---|---|---|---|---|---|---|---|---|---|
| **Battleship** | 13 | 4 | 2 | 3 | 1 | – | **23** | 1 | 3 | 2 | **6** |
| **Battle Cruiser** | 3 | – | – | – | 1 | – | **4** | 1 | – | – | **1** |
| **Cruiser** | 13 | 5 | 2 | 3 | – | 1 | **24** | 6 | 2 | 1 | **9** |
| **Light Cruiser** | 12* | – | 1 | – | 2 | – | **15** | 18◊ | – | – | **18** |
| **Monitor** | 5 | – | – | 2 | – | – | **7** | – | 3 | – | **3** |
| **Torpedo Gunboat** | 5 | 3 | – | – | – | – | **8** | – | – | – | **–** |
| **Sloop** | 18 | – | 3 | – | – | – | **21** | – | – | 9 | **9** |
| **Destroyer** | 67 | 15 | 6 | 8 | 1 | 2 | **99** | } 109 | 6 | 1 | } 126 |
| **Torpedo Boat** | 11 | 10 | 9 | 4 | 1 | – | **35** | | 8 | 2 | |
| **Aircraft Carrier** | 3 | – | – | – | – | – | **3** | – | – | – | **–** |
| **Minelayer** | 2 | 2 | 5 | – | – | – | **9** | – | – | 1 | **1** |
| **Minesweeper** | – | – | 30 | 2 | – | 1 | **33** | 29 | – | 2 | **31** |
| **Submarine** | 54 | 14 | 12 | 11 | – | – | **91** | 178 | 7 | – | **185** |
| **Personnel: killed** | 34,650† | } 15,650 | ? | 3,170 | ? | } 8,106 | **?** | } 78,300• | 980 | ? | **?** |
| **wounded** | 4,510† | | ? | 5,250 | ? | | **?** | | 310 | ? | **?** |

*6 sunk as blockships.

† Not including c. 6,000 killed and 9,000 wounded in the R.N.A.S. and R.N.Division.

‡ One set of French figures also states that 15 battleships, 15 cruisers, 44 torpedo boats and 64 submarines were laid up because of excessive wear and tear.

◊ Includes one in Turkish service.

• Total casualties including 24,112 known killed as well as the missing and the wounded – 5,100 lost in U-boats.

Δ Not actually present at battle but sunk during pursuit phase.

** Pre-dreadnought.

**Table 6.7** Comparative Losses in Major Naval Engagements 1914-18

| BATTLE AND DATE | | SHIPS LOST | | | | |
|---|---|---|---|---|---|---|
| | | D/n. | B/Cr. | A/Cr. | Cr. | Dest. |
| **Heligoland Bight 28/8/14** | | | | | | |
| | U.K. | – | – | – | – | – |
| | Germany | – | – | – | 3 | – |
| **Coronel 1/11/14** | | | | | | |
| | U.K. | – | – | 2 | – | – |
| | Germany | – | – | – | – | – |
| **Falkland Islands 8/12/14** | | | | | | |
| | U.K. | – | – | – | – | – |
| | Germany | – | – | 2 | 2Δ | – |
| **Dogger Bank 24/1/15** | | | | | | |
| | U.K. | – | – | – | – | – |
| | Germany | – | – | 1 | – | – |

| BATTLE AND DATE | | SHIPS LOST | | | | |
|---|---|---|---|---|---|---|
| | | D/n. | B/Cr. | A/Cr. | Cr. | Dest. |
| **Jutland 31/5/16** | | | | | | |
| | U.K. | – | 3 | 3 | – | 8 |
| | Germany | 1** | 1 | – | 4 | 5 |
| **Straits of Otranto 15/5/17** | | | | | | |
| | Allies | – | – | – | – | – |
| | Austria-Hungary | – | – | – | – | – |
| **Ösel and Dragö Landings 11-19/10/17** | | | | | | |
| | Russia | 1** | – | – | – | 1 |
| | Germany | – | – | – | – | – |
| **Heligoland Bight 17/11/17** | | | | | | |
| | U.K. | – | – | – | – | – |
| | Germany | – | – | – | – | – |

**Table 6.8** Annual British and German Surface Ship Losses by Cause 1914-18 (Major Types)

| | | GUNFIRE | | TORPEDO | | MINE | | SCUTTLED | | OTHER/UNKNOWN | | MISHAP | | TOTALS | |
|---|---|---|---|---|---|---|---|---|---|---|---|---|---|---|---|
| | | U.K. | G | U.K. | G | U.K. | G | U.K. | G | U.K. | G | U.K. | G | U.K. | G |
| **Battleship** | 1914 | – | – | – | – | 1 | – | – | – | – | – | 1 | – | 2 | – |
| | 1915 | – | – | 4 | – | 2 | – | – | – | – | – | – | – | 6 | – |
| | 1916 | – | – | – | 1 | 2 | – | – | – | – | – | – | – | 2 | 1 |
| | 1917 | – | – | 1 | – | – | – | – | – | – | – | 1 | – | 2 | – |
| | 1918 | – | – | 1 | – | – | – | – | – | – | – | – | – | 1 | – |
| | **TOTAL** | – | – | 6 | 1 | 5 | – | – | – | – | – | 2 | – | 13 | 1 |
| **Battle Cruiser** | 1914 | – | – | – | – | – | – | – | – | – | – | – | – | – | – |
| | 1915 | – | – | – | – | – | – | – | – | – | – | – | – | – | – |
| | 1916 | 3 | 1 | – | – | – | – | – | – | – | – | – | – | 3 | 1 |
| | 1917 | – | – | – | – | – | – | – | – | – | – | – | – | – | – |
| | 1918 | – | – | – | – | – | – | – | – | – | – | – | – | – | – |
| | **TOTAL** | 3 | 1 | – | – | – | – | – | – | – | – | – | – | 3 | 1 |
| **Cruiser** | 1914 | 2 | 2 | 4 | – | – | 2 | – | – | – | – | – | – | 6 | 4 |
| | 1915 | – | 1 | – | 1 | – | – | – | – | – | – | 2 | – | 2 | 2 |
| | 1916 | 3 | – | – | – | 1 | – | – | – | – | – | – | – | 4 | – |
| | 1917 | – | – | 1 | – | – | – | – | – | – | – | – | – | 1 | – |
| | 1918 | – | – | – | – | – | – | – | – | – | – | – | – | – | – |
| | **TOTAL** | 5 | 3 | 5 | 1 | 1 | 2 | – | – | – | – | 2 | – | 13 | 6 |
| **Light Cruiser** | 1914 | 1 | 3 | 1 | 1 | 1 | – | – | 1 | – | 2 | – | 2 | 3 | 9 |
| | 1915 | – | 1 | – | 1 | – | 1 | – | 1 | – | – | – | – | – | 4 |
| | 1916 | – | – | 2 | 2 | 1 | – | – | – | – | 1 | – | 1 | 3 | 4 |
| | 1917 | – | – | – | – | – | – | – | – | – | – | – | – | – | – |
| | 1918 | – | – | – | – | – | 1 | 6* | – | – | – | – | – | 6 | 1 |
| | **TOTAL** | 1 | 4 | 3 | 4 | 2 | 2 | 6 | 2 | – | 3 | – | 3 | 12 | 18 |
| **Sloop/Destroyer/ Torpedo Boat** | 1914 | – | 5 | 1 | 1 | 1 | – | – | 1 | – | – | 1 | 5 | 3 | 12 |
| | 1915 | – | 4 | 3 | 1 | 4 | 11 | – | 1 | – | 1 | 6 | 6 | 13 | 24 |
| | 1916 | 10 | 4 | 3 | 1 | 4 | 10 | – | – | – | 2 | 6 | 1 | 23 | 18 |
| | 1917 | 5 | 3 | 10 | 1 | 16 | 12 | – | – | – | 2 | 5 | 1 | 36 | 19 |
| | 1918 | 1 | 2 | 7 | 1 | 4 | 24 | – | 9 | 1 | – | 13 | – | 26 | 36 |
| | **TOTAL** | 16 | 18 | 24 | 5 | 29 | 57 | – | 11 | 1 | 5 | 31 | 13 | 101 | 109 |

\* Sunk as blockships at Ostend and Zeebrugge.

**Table 6.9** Annual German U-boat Losses by Locality 1914-18

| | NORTH SEA ORKNEYS & SHETLANDS | ENGLISH CHANNEL & BELGIAN COAST | NORTH CHANNEL IRISH SEA & BRISTOL CHANNEL | NORTH ATLANTIC | SOUTH ATLANTIC (S. of Scily Isles) | BALTIC | MEDITER-RANEAN | BLACK SEA & BOSPHORUS | UNKNOWN | TOTAL |
|---|---|---|---|---|---|---|---|---|---|---|
| 1914 | 3 | 2 | – | – | – | – | – | – | – | 5 |
| 1915 | 10 | 2 | 1 | 1 | 2 | 1 | – | 1 | 1 | 19 |
| 1916 | 8 | 2 | 1 | 4 | – | 1 | 1 | 3 | 2 | 22 |
| 1917 | 13 | 13 | 4 | 25 | 5 | 1 | 2 | – | – | 63 |
| 1918 | 13 | 9 | 9 | 14 | 10† | – | 12 | – | 2 | 69 |
| **TOTAL** | 47 | 28 | 15 | 44 | 17 | 3 | 15 | 4 | 5 | 178 |

† Including one sunk off the N.American coast.

*Table 6.10* Annual German U-boat Losses by Cause 1914-18

| AGENT | 1914 | 1915 | 1916 | 1917 | 1918 | TOTAL |
|---|---|---|---|---|---|---|
| **Man-of-War** | | | | | | |
| Ram | 1 | 1 | – | – | 1 | **3** |
| **Patrol/Hunting** | | | | | | |
| Ram | 1 | – | – | 5 | 1 | **7** |
| Gunfire | – | 1 | 2 | – | 1 | **4** |
| Expl. Sweep | – | 1 | 1 | – | – | **2** |
| Depth Charge | – | – | 1 | 3 | 16 | **20** |
| Torpedo | – | 3 | 2 | 7 | 6 | **18** |
| Air | – | – | – | 1 | – | **1** |
| **Decoy Gunfire** | – | 4 | 2 | 6 | – | **12** |
| **Merchant Ship** | | | | | | |
| Ram | – | – | – | 2 | 3 | **5** |
| Gunfire | – | – | – | – | 1 | **1** |
| Explosion | – | – | – | 1 | – | **1** |
| **Escort** | | | | | | |
| Ram | – | – | – | 3 | 1 | **4** |
| Gunfire | – | – | – | – | 2 | **2** |
| Expl. Sweep | – | – | – | 1 | – | **1** |
| Depth Charge | – | – | – | 3 | 6 | **9** |
| **Mine** | 3 | 3 | 6 | 20 | 18 | **50** |
| **Accident** | – | 4 | 3 | 10 | 2 | **19** |
| **Other** | – | – | 1 | – | – | **1** |
| **Unknown** | – | 2 | 4 | 2 | 10 | **18** |
| **TOTAL** | **5** | **19** | **22** | **64** | **68** | **178** |

# PART III MERCHANT SHIPPING

*Table 6.11* **Monthly Totals of British, Allied and Neutral Merchant Shipping Lost Through Enemy Action 1914-18 (gross tonnage)***

\* Includes fishing vessels.

† British losses as percentage of total.

| | BRITISH | %† | ALLIED & NEUTRAL | TOTAL |
|---|---|---|---|---|
| **1914** | | | | |
| August | 44,692 | 61 | 18,075 | **72,767** |
| September | 89,251 | 90 | 9,127 | **98,378** |
| October | 78,088 | 89 | 9,829 | **87,917** |
| November | 9,348 | 48 | 10,065 | **19,413** |
| December | 26,815 | 61 | 17,382 | **44,197** |
| **TOTAL** | **248,194** | **79** | **64,478** | 312,672 |
| **1915** | | | | |
| January | 32,276 | 67 | 15,705 | **47,981** |
| February | 36,372 | 61 | 23,549 | **59,921** |
| March | 71,768 | 89 | 9,007 | **80,775** |
| April | 24,383 | 44 | 31,342 | **55,725** |
| May | 89,673 | 75 | 30,385 | **120,058** |
| June | 91,315 | 69 | 40,113 | **131,428** |
| July | 57,274 | 48 | 52,366 | **109,640** |
| August | 151,354 | 81 | 34,512 | **185,866** |
| September | 102,135 | 67 | 49,749 | **151,884** |
| October | 54,156 | 61 | 34,378 | **88,534** |
| November | 94,655 | 62 | 58,388 | **153,043** |
| December | 74,490 | 60 | 48,651 | **123,141** |
| **TOTAL** | **879,851** | **67** | **428,145** | **1,307,996** |
| **1916** | | | | |
| January | 62,645 | 77 | 18,614 | **81,259** |
| February | 75,928 | 65 | 41,619 | **117,547** |
| March | 99,696 | 60 | 67,401 | **167,097** |
| April | 141,409 | 74 | 50,258 | **191,667** |
| May | 64,722 | 50 | 64,453 | **129,175** |
| June | 36,976 | 34 | 71,879 | **108,855** |
| July | 85,228 | 72 | 32,987 | **118,215** |
| August | 45,026 | 28 | 117,718 | **162,744** |
| September | 109,263 | 47 | 121,197 | **230,460** |
| October | 177,386 | 50 | 176,274 | **353,660** |
| November | 170,409 | 55 | 141,099 | **311,508** |
| December | 182,728 | 51 | 172,411 | **355,139** |
| **TOTAL** | **1,251,416** | **54** | **1,075,910** | **2,327,326** |
| **1917** | | | | |
| January | 155,686 | 42 | 212,835 | **368,521** |
| February | 316,964 | 59 | 223,042 | **540,006** |
| March | 357,064 | 60 | 236,777 | **593,841** |
| April | 551,202 | 63 | 329,825 | **881,027** |
| May | 353,737 | 59 | 242,892 | **596,629** |

| | BRITISH | % | ALLIED & NEUTRAL | TOTAL |
|---|---|---|---|---|
| **1917 cont.** | | | | |
| June | 419,267 | 61 | 268,240 | **687,507** |
| July | 367,594 | 66 | 190,394 | **557,988** |
| August | 330,052 | 64 | 181,678 | **511,730** |
| September | 196,457 | 56 | 155,291 | **351,748** |
| October | 276,359 | 60 | 182,199 | **458,558** |
| November | 173,647 | 60 | 115,565 | **289,212** |
| December | 253,500 | 64 | 145,611 | **399,111** |
| **TOTAL** | **3,751,529** | **60** | **2,484,349** | **6,235,878** |
| **1918** | | | | |
| January | 180,348 | 59 | 126,310 | **306,658** |
| February | 227,582 | 71 | 91,375 | **318,957** |
| March | 199,751 | 58 | 142,846 | **342,597** |
| April | 215,784 | 77 | 62,935 | **278,719** |
| May | 192,938 | 65 | 102,582 | **295,520** |
| June | 163,629 | 64 | 91,958 | **255,587** |
| July | 166,004 | 56 | 130,963 | **296,967** |
| August | 147,257 | 52 | 136,558 | **283,815** |
| September | 137,001 | 73 | 50,880 | **187,881** |
| October | 59,229 | 50 | 59,330 | **118,559** |
| November | 10,220 | 58 | 7,462 | **17,682** |
| **TOTAL** | **1,699,743** | **64** | **967,199** | **2,666,942** |
| **GRAND TOTAL** | **7,830,733** | **61** | **5,020,081** | **12,850,814** |

**Table 6.12** Annual British and Aggregate Allied and Neutral Merchant Shipping Losses by Cause 1914-18 (gross tonnage)

* Losses to submarines as percentage of total losses.

| | | SURFACE SHIP etc. | SUBMARINE | %* | MINE | AIRCRAFT | TOTAL |
|---|---|---|---|---|---|---|---|
| U.K. | 1914 | 203,139 | 2,950 | 1 | 35,112 | – | 241,201 |
| | 1915 | 29,685 | 748,914 | 88 | 77,122 | – | 855,721 |
| | 1916 | 103,352 | 888,689 | 72 | 244,623 | 970 | 1,237,634 |
| | 1917 | 100,693 | 3,325,534 | 89 | 296,616 | 6,942 | 3,729,785 |
| | 1918 | 5,833 | 1,668,972 | 98 | 19,944 | – | 1,694,749 |
| | **TOTAL** | **442,702** | **6,635,059** | **86** | **673,417** | **7,912** | **7,759,090** |
| France | | 52,905 | 812,309 | 90 | 34,144 | – | 899,358 |
| Russia | | 5,041 | 160,960 | 88 | 17,082 | – | 183,083 |
| Italy | | 6,016 | 803,092 | 95 | 37,280 | – | 846,388 |
| Japan | | 6,557 | 108,648 | 90 | 4,971 | – | 120,176 |
| U.S.A. | | 8,428 | 364,200 | 92 | 24,431 | – | 397,059 |
| Belgium | | 6,752 | 70,129 | 82 | 8,877 | – | 85,758 |
| Portugal | | – | 94,946 | 100 | – | – | 94,946 |
| Rumania | | – | 3,688 | 93 | 285 | – | 3,973 |
| Greece | | 724 | 334,408 | 97 | 10,384 | – | 345,516 |
| Brazil | | – | 25,464 | 100 | – | – | 25,464 |
| Norway | | 15,172 | 1,043,077 | 88 | 122,067 | – | 1,180,316 |
| Sweden | | 8,185 | 142,493 | 71 | 50,598 | – | 201,276 |
| Denmark | | 4,834 | 201,394 | 83 | 37,479 | – | 243,707 |
| Holland | | 5,584 | 131,948 | 62 | 74,310 | 127 | 211,969 |
| Spain | | – | 152,387 | 90 | 16,104 | – | 168,491 |
| Argentina | | – | 4,275 | 100 | – | – | 4,275 |
| Peru | | – | 1,419 | 100 | – | – | 1,419 |
| Uruguay | | – | 6,027 | 100 | – | – | 6,027 |
| | **TOTAL** | **562,900** | **11,095,923** | **87** | **1,111,429** | **8,039** | **12,778,291** |

**Table 6.13** Aggregate Ships Lost in Allied Homeward and Outward Ocean and Short Sea Convoys 1917-18

† Tonnage of ships escorted safely.

‡ Ships lost to U-boats as percentage total sailings. Except Short Sea Convoys where it is expressed as a percentage of total ships lost.

| FROM | No. CONVOYS | No. SAILINGS | GROSS TONNAGE† | No. SHIPS LOST | No. LOST TO U-BOATS | %‡ |
|---|---|---|---|---|---|---|
| **HOMEWARD OCEAN** | | | | | | |
| Halifax | 80 | 867 | 9,241,785 | 4 | 3 | 0.34 |
| New York | 89 | 1,630 | 9,690,581 | 11 | 7 | 0.43 |
| Hampton Rds. | 78 | 1,609 | 7,572,804 | 13 | 13 | 0.81 |
| Rio | 22 | 307 | 1,466,097 | 2 | 2 | 0.65 |
| Bay | 20 | 347 | 1,768,015 | 5 | 4 | 1.15 |
| Sierra Leone | 56 | 424 | 2,928,020 | 3 | 2 | 0.47 |
| Dakar | 57 | 599 | 2,507,040 | 3 | 3 | 0.50 |
| Gibraltar | 119 | 1,750 | 5,516,483 | 18 | 16 | 0.91 |
| Sydney | 63 | 1,439 | 6,744,592 | 7 | 4 | 0.28 |
| **TOTAL** | **607** | **9,323** | **49,541,313** | **73** | **61** | **0.65** |
| **OUTWARD OCEAN** | | | | | | |
| Liverpool | 72 | 580 | 5,197,522 | 9 | 9 | 1.55 |
| Falmouth | 57 | 796 | 2,846,043 | 5 | 5 | 0.63 |
| Devonport | 136 | 1,721 | 10,057,339 | 6 | 6 | 0.35 |
| Milford | 113 | 2,652 | 9,961,655 | 10 | 8 | 0.30 |
| Queenstown | 29 | 209 | 954,503 | – | – | – |
| Lamlash | 85 | 954 | 5,169,290 | 9 | 8 | 0.84 |
| Channel | 10 | 93 | 777,459 | – | – | – |
| Med. Through | 12 | 103 | 616,364 | – | – | – |
| **TOTAL** | **527** | **7,334** | **36,832,412** | **45** | **41** | **0.56** |

*Table 6.13* Aggregate Ships Lost in Allied Homeward and Outward Ocean and Short Sea Convoys 1917-18 continued

| FROM | No. CONVOYS | No. SAILINGS | GROSS TONNAGE | No. SHIPS LOST | No. LOST TO U-BOATS | % |
|---|---|---|---|---|---|---|
| **SHORT SEA** | | | | | | |
| Coastal | ? | 3,304 | ? | 2 | ? | 0.06 |
| E.Coast | ? | 19,756 | ? | 69 | ? | 0.35 |
| French Coal | ? | 39,352 | ? | 53 | ? | 0.13 |
| Dutch | ? | 1,861 | ? | 6 | ? | 0.32 |
| Scandinavian | ? | 7,653 | ? | 55 | ? | 0.72 |
| Mediterranean | ? | 10,464 | ? | 127 | ? | 1.21 |
| **TOTAL** | ? | **82,390** | ? | **312** | ? | **0.38** |

*Table 6.14* Annual U-boat Successes against Merchant Shipping by Regional Flotilla Group 1914-18 (gross tonnage)*

| | HIGH SEAS FLEETS | | FLANDERS FLOTILLA | | MEDITERRANEAN | | BOSPHORUS/ BLACK SEA | | BALTIC | | U-CRUISERS | | TOTAL | |
|---|---|---|---|---|---|---|---|---|---|---|---|---|---|---|
| | No. | Tonnage | No. | Tonnage | No. | Tonnage | No. | Tonnage | No. | Tonnage | No. | Tonnage | No. | Tonnage |
| 1914 | 3 | 2,950 | – | – | – | – | – | – | – | – | – | – | 3 | 2,950 |
| 1915 | 390 | 700,782 | 131 | 90,925 | 102 | 350,853 | 9 | 44,520 | 4 | 5,254 | – | – | 636 | 1,191,704 |
| 1916 | 350 | 508,745 | 512 | 604,151 | 415 | 1,045,058 | 11 | 20,777 | 21 | 7,731 | – | – | 1,309 | 2,186,462 |
| 1917 | ? | 2,895,983 | ? | 1,607,389 | ? | 1,514,050 | ? | 18,966 | ? | 13,510 | ? | 98,721 | ? | 6,149,070 |
| 1918 | 435 | 1,044,822 | 327 | 558,760 | 325 | 761,060 | 57 | 32,830 | – | – | 161 | 356,680 | 1,305 | 2,754,152 |
| TOTAL | ? | 5,153,282 | ? | 2,860,595 | ? | 3,671,021† | ? | 117,093 | ? | 26,495 | ? | 455,401 | ? | 12,284,338 |

*Table 6.15* German and Austro-Hungarian Merchant Shipping Rendered Unavailable from all Causes to 31/1/15 (gross tonnage)‡

| | GERMANY | AUSTRIA-HUNGARY | TOTAL |
|---|---|---|---|
| **Sunk & Captured at Sea** | 286,200◊ | 22,300 | **308,500** |
| **Seized in Allied Ports** | 103,600 | 89,300 | **192,900** |
| **Blockaded in Belgian & Turkish Ports** | 172,600 | 42,900 | **215,500** |
| **Sheltering in Neutral Ports•** | 2,307,500 | 355,500 | **2,663,000** |
| **TOTALΔ** | **2,869,900** | **510,000** | **3,379,900** |

*Table 6.16* Merchant Seamen Lost on Ships Sailing under British Flag 1914-18 **

| 1914 | 1915 | 1916 | 1917 | 1918 | TOTAL |
|---|---|---|---|---|---|
| 69 | 2,470 | 1,177 | 6,408 | 4,163 | **14,287††** |

\* These are German figures and include vessels sunk by mines laid by U-boats.

† In addition, Austrian U-boats sank 171,154 tons of merchant shipping in the Mediterranean and Adriatic, in 1917 and 1918.

** Figures for Allied & Neutral lives lost are not available. However, an equivalent pro-rata figure, based on lives lost per ton sunk, would be 9,375.

†† Plus 434 lost on fishing boats sunk by enemy action.

‡ The only figures we have come across for Turkish merchant shipping losses give a total of 23 steamers and 122 sailing ships sunk in the Black Sea by Russian submarines.

◊ Once war was declared ships in German ports mainly remained there for the duration. Those that did venture forth were restricted to the Baltic, being mainly involved in coastal traffic and the vital Swedish iron-ore trade.

• In July 1914, all German and Austrian merchant ships that could took to neutral ports, hoping to sit out Germany's swift victory. In the event they remained in these ports either until the Armistice or until seized by those countries that later sided with the Allies. The most important blocks of such shipping were located in the Mediterranean (250,000 tons); Spain and Portugal (380,000 tons); Holland (160,000 tons); United States (600,000 tons) and Brazil (233,000 tons).

Δ Totals for ships sunk and captured during the rest of the war remain elusive. The most reliable source gives a total of 300,000 tons of German shipping sunk (including mishap) and an all-in total of 360,000 tons of Austro-Hungarian shipping sunk, captured and transferred to foreign flag. (Another source gives a total of 92,000 gross tons of German shipping sunk in the Baltic by Russian mines and submarines).

# PART IV AIR FORCES

The enormous growth of the air forces in the First World War rather outstripped their book-keeping resources and figures for aircraft losses are elusive as well as being extremely unreliable even when they are presented. The following table, therefore, is riddled with question-marks and even the figures given should be treated with the utmost caution.

### *Table 6.17* Aggregate Aircraft and Aircrew Losses for the Major Powers 1914-18

* The first figure given is that for aircrew killed. The figure in brackets gives the total killed, wounded, missing and p.o.w.

† One estimate offers a figure of c.4,000.

‡ One estimate offers a figure of c.3,000.

◊ German claimed losses.

• Another set of figures from the Italian official history, giving casualty figures for 78 of the 120 or so squadrons that saw combat, offers total aircraft losses of 466, of which 283 were in combat, and personnel losses of 375.

Δ For a probably inflated estimate of Austro-Hungarian losses see Russian and Italian figures in the Claims column.

|  | TOTAL AIRCRAFT LOST | LOST IN COMBAT | AIRCREW LOST IN COMBAT* | ENEMY AIRCRAFT CLAIMED |
|---|---|---|---|---|
| U.K. | 35,970 | ?† | 6,170 (16,620) | – |
| France | 52,640 | ?‡ | 2,870 (7,250) | – |
| Russia | ? | 358◊ | ? | 200 |
| Italy• | c.900 | c.300 | ? | 600+ |
| U.S.A. | ? | 289 | 235 (513) | 781 |
| Germany | 27,640 | 3,130 | 5,950 (16,050) | – |
| Austria-HungaryΔ | ? | ? | ? | – |
| Turkey | ? | ? | ? | 28 |

### *Table 6.18* Annual Number Casualties Inflicted in German Zeppelin and Bomber Raids on England 1914-18

|  | AIRCRAFT LOST | CIVILIAN CASUALTIES KILLED | CIVILIAN CASUALTIES INJURED |
|---|---|---|---|
| **Zeppelin Raids** |  |  |  |
| 1914 | – | 4 | 16 |
| 1915 | – | 204 | 505 |
| 1916 | 9 | 293 | 691 |
| 1917 | 6 | 40 | 75 |
| 1918 | 1 | 16 | 59 |
| **TOTAL** | **16** | **557** | **1,346** |
| **Aircraft Raids (Day)** |  |  |  |
| 1914 | – | – | – |
| 1915 | – | 2 | 6 |
| 1916 | – | 19 | 61 |
| 1917 | 32 | 337 | 774 |
| 1918 | – | – | – |
| **TOTAL** | **32** | **358** | **841** |
| **A/craft Raids (Night)** |  |  |  |
| 1914 | – | – | – |
| 1915 | – | – | – |
| 1916 | – | 2 | 8 |
| 1917 | 13 | 279 | 570 |
| 1918 | 7 | 172 | 430 |
| **TOTAL** | **20** | **453** | **1,008** |
| **GRAND TOTAL** | **68** | **1,368** | **3,195** |

### *Table 6.19* Losses in Other 'Strategic' Bombing Offensives 1915-18

In Franco-British bombing raids on Germany, from 1915-18, 746 Germans were killed and 1,843 wounded. British squadrons lost 348 men killed and missing and 91 wounded and injured. The British also lost 458 aircraft, only 138 of them to enemy action.

During the German offensive against Paris, in January-September 1918, 257 airplanes took off in 17 raids which killed 303 people and injured 533. The Germans lost 11 planes.

During 42 Austrian bomber raids on Venice, from 1915-18, over 250 sorties dropped a little over 1,000 bombs which killed over 50 people and injured about 90.

# SECTION 7

# PRODUCTION

# PART I RAW MATERIALS

In the following tables aggregate figures are given for Allied and Central Powers' production. Individual countries' output are only included for those periods when they were formally at war and industrial production was specifically geared to the war-effort. But it should be borne in mind that even countries not at war were able to export raw materials and finished goods to the belligerents. Such foreign trade was of particular value to the Allies whilst the Central Powers were seriously affected by the swiftly imposed economic blockade.

### Table 7.1 Annual Production of Coal by Selected Countries 1913-18 (millions of metric tons)

|  | U.K. | FRANCE | RUSSIA | ITALY | RUMANIA | U.S.A. | TOTAL* | BELGIUM (occupied) | GERMANY | AUSTRIA-HUNGARY† | TURKEY | BULGARIA | TOTAL |
|---|---|---|---|---|---|---|---|---|---|---|---|---|---|
| 1913 | 292.0 | 40.8 | 29.0 | 0.7 | 0.2 | 478.4 | – | (22.8) | 277.3 | 43.8 | 0.8 | 0.4 | – |
| 1914 | 269.9 | 27.5 | 31.9 | 0.8 | 0.2 | 422.7 | **329.3** | 16.7 | 245.3 | 39.2 | 0.7 | 0.4 | **310.3** |
| 1915 | 257.3 | 19.5 | 31.4 | 0.9 | 0.3 | 442.6 | **309.1** | 14.2 | 234.8 | 38.1 | 0.4 | 0.5 | **288.0** |
| 1916 | 260.5 | 21.3 | 34.5 | 1.3 | 0.3 | 502.5 | **317.6** | 16.8 | 253.3 | 40.8 | 0.4 | 0.6 | **311.9** |
| 1917 | 252.5 | 28.9 | 31.3 | 1.7 | ? | 551.7 | **866.1** | 14.9 | 263.2 | 39.4 | 0.1 | 0.8 | **318.4** |
| 1918 | 231.4 | 26.3 | 13.1 | 2.1 | ? | 579.4 | **839.2** | 13.9 | 258.6 | 17.7 | 0.2 | 0.7 | **291.1** |

*\* Rumania omitted; Includes Italy from 1915; U.S.A. 1917 and 1918 only; Russia to 1917 only*

*† Does not include imports, which some figures for Austria-Hungary seem to do.*

### Table 7.2 Annual Production of Crude Petroleum by Selected Countries 1913-18 (millions of metric tons)

|  | RUSSIA | PERSIA | U.S.A. | RUMANIA | TOTAL ‡ | GERMANY | AUSTRIA-HUNGARY | TOTAL |
|---|---|---|---|---|---|---|---|---|
| 1913 | 9.2 | 0.3 | 32.8 | 1.8 | – | 0.1 | 1.1 | – |
| 1914 | 9.2 | 0.5 | 35.1 | 1.8 | **11.5** | 0.1 | 0.7 | **0.8** |
| 1915 | 9.4 | 0.5 | 37.1 | 1.6 | **11.5** | 0.1 | 0.6 | **0.7** |
| 1916 | 10.0 | 0.6 | 39.7 | 0.9 | **11.5** | 0.1 | ? | **?** |
| 1917 | 8.8 | 1.0 | 44.3 | 0.7 | **54.8** | 0.1 | ? | **?** |
| 1918 | 4.1 | 1.2 | 47.0 | 10.0 | **62.3** | 0.1 | ? | **?** |

*‡ Excludes Rumania. Includes U.S.A. 1917 and 1918 only.*

*◊ Includes U.S.A. 1917 and 1918 only.*

### Table 7.3 Annual Production of Iron Ore by Selected Countries 1913-18 (millions of metric tons)

|  | U.K. | FRANCE | RUSSIA | ITALY | U.S.A. | TOTAL◊ | LUX. | SWEDEN• | GERMANY | AUSTRIA-Δ HUNGARY | TOTAL** |
|---|---|---|---|---|---|---|---|---|---|---|---|
| 1913 | 16.3 | 21.9 | 9.2 | 0.6 | 62.0 | – | (7.3) | 7.5 | 28.6 | 3.3 | – |
| 1914 | 15.1 | 11.3 | 7.7 | 0.7 | 41.4 | **34.8** | 4.9 | 6.6 | 20.5 | 2.5 | **31.9** |
| 1915 | 14.5 | 0.6 | 5.9 | 0.7 | 55.5 | **30.7** | 6.1 | 6.9 | 17.7 | 2.9 | **35.7** |
| 1916 | 13.7 | 1.7 | 7.2 | 0.9 | 75.2 | **23.5** | 6.9 | 7.0 | 21.3 | 3.9 | **39.1** |
| 1917 | 15.1 | 2.0 | 5.3 | 1.0 | 75.3 | **98.7** | 4.5 | 6.2 | 22.5 | 2.8 | **36.0** |
| 1918 | 14.8 | 1.7 | 0.6 | 0.7 | 69.7 | **87.5** | 3.1 | 6.6 | 18.4 | ? | **?** |

*• Neutral but major exporter to Germany. This ore was a small proportion of German production but was of much better quality than that produced at home and by 1916, indeed, was the only ore suitable for the production of high-grade military steel. (This was because Germany had by then run out of the manganese needed to convert her phosphorous-heavy iron ore into suitable steel.)*

*Δ Austria only.*

*\*\* Includes 4m. tons Swedish ore.*

### Table 7.4 Annual Production of Crude Steel by Selected Countries 1913-18 (millions of metric tons)

|  | U.K. | FRANCE | RUSSIA | ITALY | U.S.A. | TOTAL†† | BELGIUM | LUX. | GERMANY | AUSTRIA-HUNGARY | TOTAL |
|---|---|---|---|---|---|---|---|---|---|---|---|
| 1913 | 7.8 | 4.7 | 4.2 | 0.9 | ? | – | 2.5 | 1.3 | 17.6 | 2.6 | – |
| 1914 | 8.0 | 2.8 | 4.5 | 0.9 | 2.6 | **16.2** | 1.4 | 1.1 | 13.8 | 2.2 | **18.5** |
| 1915 | 8.7 | 1.1 | 4.1 | 0.9 | 32.2 | **14.8** | 1.0 | 1.0 | 12.3 | 2.7 | **17.0** |
| 1916 | 9.1 | 1.8 | 4.3 | 1.0 | 42.8 | **16.2** | 1.0 | 1.3 | 14.9 | 3.6 | **20.8** |
| 1917 | 9.9 | 2.0 | 3.1 | 1.3 | 45.1 | **61.4** | 0.1 | 1.1 | 15.5 | 3.1 | **19.8** |
| 1918 | 9.7 | 1.8 | 0.4 | 1.3 | 44.5 | **57.3** | 0.1 | 0.9 | 14.1 | 1.9 | **17.0** |

*†† Includes U.S.A. 1917 and 1918 only. Russia excluded 1918. Italy included from 1915.*

**Table 7.5** Annual Electric Energy Production in Selected Countries 1913-18 (gigawatt hours)

|      | U.K. | FRANCE | RUSSIA | ITALY | GERMANY | AUSTRIA-HUNGARY |
|------|------|--------|--------|-------|---------|-----------------|
| 1913 | 2.5  | 1.8    | 2.4    | 2.0   | 8.0     | ?               |
| 1914 | 3.0  | 2.1    | ?      | 2.2   | 8.8     | ?               |
| 1915 | 3.5  | 1.9    | ?      | 2.6   | 9.8     | ?               |
| 1916 | 4.1  | 2.2    | 2.6    | 2.9   | 11.0    | ?               |
| 1917 | 4.7  | 2.4    | ?      | 3.4   | 12.0    | ?               |
| 1918 | 4.9  | 2.7    | ?      | 4.0   | 13.0    | ?               |

**Table 7.6** Annual Railway Freight Traffic in Selected Countries 1913-18 (million metric tons) and Railway Line Open and Rolling Stock Available 1914

|      | U.K. | FRANCE | RUSSIA | ITALY | RUMANIA | SERBIA | GERMANY | AUSTRIA-* HUNGARY | BULGARIA | TURKEY |
|------|------|--------|--------|-------|---------|--------|---------|-------------------|----------|--------|
| 1913 | 570.5 | 136.0 | 132 | 41.4 | ? | ? | 676.6 | 160.5† | 1.9 | ? |
| 1914 | ? | 88.2 | 123 | 37.7 | 5.6 | ? | 528.9 | ? | 2.5 | ? |
| 1915 | ? | 71.5 | 126 | 38.3 | 5.9 | ? | 367.6 | 67.9 | 2.0 | ? |
| 1916 | ? | 79.7 | 147 | 40.5 | 6.5 | ? | 415.6 | 78.2 | 2.8 | ? |
| 1917 | ? | 83.7 | 115 | 38.6 | 6.0 | ? | ? | 74.8 | 3.5 | ? |
| 1918 | ? | 64.7 | 37 | 39.0 | 5.5 | ? | 387.0 | 74.5 | 2.9 | ? |
| **Length of Railway Line Open 1914 (km.) ‡** | | | | | | | | | | |
| | 32,623 | 37,400 | 62,300 | 19,125 | 3,588 | 1,598 | 61,749 | 22,981 | 2,124 | 6,250 |
| | 10.4 | 6.9 | 0.28 | 6.7 | 2.6 | 1.8 | 11.7 | 3.9 | 1.9 | 0.35 |
| **Number Locomotives 1914** | | | | | | | | | | |
| | 23,000 | 14,500 | 17,200 | 6,000 | ? | ? | 28,000 | 12,000 | ? | 280 |
| **Number Wagons and Carriages 1914** | | | | | | | | | | |
| | 1,461,000 | 397,000 | 390,000 | 124,000 | ? | ? | 660,000 | 298,000 | ? | 5,200 |

\* For 1915-18 figures are for Hungary only. In the five years before the war Hungarian freight traffic averaged just over 50% of the Austro-Hungarian total.

† In 1912.

‡ Lower figure indicates km. of railway per 100 sq.km. national territory.

# PART II MUNITIONS AND SHIPPING

It is extremely frustrating for the authors that the following sub-section finds the first two tables seriously weakened by the absence of any comprehensive figures for German artillery and machine-gun production. Despite consulting official histories, inter-war German monographs and modern academic overviews, we have been unable to find any sets of figures that offer more than fragmentary annual and monthly totals. (As stated in the foreword, we would be delighted to hear from anyone who has proved more assiduous and can fill in any or all of the blanks in the German columns below.)

**Table 7.7** Annual Artillery Production by the Major Belligerents 1914-18 (units)

|       | U.K.   | FRANCE  | RUSSIA  | ITALY  | U.S.A. | GERMANY | AUSTRIA-HUNGARY |
|-------|--------|---------|---------|--------|--------|---------|-----------------|
| 1914  | 91     | ?       | 355     | ?      | –      | } 3,500 | 219             |
| 1915  | 3,226  | ?       | 2,065   | ?      | –      |         | 1,463           |
| 1916  | 4,551  | ?       | 8,284*  | ?      | –      | ?       | 3,650           |
| 1917  | 6,483  | ?       | 4,302   | ?      | –      | c.12,000| 4,191           |
| 1918  | 10,680 | ?       | ?       | ?      | 1,826  | ?       | 2,038           |
| TOTAL | 25,031 | 24,022† | 15,006‡ | 11,789 | 1,826◊ | ?       | 11,561          |

**Table 7.8** Annual Machine Gun Production by the Major Belligerents 1914-18 (units)

|       | U.K.    | FRANCE   | RUSSIA | ITALY  | U.S.A.   | GERMANY  | AUSTRIA-HUNGARY |
|-------|---------|----------|--------|--------|----------|----------|-----------------|
| 1914  | 274     | ?        | 833    | ?      | –        | c.1,000  | 1,200           |
| 1915  | 6,064   | ?        | 4,251  | 300    | –        | 6,100    | 3,700           |
| 1916  | 33,200  | ?        | 11,072 | ?      | –        | ?        | 6,300           |
| 1917  | 79,438  | ?        | 11,320 | ?      | –        | ?        | 15,500          |
| 1918  | 120,864 | ?        | ?      | 14,400 | 226,557  | ?        | 12,200          |
| TOTAL | 239,840•| 312,000∆ | 26,634 | 31,030 | 226,557**| ?        | 38,900          |

**Table 7.9** Annual Tank Production by the Major Belligerents 1914-18 (units)

|       | U.K.    | FRANCE  | RUSSIA | ITALY | U.S.A. | GERMANY | AUSTRIA-HUNGARY |
|-------|---------|---------|--------|-------|--------|---------|-----------------|
| 1914  | –       | –       | –      | –     | –      | –       | –               |
| 1915  | –       | –       | –      | –     | –      | –       | –               |
| 1916  | 150     | ?       | –      | –     | –      | –       | –               |
| 1917  | 1,277   | ?       | –      | –     | –      | } 20    | –               |
| 1918  | 1,391   | ?       | –      | 6     | 64     |         | –               |
| TOTAL | 2,818†† | 5,300‡‡ | –      | 6     | 64     | 20      | –               |

**Table 7.10** Annual Production of Airframes and Aircraft Engines by the Major Belligerents 1914-18 (units)

|       | U.K. A/f. | U.K. E. | FRANCE A/f. | FRANCE E. | RUSSIA† A/f. | RUSSIA† E. | ITALY A/f. | ITALY E. | U.S.A. A/f. | U.S.A. E. | GERMANY• A/f. | GERMANY• E. | AUSTRIA-HUNGARY A/f.** | AUSTRIA-HUNGARY E.** |
|-------|-----------|---------|-------------|-----------|--------------|------------|------------|----------|-------------|-----------|---------------|-------------|-----------|-----------|
| 1914  | ?         | ?       | 541         | 860       | c.170        | c.25       | ?          | ?        | –           | –         | 1,348 / 694   | 848 / ?     | 64        | 72        |
| 1915  | 1,680     | 1,721   | 4,489       | 7,086     | 722          | ?          | 382        | 606      | –           | –         | 4,532 / 2,950 | 5,037 / 6,007∆ | 281    | 440       |
| 1916  | 5,716     | 5,363   | 7,549       | 16,785    | 1,384        | 1,398      | 1,255      | ?        | –           | –         | 8,182 / 7,112 | 7,822 / 7,823 | 732     | 854       |
| 1917  | 14,382    | 11,763  | 14,915      | 23,092    | ?            | 450        | 3,861      | 6,276    | –           | 31        | 19,746 / 13,997 | 11,200 / 12,029 | 1,272 | 1,230     |
| 1918  | 32,536    | 22,088  | 24,652      | 44,563    | ?            | ?          | 6,488      | 14,840   | 4,089       | 16,294    | 14,123 / 20,971 | 15,542 / 15,153 | 1,989 | 1,750     |
| TOTAL | 54,314    | 40,935* | 52,146      | 92,386    | ?            | ?          | 11,986     | ?        | 4,089‡      | 16,325◊   | 47,931 / 45,704 | 40,449 / 41,012 | 4,338 | 4,346     |

### Table 7.11 Naval Shipbuilding by the Major Belligerent Powers 1914-18

| | U.K. | FRANCE | RUSSIA | ITALY | JAPAN | U.S.A. | GERMANY | AUSTRIA-HUNGARY |
|---|---|---|---|---|---|---|---|---|
| **Dreadnought** | 13 | 3 | 7 | 3 | 4 | 6 | 6 | 1 |
| **Battle Cruiser** | 5 | – | – | – | 2 | – | 5 | – |
| **Cruiser** | – | – | – | 2 | – | – | – | – |
| **Light Cruiser** | 54 | – | – | – | – | – | 14 | 3 |
| **Monitor** | 39 | – | – | 10 | – | – | – | – |
| **Aircraft Carrier*** | 16 | 4 | 7 | 1 | – | – | – | – |
| **Destroyer** | 329 | 6 | 36 | 28 | 38 | 77 | 107 | 5 |
| **Torpedo Boat** | – | 7 | – | 32 | – | – | 92 | 21 |
| **Sloop** | 134 | 45 | – | – | – | – | – | – |
| **Minelayer** | – | – | 11 | – | 11 | – | – | – |
| **Minesweeper** | 156 | 52 | 8 | 37 | – | 42 | 148 | – |
| **Submarine** | 98 | 25 | 40 | 46 | 2 | 55 | 346 | 17 |

\* Mostly converted merchantmen.

### Table 7.12 Monthly Total German U-Boats Commissioned 1914-18

| MONTH | | No. COMM. | MONTH | | No. COMM. | MONTH | | No. COMM. | MONTH | | No. COMM. |
|---|---|---|---|---|---|---|---|---|---|---|---|
| **1914** | Aug | 3 | | Oct | 2 | | Dec | 12 | **1918** | Jan | 3 |
| | Sept | 3 | | Nov | 2 | | TOTAL | 108 | | Feb | 6 |
| | Oct | 1 | | Dec | 6 | **1917** | Jan | 10 | | March | 9 |
| | Nov | 2 | | TOTAL | 52 | | Feb | 4 | | April | 9 |
| | Dec | 2 | **1916** | Jan | 3 | | March | 5 | | May | 11 |
| | TOTAL | 11 | | Feb | 5 | | April | 5 | | June | 9 |
| **1915** | Jan | 2 | | March | 9 | | May | 5 | | July | 9 |
| | Feb | 4 | | April | 8 | | June | 8 | | Aug | 8 |
| | March | 7 | | May | 9 | | July | 11 | | Sept | 10 |
| | April | 6 | | June | 8 | | Aug | 20 | | Oct | 12 |
| | May | 8 | | July | 9 | | Sept | 8 | | Nov | 2 |
| | June | 6 | | Aug | 10 | | Oct | 13 | | TOTAL | 88 |
| | July | 5 | | Sept | 10 | | Nov | 5 | | GRAND TOTAL | 359 |
| | Aug | 2 | | Oct | 12 | | Dec | 6 | | | |
| | Sept | 2 | | Nov | 13 | | TOTAL | 100 | | | |

### Table 7.13 Annual Production Merchant Shipping by Selected Countries 1913-18 (millions of gross tons launched)

| | U.K. | FRANCE | ITALY | JAPAN | U.S.A. | GERMANY | HOLLAND | WORLD† |
|---|---|---|---|---|---|---|---|---|
| **1913** | 1.93 | 0.18 | .5 | 0.06 | 0.23 | 0.46 | 0.10 | 3.26 |
| **1914** | 1.68 | 0.11 | 0.04 | 0.09 | 0.16 | 0.39 | 0.12 | 2.79 |
| **1915** | 0.65 | 0.03 | 0.02 | 0.05 | 0.16 | ? | 0.11 | 1.17 |
| **1916** | 0.61 | 0.04 | 0.06 | 0.15 | 0.38 | ? | 0.18 | 1.56 |
| **1917** | 1.16 | 0.02 | 0.04 | 0.35 | 0.82 | ? | 0.15 | 2.73 |
| **1918** | 1.35 | 0.01 | 0.06 | 0.49 | 2.60 | ? | 0.07 | 4.97 |
| **TOTAL** | 5.45 | 0.21 | 0.22 | 1.13 | 4.12 | ? | 0.63 | 13.22 |

† Countries listed plus rest of world.

# SECTION 8

# HARDWARE

In this section will be found details about the weaponry of the First World War. However, it has been necessary to limit individual entries to only the most essential information about a particular weapon. It should be noted therefore that

— Only the most widely used weapons are listed and there is little mention of the numerous failures and eccentricities that regularly cluttered up the production lines.
— Details about weapons are limited to their combat performance and to the number produced. Supplementary details, notably size specifications and external appearance, must be sought in the more compendious, specialised works listed in the Bibliography.

### COMBAT AIRCRAFT
Several additional points should be borne in mind here:

— Stated performance figures are usually the maximum in ideal conditions. In actual operations the infinite permutations of weight of fuel carried, weight of payload, height flown, atmospheric conditions, general climate, mechanical backup and quality of manufacture would have a marked effect on airplane performance. (With regard to payload it is frustrating to note that very few of the sources used indicate whether a bomber's performance is with payload or without.)
— Each entry gives the details for an airplane fitted with a particular engine, the horsepower of which is given in the second column. Most airplanes that went into mass production utilised various engine types, and precise performance details usually varied slightly from type to type. Wherever possible this listing shows the most common engine type though occasionally two equally prolific types are both shown. However, production and unit allocation figures normally refer to all aircraft of a particular type, regardless of engine.
— Disagreements on the capabilities and performance of First World War airplanes are multifarious and often encompass strikingly divergent figures. Often these differences simply cannot be reconciled and we have been obliged to rely on what seems to be the most reliable source.
— It should be borne in mind that many airplanes produced in large numbers in the first three years of the war were used as trainers long after they had become obsolete for combat.

**Table 8.1 Combat Aircraft**

**Fighters ***

| TYPE | H.P. | DATE IN SERVICE | SPEED (km./hr. at m.) | DURATION (hr.) RANGE (k.) | CEILING (m.) | RATE OF CLIMB (min./sec. to m.) | ARMAMENT | NUMBER PRODUCED | UNITS EQUIPPED† |
|---|---|---|---|---|---|---|---|---|---|
| **AUSTRIA-HUNGARY** | | | | | | | | | |
| Aviatik (Berg) D.I ‡ | 200 | 2/17 | 185 at sea level | 2.5 | 6,200 | 11/15 to 4,000 | 2 x m.g. | 615 accepted | ? |
| Hansa-Brandenburg D.I ‡ | 160 | 9/16 | 187 at sea level | 2.5 | 5,000 | ? | 1 x m.g. | 70 accepted | ? |
| Phönix D.I/II/III | 200 | late 1917 | 180 at sea level | 3 | 5,000 | ? | 2 x m.g. | 213 accepted | ? |
| **AUSTRALIA** | Had no indigenous aircraft industry and its small air force used exclusively British types. The two fighter squadrons flew Royal Aircraft Factory S.E.5s and Sopwith Snipes (latter not listed). | | | | | | | | |
| **BELGIUM** | Belgian fighter squadrons employed the whole gamut of Nieuport and SPAD models as well as Hanriot HD.Is (not listed), Sopwith Camels and a few Pups. | | | | | | | | |
| **BULGARIA** | Used mainly obsolete German and Austro-Hungarian types. | | | | | | | | |
| **CANADA** | No Canadian squadrons fought in the war. A fighter squadron in training in November 1918 was equipped with Royal Aircraft Factory S.E.5s. | | | | | | | | |
| **FRANCE** | | | | | | | | | |
| Caudron R.11 (3-seat long-range escort) | 2 x 215 | 2/18 | 183 at 2,000 178 at 3,000 164 at 5,000 | 3 600 | 6,000 | 8/10 to 2,000 14/30 to 3,000 39 to 5,000 | 5 x m.g. | 370 | 6 |
| Morane-Saulnier AI | 150 | 2/18 | 220 at 2,000 216 at 3,000 201 at 5,000 | 1.75 | ? | 4/25 to 2,000 7/25 to 3,000 15/50 to 5,000 | 1 or 2 x m.g. | 1,100 | 3 |
| Nieuport 11 | 80 | 1/16 | 162 at 2,000 | 2.5 | 5,000 | 8/50 to 2,000 15 to 3,000 | 1 x m.g. | ? | 23 |
| Nieuport 17 | 110 | 9/16 | 160 at 2,000 154 at 3,000 137 at 4,000 | 1.7 | 5,300 | 6/50 to 2,000 11/30 to 3,000 18/5 to 4,000 | 1 to 3 x m.g. | ? | 31 |

* All planes are single-engined, single-seater biplanes unless otherwise stated.

† British squadrons, French *escadrilles*, German *Fliegerabteilungen* or *Staffeln*, Italian *squadriglie*, Austro-Hungarian *Fliegerkompagnien*. Unless otherwise stated figures refer only to the air force of the home nation. (It should be borne in mind that during the first two to three years of the war few units were wholly equipped with one type).

‡ German designs but all produced in Austria-Hungary.

**Fighters (continued)**

| TYPE | H.P. | DATE IN SERVICE | SPEED (km./hr. at m.) | DURATION (hr.) RANGE (k.) | CEILING (m.) | RATE OF CLIMB (min./sec. to m.) | ARMAMENT | NUMBER PRODUCED | UNITS EQUIPPED |
|---|---|---|---|---|---|---|---|---|---|
| **FRANCE continued** | | | | | | | | | |
| Nieuport 24 | 130 | 6/17 | 171 at 2,000<br>169 at 3,000<br>163 at 4,000 | 2.25 | 6,900 | 5/40 to 2,000<br>9/25 to 3,000<br>21/30 to 5,000 | 1 or 2 x m.g. | ? | 72 |
| Nieuport 27 | 130 | 1/18 | 170 at 2,000<br>167 at 3,000<br>166 at 4,000 | 2.25<br>250 | 6,850 | 5/40 to 2,000<br>9/25 to 3,000<br>21/30 to 5,000 | 1 or 2 x m.g. | ? | 44 |
| SPAD* SA.2 (2-seat) | 110 | 9/15 | 140 at sea level | 3 | 4,000 | 12/30 to 2,000<br>23/30 to 3,000 | 1 x m.g. | 52 for French A.F. | ? |
| SPAD 7 | 150 | 3/17 | 187 at 2,000<br>180 at 3,000<br>174 at 4,000 | 2.7<br>400 | 5,500 | 6/40 to 2,000<br>11/20 to 3,000 | (20kg. bombs)<br>1 x m.g. | 3,500 | 65 |
| SPAD 13 | 200 | 4/18 | 208 at 2,000<br>205 at 3,000<br>190 at 5,000 | 2 | 6,800 | 5/17 to 2,000<br>8/45 to 3,000<br>20/10 to 5,000 | 2 x m.g. | 8,472 in France | 90 |
| **GERMANY** | | | | | | | | | |
| Albatros D I/II | 160 | 9/16 | 175 at sea level | 1.5 | 5,200 | 5 to 1,000 | 2 x m.g. | c.400 | ? |
| Albatros D III | 175 | 2/17 | 175 at 1,000 | 2 | 5,500 | 4 to 1,000 | 2 x m.g. | ? | 43 |
| Albatros D V/Va | 180 | 5/17 | 187 at 1,000 | 2 | 5,700 | 4 to 1,000 | 2 x m.g. | ? | 42 |
| Fokker E III (monoplane) | 100 | 2/16 | 140 at sea level | 1.5 | 3,500 | 5 to 1,000<br>30 to 3,000 | 1 x m.g. | 140 | to individual pilots |
| Fokker Dr I (triplane) | 110 | 8/17 | 165 at 4,000 | 1.5 | 6,100 | 2/55 to 1,000 | 2 x m.g. | 320 | 43 (most partial only) |
| Fokker DVII | 160 | 4/18 | 186 at 1,000<br>167 at 4,000<br>153 at 5,000 | 1.5 | 5,500 | 4/15 to 1,000<br>18/50 to 3,000<br>38/30 to 5,000 | 2 x m.g. | } 412 delivered | } 44 |
| | 185 | ?/18 | 186.5 at 1,000<br>182.5 at 2,000 | 1.5 | 7,000 | 3/50 to 1,000<br>31/30 to 5,000 | 2 x m.g. | | |
| L.F.G. D II/IIa † | 160 | 3/17 | 180 at sea level | 2 | 5,000 | 21 to 5,000 | 2 x m.g. | c. 300 | 32 |
| Pfalz E II (monoplane) | 100 | 1915 | 150 at sea level | 2 | ? | 2/45 to 800<br>9/45 to 2,000 | 1 x m.g. | ? | ? |
| PfalzD III/IIIa | 180 | 9/17 | 102 at 3,000<br>92 at 4,500 | 2.5 | 5,200 | 3/15 to 1,000<br>11/45 to 3,000<br>41/20 to 4,500 | 2 x m.g. | c. 900 | 33 |
| **GREECE** | The Greek Air Force used mainly French types throughout the war, the main fighters being Nieuport 24s and SPAD 7s and 13s. | | | | | | | | |
| **ITALY** | By 1918 the Italian aircraft industry was beginning to turn out substantial numbers of all types of airplane. It's two main fighter types are listed below but these were perhaps the least impressive products of native aviation skills and the fighter units were reliant throughout the war on foreign types, almost exclusively French. Hanriot HD–1s (not listed), Nieuport 11s and 17s, and SPAD 7s and 13s were the most common types purchased and built under license. | | | | | | | | |
| Ansaldo A–1 | 220 | 8/17 | 220 at 2,000 | 1.5 | 5,000 | 8 to 3,000 | 2 x m.g. | 130 | ? |

*\* Société Anonyme pour l'Aviation et ses Dérivés.*

*† Luftfahrzeug Gesellschaft*

**Fighters (continued)**

| TYPE | H.P. | DATE IN SERVICE | SPEED (km./hr. at m.) | DURATION (hr.) RANGE (k.) | CEILING (m.) | RATE OF CLIMB (min./sec. to m.) | ARMAMENT | NUMBER PRODUCED | UNITS EQUIPPED |
|---|---|---|---|---|---|---|---|---|---|
| **ITALY continued** | | | | | | | | | |
| Pomilio PE (2-seat) | 260 | 1918 | 194 at sea level | 3.5 | 5,000 | ? | 2 x m.g. | 1,500 (all P. types) | 30 (all P. types) |
| **JAPAN** | During the war a limited number of Nieuport 24s and SPAD 7s were purchased. None saw combat. | | | | | | | | |
| **NEW ZEALAND** | No New Zealand air units were formed. | | | | | | | | |
| **PORTUGAL** | Portugese pilots on the French front were mainly attached to French squadrons. | | | | | | | | |
| **RUMANIA** | Had a small indigenous aircraft industry producing a few Vlaicu monoplanes but almost entirely reliant upon French types: mainly Morane-Saulnier LAs and Nieuport 11s and 17s. | | | | | | | | |
| **RUSSIA** | The Russian aircraft industry produced no fighter types of note and the air force was mainly reliant on foreign types, mostly French. The most used, both purchased and built under license, were the Nieuport 7, 11, 21 and 23 (last two are not listed), and the SPAD SA-2, SA-4 (not listed), and 7. | | | | | | | | |
| **SERBIA** | The first fighters in the Serbian Air Force were those of three French squadrons sent to fight with the exiled Serbian forces in Macedonia in 1916. These units employed the usual sequence of Nieuport 17s and 24s followed by SPAD 13s. | | | | | | | | |
| **S. AFRICA** | No fighters flew with the short-lived South African Aviation Corps. | | | | | | | | |
| **TURKEY** | The Turks had originally depended on the French for both airplanes and technical support but by their entry into the war hardly any French planes were still operational and they found themselves entirely reliant on the Germans. The main types supplied for their own fighter units and those of the German air force despatched to the Middle East were Fokker E IIIs, Albatros D IIIs and Halberstadt D IIIs and IVs (not listed). | | | | | | | | |
| **UNITED KINGDOM** | | | | | | | | | |
| Airco D.H.2 | 100 | 1/16 | 145 at 1,400 124 at 3,000 | 2.75 | 4,250 | 12 to 2,000 24/45 to 3,000 | 1 x m.g. | 400 | 10 |
| Bristol Scout 'D' | 80 | 8/14 | 143 at 2,000 139 at 3,000 | 2.5 | 4,700 | 10/48 to 2,000 21/20 to 3,000 50 to 4,500 | 1 x m.g. (from 1915) | 236 | 23 (all types) |
| Royal Aircraft Factory B.E.12 * | 160 | 5/16 | 156 at 2,000 149 at 3,000 | 3 | 3,800 | 11/05 to 1,500 33 to 3,000 | 2 or 4 x m.g. | 470 | 20 |
| R.A.F. S.E.5a | 200 | 7/17 | 212 at 2,000 206 at 3,000 186 at 4,500 | 2.5 545 | 6,000 | 6 to 2,000 11/20 to 3,000 22/55 to 4,500 | (45kg. bombs) 2 x m.g. | 4,000 | 29 |
| Sopwith F.1 Camel | 110 | 6/17 | 180 at 4,500 | ? | 7,300 | 5/10 to 2,000 9/10 to 3,000 16/50 to 4,500 | } (45kg. bombs) 2 x m.g. | 5,500 | 21 |
| | 130 | 6/17 | 183 at 4,500 | 2.5 | 7,300 | 5 to 2,000 8/30 to 3,000 15/45 to 4,500 | | | |
| Sopwith Scout "Pup" | 80 | 9/16 | 171 at 2,000 168 at 3,000 165 at 5,000 | 3 | 5,600 | 8 to 2,000 14/25 to 3,000 30 to 4,500 | 1 x m.g. | 1,800 | 9 |
| **UNITED STATES** | No American-produced fighters flew in the war. The American pursuit squadrons in France were almost entirely reliant on French types, notably the SPAD 13 and some Nieuport 28s (not listed). | | | | | | | | |

* Intended as a single-seat fighter, the B.E.12's inadequate performance led to it soon being 'demoted' to a light-bombing role. Some were later used in home-defence fighter squadrons.

## RECONNAISSANCE

The classification 'reconnaissance' is a very loose one which applies essentially to all two-seater planes not designed as dedicated bomber-types. Proper reconnaissance flights were one of their major tasks but these aircraft also assumed escort, ground attack, light bombing or home defence duties. All planes are single-engined two-seater biplanes unless otherwise stated.

**Reconnaissance**

| TYPE | H.P. | DATE IN SERVICE | SPEED (km./hr. at m.) | DURATION (hr.) RANGE (k.) | CEILING (m.) | RATE OF CLIMB (min./sec. to m.) | ARMAMENT | NUMBER PRODUCED | UNITS EQUIPPED |
|---|---|---|---|---|---|---|---|---|---|
| **AUSTRIA-HUNGARY** | | | | | | | | | |
| Lloyd C.II | 145 | 1915 | 128 at sea level | 2 | 3,000 | ? | 1 x m.g. | 94 accepted | ? |
| III | 160 | 1916 | 140 at sea level | 3.5 | 6,000 | ? | 1 x m.g. | 52 accepted | ? |
| Phönix C.I | 230 | 5/18 | 177 at sea level | 3.5 | 5,400 | ? | (50kg. bombs) 2 x m.g. | 98 accepted | ? |
| UFAG C.I * | 230 | 4/18 | 190 at sea level | 3 | 4,900 | ? | 2 or 3 x m.g. | 166 accepted | ? |
| **AUSTRALIA** | See **Fighters**. The two reconnaissance squadrons flew Royal Aircraft Factory R.E.8s and Bristol F.2Bs. | | | | | | | | |
| **BELGIUM** | At the start of the war the *Aviation Militaire* was entirely equipped with Farman HF 20s and by the end its reconnaissance squadrons were still using some Farmans (HF 40s) as well as Breguet 14s. | | | | | | | | |
| **BULGARIA** | Ago CI (German) not listed. (Early type). | | | | | | | | |
| **CANADA** | No Canadian squadrons fought in the war. | | | | | | | | |
| **FRANCE** | | | | | | | | | |
| A.R.1/2 (Dorand) | 190 | 4/17 | 152 at 2,000 147 at 3,000 141 at 4,000 | 375 | 5,500 | 11/0 to 2,000 22/20 to 3,000 39/0 to 4,000 | (4 x 120mm. bomb) 2 or 3 x m.g. | 1,435 | 49 |
| Blériot 11-2 (monoplane) | 70 | 1913 | 100 max | 330 | ? | 12 to 1,000 | personal | 130 | ? |
| Breguet 14 A2 | 300 | 8/17 | 184 at 4,000 | 2.75 | 6,100 | 6/50 to 2,000 11/35 to 3,000 29/30 to 5,000 | (4 x 120mm. bomb) 3 x m.g. | 800 | 72 |
| Caudron G.4 | 2 x 80 | 8/15 | 125 at 2,000 124 at 3,000 | 5 | 4,300 | 6/30 to 1,000 15/0 to 2,000 | 1 x m.g. | 1,358 | 47 |
| Caudron G.6 | 2 x 110 | 7/16 | 145 at 2,000 | 3 275 | 4,400 | 7/30 to 2,000 | 2 x m.g. | 512 | 43 |
| Farman H.F.20 | 80 | 1912 | 165 max | 3 315 | ? | 22 to 2,000 | (some 75mm. bombs) 1 x m.g. | 3,310 H.F.20 through H.F.27 | 6 |
| Farman M.F.7 | 70 | 1913 | 95 max | 3.25 | 4,000 | ? | (some bombs) 1 x m.g. | 358 | 11 |
| Farman M.F.11 | 110 | 2/15 | 118 max | ? | ? | ? | 1 x m.g. | ? | 40 |
| Farman F.40 | 130 | late 1915 | 135 at 2,000 | 2.3 420 | 4,000 | 15 to 2,000 | (240kg. bombs) 1 x m.g. | ? | 56 |

* Ungarische Flugzeugfabrik A.G.

**Reconnaissance (continued)**

| TYPE | H.P. | DATE IN SERVICE | SPEED (km./hr. at m.) | DURATION (hr.) RANGE (k.) | CEILING (m.) | RATE OF CLIMB (min./sec. to m.) | ARMAMENT | NUMBER PRODUCED | UNITS EQUIPPED |
|---|---|---|---|---|---|---|---|---|---|
| **FRANCE continued** | | | | | | | | | |
| Nieuport 10 | 80 | 4/15 | 115 max | 250 | ? | 16 to 2,000 | 1 x m.g. | 7,000 (10s and 12s) | 13 |
| Nieuport 12 | 110 | early 1916 | 146 at 2,000 | 3 400 | 4,000 | 5/30 to 1,000 14/20 to 2,000 | 2 x m.g. | (see above) | 26 (mostly partially) |
| Salmson 2 A2 | 230 | 10/17 | 186 at 2,000 181 at 3,000 168 at 5,000 | 500 | 6,250 | 3/20 to 1,000 7/20 to 2,000 27/30 to 5,000 | 3 x m.g. | 3,200 | 55 |
| Spad 11 * | 220 | 11/17 | 185 at sea level 172 at 4,000 | 2.25 | 6,300 | 7/30 to 2,000 12/35 to 3,000 17 to 4,000 | (70kg. bombs) 2 x m.g. | c. 1,000 | 12 |
| Spad 16 | 240 | early 1918 | 180 at sea level 175 at 2,000 170 at 3,000 | ? | ? | 4/30 to 1,000 9/15 to 2,000 29/30 to 4,000 | (70kg. bombs) 2 or 3 x m.g. | c. 1,000 | 32 |
| **GERMANY** | | | | | | | | | |
| A.E.G. C IV † | 175 | 4/16 | 158 max | 4 | 5,000 | 6 to 1,000 | 2 x m.g. | c. 500 | 18 Staffeln |
| Albatros SS B II | 100 | pre-war | 105 max | 4 | 3,000 | 10 to 800 | — | ? | ? |
| Albatros C I | 150 | 4/15 | 140 max | 2.5 | 3,000 | 9/45 to 1,000 | (90kg. bombs) 1 x m.g. | ? | ? |
| Albatros C III | 150 | 11/16 | 140 at sea level | 4 | 3,400 | 9 to 1,000 | (90kg. bombs) 1 or 2 x m.g. | ? | 53 Fl. Abts. |
| Albatros C VII | 200 | 12/16 | 170 at sea level | 3.3 | 5,000 | 8 to 1,000 | (90kg. bombs) 2 x m.g. | ? | ? |
| Albatros C X | 260 | 2/17 | 175 at sea level | 3.4 | 5,000 | 5 to 1,000 | (90kg. bombs) 2 x m.g. | ? | ? |
| Albatros C XII | 260 | 1918 | 175 at sea level | 3.2 | 5,000 | 5 to 1,000 | (90kg. bombs) 2 x m.g. | ? | ? |
| Aviatik C I | 160 | 3/15 | 142 at sea level | 3 | 3,500 | 12 to 1,000 | 1 x m.g. | ? | ? |
| Aviatik C III | 160 | 1916 | 160 at sea level | 3 | 4,500 | 7 to 1,000 | 2 x m.g. | ? | ? |
| D.F.W. C V ‡ | 200 | 12/16 | 155 at sea level | 3.5 | 5,000 | 4 to 1,000 | 2 x m.g. | 4,000+ | 54 Fl. Abts. |
| Halberstadt C V | 220 | 7/18 | 170 max | 3.5 | ? | 3/10 to 2,000 23 to 5,000 | 2 x m.g. | ? | ? |
| L.F.G. Roland C II ◊ | 160 | 1/16 | 165 max | 4.5 | 4,000 | 6 to 1,000 12 to 2,000 45 to 4,000 | 2 x m.g. | ? | 26 Staffeln |

*Société Anonyme pour l'Aviation et ses Dérivés.*

†*Allgemeine Elektrizitäts Gesellschaft.*

‡*Deutsche Flugzeug-Werke.*

◊*Luftfahrzeug Gesellschaft.*

## Reconnaissance (continued)

| TYPE | H.P. | DATE IN SERVICE | SPEED (km./hr. at m.) | DURATION (hr.) RANGE (k.) | CEILING (m.) | RATE OF CLIMB (min./sec. to m.) | ARMAMENT | NUMBER PRODUCED | UNITS EQUIPPED |
|---|---|---|---|---|---|---|---|---|---|
| **GERMANY continued** | | | | | | | | | |
| L.V.G. C V * | 230 | 8/17 | 177 at sea level 164 at 2,000 150 at 4,000 | 3.5 | ? | 35 to 4,000 | 2 x m.g. | ? | 54 Fl. Abts. |
| L.V.G. C VI | 230 | 1918 | 170 max | 3.5 | 6,500 | 4 to 1,000 8 to 2,000 15 to 3,000 | 2 x m.g. | c. 1,000 | ? |
| Rumpler C I/Ia | 160 | 2/15 | 152 max | 4 | 5,000 | ? | (100kg. bombs) 2 x m.g. | c. 400 | ? |
| Rumpler C IV | 260 | 1917 | 169 at 2,000 165 at 3,000 94 at 5,000 | 3.5 | 6,400 | 3/45 to 1,000 8/25 to 2,000 38 to 5,000 | (100kg. bombs) 2 x m.g. | ? | ? |
| Rumpler C VII | 240 | 11/17 | 175 at 1,000 160 at 6,000 | 3.5 | 7,300 | 2/20 to 1,000 8 to 3,000 33 to 6,000 | 2 x m.g. | ? | ? |
| **GREECE** | Two Greek squadrons combined Bombing and Reconnaissance duties and were mainly equipped with Dorand A.R.Is and Breguet 14s. | | | | | | | | |
| **ITALY** | See **Fighters**. The Reconnaissance types listed below were standard Italian equipment by 1918 but hitherto they had been very reliant on French types such as the Caudron G III and IV (former not listed) and the Farman 11. | | | | | | | | |
| Ansaldo S.V.A.5 | 220 | 2/18 | 230 at sea level | 5 | 6,000 | ? | 2 x m.g. | 1,250 (5, 9 & 10s) | ? |
| S.A.M.L. 1 † | 260 | 1917 | 162 at sea level | 3.5 | 5,000 | ? | (40kg. bombs) 2 x m.g. | 660 (1 & 2s) | ? |
| S.I.A. 7B ‡ | 300 | 11/17 | 190 at sea level | 500 | 7,000 | ? | (250kg. bombs) 2 x m.g. | 500 (7B 1) | 13 |
| **JAPAN** | The only aircraft to see any kind of combat were some Farman M.F. 7s, a Nieuport NG2 (not listed) and a few Farman sea planes (not listed). The main types acquired later in the war were the Sopwith 1½ Strutter and the SPAD 11. | | | | | | | | |
| **NEW ZEALAND** | See **Fighters**. | | | | | | | | |
| **PORTUGAL** | See **Fighters**. | | | | | | | | |
| **RUMANIA** | See **Fighters**. Main reconnaissance types used were Henry Farman 20, 27 and 40. | | | | | | | | |
| **RUSSIA** | See **Fighters**. The most important foreign types imported and built under license were the Farman 30, Morane-Saulnier G, L and LA (not listed), the Caudron GIV and the Sopwith 1½ Strutter. | | | | | | | | |
| Anatra D & DS | 150 | 7/16 | 143 at sea level | 3.5 | 4,300 | ? | 2 x m.g. | 305 | ? |
| Lebed 12 | 150 | 10/16 | 134 at 2,000 | 3 | 3,500 | ? | (90kg. bombs) 1 or 2 x m.g. | 225 | ? |
| **SERBIA** | In July 1914 the small Serbian air force consisted of Bleriot XIs, Farman HF 20s and Deperdussins (not listed). After being driven out of their country the Serbs were entirely dependent on French reconnaissance squadrons employing Farman F. 40s and Breguet 14s. | | | | | | | | |
| **S. AFRICA** | The short-lived South African Aviation Corps operated Farman 27s (not listed) and Royal Aircraft Factory B.E.2c's. Just the same types were used by 26 (South Africa) Squadron RFC. | | | | | | | | |
| **TURKEY** | See **Fighters**. The main reconnaissance types used were the Albatros C III and the A.E.G. C IV. | | | | | | | | |

*Side notes:*

* Luft-Verkehrs Gesellschaft.

† Società Aeronautica Meccanica Lombarda.

‡ Società Italiana Avazione. Unfortunately, although the 7B 1 was by far the most common I have only been able to find technical details for the 7B 2.

**Reconnaissance (continued)**

| TYPE | H.P. | DATE IN SERVICE | SPEED (km./hr. at m.) | DURATION (hr.) RANGE (k.) | CEILING (m.) | RATE OF CLIMB (min./sec. to m.) | ARMAMENT | NUMBER PRODUCED | UNITS* EQUIPPED |
|---|---|---|---|---|---|---|---|---|---|
| **UNITED KINGDOM** | | | | | | | | | |
| Bristol F.2B | 275 | 4/17 | 180 at 3,000<br>170 at 4,500 | 3 | 6,100 | 11/15 to 3,000<br>21/20 to 4,500 | (130kg. bombs)<br>2 x m.g. | 3,100 | 20 |
| R.A.F. B.E.2a/b | 70 | pre-war | 113 at sea level<br>105 at 2,000 | 3 | 3,000 | 9 to 900<br>35 to 2,000 | (45kg. bombs)<br>personal<br>weapons | 100 | ? |
| c/d | 90 | 1/15 | 116 at 2,000<br>110 at 3,000 | 3.25 | 3,100 | 20 to 2,000<br>45/15 to 3,000 | (100kg. bombs)<br>1 to 4 x m.g. | 1,300 | 28 |
| e | 90 | 6/16 | 145 at sea level<br>132 at 2,000<br>120 at 3,000 | 4 | 3,300 | 23/50 to 2,000<br>53 to 3,000 | (100kg. bombs)<br>1 to 4 x m.g. | 1,800 | 35 |
| R.A.F. F.E.2b | 120 | 10/15 | 130 at sea level<br>117 at 2,000<br>116 at 3,000 | 3 | 2,750 | 19/30 to 2,000<br>43/50 to 3,000 | (160kg. bombs)<br>2 or 3 x m.g. | 2,000 | 20 |
| R.A.F. R.E.8 | 150 | 11/16 | 158 at 2,000<br>150 at 3,000 | 4.25 | 4,000 | 21 to 2,000<br>39/50 to 3,000 | (100kg. bombs)<br>2 x m.g. | 4,000 | 29 |
| Sopwith 1A2 (or LCT) (1½ Strutter) | 130 | 5/16 | 170 at sea level<br>160 at 2,000<br>140 at 4,500 | 3.75 | 4,600 | 8/50 to 1,500<br>9/10 to 2,000<br>17/50 to 3,000 | (45kg. bombs)<br>2 x m.g. | 1,500<br>+ 4,200<br>French-built | 16 |
| Vickers F.B.5 | 100 | 2/15 | 113 at 1,500 | 4.25<br>330 | 2,750 | 5 to 450<br>16 to 1,500 | 2 x m.g. | 115 | 6 |
| Vickers F.B.9 | 100 | 12/15 | 130 at 1,500<br>127 at 2,000<br>122 at 3,000 | 5<br>360 | 3,350 | 15 to 1,500<br>19 to 2,000<br>51 to 3,000 | 2 x m.g. | 95 | 6 |
| **UNITED STATES** | | | No American-produced reconnaissance aircraft flew in the war. The observation squadrons were mainly equipped with French types, notably the Salmson 2 A2. | | | | | | |

## GROUND ATTACK

Whilst ground attack missions became increasingly common as the war went on these were usually undertaken by fighters and all-purpose reconnaissance types. Only two countries produced aircraft that could reasonably be regarded as dedicated ground attack aircraft.

### Ground Attack

| TYPE | H.P. | DATE IN SERVICE | SPEED (km./hr. at m.) | DURATION (hr.) RANGE (k.) | CEILING (m.) | RATE OF CLIMB (min./sec. to m.) | ARMAMENT | NUMBER PRODUCED | UNITS EQUIPPED |
|---|---|---|---|---|---|---|---|---|---|
| **FRANCE** | | | | | | | | | |
| Voisin 4 (2-seater) | 120 | 4/15 | 90 at 2,000 | ? | ? | 35 to 2,000 | 1 x 37mm cannon | 100 | 5 |
| **GERMANY** | | | | | | | | | |
| A.E.G. J I/J II | 200 | late 1917 | 150 max | 2.5 | 4,500 | 6 to 1,000 | 3 x m.g. (2 fixed to fire downward) | 609 | ? |
| Albatros J I | 200 | 1917 | 140 max | 2.5 | ? | 11/20 to 1,000 50 to 3,000 | 3 x m.g. (2 fixed to fire downward) | ? | ? |
| Halberstadt CL II | 160 | 7/17 | 155 at 3,000 | 3 | 5,100 | 5 to 1,000 39/30 to 5,000 | (50kg. bombs) 2 or 3 x m.g. | ? | 24 *Staffeln* |
| Halberstadt CL IV | 160 | 2/18 | 165 max | 3.25 | ? | 32 to 5,000 | (50kg. bombs) 2 or 3 x m.g. | ? | ? |
| Hannover CL IIIa | 180 | 10/17 | 165 at 5,000 | 3 | 4,600 | 5/20 to 1,000 29/45 to 4,000 | 2 x m.g. | 540 | 24 *Staffeln* |
| Junkers J I | 230 | 9/17 | 155 at 1,500 | 2 | 4,000 | 32 to 2,000 | 3 x m.g. | 230 | ? |

### Bombers

| TYPE | H.P. | DATE IN SERVICE | SPEED (km./hr. at m.) | DURATION (hr.) RANGE (k.) | CEILING (m.) | RATE OF CLIMB (min./sec. to m.) | ARMAMENT | NUMBER PRODUCED | UNITS EQUIPPED |
|---|---|---|---|---|---|---|---|---|---|
| **AUSTRALIA** | The Australian Flying Corps operated no bombers. | | | | | | | | |
| **AUSTRIA-HUNGARY** | Operated German types. | | | | | | | | |
| **BELGIUM** | One Belgian squadron undertook (night) bombing operations along with its night reconnaissance duties and was equipped with Breguet 14s. | | | | | | | | |
| **BULGARIA** | Operated no bombers. | | | | | | | | |
| **CANADA** | No Canadian squadrons fought in the war. A light-bomber squadron in training in November 1918 was equipped with Airco D.H. 9s. | | | | | | | | |
| **FRANCE** | | | | | | | | | |
| Breguet 14 B2 (2-seater) | 300 | 8/17 | 165 at 4,000 | 2.75 | 6,200 | 26 to 4,000 | 355kg. bombs 3 x m.g. | ? | 16 |
| Breguet-Michelin 4 (2-seater) | 220 | 4/16 | 135 max | 675 | 3,900 | 28 to 2,000 | 320kg. bombs 1 x m.g. | 200 | 5 |
| Farman F.50 (2-seater) | 2 x ? | 7/18 | 150 at 1,000 | 420 | 4,750 | 12 to 2,000 | 400kg. bombs 2 x m.g. | ? | 3 |
| Voisin 3 | 120 | pre-war* | 98 at 2,000 | 200 | 3,000 | 24/30 to 2,000 | 150kg. bombs 2 x m.g. | c. 1,000 | 12 |
| Voisin 5 (2-seater) | 150 | 9/15 | 109 at 2,000 | 3.5 | 3,500 | 22 to 2,000 | 160kg. bombs 2 x m.g. | 300 | 10 |

\* September 1914 as a bomber.

**Bombers (continued)**

| TYPE | H.P. | DATE IN SERVICE | SPEED (km./hr. at m.) | DURATION (hr.) RANGE (k.) | CEILING (m.) | RATE OF CLIMB (min./sec. to m.) | ARMAMENT | NUMBER PRODUCED | UNITS EQUIPPED |
|---|---|---|---|---|---|---|---|---|---|
| **FRANCE continued** | | | | | | | | | |
| Voisin 8 (2-seater) | 220 | 11/16 | 118 at 2,000 | 350 | 4,300 | 17 to 2,000 | 180kg. bombs 1 x m.g. | 1,100 | 5 |
| Voisin 10 (2-seater) | 280 | 10/17 | 135 at 2,000 | 5 350 | ? | 20 to 2,000 | 300kg. bombs 1 x m.g. | 900 | 14 |
| **GERMANY** | | | | | | | | | |
| A.E.G. G IV (2-seater) | 2 x 260 | 11/16 | 165 max | 3.25 | 4,500 | 5 to 1,000 | 400kg. bombs 2 x m.g. | c. 500 | 18 *Staffeln* |
| Friedrichshafen G III (3-seater) | 2 x 260 | early 1917 | 135 at 1,000 | 4.5 | 4,000 | 6 to 1,000 | 1,500kg. bombs 2 or 3 x m.g. | 340 | 18 *Staffeln* |
| Gotha G IV/V (3-seater) | 2 x 260 | 5/17 | 140 at sea level 115 at 3,500 | 4 490 | 6,500 | 28 to 3,000 52/30 to 6,500 | 3-500kg. bombs 2 x m.g. | 230 (IVs) | 18 *Staffeln* |
| Zeppelin Staaken R VI (7-seater) | 4 x 245 | 12/17 (first raid) | 135 max | 7-10 | 4,300 | 43 to 3,000 | c. 2,000kg. max (long-range usually 1,000kg.) 4 x m.g. | 18 | 2 *Abteilungen* |
| **GREECE** | See **Reconnaissance**. | | | | | | | | |
| **ITALY** | Unlike their one-and two-seaters (see **Fighters** and **Reconnaissance**) the Italian air force found the Caproni bomber listed below entirely adequate to their requirements. | | | | | | | | |
| Caproni 3 (4-seater) | 3 x 150 | 4/15 | 140 max | ? | 4,800 | 8 to 1,000 40 to 4,000 | 455kg. bombs ? x m.g. | 270 | 22 |
| **JAPAN** | No bomber types were acquired during the war. | | | | | | | | |
| **NEW ZEALAND** | See **Fighters**. | | | | | | | | |
| **PORTUGAL** | See **Fighters**. | | | | | | | | |
| **RUMANIA** | See **Fighters**. Main bombing types used were Voisin 3, Caudron G4 and Breguet-Michelin 4. | | | | | | | | |
| **RUSSIA** | See **Fighters**. Russian 'strategic' bombing requirements were satisfied by the Ilya Mourometz listed below but for tactical bombing they were heavily dependant on license-built French Voisin 3s. | | | | | | | | |
| Sikorsky 'Ilya Mourometz' (7-seater) | 2 x 200 2 x 135 | 1914 | 95 at 2,000 (B-type) | 5 (B-type) 550 (V-type) | 2,000 (B-type) | 44 to 3,000 (E-type) | 500kg. bombs (B-type) 800kg. bombs (E-type) | 80 inc: 32 x V 30 x G 12 x E | ? |
| **SERBIA** | No bomber aircraft served with the Serbian Air Force. | | | | | | | | |
| **S. AFRICA** | No bomber aircraft served with the short-lived South African Aviation Corps. | | | | | | | | |
| **TURKEY** | See **Fighters**. The Ottoman air force maintained no bomber units nor were any provided by the Germans. | | | | | | | | |
| **UNITED KINGDOM** | | | | | | | | | |
| Airco D.H.4 (2-seater) | 230 | 3/17 | 188 at 2,000* 180 at 3,000 160 at 4,500 | 3.5 | 5,300 | 8/55 to 2,000* 16/25 to 3,000 36/40 to 4,500 | 200kg. bombs 2 x m.g. | ? | 18 |
| Airco D.H.9 | 230 | 2/18 | 180 at 3,000* 157 at 4,500 | 4.5 | 5,300 | 10 to 2,000* 20 to 3,000 45 to 4,500 | 210kg. bombs 2 or 3 x m.g. | 2,150 | 23 |
| 9a | 375 | 9/18 | 183 at 3,000* 170 at 4,500 | 5.75 | 5,000 | 8/55 to 2,000* 15/40 to 3,000 33 to 4,500 | 210kg. bombs 2 x m.g. | 272 in service 11/18 | 4 |
| Handley-Page 0/400 (4-seater) | 2 x 275 | 10/17 (as bomber) | 157 at sea level* 136 at 2,000 130 at 3,000 | 8 | 2,600 | 30 to 2,000* 45 to 3,000 | 900kg. bombs 5 x m.g. | 500 | 9 |

* Most listed specifications do not distinguish between loaded and unloaded bomber performance. British ones usually do but we have had to settle for unloaded figures for the D.H.4 and loaded for the D.H.9/9a and the Handley-Page. The Martinsyde is uncertain.

**Bombers (continued)**

| TYPE | H.P. | DATE IN SERVICE | SPEED (km./hr. at m.) | DURATION (hr.) RANGE (k.) | CEILING (m.) | RATE OF CLIMB (min./sec. to m.) | ARMAMENT | NUMBER PRODUCED | UNITS EQUIPPED |
|---|---|---|---|---|---|---|---|---|---|
| **UNITED KINGDOM** | | | | | | | | | |
| Martinsyde G.102 (single-seater) | 160 | 7/16 | 164 at 2,000 160 at 3,000 150 at 4,500 | 4.5 | 5,000 | 8/35 to 2,000 15/10 to 3,000 | 150kg. bombs 2 x m.g. | 170 | 7 |
| **UNITED STATES** | The nearest thing to an American landplane in World War One was the so-called 'Liberty Bomber', a D.H.4 fitted with the superb American 420h.p. Liberty engine. These were produced in quantity but relatively few reached the front before the Armistice. Nevertheless, these were sufficient to equip the nine Army and Marine bomber squadrons that served in France. | | | | | | | | |

**Maritime (Major Powers only)**

| TYPE | H.P. | DATE IN SERVICE | SPEED (km./hr. at m.) | DURATION (hr.) RANGE (k.) | CEILING (m.) | RATE OF CLIMB (min./sec. to m.) | ARMAMENT | NUMBER PRODUCED | UNITS EQUIPPED |
|---|---|---|---|---|---|---|---|---|---|
| **AUSTRIA-HUNGARY** | The main Austrian flying-boat type was a domestic design, but for most of its other seaplanes the Navy was heavily reliant on German types license-built in Austria, notably the Hansa-Brandenburg CC and W13. | | | | | | | | |
| Lohner Type L (3-seat flying-boat) | 160 | 1915 | 105 max | 4 | 4,000 | 20 to 1,000 | 200kg. bombs 1 x m.g. | 150+ | — |
| **FRANCE** | | | | | | | | | |
| Donnet-Denhaut D.D.2 (2-seat flying-boat) | 150 | 1916 | 160 max | 450 | ? | ? | 100kg. bombs 1 x m.g. | 365 | — |
| Donnet-Denhaut D.D.8 (3-seat flying-boat) | 200 | 1917 | 140 max | 500 | ? | 15 to 2,000 | 100kg. bombs 2 x m.g. | 500 | — |
| F.B.A.* Type H (3-seat flying-boat) | 150 | 5/16 | 150 max | 450 | 4,900 | ? | 70kg. bombs 1 x m.g. | ? | — |
| **GERMANY** | | | | | | | | | |
| Albatros W IV (single-seat float-plane) | 160 | 10/16 | 160 max | 3 | 3,000 | 5 to 1,000 | 1 or 2 x m.g. | 118 | ? |
| Friedrichshafen FF 33e (2-seat float-plane) | 150 | 3/15 | 119 max | 5.5 | ? | 17.5 to 1,000 | none | 188 | ? |
| Hansa-Brandenburg CC (single-seat flying-boat) † | 185 ‡ | mid-1916 | 175 max | ? | ? | 5 to 1,000 | 1 x m.g. | 37 (operational in Austro-Hungarian Navy) | — |
| Hansa-Brandenburg W12 (two-seat float-plane) † | 150 | early 1917 | 160 max | 3.5 | 5,000 | 7 to 1,000 19 to 2,000 | 2 or 3 x m.g. | 146 | ? |
| Hansa-Brandenburg W13 (two-seat flying boat) | 350 | ? | ? | ? | ? | ? | 1 x m.g. | 80 (operational in Austro-Hungarian Navy) | — |
| **ITALY** | The F.B.A. type listed below is a French design built under license but, as it had a different, Italian engine, it has been given a separate listing. | | | | | | | | |
| F.B.A. Type H (3-seat flying-boat) | 170 | 1916 | 140 max | 600 | 5,000 | 8 to 1,000 18 to 2,000 31 to 3,000 | ? | 982 | 30 |
| Macchi M.5 (single-seat flying-boat) † | 160 | 1917 | 190 max | 4.5 | 5,000 | 20 to 4,000 | 120kg. bombs 2 x m.g. | 240 | 9 |

\* Franco-British Aviation (but hardly British at all).

† Fighter

‡ Austro-Hungarian planes only.

**Maritime (continued)**

| TYPE | H.P. | DATE IN SERVICE | SPEED (km./hr. at m.) | DURATION (hr.) RANGE (k.) | CEILING (m.) | RATE OF CLIMB (min./sec. to m.) | ARMAMENT | NUMBER PRODUCED | UNITS EQUIPPED |
|---|---|---|---|---|---|---|---|---|---|
| **UNITED KINGDOM**  The RNAS also made considerable use of the American Curtiss H-12 flying-boat. | | | | | | | | | |
| Felixstowe F.2A (4-seat flying-boat) | 2 x 345 | early 1918 | 154 at 600 130 at 3,100 | 6 | 2,900 | 3/30 to 600 39/30 to 3,100 | 210kg. bombs 4 to 7 x m.g. | 100 | 2 complete & many mixed |
| Short Type 184 (2-seat float-plane) | 260 | 6/15 | 142 at 600 135 at 2,000 | 2.75 | 2,750 | 8/30 to 600 33/30 to 2,000 | 225kg. bombs or 1 x 14" torpedo 1 x m.g. | 650+ | 5 complete & many mixed |
| **UNITED STATES** | | | | | | | | | |
| Curtiss F-5L (4-seat flying-boat) | 2 x 400 | 1918 | 145 max | 1,335 | 1,680 | 10 to 650 | 420kg bombs 6 to 8 x m.g. | 165 | ? |
| Curtiss HS-1L (2 or 3-seat flying-boat) | 350 | 5/18 (France) | 133 max | 830 | 1,600 | 10 to 700 | 160kg. bombs 1 x m.g. | 160 | ? |
| Curtiss H12 (4-seat flying-boat) | 2 x 275 | 5/17 | 138 at 600 | 6 | 3,300 | 3/20 to 600 29/50 to 3,100 | 210kg. bombs 4 x m.g. | 71 (used by RNAS) | ? |
| Curtiss H16 (4-seat flying-boat) | 2 x 320 | 1918 | 158 at 600 153 at 2,000 148 at 3,100 | 6 | 3,800 | 3/40 to 600 14/30 to 2,000 28 to 3,100 | 210kg. bombs 4 to 6 x m.g. | 274 (used by USN) | ? |
| Curtiss R-6L (2-seat float-plane) | 400 | 1/18 | 160 max | 900 | 3,700 | 10 to 1,800 | ? | 40 | ? |

---

**Table 8.2 Artillery**

Only the main belligerents are listed below as only these countries were capable of manufacturing their own artillery. Moreover, only the most common types of gun are listed. A complete inventory of First World War artillery would run into dozens of pages.

* Calibre is given in centimetres, millimetres or inches according to national custom.

† Mt.= mountain. A.A.= Anti-aircraft.

‡ Normal 'planning' or 'fighting' range was taken to be between 65 and 75 per cent of the maximum.

| PIECE* | | GUN or HOWITZER† | WEIGHT IN ACTION (kg.) | LENGTH GUN (mm.) | WEIGHT SHELL (kg.) | MAX. MUZZLE VELOCITY (m.per sec.) | MAX. ‡ RANGE (m.) |
|---|---|---|---|---|---|---|---|
| **AUSTRIA-HUNGARY** | | | | | | | |
| 8cm. | M5 | G | 1,020 | 2,295 | 6.7 | 500 | 7,300 |
| | M14 | H | 1,200 | 1,768 | 14.7 | 320 | 7,800 |
| 15cm. | M15 | H | 2,500 | 2,086 | 31.9 | 293 | 6,200 |
| 15.2cm. | M15 | G | 10,000 | 6,096 | ? | 700 | 16,000 |
| 7.5cm. | M15 | G (Mt) | 620 | 1,125 | 6.3 | 350 | 7,000 |
| 10.4cm. | M8 | H (Mt) | 1,100 | 1,352 | 15.5 | ? | 8,000 |
| 7cm. | | A.A. | ? | 2,175 | 4.7 | ? | ? |
| **FRANCE** | | | | | | | |
| 75mm. | M1912 | G | 965 | 2,320 | 7.25 | 500 | 7,500 |
| 105mm. | M1913TR | G | 2,300 | 2,980 | 16.0 | 550 | 12,700 |
| 145mm. | M1916 | G | 12,500 | 7,360 | 33.7 | 785 | 18,500 |

**Artillery (continued)**

| PIECE* | | GUN or HOWITZER† | WEIGHT IN ACTION (kg.) | LENGTH GUN (mm.) | WEIGHT SHELL (kg.) | MAX. MUZZLE VELOCITY (m.per sec.) | MAX. ‡ RANGE (m.) |
|---|---|---|---|---|---|---|---|
| **FRANCE continued** | | | | | | | |
| 155mm. | M1917 | G | 8,956 | 4,940 | 43.2 | 650 | 16,000 |
| 155mm. | GPF | G | 10,750 | 5,920 | 43.1 | 735 | 16,200 |
| 155mm. | M1915 | H | 3,040 | 2,330 | 43.5 | 450 | 11,500 |
| 75mm. | autocannon | A.A. | 460/3,995◊ | 2,720 | 5.56 | 550 | 5,000 |
| **GERMANY** | | | | | | | |
| 7.7cm. | M96nA | G | 925 | 2,102 | 6.85 | 465 | 7,800 |
| 7.7cm. | M1916 | G | 1,397 | 2,695 | 7.0 | 479 | 8,688 |
| 10cm. | M1914• | G | 3,200 | 3,675 | 20.9 | ? | 12,085 |
| 10.5cm. | M1916 | H | 1,450 | 2,310 | 15.6 | 405 | 9,186 |
| 13cm. | QF | G | 5,791 | 4,725 | 40.3 | 695 | 14,394 |
| 15cm. | long | G | 10,800 | 4,491 | 42.8 | 500 | 10,936 |
| 15cm. | M1913 | H | 2,200 | 2,096 | 41.7 | 365 | 8,497 |
| 21cm. | "mortar" | H | 6,680 | 2,296 | 113.0 | 393 | 11,100 |
| 7.7cm. | L/35 | A.A. | ? | ? | 6.8 | ? | 7,197 |
| **ITALY** | | | | | | | |
| 75mm. | M1906 (German) | G | 1,032 | 2,250 | 6.5 | 510 | 6,800 |
| 75mm. | M1911 (French) | G | 1,076 | 2,020 | 6.5 | 510 | 7,600 |
| 65mm. | M1911 | G(Mt) | 570 | 1,150 | 4.1 | 355 | 6,400 |
| 75mm. | M1906/15△ | A.A. | 4,600 | 2,280 | 6.5 | 510 | 4,575 |
| The Italians also made widespread use of the British 6 inch and 12 inch howitzers (see below) and of the French 155mm. M1917 gun (see above). | | | | | | | |
| **RUSSIA** | | | | | | | |
| 76.2mm. | M1902 | G | 1,040 | 2,280 | 6.5 | 588 | 6,600 |
| 85mm. | M1902 | G | 1,930 | 2,900 | 10.0 | 555 | 6,400 |
| 6in. | M1909 | H | ? | ? | 41.0 | ? | 8,700 |
| 76.2mm. | M1904 | G(Mt) | 426 | 1,010 | 6.5 | 295 | 4,160 |
| Most Russian production was made up of a wide variety of Schneider and Krupp models from the first decade of the century built under license. The list included two 107mm. guns, two 122mm. howitzers, two 152mm. guns and three 155mm. howitzers. | | | | | | | |
| **TURKEY** The Turks relied entirely on foreign-designed artillery and mainly employed Krupp and some Schneider pre-war types. | | | | | | | |
| 7.5cm. | M1903 (Krupp) | G | 1,070 | 2,250 | 6.5 | 500 | 8,000 |
| 12cm. | M1905 (Krupp) | H | 1,125 | 1,445 | 20.0 | 275 | 5,800 |
| 15cm. | M1913 (Krupp) | H | see Germany above | | | | |

* Calibre is given in centimetres, millimetres or inches according to national custom.

† Mt.= mountain. A.A.= Anti-aircraft.

‡ Normal 'planning' or 'fighting' range was taken to be between 65 and 75 per cent of the maximum.

◊ Unmounted and mounted (on truck).

• *sic.* In fact, a 10.5cm. calibre gun.

△ Hybrid of German and French equipment.

## Artillery (continued)

| PIECE | GUN or HOWITZER | WEIGHT IN ACTION (kg.) | LENGTH GUN (mm.) | WEIGHT SHELL (kg.) | MAX. MUZZLE VELOCITY (m.per sec.) | MAX. RANGE (m.) |
|---|---|---|---|---|---|---|
| **TURKEY continued** | | | | | | |
| 7.5cm. M1905 (Krupp) | G(Mt) | ? | ? | ? | ? | ? |
| **UNITED KINGDOM** | | | | | | |
| 18pdr. Mk.I* | G | 1,278 | 2,463 | 8.4 | 493 | 5,963 |
| 4.5in. Mk.I | H | 1,364 | 1,778 | 15.8 | 308 | 6,672 |
| 60pdr. Mk.I† | G | 4,465 | 4,267 | 27.2 | 634 | 11,242 |
| 6in. (26cwt) | H | 3,689 | 2,222 | 30.5 | 376 | 8,683 |
| 8in. Mk.VI | H | 8,670 | 3,251 | 90.6 | 396 | 9,835 |
| 9.2in. Mk.II | H | 16,510 | 4,318 | 131.4 | 488 | 12,736 |
| 12in. Mk.II | H | 37,185 | 4,432 | 339.7 | 365 | 10,364 |
| 3.7in. | H(Mt) | 729 | 1,189 | 9.6 | 297 | 5,392 |
| 13pdr. (9cwt) Mk.I | A.A. | 7,260‡ | 2,464 | 5.9 | 656 | 17,366 |
| **UNITED STATES** | | | | | | |
| 75mm. M1917◊ | G | 1,204 | 2,240 | 6.1 | 579 | 8,103 |

The American 75mm. M1916 arrived too late to see active service and right up to the Armistice American artillery units were mainly reliant on the French 75mm. gun and the British 6in. gun and 8in. and 9.2in. howitzers (see above).

## *Table 8.3* Machine Guns ●

| TYPE | COOLANT | CALIBRE (mm.) | WEIGHT△ (kg.) | RATE OF FIRE (rds. per min.) | MUZZLE VELOCITY (m.per sec.) | AMMO FEED |
|---|---|---|---|---|---|---|
| **AUSTRIA-HUNGARY** | | | | | | |
| Schwarzlose | Water | 8 | 19.9 | 400 | 625 | 250 rd. belt |
| **FRANCE** | | | | | | |
| Hotchkiss | Air | 8 | 23.6 | 600 | 725 | 24 or 30 rd. strip |
| Chauchat | Air | 8 | 9.1 | 250 | 700 | 20 rd. box |
| **GERMANY** | | | | | | |
| Maxim MG08** | Water | 7.92 | 26.4 | 300 or 450 | 892 | 250 rd. belt |
| **ITALY** | | | | | | |
| Fiat-Revelli | Water | 6.5 | 17.0 | 400 | 640 | 50 rd. strip |
| **RUSSIA** | | | | | | |
| Maxim M1910 | Water | 7.62 | 23.8 | 520 to 580 | 863 | 250 rd. belt |
| **UNITED KINGDOM** | | | | | | |
| Vickers MkI. | Water | 0.303in. | 18.1 | 450 | 745 | 250 rd. belt |
| Lewis | Air | 0.303in. | 11.8 unloaded | 550 | 745 | 47 rd. pan |
| **UNITED STATES††** | | | | | | |
| Browning | Water | 0.30in. | 14.97 (w/out coolant) | 500 | 853 | 250 rd. belt |

*Sidebar (left margin):*

* 3.3in. calibre.

† 5in. calibre.

‡ Truck-mounted.

◊ U.S. manufactured British 18pdr.

● Range data for machine guns is rarely given. However, the British Vickers might be taken as a typical example, whose maximum range providing plunging indirect fire was roughly 4,500 yards.

△ Includes the water where relevant (roughly 4 litres) but not the mount. Those for heavy machine guns usually weighed more than the gun. The Vickers tripod, for example, weighed 21.8 kg. and the wheeled mount for the Russian Maxim 49.8kg. The Chauchat and Lewis bipod mounts weighed only 1kg. or so.

** The MG 08/15, a stripped down version, weighed only 18kg. and fired a 50-round belt.

†† The Browning was not used in action until 9/18. Prior to that the Americans had to rely on British and French guns, including the execrable Chauchat which the French were only too happy to off-load.

### Table 8.4 Tanks

| TYPE | DATE: in service in action | BATTLE WEIGHT (tons) | ENGINE (h.p.) | MAX. SPEED (k.p.h.) | RADIUS (km.) | ARMAMENT | ARMOUR THICKNESS (mm.) Turret | Hull front | Hull side | No. PRODUCED (to 11/18) |
|---|---|---|---|---|---|---|---|---|---|---|
| **FRANCE** | | | | | | | | | | |
| Renault FT | 3/18 5/18 | 6.3 | 35 | 7.7 | 35.4 | 1 x 37mm. gun 1 x m.g. | 22 max | 16 | 8 | 3,177 |
| Saint Chamond | ? 5/17 | 23 | 90 | 8.5 | 59.5 | 1 x 75mm. gun 4 x m.g. | — | 5 to 17 max. | | 400 |
| Schneider C.A. | 12/16 4/17 | 14.6 | 55 | 6.0 | 48.3 | 1 x 75mm. gun 2 x m.g. | — | ? | 11.5 19.5* | 402 |
| **GERMANY\*** | | | | | | | | | | |
| A7V | 10/17 3/18 | 33 | 2 x 100 | 12.9 | 40.3 | 1 x 57mm. gun 6 x m.g. | — | 30 | 15 | 20 |
| **UNITED KINGDOM** | | | | | | | | | | |
| Vickers MkI/II | 6/16 9/16 | 27 (female)‡ 28 (male)‡ | 105 | 6.0 | 38.0 | 2 x 6pdr. gun (male) 4 x Vickers m.g. (fem) plus 2 x Hotchkiss m.g. (both) | — | 12 | 10 | 150 x I 50 x II |
| MkIII | 2/17 4/17 | 27 (female) 28 (male) | 105 | 6.0 | 38.0 | 2 x 6pdr. gun (male) 4 x Vickers m.g. (fem) plus 2 x Hotchkiss m.g. (both) | — | 12 | 12 | 50 |
| MkIV | 4/17 6/17 | 27 (female) 28 (male) | 105 | 6.0 | 38.0 | 2 x 6pdr. gun (male) 4 x Lewis m.g. (male) 6 x Lewis m.g. (female) | — | 12 | 12 | 1,015 |
| MkV | 5/18 ? | 28 (female) 29 (male) | 150 | 7.4 | 72.5 | as above except Hotchkiss m.g.s | — | 16 | 12 | 400 |
| Whippet Mk. A | 2/18 3/18 | 14 | 2 x 45 | 13.4 | 130 | 3 x Hotchkiss m.g. | 5 to 14 max. | | | 45 |

**UNITED STATES**

The three American light tank battalions used French-built Renault FT tanks, first seeing action in 9/18. The single heavy tank battalion used British-built Vickers Mk.Vs, and was first in action in late 9/18. American production of Renault tanks got under way but none arrived in France before the Armistice.

\* 19.5mm. in later models.

† Low production meant that the Germans relied heavily on untilising captured tanks. In 7/18 five out of the eight existing tank detachments were equipped with British tanks.

‡ The all-machine gun females were to provide additional protection against enemy infantry.

## SHIPS

### Classes Listed

The multiplicity of small classes in many First World War navies, many of them obsolete or obsolescent, makes it impossible to list all such classes. Broadly speaking we have listed classes shown as new construction from *Conway's All The World's Fighting Ships 1906-1921* and ignored all earlier classes. An exception is that we have listed some older armoured cruiser types where countries had little or no post-1906 light cruiser construction (e.g. France, Italy and, surprisingly, the United States).

Even with this restriction there are still too many classes to be listed in full. The following has been our policy:–

(1) This being the 'Dreadnought' era *all* Dreadnought type battleships and battle cruisers have been listed.

(2) For all other types we have tried to give a representative selection of classes. We make no apology for giving a heavier emphasis to Britain and Germany here. These two countries were involved in virtually all fleet encounters, whilst U-boat warfare was crucial in the latter part of the war. Thus we have listed virtually all British escort classes. They also sustained by far the heaviest loss rates of the belligerent powers.

(3) We have not listed any aircraft carriers as carrier aviation was in its infancy in World War I.

(4) Classes with no ships complete before November 1918 have been omitted.

### Explanatory Notes to Tables

**Completed Column**

Gives period over which ships entered service up to Nov. 1918. Ships completed post-armistice are usually noted in Comments column.

**Displacement**

Figure quoted is full load unless otherwise noted.

Upper and lower figures quoted in Displacement, Speed and Crew columns reflect variations within individual classes.

**Submarine Section**

Where two tonnages and speeds are quoted, the upper figure is for surfaced condition and the lower for submerged condition.

**Armament column**

Only main weapons systems are specified.

**Number completed**

Reflects ships completed by *11th November 1918*. Comments column usually makes brief reference to ships completed after this date.

**Number lost**

Covers ships lost in period August 1914-November 1919. Normally we note the number lost by collision, scuttling etc. A note is usually made of losses in 1919 related to operations during the Russian revolution for powers *other than* Russia itself. A note is also made of ships scuttled at Scapa Flow on 21 June 1919.

---

### *Table 8.5* Ships

**Battleships and Battle Cruisers** (Battle Cruisers shown thus *)

| CLASS | COMPLETED | DISPLACEMENT | SPEED (knots) | CREW | MAIN ARMAMENT | NUMBER COMPLETED | NUMBER LOST (Comments) |
|---|---|---|---|---|---|---|---|
| **AUSTRIA-HUNGARY** | | | | | | | |
| Tegetthoff | 1912-1915 | 21,595 | 20.3 | 1,087 | 12 x 12"<br>12 x 5.9"<br>4 x 21" T.T. | 4 | Szent Istvan (10.6.18)<br>Vinibis Unitis (1.11.18) |
| **FRANCE** | | | | | | | |
| Courbet | 1913-1914 | 25,000-26,000 | 20.0 | 1,085-1,108 | 12 x 12"<br>22 x 5.4"<br>4 x 17.7" T.T. | 4 | |
| Bretagne | 1915-1916 | c.25,000 | 20.0 | 1,124-1,133 | 10 x 13.4"<br>22 x 5.4"<br>4 x 17.7" T.T. | 3 | |
| **GERMANY** | | | | | | | |
| Nassau | 1910 | 21,000 | 19.5 | 1,008 (later 1,124-1,139) | 12 x 11.1"<br>12 x 5.9"<br>6 x 17.7" T.T. | 4 | |
| Helgoland | 1911-1912 | 25,200 | 20.3 | 1,113 (later 1,284-1,390) | 12 x 12"<br>14 x 5.9"<br>6 x 19.7" T.T. | 4 | |
| Kaiser | 1912-1913 | 27,400 | 21 | 1,084 (later 1,249-1,278) | 10 x 12"<br>14 x 5.9"<br>5 x 19.7" T.T. | 5 | (All scuttled 21.6.19) |
| König | 1914-1915 | 29,200 | 21 | 1,136 (later 1,284-1,315) | 10 x 12"<br>14 x 5.9"<br>5 x 19.7" T.T. | 4 | (All scuttled 21.6.19) |
| Bayern | 1916-1917 | 31,690 | 21 | 1,187-1,271 | 8 x 15"<br>16 x 5.9"<br>5 x 23.6" T.T. | 2 | (Bayern scuttled 21.6.19) |
| Von der Tann* | 1911 | 21,700 | 24.75 | 923 (later 1,174) | 8 x 11.1"<br>10 x 5.9"<br>4 x 17.7" T.T. | 1 | (Scuttled 21.6.19) |
| Moltke* | 1912 | 25,300 | 25.5 | 1,053 (later 1,355) | 10 x 11.1"<br>12 x 5.9"<br>4 x 19.7" T.T. | 2 | (Moltke scuttled 21.6.19)<br>(Goeben transferred to Turkey 16.8.14 as Yavuz Sultan Selim) |
| Seydlitz* | 1913 | 28,100 | 26.5 | 1,068 (later 1,425) | 10 x 11.1"<br>12 x 5.9"<br>4 x 19.7" T.T. | 1 | (Scuttled 21.6.19) |
| Derfflinger* | 1914-1916 | 30,700 | 26.5 | 1,112 (later 1,391) | 8 x 12"<br>12 x 5.9" (Lützow 14 x 5.9")<br>4 x 19.7"/23.6" T.T. | 2 | Lützow (1.6.16)<br>(Derfflinger scuttled 21.6.19) |

**Battleships and Battle Cruisers** (Battle Cruisers shown thus *) **continued**

| CLASS | COMPLETED | DISPLACEMENT | SPEED (knots) | CREW | MAIN ARMAMENT | NUMBER COMPLETED | NUMBER LOST (Comments) |
|---|---|---|---|---|---|---|---|
| **GERMANY continued** | | | | | | | |
| Hindenburg* | 1917 | 31,000 | 27.5 | 1,182 | 8 x 12"<br>14 x 5.9"<br>4 x 23.6" T.T. | 1 | (Scuttled 21.6.19) |
| **ITALY** | | | | | | | |
| Dante Alighieri | 1913 | 21,600 | 22.8 | 981 | 12 x 12"<br>20 x 4.7"<br>3 x 17.7" T.T. | 1 | |
| Conte di Cavour | 1914-1915 | 24,250-24,677 | 21.5-22.2 | 1,232 | 13 x 12"<br>18 x 4.7"<br>3 x 17.7" T.T. | 3 | Leonardo da Vinci (2.8.16) |
| Andrea Doria | 1915-1916 | 24,729 and 24,715 | 21-21.3 | 1,233 | 13 x 12"<br>16 x 6"<br>3 x 17.7" T.T. | 2 | |
| **JAPAN** | | | | | | | |
| Settsu | 1912 | 21,433 | 20 | 986-999 | 12 x 12"<br>10 x 6"   8 x 4.7"<br>5 x 18" T.T. | 2 | Kawachi (12.7.18) |
| Fuso | 1915-1917 | 35,900-39,154 | 22.5 | 1,193 | 12 x 14"<br>16 x 6"<br>6 x 21" T.T. | 2 | |
| Ise | 1917-1918 | 36,500 | 23 | 1,360 | 12 x 14"<br>20 x 5.5"<br>6 x 21" T.T. | 2 | |
| Tsukuba* | 1907-1908 | 15,400 | 20.5 | 879 | 4 x 12"<br>12 x 6"   12 x 4.7"<br>3 x 18" T.T. | 2 | Tsukuba (14.1.17)<br>(Originally classed as armoured cruisers. Re-classified 1912) |
| Ibuki* | 1909-1911 | 15,595 | 20.5-21.5 | 844 | 4 x 12"<br>8 x 8"   14 x 4.7"<br>3 x 18" T.T. | 2 | |
| Kongo* | 1913-1915 | 32,200 | 27.5 | 1,221 | 8 x 14"<br>16 x 6"<br>8 x 21" T.T. | 4 | |
| **RUSSIA** | | | | | | | |
| Gangut | 1914 | 25,850 | 23 | 1,126 | 12 x 12"<br>16 x 4.7"<br>4 x 18" T.T. | 4 | |
| Imperatritsa Mariya | 1915-1917 | 24,000-24,960 | 21 | 1,220 | 12 x 12"<br>18/20 x 5.1"<br>4 x 18" T.T. | 3 | Imp. Mariya (20.10.16)<br>Imp. Ekaterina Velikaya (18.6.18) |
| **UNITED KINGDOM** | | | | | | | |
| Dreadnought | 1906 | 21,845 | 21 | 699-773 | 10 x 12"<br>27 x 12pdr. (later 10)<br>5 x 18" T.T. (later 4) | 1 | |
| Bellerophon | 1909 | 22,102 | 20.75 | 733 | 10 x 12"<br>16 x 4"<br>3 x 18" T.T. | 3 | |
| St. Vincent | 1909-1910 | 23,030 | 21 | 718 | 10 x 12"<br>20 x 4"<br>3 x 18" T.T. | 3 | Vanguard (9.7.17) |
| Invincible* | 1908-1909 | 20,078 | 25.5 | 784 | 8 x 12"<br>16 x 4"<br>5 x 18" T.T. | 3 | Invincible (31.5.16) |
| Neptune | 1911 | 22,720 | 21 | 759 | 10 x 12"<br>16 x 4"<br>3 x 18" T.T. | 1 | |
| Colossus | 1911 | 23,050 | 21 | 755 | 10 x 12"<br>16 x 4"<br>3 x 21" T.T. | 2 | |
| Indefatigable* | 1911-1913 | 22,080-22,110 | 25 | 800 | 8 x 12"<br>16 x 4"<br>3 x 21" T.T. | 3 | Indefatigable (31.5.16)<br>(Australia and New Zealand†) |
| Orion | 1912 | 25,870 | 21 | 752 | 10 x 13.5"<br>16 x 4"<br>3 x 21" T.T. | 4 | |
| Lion* | 1912 | 29,680 | 27 | 997 | 8 x 13.5"<br>16 x 4"<br>2 x 21" T.T. | 2 | |
| King George V | 1912-1913 | 25,700 | 21 | 782 | 10 x 13.5"<br>16 x 4"<br>3 x 21" T.T. | 4 | Audacious (27.10.14) |

† Built for Australian and New Zealand navies. New Zealand presented to R.N. on completion)

**Battleships and Battle Cruisers** (Battle Cruisers shown thus *) **continued**

| CLASS | COMPLETED | DISPLACEMENT | SPEED (knots) | CREW | MAIN ARMAMENT | NUMBER COMPLETED | NUMBER LOST (Comments) |
|---|---|---|---|---|---|---|---|
| **UNITED KINGDOM continued** | | | | | | | |
| Queen Mary* | 1913 | 31,650 | 27.5 | 997 | 8 x 13.5"<br>16 x 4"<br>2 x 21" T.T. | 1 | Queen Mary (31.5.16) |
| Iron Duke | 1914 | 29,560 | 21.25 | 995-1,022 | 10 x 13.5"<br>12 x 6"<br>4 x 21" T.T. | 4 | |
| Tiger* | 1914 | 35,710 | 28 | 1,121 | 8 x 13.5"<br>12 x 6"<br>4 x 21" T.T. | 1 | |
| Queen Elizabeth | 1915-1916 | 31,500 | 23 | 925-951 | 8 x 15"<br>14/16 x 6"<br>4 x 21" T.T. | 5 | (+1 cancelled 8.14) |
| Revenge | 1916-1917 | 31,000 | 23 | 908-997 | 8 x 15"<br>14 x 6"<br>4 x 21" T.T. | 5 | (+2 suspended & re-ordered as Battle Cruisers)<br>(+1 cancelled 8.14) |
| Erin | 1914 | 25,250 | 21 | 1,070 | 10 x 13.5"<br>16 x 6"<br>4 x 21" T.T. | 1 | (Turkish Reshadieh, building in U.K., seized 8.14) |
| Agincourt | 1914 | 30,250 | 22 | 1,115 | 14 x 12"<br>20 x 6"<br>3 x 21" T.T. | 1 | (Ordered for Brazil, sold to Turkey 1914. Seized 8.14)<br>(Rio de Janeiro - Sultan Osman I) |
| Canada | 1915 | 32,120 | 22.75 | 1,167 | 10 x 14"<br>16 x 6"<br>4 x 21" T.T. | 1 | (Chilean Almirante la Torre building in U.K., purchased 1914) † |
| Renown* | 1916 | 30,835 | 30 | 1,000-1,250 | 6 x 15"<br>17 x 4"<br>2 x 21" T.T. | 2 | (Originally ordered as Revenge Class Battleships)<br>(Re-ordered 4.15) |
| Courageous*<br>Light Battlecruiser | 1917 | 22,690 | 32 | 828-842 | 4 x 15"<br>18 x 4"<br>2 x 21" T.T. (+ 12 x 21" T.T. 1917) | 2 | (Both converted to Aircraft Carriers post-war) |
| Furious*<br>Light Battlecruiser | 1917 | 22,890 | 31.5 | 880 | 2 x 18"<br>11 x 5.5"<br>2 x 21" T.T. (see comments) | 1 | (Completed 7.17 with 1 x 18" and converted to Aircraft Carrier. 12, then 6 x 21" T.T. added) |
| **UNITED STATES** | | | | | | | |
| South Carolina | 1910 | 17,617 | 18.5 | 869 | 8 x 12"<br>22 x 3"<br>2 x 21" T.T. | 2 | |
| Delaware | 1910 | 22,440 | 21 | 993 | 10 x 12"<br>14 x 5"<br>2 x 21" T.T. | 2 | |
| Florida | 1911 | 23,033 | 20.75 | 1,001 | 10 x 12"<br>16 x 5"<br>2 x 21" T.T. | 2 | |
| Wyoming | 1912 | 27,243 | 20.5 | 1,063 | 12 x 12"<br>21 x 5"<br>2 x 21" T.T. | 2 | |
| New York | 1914 | 28,367 | 21 | 1,042 | 10 x 14"<br>21 x 5"<br>4 x 21" T.T. | 2 | |
| Nevada | 1916 | 28,400 | 20.5 | 864 | 10 x 14"<br>21 x 5"<br>2 x 21" T.T. | 2 | |
| Pennsylvania | 1916 | 32,567 | 21 | 915 | 12 x 14"<br>22 x 5"<br>2 x 21" T.T. | 2 | |
| New Mexico | 1917-1918 (2) | 33,000 | 21 | 1,084 | 12 x 14"<br>14 x 5"<br>2 x 21" T.T. | 3 | (1 completed 1919) |

† Sister ship completed as Aircraft Carrier Eagle.

**Cruisers** All Classes are Light Cruisers except those shown thus (A.C.) which are Armoured Cruisers

| CLASS | COMPLETED | DISPLACEMENT | SPEED (knots) | CREW | MAIN ARMAMENT | NUMBER COMPLETED | NUMBER LOST (Comments) |
|---|---|---|---|---|---|---|---|
| **AUSTRIA-HUNGARY** | | | | | | | |
| Modified Admiral Spaun | 1914-1915 | 4,010 | 27 | 340 | 9 x 3.9"<br>Added 1917 6 x 21" T.T. | 3 | |

**Cruisers continued** All Classes are Light Cruisers except those shown thus (A.C.) which are Armoured Cruisers

| CLASS | COMPLETED | DISPLACEMENT | SPEED (knots) | CREW | MAIN ARMAMENT | NUMBER COMPLETED | NUMBER LOST (Comments) |
|---|---|---|---|---|---|---|---|
| **FRANCE** | | | | | | | |
| Leon Gambetta (A.C.) | 1903-1906 | 11,959-13,108 | 22 | 734 | 4 x 7.6"<br>16 x 6.4"<br>2 x 18" T.T. | 3 | 1 |
| Jules Michelet (A.C.) | 1908 | 13,105 | 22.5 | 770 | 4 x 7.6"<br>12 x 6.4"<br>2 x 18" T.T. | 1 | |
| Edgar Quinet (A.C.) | 1911 | 13,847-13,995 | 23 | 859-892 | 14 x 7.6"<br>2 x 18" T.T. | 2 | |
| **GERMANY** | | | | | | | |
| Königsberg | 1907-1908 | 3,814-4,002 | 23/24 | 322 | 10 x 4.1"<br>2 x 17.7" T.T. | 4 | 2 (of which 1 scuttled)<br>(1 converted to Seaplane Carrier 1918) |
| Dresden | 1908-1909 | 4,268 | 24 | 361 | 10 x 4.1"<br>2 x 17.7" T.T. | 2 | 2 (of which 1 scuttled) |
| Kolberg | 1909-1911 | 4,915 | 25.5-26.7 | 367 | 12 x 4.1" (2 ships later 6 x 5.9")<br>2 x 17.7" T.T. (2 later 4)<br>100 mines | 4 | 2 |
| Magdeburg | 1912 | 5,587 | 27.5-28.2 | 354 | 12 x 4.1" (2 ships later 7 x 5.9")<br>2 x 19.7" T.T. (2 later 4)<br>120 mines | 4 | 2 (including ex-Breslau)<br>(Breslau to Turkey 8.14 as Midilli) |
| Karlsruhe | 1914 | 6,191 | 27 | 373 | 12 x 4.1"<br>2 x 19.7" T.T.<br>120 mines | 2 | 2 |
| Graudenz | 1914-1915 | 6,382 | 28 | 385 | 12 x 4.1" (later 7 x 5.9")<br>2 x 19.7" T.T. (later 4) | 2 | 2 |
| Brummer (Minelayer) | 1916 | 5,856 | 28 | 309 | 4 x 5.9"<br>2 x 19.7" T.T.<br>400 mines | 2 | Both scuttled 21.6.19. |
| Pillau | 1914-1915 | 5,252 | 27.5 | 442 | 8 x 5.9"<br>2 x 19.7" T.T.<br>120 mines | 2 | 1 (scuttled)<br>(Originally ordered for Russia, taken over 8.14) |
| Wiesbaden | 1915 | 6,601 | 27.5 | 474 | 8 x 5.9"<br>4 x 19.7" T.T.<br>120 mines | 2 | 1 |
| Königsberg (ii) | 1916-1917 | 7,125 | 27.5 | 475 | 8 x 5.9"<br>4 x 19.7" T.T.<br>120 mines | 4 | 1 scuttled 21.6.19. |
| Cöln (ii) | 1918 | 7,486 | 27.5 | 511-552 | 8 x 5.9"<br>4 x 23.6" T.T.<br>120 mines | 2 | Both scuttled 21.6.19.<br>(5 more not completed) |
| **ITALY** | | | | | | | |
| Pisa (A.C.) | 1909 | 10,600 | 23.6 | 684-687 | 4 x 10"<br>8 x 7.5"<br>3 x 17.7" T.T. | 2 | 1 |
| San Giorgio (A.C.) | 1910-1911 | 11,300-11,900 | 23.2-23.7 | 698-705 | 4 x 10"<br>8 x 7.5"<br>3 x 17.7" T.T. | 2 | |
| Campania | 1917 | 3,187 | 15.5 | 204 | 6 x 6" | 2 | |
| Bixio | 1914 | 4,141 | 26.8 | 296 | 6 x 4.7"<br>2 x 17.7" T.T.<br>200 mines | 2 | (Scout Cruisers) |
| **JAPAN** | | | | | | | |
| Yodo | 1908 | 1,250-1,350 (normal) | 22-23 | 180 | 2 x 4.7"<br>2 x 18" T.T. | 2 | (Rated as Dispatch Vessels) |
| Tone | 1910 | 4,900 | 23 | 370 | 2 x 6"<br>10 x 4.7"<br>3 x 18" T.T. | 1 | |
| Chikuma | 1912 | 5,040 | 26 | 414 | 8 x 6"<br>3 x 18" T.T. | 3 | |
| **RUSSIA** | | | | | | | |
| Bayan (A.C.) | 1908-1911 | 7,775 | 21-22.5 | 568-593 | 2 x 8"<br>8 x 6"<br>2 x 18" T.T. | 3 | 1* |

* Additionally an earlier unit of this class was taken as a prize by Japan in 1904/5.

**Cruisers continued** All Classes are Light Cruisers except those shown thus (A.C.) which are Armoured Cruisers

| CLASS | COMPLETED | DISPLACEMENT | SPEED (knots) | CREW | MAIN ARMAMENT | NUMBER COMPLETED | NUMBER LOST (Comments) |
|---|---|---|---|---|---|---|---|
| **RUSSIA continued** | | | | | | | |
| Rurik (A.C.) | 1908 | 15,190 | 21 | 899 | 4 x 10"    8 x 8" 20 x 4.7"    2 x 18" T.T. (and 400 mines on occasions) | 1 | |
| **UNITED KINGDOM** | | | | | | | |
| Bristol | 1910 | 5,300 | 25 | 480 | 2 x 6" 10 x 4" 2 x 18" T.T. | 5 | |
| Weymouth | 1911-1912 | 5,800 | 25 | 475 | 8 x 6" 2 x 21" T.T. | 4 | 1 |
| Active | 1911-1913 | 4,000 | 25 | 321-325 | 10 x 4" 2 x 18" T.T. (2 ships later 8 x 4") | 3 | (Scout Cruisers) 1 |
| Chatham | 1912-1913 (one in 1916) | 6,000 | 25.5 | 475 | 8 x 6" 2 x 21" T.T. | 6 | (3 for Australian Navy) (1, completed in 1916, built in Australia) |
| Birmingham | 1914 | 6,040 | 25.5 | 480 | 9 x 6" 2 x 21" T.T. | 3* | 1 |
| Arethusa | 1914-1915 | 4,400 | 28.5 | 276-282 | 2 x 6" 6 x 4" 4 x 21" T.T. (later 8) | 8 | 1 (5 re-armed in 1918 – 3 x 6", 4 x 4") |
| Caroline | 1914-1915 | 4,733 | 28.5 | 301 | 2 x 6" 8 x 4" 4 x 21" T.T. (later 8) | 6 | (Later re-armed with [1] 3 x 6", 5 x 4" then [2] 4 x 6", 2 x 3") |
| Calliope | 1915 | 4,695 | 29.5 | 368 | 2 x 6" 8 x 4" 2 x 21" T.T. (later 6) | 2 | (Later re-armed as Caroline Class) |
| Birkenhead | 1915-1916 | 5,795-5,845 | 25.5-26.5 | 450-500 | 10 x 5.5" 2 x 21" T.T. | 2 | (Building for Greece, purchased early 1915) |
| Cambrian | 1915-1916 | 4,799 | 28.5 | 368 | 2 x 6" 8 x 4" 2 x 21" T.T. (later 6) | 4 | (Later re-armed as Caroline Class) |
| Centaur | 1916 | 4,870 | 29 | 437 | 5 x 6" 2 x 21" T.T. | 2 | (Replaced orders and used materials assigned to 2 Turkish cruisers) |
| Caledon | 1917 | 4,950 | 29 | 400-437 | 5 x 6" 8 x 21" T.T. | 4 | 1 lost in Baltic in 12.18. |
| Ceres | 1917-1918 | 5,020 | 29 | 460 | 5 x 6" 8 x 21" T.T. | 5 | |
| Danae (1st Group only) | 1918 | 5,870 | 29 | 450-469 | 6 x 6" 12 x 21" T.T. | 3 | (5 completed and 4 more cancelled post-war) |
| **UNITED STATES** | | | | | | | |
| Tennessee (A.C.) | 1906-1908 | 15,715-15,981 | 22 | 856-914 | 4 x 10" 16 x 6" 4 x 21" T.T. | 4 | 1 (Wrecked 8.16) (Re-named in 1916 and 1920 after cities) |
| Chester | 1908 | 4,687 | 24 | 359 | 2 x 5" 6 x 3" 2 x 21" T.T. | 3 | |

* 4th unit for R.A.N. not complete until 1922, not included)

**Destroyers**

| CLASS | COMPLETED | DISPLACEMENT | SPEED (knots) | CREW | MAIN ARMAMENT | NUMBER COMPLETED | NUMBER LOST (Comments) |
|---|---|---|---|---|---|---|---|
| **AUSTRIA-HUNGARY** | | | | | | | |
| Huszar (1st and 2nd Groups) | 1st Group 1905-1907 2nd Group 1908-1909 | 414 | 28.4 | 65-70 | 6 x 2.6" 2 x 17.7" T.T. 10-12 Mines | 13† | 2+1 wrecked pre-war |
| Tatra | 1913-1914 | 1,050 | 32.6 | 105 | 2 x 3.9" 6 x 2.6" 4 x 17.7" T.T. | 6 | 2 |

† Includes 1 completed in 1911 to replace pre-war loss.

**Destroyers continued**

| CLASS | COMPLETED | DISPLACEMENT | SPEED (knots) | CREW | MAIN ARMAMENT | NUMBER COMPLETED | NUMBER LOST (Comments) |
|---|---|---|---|---|---|---|---|
| **FRANCE** | | | | | | | |
| Spahi | 1909-1912 | 550 | 28 | 77-79 | 6 x 2.6" (65mm.)<br>3 x 17.7" T.T. | 7 | 1 |
| Chasseur | 1909-1911 | 520 | 28 | 77-79 | 6 x 2.6" (65mm.)<br>3 x 17.7" T.T. | 4 | 1 |
| Bouclier | 1911-1913 | 720-756 (normal) | 30 | 80-83 | 2 x 3.9"<br>4 x 2.6" (65mm.)<br>4 x 17.7" T.T. | 12 | 4 |
| Bisson | 1913-1914 | 855 | 30 | 80-83 | 2 x 3.9"<br>4 x 2.6" (65mm.)<br>4 x 17.7" T.T. | 6 | 1 |
| **GERMANY** | | | | | | | |
| G7-G12 | 1912 | 719 | 32 | 74 | 2 x 3.45"<br>4 x 19.7" T.T. | 6 | 2 |
| S13-S24 | 1912-1913 | 695 | 32.5 | 74 | 2 x 3.45"<br>4 x 19.7" T.T. | 12 | 8 |
| V25-V30 | 1914 | 975 | 33.5 | 83 | 2 x 3.45"<br>6 x 19.7" T.T.<br>24 mines | 6 | 4 (Including 1 en route to internment at Scapa) |
| S31-S36 | 1914-1915 | 971 | 33.5 | 83 | 2 x 3.45"<br>6 x 19.7" T.T.<br>24 mines | 6 | 4 (+2 scuttled 21.6.19) |
| V47-V48 | 1915 | 1,188 | 33.5 | 87 | 2 x 3.45"<br>6 x 19.7" T.T.<br>24 mines | 2 | 2 (Including 1 scuttled) |
| S53-S66 | 1916-1917 | 1,170 | 34-35 | 87 | 3 x 3.45" (S57-66 – 3 x 4.1")<br>6 x 19.7" T.T.<br>24 mines | 14 | 7 (Including 1 scuttled) + (6 scuttled 21.6.19) |
| V67-V84 | 1915-1916 | 1,118 | 34-36.5 | 85 | 3 x 3.45" (1916 re-armed with 3 x 4.1")<br>6 x 19.7" T.T.<br>24 mines | 18 | 9 (Including 4 scuttled) + (7 scuttled 21.6.19) |
| G85-G95 | 1916 | 1,147 | 33.5 | 85 | 3 x 3.45" (1916 re-armed with 3 x 4.1")<br>6 x 19.7" T.T.<br>24 mines | 11 | 6 (+4 scuttled 21.6.19) |
| G101-G104 | 1915 | 1,734 | 33.5 | 104 | 4 x 3.45" (1916 re-armed with 4 x 4.1")<br>6 x 19.7" T.T.<br>24 mines | 4 | (Originally ordered for Argentina. Seized 1914) (All scuttled 21.6.19) |
| B109-B112 | 1915 | 1,843 | 36.5 | 114 | 4 x 3.45" (1916 re-armed with 4 x 4.1")<br>6 x 19.7" T.T.<br>24 mines | 4 | (All scuttled 21.6.19) |
| V125-V130 | 1916-1917 | 1,118 | 34.5 | 105 | 3 x 4.1"<br>6 x 19.7" T.T.<br>24 mines | 6 | (5 scuttled 21.6.19, but 4 beached) |
| S131-S139 | 1917-1918 | 1,170 | 34 | 105 | 3 x 4.1"<br>6 x 19.7" T.T.<br>24 mines | 9 | (4 scuttled 21.6.19) |
| H145-H147 | 1918 | 1,147 | 34 | 105 | 3 x 4.1"<br>6 x 19.7" T.T.<br>24 mines | 3 | (1 scuttled 21.6.19) |
| **ITALY** | | | | | | | |
| Mirabello | 1916-1917 | 1,972 | 35 | 169 | 8 x 4" (or 1 x 6" 7 x 4")<br>4 x 17.7" T.T.<br>100 mines | 3 | (Flotilla Leaders) (1 mined in 1920) |
| Soldati (2 Groups) | 1907-1910 | 412-424 | 28.7-29 | 50-55 | 4 x 3"<br>3 x 17.7" T.T.<br>10 mines | 10 | 1 |
| Indomito | 1913-1914 | 770 | 35.7 | 70-79 | 1 x 4.7"  4 x 3"<br>2 x 17.7" T.T.<br>(Later 4 T.T. and 10 mines) | 6 | 2 |
| Pilo | 1915-1916 | 850 | 30-33.8 | 70-79 | 4 x 3" (+ 2 x 3: A.A.)<br>4 x 17.7" T.T.<br>(10 mines on occasions) | 8 | |
| Sirtori | 1916-1917 | 850 | 33.6 | 85 | 6 x 4"<br>4 x 17.7" T.T.<br>10 mines | 4 | |

**Destroyers continued**

| CLASS | COMPLETED | DISPLACEMENT | SPEED (knots) | CREW | MAIN ARMAMENT | NUMBER COMPLETED | NUMBER LOST (Comments) |
|---|---|---|---|---|---|---|---|
| **ITALY continued** | | | | | | | |
| La Masa | 1917-1918 | 851 | 33.6 | 78 | 4 x 4"<br>4 x 17.7" T.T. | 6 | 1<br>(2 more completed in 1919) |
| **JAPAN** | | | | | | | |
| Asakaze | 1905-1909 | 450 | 29 | 70 | 6 x 3.1"<br>2 x 18" T.T. | 32* | 1 |
| Kaba | 1915 | 850 | 30 | 92 | 1 x 4.7"<br>4 x 3.1"<br>4 x 18" T.T. | 10 | |
| Momo | 1916-1917 | 1,080 | 31.5 | 110 | 3 x 4.7"<br>6 x 18" T.T. | 4 | |
| Enoki | 1918 | 1,100 | 31.5 | 110 | 3 x 4.7"<br>6 x 18" T.T. | 6 | |
| Isokaze | 1917 | 1,570 | 34 | 128 | 4 x 4.7"<br>6 x 18" T.T. | 4 | 1 (Wrecked)<br>(re-raised and returned to service) |
| **RUSSIA** | | | | | | | |
| Novik | 1913 | 1,280 (normal) | 36 | 130 | 4 x 4"<br>8 x 18" T.T.<br>60 mines | 1 | |
| Bespokoiny | 1914-1916 | 1,320-1.460 | 34 | 125 | 3 x 4"<br>10 x 18" T.T.<br>80 mines | 9 | 2 (Scuttled) |
| Izyaslav | 1916-1917 | 1,350 (normal) | 33 | 150 | 5 x 4"<br>9 x 18" T.T.<br>80 mines | 2 | + 1 completed 1927 and 2 incomplete, broken up |
| Kerch | 1917-1918 | 1,570 | 33 | ? | 4 x 4"<br>12 x 18" T.T.<br>80 mines | 4 | 4 (1 accidental, 3 scuttled)<br>(+ 4 completed post-war) |
| **UNITED KINGDOM** | | | | | | | |
| F (Tribal) | 1909-1911 | 1,000-1,200 | 33 | 68 | 1st Group 3/5 x 12pdr.<br>2nd Group 2 x 4"<br>2 x 18" T.T. | 12<br>+ 1 Hybrid | 2<br>+2 damaged, rebuilt as Zubian (from Zulu and Nubian) |
| I (Acheron) | 1912-1913 | 990 | 27-29 | 70 | 2 x 4"<br>2 x 12pdr.<br>2 x 21" T.T. (3 x 18" T.T. in R.A.N. units) | 29 | 3<br>(Includes 6 R.A.N. and 9 'Specials') |
| K (Acasta) | 1913-1914 | 1,300 | 29 | 73 | 3 x 4"<br>2 x 21" T.T. | 20 | 7 |
| L (Laforey) | 1914 | 1,150-1,300 | 29 | 73 | 3 x 4"<br>2 x 21" T.T. | 22 | 3 (Including 1 wrecked)<br>(Includes 2 Emergency War Programme Units) |
| M (All types)† | 1915-1917 | 990-c.1,100 | 34-35 | 76-80 | 3 x 4"<br>4 x 21" T.T. | 107 | 12 (Including 3 in collision and 2 wrecked) |
| R (All types)‡ | 1916-1917 | 1,173 (Admiralty Boats) | 36 | 82 | 3 x 4"<br>4 x 21" T.T. | 62 | 9 (Including 1 in collision) |
| V | 1917-1918 | 1,490-1,512 | 34 | 134 | 4 x 4"<br>1 x 3"<br>4 x 21" T.T. | 30 | 1 (+ 2 in 1919)<br>(Includes 5 Flotilla Leaders and 2 Thornycroft boats) |
| W◊ (or Repeat V) | 1918 | 1,490-1,512 | 34 | 134 | 4 x 4"<br>1 x 3"<br>6 x 21" T.T. | 21 | (Includes 2 Thornycroft boats)<br>(2 further units were cancelled) |
| S | 1918 | 1,075 (normal) | 36 | 90 | 3 x 4"<br>4 x 21" T.T.<br>(+ 2 x 18" T.T. in Thornycroft boats) | 20•<br>(by 11.11.18) | |
| Marksman/Imp. Marksman | 1915-1917 | 1,700-1,900 (Imp.) | 34 | 104<br>116 (Imp.) | 4 x 4"<br>4 x 21" T.T.<br>(+ 2 x 14" T.T. in 2 units) | 13 | 1 lost<br>(Flotilla Leaders)<br>(3 units fitted for minelaying) |
| Shakespeare | 1918 | 2,009 | 36 | 183 | 5 x 4.7"<br>1 x 3"<br>6 x 21" T.T. | 2 | (Flotilla Leaders)<br>+ (3 units completed post-war)<br>(4 further units were cancelled) |
| Scott | 1918 | 2,050 | 36 | 164 | 5 x 4.7"<br>1 x 3"<br>6 x 21" T.T. | 4 | 1 lost<br>(Flotilla Leaders)<br>+ (4 units completed post-war) |

* Includes 1 wrecked pre-war.

† 4 Ex-Greek, 7 Yarrow and 4 Thornycroft.

‡ 5 Thornycroft, 7 Yarrow, 11 Modified R.

◊ No modified W Class units were completed in 1918.

• 67 completed in all from 1918 - 1924. 2 further units were cancelled, 5 were Thornycroft and 7 Yarrow types.

## Destroyers continued

| CLASS | COMPLETED | DISPLACEMENT | SPEED (knots) | CREW | MAIN ARMAMENT | NUMBER COMPLETED | NUMBER LOST (Comments) |
|---|---|---|---|---|---|---|---|
| **UNITED STATES** | | | | | | | |
| Paulding-Monoghan | 1910-1912 | 887 | 29.5 | 86-89 | 5 x 3"<br>6 x 18" T.T. | 21 | |
| Cassin-O'Brien | 1913-1919 | 1,171 (O'Brien) - 1,235 (Cassin) | 29 | 98-101 | 3 or 4 x 4"<br>8 x 18" T.T.<br>(8 x 21" T.T. in O'Briens) | 14 | |
| Tucker-Sampson | 1915-1917 | 1,205-1,225 | 29.5 | 99 | 4 x 4"<br>8 x 21" T.T.<br>(12 x 21" T.T. in Sampsons) | 12 | 1 |
| Caldwell | 1917-1918 | 1,187 | 30 | 100 | 4 x 4"<br>12 x 21" T.T. | 6 | (First of the 'Flush Deckers') |
| Wickes | 1918 | 1,247 | 35 | 114 | 4 x 4"<br>1 x 3"<br>12 x 21" T.T. | 36<br>(by 11.11.18) | (111 completed in all by 1920) |

## Submarines

| CLASS | COMPLETED | DISPLACEMENT | SPEED (knots) | CREW | MAIN ARMAMENT | NUMBER COMPLETED | NUMBER LOST (Comments) |
|---|---|---|---|---|---|---|---|
| **AUSTRIA-HUNGARY** | | | | | | | |
| U 10 | 1915 | 127 / 141 | 6.5 / 5.5 | 16 | 2 x 17.7" T.T. | 5 | 1 (mined, later salvaged)<br>German-built UB coastal type<br>(2 transferred from German navy) |
| U 27 | 1917 | 278 / 312 | 9 / 5.7 | 19 | 1 x 75mm.<br>2 x 17.7" T.T. | 7 | 2 (1 later salvaged)<br>German U8-II coastal type |
| **FRANCE** | | | | | | | |
| Pluviôse | 1908-1911 | 398 / 550 | 12 / 8 | 24 | 1 x 17.7" T.T. | 17 | 5 (Includes 3 by collision) |
| Brumaire | 1913-1914 | 397 / 551 | 13 / 8.8 | 29 | 1 x 17.7" T.T. | 16 | 3 |
| Amphitrite | 1915-1918 | 414 / 609 | 12-13 / 9.5 | 29 | 1 x 75mm. (added later)<br>8 x 17.7" Torpedoes<br>(2 fitted for minelaying) | 8 | 1 |
| Diane | 1916-1917 | 633 / 891 | 17 / 11.5 | 43 | 1 x 75mm.<br>10 x 17.7" T.T. | 2 | 1 |
| Dupuy de Lôme | 1916 | 833 / 1,287 | 17 / 11 | 43 | 1 x 75mm.<br>1 x 47mm.<br>8 x 17.7" T.T. | 2 | |
| **GERMANY** | | | | | | | |
| U 31<br>(U 31 – U 41) | 1914-1915 | 685 / 878 | 16.7 / 9.7 | 35 | 1 x 3.4"<br>4 x 19.7" T.T. | 11 | 7 (+ 1 interned in Spain) |
| U 43<br>(U 43 – U 50) | 1915-1916 | 725 / 940 | 15.2 / 9.7 | 35 | 1 x 3.4"<br>4 x 19.7" T.T. | 8 | 6 (Including 2 scuttled) |
| U 51<br>(U 51 – U 56) | 1916 | 712 / 902 | 17 / 9 | 35 | 2 x 3.4"<br>4 x 19.7" T.T.<br>(some later 1 x 4.1" and 1 x 3.4") | 6 | 2 |
| U 66<br>(U 66 – U 70) | 1915 | 791 / 933 | 16.8 / 10.3 | 36 | 1 x 3.4"<br>(1917 1 x 4.1" in lieu)<br>5 x 19.7" T.T. | 5 | 4<br>(Building for Austria-Hungary.<br>Taken over by German navy) |
| U 81<br>(U 81 – U 86) | 1916 | 808 / 946 | 16.8 / 9.1 | 35 | 1 x 4.1"<br>or 2 x 3.4"<br>6 x 19.7" T.T. | 6 | 4 |
| U 117<br>(U 117 – U 121) | 1918 | 1,164 / 1,512 | 14.7 / 7 | 40 | 1 x 5.9" (U 117 also 1 x 3.4")<br>4 x 19.7" T.T.<br>42 mines | 5 | (Class UE-II Minelayers) |
| U 139<br>(U 139 – U 141) | 1918 | 1,930 / 2,438 | 15.8 / 7.6 | 62 | 2 x 5.9" (U 139)<br>2 x 5.9" + 2 x 3.4" (others)<br>6 x 19.7" T.T. | 3 | (Ocean-Going Cruiser type) |
| U 151<br>(U 151 – U 157) | 1916-1917 | 1,512 / 1,875 | 12.5 / 5.2 | 56 | 2 x 5.9"<br>2 x 3.4"<br>2 x 19.7" T.T. | 7 | (Submarine Cruisers*)<br>2 + 1 interned in Norway |

\* Originally designed as mercantile submarine freighters.

**Submarines continued**

| CLASS | COMPLETED | DISPLACEMENT | SPEED (knots) | CREW | MAIN ARMAMENT | NUMBER COMPLETED | NUMBER LOST (Comments) |
|---|---|---|---|---|---|---|---|
| **GERMANY continued** | | | | | | | |
| UB 18 (UB 18 – UB 47) | 1915-1916 | 263-272 / 292-305 | 8.8-9 / 5.8-6.2 | 23 | 1 x 4pdr. (UB 18-29) 1 x 3.4" (UB 30 -47) 2 x 19.7" T.T. | 30 | 21 (inc. 1 scuttled) + 1 interned in Spain (UB II Series Coastal type)* |
| UB 48 (UB 48 – 155 series) | 1917-1918 | 512-533 / 639-656 | 13.6 / 7.6-8 | 34 | 1 x 3.4" or 1 x 4.1" 5 x 19.7" T.T. | 90 | 40 (inc. 3 scuttled) + 2 interned in Sweden (UB III Series Coastal type)† |
| UC 1 (UC 1 – UC 15) | 1915 | 168 / 183 | 6.25-6.5 / 5.25-5.7 | 14 | 6 mine tubes 12 mines | 15 | 14 (inc. 1 scuttled) + 1 interned in Holland (Coastal Minelayers) |
| UC 16 (UC 16 – UC 79) | 1916-1917 | 410-434 / 493-511 | 11.6-12 / 6.7-7.4 | 26 | 1 x 3.4" 3 x 19.7" T.T. 6 mine tubes 18 mines | 64 | 43 (inc. 4 scuttled) + 1 interned in Spain (Coastal Minelayers) |
| UC 90 (UC 90 – UC 114) | 1918 | 491 / 571 | 11.5 / 6.6 | 32 | 1 x 3.4" or 4.1" 3 x 19.7" T.T. 6 mine tubes 14 mines | 25 | 1 interned in Spain (Coastal Minelayers) (34 more not completed) |
| **ITALY** | | | | | | | |
| Micca | 1918 | 842 / 1,244 | 14.5 / 11 | 40 | 2 x 3" 6 x 17.7" T.T. | 4 | (+ 2 completed in 1919) |
| Provana | 1918 | 762 / 924 | 16 / 9.8 | 40 | 2 x 3" 6 x 17.7" T.T. | 2 | (+ 2 completed in 1919) |
| Medusa | 1912-1913 | 248-252 / c.305 | 12 / 8 | 21-22 | 2 x 17.7" T.T. | 8 | 2 |
| F | 1916-1918 | 262 / 319 | 12.5 / 8.2 | 26 | 1 x 3" 2 x 17.7" T.T. | 21 | 1 (On trials, salvaged and put into service) |
| **JAPAN** | | | | | | | |
| Vickers C1-C2-C3 | 1909 | 286 / 321 | 12 / 8.5 | 26 | 2 x 18" T.T. | 7 (C1 - 2) (C2 - 3) (C3- 2) | |
| S1 | 1917 | 418 / 665 | 17 / 10 | c.30 | 1 x 2pdr. 2 x 18" T.T. | 1 | (Built in France) (+1 taken by France, replacement built in Japan not completed until 1926) |
| Holland | 1905 | 103 / 124 | 8 / 7 | 13 | 1 x 18" T.T. | 5 | |
| **RUSSIA** | | | | | | | |
| Holland | 1904-1907 | 105 / 122 | 8.5 / 6 | 22 | 1 x 15" T.T. | 7 | 5 (all scuttled 2.18) (+2 scuttled 4.19) |
| Kaiman | 1910 | 409 / 482 | 10.5 / 7 | 34 | 4 x 18" T.T. | 4 | 4 (all scuttled 2.18) |
| Narval | 1912-1916 | 621-673 / 994-1,045 | 9.6 / 11.3 | 47 | 1 x 75mm. 1 x 63mm. 4 x 18" T.T. | 3 | (All scuttled 4.19) |
| Bars | 1915-1918 | 650 / 780 | 18 / 10 | 33 | 1 x 63mm. 4 x 18" T.T. | 24 | 4 (+ 4 scuttled 4.19) |
| AG | 1916-1918 | 355 / 433 | 12 / 10 | 30 | 1 x 47mm. 4 x 18" T.T. | 6 | 2 (+ 1 foundered, re-raised) 3 scuttled 4.18, inc. re-raised boat (1 scuttled 4.19) ‡ |
| **UNITED KINGDOM** | | | | | | | |
| C | 1906-1910 | 287-290 / 316-320 | 13 / 7.5 | 16 | 2 x 18" T.T. | 38 + 2 R.C.N. | 10 (Includes 1 lost pre-war) (2 R.C.N. taken over from Chile) |
| E | 1913-1917 | 655-667 / 796-807 | 15 / 9 | 30 | 1 x 12pdr. (E1-8) – 4 x 18" T.T. (E9-56) – 5 x 18" T.T. (6 Minelayers) – 3 x 18" T.T. 20 mines | 55 + 2 R.A.N. | (+ 1 unit cancelled) 25 (including 4 scuttled and 1 wrecked) + 2 R.A.N. + 1 interned in Denmark |
| G | 1915-1917 | 703 / 837 | 14.25 / 9 | 30 | 1 x 3" 1 x 21" T.T. 4 x 18" T.T. | 14 | 3 (+ 1 unit cancelled) |
| H/Imp. H | 1915-1918 | 364-423 / 434-510 | 13 / 11.0 / 11.5 / 10.9 | 22 | 4 x 18" T.T. (Imp. H) 4 x 21" T.T. | 26 (by 11.18) | 3 (1 in collision) + 1 interned in Holland (44 completed in all, of which 6 ceded to Chile in 1917) (10 further units cancelled) |

*Margin notes:*

* 2 transferred to Austria-Hungary.

† 18 more not completed.

‡ Plus 5 completed 1919-23 and 6 taken over by U.S.Navy.

## Submarines continued

| CLASS | COMPLETED | DISPLACEMENT | SPEED (knots) | CREW | MAIN ARMAMENT | NUMBER COMPLETED | NUMBER LOST (Comments) |
|---|---|---|---|---|---|---|---|
| **UNITED KINGDOM continued** | | | | | | | |
| K | 1916-1918 | 1,980 / 2,566 | 24 / 9.5 | 59 | 2 x 4"<br>1 x 3"<br>10 x 18" T.T. | 17 (by 11.18) | 3 (all by collision) + 1 foundered, salved and re-numbered* |
| L1-L33 | 1918 | 890-891 / 1,074-1,084 | 17 / 10.5 | 35-38 | L1-8: 1 x 4", 6 x 18" T.T.<br>L9-33: 4 x 21"T.T., 2 x 18" T.T.<br>(5) Minelayers 4 x 21" T.T. | 18 (by 11.18) | 1 (+ 1 in 6.19)<br>(34 completed in all, 40 further units cancelled or not ordered) |
| L50-L71 | 1918-1919 | 960 / 1,150 | 17 / 10.5 | 44 | 2 x 4"<br>2 x 21" T.T. | | |
| **UNITED STATES** | | | | | | | |
| F | 1912-1913 | 330 / 400 | 13.5 / 11.5 | 22 | 4 x 18" T.T. | 4 | 1 (collision)<br>(+ 1 foundered before U.S.entered war) |
| H | 1913-1914 and 1918 | 358 / 467 | 14 / 10.5 | 25 | 4 x 18" T.T. | 9 | |
| L | 1916-1918 | 450-456 / 548-524 | 14 / 10.5 | 28 | 1 x 3"<br>4 x 18" T.T. | 11 | |
| O | 1918 | 521 / 629 and 491 / 566 | 14 / 10.5 | 28 | 1 x 3"<br>4 x 18" T.T. | 16 | |

\* 1 further unit completed 1923, 5 further units cancelled.

## Miscellaneous Classes

| CLASS | COMPLETED | DISPLACEMENT | SPEED (knots) | CREW | MAIN ARMAMENT | NUMBER COMPLETED | NUMBER LOST (Comments) |
|---|---|---|---|---|---|---|---|
| **FRANCE** | | | | | | | |
| Marne (Sloop) | 1917-1918 | 566 (Marne only 601) | 20-21 | 113 | 2 x 65mm. | 6 | |
| **GERMANY** | | | | | | | |
| A1 (Torpedo Boat) | 1915 | 137 | 19-20 | 28 | 1 x 4pdr. (2")<br>2 x 17.7" T.T.<br>Fitted for minesweeping | 25 | 8 (+ 1 scuttled)<br>+ 1 interned in Holland<br>(Coastal Torpedo Boats) |
| A26 (Torpedo Boat) | 1916-1917 | 250 | 25.8 | 29 | 2 x 3.45"<br>1 x 17.7" T.T.<br>Fitted for minesweeping | 24 | |
| M7 (Minesweeper) | 1915-1916 | 476 | 16.5 | 40 | 1 x 3.45"<br>later 2 x 3.45"<br>30 mines | 20 | 10 |
| M27 (Minesweeper) | 1915-1916 | 507 | 16.5 | 40 | 2 x 4.1"<br>(2 had 3 x 3.45")<br>30 mines | 18 | 6 (including 1 in collision) |
| M57 (Minesweeper) | 1917-1918 | 539 | 16 | 40 | M57-66: 2 x 4.1"<br>M67-70: 2 x 3.45")<br>All 30 mines | 14 | 4 |
| **ITALY** | | | | | | | |
| Pegaso (Torpedo Boat) | 1906-1909 | 210-216.5 | 25-26.5 | 39-42 | Varied:– 3 x 57mm. 1 x 47mm.<br>or 3 x 47mm. or, later, 1 or 2 x 3"<br>3 (later 2) x 17.7" T.T. | 18 | 1 + 1 wrecked, salved and put back in service (Built in 3 series of 4, 8 and 6 units) |
| RD 7 (Minesweeper) | 1917 | 215.6 | 14 | 22 | 1 x 3" | 3 | |
| RD 15 (Minesweeper) | 1916-1917 | 200.8 | 12.6-13.6 | 22 | 1 x 3" | 6 | |
| **UNITED KINGDOM** | | | | | | | |
| Lord Clive (Monitor) | 1915 | 6,150 | 6.5 | 194 | 2 x 12"<br>2 x 12pdr. | 8 | |
| Marshall Ney (Monitor) | 1915 | 6,900 | 9 | 187 | 2 x 15"<br>2 x 12pdr. | 2 | |

## Miscellaneous Classes continued

| CLASS | COMPLETED | DISPLACEMENT | SPEED (knots) | CREW | MAIN ARMAMENT | NUMBER COMPLETED | NUMBER LOST (Comments) |
|---|---|---|---|---|---|---|---|
| **UNITED KINGDOM continued** | | | | | | | |
| M 15 (Coastal Monitor) | 1915 | 650 | 11 | 69 | 1 x 9.2" 1 x 12pdr. | 14 | 3 (+ 2 scuttled 9.19) |
| Acacia (Minesweeping Sloop) | 1915 | 1,200 (normal) | 16.5 | 90 | 2 x 12pdr. | 24* | 2 (+ Azalea 1 lost in collision and 1 lost in 7.19) |
| Arabis (Minesweeping Sloop) | 1915-1916 | 1,250 (normal) | 16 | 90 | 2 x 4.7" (2 x 4" in 6 units) | 36† | 6 (+ 1 mined in 7.19) |
| Aubrietia (Convoy Sloop) | 1916 | 1,250 (normal) | 17.5 | 92 | 2 x 4" (as built) (originally to be 3 x 12pdr.) | 12 | 3 (1 transferred to French navy) |
| Anchusa (Convoy Sloop) | 1917-1918 | 1,290 (normal) | 16.5-17.5 | 92 | 2 x 4" 2 x 12pdr. Depth charges | 28 | 6 |
| 24 (Fleet Sweeping Sloops) | 1918 | 1,320 (normal) | 17 | 82 | 2 x 4" 39 depth charges | 10 (by 11.18) | (12 further units completed post-war and 2 more cancelled) |
| P (Patrol Boats) | 1916-1918 | 613 (normal) | 20 | 50-54 | 1 x 4" 2 x 14" T.T. (P52 only – 2 x 4" No T.T.) | 44 | 2 (inc. 1 in collision) |
| PC (Decoy Patrol Boats) | 1917-1918 | 682-694 (normal) | 20 | 50-55 | 1 x 4" 2 x 12pdr. | 20 | Initially known as PQ Boats |
| Kil (Patrol Gunboats) | 1917-1918 | 895 (normal) | 13 | 39 | 1 x 4" 6+ depth charges (11 fitted for minesweeping) | 29‡ (by 11.11.18) | (31 further units cancelled) |
| Ascot (Paddle Minesweepers) | 1916-1918 | 810-820 (normal) | 14.5 | 50 | 2 x 6pdr. | 32 | 5 (last 8 were of an improved type) |
| Hunt (Minesweepers) | 1917 | 750 (normal) | 16 | 71 | 1 or 2 x 12pdr. | 20 | 1 |
| Later Hunt or Abedare (Minesweepers) | 1918 | 800 (normal) | 16 | 74 | 1 x 4" 1 x 12pdr. | 32◊ (by 11.11.18) | 0 (but 3 mined in 1919) |
| **UNITED STATES** | | | | | | | |
| Eagle Boats (Patrol Vessels) | 1918 | 615 | 18.3 | 61 | 2 x 4" 1 x 3" 1 x Y gun | 7 (by 11.11.18) | (53 completed post-war in 1919) (62 further units cancelled) |
| SC (110ft) (Submarine Chasers) | 1917-1918 | 85 | 18 | 27 | 1 x 3" 1 x Y gun | 302• (by 11.11.18) | 6 |

Side notes (left margin):

* Azalea class of 12 units similar, except 2 x 4.7".

† 8 further units were built for French navy.

‡ 25 further units completed 1918-1920.

◊ 61 completed post-war, 2 broken up incomplete and 36 cancelled.

• Additionally 100 built for France, 4 transferred to Cuba, 35 completed post-war and 7 cancelled.

# BIBLIOGRAPHY

The following are the titles we have found most useful whilst compiling this book. They are mostly also the ones to which anyone seeking more detail on a particular topic should turn.

All books are published in London unless otherwise stated.

## A

P. ADAM-SMITH, *The Anzacs*, Hamish Hamilton, 1976

ADMIRALTY, *Navy Losses 1914-18*, H.M.S.O., 1919
– *Merchant Shipping (Losses) 1914-18*, H.M.S.O., 1919

W.E.D. ALLEN & P. MURATOFF, *Caucasian Battlefields: a History of the Wars on the Turco-Caucasian Border 1828-1921*, C.U.P., 1953

L. ANDERSON, *Soviet Aircraft and Aviation 1917-41*, Putnam, 1994

ANNUAL REGISTER 1914-1919, Longmans Green

ANON, 'Oil-Well Top Cover: 60 Years of Rumanian Military Aviation', in *Air Enthusiast*, March-August 1998
- *Die Deutsche Wehrmacht 1914-39*, E.S. Mittler und Sohn, Berlin, 1939

C.F. ASPINALL-OGLANDER (see Imperial Defence Committee)

L.P.AYRES, *The War with Germany: a Statistical Summary*, G.P.O., Washington, 1919

A. AYVAZIAN, *Armenian Victories*, St.Vortan Press, New York, 1985

## B

A. BANKS, *A Military Atlas of the First World War*, Heinemann, 1975

A.J. BARKER, *The Neglected War: Mesopotamia 1914-18*, Faber, 1967

C.W.E. BEAN, 'The First A.I.F.', in *Australian Encyclopedia*, Angus & Robertson, 1958

A.F. BECKE (see Imperial Defence Committee)

D.J. BERCUSON & J.E. GRANATSTEIN; *Dictionary of Canadian Military History*, O.U.P., 1992

R. BIDWELL, *Bidwell's Guide to Government Ministers 1900-1972*, vols 1 & 2, Cass 1973 and 1974

A.G. BLUME, 'History of the Serbian Air Force' (Pts 1-3), in *Cross and Cockade*, v.8, 1967

W.V. BRELSFORD, *The Story of the N.Rhodesia Regiment*, (1954), Galago, Bromley, 1990

J.M. BRUCE, *The Aeroplanes of the Royal Flying Corps (Military Wing)*, Putnam, 1992

J. BUCHAN, *Nelson's History of the War*, 26 vols, Nelson, n.d.

D.L. BULLOCH, *Allenby's War*, Blandford, 1988

BUNDESMINISTERIUM FÜR LANDESVERTEIDIGUNG, *Österreich-Ungarns*

*Letzter Krieg 1914-18*, 7 vols, (each with separate appendices and maps) + Index, Verlag der Militärwissenschaftlichen Mitteilungen, Vienna, 1930-38

H.BUSCHE, *Formationsgeschichte der deutschen Infanterie im Ersten Weltkrieg*, Forschungsstelle für deutsche Adelsgeschichte, Owschalg, 1997

J.R. BUSHBY, *Air Defence of Great Britain*, Ian Allan, Shepperton, 1973

D. BUTLER & J. FREEMAN, *British Political Facts 1900-1960*, Macmillan, 1964

## C

de CHAMBRUN & de MARENCHES, *The American Army in the European Conflict*, Macmillan, New York, 1919

R. CHESNAU, *Aircraft Carriers of the World 1914 to the Present*, Arms & Armour Press, 1984

A. CLAYTON, *France, Soldiers and Africa*, Brassey's, 1988

R. CLOGG, *A Short History of Modern Greece*, C.U.P., 1979

C. COLE & E.F. CHEESEMAN, *The Air Defence of Britain 1914-18*, Putnam, 1984

P. CONRAD & A. LASPEYRES, *La Grande Guerre 1914-18*, EPA Editions, Paris, 1989

*Conway's All the World's Fighting Ships 1906-21*, Conway Maritime Press, 1985

C.COOK & J. PAXTON, *European Political Facts 1848-1918*, Macmillan, 1978

J.S. CORBET, (see Imperial Defence Committee)

H. CRON, *Geschichte des deutschen Heeres im Weltkrieg 1914-18*, (1937), Biblio Verlag, Osnabrück, 1990

D. CROW *et al*, *Armoured Fighting Vehicles of World War One*, Profile Publications, Windsor, 1970

J.B. CYNK, *The History of the Polish Air Force 1918-68*, Osprey, 1972

## D

N. DAVIES, *God's Playground: a History of Poland*, v.2, Clarendon, Oxford, 1981

J.J. DAVILLA & A.M. SOLTAN, *The French Aircraft of the First World War*, Flying Machines Press, Stratford (Conn.), 1997

P. DENNIS *et al*, *Oxford Companion to Australian Military History*, O.U.P., 1995

W. DIECKMANN, *Die Behördenorganisation in der deutschen Kriegswirtschaft 1914-18*, Hanseatische Verlagsanstalt, Hamburg, 1937

F.J. DITMAR & J.J. COLLEDGE, *British Warships 1914-19*, Ian Allan, Shepperton, 1972

A. DUSKOTA *et al*, *The Imperial Russian Air Service: Famous Pilots and Aircraft of World War I*, Flying Machines Press, Stratford (Conn.), 1995

# E

W. von EBERHARDT (ed.), *Unsere Luftsreitkräfte 1914-18*, C.A.Weller, Berlin, 1939

J.E. EDMONDS (see Imperial Defence Committee)

*Encyclopedia Britannica* (14th ed.), 1929

E.J. ERICKSON, *Ordered to Die: The History of the Ottoman Army in the First World War*, Greenwood Press, Westport (Conn.), 2000\*

V.J. ESPOSITO, *The West Point Atlas of American Wars*, v.2, Praeger, New York, 1959

# F

C.FALLS (see Imperial Defence Committee)

C.E. FAYLE (see Imperial Defence Committee)

A. FRACCAROLI, *Italian Warships of World War I*, Ian Allan, Shepperton, 1970

N. FRANKS *et al*, *Above the War Fronts*, Grub Street, 1997
– *The Jasta Pilots*, Grub Street, 1996

J.B.M. FREDERICK, *Lineage Book of British Land Forces 1660-1978*, 2 vols, Microform Academic Publishers, Wakefield, 1984

B. FRIEDHAG, *Führer durch Herr und Flotte 1914,* (1913), Verlag 'Heere und Vergangenheit', J. Olmes, Krefeld, 1974

# G

B. GARDNER, *German East: The Story of the First World War in East Africa*, Cassell, 1963

R. GENTILI & P. VARRIALE, *I Reparti dell'Avizzione Italiana nella Grande Guerra*, Ufficio Storico dello Stato Maggiore dell'Aeronautica, Rome, 1999

T. GERMAN, *The Sea is our Gate: the History of the Canadian Navy*, McClelland & Stewart, Toronto, 1990

E. GOLDSCHMID, *Die Wirtschaftlichen Kriegsorganisationen Osterreichs*, Staatsdrückerei, Vienna, 1919

N.N. GOLOVINE, *The Russian Army in the World War*, Yale University Press, New Haven, 1931

R.M. GRANT, *U-Boat Intelligence 1914-18*, Putnam, 1969
– *U-Boats Destroyed: The Effect of Anti-Submarine Warfare 1914-18*, Putnam, 1964

P. GREY & O.THETFORD, *German Aircraft of the First World War*, Putnam, 1962

R. GRAY, *Chronicle of the First World War*, 2 vols, Facts on File, Oxford, 1990

R. GREGER, *Austro-Hungarian Warships of World War I*, Ian Allan, Shepperton, 1976
– *The Russian Fleet 1914-17*, Ian Allan, Shepperton, 1972

P.M. GROSZ *et al*, *Austro-Hungarian Aircraft of World War One*, Flying Machines Press, Stratford (Conn.), 1996

L. GUICHARD, *The Naval Blockade 1914-18*, P. Allan, 1930

# H

G.W. HADDOW & P.M. GROSZ, *The German Giants: the Story of the R-Planes 1914-19*, Putnam, 1962

P.G. HALPERN, *A Naval History of World War I*, UCL Press, 1994
– *The Naval War in the Mediterranean 1914-18*, Allen & Unwin, 1987

P.J. HAYTHORNWAITE, *The World War One Source Book*, Arms & Armour Press, 1992

H.H. HERWIG, *The First World War: Germany and Austria-Hungary 1914-18*, Arnold, 1997
– *The German Naval Officer Corps: A Social and Political History 1890-1918*, Clarendon, Oxford, 1973
– *'Luxury' Fleet: the Imperial German Navy 1888-1918*, Allen & Unwin, 1980
- and N.M. HEYMAN, *Biographical Dictionary of World War I*, Greenwood Press, Westwood (Conn.), 1982

E. von HOEPPNER, *Deutschlands Krieg in der Luft*, K. F.Koehler, Leipzig, 1921

I.V. HOGG, *Allied Artillery of World War One*, Crowood Press, Markborough, 1998
– and J. WEEKS, *Small Arms of the Twentieth Century*, Cassell, 1991

PRINZ von HOHENZOLLERN-EMDEN, *Emden: the Last Cruise of a Chivalrous Raider 1914*, Lyon, Brighton, 1989

E.G. von HORSTENAU & R. KISZLING (see Bundesministerium)

R. HOVANNISIAN, *Armenia on the Road to Independence 1918*, University of California Press, Los Angeles, 1967

# I

A. IMRIE, *Pictorial History of the German Air Service 1914-18*, Ian Allan, Shepperton, 1971

IMPERIAL DEFENCE COMMITTEE (Historical Section), *Official History of the War*, 57 vols, H.M.S.O and (occasionally) Heinemann, John Murray and Longmans Green 1923- . We have consulted the following volumes:
**Military Operations**
(Edmonds) *France and Belgium*, 14 vols
(Macmunn & Falls) *Egypt and Palestine*, 2 vols
(Moberley) *Mespotamia*, 4 vols, *Persia*
(Aspinall-Oglander) *Gallipoli*, 2 vols
(Falls) *Macedonia*, 2 vols
(Edmonds *et al*) *Italy*

**Order of Battle**
(Becke), 6 vols
see also F.W. Perry below

\* Unfortunately, the authors came across this excellent book too late to make anything but cursory use of it.

**Medical**
(T. Mitchell) *Casualties and Medical Statistics*

**Naval Operations**
(Corbett and Newbolt), 5 vols

**Seaborne Trade**
(Fayle), 3 vols

# J

E. A JAMES, *British Regiments 1914-18*, Samson Books, 1978
– *A Record of the Battles and Engagements of the British Armies in France and Flanders 1914-18*, London Stamp Exchange, 1990

C.G. JEFFORD, *RAF Squadrons*, Airlife, Shrewsbury, 1988

H. JENTSCHURA *et al*, *Warships of the Imperial Japanese Navy 1869-1945*, Arms & Armour Press, 1977

H.A. JONES, *The War in the Air*, 6 vols, O.U.P., 1928-37

R.E. JONES *et al*, *The Fighting Tanks from 1916 to 1933*, (1933) W.E. Inc., Old Greenwich (Conn.), 1969

# K

J. KAYALOFF, *The Battle of Sardarahab*, Mouton, The Hague, 1973

P. KILDUFF, *Germany's First Air Force 1914-18*, Arms & Armour Press, 1991

B. KING, *The Royal Naval Air Service 1912-18*, Hikoki Publications, 1997

W.M.G. St.G. KIRKE, 'An Outline of the Rumanian Campaign', in *RUSI Journal*, v. LXIX, Nov 1924

A. KNOX, *With The Russian Army 1914-17*, 2 vols, Hutchinson, 1921

F.KOCH, *Beutepanzer im Ersten Weltkrieg*, Podzun-Pallas, Freiburg, 1994

# L

J. LAYBAYLE-COUHAT, *The French Navy of World War I*, Ian Allan, Shepperton, 1974

H.M. LE FLEMING, *Warships of World War I*, Ian Allan, Shepperton, 1970

R.F. LESLIE, *The History of Poland since 1863*, C.U.P., 1980

A. LIVESEY, *Viking Atlas of World War I*, Viking, 1994

C. LUCAS, *The Empire at War*, 5 vols, O.U.P., 1922-6

J.S. LUCAS, *Austro-Hungarian Infantry 1914-18*, Almark, New Malden, 1973
– *Fighting Troops of the Austro-Hungarian Army 1868-1914*, Spellmount, Tunbridge Wells, 1987

# M

G. MACMUNN & C. FALLS (see Imperial Defence Committee)

G. MANNERHEIM, *The Memoirs of Marshal Mannerheim*, Cassell, 1953

A. MARDER, *From the Dreadnought to Scapa Flow*, 5 vols, O.U.P., 1961-1970

C. McCARTHY, *The Somme: The Day-by-Day Account*, Arms & Armour Press, 1993
– *Passchendaele: the Day-by-Day Account*, Arms & Armour Press, 1995

A.H. McCLINTOCK, *An Encyclopedia of New Zealand*, vol. 3, Government Printers, Wellington, 1966

A.H. MICHELSEN, *Der U-Bootskrieg 1914-18*, Leipzig, 1925

R. C. MIKESH & S. ABE, J*apanese Aircraft 1910-41*, Putnam, 1990

B.R. MITCHELL, *European Historical Statistics 1750-1975*, Facts on File, New York, 1981

D.W. MITCHELL, *History of the Modern American Navy*, John Murray, 1947

T. MITCHELL, (see Imperial Defence Committee)

F. MOBERLEY, (see Imperial Defence Committee)

A. MORRIS, *The First of the Many: The Story of the Independent Force, RAF*, Jarrolds, Norwich, 1968

J.H. MORROW, *German Air Power in World War I*, University of Nebraska Press, Lincoln, 1982
– *The Great War in the Air: Military Aviation from 1909 to 1921*, Airlife, Shrewsbury, 1993

L. MOVAREAU *et al*, *L'Aviation Maritime Francaise pendant la Grande Guerre*, Association pour la Recherche de Documentation sur l'Histoire de l'Aeronautique Navale, October 1999

P. MOYES, *Bomber Squadrons of the R.A.F. and their Aircraft,* Macdonald & Janes, 1964

K. MUNSON, *Aircraft of World War I*, Ian Allan, Shepperton, 1967

C.C.R. MURPHY, 'The Turkish Army in the Great War', a *Pallas Armata* reprint. Source of orignal not known.

# N

D. NASH (ed.), *German Army Handbook April 1918*, (1918), Arms & Armour Press, 1977
– *Imperial German Army Handbook 1914-18*, Ian Allan, Shepperton, 1980

H. NEWBOLT (see Imperial Defence Committee)

D. NICOLLE, *Lawrence and the Arab Revolts*, Osprey, 1989
– *The Ottoman Army 1914-18*, Osprey, 1994
– 'Young Turks: Ottoman Turkish Fighters 1915-18', in *Air Enthusiast*, March-August 1998

G.W.L. NICHOLSON, *The Canadian Expeditionary Force 1914-19*, (Official History of the Canadian Army in the First World War), Queen's Printers, Ottawa, 1962

# O

H.C. O'NEILL, *History of the War*, Jack, 1920

# P

M. PAGE, *KAR: a History of the King's African Rifles*, Leo Cooper, 1998

H. PEMSEL, *Atlas of Naval Warfare*, Arms & Armour Press, 1977

H. PENROSE, *British Aviation: the Great War and the Armistice*, Putnam, 1969

F.W. PERRY, *Order of Battle of Divisions*, (Parts 5A & 5B), Ray Westlake, Newport, 1991-93

J.J. PERSHING, *My Experiences in the World War*, Hodder & Stoughton, 1931

S. POPE & E. WHEAL, *Macmillan Dictionary of the First World War*, Macmillan, 1995

H. POPHAM, *Into the Wind: a History of British Naval Flying*, Hamish Hamilton, 1969

H. POTGEITER & W. STEENKAMP, *Aircraft of the South African Air Force*, Janes, 1981

PURNELL, *History of the First World War*, (part-work), Purnell, 1969-71

# R

H. ROOS, *A History of Modern Poland*, Eyre & Spottiswoode, 1966

W. RUTHERFORD, *The Russian Army in World War I*, Gordon Cremonesi, 1975

# S

C. SCHAEDEL, *Men and Machines of the Australian Flying Corps 1914-19*, Kookabura Publications, Victoria, 1972

W. SCHMIDT-RICHBERG & E. von MATUSCHKA, *Handbuch zur deutschen Militargeschichte 1648-1939*, v. 5, Bernhard & Graefe, Frankfurt, 1968

M. SCHWARTE (ed.), *Der Weltkampf um Ehre und Recht*, vol.1, Ernst Finking, Leipzig, n.d.

E. SEKIGAWA, *Pictorial History of Japanese Military Aviation*, Ian Allan, Shepperton, 1974

SERVICE HISTORIQUE DE L'ARMEE, *Les Armées francaises pendant la Grande Guerre 1914-18*, tome X, vols. 1 & 2, (Ordre de Bataille des Grandes Unités), Paris, 1934

H. SHURMAN (ed.), *The Blackwell Encyclopedia of the Russian Revolution*, Blackwell, Oxford, 1988

P.H. SILVERSTONE, *U.S. Warships of World War I*, Ian Allan, Shepperton, 1970

H.H.SOKOL, *Osterreich-Ungarns Seekrieg 1914-18*, Amalthea-Verlag, Vienna, 1935

*Statesman's Yearbook* 1914-1919

R.SHERROD, *History of Marine Corps Aviation in World War II*, (1952), Presidio Press, San Rafeal (Ca.), 1980

Stato Maggiore dell'Esercito (Ufficio Storico), *L'Esercito e sui Corpi: Sintesi Storica*, vol.1, Rome 1971
– *L'Esercito Italiano nella Grande Guerra*, vols. 1 & 1 bis, Rome, 1927

N.STONE, *The Eastern Front 1914-17*, Hodder & Stoughton, 1975

I.SUMNER, *The French Army 1914-18*, Osprey, 1995

G.SWANBOROUGH & P.M.BOWERS, *U.S.Navy Aircraft since 1911*, Putnam, 1976 (2nd Ed.)

# T

R.L.TARNSTROM, *Balkan Battles*, Trogen Books, Lindsborg (Kansas), 1998
– *Poland and the Baltic Republics*, Trogen Books, Lindsborg (Kansas), 1990
– *The Sword of Scandinavia*, Trogen Books, Lindsborg (Kansas), 1996
– *The Wars of Japan*, Trogen Books, Lindsborg (Kansas), 1992

V.E.TARRANT, *The U-Boat Offensive 1914-45*, Arms & Armour Press, 1989

J.C.TAYLOR, *German Warships of World War I*, Ian Allen, Shepperton, 1969

C.THETFORD, *British Naval Aircraft since 1912*, Putnam, 1971

A.THOMAZI, *La Guerre Navale dans l'Adriatique*, Payot, Paris, 1927
– *La Guerre Navale dans la Méditerranée*, Payot, Paris, 1929
– *La Guerre Navale dans la Zone des Armées du Nord*, Payot, Paris, 1925

S.H.THOMPSON, *Czechoslavakia in European History*, Cass, 1965

S.C.TUCKER (ed.), *The European Powers in the First World War*, Garland, New York, 1996

# U

U.S. AIR FORCE (Office of Air Force History), *The U.S. Air Service in World War I*, vol. 1 (*Final Report* and *Tactical History*), G.P.O., Washington, 1978

U.S.ARMY SURGEON GENERAL, *Report*, G.P.O., Washington, 1920

U.S.ARMY WAR COLLEGE, *Order of Battle of the U.S. Forces in the World War: American Expeditionary Forces*, vols. 1 & 2, G.P.O., Washington, 1937

U.S.GENERAL STAFF (Intelligence Section), *Histories of the 251 Divisions of the German Army which participated in the War (1914-18)*, (1920), London Stamp Exchange, 1989

# W

W.WAGNER, *Die Oberster Behörden der k.u.k. Kriegsmarine*, Verlag Ferdinand Berger, Vienna, 1961

P.S.WANDYCZ, *The Lands of Partitioned Poland*, University of Washington Press, Seattle, 1964